Windows Server® 2008 Terminal Services Resource Kit

Christa Anderson and Kristin L. Griffin
with the Microsoft Presentation Hosted
Desktop Virtualization Team

PUBLISHED BY
Microsoft Press
A Division of Microsoft Corporation
One Microsoft Way
Redmond, Washington 98052-6399

Library of Congress Control Number: 2008938213

Printed and bound in the United States of America.

1 2 3 4 5 6 7 8 9   QWT   3 2 1 0 9 8

Distributed in Canada by H.B. Fenn and Company Ltd.

A CIP catalogue record for this book is available from the British Library.

Microsoft Press books are available through booksellers and distributors worldwide. For further information about international editions, contact your local Microsoft Corporation office or contact Microsoft Press International directly at fax (425) 936-7329. Visit our Web site at www.microsoft.com/mspress. Send comments to rkinput@microsoft.com.

Microsoft, Microsoft Press, Active Directory, Excel, Hyper-V, MS, MSDN, Visio, Windows, Windows PowerShell, Windows Server, and Windows Vista are either registered trademarks or trademarks of the Microsoft group of companies. Other product and company names mentioned herein may be the trademarks of their respective owners.

The example companies, organizations, products, domain names, e-mail addresses, logos, people, places, and events depicted herein are fictitious. No association with any real company, organization, product, domain name, e-mail address, logo, person, place, or event is intended or should be inferred.

This book expresses the author's views and opinions. The information contained in this book is provided without any express, statutory, or implied warranties. Neither the authors, Microsoft Corporation, nor its resellers, or distributors will be held liable for any damages caused or alleged to be caused either directly or indirectly by this book.

Acquisitions Editor: Martin DelRe
Project Editor: Victoria Thulman
Editorial Production: Custom Editorial Productions, Inc.
Technical Reviewer: Bob Hogan; Technical Review services provided by Content Master, a member of CM Group, Ltd.
Cover: Tom Draper Design

Body Part No. X15-04071

Contents at a Glance

Table of Contents

What do you think of this book? We want to hear from you!

Microsoft is interested in hearing your feedback so we can continually improve our books and learning resources for you. To participate in a brief online survey, please visit:

www.microsoft.com/learning/booksurvey

What do you think of this book? We want to hear from you!

Microsoft is interested in hearing your feedback so we can continually improve our books and learning resources for you. To participate in a brief online survey, please visit:

www.microsoft.com/learning/booksurvey

Acknowledgments

We were both pretty busy while writing this book. It was written while its authors were moving, selling houses, buying houses, working full time, and getting married—not quite all at once, but sometimes pretty close. This book isn't just the work of two people. We owe many thanks to the combined efforts of a lot of people at Microsoft, our terrific set of editors, and the greater community. (All this said, any errors in this book are the sole responsibility of the authors.)

Throughout this book, you'll find From the Source sidebars contributed by members of the product team. In addition to the contributors of the From the Source sidebars, we must give our heartfelt thanks to the members of the product team who sat down with us to explain the finer details of how something worked. From the Presentation Hosted Desktop Virtualization (PHDV) product group, we'd like to thank Geanina Andreiu, James Baker, Alex Balcanquall, Ara Bernardi, Tad Brockway, Hammad Butt, Rong Chen, Gaurav Daga, Munindra Das, Samim Erdogan, Graham Fagg, Costin Hagiu, Al Henriquez, Olga Ivanova, Gopikrishna Kannan, Ramesh Kasturi, Harish Kumar Poongan Shanmugam, Alice Kupchick, Anubhav Kushwaha, Sergey Kuzin, Rob Leitman, Meher Malakapalli, Ayesha Mascarenhas, Josh Moyer, Roman Porter, Subashini Raghunathan, Sriram Sampath, Elton Saul, Aruna Somendra, NK Srivinas, Soo Kuan Teo, Janani Venkateswaran, Prasad Wagle, Sudarshan Yadav, and Ratnesh Yadav for all their help. Even people from other teams got involved: Thank you, Prabu Ambravaneswaran and Makarand Patwardhan, for your invaluable assistance. Each and every one of these people was instrumental in helping us understand how part of Terminal Services or a related technology works. We'd also like to thank Christa's manager, Ashwin Palekar, for his support during this project, as well as Chandra Shekaran, general manager for the PHDV team, for contributing a foreword to this book.

People outside the PHDV product group also pitched in with their knowledge of Terminal Services in From the Field sidebars and in reviewing content. Many thanks go to Jeff Heaton, Timothy Newton, James Owusu, Bohdan Velushchak, Oliver Weindl, Naren Wicaksono, and Jon Wojan. Tom Bailey from Product Support Services helped us track down a mystery tool. Catherine Wrightsman from Microsoft's legal department also pitched in to help create an end user license agreement for one of the tools that needed one. Thank you all!

The MVP community was also a huge asset during the writing of this book. We bounced ideas off Brian Madden, Michael Smith, and Benny Tritsch, and all three volunteered their expertise in contributing From the Field sidebars.

Several independent software vendors contributed freeware to the Resource Kit. Many thanks to AppSense, Ericom, Immodio, Quest Software, and visionapp!

The great team at Microsoft Press had a huge hand in turning this project from an idea into the book you hold in your hands. We'd like to thank Martin Del Re for asking us to write the book in the first place, Victoria Thulman for great editing and project management, Melissa von Tschudi-Sutton for project management vacation backup, and Bob Hogan for tech editing the book. The editorial team at Custom Editorial Productions, Inc. did a terrific job of copyediting and proofing this text.

Finally, we'd like to thank our friends and families for their support during this big project. We couldn't have done it without you.

Foreword

Windows Server 2008 Terminal Services presentation virtualization has been a significant part of my life for five years. During this time, there have been three platform releases culminating with the launch of Windows Server 2008. Building Terminal Services (TS) is a fascinating and challenging experience as we continually work toward making the remote end user experience closer to the local desktop experience and providing the administrator with better tools to ease the task of managing a Terminal Services deployment.

This latest TS update represents the largest incremental platform enhancement to date in our ongoing quest to accelerate application deployment, improve remote worker efficiency, and help organizations secure corporate data and applications. The following features are of particular interest.

- Terminal Services RemoteApp (TS RemoteApp) applications appear to be no different from local applications including tight integration with the client desktop taskbar. TS RemoteApp helps improve end-user productivity and reduces training requirements.

- Terminal Services Gateway (TS Gateway) securely connects applications and data to users outside the firewall. It provides simple and secure delivery of critical applications and data to mobile employees without a virtual private network (VPN).

- Terminal Services Web Access (TS Web Access) simplifies application deployment by making applications available from a Web page or a SharePoint portal without installing them on the local PC. This quickly connects users to the applications they need.

- Terminal Services Easy Print utilizes the client-side print driver (no server-side driver need be installed) to enable fast and reliable printing to a local printer or a network-attached printer. End users can work more productively from remote locations.

- Terminal Services Session Broker (TS Session Broker) provides load-balancing and brings better uptime and performance to your TS environment. It also enables independent software vendors (ISVs) to build "connection brokers" to access virtual desktop infrastructure (VDI) deployments (wherein applications are hosted on guest virtual machines running a Windows desktop OS and accessed remotely using a TS client). This enables organizations to accrue the scalability benefits of TS along with the isolation benefits of VDI in a single, seamless deployment.

Windows Server 2008 Terminal Services Resource Kit describes how to deploy and use Terminal Services. It also gives a high-level view of how TS works. Readers will come away with an understanding of a range of topics.

- How Terminal Services is used and how the role services support the business cases

- How to determine the number of people who can use a terminal server and how to monitor usage increases

- How each of the role services and main features works so that people understand the dependencies

- How key components of the OS (CPU scheduling, memory allocation, and disk I/O) work

- How to install and configure all TS role services

- How to use virtualization with TS role services—where virtualization works and where it is less useful

- How to make TS work with user profiles/folder redirection and Group Policy to set up the user environment

- How to create scripts that use TS interfaces to get new information about the TS ecosystem and its usage

Christa and Kristin have done a superb job describing the inside story of Windows Server 2008 Terminal Services. The book includes sidebars from members of my team who built the product, Microsoft field engineers, and Microsoft Most Valuable Professionals (MVPs). The sidebars describe various product features or usage tips/tricks to improve the experience of IT professionals and end users. Several ISVs have also contributed TS-related freeware.

It has been quite a journey for those of us involved in building Terminal Services. This book is part of our effort to facilitate maximizing the benefit of Terminal Services to our users. So, start reading and realizing the value of centralized desktop and application deployment.

Chandra Shekaran

General Manager, Microsoft Presentation Hosted Desktop Virtualization Team

Introduction

Welcome to the *Windows Server 2008 Terminal Services Resource Kit*! This is a detailed technical resource for planning, deploying, and running Microsoft Terminal Services. Because so many features of Terminal Services are brand new, this book is valuable both for those completely new to Terminal Services and those who have used Terminal Services in previous versions of Microsoft Windows.

Within this resource kit, you'll find in-depth information about the improvements in Terminal Services introduced in Windows Server 2008. This book combines underlying architectural concepts with practical hands-on instructions that allow you to set up a working Terminal Services ecosystem, understand *why* it's working, and give you some guidance about how to fix it when it's not. You'll also find detailed information and task-based guidance on managing all aspects of Terminal Services, including deploying terminal servers, integrating Terminal Services roles with other key parts of the Windows Server 2008 operating system, and extending the reach of the terminal servers to outside the corporate network. Finally, the companion media includes additional tools and documentation that you can use to manage and troubleshoot Terminal Services servers.

Although we mention some third-party tools in the course of this book (and some Terminal Services independent software vendors [ISVs] have kindly agreed to make tools available through the companion media), this book is fundamentally about running a terminal server farm using only the tools found in the operating system. You can do what we've done here using *only* Windows Server 2008. Nor do we get into extensive discussion of any of the third-party tools that many people use with native Terminal Services. Citrix's XenApp, for example, is management software in use on many high-complexity server farms, but we don't discuss it here because it's not included with the operating system.

> **On the Companion Media** See the team partner page at *http://www.microsoft.com/windowsserver2008/en/us/ts-partners.aspx* for a list of companies that make products complementing or expanding on Terminal Services in Windows Server 2008.

What's New in Terminal Services in Windows Server 2008?

Terminal Services has changed a lot in this version of the operating system. Previous versions offered basic connectivity—a terminal server and a license server to manage connections to it. Today, it's become a much more comprehensive solution in terms of what comes with the operating system and how third parties can build on top of it through new application programming interfaces (APIs). Among its many improvements, Terminal Services in Windows Server 2008 delivers the following:

- Integrated application delivery

  Previous versions of Terminal Services presented all remote applications from their own desktop, completely separating the display of local and remote applications. TS RemoteApps in Windows Server 2008 launch from a terminal server, but look like they're running locally.

- Connection brokering to enable terminal server farms

  The Session Directory service in Windows Server 2003 offered the beginning of farm support, but was only available for Enterprise SKUs and didn't include any load-balancing—it just kept track of where connections had gone. In Windows Server 2008, TS Session Broker is available on the Standard SKU, supports load balancing, and can even be extended to support brokering connections to endpoints other than sessions on a terminal server. To connect to servers in a terminal server farm, users must provide only the farm's name, and TS Session Broker determines where the connection should go.

- Built-in support for secure Internet access

  One of the key benefits of Terminal Services is its ability to support mobile workers; it allows them to use their current data without worrying about it getting out of sync with the information in the data center. In previous versions of Windows, Terminal Services didn't support secure Internet access except across virtual private networks. In Windows Server 2008, Terminal Services supports connectivity over Secure Sockets Layer (SSL) via the Terminal Services Gateway (TS Gateway). TS Gateway allows you to set up different rules for local and remote access and does not require any client-side work or setup.

- Simplified printing

  Printing support is one of the banes of the terminal server administrator's life. With Terminal Services Easy Print, you don't need to install printer drivers on the terminal server to let people print. For those users who can't use Easy Print for any reason, the Printer Management Console makes it easier to manage and distribute tested printer drivers.

- Presentation of applications and desktop access through a Web page or online application

  One of the questions for enabling remote access is how to get the most complete and up-to-date set of remote resources to your user base. This is especially true when you're providing access to individual applications, not to a full desktop. Using Terminal Services Web Access (TS Web Access), you can present links to individual applications or to entire desktops and know that these links will always be up to date.

- Support for additional device redirection

  Part of the rich remote work experience is using local devices. Support for local devices in the new version of Terminal Services has been expanded through the Plug and Play Device Redirection Framework.

- Per-user Terminal Services client access license (TS CAL) tracking and reporting

  Per-user licensing was introduced in Windows Server 2003, but didn't include any tracking, so you couldn't easily tell if you were in compliance. Windows Server 2008 introduces ways to track per-user TS CAL usage. Additionally, a new Licensing Diagnostics feature can help you resolve licensing issues.

- Many new APIs to support extensibility

  Terminal Services is a product in itself, but it's also the starting point for a lot of third-party applications to address more complex scenarios or specific problems. Using the APIs published on MSDN, you can manipulate data in ways that the graphical user interfaces don't plan for, automate configurations, or even build new user interfaces for pieces of Terminal Services such as TS RemoteApps.

This is only a partial list—Chapter 1 (and the rest of this book) highlights new Terminal Services features in Windows Server 2008 and how to use them. But these are some of the highlights that show how the role has expanded in management and user experience.

> **On the Companion Media** The authors will post data that is relevant to the *Windows Server 2008 Terminal Services Resource Kit* on the book's blog, located at *http://blogs.technet.com/tsresourcekit/default.aspx*. You can find this link on the companion CD.

How This Book Is Structured

Our goal in writing this book is to help you set up a working Terminal Services farm using all the pieces in the operating system, while understanding the greater context of the circumstances under which Terminal Services is useful, how it works, and how Windows Server 2008 compares to previous versions. This book has nine chapters:

- Chapter 1, "Introducing Terminal Services in Windows Server 2008," provides the background of where Terminal Services came from, what it's for, and how it's available as both a feature in itself and as a development platform.

- Chapter 2, "Planning the Terminal Server Ecosystem," discusses key operating system architecture as it relates to Terminal Services, including processor, memory, and disk.

- Chapter 3, "Installing the Core Terminal Server Environment," introduces the basics of Terminal Services—the terminal server and license server—and explains how to install them and how they work.

- Chapter 4, "Creating the User Work Environment," explains how to set up user profiles with Terminal Services. It also introduces Group Policy in this environment.

- Chapter 5, "Fine-Tuning the User Experience," discusses the user environment, including device redirection, server lockdown, and the use of Group Policy for tweaking the user experience.

- Chapter 6, "Installing and Publishing Applications," focuses on application presentation. This chapter covers how applications install on a terminal server, how to set them up, how to publish TS RemoteApps and how to integrate them with a browser using TS Web Access.

- Chapter 7, "Multi-Server Deployments and Securing Terminal Server Connections," expands the terminal server beyond the single server to include TS Session Broker and support for farms. It also expands the reach beyond the corporate network to add TS Gateway and enable secure Internet access to terminal servers and other approved computers.

- Chapter 8, "Managing the Terminal Server Runtime Environment," discusses real-time management using Terminal Services Manager and the command-line tools. It also explains how to use these tools in scripts to enable functionality that doesn't exist through the graphical tools, but is accessible to anyone with very basic scripting abilities.

- Chapter 9, "Terminal Services Ecosystem Management," steps back from the details of the Terminal Services roles to discuss long-term management, including change management strategies, key server backup and restoration techniques, and some capacity planning tips to let you know when to add more capacity to the server farm.

Document Conventions

The following conventions are used in this book to highlight special features or usage.

Reader Aids

The following reader aids are used throughout this book to point out useful details.

Reader Aid	Meaning
Caution	Warns you that failure to take or avoid a specified action can cause serious problems for users, systems, data integrity, and so on
Note	Underscores the importance of a specific concept or highlights a special case that might not apply to every situation
On the Companion Media	Calls attention to a related script, tool, template, job aid, or URL on the companion CD that helps you perform a task described in the text

Sidebars

The following sidebars are used throughout this book to provide added insight, tips, and advice concerning different Windows Server 2008 Terminal Services features.

> **Note** Sidebars are provided by individuals in the industry as examples for informational purposes only and may not represent the views of their employers. No warranties, express, implied or statutory are made as to the information provided in sidebars.

Sidebar	Meaning
Direct from the Source	Contributed by experts from the product group who provide "from-the-source" insight into how Terminal Services works, best practices, and troubleshooting tips.
Direct from the Field	Contributed by experts external to the product group who have real-world experience working with Terminal Services. Some experts are Microsoft field engineers; others are Microsoft MVPs or other experts.
How It Works	Provides unique glimpses of Terminal Services features and how they work.

Command-Line Examples

The following style conventions are used in documenting command-line examples throughout this book.

Style	Meaning
Bold font	Used to indicate user input (characters that you type exactly as shown)
Italic font	Used to indicate variables for which you need to supply a specific value (for example, *file name* can refer to any valid file name)
`Monospace font`	Used for code samples and command-line output
%VariableName%	Used for environment variables

Companion Media

In addition to the book itself, you also get a CD that contains some great tools and other resources. System requirements for running the CD are at the back of this book. The CD includes the following resources.

Links

The companion media includes many links to URLs that lead to more information about Terminal Services-related topics, Terminal Services resources, partner Web sites, and more. Some of the URLs are referenced throughout the book and some are not.

Add-on Tools

Several of the third-party Terminal Services vendors have kindly provided versions of their tools that you can use to extend the role's core functionality and address new situations not covered in the core product. Some of these tools are mentioned in the course of the chapters; some are not.

Management Scripts

On the companion media, you will find a collection of scripts illustrating ways to work with Terminal Services using Windows PowerShell and VBScript. We've also included listings in relevant locations in the book so that you can better understand how these scripts support the functionality you're looking for. Although these scripts are intended as samples instead of finished products, they do useful work such as allowing you to easily determine the shadowing permissions on a server or providing application-usage metering not provided in the GUI.

> **Find Additional Content Online** As new or updated material becomes available that complements your book, it will be posted online on the Microsoft Press Online Windows Server and Client Web site. The type of material you might find includes updates to book content, articles, links to companion content, errata, sample chapters, and more. This Web site is available at *http://microsoftpresssrv.libredigital.com/serverclient/,* and is updated periodically.

> **Digital Content for Digital Book Readers:** If you bought a digital-only edition of this book, you can enjoy select content from the print edition's companion CD.
> Visit **http://go.microsoft.com/fwlink/?LinkId=130247** to get your downloadable content. This content is always up-to-date and available to all readers.

Resource Kit Support Policy

Every effort has been made to ensure the accuracy of this book and the companion media content. Microsoft Press provides corrections to this book through the Web at the following location:

http://www.microsoft.com/learning/support/search.asp

If you have comments, questions, or ideas regarding the book or companion CD content, or if you have questions that are not answered by querying the Knowledge Base, please send them to Microsoft Press by using either of the following methods:

E-mail:

rkinput@microsoft.com

Postal Mail:

Microsoft Press
Attn: *Windows Server 2008 Terminal Services Resource Kit* Editor
One Microsoft Way
Redmond, WA 98052-6399

Please note that product support is not offered through the preceding mail addresses. For product support information, please visit the Microsoft Product Support Web site at the following address:

http://support.microsoft.com

Chapter 1
Introducing Terminal Services in Windows Server 2008

You may be reading this for any of a number of reasons. Perhaps you're an old hand at Terminal Server and are interested in seeing what Terminal Services in Windows Server 2008 can do for you. You may have Windows Server 2008 and be interested in what all these Web accesses and gateways and terminal servers do. Or you may have heard about Terminal Services for years and are interested in how you might benefit by incorporating Terminal Services into your environment. The question is: What can Terminal Services do for you that you can't do with managed desktops?

Whichever reason sounds closest, this book is for you.

This chapter sets the stage for the rest of the book. To understand the evolution of Terminal Services, you have to understand where it came from and the ecosystem in which it operates. To understand what you can do with the roles and role services, you have to understand the essential goals of Terminal Services in Windows Server 2008 and the scenarios that it's designed for. And, since Terminal Services isn't an end in itself but a piece of the broader Windows infrastructure, you'll see how Terminal Services roles interact with other roles.

After reading this chapter, you'll understand:

- What Windows Server 2008 includes for supporting a Terminal Services environment

- What scenarios the Terminal Services role services are intended to support

- How Terminal Services role services interact with each other

- How Terminal Services role services can work with other Windows Server roles

- What interfaces are available for independent software vendors (ISVs) and customers who want to create custom solutions on top of Terminal Services and the capabilities these interfaces can provide

Where Did Terminal Server Come From?

If you're looking at Terminal Services for the first time with Windows Server 2008, you'd hardly recognize its earliest incarnations. Like Windows Server itself, Terminal Services has changed a *lot* over the years. It's not important to go through an exhaustive feature list for each edition, but it's useful to see how multi-user Windows has developed since its inception in the middle 1990s and how ownership has evolved.

The original MultiWin architecture was designed by Citrix, who licensed the Windows NT 3.51 source code from Microsoft to create multi-user Windows. (MultiWin was originally going to be based on IBM Operating System/2 [OS/2] when Microsoft was part of the OS/2 project. Windows won out.) Citrix created its own product called WinFrame, which was a multi-user version of Windows NT 3.51 and totally separate from the operating system that Microsoft produced.

A First Experience with Multi-User Windows

Christa first experienced multi-user Windows through WinFrame 1.7 in 1997 at an IBM training center in New York's Hudson River Valley. Originally, the training center provided a PC in each guest room (training lasted multiple days, so there were hotel rooms in the training center) and staff had to deal with the maintenance headaches of that setup. They'd moved to setting up thin clients (connected to the WinFrame servers) in all guest rooms so that guests could check e-mail and work from their rooms. When attendees checked in, a script automatically created a user account for that person. Totally predictable now, of course, but at the time it was heady stuff and a big change from the desktop-centric model of Windows.

The catch to WinFrame, of course, is that it was built on Windows NT 3.51. Microsoft licensed MultiWin back from Citrix in 1995 and plugged this multi-user core into the base operating system to make a new product: Windows Server with multi-user capabilities. The end result was Windows NT, Terminal Server Edition. Citrix no longer provided a standalone product but released MetaFrame, which ran on top of Terminal Server Edition in much the same way that Citrix Presentation Server runs on Windows Server now.

Terminal Server Edition was very much a starting point. The operating system was pretty basic, to put it mildly. Almost every installation of Terminal Server Edition ran MetaFrame on top of it because the base product did little more than provide a multi-user operating system. Even basic functionality such as clipboard mapping was not included. That Terminal Server Edition and the core operating system were different products wasn't great for either Microsoft or its customers. Microsoft had to deal with two sets of operating system service packs, while customers had to purchase a separate product to test server-based computing *and* juggle two different service packs that were not released at the same time. (On the plus side, when there was a problem with Service Pack 6 for Windows NT 4.0, by the time SP 6 for Terminal Server Edition was released, the problem was solved.)

The first real breakthrough in Microsoft Terminal Services was in Windows 2000 Server. For the first time, Terminal Services was a server role in the base server operating system, not a separate product. Why did this matter? There are several reasons. First, the game of juggling incompatible service packs for single-user and multi-user operating systems was over. Second, there was a fundamental change in the way that server-based computing and remote access were perceived. Before Windows 2000, if you wanted to manage a Windows server from the graphical user interface (GUI) you generally sat down in front of it—there was no capability for remote management using Microsoft Remote Desktop Protocol (RDP). The problem: There's a limit to the number of servers that you can sit in front of during the day, especially when those servers are in different buildings—or even in different cities. Windows 2000 Server introduced Remote Administration as an optional component, allowing server administrators to manage servers they *weren't* sitting in front of, even servers in a different building. Not only did this make server administration a lot easier, it also came to the aid of Terminal Services, because it gave people a good use case for remote usage and multi-user computing.

Having Terminal Services in Application Server mode available in the core operating system also meant that trying out Terminal Server for end users required comparatively little effort—setting up a basic pilot could be done with as little effort as installing the role in Application Server mode and letting people use Notepad. And, since RDP in Windows 2000 Server added some basic functionality such as client printer redirection and a shared clipboard between local and remote sessions, trying out Terminal Server and getting a feel for how end users could benefit from shared computing was possible even with only the tools in the core operating system.

The next big step was Windows Server 2003, which took some of the decisions made in the Windows 2000 Server time frame to the next logical conclusion. If Remote Administration is a good thing, why should it be an optional component? Instead, enable it for all Windows server roles and make it an option for the client. And while the basic functionality in Windows 2000 Terminal Server is useful, it doesn't provide a sufficiently rich client experience. Let's enable drive mapping, full color, sound, and other features previously only possible with third-party products to make the remote experience a lot more like the local desktop experience.

Another big change to Windows Server 2003 was in the management sphere. Windows 2000 terminal servers could only be managed singly. You could configure them remotely, but not collectively. Windows Server 2003 introduced some Group Policy settings for configuring and managing terminal servers, and Terminal Server Manager supported management of remote servers.

Although this book focuses on the server shared-computer experience, not the client, it is important to know that Terminal Services also changed on the client side during this period. Windows 2000 Professional did not support incoming remote access connections (nor did Windows 9.*x*), but Windows XP did, and Windows Vista does. Supporting incoming remote connections enables several new ways to use Windows clients, including:

- Remote access from home or another area of the building
- Remote Assistance
- Virtual desktop hosting

Remote access from another computer is a reflection of the reality that many people use more than one computer—that even a home might have more than one computer. Remote Assistance utilizes the remote control feature of Terminal Services—the ability to permit a second person to see or even take over a remote session—for enabling help desk support even on desktops. And virtual desktop hosting has been one of the chief competitors to Terminal Services for providing a hosted application environment when a shared computer isn't a viable option.

Terminal Services shows up in the client versions of Windows even when you don't expect it. It's the technology that enables Fast User Switching and Remote Assistance, to name just two.

In short, the story of Terminal Services is the story of how multi-user computing has become less of a niche technology and more of a strategy for enabling various scenarios that blur the line between the PC and the data center. Even when they're not called Terminal Services, multi-user computing and the remote desktop protocol have become crucial parts of the core Windows platform.

What Can You Do with Terminal Services?

The preceding section provides a (very fast) look at where server-based Windows came from and how it became part of the core Windows platform for both client and server. But what do you *do* with it?

Fundamentally, Terminal Services breaks the hard links between location and capability. With a PC, you are absolutely tied to what that computer can do. With server-based computing, the capabilities are more flexible. This has benefits for security, location, and device independence.

Improve Security for Remote Users

Totally PC-based computing has problems with data security. More and more people work on laptops, and laptops are meant to be taken places. But laptops with data stored on them are a security risk, even if you password-protect the laptop. Unless you take the laptop with you *everywhere*, including lugging it along to dinner instead of leaving it in the hotel room when you're on the road, the data on your laptop is vulnerable to theft. And if someone *really* wants the laptop, it doesn't matter if you take it with you. This doesn't even address the dilemma of leaving the laptop in a taxi or on a train by accident. It happens.

If the data's on the laptop and you lose the laptop, the data's gone. Obvious solution: Don't keep the data on the laptop—instead store it in the data center. But if you're accessing the data center from a remote location and working with large files (in this day of heavy-duty formatting, what file *isn't* large?), it's tempting to keep the file on the local drive while working on it remotely and then copy it back to the network when you're done with it. End result: the data's on the local drive and you're back where you started.

Information Insecurity

It's not practical to make sensitive information accessible only to people within the four walls of the office, but it's been shown again and again what happens when that information leaves the data center. In November 2007, one British government agency sent two CDs of sensitive information to another agency using interoffice mail. The two CDs, containing details such as people's names and dates of birth, spouse's and children's names, home addresses, and bank account details, were lost and have not yet been recovered. Nor is this the first time that sensitive data has been lost to a misplaced laptop or other portable media.

It's not always feasible to store sensitive information only in the data center, accessible solely via secure connection to a terminal server behind the perimeter network. Sometimes, the information must be available even when a network connection isn't. But when it is feasible, it's much more secure to keep information where it's least likely to be compromised, stolen, or lost: in the data center.

One solution to this dilemma is to keep *everything* in the data center, including the applications required to edit the confidential documents. If both the applications and the confidential data are on the network, then it's either impossible to edit the data locally (because no application for doing the editing is installed locally) or not as desirable to do so because there's no reason to download the remote file to the local computer for a more responsive experience. No sensitive data ends up on the client computer; it all stays within the boundaries of the data center.

> **Note** Given a sufficiently long distance or sufficiently slow Internet connection, the remote connection will also be slow, and if the network connection isn't totally reliable it may be frustrating as the session disconnects. As we know all too well, even high-speed networks experience some latency when you're working on one continent and the data center is on another one. But these problems apply to any remote-access scenario and have less chance of accidentally corrupting the original document by attempting to write to it over a slow connection. A disconnected session doesn't lead to data loss—it's just there waiting for its user to reconnect to it.

What if you want people to be able to edit confidential documents when they are in a secure location but not when they're accessing the corporate network from the local coffee shop? Using Terminal Services in Windows Server 2008, it's possible to set up rules for remote access that determine which applications a remote user has access to, whether or not the user has any local drives mapped, and even if it's possible to cut and paste text between local and remote applications. Security needs can determine the restrictions placed on remote access while still keeping the data easily available when it should be.

Enable Remote Work

Related to security for mobile workers is the general theme of remote work. Telecommuting is becoming more common in the workplace. Some help desk suppliers and U.S. government agencies don't even have desks for all their workers, since their workplaces are designed for most people to be working from home most of the time. Nor is telework a solely North American phenomenon. According to "IT and the Environment," a 2007 paper by the Economist Intelligence Unit, in 39 percent of western European companies, at least some people work at home at least part of the time.

But working from home has its own set of challenges, not least being the question of how the company can support the desktop environment. Home-based computers can't be easily managed by Group Policy, they can break down with no IT staff immediately available to provide assistance, and people working from home can't always readily talk through a computer-based problem with help desk staff. And how do you update an application when it's time to move from, say, Microsoft Office 2003 to Microsoft Office 2007? If you've worked remotely for even a brief span of time, you probably have experienced the advantages of mobility and the disadvantages of lack of local support. Although it's great being able to work from the coffee shop or hotel or airport lobby, it's not so great acting as your own help desk. Server-based computing helps enable remote scenarios in several ways. You don't have to worry about home users installing applications they shouldn't run on the terminal servers if you follow basic security procedures (more later on this topic). Since the applications are stored on the terminal servers, they're installed and updated there, not on the client computers. And, as discussed earlier, using Terminal Services allows the administrator to determine the kind of resource sharing the local and remote computers should do and which applications are available depending on where a user is connecting from.

Bringing Windows to PC-Unfriendly Environments

Although the client emphasis for Terminal Services in Windows Server 2008 is the full desktop, the ability to get Windows Server 2008-like capabilities out of a computer that can't run Windows Server 2008 is valid and has its devotees. One example is electronics firms. If you're making circuit boards, you make them within what's called a *clean room*, a room with no dust and which requires a time-consuming process to enter. If you need to use Windows applications in a clean room, you can't use PCs—the fans inside the case kick up dust inside the computer and spread it into the room. Additionally, it's not practical to have PCs that might need servicing in any room that takes extensive preparation to enter, as a clean room does. Therefore, you need Terminal Services to provide Windows applications to the terminals.

Thin clients are also good for environments where you want access to Windows applications but the circumstances are not PC-friendly—they've got too much dust or vibration to be good for the PC. Small terminals that can be wall-mounted or carried work better in these circumstances than PCs do. But since these small terminals have very limited memory and CPU power and no disks, you can't run Windows Vista on them. To get access to the latest operating system and applications, you need a terminal server for the terminals to connect to.

PC-less Windows environments include places such as upscale health clubs or city apartment lobbies. Management wants to attract customers by offering the convenience of a personal computer in the lobby or café but doesn't want to support computers in these locations. (Bulk can also be an issue when you're trying to squeeze five user work areas into a small counter space.) Windows terminals can connect to a terminal server and present the applications; besides, they're smaller, cooler, and more reliable than PCs that may get misconfigured.

We've heard it said that there's no point to getting thin clients because if you buy PCs you get more power for the same money. With thin clients you're not paying for the computing power—you're using very little, comparatively speaking. You're paying for the reduced administration and smaller physical footprint and energy use. This solution is not for everyone, but sometimes thin clients are a better choice than PCs.

Supporting Green Computing

One of the hot topics (no pun intended) these days is how to make companies and governments greener—how to help them use less energy. IDC, a market-research firm, says power consumption is now one of systems managers' top five concerns. Companies now spend as much as 10 percent of their technology budgets on energy, says Rakesh Kumar of Gartner, a consultancy. (Only about half of this is used to run computers; much of it goes toward cooling, since for every dollar used to power a server you spend a dollar to cool it.) Dropping power usage is a win-win situation, really—because companies have to pay for their power, using less energy means that they spend less money on power.

> **Note** A December 2007 paper from McKinsey & Company, "Reducing U.S. Greenhouse Gas Emissions: How Much at What Cost?" (*http://www.mckinsey.com/clientservice/ccsi/pdf/US_ghg_final_report.pdf*) shows the marginal costs of reducing carbon dioxide emissions. The cost of reducing the carbon emissions for combined heat and power in commercial buildings is negative. That is, it pays companies to go green.

There's a *lot* of waste in desktop-centric computing. According to IDC, average *server* utilization levels range from 15 to 30 percent. Average resource utilization rates for *PCs* have been estimated at less than 5 percent. Since you have to power the processor and memory whether you're using them or not, this represents a lot of waste. Therefore, depending on the needs of the client, there may be quite a bit of room for people accessing their desktops, or at least their applications, from a terminal server. For companies that can reasonably exchange desktop computers for Windows-based terminals, this can represent a huge savings, both in terms of the power drawn by the full desktops as well as the air-conditioning required to cool the building heated by hundreds of powerful PCs.

Terminal Services for Windows Server 2008: The Big Picture

This has been an overview of some of the ways you might apply server-based computing to meet your company's needs for supporting remote workers or PC-unfriendly environments. And there are many new features in Windows Server 2008 to help you support these scenarios specifically. This book is devoted to letting you know what's new in Terminal Services and how to use it. In this section, we'll discuss some of the features and how this version of Terminal Services differs from previous versions in ways larger than individual features.

The Changing Character of Terminal Server Usage

One Terminal Services change in Windows Server 2008 is in the usage assumptions. Windows Server 2003, for example, assumes that administrators will generally run individual servers from the corporate local area network (LAN), and probably only one or two of them, since the session brokering piece is available only in the enterprise edition. The features included in Windows Server 2008 assume the following:

- Many end users access the corporate LAN from the Internet at least some of the time.

- End users don't always log on from domain-joined computers.

- End users are more likely to run a full desktop (with some locally installed applications) than a terminal device.

- End users may work from a branch office but still are connected to the domain.

- Administrators need more application-serving capacity than a single server—they must be able to add some redundancy.

We'll introduce some Terminal Services role services here, but a technical walkthrough of these features is less important right now than understanding the business problems they're designed to solve.

Supporting Telecommuters and Mobile Workers

The way that people work in information fields has changed a great deal over the years. At one time, most information workers (the best way to describe people who need regular access to a shared pool of data to do their jobs) went to where the information was: they went to the office. When they left the office, they stopped working on anything that depended on that central pool of information. Similarly, when they were in the office, they could easily add to this central pool of information—after all, all this information is created by people—and when they left, they could not continue adding to the central pool of information.

Laptops changed this by giving telecommuters a computer they could easily take with them, but laptops still didn't have access to the central pool of information that people could access at the office. Widespread Internet access combined with the increasing use of e-mail as a personal information store gave additional access, but e-mail doesn't include *everything* your company knows—just that information included within e-mails you've sent or received.

The next stage was securely connecting to the corporate network, retrieving the information required, and then downloading it to the laptop computer. This, of course, required both broad access to high-speed networks for downloading the documents to the local computer and also for the application to be installed locally. It also meant that people needed some way for the laptop to access the data center without creating a security breach or spreading a virus on the corporate network.

Much of the industrialized world today has access to the necessary components: laptops and high-speed networks that are available both at home and in public places such as airports and hotels. The tricky problems that arise include how to regulate which computers are allowed access to the network and how to keep sensitive data off computers vulnerable to theft or loss. There's also the problem of gaining access to the data that mobile workers create while on the road. This data won't make it back to the corporate network until the road warriors get back from the trip or at least get some free time to upload all their new data to the central data pool.

Terminal Services has long held promise in supporting telecommuters and mobile workers, but the solution included with the operating system hasn't had all the tools needed to make this work. Windows Server 2008 Terminal Services changes this, introducing Terminal Services Gateway (TS Gateway). This role service enables users to securely access the corporate network—and the centralized data pool— via HTTP Secure Sockets Layer (SSL or HTTPS) from the hotel or airport or even the beach (if you can keep sand out of your laptop). When combined with RDP file signing and server authentication, TS Gateway provides secure Internet access, thus giving end users some assurance that the RDP file they receive in e-mail is a legitimate resource and not a spoofed server set up to capture their logon credentials.

> **Note** TS Gateway and SSL aren't the only ways to create a secure connection to the data center from a remote location—virtual private networks (VPNs) are another option. But TS Gateway has some advantages over VPNs, including granular access to resources, which we'll discuss in detail in Chapter 7, "Multi-Server Deployments and Securing Terminal Server Connections."

Using Public Computers

The previous section discussed personal laptops, and that's what most people will be using, but it's not reasonable to expect that people will *never* log on except from a computer that they own. For example, you may connect to the corporate terminal servers from a computer at your family's home in Tucson or from a kiosk at an Internet café in Darmstadt. In both cases, you need a way to access work resources without leaving any personal data cached on those computers. Terminal Services Web Access (TS Web Access) has features that enable you to do this.

Integrated Desktop and Remote Workspaces

Terminal Services in Windows Server 2008 doesn't require a specific client operating system to work—you can connect using clients as far back as RDP 5.2. (Previous versions of RDP aren't supported because of security improvements in RDP 5.*x*.) That said, this version of Windows Server 2008 shows a new interdependence between client and server for support-ing the multi-user experience. The new scenarios that Windows Server 2008 enables, such as single sign-on and RemoteApps, require the most recent version of the RDP client (6.1), which is supported only on Windows Vista SP1 and Windows XP SP3. This is an effort to make Terminal Services an extension of the Windows desktop, not a full replacement of it (and recognizing that this has generally been the case since Windows Terminal Services first became available). Terminal Services in Windows Server 2008 is blurring the line between desktop and terminal server.

Working from Branch Offices

Working remotely isn't a label just for those working from home or while on the road. "Remote" workers may operate in a separate office—but one with resources similar to the corporate office. In this scenario, the network is reliable, the computers are domain-joined . . . but the data center is not in the same physical location as the branch office workers, and onsite IT staffing may be minimal.

Larger Server Farms

Terminal Server deployments don't consist of just one or two servers anymore, but the tools available in Windows Server 2003 didn't really support farms. (Session Directory Server was available only on the enterprise edition.) Windows Server 2008 Terminal Services is more suited to managing access to multiple servers because it adds additional group policies for server management and the improved Session Broker in the standard edition of Windows Server 2008 for enabling end users to connect to farms rather than having to specify particular servers.

> ### Direct from the Source: Other Business Cases for Terminal Services
>
> Administrators benefit from Terminal Services, too.
>
> #### Regulatory Compliance Requirements
> For the IT department, data security and the ability to meet regulatory requirements both remain top priorities. Terminal Services helps secure an application and its data in a central location, reducing the risk of accidental data loss caused by, for example, the loss of a laptop. Key features of Terminal Services such as Terminal Services Gateway (TS Gateway) and Terminal Services RemoteApp (TS RemoteApp) help ensure that partners, or users, who do not need full access to a company network or computers can be limited to a single application, if needed.
>
> #### Complex Applications
> In an environment with complex applications such as line of business (LOB) or customized legacy software, or in situations in which large and complex applications are frequently updated but are difficult to automate, Terminal Services can help simplify the process by reducing the burden of running multiple applications across the entire environment. The client machines can access the applications they require from a central source, rather than requiring applications to be installed locally.

> ### Merger Integration or Outsourcing
>
> In the case of a merger, the affected organizations will typically need to use the same LOB applications, although they may be in a variety of configurations and versions. Additionally, organizations may also find that they are working with outsourced or partner organizations requiring access to specific LOB applications but not to the full corporate network. Rather than performing a costly deployment of the entire set of LOB applications across the extended infrastructure, these applications can be installed on a terminal server and made available to the employees and business partners who require access, when they need it.
>
> *Alex Balcanquall*
>
> *Product Manager*

Cool New Stuff for Terminal Services in Windows Server 2008

New features of Terminal Services in Windows Server 2008 do a lot to improve the end user experience. Fat clients have become really capable when it comes to display and desktop experience, and server-based computing has had to stay competitive.

Getting the *Really* Big Picture with Multi-Monitor Support

The Windows Server 2003 display looked pretty good: At a maximum display size of 1600 × 1200, support for 32-bit color, and mapped drives, it was a big improvement over Windows 2000 Server. But now, many users are accustomed to multiple monitors and types of client-side hardware that weren't common five years ago. Remote connections using RDP 6.1 can connect to a Windows Server 2008 terminal server and use a display much like the one they can get locally, including:

- Support for multiple monitors of the same resolution and oriented side by side
- Support for custom display resolutions
- Support for larger screen size (up to 4096 × 2048)

> **Note** Unfortunately, Terminal Services in Windows Server 2008 does not support the Aero Glass view that Vista does.

We'll talk more about how to configure client display settings and some things to watch out for when enabling monitor-spanning support in Chapter 4, "Creating the User Work Environment."

Broader Support for Client-Side Device Redirection

When Terminal Services was introduced, the important client-side devices needing support were keyboards and mouse devices. The next demand was for printers so that end users could print to a printer connected to the client. Local drives became a priority so that end users could copy files to and from their local drives and even save files locally from the beginning if desired.

In today's working environment, there are even more devices to support. Two important consumer devices are media players and digital cameras. If you're working in a completely remote environment, you must be able to control these devices from the remote session and to copy data to and from the remote devices. Using Windows Server 2008 Terminal Services with Remote Desktop Client (RDC) 6.1, you can map devices that use the Media Transfer Protocol (MTP) for media players and digital cameras that use the Picture Transfer Protocol (PTP).

Consumer devices aren't alone in needing support. In Windows Server 2008, support for client-side Point of Service (POS) devices is also available for retailers. We'll talk about supporting and configuring client-side device redirection in Chapter 5, "Fine-Tuning the User Experience."

Note Support for POS redirection requires that the server be an x86 computer and that the device use .NET Framework 1.1 or later.

Direct from the Source: Why Plug and Play?

Plug and Play devices are becoming the norm in Windows these days. This means that locally attached Plug and Play devices should work seamlessly during remote sessions. We introduced an infrastructure piece called Terminal Server Plug and Play Device Redirection Framework, to help redirect all those locally attached Plug and Play devices that are not already covered by existing device redirections in the Terminal Services world. The framework, coupled with simple guidelines for Plug and Play device driver writers that are published as part of the Windows Vista and Windows Server 2008 logo program, allows any third-party Plug and Play device to be available in remote sessions if the device drivers are authored correctly.

As a proof of concept, we chose to provide core support for two classes of devices: Windows Portable Devices (Media Transfer Protocol-based digital still cameras and media players) and Point of Service (POS) devices based on the Microsoft POS for the .NET Framework 1.1 stack. One key point to note is that this feature provides redirection of any logo guidelines compliant Plug and Play device regardless of its connectivity mechanism; that is, this is not just universal serial bus (USB) device redirection.

Gaurav Daga

Program Manager

Single Sign-On

Single sign-on, or having to present a password only once to use resources from your computer, is obviously good for end users. Imagine coming to work in the morning and logging into your computer. Then you click an icon and need to present credentials again. Then you click another icon and need to present credentials again. By 10 A.M., you're probably ready to just go for coffee and skip working, since productivity clearly isn't happening if you have to log on every time you start an application.

That is what *could* happen with Terminal Services without single sign-on. You come to work in the morning and log on to your computer, but you need to authenticate to the terminal server to use remote applications. Every time you connect to a terminal server, you must authenticate yourself again. If you're connecting via the Internet, you'll need to get authenticated to the gateway server that controls who's allowed to use terminal servers from outside the corporate LAN.

To avoid wasting your entire day logging on or creating a head-shaped dent in your keyboard when you bang your head on your desk, you need some mechanism to log on once and forget about it. Mercifully, you have one: Windows Server 2008 supports single sign-on for credential passing from domain-joined Windows Vista or Windows XP SP3 clients so that every time you need to present your credentials to a terminal server, it's done for you. We'll discuss how to set this up in Chapter 7.

Eliminating Printer Drivers

Printer drivers have long been the bane of the terminal services administrator's life. At first, supporting printer drivers was a gamble in which, if the driver didn't crash the terminal server, you'd won. Supporting client-side printers increased the exposure to error-prone drivers by lessening the administrator's control over the drivers installed. When supporting Windows NT drivers on the terminal servers and non-Windows NT drivers on the client (for example, when using Windows 98 as a client to a Windows 2000 Server terminal server), the drivers might not have the same name. This would require the administrator to create driver mapping files that basically say, "When the system refers to *this* driver from within the client session, *that* driver on the terminal server should be used." Otherwise, the print job would not print.

Over time, the drivers got more reliable as the problem became better understood. When both the client and terminal server were based on Windows NT technology, the driver name mismatch problem ceased to be an issue. Then Windows Server 2003 introduced a new Group Policy that permitted only user-mode drivers by default. This removed the chance of installing a poorly written kernel-mode driver that could crash the server, but still meant that terminal server administrators had to test, maintain, and support a variety of drivers for both corporate printers and mapped client printers (although some companies stopped supporting mapped client printers just to avoid the driver problems).

How It Works: Why Does It Matter Whether Drivers Are User-Mode or Kernel-Mode?

If it's not obvious to you why a policy to permit only user-mode drivers might be necessary or desirable, read on.

Every component of the Windows operating system is designed to call on memory from a particular section of memory, which is organized into blocks. The amount of memory an operating system can access depends on the addressing scheme it supports. For example, 32-bit operating systems can call on up to 4 gigabytes (GB) of memory, and this memory is normally divided into two pieces: the upper 2 GB of kernel-mode memory and the lower 2 GB of user-mode memory. *Kernel-mode* components have access to actual physical memory structures. *User-mode* components have access only to a mapped view of these structures.

It's as if the memory structures are a set of interoffice mailboxes. The kernel-mode components have access to the mailboxes themselves—the physical bins that line the wall. User-mode components don't have access to the boxes; instead they indicate that a piece of data should go into the box belonging to Kim Abercrombie or to Michael Pfeiffer. The kernel-mode component creates the mapping that identifies which physical location is associated with Kim Abercrombie and routes the data there, so that even if the boxes are shuffled or Kim gets a new mailbox, the data ends up in the right place. Similarly, if a user-mode component needs data from a location, that component doesn't know the physical location of the data, but calls on it according to its virtual data—"I need the data stored in Kim Abercrombie's mailbox." The kernel-mode component then maps Kim Abercrombie's name to a mailbox location and retrieves the data. The area of memory that a component is designed to use depends on what that component needs to do, how quickly it needs to do it, and how likely it is to have a problem doing it. Almost everything you *see* happening on a computer occurs in user mode: applications open, windows move, characters appear on the screen as you type, and so forth. Operations running in user mode are protected from each other because they write to virtual locations, not to physical ones. Kernel-mode components ensure that these operations don't write to the same physical locations. For this reason, user mode is also called *protected mode*. If an application running in user mode crashes, it does not affect other applications.

Kernel-mode components are slightly faster than user-mode components because they don't have to translate virtual memory addresses to physical ones; however, they are more vulnerable to error. (That said, "slightly faster" in this context is not a difference that you can detect as an administrator or end user.) Kernel-mode references the physical memory structures shared among all components on the same computer, so it's possible that two applications could attempt to store information in the same memory space. When this happens, the components crash and it may crash the entire operating system. Printer drivers running in kernel-mode on a terminal server, therefore, put not just one person's workspace at risk but that of everyone using that same computer. Although printer drivers are more reliable on terminal servers than they used to be, it's best to use only user mode drivers. If you absolutely must use kernel-mode drivers, you must test them before putting them into production.

Technically speaking, the user-mode drivers are only partially user-mode, or at least are not able to do all their work from within user mode. They still communicate with a kernel-mode component that puts the data in the physical location where it must go. However, if the user-mode piece fails, this does not affect the kernel-mode area of memory.

Memory layout is important to terminal servers, so we'll be discussing this more in Chapter 2, "Planning the Terminal Server Ecosystem."

Another problem with previous iterations of printing was deciding which printers should be mapped to the remote session. If printer mapping was enabled, then all the client printers would map to the terminal server, regardless of whether or not this was appropriate. Mapping all these printers could also be time-consuming, not to mention increasing the number of drivers that needed to be installed on a terminal server.

Terminal Services in Windows Server 2008 addresses these problems in several ways. First, and simplest, a Group Policy allows administrators to map only the client's *default* printer to a terminal session. Second, Easy Print technology avoids the driver problem for Windows Vista clients running Remote Desktop Connection 6.1. Basically, Easy Print allows end users to print from a remote session without having to install any drivers on the terminal session at all. The remote session gets printer settings from the client's computer and even makes calls to the client-side GUI to show the driver configuration panes for the drivers.

To learn more about how Easy Print works and how to configure your system to use it or disable it, see Chapter 5.

Direct from the Field: Easy Print Is Easy

No matter how users traditionally got their applications, printing and printer drivers have long been the bane of Terminal Services administrators. The pain of keeping the right drivers on the right servers—while hoping and praying that none of them would cause the dreaded blue screen of death—has kept many an admin awake at night. With previous versions of Terminal Services, it was critical that the device driver on the server matched the one installed on the client. With driver names all over the place, ensuring that one-to-one mapping was correct often ended up in failure.

With Vista and Server 2008, a big portion of this pain goes away. In Server 2008's Terminal Services, the administrator no longer needs to install drivers onto the Terminal Server. This functionality works due to the incorporation of the new XPS print path built into Vista. That print path, combined with the ability to redirect the printer device down to the client means that the user can utilize their local print drivers to print to remote printers. Because the XPS print path is available by default on every Vista client, print jobs can be redirected with a maximum of confidence they'll accurately print using the client's driver.

What does this look like to the client? When a client uses Vista to connect to a Server 2008 Terminal Server and clicks to view their print properties, they'll see the same interface for printer properties they've always seen with their local driver. In fact, the UI used to configure that printer is actually run from the client machine. Clicking print creates an XPS print job on the server that is pushed down to the client where it is printed via their local connection.

Now obviously there are going to be some environments where this isn't the optimum configuration. If the print server is in network proximity to the Terminal Server instead of the client, then that job will need to traverse the network twice. Citrix has a built-in mechanism for configuring local printing on the Citrix server for these sorts of scenarios. But for most configurations, the printer is usually located right next to the client and away from the Terminal Server. So, most of us will appreciate this new feature.

Greg Shields, MCSE: Security, CCEA

"On the Server Side of Terminal Services," MCP Magazine, *January 2008*

Used with permission

Terminal Services RemoteApp

The last of the new user-experience features we'll mention is RemoteApp. Historically, native Terminal Services has been a way of "remoting" an entire desktop, not individual applications. *Remoting* a desktop involves removing extra icons from the desktop to avoid confusing or distracting users. It means that the applications running in the remote session are not well integrated with the applications running locally, that the end user needs to remember whether an application is running locally or remotely.

In previous versions of Terminal Server, it was possible to make an RDP file point to only a single application, ending the remote session when the end user closed the application. In practice, this approach had several downfalls:

- The application ran in a frame for a remote session and didn't look like an application running locally.

- The application's icon in the taskbar was for a remote session, not for the application itself, meaning that users running more than one application in this manner couldn't tell their application windows apart when minimized.

- Each application displayed in this way had its own session. Therefore, the terminal server had to maintain an entire session for each individual application presented this way, increasing its memory overhead. It also meant that every application opened in this way had its own copy of the user's terminal server profile open, leading to lost changes to the profile.

- Administrators had to create and maintain RDP files for these individual applications with the connection name hard-coded into the file. If an application was updated, then the RDP file would need to be updated.

In short, there's a reason why not many people displayed single applications from a pre-Windows Server 2008 terminal server.

Windows Server 2008 introduces RemoteApps for the Terminal Services platform for use with RDP 6.1. RemoteApps display single applications, but without a lot of the drawbacks of the workaround of creating an RDP file intended to show only a single application:

- The application has the same title bar that it would if running locally and is identified in the taskbar by its name. This makes it easy to find and it integrates well with local applications.

- All applications launched from the same terminal server share the same session, reducing the strain on the server and allowing all applications to use the same copy of the user profile.

- RemoteApps can be integrated with Terminal Services Web Access (TS Web Access) to display application icons in a browser and create the connection settings on demand so that they'll never be stale.

You can learn more about RemoteApps and how to use them with TS Web Access in Chapter 6, "Installing and Publishing Applications."

Terminal Services Roles in Windows Server 2008

Another way that Terminal Services in Windows Server 2008 differs from previous versions is that the role is designed to address many more issues than the two addressed in previous versions. Previously, Terminal Services was the answer to the questions, "How can I run these applications on a shared server and how can I license access to this shared server?" Now, it's broader than that. Terminal Services answers questions such as:

- How do I host applications for many people to use at the same time?

- How do I present these applications in a Web browser to ensure that my end users have the most current client connection settings?

- How do I easily provide access to redundant shared servers?

- How do I make the shared servers accessible to people working from locations outside the office?

- How can I secure remote access to shared servers located on my local area network?

Each of these questions is answered by one of the five role services of Terminal Services in Windows Server 2008 (see Figure 1-1).

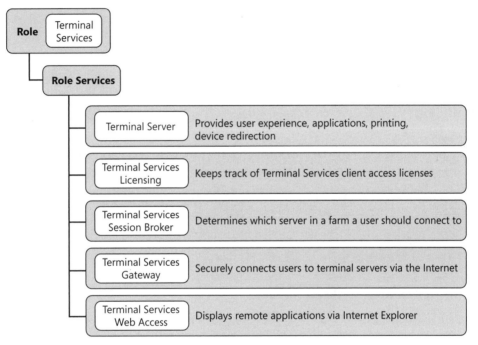

FIGURE 1-1 The Terminal Services role has five role services.

Read on to learn more about the five role services of Terminal Services:

- Terminal Server

- TS Licensing

- TS Session Broker

- TS Gateway

- TS Web Access

Terminal Server

As in earlier versions, the Terminal Server remains the core piece of the Terminal Services architecture. At the end of the day, all the applications run here: Users connect to the terminal servers and run applications that have been installed on them.

A terminal server is different from other types of Windows servers in several ways. Fundamentally, it works a lot more like a workstation than a server.

For example, other server roles are designed to serve one general purpose, such as handle e-mail or database queries. Their priorities are clear: Whatever is at the foreground of that server's purpose gets the lion's share of the processor. A shared server is different. Many people are using it at the same time, so it can't just assume that whichever application is in the foreground is the one that should get all the processing time—which foreground of the 40 or so sessions should it pick? Therefore, all user processes on a terminal server have the same priority so that they share the processor more or less evenly among all remote users.

End users connect to a terminal server via an RDP file that stores connection information for the server or its farm, or via TS Web Access that displays application icons in a browser to quickly create an RDP file. When a user launches a remote session, it's protected from other remote sessions running on that computer. End users can't see each other's sessions. They may have an impact on each other inadvertently (for example, by using demanding applications that take processor cycles or memory away from other users) but there's no security risk in having multiple people running sessions on the same terminal server.

Terminal servers have a heavy workload supporting all the remote client sessions, so it's generally best to reserve terminal servers only for that use.

Terminal Services Web Access

Terminal Services Web Access (TS Web Access) integrates with Internet Information Services (IIS) to display selected icons of published applications in a portal displayed in Internet Explorer. A user authorizes against the portal and can see the application icons. When he or she clicks an icon, it creates and launches a RemoteApp application in much the same way it would if the RDP file were stored on the end user's computer.

TS Web Access is a role service to the Terminal Services role that lets you make RemoteApp programs and is also a link to the terminal server desktop, available to users from Internet Explorer. Additionally, TS Web Access enables users to connect from a Web browser to the remote desktop of any server or client computer where they have the appropriate access.

With TS Web Access, users can visit a Web site (either from the Internet or from an intranet) to access a list of available RemoteApp programs. When a user starts a RemoteApp program, a Terminal Services session is started on the Windows Server 2008–based terminal server that hosts the RemoteApp program. The TS Web Access server does not launch the application. As shown in Figure 1-2, it just displays the application icon, creates the RDP file for that application when the end user double-clicks that icon (1), and then passes the RDP file to the end user to launch the application from the terminal server (2). RemoteApps and desktops launched via TS Web Access do not display in the browser but in their own windows (3), and are independent of the browser window.

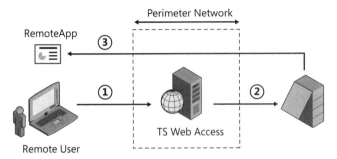

FIGURE 1-2 TS Web Access displays application icons in a browser for the convenience of end users.

TS Web Access has many benefits, including the following:

■ Users can access RemoteApp programs from a Web site over the Internet or from an intranet. To start a RemoteApp program, they just double-click the program icon.

■ If a user starts more than one RemoteApp program through TS Web Access and the programs are running on the same terminal server, the RemoteApp programs run within the same Terminal Services session. This keeps only a single copy of the user's profile open and reduces overhead on the terminal server.

■ By using TS Web Access, there is much less administrative overhead than that required to maintain and distribute RDP files for connecting to a terminal server farm. You can easily deploy programs from a central location and don't have to worry about ensuring that RDP files containing connection information are up to date. Additionally, programs are running on a terminal server and not on the client computer so they are easier to maintain.

■ TS Web Access includes Remote Desktop Web Connection, which enables users to connect remotely to the desktop of any computer where they have Remote Desktop access from the TS Web Access portal.

■ TS Web Access works with minimal configuration, but the TS Web Access Web page includes a customizable Web Part, which can be incorporated into a customized Web page or a Microsoft SharePoint site.

We'll talk more about how to configure and use TS Web Access—and what its limitations are—in Chapter 6.

Terminal Services Session Broker

For the sake of redundancy, it's good practice to have more than one terminal server hosting your remote application set and to load-balance your servers. That allows you to spread the user load out and eliminates the possibility that one server could go down and take out your ability to serve centralized applications. Trouble is, connections are fundamentally made to individual terminal servers, not to groups of them—that is, at the end of the day the final connection is made to the terminal server named TS01 or whatever other original name you've given it. But if your RDP files include the names of individual terminal servers, they won't be load-balanced. Nor will they be flexible enough to determine that a user really should be connecting to another terminal server when launching a new application, because he or she already has an application open there.

Terminal Services Session Broker (TS Session Broker) is responsible for determining which terminal server an incoming connection should be connected to when the user connects to a farm, as shown in Figure 1-3. TS Session Broker makes this decision according to several criteria, including:

- Which farm the incoming request was attempting to connect to.

- Whether or not the person making the connection request already has an existing (active or disconnected) session on that farm.

- Which terminal server has the lowest number of sessions.

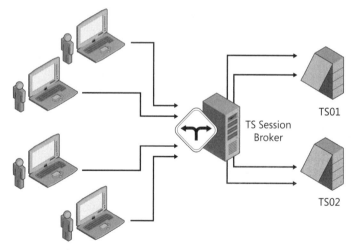

FIGURE 1-3 The Terminal Services Session Broker routes incoming connections to the appropriate server.

The TS Session Broker includes only one form of load balancing—keeping track of how many sessions terminal servers have—but it can be integrated with third-party load balancers that support other criteria such as processor or memory load, time of day, application, or others. We'll talk more about how to use TS Session Broker in Chapter 7.

Terminal Services Gateway

In the dark days before Windows Server 2008, if you wanted to connect to a terminal server from the outside world using only the tools in the box, you might have considered opening port 3389 (the port that Remote Desktop Protocol [RDP] listens on) so that the terminal server could accept incoming connections. Most people didn't do this because of the security hole it opened up via the additional port.

One of the role services of Terminal Services in Windows Server 2008 is Terminal Services Gateway (TS Gateway). TS Gateway enables authorized remote users to connect to resources on an internal corporate or private network, from any Internet-connected device, whether originally part of the domain or a public kiosk. As shown in Figure 1-4, the network resources can be terminal servers supporting full desktops, terminal servers running RemoteApp programs, or computers with Remote Desktop enabled. In other words, people accessing the corporate network from the Internet can use full desktops, individual applications, or even their own desktop computers—it all depends on what the administrator has set up.

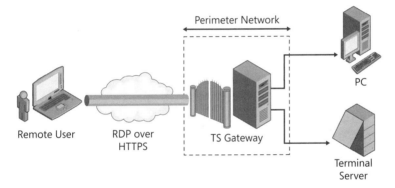

FIGURE 1-4 Terminal Services Gateway provides secure access to the corporate network from the Internet.

TS Gateway uses RDP over HTTPS to establish a secure encrypted connection between remote users on the Internet and the internal network on which their applications run; this requires only port 443 to be open (which it already is for secure Internet connectivity). By doing this, TS Gateway does the following:

- Enables remote users to connect to internal network resources over the Internet by using an encrypted connection, without needing to configure virtual private network (VPN) connections.

- Provides a comprehensive security configuration model that enables you to control access to specific internal network resources.

- Provides a point-to-point RDP connection that can be limited, rather than allowing remote users access to all internal network resources.

- Enables most remote users to connect to internal network resources that are hosted behind firewalls in private networks and across network address translators (NATs). With TS Gateway, you do not need to perform additional configuration for the TS Gateway server or clients for this scenario.

The TS Gateway Manager snap-in console enables you to configure authorization policies to define conditions that must be met for remote users to connect to internal network resources. For example, you can specify:

- Who can connect to network resources (in other words, the user or computer groups who can connect).

- Which network resources (computer groups) users can connect to.

- If device and disk redirection is allowed.

- Whether clients must use smart card authentication or password authentication, or whether they can use either method.

You can configure TS Gateway servers and Terminal Services clients to use Network Access Protection (NAP) to further enhance security. NAP is a health policy creation, enforcement, and remediation technology included in Windows XP Service Pack 3 (Windows XP SP3), Windows Vista, and Windows Server 2008. Using NAP, system administrators can enforce health requirements, which can include software requirements, security update requirements, required computer configurations, and other settings.

> **Note** Computers running Windows Server 2008 cannot be used as NAP clients when TS Gateway enforces NAP. Only computers running Windows XP SP3 and Windows Vista can be used as NAP clients when TS Gateway enforces NAP.

You can also use TS Gateway server with Microsoft Internet Security and Acceleration (ISA) Server to enhance security. In this scenario, you can host TS Gateway servers in a private network rather than a perimeter network and host ISA Server in the perimeter network. The SSL connection between the Terminal Services client and ISA Server can be terminated at the Internet-facing ISA Server.

The TS Gateway Manager snap-in console provides tools to help you monitor TS Gateway connection status, health, and events. With TS Gateway Manager, you can specify events (such as unsuccessful connection attempts to the TS Gateway server) that you want to monitor.

TS Gateway can be used with just a terminal server farm and RDP files stored on client computers or with TS Web Access. Combined with TS Web Access, you can set up a remote workspace that presents a Web site with the application icons and then makes sure that the person connecting or the computer they're connecting from meets the TS Gateway rules.

TS Gateway uses few resources and can support hundreds of incoming users, so it can safely be combined with other roles that may be in the perimeter network.

Terminal Services Licensing

The Terminal Services Licensing (TS Licensing) role service is responsible for keeping track of who has a license to use the terminal server. Not who's authorized to use the terminal server—Active Directory user rights and/or Terminal Services Gateway make that call, depending at what level the administrator is authorizing this connection. TS Licensing is the license management system that enables terminal servers to obtain and manage Terminal Services client access licenses (TS CALs) for devices and users that are connecting to a terminal server.

> **Note** TS Licensing supports terminal servers that run Windows Server 2008 as well as terminal servers running Windows Server 2003 or Windows Server 2000. The operating system supports two concurrent connections to remotely administer a computer, so you do not need a license server for these connections.

We'll talk more about the details of TS Licensing in Chapter 3, "Installing the Core Terminal Server Environment," but the basic story is this: The terminal server determines if the user or the computer connecting to it has a valid license. If it does, then the terminal server grants the connection. If it does not, then the terminal server attempts to contact a license server to see if a license for that device or user is available. The license server then either allocates a license to the device or edits the properties of the user's account in Active Directory to show that a license has been used. If the terminal server cannot connect to a TS Licensing server, it will issue a temporary license if the terminal server is within its grace period. This temporary license will only be valid for 120 days.

Servers supporting the TS Licensing role maintain a database that tracks how TS CALs have been issued. For per-device TS CALs, the license is assigned to a computer. For per-user licenses, the license is not actually assigned but its usage is tracked.

TS Licensing is a low-impact service, requiring very little CPU or memory for regular operations. Memory usage is less than 10 megabytes (MB). Its hard disk requirements are small, even for a significant number of clients: The license database grows in increments of 5 MB for every 6,000 TS CALs issued. The license server is only active when a terminal server is requesting a TS CAL, and its impact on server performance is very low, even in high-load scenarios. Therefore, in smaller deployments, the TS Licensing role service may be installed on the same computer as the Terminal Server role service. In larger deployments, the TS Licensing role will often be on a separate computer.

We'll talk more about TS Licensing in Chapter 3.

Understanding the Windows Server 2008 TS Environment

The Terminal Services role doesn't exist in a vacuum. Several roles help to support the various role services of Terminal Services, and without them, the solution doesn't work. In addition to the core Terminal Services role services and their relationship with each other, it's important to understand their relationship with other Windows Server roles. This section covers what these roles are and how they support Terminal Services functionality.

What are the roles and how do they fit together? How do they fit with the other non-TS parts of the Windows infrastructure (IIS, certificates, Active Directory, etc.)? This is a system architecture description, not a deployment guide.

The Client Connection

Obvious, yes, but still worth looking at: The way the client interacts with the role services of Terminal Services defines what the user experience will be.

The fundamental relationship between client and server has three parts: the RDC client, the RDP connection, and the server:

> **Note** Why the distinction between RDP and RDC? RDP is the Remote Desktop Protocol, the protocol that passes user input and application output between client and server. RDC is the Remote Desktop Connection, the client component that initiates and manages the RDP connection.

- The RDC client component initiates the connection to the server and receives the data that the server sends to it.

- The server component interacts with the core operating system and takes the information received (e.g., sounds being produced, bitmaps being displayed), converts it to RDP commands, and serializes it to be passed to the client.

- The protocol enables the connection between the client and the server; it defines the kind of information that is passed between them via virtual channels.

In short, the client requests the connection, the server formats the calls to the applications and operating system in a way that the client (or server, depending on which way the information flow is working for a particular transaction) can understand, and RDP passes let the user communicate with the applications on the server as though they were running locally.

Virtual channels are bi-directional connection streams provided through RDP. They establish a data pipe between the RDC client and the terminal server to pass specific kinds of information, such as device redirection or sound, between client and server. Virtual channels are a way to extend the functionality of RDP in Windows 2000 and are also used by some features of Terminal Services, such as device and sound redirection.

But a lot has changed since Windows 2000 Server, and one of the components that's changed is that the 32 virtual channels originally made available with RDP 5.1 aren't enough anymore. More kinds of data are now available, and it's clear that there may be more not yet considered. Additionally, virtual channels had a problem: They were created at the beginning of the connection and torn down at the end. If you added a device while using the RDP client, it couldn't use virtual channels unless you terminated the connection and then reconnected.

 Note Terminating a connection ended it completely on the server. A disconnected session could still be connected to.

Therefore, Terminal Services in Windows Server 2008 supports *dynamic channels*, virtual channels that the client creates on demand and then shuts down when it's done with them. If you're curious about the interfaces to make dynamic virtual channels work for you (or how they work at all), see the section titled "New Functionality for Terminal Services Partners" later in this chapter.

Authenticating Servers and Client Machines with Certificates

One of the curious things about Terminal Services is the trust required between client and server. Obviously, the server has to trust the client, since the server is a partial porthole to the corporate network. But the client has to trust the server as well. The client is providing the user name and password for the corporate network, so it's important that the server the client is connecting to is a legitimate terminal server and not a rogue server set up to steal logon credentials.

To ensure that a client is who it says it is and a server is who it says it is, you can install a certificate on the server and on the client. To do this, you'll need a Certificate Server to manage the certificates, or you'll need to purchase certificates from a public Certificate Authority.

Note All terminal servers in the same farm will use the same certificate. Today, it's the only way to make them able to authenticate themselves the same way to the client.

Displaying RemoteApps for Terminal Services Web Access

Terminal Services doesn't have a Web component for displaying applications in a portal. To make TS Web Access work, you'll need to set up an IIS server to host the site displaying the portal.

Updating User and Computer Settings

Active Directory is such an obvious choice for a support role that you may not have thought of it, but it's crucial to a functioning centralized computing infrastructure in several ways—not all of which you may have expected. Active Directory manages:

- The group policies that configure terminal servers and the user sessions running on them.

- Whether or not a user has the right to connect to a terminal server.

- The process of showing that a user has consumed a per-user TS CAL.

New Functionality for Terminal Services Partners

It's crucial to understand that Terminal Services is not just a product—although it's definitely that—but it's also a development platform for both ISVs and consultants creating custom solutions. Given that, this section will explain the functionality Windows Server 2008 Terminal Services offers for customization in the form of public interfaces.

> **Note** Public interfaces (also known as application programming interfaces, or APIs) are interfaces that are, well, publicly available and documented on MSDN so that consultants and ISVs can easily make use of them. Private interfaces are not documented. The main difference is supportability. A private interface may change at any time if required by the people who developed it (in this case, Microsoft). An API won't change without notice. In contrast, if you built on private interfaces, you'd never know when the tool you'd worked so hard to create would break due to a code change in the operating system. Even if you had the option to build solutions based on private interfaces, it would be better to build on the public APIs than on private ones.

Terminal Services APIs

Strictly speaking, APIs for terminal services aren't new. The first set of public interfaces Microsoft made available were the Windows Terminal Server (WTS) interfaces, first introduced in Service Pack 4 for Windows Server NT 4.0 Terminal Server Edition, and made public in Windows 2000 Server. They've been around for a long time and are the basis for the Terminal Services command-line tools such as Qwinsta.exe and Query.exe. There are four groups of WTS APIs:

- **Session Administration**   Used for enumerating and managing sessions and processes on a terminal server. They also allow you to connect to other terminal servers in the domain.

- **Client/Server Communication**   Use Terminal Services virtual channels to communicate between client and server components of an application on two different computers.

- **Virtual Channels**   Used for enhancing client/server applications in a Terminal Services environment.

- **User Configuration**   Used for setting and retrieving Terminal Services–specific user configuration information.

Session Administration APIs

Session Administration APIs really haven't changed since the WTS APIs first became available; Table 1-1 references them and their functions. If you've used Terminal Services for a while, you may recognize the functionality from the command-line tools and Terminal Services Manager.

TABLE 1-1 WTS APIs in Windows Server 2008

API	Description	Used By
WTSDisconnectSession	Disconnects the client from a specified session. The session remains active and the user can log on again to connect to the same session.	Tsdiscon; Disconnect operation of Terminal Services Manager.
WTSEnumerateSessions	Returns a list of sessions on the specified Terminal Server.	Query session; Session tab of Terminal Services Manager.
WTSEnumerateProcesses	Returns a list of processes on the specified Terminal Server.	Query process; Process tab of Terminal Services Manager.
WTSLogoffSession	Logs off the specified session.	
WTSQuerySessionInformation	Returns information about the specified session on the specified Terminal Server.	Query session; Session tab of Terminal Services Manager.
WTSSendMessage	Shows a message box on the client display of a specified session or sessions.	Msg; Send Message function of Terminal Services Manager.
WTSShutdownSystem	Shuts down and optionally restarts a specified Terminal Server.	Used to be associated with tsshutdn, but that command is no longer available.
WTSTerminateProcess	Terminates a specified process on a specified Terminal Server.	Tskill; Processes tab of Terminal Services Manager.
WTSVirtualChannelOpen	Opens a handle to the server end of a specified virtual channel. For more information about virtual channels, see "The Client Connection" in this chapter.	
WTSWaitSystemEvent	Waits for an event, such as the creation of a client session or a user logging on to the Terminal Server.	

Client/Server Communication APIs

The main client/server need in interfaces from a Terminal Services perspective is ensuring that communication is established between the correct instance of the client running on the terminal server and the back-end server. The server component may also use public interfaces to send messages to the client. See Table 1-2 for the function and interfaces that enable these capabilities.

TABLE 1-2 APIs Enabling Client/Server Communication in a Terminal Services Environment

API/Function	Description	Used For
ProcessIdToSessionId	Maps the PID of the client component to a specific session.	Used by the client component of a client-server application to get the session ID so it can pass this information to the server component. The server component can then use this information to set up a private communications channel.
WTSQuerySessionInformation	Returns information about the specified session on the specified Terminal Server.	In this case, used by the server component to retrieve additional information about the client.
WTSSendMessage	Shows a message box on the client display of a specified session or sessions.	In this case, may be used by the server component to send a message to the client component.

Virtual Channel APIs

The virtual channel APIs listed in Table 1-3 are most likely to be used by developers, not terminal server consultants creating scripted solutions. The ones listed here are for static channels that are created at the beginning of a session and torn down at the end of it. Terminal Services in Window Server 2008 also supports dynamic virtual channels, which may be created and destroyed during the course of the session to accommodate changes to the environment (such as a client-side device being plugged in). Dynamic virtual channels are supported by the IWTSPlugin interface used to set up and take down the virtual channels.

TABLE 1-3 Virtual Channel APIs

API	Description
WTSVirtualChannelClose	Closes an open virtual channel handle.
WTSVirtualChannelPurgeInput	Purges all queued input data sent from the client to the server on a specific virtual channel.
WTSVirtualChannelPurgeOutput	Purges all queued output data sent from the server to the client on a specific virtual channel.
WTSVirtualChannelQuery	Returns information about a specified virtual channel.
WTSVirtualChannelRead	Reads data from the server end of a virtual channel.

TABLE 1-3 Virtual Channel APIs

API	Description
WTSVirtualChannelWrite	Writes data to the server end of a virtual channel.
VirtualChannelInit	Registers the names of the virtual channels to be used by the client and provides a VirtualChannelInitEvent callback function through which Terminal Services notifies the client about events that affect the client connection.
VirtualChannelOpen	Opens the client end of a specified virtual channel and provides a path through which Terminal Services notifies the client about events that affect the virtual channel.
VirtualChannelWrite	Writes data to a virtual channel. Terminal Services sends this data to the server end of the virtual channel where the server will read the data.
VirtualChannelClose	Closes a virtual channel.

User Configuration APIs

The WTS_CONFIG_CLASS configures session properties for many session settings (e.g., drive redirection, whether or not the client's default printer becomes the default printer for the session, and the settings determining what happens if the session is disconnected), establishing them on a user basis instead of a per-server basis. To *set* these properties, use IADsTSUserEx.

Windows Management Instrumentation

This isn't really the place for an exhaustive primer on Windows Management Instrumentation (WMI), but a little background is helpful. If you're completely new to WMI, you may want to study it more completely before attempting to use these interfaces for Terminal Services management. The "Windows Management Instrumentation" page on Microsoft's MSDN site (currently at *http://msdn2.microsoft.com/en-us/library/aa394582(VS.85).aspx*) is a good place to start learning about WMI.

WMI is essentially a way of describing a computer, both in hardware (like network cards, hard disks) and in software (including services) terms. At a high level, you can describe the items in a computer in terms of classes such as "hard disks" or "TS Gateway servers." At a lower level, you can get more specific about the individual instances of those hard disks or a connection to one of those TS Gateway servers.

Strictly speaking, support for WMI isn't new to Windows Server 2008 either. But although Terminal Services in Windows Server 2003 included some WMI objects for managing the Terminal Services environment, Windows Server 2008 added many more, including entirely new classes for TS Licensing, TS Gateway, and RemoteApps. The following sections and tables provide a quick reference to show you what the classes are for and what's new in Windows Server 2008. If you're interested in more details about how to use these classes, MSDN documents all of them. But for now, it's worth reading through the tables to get an idea of what you can do with these interfaces. Where applicable in this book, we'll show you how to do scripting.

> **Note** Although WMI has historically been used through scripting languages such as VBScript, we find it to be more accessible through Windows PowerShell. This also gives you the ability to combine WMI interfaces with the built-in functionality of Windows PowerShell.

Terminal Server Configuration Classes

There are no new Terminal Server configuration classes in Windows Server 2008. As you can see in Table 1-4, however, there are quite a few changes to the ones that exist. In particular, there's the new ability to determine the source of a configuration setting—the server itself or a group policy applied to it. The Session Directory class also has many more methods and properties in Windows Server 2008 than it did in Windows Server 2003.

TABLE 1-4 Terminal Services Configuration Classes in Windows Server 2008 and Changes from Windows Server 2003

WMI Class	Description	Changes Since Windows Server 2003
Win32_TerminalService	The *Win32_TerminalService* class is a subclass of the *Win32_Service* class and inherits all its properties and methods. *Win32_TerminalService* also represents the *Element* property of the *Win32_TerminalServiceToSetting* association.	None
Win32_TSSessionDirectory	Defines the configuration for *Win32_TSSessionDirectorySetting*, including properties such as *Session Directory store* and *Cluster Name*.	This class didn't have much to do in Windows Server 2003, so there are many changes since WS03, including the new methods *GetCurrentRedirectable Addresses*, *SetCurrentRedirectable Addresses*, *GetRedirectable Addresses*, *PingSessionDirectory*, *SetLoadBalancingState*, and *SetServerWeight*. All the related properties are also new to Windows Server 2008.

TABLE 1-4 Terminal Services Configuration Classes in Windows Server 2008 and Changes from Windows Server 2003

WMI Class	Description	Changes Since Windows Server 2003
Win32_TerminalServiceSetting	Defines the configuration for *TerminalServerSetting*, including properties such as *TerminalServerMode*, *Licensing*, and *ActiveDesktop*. Other properties included are *Permissions Capability*, *Deletion of Temporary folders*, and *per-session Temporary folders*.	This class has several new properties: *LimitedUserSessions*, *PossibleLicensingTypes*, *SessionBrokerDrainMode*, and several policy source properties for determining whether the source of a particular configuration is Group Policy or a local server configuration. It also supports several new methods, including *CreateWinStation*, *PingLicenseServer*, and *UpdateDirectConnectLicenseServer*.
Win32_Terminal	Associates a *TerminalSetting* and its several configuration setting classes in this table such as: *General, Logon, Session, Environment, Remote Control, Client, Network Adapter,* and *Permission*.	The *Create* and *Delete* methods for this class are new in Windows Server 2008.
Win32_TSGeneralSetting	Defines properties such as *Protocol, Transport, Comment, Windows Authentication,* and *Encryption Level*.	Support for the *SetSecurityLayer* method was added in Windows Server 2003 SP1; support for the *SetUserAuthenticationRequired* is new in Windows Server 2008.
Win32_TSLogonSetting	Defines properties such as *ClientLogonInfoPolicy, UserName, Domain,* and *Password*.	*ClientLogonInfoPolicy* is not used in Windows Server 2003 but is in Windows Server 2008. Several policy source properties for determining whether the source of a particular configuration is Group Policy or a local server configuration are also new in Windows Server 2008.
Win32_TSSessionSetting	Defines properties such as the time limit policy for connections and session limits for active, idle, and disconnected sessions.	Several policy source properties for determining whether the source of a particular configuration is Group Policy or a local server configuration are new in Windows Server 2008.
Win32_TSEnvironmentSetting	Defines properties such as initial program policy, initial program path, start in, and client wallpaper.	Several policy source properties for determining whether the source of a particular configuration is Group Policy or a local server configuration are new in Windows Server 2008.

TABLE 1-4 Terminal Services Configuration Classes in Windows Server 2008 and Changes from Windows Server 2003

WMI Class	Description	Changes Since Windows Server 2003
Win32_TSRemoteControlSetting	Defines properties such as *Remote Control* policy and level of control.	Several policy source properties for determining whether the source of a particular configuration is Group Policy or a local server configuration are new in Windows Server 2008.
Win32_TSClientSetting	Defines properties such as *Connection* policy, Windows printer mapping, PNP redirection, and COM port mapping.	The *PNPRedirection* property is new to Windows Server 2008, as are several policy source properties for determining whether the source of a particular configuration is Group Policy or a local server configuration.
Win32_TSNetworkAdapterSetting	Defines properties such as LAN adapter and maximum number of connections.	Quite a bit of information about network adapters is newly available in Windows Server 2008, including *DeviceIDList, NetworkAdapterList,* and *NetworkAdapterLanaID.* The property determining the policy source for the maximum connections count is also new.
Win32_TSNetworkAdapterList Setting	Enumerates the list of network adapters configurable for Win32_Terminal based on the Terminal Protocol and Transport. The properties include: *TerminalProtocol, Transport, NetworkAdapterID,* and *Description.*	None
Win32_TSPermissionsSetting	Represents an association between a Win32_Terminal and its configuration settings (Win32_TSAccount). Contains properties for adding accounts to defined permission sets and restoring default permissions.	The *StringSecurityDescriptor* and *DenyAdminPermissionForCustomization* properties are new to Windows Server 2008, as is a policy source property for determining whether the source of a particular configuration is Group Policy or a local server configuration.
Win32_TSAccount	Defines properties such as SID, allowed and denied permissions.	None

Terminal Services Session Broker Classes

Although TS Session Broker has a new name and new functionality in Windows Server 2008, its WMI interfaces described in Table 1-5 are similar to those for Session Directory in Windows Server 2003. One obvious difference is nomenclature; for example, in Windows Server 2003, a collection of servers is called a *cluster*, and in Windows Server 2008 a collection of like servers managed by a Session Broker is called a *farm*. Additionally, some properties defined in *Win32_SessionDirectoryServer* are not supported in Windows Server 2003.

> **Note** When referring to a farm in this book, we mean a set of *homogenous* terminal servers that are load-balanced. You can safely assume that although the hardware may differ slightly, all the terminal servers in a farm are assumed to have the same configuration and application set.

TABLE 1-5 WMI Interfaces for Session Broker in Windows Server 2008

Class	Description	Functionality
Win32_SessionDirectoryCluster	Represents a farm in TS Session Broker.	Gets the name of the terminal server farm, how many servers are in it, and whether or not the farm is in single-session mode (allows users to have only a single session, so that if they reconnect while having a disconnected session they will be reconnected to that session).
Win32_SessionDirectoryServer	Represents a TS Session Broker server.	Describes the current state of the Session Broker, including its name, IP address, number of sessions pending reconnections, the number of sessions, and server weight.
Win32_SessionDirectorySession	Represents a TS Session Broker session.	Describes the session itself, including the session ID, user name, and domain name of the end user with the connection, the time when the session was created (and disconnected, if applicable), and the appearance of the session (color depth and resolution).

The remaining classes are all new to Windows Server 2008.

> **Note** WTS interfaces for extending TS Session Broker capability are also available, although only useful if you plan to build extensions to TS Session Broker (not for managing what's there). See *http://msdn.microsoft.com/en-us/library/cc644953(VS.85).aspx* for more details.

Terminal Services Gateway Classes

The TS Gateway classes shown in Table 1-6 allow you to control the connections, policies, and TS Gateway configurations and relationships. The Functionality column doesn't include a complete list of all properties and methods, but it is representative of what that particular class is for.

TABLE 1-6 WMI Classes for TS Gateway

Class	Description	Functionality
Win32_TSGatewayConnection	Represents a connection from a client computer to a Terminal Services Gateway (TS Gateway) server.	Checks connection status and selectively terminates sessions. Identifies information about the connection, including how long it's been active and the farm or server the end user is connected to.
Win32_TSGatewayConnection AuthorizationPolicy	Represents a Terminal Services connection authorization policy (TS CAP).	Defines which user groups are allowed to make connections and the authorization methods open to them (e.g., smartcard, password). It also defines the limitations on the connection, such as whether or not clipboard mapping is permitted. A TS Gateway can have more than one CAP, so this class also allows you to assign unique names to the CAPs.
Win32_TSGatewayLoadBalancer	Represents a set of TS Gateway load-balancing servers.	Manages TS Gateway load-balancing membership. Adds, deletes, or queries load-balancing members.
Win32_TSGatewayRADIUSServer	Describes and manages a RADIUS server managing the CAPs.	Changes RADIUS server priority or name, edits shared secret information.
Win32_TSGatewayResource AuthorizationPolicy	Represents a Terminal Services resource authorization policy (TS RAP).	Edits the TS RAP name or description, adds user groups to or deletes user groups from it. Also allows you to create new TS RAPs or delete them.
Win32_TSGatewayResourceGroup	Represents a *resource group* (set of computer names to which anyone with the corresponding TS RAP has access).	Edits a resource group's name or description, adds resources to or deletes resources from a resource group.

TABLE 1-6 WMI Classes for TS Gateway

Class	Description	Functionality
Win32_TSGatewayServer	Used for TS Gateway server-specific operations such as importing and exporting configuration or creating certificates.	Imports or exports configuration settings stored in an XML file or creates a self-signed certificate.
Win32_TSGatewayServerSettings	Represents the configuration of a TS Gateway server.	Configures event logging, if a central CAP server sets policy, if a statement of health (from the client trying to connect) is required, and the maximum number of connections required.

Terminal Services Licensing Server Classes

Even though the TS Licensing role is not new in Windows Server 2008, the classes related to this role and described in Table 1-7 did not exist in Windows Server 2003.

> **Note** Notice that per-device and per-user TS CALs are managed separately.

TABLE 1-7 WMI Classes for TS Licensing in Windows Server 2008

Class	Description	Functionality
Win32_TSIssuedLicense	Describes instances of per-device TS CALs issued from a Terminal Services license server.	Revokes a TS CAL or gets information about its expiration date, KeyPackID, the type of license (active, temporary, revoked, etc) and issues identifiers for the machine to which it's assigned.
Win32_TSLicenseKeyPack	Provides methods and properties for viewing and installing Terminal Services license key packs.	Installs various types of license key packs and determines the number of TS CALs in the pack, the product version of the TS CAL (back to Windows 2000 TS CALs), and whether they're per-user or per-device.
Win32_TSLicenseReport	Reports on usage of per-user TS CALs for that license server.	Generates and manages reports of per-user TS CAL usage. The reports generated using WMI appear in the TS Licensing Manager.

TABLE 1-7 **WMI Classes for TS Licensing in Windows Server 2008**

Class	Description	Functionality
Win32_TSLicenseReportEntry	Provides details of an issued per-user TS CAL.	Gets details about the expiration date of a per-user TS CAL.
Win32_TSLicenseServer	Provides methods and properties to view and configure a Terminal Services license server.	Sets the configuration information for activating a license server, including the company information. This class also includes methods for activating, deactivating, and reactivating a license server.

Note Although one option for the *Win32_TSLicenseReportEntry* class is determining which version of Terminal Server a per-user TS CAL can be used to connect to, and Windows 2000 Server is one valid return value for this property, there are no per-user TS CALs for Windows Server 2000 Terminal Services.

Terminal Services RemoteApp Classes

The RemoteApps are managed separately from the terminal server settings, even though the terminal server makes the RemoteApps available. Their WMI APIs are described in Table 1-8.

TABLE 1-8 **WMI Interfaces for RemoteApps**

Class	Description	Functionality
Win32_RemoteAppChangeEvent	Represents a change to RemoteApp settings on the terminal server.	No properties or methods are defined for this class—it's a pointer elsewhere.
Win32_TSPublishedApplicationList	Represents the list of programs that are in the RemoteApp programs list on a terminal server.	No properties or methods are defined for this class. You can determine whether the terminal server allows users to begin the connection using any application installed on it or only those that the administrator has designated as published applications and added to the allow list.

TABLE 1-8 WMI Interfaces for RemoteApps

Class	Description	Functionality
Win32_TSPublishedApplication	Defines the applications that are made available for remote use through TS RemoteApp.	Lists the applications published on the terminal server and get details such as path (actual and virtual), icon, whether or not the application will appear in TS Web Access, and any restrictions on or requirements for using command-line options to launch the application.
Win32_TSRemoteDesktop	Describes the Remote Desktop connection to the terminal server that can be made available through TS Web Access.	Returns the names, icons, and paths of applications authorized to be displayed in TS Web Access.
Win32_TSDeploymentSettings	Defines the deployment settings for RemoteApp programs.	
Win32_TSStartMenuApplication	Describes the applications that are on the Start menu of a terminal server.	
Win32_TSApplicationFileExtensions	Describes the file extensions that are handled by an application on a terminal server.	
Win32_TSExpandEnvironmentVariables	Expands system-defined environment variables.	

Note *Win32_TSPublishedApplicationList* applies only to the initial program a user runs on a terminal server. When the connection has been established, the end user can, if not prevented otherwise, run any application installed on the terminal server.

Summary

This chapter introduced you to Windows Server 2008 Terminal Services. At this point, you should understand how this role has developed since it became part of Windows 10 years ago, and what Terminal Services is used for. We also discussed the new business cases that Windows Server 2008 Terminal Services now supports and the roles that support these new business cases and how they interact. You should also have a broad overview of the other Windows roles that directly support Terminal Services functionality. Finally, we talked about how Terminal Services is built to be not just a feature set but a platform on which ISVs and consultants can develop custom solutions and scripts; we explained how this platform has evolved from the one in Windows Server 2003. In the next chapter, we'll move on from understanding this set of roles to planning your Terminal Server environment.

Additional Resources

This chapter has introduced you to a number of concepts that we'll expand on in the course of this book.

- For more information about memory usage on terminal servers, see Chapter 2, "Planning the Terminal Server Ecosystem."

- For more information about the core Terminal Server role and TS Licensing, see Chapter 3, "Installing the Core Terminal Server Environment."

- For more information about printing with Terminal Services, see Chapter 5, "Fine-Tuning the User Experience."

- For more information about TS Web Access, see Chapter 6, "Installing and Publishing Applications."

- For more information about TS Session Broker, see Chapter 7, "Multi-Server Deployments and Securing Terminal Server Connections."

- For more information about TS Gateway, see Chapter 7, "Multi-Server Deployments and Securing Terminal Server Connections."

Chapter 2
Planning the Terminal Server Ecosystem

Before you start installing Terminal Services (TS), you must understand the business and technical decisions you'll need to make. This chapter addresses planning and also the system internals that can help you understand why Terminal Services works in the way it does; knowing this will let you better scope out the resources required to support what you want to do. We'll cover such topics as:

- Windows Server 2008 internals particularly relevant to Terminal Services (TS) roles

- Server sizing recommendations and base hardware requirements

- The client requirements for using some new features of Windows Server 2008 Terminal Services

- Characteristics of an application that will run properly on a terminal server

- Technology decisions rooted in business needs, such as the licensing mode or the kinds of clients that make the best business sense for your company

Note In parts of this chapter, we'll be talking about how to do performance scaling on an existing terminal server. We debated how to order the chapters and decided to put planning before installing. For details of the installation process, see Chapter 3, "Installing the Core Terminal Server Environment."

Know Your Terminal Server

Before getting too deeply into the question of the internals of memory architecture or tips for server sizing, you need to know what a terminal server does. Understanding this is essential to understanding sizing guidelines.

A terminal server is the workstation for multiple users. When in use, the terminal server launches applications and loads files into memory. It saves users' files. When users log on to a terminal server, it loads their profile so that they get the customized work environment that they've come to know and love. It does everything a workstation does . . . but it does it for many users simultaneously.

In practical terms, this means that a terminal server must:

- Try to spread the use of processor time across all sessions so that one session isn't consuming all of it.

- Support new users as they log on while still maintaining current users.

- Run many instances of the same applications as efficiently as possible.

- Keep track of how much physical memory is available and use it as efficiently as possible for the greater good of the entire server.

The terminal server's role as a desktop to a large number of users involves a bit of juggling. Your job is to give it enough resources to juggle as efficiently as possible. To do your job, it's helpful to know how the terminal server does all these things.

Understanding Key Terminal Server Internals

In this section, we'll discuss the internal workings of some system components that are most helpful to understanding how a terminal server allocates system resources to the sessions it's hosting.

How Does the Terminal Server Dole Out Processor Cycles?

Nothing happens on a computer without a processor. When a workstation serves dozens of users, there's a lot of competition for any available processor cycles. Here, we'll talk about how the terminal server decides who's going to get processor time.

Users run applications, but operating systems don't know anything about applications. The operating system deals with processes and threads that support through the application executable. A *process* defines the working environment for an application, including its priority when it comes to being allocated processor time, the image name of the application associated with the process (e.g., Winword.exe), the process identifier (process ID, or PID) that the operating system uses to uniquely identify the process, the memory regions allocated to this process by the memory manager, links to parent processes that spawned this new process, and the like.

> **Note** Why does a process need both an image name (this is the same as the executable name) and a process identifier (PID)? Image names are not necessarily unique on a server. Particularly on a terminal server, it's highly likely that more than one instance of the same application will be running, and it is guaranteed that more than one instance of required system processes will be running (see Chapter 3 for more information about the processes common to all sessions). Since more than one instance could be running in the same session, you can't identify the processes by session. To give Windows and the administrator more control over individual processes, the process manager creates new processes with a PID. You'll often work with PIDs when using the Terminal Server Manager and query process tools.

Processes don't do anything themselves. Rather, they define the environment and relationships that the executable part of a process, the *thread*, must know about. Threads know details such as the process they're associated with, as well as their security information such as their access token and impersonation information. They also keep track of their pending I/O requests. Like processes, threads have a priority. They inherit their priority range from their process but may adjust their own priority within that range.

One key property of a process or thread is its priority, since that determines how often a thread gets some processor cycles. As you might guess, the higher the priority, the more often a thread gets processor time. Since nothing happens on a computer without processor time to execute instructions, this is critical.

> **Note** If you're curious to see how a processor thread priority compares to that of other types of processes, use the Process: Priority Current or Thread: Priority Current performance counters in the Reliability and Performance Monitor. For example (and not surprisingly), the Win32 SubsystemCsrss.exe process has a higher base priority than user applications, so it will get more processor time. This is a good thing, as it doesn't matter if an application is responsive if Windows isn't.

One way in which terminal servers differ from other type of servers is in their use of process priority. Other types of servers are generally designed to do one thing really well: they search databases, or manage e-mail, or support Web sites. Their priorities are clear: the application in the foreground is the one to support. Therefore, the processes and threads belonging to the application in the foreground have a higher priority than those in the background.

> **Note** Just because the application in the foreground is the main one supported doesn't mean that the foreground application processes have the highest priority. See *Microsoft Windows Internals, Fourth Edition*, by Mark E. Russinovich and David A. Solomon (Microsoft Press, 2004), for more background on the relative priority of various types of processes. (At the time of this writing, a fifth edition of this book is slated to be available in early 2009.)

Terminal servers are conflicted, meaning that they don't have one clear priority ("I *must* get the mail through."). Rather, they have dozens of priorities. Therefore, the only way for a server with the Terminal Server role installed to cope is to prioritize all user application processes and threads equally. Because the processes backing user applications have the same priority, you can approximate the load a server can take by determining how much of the total processor time a user session will require. We'll explain more about *how* to do this with the Performance Monitor later in this chapter. But a key takeaway here is that the action of installing the Terminal Server role optimizes the operating system for playing this role in your network. A terminal server does not prioritize processes in the same way as a database server because the needs of a terminal server are different.

How Do Terminal Servers Maximize Memory Efficiency?

Terminal servers spread processor time among individual sessions by prioritizing all user application processes in the same way. Next, let's discuss how memory works on a terminal server. We touched on memory layout in Chapter 1, "Introducing Terminal Services in Windows Server 2008," when explaining why kernel-mode printer drivers were best avoided. We'll expand on that rationale now, including:

- The differences between user mode and kernel mode
- The relationship between physical storage and virtual memory
- The role of the page file in providing additional physical storage
- How the memory manager optimizes the use of memory
- How memory usage, disk reads/writes, and processor time are related
- Some changes to memory management in Windows Server 2008 that affect terminal servers
- How—and why—you could use more than 4 gigabytes (GB) of RAM in a terminal server running 32-bit Windows Server 2008

Understanding User-Mode and Kernel-Mode Virtual Address Space

You can't do anything on a computer without a processor, but the threads getting processor time can't do anything without memory to store data in. Operating systems store data that they're currently working with in memory. (Data that they are not currently working with, such as files you've saved and don't currently have open, are stored on the hard disk.) This data may include user data such as files or applications, or system data such as pointers to where data is stored in memory. (Memory is big. *Really* big. Even the operating system needs a map to avoid getting lost.)

There are two kinds of memory in your computer. One is physical memory, determined by the amount of RAM installed in the computer. If you have 2 GB of RAM, there are 2 GB of physical memory available to the operating system. The other is virtual memory, which is determined by the size of the operating system addressing structure. All 32-bit operating systems have a 4-GB virtual memory address space; 64-bit operating systems have a 16-terabyte virtual memory address space—8 terabytes for user-mode processes and 8 terabytes for kernel mode. (If you've heard it said that the 64-bit OS removes the memory limitation on a terminal server but weren't quite sure what that meant, this should make it more clear.) We'll use the 4-GB model in our explanation. Virtual memory is supported by two physical storage places: the physical memory of RAM and an area on the hard disk called the *page file* or *swap file*. Therefore, even if a computer has only 1 GB of RAM installed, it still has a 4-GB range of virtual addresses for data storage.

> **Note** If you've done the math, you'll notice that 2 to the 64th power is more than 8 terabytes—it's actually 16 exabytes. Windows (and currently available processors) don't currently support 2^{64} bytes, however— they only support up to 2^{44}, or 16 terabytes split evenly between kernel mode and user mode.

This 4-GB virtual memory address space is divided into two regions: kernel space and user space, and the processes that store data in each region are called user-mode or kernel-mode processes. Kernel space, the upper 2 GB, is shared by all processes that store data here. User space is specific to each user-mode process. Conceptually, the memory layout looks like that shown in Figure 2-1. All kernel-mode processes know they must share a memory region, but all user-mode processes think they have their own personal 2 GB of user-mode storage. Because this means that virtual memory addresses are duplicated from process to process, one key job of the memory manager is to make sure that user-mode processes don't impact each other when storing memory in their view of user-mode memory.

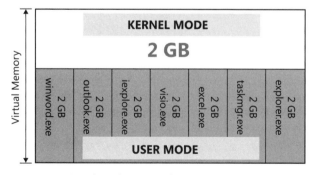

FIGURE 2-1 Kernel-mode memory is common to all processes that store information there; user-mode memory appears specific to each process.

> **Note** You may have heard of booting with the /3 GB switch to change the proportion of user-mode memory to kernel-mode memory from 2:2 to 3:1—halving the kernel-mode address area to enlarge user-mode. This is also called 4-GB tuning, or 4GT. Don't bother doing this on a terminal server. You'd need an application that actually could use 3 GB of memory to take advantage of this, and most user applications of the type you'd run on a terminal server couldn't. (*Why* they couldn't is complicated, but it basically comes down to their expecting their upper memory address to be a specific value.) More important, you'd be shorting yourself of space to store kernel-mode structures that are very important to a terminal server's functioning: page table entries (PTEs). We'll talk more about why PTEs are important and how Windows Server 2008 maximizes the memory available to these key structures shortly.

Understanding both user-mode and kernel-mode storage is important to understanding how a terminal server uses memory.

The Role of the Memory Manager

How does all this paging take place? Who's in charge of mapping virtual address space to physical memory so that when you try to bring a file into memory you get the right one? How is it possible that each user-mode process thinks that it has its own 2 GB of user-mode memory? All this is handled by a key part of the operating system called the *memory manager*.

The memory manager has four main jobs:

- Mapping the virtual address space into physical memory
- Protecting the address space of processes from each other and from the operating system
- Paging data to and from disk
- Managing key system resources such as the paged and non-paged memory pools and system cache

The memory manager works with the I/O manager (responsible for writing to and reading from disk) and the cache manager (some storage for the system cache) to ensure that processes have the data they need as quickly as possible.

In the next sections, we'll talk more about how the memory manager does its job.

Mapping Virtual Memory to Physical Memory

A 32-bit operating system can see 4 GB of RAM, but the computer in which the operating system is running may not have exactly 4 GB of storage space. Not only that, but each user-mode process thinks it has a dedicated 2 GB of storage. Something has to sort out where the data that a process thinks it stored at a particular location is really located. That function is handled by the memory manager.

Note The following section applies to user-mode code. Kernel-mode processes don't have the same storage retrieval problem as user-mode processes because there is only one view of kernel-mode memory. It's easy for a kernel-mode process to know which area of physical storage maps to a virtual memory address because there's only one possibility. Kernel-mode processes are (infinitesimally) faster than user-mode processes because they don't rely on the memory manager to map the addresses. It's also the reason why kernel-mode drivers are so potentially dangerous; they can bypass the memory manager, be wrong about the mapping, and inadvertently overwrite the memory being used by another kernel-mode process.

The way the memory manager keeps track of how virtual addresses correspond to physical locations is much the way you'd do it if someone gave you the same job: it maintains lists mapping each virtual address to a physical location. These lists are called *page tables*. The collection of page tables is organized in the *page table directory*. (A *page* is a contiguous block of memory and the smallest unit of data that the memory manager can work with.) An individual entry on the page table is called a *page table entry (PTE)*. A PTE contains the pointer to an area of physical memory. If you find page directories and PTEs confusing, think of it this way: The page table directory is like a telephone book for each process. Within the telephone book are the pages of listings—the pages are the page tables. Individual addresses on the page tables are the page table entries. With any one of the addresses, you can find a physical location for the information.

Note The amount of physical memory a process is using at any given time is called its *working set*.

Page tables and page table directories are stored in an area of kernel-mode memory reserved for this memory mapping information. The relationship between virtual memory, PTEs, and physical storage is shown in Figure 2-2.

32-bit Windows maintains a two-level page table structure of page table directories and page tables. Each process has its own page table directory. Within that page directory are the page tables listing the pages. (A process has to have more than one page table—and hence the page table directory—because the page tables are limited in size.) Within the page tables, the entries are indexed according to where they are on the page. The value of the index tells the memory manager which area of physical storage a virtual memory address points to. A virtual address contains a pointer to the correct page table directory, indexing information that points to the correct page table, and indexing information pointing to the correct PTE, as shown in Figure 2-3.

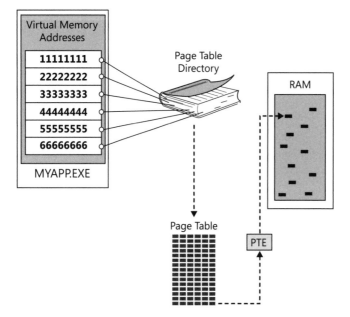

FIGURE 2-2 Mapping virtual addresses to physical locations with PTEs

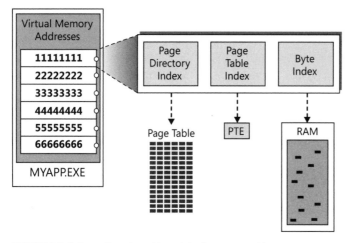

FIGURE 2-3 Information stored in a virtual memory address

> **Note** When mapping virtual memory to amounts of RAM greater than 4 GB using Physical Address Extension (PAE), the structure has three levels. We'll talk more about PAE in the section titled "Physical Address Extension" later in this chapter.

One of the limitations of Terminal Services on 32-bit Windows is that the telephone book can only be so big, because there's a limited amount of space to store the pages. It's as if the size of a community were limited by the size of the telephone book that would fit in each mailbox. No more space available indicates there can be no additional pages in the telephone book. This means you'll never be able to visit the new family in the neighborhood, because they have no entry in the telephone book and you can't find them. In the same way, the size of the space available to store PTE records limits the number of processes that can run even if you have all of the RAM in the world available. The number of virtual memory addresses available to user-mode processes appears enormous since each process sees the entire 2-GB area. But for this area to be useful, the memory manager must be able to map the virtual address to a physical location, which means creating a page directory, page tables, and page table entries for each process. If the memory manager can't do the mapping, then the process can't start.

In previous versions of Windows, the area of kernel-mode memory dedicated to PTEs was fixed in size. In Windows Server 2008, kernel-mode memory for these storage structures is dynamically allocated, so that if the memory isn't needed for one structure it may be available to another. Windows Server 2008 uses more memory than Windows Server 2003 due in part to some changes in the user shell. But if Windows Server 2003 Terminal Server was constrained by the amount of space available for PTEs, it's possible that on the same hardware, the Windows Server 2008 Terminal Server could support more users.

How Virtual Memory Is Supported

Ideally, the virtual memory a process uses to organize its storage will map to the RAM committed to that process. But RAM is finite, and sometimes it's necessary to store that data elsewhere and then add it to the process working set when required. "Elsewhere" translates to the page file or another area of memory. We'll start with the page file.

The page file is one of those pieces of the memory structure that you've probably heard is very important but perhaps aren't quite sure how. Basically, the page file helps makes virtual memory work by adding data storage to the server above and beyond what physical RAM supplies. When RAM gets full, data that isn't being used gets moved to the area of hard disk called the *page file* or *swap file*—that is, the data is paged to disk. When this data written to disk is called on, this produces a *hard page fault*. When a process searches for that data, it goes to where the data was last stored in virtual memory. The memory manager intercepts this request and retrieves the requested data from its location in the page file, paging the data back into physical memory where the process can access it. The page file increases the amount of physical storage for the virtual address space the operating system recognizes and can use to store the data, but keep in mind that swapping data to and from the hard disk takes some time. When memory is on the hard disk, retrieving it takes slightly longer than if the data is stored in RAM when called for. "Slightly longer" isn't perceptible to a user, but paging still takes a toll. Each page fault takes processor cycles to complete. Each request to read or write to disk has to get in the input/output (I/O) queue for the hard disk (more about this shortly). The system slowdowns do add up.

This isn't sounding like much of a bargain, is it? You may be wondering why the page file is important if a 32-bit operating system can address 4 GB of virtual memory. It may seem as if the simplest action is to install 4 GB of RAM. Then the operating system will have plenty of very fast RAM to store data, instead of swapping data between the RAM and the page file.

If all memory worked like kernel-mode memory, this assumption would be correct. But user-mode processes, remember, each think that they have their very own 2-GB area of user-mode virtual memory. If, for example, Microsoft Office Word needs 1 GB to support all the files you've opened, a PDF reader needs 1 GB for all those e-books, and Microsoft Office PowerPoint files with lots of flashing animations need 1.5 GB, you've already exceeded the amount of physical memory able to handle that 2 GB of per-user space. Multiply all this by 50 users or more on the same computer, and you can see that you need a lot more memory than just 4 GB of RAM to back the 4 GB of addresses the operating system can address.

> **Note** Microsoft's best practices for terminal servers suggest that your page file should be two to three times the size of the installed RAM to support all the individual user-mode memory areas for each process. The reasoning is that process creation is expensive, two or three times more so than maintaining the process in memory. Because many people are using the same computer, it's likely that the computer will be creating a lot of processes for all those people. Therefore, every time a user launches an application, they're engaging in this expensive activity. To keep the terminal server running smoothly, you need more memory than just enough to keep the processes running.

How It Works: Improvements to the Page File System in Windows Server 2008

One change to memory management in Windows Server 2008 lies in the way the page file works. It's designed to be more efficient than previous versions of Windows in two important ways that allow it to write less often.

First, the fewer write actions the operating system has to take, the better, because every action has a cost. To reduce the number of necessary write options in Windows Server 2003, the memory manager could only write up to 64 kilobytes (KB) of data in a single action. Today, that limit has been removed so the memory manager can write data in larger chunks. Most write operations now are approximately 1 megabyte (MB).

Another improvement to the page file in Windows Server 2008 is that it takes the amount of free physical memory into account before writing to the page file. In previous versions of Windows, the decision to write to the page file was based on the number of *dirty pages* in RAM, or areas where data had been modified. Now, if there's no shortage of RAM, the memory manager will leave the modified data in RAM.

Not all data can be paged to disk, however. Some important data (important to the functioning of the operating system, not important to a user) must be maintained in RAM at all
times. Data that never gets paged is stored in an area of kernel-mode memory called the
non-paged pool. Kernel-mode processes that store data that can be paged to disk store it in
the paged pool. In previous versions of Windows, paged pool and non-paged pool had fixed
sizes depending on the amount of RAM installed on the server; however, in Windows Server
2008 (and Windows Vista), these memory areas have no fixed size but can fluctuate based on
the needs of the operating system at run time (see Figure 2-4).

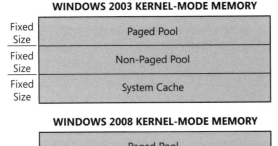

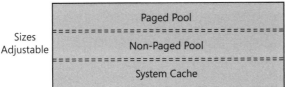

FIGURE 2-4 Kernel-mode memory areas supporting important system structures are dynamically sized in
Windows Server 2008.

Not all page faults are hard page faults. Sometimes, the data is still stored in RAM, but not in
the process working set. For example, the data may be being used by another process (see
the next section, "Memory Sharing and Copy-on-Write"). Soft page faults cost little in terms
of time or system resources, so you don't need to worry about them. Hard page faults, where
the memory manager has to initiate a process to retrieve the data from disk, are much more
expensive. When a computer is very low on available RAM and must store a lot of data in the
page file, the constant reads and writes are called *thrashing*.

To sum up this section:

- A user process expects to find the data it's looking for in its working set.

- If the data is not in the working set, then memory manager will check to see if it's
  stored anywhere else in RAM and add it to the process working set (a soft page fault).

- If the data is not in memory, then the memory manager prompts the I/O manager to
  find the data in the page file on hard disk so it can be added to the process working set
  (a hard page fault).

Memory Sharing and Copy-on-Write

We mentioned earlier that all user-mode processes think they have a 2-GB user-mode memory area to themselves. We also mentioned that this forces the need for a page file to back the virtual memory addresses, since there's no way RAM can do it. But the memory load of many modern applications is quite large. On a terminal server running many memory-hungry applications that are not designed to be efficient with memory (since applications are typically designed for a single-user computer), how do you avoid running out of page file as well as RAM?

One way, of course, is to ensure that you've got enough page file. Another way that doesn't require any work on your part is a memory-sharing technique implemented in Windows that allows processes to share memory space—sometimes. This technique is called *copy-on-write* and is related to *shared memory*.

At the basis of copy-on-write is the fact that there's a lot of redundancy in a computer. If two processes need to use the same Dynamic Link Library (DLL), for example, it is better if they can use the same one—if one can "read over the shoulder" of the other. So long as neither process is modifying the data, this works fine, and it decreases the amount of data that a process must store in memory to support all its threads.

The tricky bit comes when a piece of data that two processes are using needs to be changed by one of them. There are two ways you can avoid having a change by Process B make an impact on Process A. One way is to make a copy of the data for Process B as soon as Process B accesses the shared memory area. This can be wasted effort, though—what if the second process won't change the shared data?

Another way that avoids this wasted effort is the approach that Windows takes: When Process B needs to change the data at the shared location, the memory manager copies the edited data to a new location. The original data is not affected, and the process that must change the data can continue, now using its own copy, as shown in Figure 2-5. Windows works like this; other operating systems may make a copy of the page at the time the second process must access the same data as the first process.

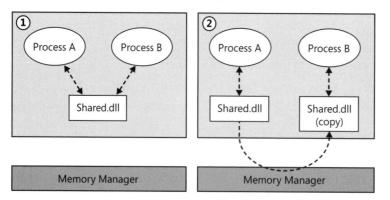

FIGURE 2-5 Copy-on-write allows for more efficient use of physical memory.

The catch to copy-on-write is that applications must be written in a way that allows them to take advantage of it. The Windows operating system can use copy-on-write for itself, but developers must plan for its use in user applications.

How Can I Use More Than 4 GB of RAM?

A 32-bit operating system supports up to 4 GB of virtual address space, meaning that no matter how much physical storage in the form of RAM you put in the server, the operating system can only "see" 4 GB. A 64-bit operating system supports up to 8 terabytes of virtual address space. It would be hard (maybe impossible) to install too much physical memory into 64-bit server, but 4 GB is a lot less than it used to be. Are you limited to maxing out the server at 4 GB if you're running the 32-bit version of Windows Server 2008?

You're not. There are two ways in which Windows Server 2008 can be convinced to use more than 4 GB of physical memory: one that applies to the entire operating system and one that applies to individual processes (but does not affect the amount of kernel-mode space available, as the /3 GB switch does). 32-bit Windows can't see more than 4 GB of virtual addresses no matter what you do, but you can use up to 64 GB of *physical* memory with 32-bit Windows Server 2008 (standard edition) or up to 2 terabytes with enterprise or datacenter editions. (Where did I put those 1-terabyte DIMMs?)

Let's review very quickly why it matters that you might not be able to install more physical memory than the server can address. Kernel-mode memory, the upper 2 GB of virtual memory, is shared among all components that store data in that region. User-mode memory, the lower 2 GB of virtual memory addresses, is unique to each process—or so the processes think. Therefore, to back 4 GB of virtual memory, you need a lot more than 4 GB of RAM. The common way to do this is to use the page file to enlarge the physical storage backing the virtual address space, and you'll continue to do that. But paging, as we discussed earlier, uses processor cycles you could be using elsewhere, and reading data back from the hard disk is slower than reading it from RAM.

Why not just use the 64-bit version of Windows Server 2008 and install as much RAM as you need? That is absolutely an option and will avoid the need to worry about any of the advanced address translation mechanisms. But from what we've seen in our testing on the Terminal Server team (and confirmed by outside research as well), using 64-bit usually begins to make sense when the server has more than 16 GB of RAM installed. (This isn't a universal rule, but it's fairly consistent.) Before that point, the larger memory use required by the more memory-hungry processes in 64-bit Windows means that it's to your advantage to run 32-bit; 16 GB is about where you break even.

> ## Direct from the Field: How Does 64-Bit Windows Perform as a Terminal Server?
>
> We have recently moved to 64-bit on many of our servers. We see that the same physical server that could support say, 55 users in 32-bit mode with 4 GB of RAM, can support 150 users with little stress on 64-bit with 8 GB of RAM. The 64-bit solution seems to work extremely well and I suspect in our environment we could scale up further just by adding more RAM. Some servers have seen more than 300 sessions with no performance issues.
>
> We find that with our application the workload is variable by region for the same application, because users have different work patterns in the different regions. The European folks are heavy hitters, whereas the U.S. and Far East folks give the TS farms an easier time.
>
> *Jeff Heatton*
>
> *Operations Engineer*

So, assuming that you'd like to install something less than 32 GB of RAM on the server but more than 4 GB—let's see what your options are.

Physical Address Extension

Your primary option for expanding the amount of memory available to 32-bit processes is called Physical Address Extension (PAE). Turning this on (you have to turn on PAE explicitly, even on computers that support it) enables a 32-bit operating system to use 36-bit addressing. Basically, PAE extends the memory manager's vocabulary so it's able to access areas of memory beyond 4 GB, up to 64 GB of RAM

Note Windows Server 2008 standard edition only supports up to 4 GB of RAM, so PAE won't help you below Windows Server 2008 enterprise or datacenter editions, which both support up to 64 GB. The kernel isn't any different—this is a licensing difference, not a technical one.

Intel originally developed PAE to allow its processors to address more memory. Originally, the processors could only support up to 2 to the 32nd power number of addresses. Intel updated the processors to support up to 2 to the 36th power, which translates to up to 64 GB of physical memory. The operating system has to change to accommodate this, as does the kernel to support 36 bits of addresses, so to use PAE you must boot the operating system with the /PAE switch.

Ordinary virtual address translation has two pieces: the page directory for each process and the page tables listed in the page directory. PAE adds another layer to support the greater description possible with 64-bit addressing. Rather than a page directory for each process, there's one *page directory pointer* for each process. The page directory pointer locates the right page directory. From there, the process is the same: the memory manager looks up the correct page table and the right page entry. Because of the additional layers of translation, virtual addresses in PAE-enabled servers contain more fields than the usual, as shown in Figure 2-6.

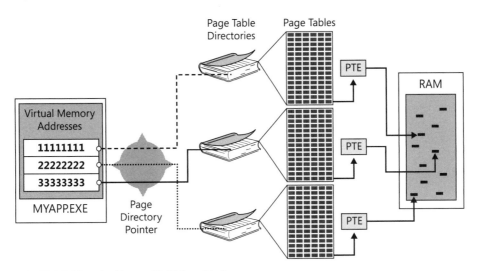

FIGURE 2-6 Virtual address with PAE enabled

The end result of PAE is that now, instead of one telephone book (see the previous section on mapping virtual addresses to physical ones), a process can have several telephone books. It's gone from being the small town with just one telephone book to the metropolitan region with a telephone book for each region. The first step in mapping virtual addresses to physical locations is no longer to pick up the telephone book, but to pick up the *correct* telephone book.

So what's the downside to PAE? A computer using PAE needs more PTEs to map a virtual address to the RAM it's using, so you'll need to balance the benefit of more RAM against the greater amount of kernel-mode memory needed to store the pointers.

Used on its own, PAE does not allow user applications to address large memory configurations to give themselves more RAM. However, the operating system can use the larger amount of RAM to increase the size of the system cache and other areas in RAM where data isn't part of a process working set but is still stored in RAM. And frankly, most applications that can use large memory configurations aren't usually run on a terminal server anyway.

Address Windowing Extensions

What if you *do* have an application that would benefit from a storage space in RAM larger than 2 GB, but you've already eliminated 4 GB tuning (4GT), also known as the /3 GB switch, because of the detrimental effect it would have on the operating system performance and knowing that only one application needs this much storage space? In that case, you might consider using Address Windowing Extensions (AWE) in addition to PAE. AWE is more relevant to database servers than terminal servers, but since it comes up in discussions of how to use more than 4 GB of RAM, it's useful to know how it differs from PAE and how it can complement PAE.

> **Note** AWE does not depend on PAE, but without PAE, AWE cannot reserve memory above 4 GB of RAM. On a Windows Server 2008 Terminal Server, it's unlikely that you'll need or want to use AWE at all, and never without PAE.

In Robert Silverberg's science fiction novella *Nightwings* (I Books, 2003), some people have personal storage containers called *overpockets* that are pockets with access to another dimension. When they travel and have more baggage than they can carry, they put it in their overpocket and forget about it—the items go to the other dimension and it's as if the character isn't carrying it. It's a handy way to tote anything that isn't practical for a human to carry. Overpockets are also safe, because the backing dimension is somehow exclusive to each person's overpocket.

AWE works like an overpocket for 32-bit applications. An application allocates an area of physical memory (RAM, not a virtual address space) that it will use. It then defines a region of its virtual memory to act as a window to this region of physical memory. This area of RAM is now an overpocket to the process 2-GB user area. Although the process loses a little memory area by dedicating it as a window to its overpocket region (the larger the area of RAM backing the window, the bigger the window needs to be), that loss of memory area is made up for by having a data cache stored in RAM.

For example, let's say that you want to dedicate an additional 4 GB of RAM to a user-mode process. When a process is launched, a certain area of physical memory is allocated to this process. The process can define a 256-MB area to be a window on the 4-GB region of RAM. Figure 2-7 is an illustration of how this works.

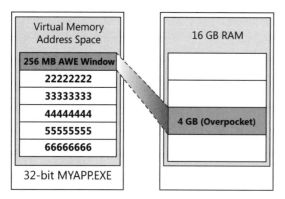

FIGURE 2-7 How AWE enables use of physical memory beyond 4 GB

Despite the positive attributes of AWE, it's not likely to be the best fit on most terminal servers for the following reasons:

- It only benefits applications that store a lot of fairly static data in memory at one time. How often do you run large databases or mail servers on terminal servers? (Not often, one hopes.)

- Any data stored in the overpocket region (going back to our analogy about how this window into another region of memory is like the overpocket in the Silverberg story) cannot be shared between processes. The dimension backing the overpocket is exclusive to its user, and the same holds true for AWE. This includes any child processes the original process spawns.

- Since the data in the area of RAM dedicated to supporting this window is never paged to disk, this area of physical storage is not available to any other process—ever. Using AWE with processes on a terminal server could lead you to quickly run out of RAM.

How Does Disk Performance Affect a Terminal Server?

The last item in our terminal server internals roundup is disk performance. Although not everyone thinks of hard disks as a consideration in designing a terminal server, for best results it's important to keep them in mind.

Arranging Data Storage

Terminal servers should be as generic as possible. All load-balanced servers should contain the same application set so that end users don't see any difference regardless of which server the Terminal Services Session Broker sends them to. They should never contain any user-specific data at all. Only three types of data should be stored on a terminal server:

- The page file
- The cached user profiles currently in use (while the profiles themselves are stored on a separate file server)
- The operating system and application files

> **Note** User profiles should not be stored on a terminal server, but rather on a central file share so that there's only one copy of the profile. However, the profile will be cached on the terminal server for the duration of the session it's supporting. See Chapter 4, "Creating the User Work Environment," for more details about combining profiles and terminal services.

One approach to storing all this data is to get one big hard disk and keep all the data on it. That way, you can mirror the hard disk and have a backup configuration. For small environments or pilot programs, this may work fine. But generally best practice is to divide up the three types of data among three separate hard disks, to avoid waits for disk I/O requests. The problem is that all user activity requires a lot of disk reads and writes. Beginning a user connection, loading a user profile, launching an application, paging some data in memory to disk (or reading data previously paged to disk back into memory)—these are just some of the events that generate disk I/O requests. If these requests begin to stack up, users will see delayed response times. Paging data back into memory from disk, for example, is already relatively slow compared to accessing the same data from physical memory.

Processors and memory are extremely fast. Disks, although fast, are much slower than either RAM or processors. (If you'll recall from the section titled "How Virtual Memory Is Supported" earlier in this chapter, this is why it's good to minimize use of the page file, even though it's critical to your server functioning well.) Ideally, try to have one hard disk spindle for every 20 end users on a given terminal server. That way, the users' disk requests will be less likely to delay each other.

Understanding the System Cache

As we've seen, writing data to the page file or reading from it is expensive and relatively slow. What if you'll use the data again soon but need to free up some RAM now? What if a user requests one piece of data but is likely to need related pieces close to it in storage? In either case, the process (or, rather, part of the operating system called the memory manager, which we'll discuss soon) can store some data in an area of kernel-mode memory called the *system cache*.

The file system cache holds data pulled from disk. Without getting too deeply into the minute details of the decision tree (see the Additional Resources section at the end of this chapter for some extremely detailed references), when a process requests some data, the request goes first to the area in virtual memory where the process stored the data. If the data is in RAM, then the process can continue with whatever it was doing.

If the data is not in the RAM mapped to the user's virtual address space, the next stop is the system cache, which is a collection of virtual addresses backed by RAM. If the entire request can be satisfied from the system cache (that is, if the process has asked for data A through E, and the cache contains A, B, C, D, and E), then the request never gets as far as the file system. If only part of the data is in the system cache (say, A and B), then the cache manager forwards the request to the memory manager, which then generates a hard page fault and gets the data from the page file or from disk as appropriate.

The larger the system cache, the more efficient the process of retrieving data is. So how much storage space is in the cache? In previous versions of Windows, the system cache had a preset limit. When you booted the system, the system cache was created based on the amount of memory—by default, 64 MB of kernel-mode virtual address space. This was the limit for servers with up to 16 GB of RAM installed. (After 16 GB, as more RAM was installed, the cache had a baseline of 128 MB plus 64 MB for each 4 GB of RAM, but for our purposes the effective system cache size was 64 MB.) The system cache also always started at exactly the same location in memory. It was possible to edit the registry to change the size of the system cache or the space devoted to other storage in kernel-mode, but this had its own dangers, as an administrator might get the proportions wrong and affect system performance (or crash the system).

In Windows Server 2008, the system cache (and the other storage areas in kernel mode) no longer has a fixed size, but all compete for space as shown in Figure 2-4. Instead, it now grows as it needs to, limited only by the amount of virtual address space available. If the system cache needs to get larger and another storage structure doesn't require a lot of space, the cache can grow. For this reason, Windows Server 2008 and Windows Vista will ignore any registry keys specifying the size of kernel-mode structures. If you boot your servers with PAE, then you can use more memory and increase the size of the system cache.

How Does RAID Affect Disk Performance?

What about RAID? RAID (Redundant Array of Independent Disks) is one way to increase the uptime of your servers by decreasing the likelihood of a disk failure. The basic idea of RAID is that, rather than using a monolithic disk for all your storage, you combine partitions on multiple disks into a single logical unit. The partition may encompass the entire physical disk or only part of it.

The purpose for combining the multiple disks depends on the scenario. Some forms of RAID are intended for data security by linking two or more disks in a way that maintains a copy of your data. Some increase disk throughput by letting you use two or more I/O paths to support a single logical disk (one spanning multiple physical disks).

> **Note** Not all forms of RAID increase server reliability. Some even reduce it by linking two physical disks and making a volume spanning both, so that if one disk fails the entire volume is inaccessible. For our purposes here, we're talking only about the fault-tolerant forms of RAID.

There are two basic kinds of fault-tolerant RAID: disk mirroring (RAID 1) and stripe sets with parity (RAID 5). (RAID 10 is fault tolerant, but essentially combines 5 and 1.) There is an obvious winner when it comes to terminal servers, but we'll review both to make it clear why one is a better choice.

Disk Mirroring   Disk mirroring is the preferred configuration for a terminal server. In this RAID configuration, you have two disks backing a single logical volume. One disk contains the primary partition, and one contains the mirror partition. Each time you write data to the primary partition, it's also written to the mirror partition. When you read data from the primary partition, it can be read simultaneously, on some implementations, from the mirror partition. This means that reads from a RAID 1 configuration could theoretically be twice as fast as reading from a volume encompassing only a single physical disk. Writes do not take twice as long because they can happen asynchronously.

If one disk of a mirror set fails, then a perfect and always up-to-date copy remains on the other disk. If one disk fails, you can easily restore redundancy by breaking the mirror set and replacing the failed disk, then adding the new disk to the mirror set. The disks will recreate the information on the existing disk onto the one you've just added to the mirror set.

RAID 1 reduces the time required to read from disk while not really affecting the write time. It also makes it easy to recover from a disk failure since the data is already fully assembled. About the only disadvantage is that it does not make very efficient use of space, because there are two full copies of all data.

Stripe Sets with Parity   The other contender for a fault-tolerant system is RAID 5, for stripe sets with parity. RAID 5 works differently than RAID 1. Whereas RAID 1 maintains a perfect copy of all the data on a partition on a second disk partition, RAID 5 takes a more space-efficient approach. It writes a slice of data to each disk in the array (a minimum of three disks), but only once across the entire array. Each physical partition then contains both actual data and parity information for data stored on another drive. Therefore, so long as no more than one disk fails, you have either the original data or the parity information required to create the original data. (Be aware: If a second disk fails before you replace one failed disk in a stripe set, you're in trouble.)

RAID 5 has its advantages. It can take many more disks than RAID 1, and it is more efficient in the way that it stores data, since it's not maintaining duplicates of all data—just parity information needed to recreate it in case of disk failure. It can also be more efficient for reads, since more than one I/O path may be used. But writing data takes more time with RAID 5, because every time you write data, you must also calculate and write its parity information.

One caution about using RAID on a terminal server: Don't use software RAID. Especially don't use software RAID 5 (stripe sets with parity), because the calculations required will utilize processor cycles that could be used more profitably elsewhere. Hardware RAID systems have their own processor and will increase disk performance.

> **Note** Not sure why a terminal server should contain no user data? If there's only one terminal server, then you *can* store user profiles and even data on it if you must, just as you do with a single workstation. If there's more than one terminal server in the farm, however, then storing per-user data on a terminal server leads to an inconsistent user experience, because the server a user is connected to will determine what the data and settings are. This isn't ideal for the users or the IT staff supporting them, so it's best to store user-specific data off the terminal servers and make it accessible to their sessions via the network.

Determining System Requirements for Terminal Servers

We've looked at disk, processor, and memory internals in some detail. Armed with your newfound knowledge, answer this: If you have a server running 32-bit Windows Server 2008 standard edition with 16 GB of RAM with PAE enabled, a 3-disk array, 2 dual-core processors, and a gigabit network, how many end users can this terminal server support?

The answer, of course, is that it depends on what those end users are doing.

Many times, when you're choosing hardware to support a given situation, you can take a well-established path to choose the hardware. Look at the product documentation for the operating system you plan to run and the software you want to buy, and it's easy to tell what the hardware requirements are. Follow those guidelines and you should be all right.

With terminal servers, it's not that easy. Defining hardware requirements for a terminal server is more difficult than defining them for a Microsoft Exchange Server, for example. A Microsoft Exchange Server load is more predictable: It sends mail and it receives mail. The mailboxes can be of a predetermined size limit, and the process of sending or receiving an e-mail takes a predictable number of processor cycles. Given all that, if you know how many users are utilizing the server, you can determine what hardware to buy.

Terminal servers, in contrast, support individuals who may be doing various kinds of activities with differing types of applications. It's possible to predict the hardware profile required to support 50 users getting e-mail with a fair degree of accuracy. It's much harder to predict the hardware needed to support 50 users on a terminal server who are using a combination of the thousands (to be conservative) of business applications available. To know the load a terminal server can manage, you must have a very good idea what the individuals using it will be doing.

This may be frustrating to hear, but the most reliable way to determine how many people can use a terminal server simultaneously is to try it out: install the server and the applications, get a representative group of end users together, and keep adding users until performance slows to an unacceptable level. Alternatively, you can make some guesses based on a test run or on information derived from one session. Read on for more details about doing a test run or extrapolating usage information from a single representative session.

Baseline Server Requirements

Saying that you can't know how many people can use a terminal server at the same time given a certain hardware profile isn't to say that there are no guidelines at all. Before getting into some procedures for load testing, let's look at some basic recommendations for terminal server hardware.

Memory

Load up on memory. This is always true for a terminal server, because many people will be using applications and loading data into memory at the same time, all in parallel. One person working on eight Office PowerPoint presentations at the same time is bad enough, but 50 individuals doing the same thing can take quite a toll on a server.

Memory was an issue with terminal servers running Windows Server 2003, but will be more of an issue for servers running Windows Server 2008. The base operating system uses more memory now, for reasons that have nothing to do with Terminal Services. First, the server operating system runs Windows Internet Explorer 7, which uses more memory than Windows Internet Explorer 6. Any scenarios that require the Microsoft native browser will be affected by this. Second, the shell in Windows Server 2008 and Windows Vista is more memory-intensive than that in Windows Server 2003 and Windows XP. And with Windows Server 2008, these additional memory consumers will especially affect a terminal server since these programs are all about the end user experience.

We recommend that you start with 4 GB of RAM per terminal server for a small deployment and work your way up from there. You may be able to run a small pilot with 2 GB of RAM in a terminal server, but you probably won't like its performance in a production environment. If running 32-bit Windows, consider using PAE so you can hold more data in RAM.

Disk

As we discussed previously, be sure to pay attention to your physical hard disk layout. Everyone thinks about memory when sizing a terminal server, with processor power another obvious consideration. Not everyone takes disk I/O into consideration, but a server supporting reads and writes for many users needs a wide and unobstructed I/O path. Split data among multiple hard disks (20 users to a disk spindle, as a guideline) for best performance and use RAID 1 for disk fault-tolerance.

Network

Of course, network speed is important to a centralized computing environment. In-house, bandwidth should not be a problem, although you may consider a multi-homed server so you can dedicate one network card to Remote Desktop Protocol (RDP) traffic and one to serving file and print requests. Out of the corporate network, you're dependent on networks you may not be able to control. To support remote users, consider a test run to determine the usability via the networks your end users have available. What works well on the LAN may be difficult over a digital subscriber line (DSL); what works well via DSL is likely to be difficult over dial-up. Disable any features that use a large amount of bandwidth but aren't required.

Processor

Processor speed is unlikely to be your biggest bottleneck if you're running the 32-bit version of Windows Server 2008. Quad-core processors are common these days; get a motherboard that has additional sockets in case you decide to move to the 64-bit operating system before upgrading the entire box. As of this writing, processor speeds range from 1.6 gigahertz (GHz) to 3.6 GHz. The amount of cache is more critical to processor responsiveness than the processor's speed. More cache provides more space to store instructions that are quickly available to the processor to execute. Incremental changes in megahertz (MHz) made a lot more difference when we were moving from 66 MHz to 100 MHz.

Direct from the Field: RDP Network Requirements

How much network bandwidth does a typical remote session require? The answer depends on a variety of factors, including but not limited to:

- Pixel dimensions of the RDP session

- Color depth of the RDP session

- Redirected devices in the RDP session and their usage patterns

- Amount of screen redraw done by user workload/multitasking and application repaints in the RDP session

- Compression schemes being used on the RDP channel

Due to the number of factors involved, any estimate would likely be wrong for more than 90 percent of all scenarios. However, if you want to do some testing on your own, you can use a third-party application that measures network traffic. One option Tim uses is a tool called NetMeter that shows a little graph of upload and download in real time. You could then easily see how much is going up and coming down from a given client (or you could run it on the server and see the overall load).

Jon Wojan, Senior Premier Field Engineer

Timothy Newton, Support Escalation Engineer

Defining Acceptable Performance

Your goal is to create an efficient and effective user experience. That user experience will be defined subjectively by three main criteria:

- The logon process, including both how long it takes to log on, whether the server seems unresponsive or gives some feedback data, and how many times the end user needs to supply credentials. Although the ideal user experience is to avoid logons totally—just sitting down and having applications open is easiest—you can create a reasonable experience if the wait isn't unacceptably long and the process is fairly transparent.

- Application responsiveness is crucial. Users must feel as though applications are responsive from the terminal server. A little lag is normally acceptable, but if the delay is so great that end users are typing ahead of the display, the IT department will likely receive complaints.

- Files should load quickly when requested and print jobs should print. When using the centralized application model, you may get better response times than are possible with desktop-based applications.

> **Note** Consider each of these criteria separately when designing a live test. That is, don't try to measure performance data at the same time you're measuring the number of simultaneous log-ons the server can support. If you mix scenarios, the two tests will interfere with each other. How can you tell how a server will perform on a daily basis if it's stressed out at that moment from too many logons? Sort out the logon bottleneck, and *then* look to see how the servers will respond to day-to-day usage requirements.

Designing a Live Test

To create a live test, you need to know which applications are going to be run and how the users running them work so you can pick a representative group of users and applications. What is the plan for these terminal servers?

Root the Test in Reality

There's a lot of difference between running a low-impact point of sale (POS) application and running computer-assisted design (CAD) applications requiring lots of rendering. For a less extreme example, there's even a difference between running Microsoft Office 2003 and Microsoft Office 2007, since the Office 2007 interface is more resource-intensive. Test with the applications you expect to be running, not with a random or invented scenario that does not apply to your real-life expectations. If the server isn't doing the work under normal circumstances, then your results will be meaningless.

> **Note** Because of the memory sharing discussed earlier, the first terminal server session may use more memory than that of subsequent consecutive sessions. This is why running the live test helps—it shows the effect of multiple instances running.

Generate Typical User Behavior

Similarly, you need to know how your users work. Are they intensive workers who pound at their applications all day (for example, inputting data or writing a long document)? Or will they be up and down, engaging the terminal server on an occasional basis? Just checking the number of open sessions on a terminal server doesn't give you the information you need. Even if there are 100 open sessions, how many are active? How long have the inactive ones been idle?

> **Note** You may see references to knowledge workers and task-based workers when researching terminal server sizing. Knowledge workers conform to the profile we described in Chapter 1; they need access to the data stored in the data center to do their job. Knowledge workers use many business applications such as Microsoft Office. Task-based workers generally input or review discrete chunks of data, such as working a cash register displayed as a Windows application. Each profile can be light, medium, or heavy usage. Someone who's using a terminal server to check their e-mail is a knowledge worker, but a light one.

If your final environment will be running a mix of users, try to get that mix represented in your live test. Does your work group include 75 knowledge workers and 25 task-based workers? If so, select three knowledge workers for every task-based worker for your test run.

Ideally, get real workers to participate in this test so that you can receive usage data that accurately depicts typical user actions and needs throughout your workday. For instance, you may know that users typically open files located on a file server from their terminal server sessions. You may not know that these files are typically 100 MB each. It would be best if this is discovered during your test phase and not during rollout.

Executing the Tests

If your main concern is to determine how many users a terminal server can support during the day, you'll need to build a terminal server using the instructions in Chapter 3. Install the applications you intend to use and make some representative files available to the users involved in the test. These are the steps you'll follow:

1. Launch a remote instance of the Reliability And Performance Monitor, the Windows 2008 performance monitoring tool. Begin monitoring the counters that are not session-specific.

> **Note** You're launching a remote instance so that the overhead of running the performance monitoring tool doesn't affect the server. Any time you're testing server performance, you should run this tool remotely unless network performance is part of your test.

2. Have the users log on.

3. Tune the Reliability And Performance Monitor to record performance data for the activity in each of the user sessions for session-specific counters.

4. Ask logged-on users to launch applications, load files, check e-mail (if that's a part of your test), surf the Web—in short, have them work as they would normally.

5. Let the test continue for a reasonable amount of time, perhaps an hour or even longer.

6. Review the results and see the strain on the terminal server.

Using the Reliability And Performance Monitor

Most of these steps are fairly self-explanatory, but using performance counters may be new to you. If so, read on for a walk-through of how the monitoring process works.

Collecting the Data   To launch the tool, go to Start | Administrative Tools | Reliability and Performance Monitor.

Note The process name for this tool hasn't changed from previous versions of Windows Server. You can also launch it by going to Start | Run | Perfmon.exe.

First, build a data collector set. Drill down to Data Collector Sets. Right-click User Defined and select New | Data Collector Set as shown in Figure 2-8.

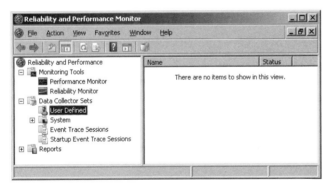

FIGURE 2-8 Start by making a new data collector set.

Note Although you can monitor the counters from the Performance Monitor, creating a data collector set makes it easier for you to reproduce your results.

Name your data collector set using a description of what you are collecting, such as TS1 User Test 1. As shown in Figure 2-9, choose Create Manually (Advanced) and click Next.

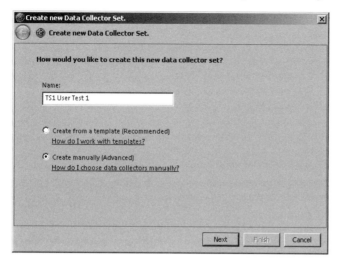

FIGURE 2-9 Manually creating a new data collector set

The goal is to log data, not initiate alerts for error conditions, so choose to create data logs based on performance counters as shown in Figure 2-10. Click Next.

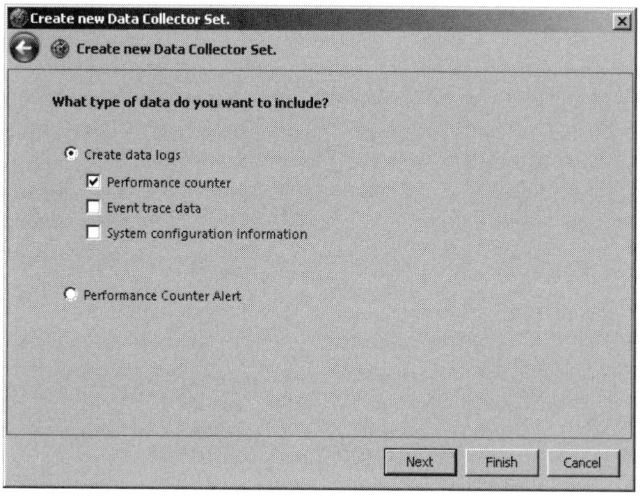

FIGURE 2-10 Creating a data log from performance counters

Next, you need to add performance counters to the collection set. What counters should you include as part of a full test pass? Since you're loading the server with many users, you can take a holistic view of the server rather than just focusing on what's happening within a single session. See Table 2-1 for an example of counters that can tell you about the strain on the server.

TABLE 2-1 Reliability And Performance Monitor Counters for a Full Test Pass

Counter	Description
Processor: % Processor Time	The percentage of elapsed time that the processor spends to execute a non-idle thread (in other words, the percentage of time the processor is doing anything useful).
Terminal Services Session: Total Bytes	Total number of bytes sent to and from this session via virtual channels. Gives an idea of the traffic coming in and out of the session due to redirected device calls.
Physical Disk: Avg. Disk Queue Length	Average number of I/O requests waiting for the disk. This number should not be more than 2.
Memory: Page Faults/Sec	The rate at which the terminal server is reading from and writing to the page file. Higher numbers indicate that the server may be low on memory for its user load.
Terminal Server Session: Working Set Peak	The peak amount of virtual memory backed by RAM for a given session. This shows the demand for physical memory.
Terminal Server Session: % Processor Time	The percentage of processor time a given session uses.

To add a counter, find the appropriate object in the list as shown in Figure 2-11. Click the icon to expand the list of counters for that object. If you're choosing a session-specific counter, choose the sessions to add it to; to choose all of them, choose <All Instances>.

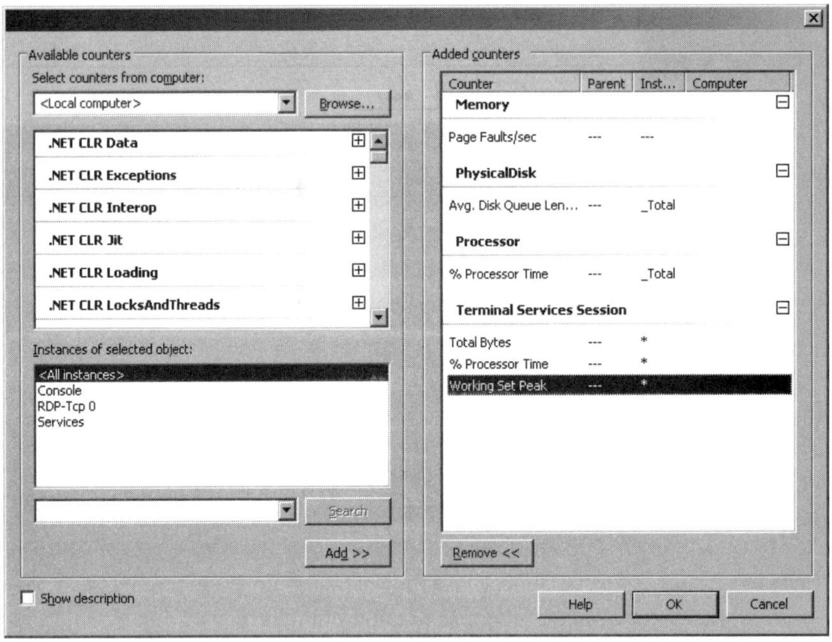

FIGURE 2-11 Choose counters for each object you want to monitor.

When you're done selecting counters, click OK to display the list of counters you're monitoring. The default sample selection should be fine. Click Next.

Choose the location where you'd like to save the data (as shown in Figure 2-12) and click Next.

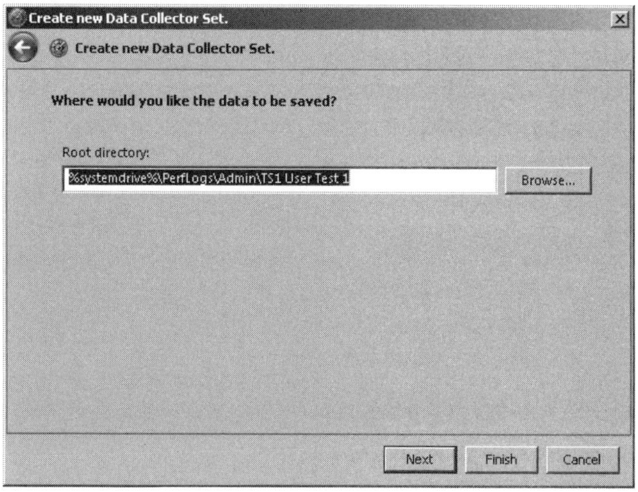

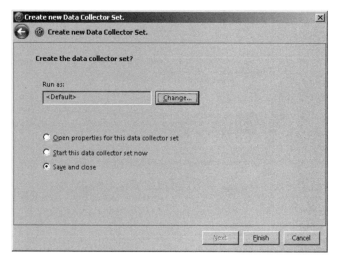

FIGURE 2-12 Specify the location to save your data collection set.

You can either save the data collector set to be initiated manually or edit the properties to set a schedule of when it should start and how long it should last. For the moment, assume that you're going to start it manually, so choose that option from the list shown in Figure 2-13 and click Finish.

FIGURE 2-13 Save the data collector set to launch it later.

When you're ready to begin testing, return to the main screen of the Reliability And Performance Monitor and choose the saved set from the folder of user-defined data collector sets. Right-click to open the context-sensitive menu and choose Start or click the green Start button as shown in Figure 2-14.

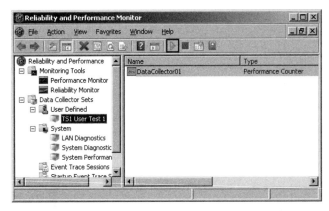

FIGURE 2-14 Start the data collector set.

When you have finished with the test, go back to the Reliability And Performance Monitor, right-click the collector set, and choose Stop, or click the square-shaped Stop button located to the right of the green Start button.

Reviewing the Data   To review the results of your test, go to the Reports area shown in Figure 2-15 to find the report identified with the name you specified.

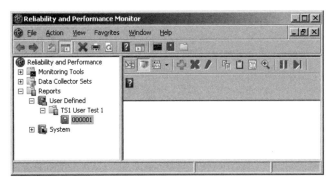

FIGURE 2-15 Find your report.

A report doesn't have to show all the counters you included in the original data collector set. To choose the counters you want to show, click the green plus sign at the top of the pane on the right to open the dialog box shown in Figure 2-16. Only the objects for which you selected counters will be available.

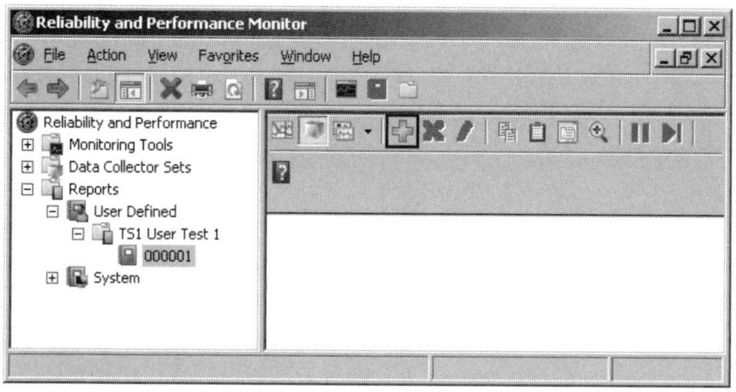

FIGURE 2-16 Choose counters to display in your report.

Choose the correct object and the counters to include, and because you are measuring the total user load, make sure that <All Instances> is selected in the Instances Of Selected Object list as shown in Figure 2-17. (<All Instances> is represented by the asterisk [*] symbol in the pane at right.) Click OK when you've chosen all the counters.

> **Note** The Total option makes a total count for all selected instances; <All instances> tabs each instance individually but monitors all of them.

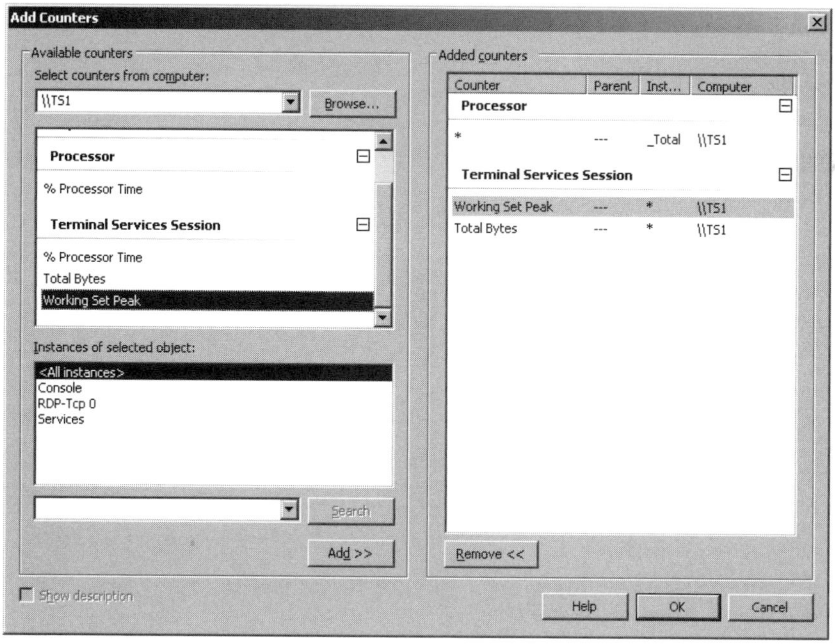

FIGURE 2-17 Choose the counters and specific object instances to display in your report.

Finally, click the Change Graph Type drop-down menu to the left of the green plus sign and choose to display the information as a report (see Figure 2-18).

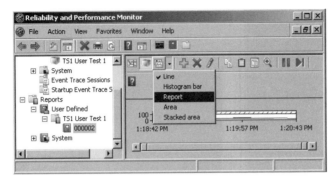

FIGURE 2-18 Change the report view to Report.

You should see data similar to Figure 2-19 displaying the results of your tests.

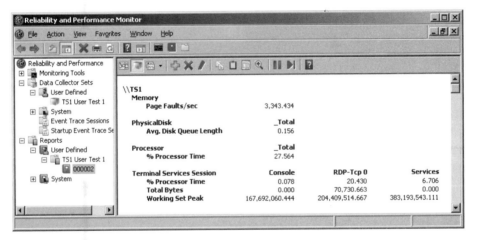

FIGURE 2-19 View the final report.

The Alternative to Full Testing: Extrapolation

Running a test pass implementation of your terminal server project is the best way for you to get a true picture of the session load your Terminal Services hardware can handle before running a full pilot program. There may be situations, however, in which you will be unable to run through a test pass. If no one is available to help you, you can do a single pass on your own, record the results with the Reliability And Performance Monitor, and extrapolate the number of users that server can handle from the results.

You will still need to set up your terminal server and load the applications that you will host. (To learn how to set up a terminal server, see Chapter 3.) Where you can save time is in user testing. Instead of mimicking your user environment with multiple user sessions and with real user help, you can make some estimates by testing with one user session and doing some math.

In this case, most of the counters we checked for the full test pass will not help you. You can't really tell much about page file usage with only one user, and with only one session you're not likely to be putting much strain on disk I/O. You can, however, tell what's going on within the session itself.

To find out, create a data collector as we discussed earlier in this chapter, including only the Terminal Server Session counters for Working Set Peak and % Processor Time.

Note Because your report doesn't have to include every counter you collect data for, you can reuse the one from the earlier walkthrough if you created it as you read.

Run the test as described previously, trying to mimic a user session. When you've finished collecting data, select the counters to view as described previously in this chapter and choose to show a report of what's happening in that session (as opposed to choosing counter data for <All instances> as we did in the test pass). View this step in Figure 2-20.

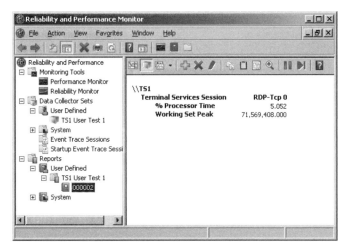

FIGURE 2-20 Report based on session extrapolation

Now that you have this report, what does it mean? You can view the data in several ways.

The data shows that the % Processor Time is approximately 5 percent. To determine the maximum users that can be supported with this processor, divide 100 percent by 5 percent; the result is 20 users.

> **Note** You may have multiple processors in your terminal server. Be aware that two processors don't render twice the power of one. Instead, there is a sliding scale:
>
> ~1.8 when going from one to two processors
>
> ~1.65 when going from two to four processors
>
> So, if you have four processors in your terminal server, you compute Max Users in this way:
>
> 100% divided by 5% = 20 users. Now take into account the other three processors: 20*1.8*1.65 = 60 users at full load

The processor isn't likely to be the main bottleneck. You must look at the peak working set for the session and weigh that against the amount of RAM in the computer. In this example, the peak working set was about 250 MB. Because it takes 1 GB to support the operating system, take the remainder and divide it by 250. As you can see, if the terminal server has 2 GB of RAM, it should be able to support four users with Microsoft Office productivity applications.

So can this server support 20 users or four users? As you might guess, for best results you should always use the lower number. On this processor, with this amount of RAM, it's safe to guess that you can reasonably support four concurrent users.

> **On the Companion Media** See the book's companion media for a new server sizing tool to help you determine how many people can use a terminal server based on your application set.

Direct from the Source: Server Sizing Tips

If detailed information about end-user activity on the terminal server is not available, then you can make some estimates about how many resources each session will need:

- Allocate a percentage of a processor to a user based on how much CPU you expect users to need for running their tasks. For example, if you expect your users to need approximately 5 percent of the CPU's capacity for their work, expect to have about 20 users per CPU.

- Allocate a working set amount of X MB per user. You can approximate the value of X by launching the applications you expect your users to open, working through a normal scenario, and noting the value of Peak Working Set from Task Manager. If this is not possible, make an estimate starting with a minimum of 50 MB per session for a 32-bit operating system and 100 MB per session for a 64-bit operating system.

- Always make sure that the paging file is three times the size of RAM (for example, if the terminal server has 4 GB of RAM, plan on a 12-GB page file).

- Allocate a disk spindle for every 20 users for best performance. User profiles, page files, and system and application files should be on separate physical volumes as far from each other as possible to avoid I/O bottlenecks.

- Install and configure Windows System Resource Manager (WSRM) for the equal per session policy to balance the load between sessions.

Each of these points will allow you to compute a number of supported users per specific resource. For example, if 5 percent of CPU capacity per user means 20 users per CPU, to compute the number of users four processors will support, the equation is 20 × 1.8 × 1.65 = 60 users at full load, for a margin of 50 percent of the maximum CPU usage, or 30 users.

For memory, 200 MB per user means approximately 15 users for a 4-GB system, where we keep 1 GB for system needs (15 = 3000/200).

You'll likely end up with different results when calculating for different resources. Always use the lowest numbers to avoid overstressing the servers. And of course, keep in mind that this is just an approximation process. There is no guarantee that the system will not run out of resources.

Costin Hagiu

Terminal Server Test Architect

How Many Servers Should You Buy?

Now that you've got a reasonable idea about load, how should you distribute it across servers? Some people question whether it's more cost-efficient to have a single large server that can handle the entire load or to spread the load among more, but less powerful, servers. Is it cheaper to buy one server with 8 GB of RAM or two servers with 4 GB of RAM each?

If initial hardware and software costs are your primary concern, then Terminal Services may not be the ideal platform for you. Using Terminal Services *will* increase your up-front costs. Consider these points:

- You won't save on application licensing. Generally each user needs a license for the applications you host on the terminal server. (Be sure to read the fine print on your application license agreements; it's possible but not likely that an application will charge you only for a single instance when run on a terminal server, even when 20 people are using that application.)

- You won't save on desktop hardware. Unless you're starting from scratch—new company, entirely new hardware, and all the rest—you're not likely to get cheaper desktops than those you already have. Client hardware is a sunk cost.

- You will have to buy terminal servers.

- You will have to buy Terminal Services client access licenses (TS CALs) for users to connect to those servers, regardless of how many servers they're connecting to. (In an interesting side effect, having a TS CAL on your computer technically—but not legally—provides access to any terminal server.) If you're using any additional management software on those terminal servers, you'll need to purchase those components as well. For example, if you install Citrix XenApp (formerly known as Citrix Presentation Server) on your terminal servers to increase manageability, you'll also need to purchase both TS CALs and per-connection licenses from Citrix.

People use Terminal Services for many, many reasons and may discover that it's possible to reduce long-term costs and increase productivity. Up-front costs aren't the best way to determine how to build a sustainable platform, however.

Nevertheless, we recommend getting the second server. Most servers have a maximum of eight memory slots, and the 4-GB DIMMs (dual inline memory modules) are significantly more expensive than the 2-GB DIMMs—currently about five times as much. Additionally, with that second server, you create some redundancy in your environment by not relying solely on one terminal server.

Other Sizing Questions

Thus far, this discussion has focused on what you need to know to size a terminal server properly when that terminal server is running on a physical computer. Let's take a look at other sizing scenarios.

What About Sizing Other Terminal Services Roles?

Do other Terminal Services role services face the same constraints as a terminal server?

The short answer is "not really." We'll talk about the internal workings of each server role as it's introduced in this book, but here's a quick overview of what those other role services are doing:

- A Terminal Services Licensing Server provides per-device TS CALs or updates Active Directory to show usage of a per-user TS CAL on a user account object, depending on whether the terminal server using the license server is in per-user mode or per-server mode.

■ A Terminal Services (TS) Gateway examines incoming connections and permits them or refuses them based on the rules that you set up. The main constraint on TS Gateway performance is the number of simultaneous incoming connections and the number of network packets in each one compared to the network speed; keep in mind that the server can maintain hundreds of connections.

■ A Terminal Services Session Broker (TS Session Broker) examines incoming connection requests and determines which terminal server they should be routed to, based on current session load and whether or not the person making the request already has a connection on another terminal server.

■ A Terminal Services Web Access server accepts incoming HTTP connections to generate RDP files on the fly. When delivered, those RDP files provide a direct connection to a terminal server.

In short, with the exception of TS Gateway, other Terminal Services role services generally handle short transactions and then pass the more substantial duties to a terminal server. The load really isn't very large except during heavy logon times when they're processing a lot of connections. Ensure that the TS Gateway (or TS Web Access, whichever users are going to first) has sufficient bandwidth to handle the expected load of concurrent incoming connections. Otherwise, the servers should be able to function well if they meet the requirements for Windows Server 2008.

Can I Run Terminal Services in a Virtual Machine?

Virtualization is one of the hot topics today. VMware has a large following, Microsoft has a Microsoft Server 2008 Hyper-V hypervisor virtualization solution for 64-bit operating systems in beta as of this writing, and IT professionals are interested in what virtualization can do for them. Does virtualization mix with Terminal Services?

The answer to the question: Maybe, but maybe not. The short answer is that it depends on what roles you want to run in virtual machines and the stress on those roles. For most role services related to Terminal Services (e.g., TS Gateway, TS Session Broker, or TS Licensing), running in a virtual computer should not cause any problems. In fact, for years Terminal Services administrators have run license servers in virtual computers to make it easier to maintain a backup. (This isn't necessarily supported depending on the virtual machine platform you use, but it is done.)

For terminal servers, it depends on how heavily used the terminal servers are. If the load is very light—say only a few users per server—then this may be practical and allow you to avoid dedicating a physical server to an undemanding role. For terminal servers with heavier usage, however, this isn't likely to be a good fit for several reasons:

■ **Disk I/O bottlenecks**   We've talked about how best practices for terminal servers recommend that you have one disk spindle—one physical disk—for each 20 users. If your virtual server is supporting five terminal servers, each supporting 20 users, you could need 15 disk spindles to conform to recommendations.

- **Memory constraints** Terminal servers are memory-hungry. A virtual machine host must have a lot of RAM to support many terminal servers. This virtual machine host could also end up being very expensive. Most servers we've seen max out at 8 slots for RAM. As of this writing, 4-GB DIMMs cost about four times as much as 2-GB DIMMs. Money-wise, you're better off with a second server than one server with twice as much RAM.

There is a place for hosting TS role services (such as a license server) on virtual computers, however. Session brokers and license servers don't need a lot of resources to keep running. The main reason not to put some servers on virtual machines is for physical isolation of roles deployed outside the firewall—just as you don't mix those with roles deployed inside the firewall on the same physical host.

> **Note** Microsoft offers both Microsoft Virtual Server and Hyper-V as virtualization options. You'll get better performance from Hyper-V, scheduled to be available within 180 days of the Windows Server 2008 release.

Supporting Client Use Profiles

We've talked a lot about servers—and specifically the Terminal Services role—in this chapter. But you also need to take the users into consideration when planning. What kinds of computers do you need? What licensing model should you follow to best support their work patterns?

PC or Thin Client?

This is another one of those "it depends" situations. The reasons that make thin client devices a requirement for some people just don't apply to all situations, and the same is true for PCs.

> **Note** For those new to Terminal Services, a *thin client* is a solid-state computer (that is, no hard disk) that is intended to act entirely or almost entirely as a client to a terminal server. Clients supporting RDP connections usually run Microsoft Windows CE or Microsoft Windows XP Embedded. (You'll see some Linux-based thin clients, but the RDP clients on Linux are not supported by Microsoft.)

Thin clients are common in places where PCs won't work well because of space, vibration, and other environmental issues, and they are also favored when the cost of maintaining individual, personalized computers is very high because of frequent user turnover. Thin clients generally only work when all applications are run from the terminal servers. It is technically possible to preload a thin client running Windows XP Embedded with applications, but this would be extremely expensive because of the amount of flash memory and RAM required to store and run those applications locally. (As of this writing, thin clients running Windows CE Embedded do not support TS RemoteApps, discussed in Chapter 6, "Installing and Publishing Applications.")

PCs are for the common scenario when not all applications will be run from the terminal server. Not all applications work well in a shared environment, and not everyone is connected to a network all the time. PCs do require more maintenance than thin clients and are harder to lock down.

What's the Best License Model?

We'll talk about Terminal Services Licensing and how it works in detail in Chapter 3, but Terminal Services client access licenses (TS CALs) are worth a mention when you're planning your terminal server environment.

Terminal servers support either per-device or per-user TS CALs. Per-device TS CALs are associated with a particular computer (can be either PC or thin client). Per-user TS CALs are associated with a particular end user.

The answer to "Which is better?" can best be answered by "Which will cost the least amount of money while still allowing us to comply with the EULA (End User License Agreement)?" To calculate the answer, just consider whether you have more computers or more end users. Organizations doing shift work, where three people may use the same computer, will benefit from the per-device model. Organizations where the ratio is one user to every computer, or even two computers to every user (for example, if many users have both a desktop computer and a laptop), will benefit from the per-user model.

Each licensing model has a limitation, or at least a consideration. Per-user licensing works only with Windows Server 2003 or later—you cannot use it in a workgroup or within a domain prior to Windows 2003. This is because the license usage is stored as a property to the user's account object. Additionally, the license server must be able to update the domain controller to write this property. Although per-device licensing does not have this limitation, the license is associated with a particular device. This can sometimes lead to complications when you retire a PC or are using a thin client that does not store the per-device TSCALs properly and keeps requesting a new one whenever it connects.

There *is* one other major difference between per-user and per-device licensing in Windows Server 2008: per-device licensing is enforced, whereas per-user licensing is only tracked. This does not mean it is okay to break the EULA. You still need to buy a per-user license for each person accessing one of your terminal servers.

Want to know more about how licensing works? See Chapter 3.

What Applications Can I Run on a Terminal Server?

Okay, you're convinced. You'd like to add terminal servers to your IT infrastructure. One question remains: Can you use terminal servers to host all your current applications?

This is a great question to which there is no definitive answer. Microsoft does not maintain a list of third-party applications tested with Terminal Services. Not all application vendors test their applications on terminal servers. How can you find out what will work well, what will work well with a little help, and what won't work at all?

Note Although application vendors may not test on terminal servers, if an application is certified to run on Windows Vista, it should run on a terminal server. Not all features may work as well as they would if the application was installed locally, but the main features of most applications certified to run on Windows Vista should be available on Windows Server 2008 Terminal Servers.

There are two main ways you can find out if an application will work on a terminal server (or what you'll need to do to it to make it work well) before actually installing it.

- Ask if the vendor supports the application on a terminal server, and ask about the recommended configuration. If the vendor has not tested the application on a terminal server, you may need to get into some details about the application design. Table 2-2 includes some of the details you should know about an application before attempting to run it on a terminal server. This is especially applicable to older or proprietary applications; most applications certified to run on Windows Vista should not have any problems running on a Windows Server 2008 Terminal Server. They may be resource-intensive, depending on the application (few application developers design with a shared computer in mind), but they will avoid the design flaws that prevent an application from running properly.

- Check to see if anyone else has successfully run the application on a terminal server. This can be as simple as doing a Web search for the name of the application plus "terminal server," or going to the Web site of an independent software vendor (ISV) who packages applications for automatic deployment on a terminal server.

Note One ISV that makes this type of information available is visionapp, located at *http://www .visionapp.com*. If you look in the Home | Resources | Download Center section and click the link for the installation packages, you'll see a long list of application packages that visionapp has tested—and deployed—for its customers. You can't use the packages without the visionapp software, but you can search to see if their consulting arm has actually deployed the application you had in mind.

TABLE 2-2 Application Design Questions

Characteristic	Background	Implications
Will the application setup automatically begin Add/Remove Programs? (Applies to non-MSI programs only.)	A terminal server has a special mode called Install Mode for installing applications properly for multi-user use, which the administrator can set from the command line or by using Add/Remove Programs. If the setup routine is launched from Windows Explorer or the command line, the terminal server should change modes.	If an application does not install in Install Mode, it will not support personalization for each person using it.
Will the application permit multiple versions to be run on the same terminal server?	Different versions of an application may use identically named but different DLLs.	If more than one version of an application is running on the same terminal server, the applications may have a DLL conflict and not run properly.
Does the application separate per-user and per-machine registry data, or does it assume that one user equates to one computer?	Applications may store configuration data in HKEY_LOCAL_MACHINE (the registry hive relating to the computer) or in HKEY_CURRENT_USER (the registry hive relating to the currently logged-in user.) Terminal servers will have one instance of HKCU for each logged-in user.	Since many people are running applications on the same terminal server, for personalization to be supported the application must separate per-machine and per-user data.
Does the application separate per-user and per-machine configuration data, or does it assume that one user equates to one computer?	Applications may store configuration data in the system files, but these may not be (and should not be) available to everyone logged on to the terminal server. Applications should store personalized data structures by user.	Since many people are running applications on the same terminal server, for personalization to be supported the application must separate per-machine and per-user data.
Does the application allow (or disallow) multiple instances of itself to run as appropriate?	Some administrative applications should only be launched once to work best (a disk-management utility that can mount or format disks is one good example). Business applications on a terminal server should launch more than once, but older ones may only permit one instance of themselves.	More than one instance of a management application could end up in inconsistencies in user or machine configuration that may result in serious problems. For business applications, if it will only run one instance, it's useless on a terminal server.

TABLE 2-2 Application Design Questions

Characteristic	Background	Implications
Does the application separate computer and user identities?	Some older network applications identify themselves by computer name or IP address, but on a shared computer this doesn't work properly. Applications that have a network presence should be user-specific (like MSN Messenger, for example), not computer-specific (like the old WinChat used to be).	If an application identifies itself by the computer it's running on, then it can't map to a specific user running that application on a shared computer. (This isn't the same thing as applications needing per-session IP addresses to communicate with the outside world. That's a legitimate need, but not one Terminal Services supports in Windows Server 2008.)
Does the application assume that the Windows Explorer shell is always present?	Applications should not assume that the Windows Desktop will be available—especially now that RemoteApps are used. (Your user configuration for File-Save Locations should *also* not assume that the Desktop is available.)	If an application assumes the Windows Explorer shell is available, then it may not work properly with RemoteApps.
How does the application communicate with any external hardware resources?	If the application needs to communicate with any external hardware resources, then it should use ports that are supported for redirection.	Hardware requiring ports that are not supported for redirection won't work from within a terminal server session.
Does the application assume that the TEMP directory is persistent?	A user's TEMP directory will be cleaned up when the user logs off a terminal server session.	If the application stores data in Temp files, then that data will be deleted with the TEMP directory when the user logs off.

What Version of Remote Desktop Connection Do I Need?

Some features of Windows Server 2008 Terminal Services require the latest version of the Remote Desktop Connection (RDC). As of this writing, the latest version is RDC 6.1, available in Windows XP Service Pack 3, Windows Vista Service Pack 1, and as a standalone package for Windows XP SP2. Table 2-3 maps the features in Windows Server 2008 and their RDC requirements. Not all features are new; this is just the feature set now available. If no requirement it listed, then the feature works with RDC 5.x and is therefore supported for version 6.x.

TABLE 2-3 Client Requirements for Features of Windows Server 2008 Terminal Services

Feature	Requires RDC 6.0	Requires RDC 6.1
Using role services		
TS Remote Desktops		
TS RemoteApp	X	

TABLE 2-3 **Client Requirements for Features of Windows Server 2008 Terminal Services**

Feature	Requires RDC 6.0	Requires RDC 6.1
TS Gateway	X	
TS Web Access		X
TS Session Broker	X	
User experience		
24-bit color		
32-bit color	X	
Display data prioritization	X	
Font Smoothing	X	
Large Resolution Support	X	
Monitor Spanning	X	
Advanced Compression	X	
Support for IPv6		
Device redirection		
Legacy Printer Redirection		
PnP Device Redirection Framework Support	X	
Serial Port Redirection		
Sound Redirection		
Basic Clipboard Redirection		
Advanced Clipboard Redirection	X	
Drive Redirection		
Security		
Smart Card Support		
FIPS 140-1 Support		
SSL Authentication		
Network Level Authentication	X (Vista only)	X (XP and Vista)
Single Sign-on using CredSSP	X (Vista only)	X (XP and Vista)
Network Access Protection Integration		X
RDP Signing		X
Wildcard SSL certificate support		X

The reason why NLA and single sign-on are version dependent is because Windows XP SP2 does not support CredSSP, required for these features. SP3 does, but with Windows XP SP3 comes RDC 6.1. (For more information about CredSSP and single sign-on, see Chapter 7, "Multi-Server Deployments and Securing Terminal Server Connections.")

What Server Role Services Do I Need to Support My Business?

Although Windows Server 2008 has several role services to support the main role of terminal services, you don't necessarily need all of them, or you may add them as your needs grow. Some of these may seem obvious, but we've been questioned about all of these subjects, so they are worth addressing directly:

- You always need a TS license server. The terminal server will not continue to accept connections without one.

- You need Terminal Services Gateway to support secure access from the Internet. You do not need TS Gateway to provide secure access within the firewall.

- You need Terminal Services Web Access (and an IIS server) if you intend to display application links in a Web browser. TS Web Access will work on both a corporate intranet and on the Internet.

- You only need Terminal Services Session Broker if you have more than one server. It's definitely worth it to have two servers, however. Having a TS Session Broker allows you to address your servers as a farm rather than as individuals.

Summary

After reading this chapter, you should have a good understanding of the internal workings of Windows Server 2008 and how they apply to terminal servers. You should also have some notion of how to design a test program or how to use the Reliability And Performance Monitor to estimate the number of users a server can support. We've covered the client requirements and discussed what server roles you'll need to support different business needs (e.g., remote workers).

Best practices for planning a Windows Server 2008 Terminal Services deployment include:

- Use the 64-bit version of the operating system if your needs will require more than 16 GB of RAM. 64-bit terminal servers can use more memory than 32-bit, and memory is the greatest constraint on a 32-bit operating system.

- Try to have one disk spindle for each 20 to 30 simultaneous users of the terminal server, to avoid I/O bottlenecks.

- Don't install the Terminal Server role service on a virtual machine. Virtual machines aren't well suited to the disk I/O and memory demands of terminal servers.

- Choose applications wisely. Applications certified for Windows Vista should run without problems on a terminal server (aside from any issues relating to resource-intensive applications). A proven track record or official support for execution on a terminal server is ideal.

- Use real-world testing to understand the system and network requirements for the applications and usage profiles you want to support. Estimates based on theory are less useful than experience.

Now that you understand the basic operations of your terminal server, the next step is to start setting it up. In Chapter 3, we'll go through the process of setting up your basic terminal server environment, including the license server.

Additional Resources

There's a lot of information covered in this chapter, and even more background is available. If you'd like more details about Windows internals that are relevant to terminal servers, please see the following:

- For some tips on capacity planning, please see the "Terminal Services Scaling and Performance on Windows Server 2008" white paper posted here: *http://go.microsoft.com/fwlink/?LinkId=128271*.

- We've scratched the surface of Terminal Services internals here. For more information about Windows Server internals, please see *Microsoft Windows Internals, Fourth Edition* by David Solomon and Mark Russinovich (Microsoft Press, 2004).

- For details of how memory management in Windows Server 2008 (and Windows Vista) differ from previous versions, see "Advances in Memory Management for Windows" posted at *http://www.microsoft.com/whdc/system/cec/MemMgt.mspx*.

- The companion media that accompanies this book includes a server sizing tool you can use to simulate usage patterns, newly developed for Windows Server 2008.

- The Performance Team's blog located at *http://blogs.technet.com/askperf/default.aspx* is also a good introduction to Windows Server 2008 internals.

Chapter 3
Installing the Core Terminal Server Environment

This chapter covers building the basic framework of a terminal server ecosystem, including a terminal server and license server. Specifically, the following topics are covered:

- How terminal servers work

- How to install the Terminal Server role

- Setting up the Windows System Resource Manager

- Configuring a terminal server

- How license servers work

- Installing and activating the license server and installing Terminal Server Client Access Licenses (TS CALs)

- Configuring the terminal server licensing settings

- Managing TS CALs and defining which terminal servers can allocate them

- Reporting on TS CAL usage

How Terminal Servers Work

You know what a terminal server *does*: It accepts incoming connections from multiple users and runs unique sessions to support those users as though they each had their own computer. What you may not know is *how* it does this. This section discusses the components of the operating system that let terminal servers do what they do. It covers both the key services directly related to supporting the multi-user remote access architecture and the components that support it for the entire operating system.

Services Supporting Terminal Services

Three services support a terminal server: Terminal Services, Terminal Services Configuration, and Terminal Services User Mode Port Redirector.

Note All three services run on both Windows Server 2008 and Windows Vista computers, since both can accept remote interactive connections. A major difference between the two is licensing. A Windows Server 2008 computer can run multiple active connections; a Windows Vista computer can only have one active connection at any given time. Even if the Windows Server 2008 computer isn't a terminal server, it can still accept multiple connections for remote administration: one remote and one local.

The Terminal Services service enables a computer to accept an interactive logon from another computer. Terminal Services Configuration enables system configuration that needs to happen in the System Context (meaning that it's highly privileged; even more so than the administrative context). The Terminal Services User Mode Port Redirector enables remote device mapping (used for printers, MP3 players, or client-side drives).

To see the impact of these three services, try stopping them.

Caution In previous versions of the operating system, the Terminal Services service could not be stopped; if you tried, you'd get an error message. In Windows Server 2008, you can stop it, even from a remote session. Unless you're prepared to either remotely restart the service using WMI or can physically get to the console to restart the service, however, you might want to skip the first experiment!

If you stop Terminal Services, all remote connections to the computer—including the one you're using (if you stop the service from a remote connection)—will immediately disconnect. That is, any applications open in a remote session will still run on the terminal server, but the remote connection is ended and anyone using that connection will need to log in again to reconnect. If you need to disconnect everyone from the terminal server immediately, stopping this service will make that happen. It will also only disconnect their sessions, not log them off, so their applications will remain open.

If you stop the Terminal Services User Mode Port Redirector, any client-side devices or drives that you have in the remote session will instantly disappear from My Computer in the remote session. Restarting the service will *not* bring the redirected resources back after stopping the service deletes them. If you restart this service, anyone who has client-side devices redirected to their terminal session must disconnect and reconnect to their session to remap those resources to the remote session. This is because when you stop the service, you're closing down the virtual channels in Remote Desktop Protocol (RDP) that support device redirection. To bring them back, simply restart the connection.

> **Note** For more about virtual channels, see Chapter 5, "Fine-Tuning the User Experience."

You'll find that stopping the Terminal Services Configuration Service does not have any effect on your ability to make configuration changes. That's because it looks like it's stopping, but it doesn't. Rather than give you an error message, the service just ignores the request. Although the Services Microsoft Management Console (MMC) snap-in will imply that the service is stopped, if you right-click the service you'll see that the active option is to stop, not start the service.

If you double-click the service while it's apparently stopped (see Figure 3-1), you'll notice that the only option is to stop it, not start it. (It takes the Services tool a few seconds to refresh; at first, it will appear that the service is truly stopped, but you won't see any change in your ability to configure the terminal sever.)

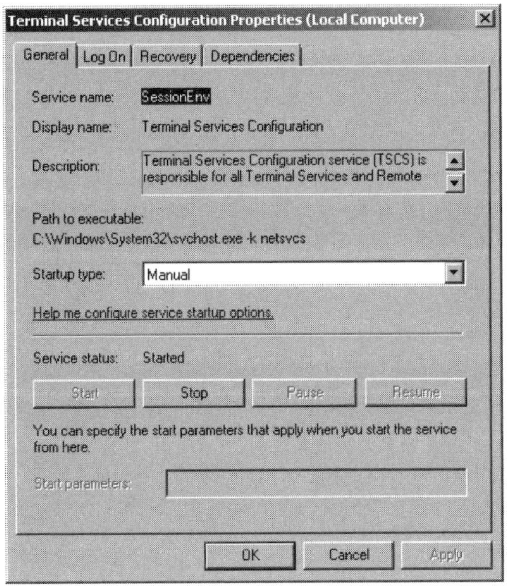

FIGURE 3-1 Stopping the Terminal Services Configuration services has no effect, even though the Services snap-in will imply on its main page that the service is stopped.

Creating and Supporting a Terminal Session

Those are the services that support Terminal Services. The operating system needs to do the following to support the sessions that those services make possible:

- Create the sessions for each person to use.

- Connect client to server via a display protocol that allows the two to share data.

- Create a Windows environment for each session.

- Route client input to the correct application on the terminal server and route client output to the appropriate client computer, including

  ❑ Windows user interface and application screens

  ❑ Mouse clicks and keystrokes

  ❑ Sound

  ❑ Redirected devices such as printers and drives

- Package the RDP data for transport over the network protocol (TCP/IP, in this case).

The pieces to support all of this come together as shown in Figure 3-2, which displays the server-side architecture of Terminal Services in Windows Server 2008. Over the next pages, we'll explore this architecture to show how these components cooperate.

In Figure 3-2, the components that are identified as being protocol dependent only operate when the Remote Desktop Protocol (RDP), included with Windows 2008 Server Terminal Services, is used. If a third-party product replaces RDP with another protocol, the rest of the session looks much the same, but those protocol-specific extensions are replaced.

Key Terminal Services Processes Loaded at Boot Time

In Windows Server 2008 and Windows Vista, key system services run in Session 0, which is not accessible to users. When you boot a terminal server, the operating system loads many new services to support itself. The ones important to Terminal Services functionality include:

- The Session Manager (Smss.exe)

- The Windows Startup Manager (Winit.exe)

- The Services And Controller Application (Services.exe)

- The Local System Authority (Lsass.exe)

- The Local Session Manager (Lsm.exe)

- The euphoniously named Desktop Window Manager Session Manager (runs inside an instance of Svchost.exe)

- The Terminal Services service (runs inside an instance of Svchost.exe)

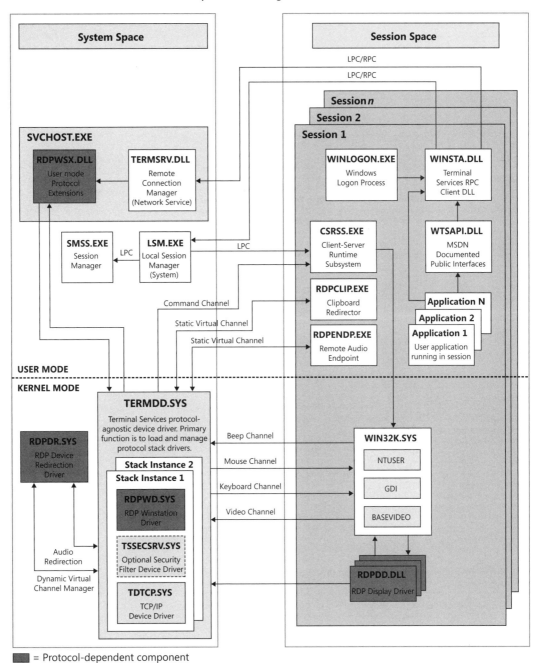

FIGURE 3-2 Windows Server 2008 Terminal Services architecture

Boot time works through a series of steps to enable Terminal Services functionality:

1. The system process loads the Session Manager.

2. The Session Manager loads another instance of itself.

3. The new Session Manager loads the Windows Startup Manager and then exits.

4. The Windows Startup Manager loads the Services and Controller Application, the Local Security Authority, and the Local Session Manager.

5. The Services and Controller Application loads instances of Svchost.exe for the Desktop Window Manager Session Manager and the Terminal Services service (among others not as relevant here).

> **Note** If you look up Winint.exe online, you'll find a lot of links saying that it's part of the Wolf virus. It's not. It's the Windows Startup Manager and it should be located in Windows\System32. Some virus processes have the same names as Windows system files to reduce their chances of detection and cleaning.

To see all this, use Process Monitor. Enable boot logging and restart the terminal server. Relaunch Process Monitor and then choose Tools | Process Tree to see the boot order. As you can see, the parent instance of the Session Manager keeps running, but after the child instance has done its jobs, it closes.

You can't easily find the TermService service (or any other service) in Process Monitor to see what it's launching, because many services run within processes called Svchost.exe (to speed logon times, in part) and you can't distinguish them by name. To find out which instance of Svchost.exe a given service is running in and learn more about it using Process Monitor, run Task Manager and turn to the Services tab. Edit the visible columns to show the Process ID for that service (for this example, TermService) and find Terminal Services in the list. Now, you can filter events in Process Monitor to show only that Process ID and easily pick out the correct instance of Svchost.exe in the process tree.

> **On the Companion Media** Download Process Monitor from the following link, available on this book's companion CD: *http://technet.microsoft.com/en-us/sysinternals/bb896645.aspx.*

Getting the services running in Session 0 sets the stage for the terminal server to begin accepting incoming sessions. The following sections will explain the roles these services play in setting up the user environment for each session.

> **Note** To see which processes run in Session 0, run Task Manager. From the Process tab, choose View | Select Columns to open the Select Process Page Columns dialog box. From the list, make sure that the box is checked for Session ID. On the Process tab, you'll now be able to see which processes run in Session 0.

Creating a New Session

Windows Server 2008 always runs at least one session for services (Session 0), and additional sessions that users can interact with. The Session Manager (Smss.exe) for the terminal server is the piece of Windows that gets the process started. A new instance of the Session Manager is created. It launches all of the processes required to support the session.

When someone attempts to log on to the system, the initial instance of Smss.exe creates another instance (of itself—that is, it launches an additional instance of Smss.exe) to configure the new session, just as it did for Session 0. On Windows Server 2008 Terminal Server systems, multiple instances of Smss.exe can run concurrently, enabling faster logons for multiple users (see Figure 3-3). The number of parallel sessions that Session Manager can create at a time depends on the number of virtual processors in the terminal server. For example, a terminal server with four quad-core processors is able to create up to 16 new sessions simultaneously.

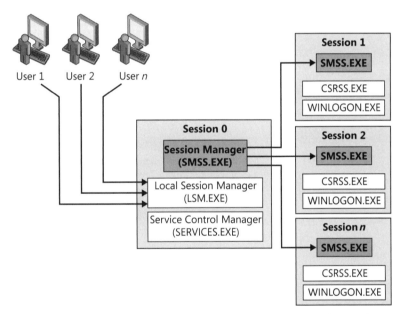

FIGURE 3-3 The Session Manager in Windows Server 2008 can launch multiple sessions at once by loading multiple copies of itself.

When the child instance of the Session Manager launches, it starts the Windows subsystem (Csrss.exe and Winlogon.exe) and then exits.

When Smss.exe enables new sessions, it does so with the help of several other services. The Local Session Manager accepts the incoming connections and helps determine whether or not a computer may connect to the server. The Terminal Services service allows a server to interact with incoming connections. All these services are managed by the Service Control Manager. To recap, see Table 3-1.

TABLE 3-1 Key System Processes for Initiating a Terminal Services Session

Function	Supporting Component	Filename
Create, destroy, enumerate, and manipulate terminal sessions. Formerly incorporated into the Terminal Services service, it is now an independent process.	Local Session Manager	Lsm.exe
Check credentials collected by the credential provider and create a token identifying the user.	Local Security Authority	Lsass.exe
Start, stop, restart, and pause Windows services.	Service Control Manager	Services.exe
Create new sessions.	Session Manager	Smss.exe
Enable multiple sessions on a server and provide the runtime interfaces for communication between client session and the operating system. Also known as the Remote Connection Manager.	Terminal Services	Termsrv.dll

Want to see more about what happens within that new session? Read on . . .

Enabling User Logons to the New Session

Having a session isn't enough. To work, you need a way to log on to it. In addition to starting the Service Control Manager and the Local Session Manager on the terminal server, the Session Manager also builds the Windows logon infrastructure in each session, including:

- The Client-Server RunTime Subsystem (CSRSS), also known as the Windows subsystem

- The Windows logon process (Winlogon.exe), which launches the Logon User Interface Host (Logonui.exe), which in turn launches the credential provider that accepts the end user's logon data.

> **Note** In versions of Windows prior to Windows Vista, Winlogon.exe launched the Graphical Identification and Authentication DLL (GINA) specified in the registry. Windows Vista and Windows Server 2008 have replaced the GINA with a credential provider, identified in HKLM\Software\Microsoft\Windows NT\CurrentVersion\Authentication\Credential Providers. It has a different name, but plays the same basic role.

In short, the logon process works by accomplishing the following steps:

1. The Windows subsystem launches the Windows logon process.

2. The Local Session Manager determines whether or not the incoming connection is allowed at all.

3. The Windows logon process presents the interface to the credential provider so a user can provide credentials (user name and password, or smart card and PIN).

4. The credential provider passes the credentials to the Local System Authority, which checks them against the security database (Active Directory for a domain account or the local computer's security account manager for a local account).

Figure 3-4 illustrates how these components work together to allow you to log onto the terminal server.

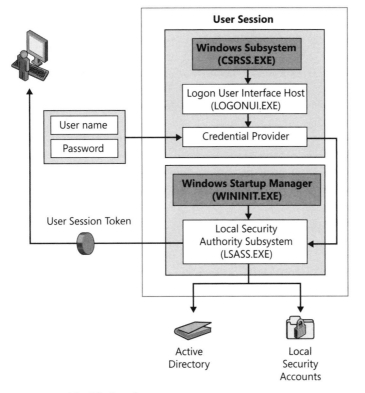

FIGURE 3-4 The Windows logon process

Creating the Base Environment in Each Session

Finally, the Windows user environment needs a shell—a user environment—even if the terminal server session will display only RemoteApps, not a full desktop. When displaying the full desktop, the usual Windows shell is Explorer. If displaying TS RemoteApps only, it's the RDP shell.

When the session begins, the Terminal Server Service and Desktop Window Manager Session Manager running in Session 0 each begin a per-session piece of themselves. Terminal Services launches Rdpclip.exe, which supports the shared Clipboard between the session and any locally running applications. The Desktop Window Manager Session Manager launches Dwm.exe, which manages the appearance of windows in the remote session.

Table 3-2 shows the user-mode processes that create the common user environment (minus the applications that you'd also expect to see running). You won't actually see all these from Task Manager.

TABLE 3-2 User-Mode Processes That Support Each Session's Windows Environment

Function	Supporting Component	Filename
Create graphical effects in Windows. Desktop Window Manager (DWM) enables Aero Glass on Windows Vista clients (and for Windows Vista remote connections), but this effect is not supported on Windows Server 2008 Terminal Services.	Desktop Window Manager	Dwm.exe
Display the Windows shell for desktops.	Explorer	Explorer.exe
Enable clipboard redirection between the session and the client.	File copy tool	Rdpclip.exe
Display TS RemoteApps.	The Windows shell for TS RemoteApps	Rdpshell.exe
Supply information to management interfaces on the terminal server.	Windows Terminal Services APIs	Wtsapi.dll

Remote sessions aren't interesting without interaction, however. That's where the last step of passing data between client and server comes in.

Passing Data Between Client and Server

A terminal server doesn't have one session, it has dozens or hundreds. A terminal services client doesn't necessarily have a single application running from the terminal server; it has perhaps four or five or more . . . and not all of those four or five applications are necessarily running on the same terminal server. How does the data passing between client and server get to the right place? The answer is threefold:

- The session structure

- The use of Session IDs and Process IDs to identify internally *which* instance of an application the system is referring to among the multiple instances running concurrently on the terminal server

- Cooperation between components on the terminal server (that is, common to all sessions) and in the client session (exclusive to one session)

Session Structure One connection to a terminal server is normally equivalent to one session. In other words, there's never any question on the client as to which session some input should go to, as each session's communication with the terminal server will be handled separately from within the terminal session. Even TS RemoteApps will all run within the same session as long as they're on the same server. The only time you'd have more than one session to the same server is if you deliberately connected to a second desktop and the terminal server was configured to permit more than one session on the same server.

Identifying Processes   If you're in a single session, how do you get the right data to the right application and send the feedback to the correct terminal session? One way is that each session has a unique identifier on the terminal server (the Session ID that you can see in the Terminal Services Manager discussion in Chapter 8, "Managing the Terminal Server Runtime Environment"). Activity within a session is identified to the terminal server by its Session ID, not by the name of the person logged on to the session. Therefore, even if one person has more than one
session open on the same terminal server, the terminal server won't confuse the sessions.

The terminal server also avoids confusion through the way the operating system identifies processes. Windows Server 2008 identifies processes running on a terminal server not only by their names but by their Process IDs. (This is true on any Windows operating system, but on a terminal server it's even more important because of the likelihood that many processes will be duplicated.) A Process ID is also unique on a terminal server. We'll talk more about Process IDs in Chapter 8 when we discuss managing user sessions and processes.

Communicating Between Session and Terminal Server   Several portions of the terminal server are responsible for making sure the right data ends up with the right session, after the ownership of Process IDs and Session IDs is sorted out:

- Rdpwsx.dll is the path between RDP and the kernel. It contains the following:
  - ❑ Generic Conference Control (GCC) to manage virtual channels, which transport specific types of data between the remote session and the client computer
  - ❑ The Multipoint Communication Service (MCS), which assigns data to virtual channels and sets the priority of each so that GCC can work with all the virtual channels as a single pipe
- The RDP stack has three jobs:
  - ❑ Rdpwd.sys transforms display data into RDP commands to be transmitted to the session.
  - ❑ Wdtshare.sys encrypts and packages the RDP stream.
  - ❑ Tdtcp.sys packages RDP for transport on TCP/IP so that the data can be passed between server and client.

The drivers and libraries supporting data-passing between the terminal server and each client session are listed in Table 3-3.

TABLE 3-3 Key Drivers and Services Supporting Terminal Services Remote Sessions for the Entire Terminal Server

Function	Supporting Component	Filename
Manage the virtual channels, allowing the creation and deletion of session connections and controlling resources provided by MCSMUX.	Generic Conference Control	GCC
Accept keyboard input from the sessions.	Keyboard driver for Terminal Services	Kbclass.sys
Assign data to virtual channels within the display protocol, set priority levels, and segment data as required. This abstracts the multiple RDP stacks into a single entity.	Multipoint Communication Service	MCSMUX
Accept mouse input from the sessions.	Mouse driver for Terminal Services	Mouclass.sys
Encode display data into RDP commands.	RDP WinStation driver	Rdpwd.sys
Communicate with kernel via I/O Control Interface; contains GCC and MCSMUX.	Interface between display protocol and kernel	Rdpwsx.Dll
Package RDP onto TCP/IP.	TCP driver	Tdtcp.sys
Coordinate and manage RDP protocol activity.	TS device driver	Termdd.sys
Handle UI transfer, compression, encryption, and framing.		Wdtshare.sys
Manage device redirection and audio.	RDP device redirection driver	Rdpdr.sys

The client also has some work to do to pass data between the session and the terminal server for processing (see Table 3-4). Win32k.sys is the kernel-mode component of the Windows subsystem that manages mouse and keyboard input and sends it to the right application. Rdpdd.sys is the display driver that packages Windows neatly to be processed by the Terminal Services Device Driver.

TABLE 3-4 Key Services and Drivers Running Within Individual Sessions on the Terminal Server

Function	Supporting Component	Filename
Manage the Windows GUI environment by taking the mouse and keyboard inputs and sending them to the appropriate application.	Kernel-mode component of the Windows subsystem	WIN32K.SYS
Capture the Windows user interface and translates it into a form that is readily converted by Rdpwd.sys into the RDP protocol.	RDP display driver	RDPDD.sys

The communication between terminal server session and client uses virtual channels. Each kind of data has its own virtual channel so that data transfer can be enabled or disabled selectively. For instance, it's possible to disable clipboard redirection while still allowing other types of data to pass between client and server.

Virtual channels may be static or dynamic. Static virtual channels are created at the beginning of a session and remain until that session is disconnected or terminated. You can't create new static channels during a session. Dynamic virtual channels are created and torn down on demand, such as when a new device is connected to a terminal session. For more information about virtual channels, see Chapter 5.

Putting It All Together

When you combine the key pieces of a working Terminal Server environment that both support a session and allow it to communicate with the terminal server, it looks like the overview shown in Figure 3-5.

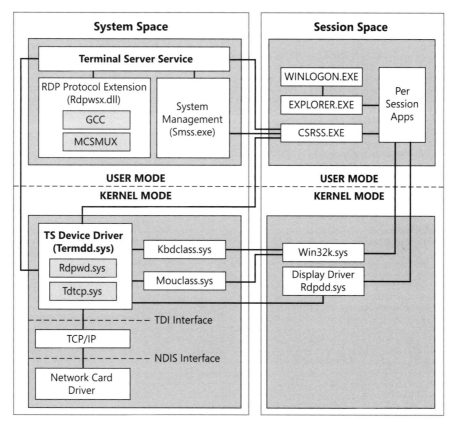

FIGURE 3-5 Components of Terminal Services architecture in Windows Server 2008

We've discussed this model in the preceding pages, but there's a lot of data here. Let's quickly separate what's happening in each quadrant of this illustration, which is broken out between system space (common to all sessions on the terminal server) and session space (unique to each session), and between kernel mode and user mode.

In the upper-left quadrant (System Space, User Mode), the terminal server is launching sessions, accepting incoming connections, and organizing virtual channels. For the sake of simplicity, this image combines the Remote Connection Manager and Local Session Manager into the Terminal Server Service.

In the upper-right quadrant (Session Space, User Mode), the terminal server session runs the following: its Windows logon processes, the Windows subsystem for presenting all aspects of the user interface (UI), its shell, and its applications.

In the lower-left quadrant (System Space, Kernel Mode), the terminal server is loading and managing the protocol-specific functionality of the session. That is, RDP is only one possible protocol that you can use to interact with a terminal server. ICA, used for connecting to terminal servers with Citrix's XenApp extensions to Terminal Server installed, is another.

In the lower-right quadrant (Session Space, Kernel Mode), the session packages the display data and input data to be processed by the display protocol when working in the kernel-mode section of system space.

When a new session is launched, the terminal server sets up the session like this:

1. The parent instance of Session Manager for the terminal server launches a child instance of itself to manage the new session.

2. The child instance of Session Manager loads the Windows subsystem and the Windows Logon Application and then exits.

3. The Windows Logon Application launches Userinit.exe.

4. The Desktop Window Manager Session Manager service for the server launches an instance of the Desktop Window Manager for that session.

5. The Terminal Services service launches Rdpclip.exe to support the shared clipboard.

6. Userinit.exe launches the shell for that session (e.g., Windows Explorer).

Installing a Terminal Server

Now that you're acquainted with the inner workings of a terminal server, it's time to become familiar with the outer workings of installing and configuring it.

> **Note** We'll spend a lot of time installing roles during the course of this book and may skip some steps to avoid unnecessary repetition, but it's worth going into detail once so you understand the processes involved.

To install the Terminal Server role, click Start | Administrative Tools | Server Manager. Right-click Roles, choose Add Roles to open the Add Roles Wizard, and then click Next to move through the opening page. When you get to the next page of the wizard, you'll see a list of available roles as shown in Figure 3-6. Choose Terminal Services by selecting it and then clicking Next. You have the option of selecting more than one check box at a time from this page.

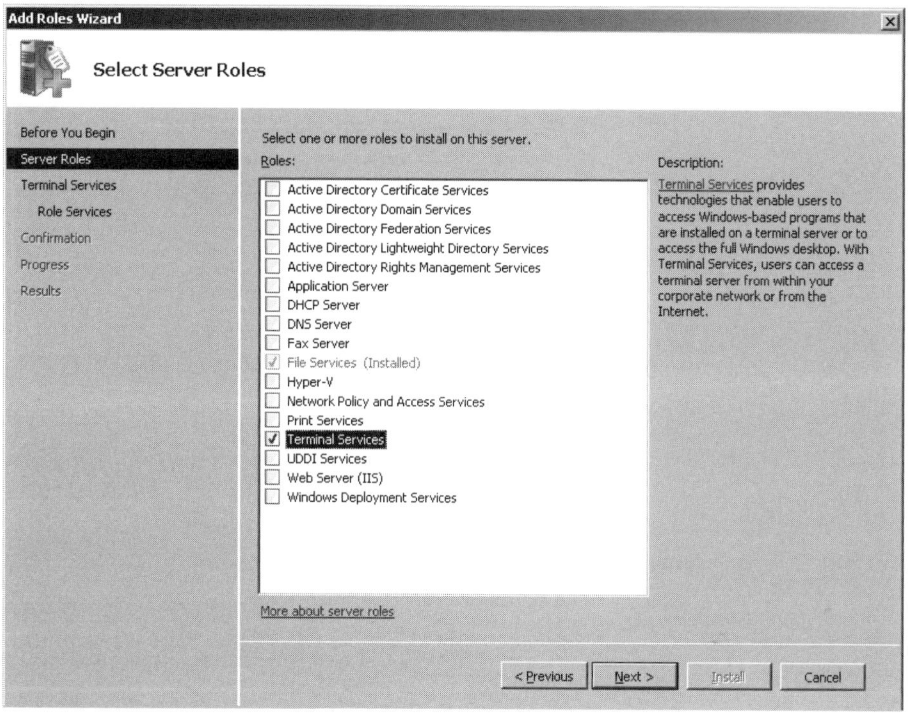

FIGURE 3-6 Choose the Terminal Services role from the list.

When you choose to install Terminal Services, the next page of the wizard offers you an overview of the service, as shown in Figure 3-7. Click Next.

Now, you can see why the Add Roles wizard only offered "Terminal Services" in the main wizard; from here (see Figure 3-8) you can choose any of the related role services. For now, stick with adding Terminal Server and click Next.

> **Note** Do not install the Terminal Server role on a server that already has the Active Directory Domain Services role installed. First, it's not good security practice to allow end users to connect to a domain controller. Second, should some problem with a user or application force you to bring down the terminal server for maintenance, you'll have a domain controller offline.

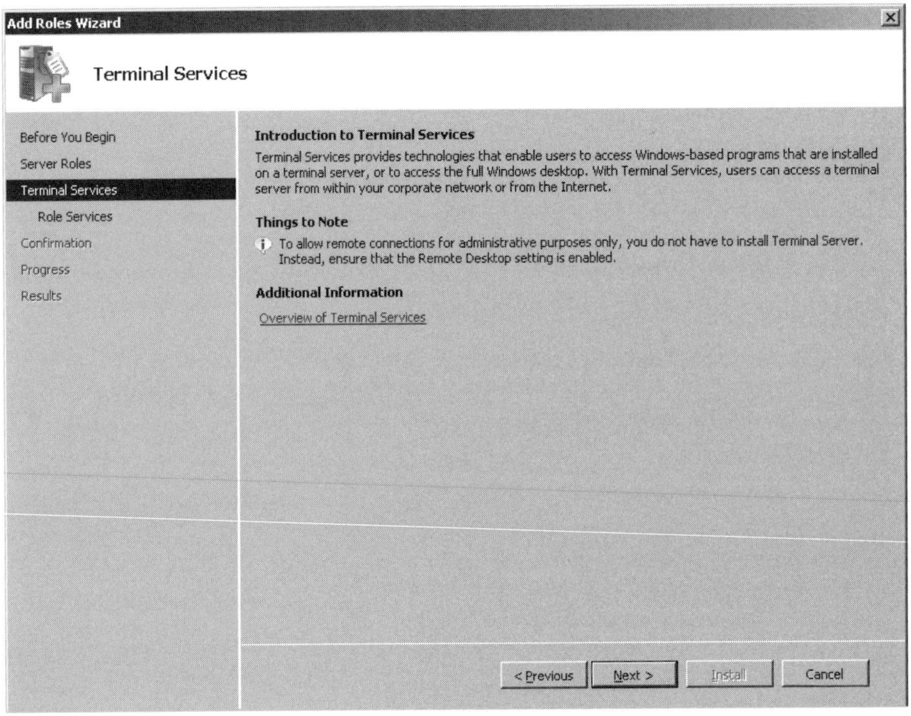

FIGURE 3-7 Windows Server 2008 explains roles before you install them.

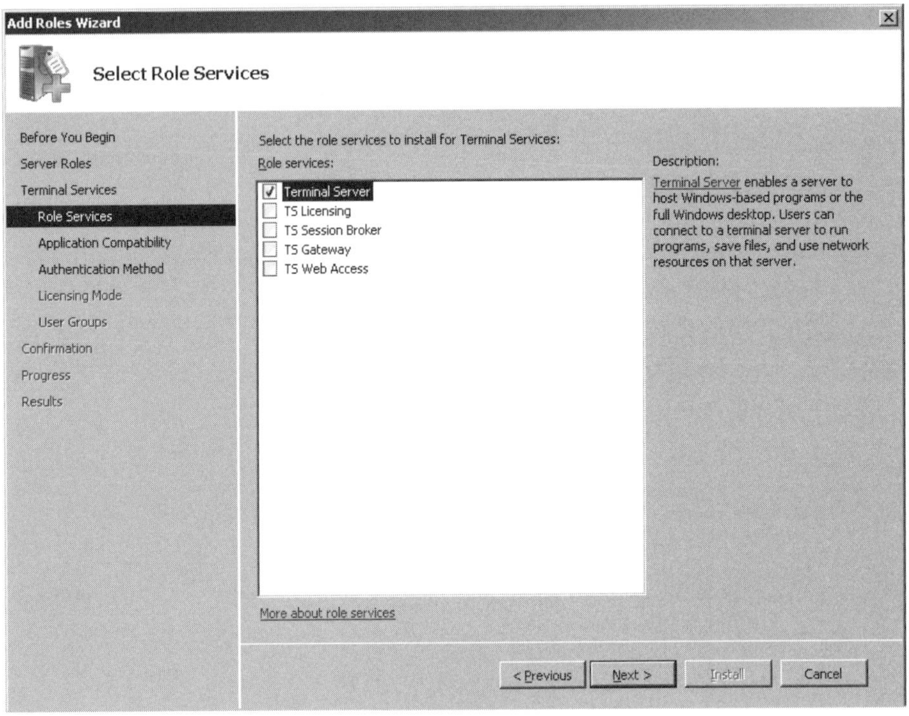

FIGURE 3-8 Choose Terminal Server from the list of Terminal Services role services.

Next, you'll see the Application Compatibility page telling you that if you installed applications on the server prior to installing Terminal Services, some of the existing applications may not work in a multiple user environment. Click Next.

Note See Chapter 6, "Installing and Publishing Applications," for the details of why you shouldn't install applications on a server before installing the Terminal Server role. Applications won't support the type of customization you'd expect for each user logging on if the applications were installed before you installed the role.

Until now, most questions have been fairly self-explanatory. As shown in Figure 3-9, you need to make a decision about whether you want computers logging into the terminal server to support Network Level Authentication (NLA). NLA is supported only for RDC 6.x and later (and only 6.0 on Windows Vista; both Windows XP SP2 and SP3 and Windows Vista SP1 support RDC 6.1). NLA works with CredSSP (which is why it requires RDC 6.1 to work with Windows Vista) to authenticate the user early in the process. We'll talk more about the details in Chapter 7, "Multi-Server Deployments and Securing Terminal Server Connections," but for now you need to know two things:

- Requiring NLA enables you to force users to authenticate themselves before they can create a connection to the terminal server.

- If you require NLA, only clients supporting CredSSP (Windows Vista or Windows XP Service Pack 3) will be able to connect to the terminal server.

Note This decision isn't final; as with many configuration settings, you can change your mind later by reconfiguring the host.

Next, you can choose the license mode of the terminal server (Figure 3-10). A terminal server can be in per-user or per-device mode—that is, it can accept either per-user licenses or per-device licenses—but not both. The incoming connection must present the kind of license that the terminal server is expecting, if the machine or user making the connection already has one. It also means that if the incoming connection *doesn't* present a TS CAL at connection time, and the terminal server has to request one from the license server (more on how this works shortly), then the licenses on the license server must be a type the terminal server is able to accept.

Note In Windows Server 2003, you had to choose the license mode when installing a terminal server. In Windows Server 2008, you can delay this decision until you are certain what types of licenses will be available. A terminal server in "configure later" mode will not ask incoming connections for a license, but a terminal server can only be in this mode during its grace period (120 days). After that, it will not accept connections without a license server and a licensing mode.

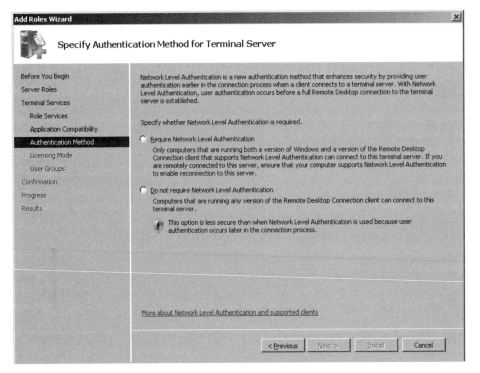

FIGURE 3-9 Choose NLA for better security or do not require it to support broader access to the terminal server.

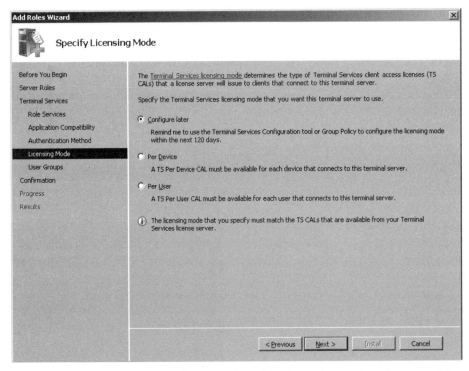

FIGURE 3-10 Choose the appropriate license mode or delay the decision until you have more information.

How It Works: Why "Configure Later"?

Why not just require people to choose a license mode when they install the terminal server? After all, they can change this mode later from the Terminal Server Configuration tools. The reason is simple: that's the way it worked in Windows Server 2003 and it caused some problems.

Before Windows Server 2003, there was only one license mode for terminal servers: per device. This model was enforced, meaning that a terminal server set up to accept per-device TS CALs would eventually stop accepting connections from computers unable to present one. This model was also the default mode for Windows Server 2003 terminal servers, but Windows Server 2003 introduced a new license mode for terminal servers: per user.

The trouble started when people installed the terminal servers without really looking at the license mode option, since this had not mattered in previous versions of Terminal Server. They installed the terminal servers in per-device mode, because that was the default, but often got per-user licenses, since that model fit their needs better. Because the terminal servers weren't set up to use or issue per-user TS CALs, the terminal servers stopped accepting connections. Although the Event Log recorded the problem and (with Service Pack 1) pop-up windows warned administrators when they logged in, this didn't entirely fix the problem.

Because terminal servers must now be in one mode or the other, part of the solution is a "configure later" option. The terminal server licensing mode will eventually need to be configured, but at least the administrator is making a conscious choice when configuring it.

Next, you'll choose who has access to the terminal server. Terminal Server access is partially determined by user membership in the Remote Desktop Users group (see Figure 3-11). Only members of this group may connect to the terminal server.

Why would you limit who is allowed to use the terminal server?

- You have a limited number of TS CALs available, and you don't want to use them for users who don't really need them.

- You have a limited number of application licenses available for applications on the terminal server, and you don't want to use them unnecessarily.

- You sized the server for a certain number of users, and you want to limit the number allowed to log on to your size limit.

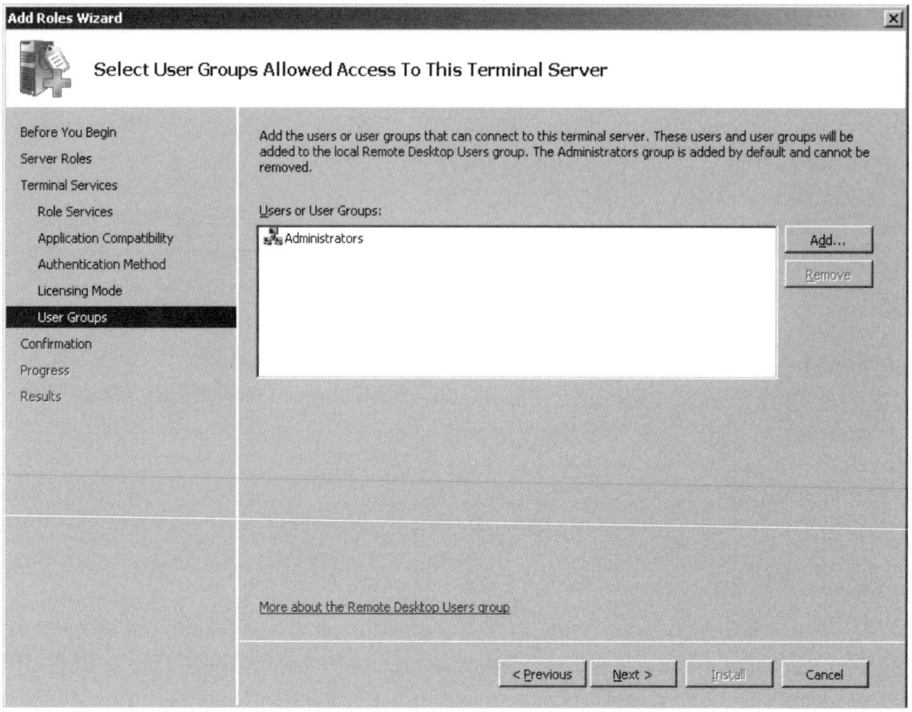

FIGURE 3-11 Add groups to the Remote Desktop Users group to enable user connections.

Note You can deny even members of the Remote Desktop Users group the right to log on by editing their user account properties in Active Directory Users and Computers (ADUC), or through Group Policy. They just can't log on if they're *not* members of the Remote Desktop Users group.

By default, the local Administrator's group is added already. To add more people to the Remote Desktop Users group, click the Add button to open the Select Users dialog box. Enter the security group or users to add, click the Check Names button to validate the name of the accounts, and then click OK. For example, you might add the Domain Users group to the Remote Desktop Users group. (You can do this because Domain Users is a global group and Remote Desktop Users a local group; global groups can be members of local groups.) Then, you can deny access to groups or users selectively.

Note If you're not sure of the name of the group or user accounts you want to add, click the Advanced button, choose the proper domain or computer to choose from, and click Find Now to populate the Search Results area. Then you can select the users or groups to add.

When you've populated the Remote Desktop Users group, the dialog box will look similar to the one shown in Figure 3-12.

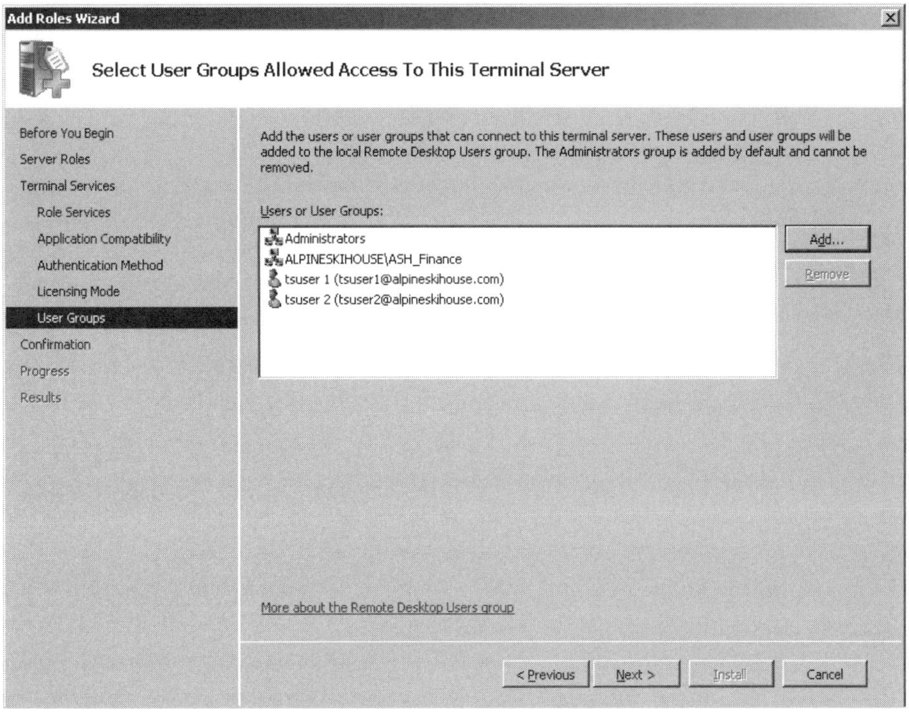

FIGURE 3-12 The Remote Desktop Users group is now populated.

Click Next. The last stage is confirming the settings that you specified during the wizard, as shown in Figure 3-13.

To save the configuration at setup, click the Print, E-mail, Or Save This Information link to create and open a simple HTML page. Particularly if you selected a licensing mode, seriously consider doing this to make a record of the basic installation. This set of information documents the way that the terminal server is set up and will be a guide to the person setting up the second server—or the twentieth—who does not want to manually inspect the terminal server configuration to make sure it's consistent across the load-balanced terminal server farm.

After you click Install, the server will take some time installing the service. When it's finished, you'll be prompted to restart the server and get a second chance at printing or saving the configuration report. When you click Close, you will be prompted to restart the server.

After rebooting, as you start up again the terminal server will spend a few minutes figuring out that you've just installed the role and making final recommendations, as shown in Figure 3-14.

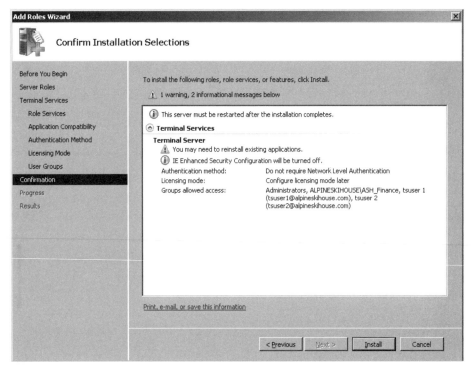

FIGURE 3-13 Confirm the settings in your setup before installing.

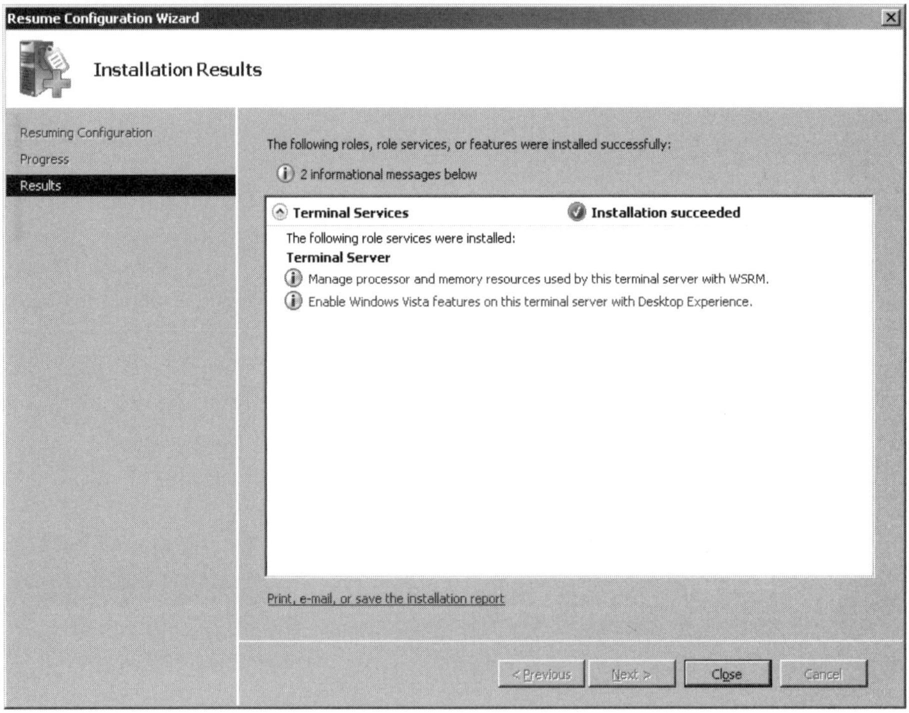

FIGURE 3-14 Complete the installation after rebooting.

Should you follow this advice? To manage processor and memory resources with Windows System Resource Manager (WSRM), you absolutely should follow the recommendations. WSRM will help prevent one person on the terminal server from taking over all the resources.

Desktop Experience is also important. As we'll discuss in Chapter 5, it's required to enable the Plug and Play framework for automatically detecting client-side plug and play devices such as cameras. If you don't install Desktop Experience, you won't be able to redirect these devices seamlessly to the remote connection.

Installing a Terminal Server from the Command Line

You can do a very basic installation from the command line by running:

```
Servermanagercmd.exe -install ts-terminal-server -restart
```

To uninstall the Terminal Server role, run the same command with *remove* instead of *install*, like this:

```
Servermanagercmd.exe -remove ts-terminal-server -restart.
```

This command doesn't give you the option of doing any configuration. When you install this way, the terminal server will be set up with all the default settings. The Remote Desktop Users group will be empty. Additionally, the server will not prompt you to install WSRM or the Desktop Experience feature.

Essential Terminal Server Configuration

After installing the service, you have some basic configuration to do before anyone uses the terminal server.

Note Not all the essential Terminal Server configuration takes place on the terminal server. To learn more about the other configuration components, see Chapter 4, "Creating the User Work Environment," and Chapter 5, for user settings, or Chapter 7, for multi-server deployments.

Allocating System Resources with Windows System Resource Manager

One of the nightmare scenarios for a shared computer is that of the end user who is such a heavy user of RAM and processor time that he impacts even the light users. This is sometimes a case for organizing terminal server users based on how much they will stress a server, and sometimes a case for not putting heavy users onto the terminal server at all.

Isolating users onto their own computers isn't always ideal or even possible, and what do you do if their use patterns change over time? A better answer is to do what you can to even out resource usage with a tool such as the Windows System Resource Manager (WSRM).

WSRM evens out processor time by monitoring processes and lowering their priority if they start impacting the performance of the processes running in other sessions. We talked about process priority in Chapter 2, "Planning the Terminal Server Ecosystem." When a process receives more processor time than others, WSRM lowers that process priority for a time so it waits for threads in other processes to execute. (It's similar to the way in which a process that isn't getting enough time may have its priority temporarily boosted to get its threads through some processor cycles.) WSRM is reactive; for it to get involved, a process must take too many processor cycles.

Using WSRM on a terminal server allows you to manage processor utilization on a per-session basis, so sessions will have equal access to these important resources. You can apply WSRM policies according to a time or date schedule, so it's possible to be more restrictive during busy hours and less so when the person running the high-impact applications really needs to get work done—even at the expense of other sessions. (Since WSRM is reactive, setting different policies for different times won't make a lot of difference in allocating resources evenly if only a heavy user is running a session.) You can even use WSRM accounting features to create, store, and view resource utilization reports. These could be useful for predicting usage trends and billing departments for terminal server time. For now, we'll talk about how to set up WSRM.

Installing WSRM

To install WSRM, start Server Manager. Right-click Features and click Add Features to start the Add Features Wizard. Scroll down the list to select Windows Server Resource Manager. When you select it, you may be prompted that you must install an additional component. WSRM requires that you have a database to store historical data, so if the Windows Internal Database isn't already installed (it could be; it's also used by several other features), you'll be prompted to add that feature. Go ahead and install it if prompted to do so by clicking the Add Required Features button.

When you click Next, you'll see a confirmation page showing the features you will install. Click Install to perform the installation.

When the installation is finished, Server Manager will show you that the two features fully installed. Close the dialog box; you don't need to reboot.

Configuring WSRM for Per-Session

By default, WSRM is not set up appropriately for a terminal server, so you'll need to configure it. To open WSRM, click Start | Administrative Tools | Windows System Resource Manager to open the Windows System Resource Manager snap-in shown in Figure 3-15. You'll first be prompted to choose the computer you want to manage; for now, choose the local server.

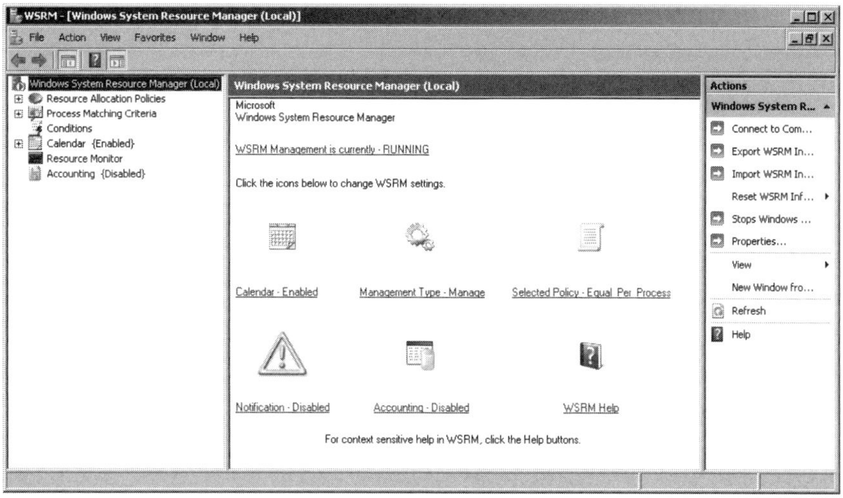

FIGURE 3-15 The WSRM management console

To begin, change the default policy to Equal Per Session to balance resource usage evenly across all sessions. (You can—and should—limit people to one connection per server using Group Policy or Terminal Services Configuration. If you do, then one session will equate to one user. See Chapter 5 for more details of how to accomplish this.) Click the Selected Policy link at the top right of the middle pane to open the dialog box in Figure 3-16.

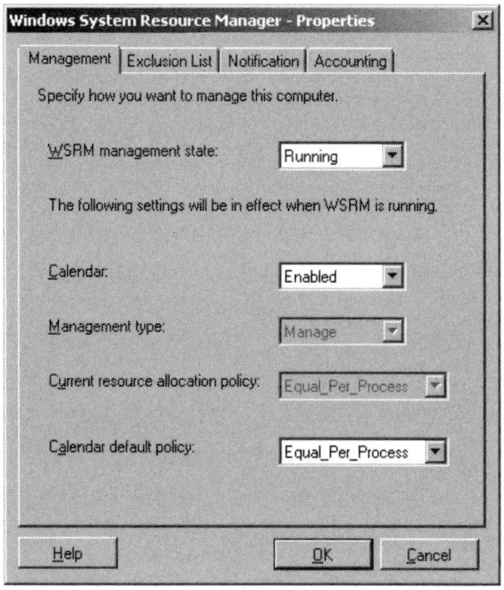

FIGURE 3-16 Set the WSRM properties.

The top setting is simple: it shows whether WSRM is running or not, which you already know from the view of the main dashboard in Figure 3-15. Leave it running.

The Calendar option must be enabled if you'd like to set up separate policies for working hours versus off hours (assuming that your terminal servers are not used 24 hours a day, as some are in global enterprises).

The current resource allocation policy is, by default, Equal_Per_Process. And the calendar default policy is also Equal_Per_Process. Choose Equal_Per_Session from the list to make it more applicable to terminal servers.

Excluding Processes from Management

WSRM does not take all processes into account when allocating processor time and memory. System services and several system processes are excluded on the Exclusion List tab (see Figure 3-17.) All the entries that begin svchost.exe -k are system services.

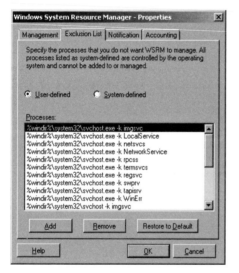

FIGURE 3-17 By default, system services are not counted by WSRM.

Most of the time, you're not going to do anything with this list. If you do have an application that you don't want to limit, click the Add button and browse to find the application executable. Just bear in mind that by adding the application to the list, you are removing it from the list of monitored processes for all sessions, not just for a single session. Since the reason to use WSRM on a terminal server is to make sure that all users have equal access during working hours, you're not likely to need to do this on a terminal server.

Note For a full-time terminal server, you won't likely find many reasons to create a calendar. As explained previously, WSRM only begins working when a process is preventing other processes from getting processor time to execute their threads, so even if one of the staff is working on a late-night processor-intensive project, having WSRM running isn't going to keep him from working.

Enabling Plug and Play Redirection with the Desktop Experience

To enable Plug and Play (PnP) redirection on the terminal server, install Desktop Experience. This feature requires no configuration and little setup. To install it, simply open the Server Manager and migrate to the list of features. Click the link to add a new feature and then walk through the wizard to select and install Desktop Experience.

You will need to reboot the terminal server after installing or uninstalling Desktop Experience.

Adjusting Server Settings with Terminal Services Configuration

After you have WSRM and Desktop Experience set up, the next step to the basic terminal server installation is reviewing the configuration settings in the Terminal Services Configuration MMC snap-in shown in Figure 3-18. This tool manages settings on a per-server basis; to manage settings for many terminal servers at a time, use Group Policy.

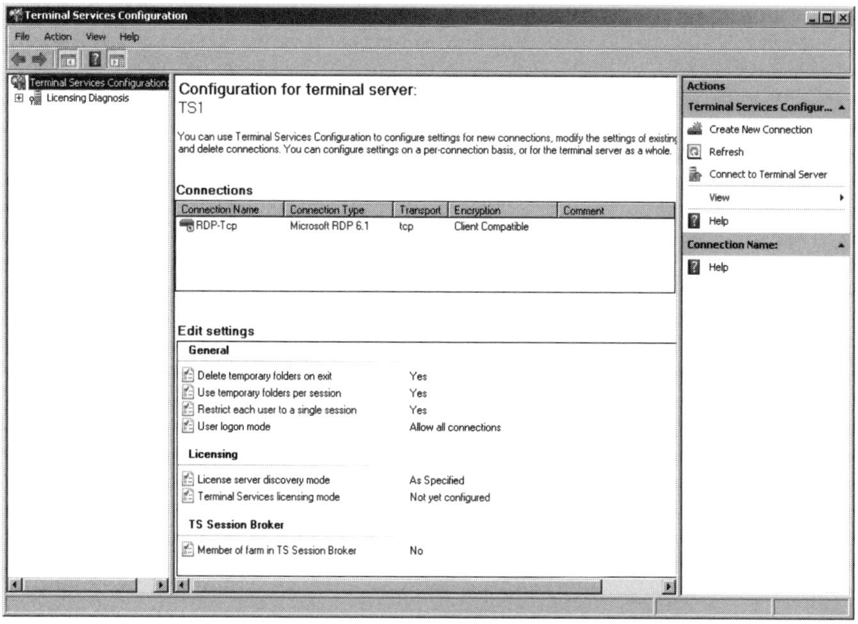

FIGURE 3-18 Use Terminal Services Configuration to edit each terminal server's configuration.

Open the Terminal Services Configuration tool by clicking Start | Administrative Tools | Terminal Services | Terminal Server Configuration. To change a setting (or settings), double-click any single entry in the Edit Settings section to open the dialog box in Figure 3-19.

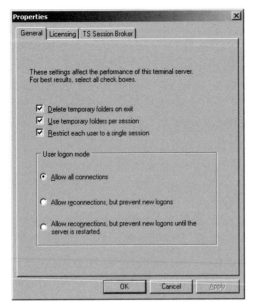

FIGURE 3-19 Clicking any setting in Terminal Services Configuration snap-in opens the same tabbed dialog box.

The following sections explain the settings found in Terminal Services Configuration. We'll come back to some of these settings within this book.

General Session Settings

Most often, you won't need to adjust any of the settings on the tab shown in Figure 3-19.

The only circumstance under which you're likely to need to change the temporary folder settings is if you are supporting an older application (or a proprietary one) that won't store temporary directories on a per-user basis, but only per-computer. There's no reason not to delete per-session temporary files when the user ends the session.

To configure temporary folder settings using Group Policy, go to Computer Configuration | Policies | Administrative Templates | Windows Components | Terminal Services | Terminal Server | Temporary Folders.

- To configure deleting the temporary folder, see Do Not Delete Temp Folder Upon Exit. When this setting isn't configured, the temp folders will be deleted unless you've specified otherwise using TS Configuration.

- To configure whether each session should have its own temp folder or all applications should use the system-wide one, see the Do Not Use Temporary Folders Per Session policy setting.

There is also generally little reason to allow users to maintain more than one session on the same terminal server. All TS RemoteApps run in the same session, so they can all use the core processes needed to support the session (e.g., Csrss.exe, Winlogon.exe) and save memory on the terminal server. Running in the same session also allows all those applications to use the same instance of the user profile. (We'll discuss profile issues in Chapter 4, but for now understand that it's good to have only one copy of your profile open.) With TS RemoteApps there's really no reason to allow most people to run multiple sessions.

To configure logon restrictions using Group Policy, go to Computer Configuration | Policies | Administrative Templates | Windows Components | Terminal Services | Terminal Server | Connections. The setting in question is Restrict Terminal Services Users To A Single Remote Session.

The settings for user logon mode depend on whether the terminal server is currently in production or you're planning on taking it down but don't want to abruptly shut everyone down. One option is applicable if you are planning for a reboot (for example, if you cyclically reboot terminal servers to fix applications with memory leaks), in which case choose the option to limit connections until the service restarts. If you're planning on longer maintenance, however, choose to limit connections until you explicitly re-enable them.

To configure the user logon mode using Group Policy, go to Computer Configuration | Policies | Administrative Templates | Windows Components | Terminal Services | Terminal Server | Connections. The setting in question is Allow Users To Connect Remotely Using Terminal Services. However, this is one situation in which Group Policy isn't the best configuration option. User Logon Mode is most appropriately set by Group Policy when you're staging a bunch of servers and don't want any of them to go online until you're done. If you're taking a terminal server offline, then it's much easier and faster to adjust this setting using the configuration tools on the server.

Terminal Server Licensing Settings

The next tab allows you to configure the licensing settings, both for the type of license you'll use and the discovery method that the server will use to locate license servers. Getting the correct settings (as shown in Figure 3-20) is crucial for the successful implementation of Terminal Services within your organization.

Terminal Services Licensing Mode   A terminal server can be in either per-device mode or per-user mode. The mode you select depends on the type of licenses you purchase, which depends mainly on the proportion of users to computers. If there are more computers than users (for example, if people using terminal servers can log in from either a work computer or from a home computer) then per-user licensing makes more sense. If there are more computers (for example, if the people using the terminal servers are shift workers and three people use the same thin client at different times of day) then per-device licensing makes more sense.

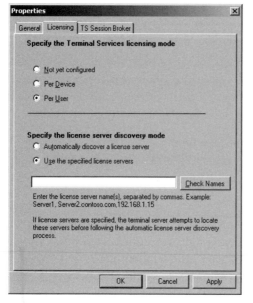

FIGURE 3-20 Terminal Services Licensing settings are critical to terminal server availability.

You can change the licensing mode, but whichever mode you pick, you must be sure that the matching license types are installed on the license server you're using. Otherwise, even if the terminal server can find a license server, it will not be able to allocate licenses to users or computers.

To configure the licensing mode using Group Policy, go to Computer Configuration | Policies | Administrative Templates | Windows Components | Terminal Services | Terminal Server | Licensing. The setting in question is Set The Terminal Services Licensing Mode. This is an excellent setting to edit using Group Policy, as all terminal servers in a farm are likely to have the same licensing mode. Using this setting avoids accidental errors.

License Server Discovery Mode   The license server discovery mode specifies the method by which terminal servers should find license servers. You have two options: to rely on license server discovery alone, or to specify license servers explicitly and supplement with license server discovery.

The details of license server discovery depend on the scope of the license server, discussed in the section titled "Changing the Scope of the License Server" later in this chapter.

- If the license server has the scope of a workgroup, then it broadcasts its availability on the local subnet to members of the same workgroup. Obviously, by definition a license server with a workgroup scope will be located on a server.

- If the license server has the scope of a domain, then it must be on a domain controller. It will announce itself as a license server along with announcing itself as a domain controller to domain members.

- If the license server has the scope of a forest, then it may be on a domain controller or a member server. Specifying this scope adds the license server to Active Directory.

Automatic discovery sounds good, but it's too complex to be reliable. A bug in the search algorithm (one that was fixed in Windows 2003 SP1) meant that a terminal server would not discover a license server located on the same computer as the terminal server. Another bug in publishing servers in Active Directory prevented license servers from being discovered across sites. Although these problems have been fixed in Windows Server 2008, the way that discovery works still introduces a number of variables into the process that can cause it to fail. For this reason, its best practice to specify at least one license server so that you're not totally dependent on discovery working.

> **Note** If the license server is located outside the terminal server forest, then you'll need to point to it explicitly as well. Discovery doesn't work outside the local forest.

Specifying at least one license server doesn't turn off automatic discovery (see "Direct from the Source: How Does Discovery Work?"), it just makes sure that the terminal server can find at least one license server. You can specify license servers either from Terminal Services Configuration or through Group Policy.

To configure TS Licensing using Group Policy, go to Computer Configuration | Policies | Administrative Templates | Windows Components | Terminal Services | Terminal Server | Licensing. The setting in question is Use The Specified Terminal Services Licensing Servers. Again, this is a good setting for Group Policy to make sure it's consistent across all terminal servers and new ones will be configured to match the existing set.

Direct from the Source: How Does Discovery Work?

What happens when a terminal server needs a license server?

A terminal server will auto-discover license servers every hour. Any license servers found are stored in the registry in HKLM\System\CurrentControlSet\Control\TerminalServer\RCM\DomainLicenseServerMulti\EnterpriseMulti keys.

If you specify a "preferred" license server for a terminal server (using Terminal Services Configuration tool), this server's name is stored in HKLM\System\CurrentControlSet\Services\TermService\Parameters\LicenseServer. Please note that you cannot set a specific order in this list.

When a client connects to the terminal server and needs a license, the terminal server chooses a random license server from the list of discovered and specified license servers, while preferring the specified license servers over the auto-discovered ones. The terminal server will then attempt to reach each license server in order, until it finds one that it can access.

If the license server has the requested type of TS CAL installed on it, then the license server allocates the license to the device or user as appropriate.

The thing to note is that when a terminal server finds a license server that it can access and sends a request to it, then after that the terminal server will not attempt further connections to other license servers directly—it will be dependent on the license server to "forward" the request to other license servers.

In short:

- If the terminal server completely fails to reach a particular license server because that server is offline or otherwise unreachable, then the terminal server will attempt to contact the next license server in the list it obtains of auto-discovered and specified license servers.

- If the terminal server succeeds in contacting a license server, then even if that license server does not have the requested TS CALs the terminal server will not query another license server in its list. Instead, it will rely on the license server it accessed to forward the license request to others.

Harish Kumar Poongan Shanmugam

Software Design Engineer, Test II

To add one or more servers, type their names in the text box and then click the Check Names button to validate the names; you should see a confirmation saying "The servers specified are valid terminal license servers." If you receive this confirmation, verify the name.

When you specify license servers, their names are added to the terminal server's registry in HKLM\SYSTEM\CurrentControlSet\Services\TermService\Parameters\LicenseServers. Again, the preferred license servers aren't the only license servers a terminal server will attempt to contact—just the ones it will contact first.

Note Make sure that any license servers you specify are activated. A license server will be a valid choice even if it is not yet activated or has no licenses installed. Since a terminal server will only request one license server if the original request gets a response (even if that response is "Hi, I'm a license server but I have no TS CALs of the type you require"), that license server should be one that can fulfill the terminal server's request.

Specifying a license server isn't always as easy as just typing in a server name:

- The license servers you specify must be Windows Server 2008 license servers. It is not possible for a Windows Server 2003 license server to issue Windows Server 2008 terminal server TS CALs. (A Windows Server 2008 license server can issue TS CALs for Windows Server 2003 terminal servers, however.)

- You can point to a license server outside the terminal server forest. However, if this license server will be issuing per-user TS CALs, there must be a trust relationship between the two domains. When issuing per-user TS CALs, the license server needs to be able to contact Active Directory on behalf of the person requesting a TS CAL.

Protocol-Specific Settings

The Connections portion of Terminal Services Configuration contains information about any protocols supported on the terminal server. In this example, we'll only see Remote Desktop Protocol, because that's the native protocol used by Terminal Services. Were Citrix XenApp extensions to Terminal Services installed, for example, there'd be another entry here for ICA, the protocol for user sessions when that software is available.

Most protocol-specific settings are controlled from the user account properties visible from Active Directory Users and Computers (ADUC), and the settings that aren't there are included in Group Policy. (If they are set using ADUC, Group Policy can still override them.) The settings in Terminal Services Configuration (see Table 3-5) are mainly advisory. In this section, we'll explain what the settings mean and how you might use them.

TABLE 3-5 Protocol Configuration Settings in Terminal Services Configuration

Tab	Settings Contained	When You'd Edit
General	Mainly security settings, including the minimum encryption level set between client and server, whether or not the server must authenticate itself to the client (RDP security layer vs. Secure Sockets Layer [SSL]), and whether or not Network Level Authentication is required. See Chapter 7 for more information about these options.	Hopefully, not often. All modern clients can support SSL connections, which reduces the chance that a rogue terminal server could intercept client authentication data. NLA works only with RDP 6.1, the most recent version of the RDP client.
Environment	Initial program path and settings.	Probably never. Since Windows Server 2008 supports RemoteApps, you don't need to specify startup applications.

TABLE 3-5 **Protocol Configuration Settings in Terminal Services Configuration**

Tab	Settings Contained	When You'd Edit
Sessions	Settings determining behavior when a session has been active, disconnected, or idle for a certain length of time.	Rarely. These settings can be set from Group Policy or ADUC and both will override the settings here. Use Group Policy to set consistent connection policies across all terminal servers; ADUC to set connection policies for individuals.
Logon Settings	Whether to use the client logon information or generic logon credentials.	Rarely. You might use this setting for a special-use terminal server supporting anonymous connections, but generally you'll want to use the user logon credentials.
Remote Control	The rules governing remote control of a user's session.	Rarely. These settings may also be set in ADUC and group policy and by default those settings take precedence. Remote Control settings may also be defined on a per-machine basis through Group Policy.
Client Settings	Maximum color depth and device redirection rules. Most supported devices are enabled by default.	Occasionally, to override client-side settings.
Network Adapter	Chooses the network adapters to support RDP traffic and limits the number of connections that the terminal server will support.	Occasionally, to limit the network adapters being used for RDP connections or to keep connections to the terminal server within the bounds of what it can support.
Security	Users and groups permitted access to the terminal server.	Rarely. As Help will remind you when you switch to this tab, it's best practice to control access via controlling the membership of the Remote Desktop Users group, as the results are more predictable.

Note There are some discrepancies between the user account properties visible in ADUC and the settings visible in Terminal Server Configuration on the Environment and Sessions tabs. The corresponding tab in ADUC shows old data; the Terminal Services Configuration console (TSCC) settings and Group Policy settings are current.

You can also configure most of these settings using Group Policy. Some of the more useful ones are described below; we'll talk about what these settings are for throughout the book. The Network Adapter and Security tabs do not have related Group Policy settings.

To configure connection security (including enabling server authentication and network-level authentication and client encryption level), go to Computer Configuration | Policies |

Administrative Templates | Windows Components | Terminal Services | Terminal Server | Security. Chapter 7 will discuss the settings in more detail, but the policies in question are:

- Set Client Connection Encryption Level
- Require Use Of Specific Security Layer For Remote (RDP) Connections
- Require User Authentication For Remote Connections Using Network Level Authentication

To configure device redirection and environment settings, go to Computer Configuration | Policies | Administrative Templates | Windows Components | Terminal Services | Terminal Server | Device And Resource Redirection. The Printer Redirection and Remote Session Environment subkeys in this same path also include policies to control the user environment, which we'll discuss in more detail in Chapter 5.

To configure the rules for Remote Control of a user's session by an administrator, go to Computer Configuration | Policies | Administrative Templates | Windows Components | Terminal Services | Terminal Server | Connections. The setting in question is Set Rules For Remote Control Of Terminal Services User Sessions. We'll discuss the use of Remote Control in Chapter 8.

License Servers

Terminal servers are useful for only a set amount of time without a license server, so soon after you install a terminal server for production, it will be time to get a license server in place.

How License Servers Assign TS CALs

When a client connects to a terminal server, the terminal server requests the type of license it is configured to understand. If the terminal server is in per-device mode, it requests a per-device license. The client presents the license from its store in the registry. If the terminal server is in per-user mode, it requests a per-user license. Per-user licenses are stored as a property on a user account object in Active Directory, so the terminal server can check this when user credentials are presented. (If you use per-user licensing in a workgroup, then per-user licenses aren't tracked.) All licenses are assigned for a random period of 52 to 89 days so that unused licenses can automatically return to the license pool. Beginning seven days before the license expires, when that license is presented at logon, the terminal server will try to renew it for another 52 to 89 days.

> **Note** With Windows Server 2008, it's possible to manually revoke a per-device license if you don't want to wait for the automatic revocation to kick in. We'll talk about how to do this in the section titled "Revoking TS CALs" later in this chapter.

If the client does not have a valid license or if the license it has is within seven days of expiring, then the terminal server must attempt to obtain a license for the client. What happens then depends on the circumstances described in Table 3-6. Notice that there are circumstances in which a terminal server in per-user mode will permit the connection when a terminal server in per-device mode will not.

TABLE 3-6 Processes When a Client Requests a License

Circumstance	Per User	Per Device
The terminal server has never found a license server but is in its grace period.	The terminal server will issue a temporary license that lasts up to 120 days.	The terminal server will issue a temporary license that lasts up to 120 days.
The terminal server has never found a license server and is out of the grace period.	The terminal server will not permit the connection.	The terminal server will not permit the connection.
The terminal server has found a license server but the license server has no TS CALs installed. The license server is in the grace period.	The license server will issue a temporary license that lasts up to 120 days.	The license server will issue a temporary license that lasts up to 120 days.
The terminal server has found a license server but the license server has no TS CALs installed. The license server is out of its grace period.	The terminal server will permit the connection.	The terminal server will not permit the connection.
The terminal server has found a license server with TS CALs available.	The terminal server will give the license server the name of the user attempting to connect to the terminal server. The license server will then contact Active Directory to set a property on that user's account object to show that the person has used a license.	The terminal server will contact the license server with the hardware ID (HWID) of the computer attempting to connect to the terminal server. The license server will then assign a TS CAL to that HWID and create a record of the assignment.

If you happen to watch a license server when a user is logging onto a terminal server in per-device mode, you may notice that before issuing a permanent license to the device, the license server will first issue a temporary license. This temporary license is given to the client device prior to the user logon. The reason is that you need a license to connect, but until the user who initiated the connection has presented credentials, the terminal server can't tell whether or not that user has permission to log on to the terminal server. Therefore, the terminal server will provide a temporary TS CAL until logon is complete.

Note Prior to Windows 2000 Service Pack 2, a terminal server issued a permanent TS CAL when the connection was initiated. Unfortunately, this meant that it was very easy for a malicious person to drain TS CALs from a license server, since the person didn't even need a domain account to attempt the connection and have a TS CAL assigned to the connecting computer.

What if the first license server the terminal server can connect to doesn't have any licenses of the right kind available? A terminal server will attempt to contact a license server only until the point at which a license server responds. When the license server responds, the terminals server doesn't check further.

It's not always that simple. If the terminal server has found a license server, but that license server has no licenses of the right type (or no licenses at all), then that won't help the terminal server issue a license. Then, the license server looks for help in fulfilling the request, forwarding the TS CAL request to another license server to see if that license server can help. If that one can't help, it forwards the request to a third, and so on, until either a license server issues a license or the last one is unable to help and the terminal server can't permit the logon. This is called *CAL request forwarding*.

For CAL request forwarding to function, the license servers must all be able to find each other using the same discovery mechanisms described for terminal servers. You can't explicitly define one license server on another license server. Therefore, CAL forwarding will only work within the same forest. If you split the distribution of TS CALs among license servers, there is a greater possibility that a license server with licenses on it will be found.

Direct from the Source: How Does CAL Request Forwarding Work?

When and how does a license server forward a request to another license server?

If the license server does not have the requested TS CAL type (if it's out of licenses of a given type), it will forward the request to another license server that it's heard of. It checks its database to find out which license servers have announced their availability of TS CALs and then forwards the request.

Like terminal servers, license servers discover other license servers hourly. When you install TS CALs on a license server, the license server announces to other license servers that a TS CAL has been installed so that others are aware that this license server has a newly installed TS CAL. But the thing to note here is that license servers announce themselves only to other license servers that they're able to discover. You cannot manually configure a license server to point to other license servers. To make request forwarding work, the license servers *must* all be able to discover each other.

To help ensure that a license server is found, at least two license servers could be placed in the same forest so that they can discover each other and forward requests among each other and licenses may be equally distributed on them.

Harish Kumar Poongan Shanmugam

Software Design Engineer, Test II

Setting Up the License Server

To set up the license server so that there is a source for TS CALs, you'll need to do the following:

1. Install the service.

2. Activate the license server (in other words, register it with the Microsoft Clearinghouse).

3. Install licenses on it.

4. Ensure that this license server is discoverable.

Installing the License Server

To install the service, go to the member server or domain controller on which you plan to install the service. If you haven't previously installed any Terminal Services roles on that computer, start Server Manager. Under Roles, choose Terminal Services. Unlike Windows Server 2003, in Windows Server 2008 there is no longer a separate first-level service for Terminal Server licensing. Terminal Server licensing is a role service of Terminal Services, so choose this option even if you don't want to install a terminal server and then click Next.

> **Note** If you are installing Terminal Services Licensing on a computer that already has Terminal Services role services installed, then you'll start from the Role Services section of Server Manager. In the Terminal Services section, the screen will show the installed role services. Click the Add Role Services button to jump to the page in the wizard where you choose to add the licensing service.

Click through the introduction to Terminal Services to open the page in Figure 3-21, where you'll choose to install TS Licensing. When prompted to select the role service to install for Terminal Services, select the box next to TS Licensing Role Service and click Next.

Next, choose the scope of the licensing server (shown in Figure 3-22). Your decision will depend on what the license server is for, not on technology. Your choices are:

- **This Workgroup**   If you're creating a lab environment in a workgroup, then only terminal servers in the lab environment should be using that license server. You could advertise that license server throughout the entire domain or enterprise and just secure it, but why would you? It makes more sense to advertise the license server only in the context of the workgroup. This option is only available outside a domain.

- **This Domain**   If your company is organized into domains that don't share financial resources (such as the money used to purchase the TS CALS installed on the server), then you can limit the scope to the domain.

- **The Forest**   If your company has more than one domain and you need to share financial resources between domains, then it makes sense to extend the scope to the entire forest of trusted domains. This is a good model if your company has, or expects to have, more than one domain—perhaps if your company is merging with another one.

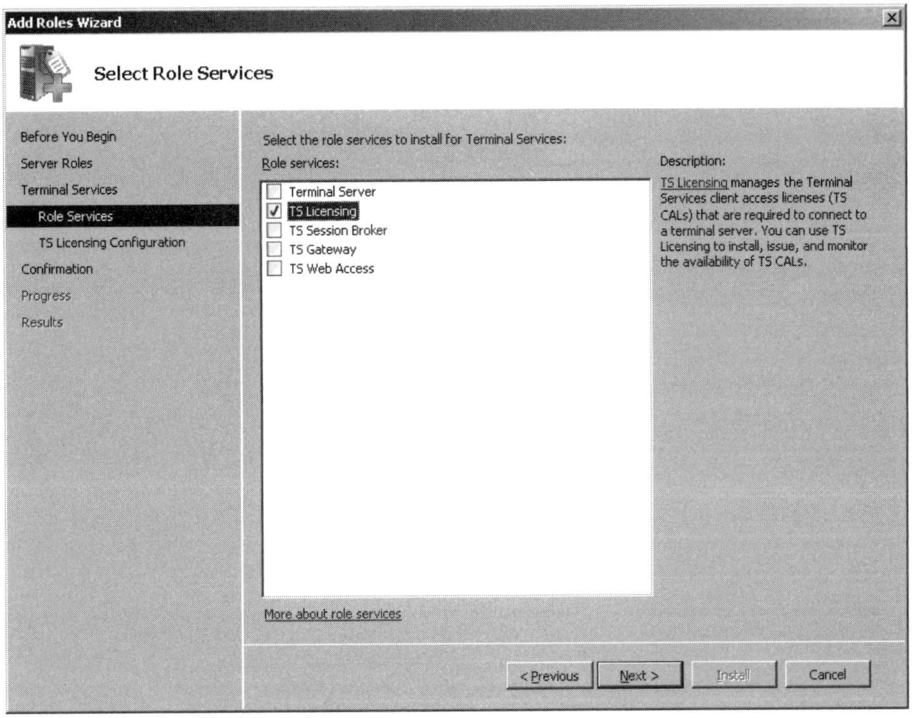

FIGURE 3-21 Select TS Licensing from the list of Terminal Services role services.

> **Note**   In Windows Server 2003, a bug in the search algorithm prevented an enterprise license server from being discoverable outside its site. This is fixed in Windows Server 2008, so now a license server can be discovered throughout its forest.

Scope is really a business question, not a technical one. Before choosing any option, know the business purpose of the license servers. Regardless of the scope of the license server, you can limit the ability to get licenses from it so that rogue terminal servers won't consume all of your TS CALs. Therefore, the recommended scope for Windows Server 2008 is the forest. If you pick this option, this will automatically publish the license server in Active Directory and the license server will be discoverable to any terminal server in the forest that has permission to obtain licenses from this license server. You can't make a license server discoverable across forests. However, you can explicitly point a terminal server to a license server located in another forest. The two domains must trust each other if you plan to use per-user licensing.

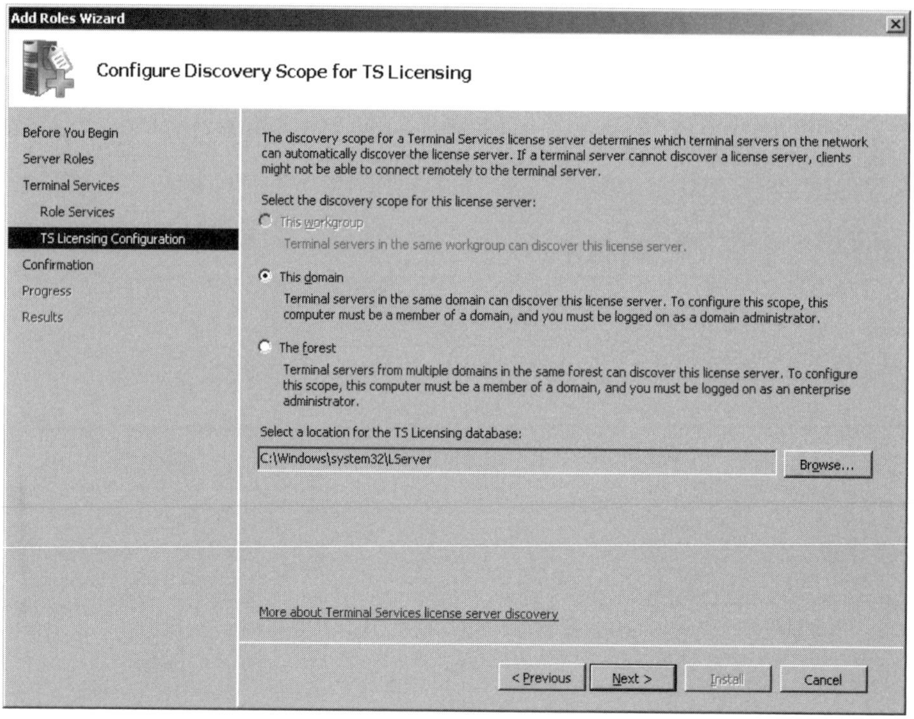

FIGURE 3-22 Choose the scope for the licensing server.

If you're logged in with an account that does not have the credentials to create a license server in the scope you request, the wizard will make this quite clear (see Figure 3-23). If you choose This Domain, then the warning will caution you that you need to log in as a member of the Domain Admins group to create that scope.

If you insist on trying to install without the required permissions, the installation will tell you about it after the installation concludes. For example, if you attempt to set the scope to the forest while logged in with an account that does not have Enterprise Admin permissions, the Installation Results screen will record this. The installation will work, but the scope will be set to the domain.

Assuming that you have all the correct permissions, when you click the Install button, the Add Role Services Wizard will show you the Installation Results screen with a message that the installation has succeeded.

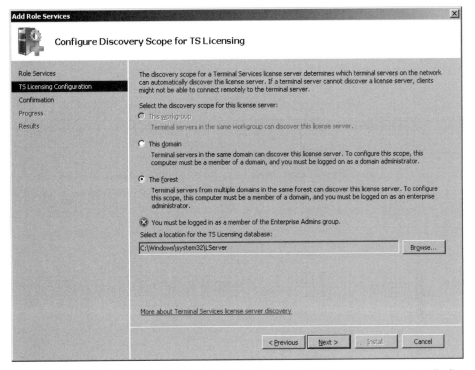

FIGURE 3-23 In Windows Server 2008, you don't have to guess whether or not you can install a license server for a particular scope.

Installing a License Server from the Command Line

You can do a very basic installation from the command line by running the following:

```
Servermanagercmd.exe -install ts-licensing
```

To uninstall the Terminal Server role, run the same command with *remove* instead of *install*, like this:

```
Servermanagercmd.exe -remove ts-licensing
```

This command doesn't give you the option of doing any configuration. When you install this way, the license server will be set up with all the default settings, will not be activated, and will have no TSCAL packs installed. The discovery scope will be Workgroup.

Activating the License Server

You're not quite ready to install license packs on the license server. If you go back to Server Manager and look at the installed services, you'll see that Terminal Services has a yellow warning icon next to it. Double-click it, and you'll open a view of the Event Log that shows only events related to this service (see Figure 3-24).

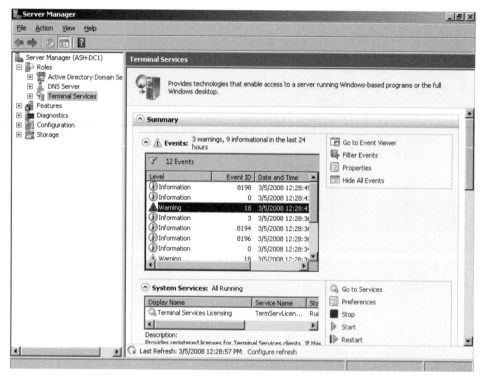

FIGURE 3-24 Check the Event Logs post-installation to see what configuration remains.

Click through these events and you should see informational events telling you that the role was successfully installed or that the license server object was successfully created in Active Directory (without this, domain-wide discovery doesn't work), and so forth. But you'll also see a warning with the Event ID of 18; this indicates that the license server has not yet been activated and therefore cannot issue permanent TS CALs.

This does not necessarily mean that you must rush to activate the server. If you're sure that you want to use this particular server for a license server, then yes, you should activate the license server; it's not going to do you a lot of good until you activate it. But if you are just experimenting with installing the role, you may not want to activate the server right away. Activating a license server registers it with the Microsoft Clearinghouse. After a server is activated, it is your license server according to the Microsoft Clearinghouse, and any licenses you install on it will be associated with that server specifically. Moving those licenses to another license server will require some cooperation from the Clearinghouse and your original license documentation.

Assuming that you *do* want to activate the license server, open the TS Licensing Manager to view the screen shown in Figure 3-25.

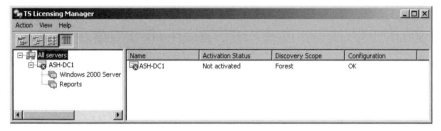

FIGURE 3-25 First view of the TS Licensing Manager

The interface here is pretty straightforward. Any license servers installed on the network and discoverable to this license server will appear under All Servers. Right now, we have only one. It's marked with a red X because it's not yet activated and therefore only capable of issuing temporary TS CALs. The Windows 2000 server built-in licenses refer to a very specific situation (see the following sidebar, "Why Are There Windows 2000 TS CALs on My Windows 2008 License Server?"), and you can't use the reports yet because you have no TS CALs on which to create reports.

Why Are There Windows 2000 TS CALs on My Windows 2008 License Server?

Because you haven't installed any TS CALs on the license server, what's that reference to Windows 2000? That's a legacy of a decision made in the Windows 2000 era. At that time, any Windows 2000 Professional computer had a license to access a Windows 2000 Server terminal server. Many people referred to this as a "built-in" license, but this is misleading; there was no license built into Windows Server 2000 Professional, just the ability to pull from the Unlimited pool on the license server.

Beginning with Windows XP and Windows Server 2003, no client operating system has been able to draw from this Unlimited pool, but it's still available if you have (a) Windows 2000 Server terminal servers using the license server and (b) Windows Server 2000 Professional clients that will be using those license servers. Otherwise, this unlimited license pool is totally irrelevant. Even if you have Windows 2000 Professional clients, they cannot draw from the Unlimited pool to access a Windows Server 2008 (or 2003) terminal server.

To activate the license server, select it, choose Action | Activate Server or right-click the license server and then choose Activate Server from the context list. This will start the Activate Server Wizard.

Click Next and then choose a method to contact the Clearinghouse to activate the server. If at all possible, use the Automatic connection option, as it's less prone to error than either the Web site or the telephone. The Microsoft Clearinghouse manages licensing for Microsoft, including activating license servers, issuing TS CALs and associating them with a license server, and recovering licenses. When you contact the Clearinghouse to activate a server, you'll receive an X.509 certificate to identity the server. Installing TS CALs on the activated server associates them with that certificate and validates their authenticity. (This does, however, mean that you can't easily move them to a new server.)

> ## Other Activation Options
>
> If you choose to activate using a Web browser, the Activate Server Wizard will show you the product ID used to identify your computer for activation purposes and prompt you to type that into the appropriate boxes at *https://activate.microsoft.com*. After you do so, you'll get the license server ID to type back into the dialog box.
>
> If you choose to activate via telephone, the wizard will prompt you for the country you're calling from to get you the right telephone number. It will then show you the number to call, the product ID, and provide a place to type the license server ID into the wizard.

Next, you'll need to provide some basic company information to the Clearinghouse to associate you with the activated server. This information is required. Type in your first name, last name, and company name, and select your country or region from the corresponding drop-down menu.

> **Note** If you're tempted to put in a false name as some people do when asked to provide contact information, be aware that this information is designed to allow the Clearinghouse to find you in their system if you need to have licenses reissued or need other support. If you put in a false name, remember it!

Next, the wizard will prompt you for some additional optional information that the Clearinghouse can use to contact you and further identify you: e-mail address, organizational unit, company address, city, state or province, and postal code.

Click Next, watch the status bar for a few seconds, and you're finished. The license server is now activated and ready for you to install TS CALs. When you go back to the TS Licensing Server console, the server will now have a green icon with a check box indicating that it is activated.

> **Note** Although the Activate Server Wizard will prompt you to install TS CALs right away, you can skip this step for now and the license server will continue to issue temporary TS CALs for 120 days or until you install some license packs.

Design a High-Availability License Server System Before Installing TS CALs

Because installing TS CALs on a license server immediately associates those licenses with that server, it's good to plan your high-availability strategy *before* you install TS CALs.

We previously discussed how license servers forward TS CAL requests to other license servers if they are unable to fulfill them. We also mentioned that terminal servers stop attempting to contact license servers after the first time they successfully contact one, even if that attempt gets them a license server that cannot provide any TS CALs of the requested type.

For best availability, you should have at least two license servers in each forest and explicitly point the terminal server to each to improve chances that the server will find one when required.

Installing TS CALs

To install the TS CAL license packs, open TS Licensing Manager and choose Actions | Install Licenses or right-click on the server to choose Install Licenses from the context menu. Click through the opening dialog box of the Install Licenses Wizard to get to the page shown in Figure 3-26.

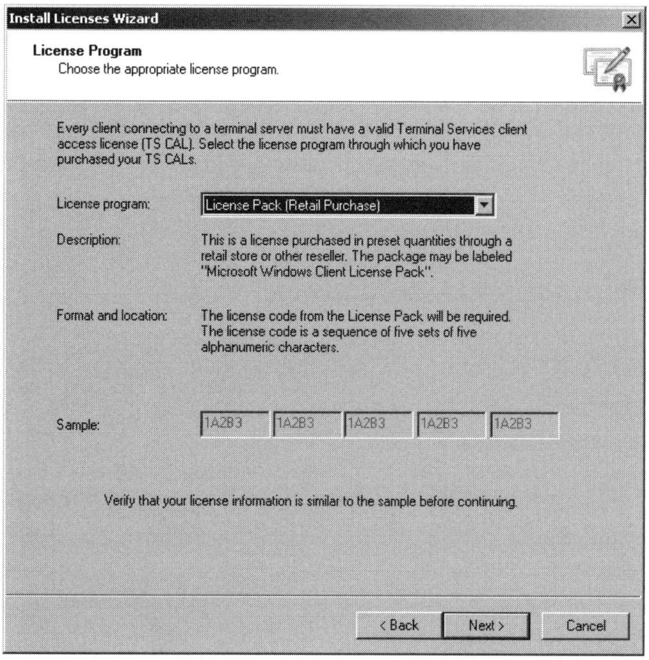

FIGURE 3-26 Choose the type of license packs you'll install.

For this example, choose to install a retail license pack. On the License Code page, you'll be prompted to add the keys for the license packs you've purchased. As you can see from Figure 3-27, you can install as many as you have available; you don't need to rerun the license installation wizard for each pack. The license codes identify both the type of license (per device or per user, for instance) and the number of licenses in the pack, although not in any human-readable form.

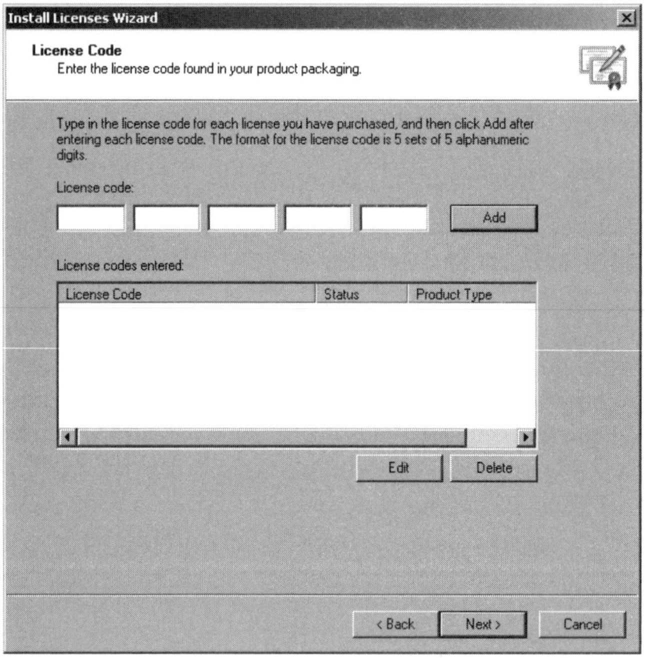

FIGURE 3-27 Enter the license codes for your license packs.

When you type in the license code and click Add, the code will show up in the list of entered license codes. You can enter as many here as you have available. When you're finished, click Next. The license server will install the licenses and then display the packs in the License Manager.

Moving TS CALs to Another License Server

When you activate a server, you're registering it with the Microsoft Clearinghouse, the back-end service that manages your licenses. When you install license packs onto a terminal server, you are stamping those license packs with that license server. You can't install them onto another license server.

We'll cover how to move licenses to a new license server in Chapter 9, "Terminal Services Ecosystem Management," but the basic actions are as follows: You deactivate the license server, call the Microsoft Clearinghouse to have them issue new license packs, and reinstall the new license packs onto the new server. You also need to change any explicit pointers to the new license server.

Changing the Scope of the License Server

What if you realize too late that you set up the license server with the wrong scope? For example, if you attempt to set up a license server on a computer to have Forest scope, but don't have Enterprise Admin privileges, the license server will set up Domain scope only, making it discoverable only to terminal servers in its own domain.

This poses a problem if the license server isn't a domain controller. To be automatically discoverable in a domain, a license server must be set up on a domain controller. If it isn't, then you can still point the terminal server to it using Terminal Server Configuration, but a terminal server will never find it if you're relying on automatic discovery. Additionally, a license server will never find it for CAL request forwarding, which relies on automatic discovery. To be discoverable, the license server must be published in Active Directory, a side effect of your choosing the Forest scope.

You don't need to reinstall the licensing service. Instead, you can edit the license server's scope either from Terminal Services Licensing Manager (the easy way) or from ASDIEDIT, which is much more complex but does not require that you have TS Licensing Manager available.

Adding a License Server to Active Directory: The Easy Way   The simplest way to publish a license server in Active Directory is to open Terminal Services Licensing Manager to view the list of available license servers. Their status will be either OK or Review. Review means that there is an inconsistency in the license server's configuration. To fix it, highlight the license server whose scope you want to edit. Choose Action | Review Configuration or right-click and choose Review Configuration from the pop-up menu to open the dialog box shown in Figure 3-28. (You can also get here by clicking the Review link in TS Licensing Manager.)

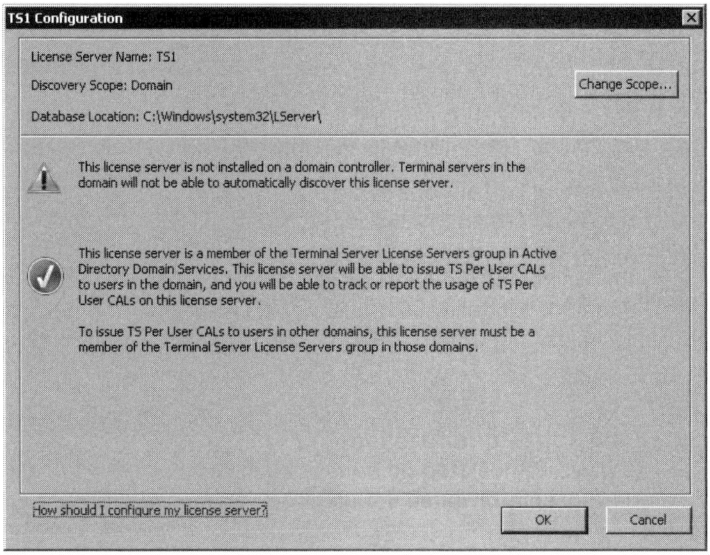

FIGURE 3-28 Review Configuration can highlight problems with a license server configuration.

This backup license server is also a terminal server, so we don't want it to be a domain controller. Therefore, the best choice is to publish this license server in Active Directory to make it visible to the entire forest. To do so, click Change Scope. You'll see a dialog box reminding you that you must have Enterprise Admins permissions to successfully change the scope of this license server.

> **Note**   Changing the scope doesn't require Enterprise Admin rights as such, but the Workgroup scope is not an option, since this server is in a domain. Therefore, the only choice remaining is changing the scope to Forest, which *does* require Enterprise Admin credentials.

Click Continue, and you'll open the TS Licensing Manager configuration page where you can choose the scope. Choose Forest and click OK. Assuming you logged in with Enterprise Admin credentials required to publish license servers in Active Directory, you'll see a confirmation dialog box confirming that the scope has been changed. When you click OK, you'll return to the original Review Configuration dialog box, which will tell you that the server is published in Active Directory and is discoverable.

Adding a License Server to Active Directory: The Painful Method   If you don't have the TS Licensing tool available, you can still publish a server in Active Directory from a domain controller. You may not enjoy this process, but it's possible to do it.

> **Note**   It is almost always easier to create a remote connection to an existing license server using Enterprise Admin credentials and then use the TS Licensing Manager to change the scope. ADSI Edit isn't known for its simple and intuitive user interface. The only reason to do it this way is if you absolutely cannot access the TS Licensing Manager.

Log on to a Windows Server 2008 domain controller using an Enterprise Admins account. From the start menu, choose Run and enter Adsiedit.msc. This will open ADSI Edit console. When you first open this, you'll be prompted to make a connection. Choose Action | Connect To or right-click ADSI Edit in the left pane and choose Connect To to open the dialog box prompting you for connection information. The easiest way to make a connection is to fill in the name of the domain, as shown in Figure 3-29, and choose Configuration from the Select A Well Known Naming Context drop-down list.

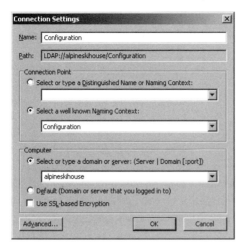

FIGURE 3-29 To connect to the appropriate domain, type its name into the text box in the Computer section.

Click OK, and you'll see the connection added to the console. From here, right-click on the connection to expand it and navigate to the site where your license server should be (for example, navigate down the branch in the left pane to CN=Configuration | CN=Sites | CN=Default-First-Site-Name).

What happens now depends on whether you've already published a license server in Active Directory or not. If you have, then in this site you should see an entry for TS-Enterprise-License-Server, as shown in Figure 3-30.

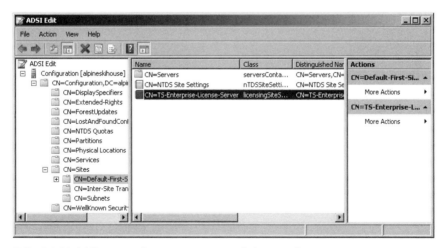

FIGURE 3-30 Adding a new license server to an existing container

Right-click on this container and choose Properties from the context menu to open the dialog box shown in Figure 3-31. Scroll down to siteServer as shown here.

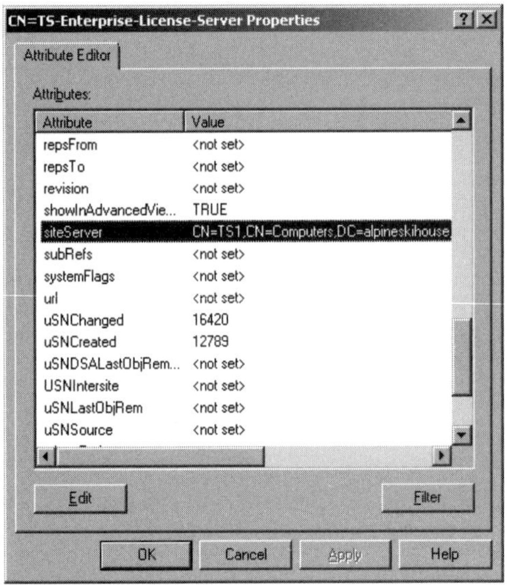

FIGURE 3-31 Find the siteServer attribute for the license server container.

From here, click Edit to open the dialog box in Figure 3-32. You now need to type the distinguished name (e.g., CN=TS1,CN=Computers,DC=alpineskihouse,DC=com) for the license server you want to publish, as shown here. When you're finished, click the Add button to add it to the list of values for this attribute. Click OK and then click OK again to exit the screen showing you the attributes for the Enterprise License Server container object.

Note If you have trouble typing distinguished names accurately, you can copy the information you need from the computer object itself. In ADSI Edit, create a connection to the Default Naming Context of the domain, which will show you the domain structure. The computer you want will be either in the Computer organizational unit (OU) or (if a domain controller) in the Domain Controller OU. Drill down to find the correct server, open its properties, search the attributes for its Distinguished Name, and copy that information to the Clipboard. From there, you can copy it into the Value To Add text box shown in Figure 3-32.

FIGURE 3-32 Type the distinguished name of the server to add and click OK.

To finish, you'll need to add the server to the site. On a domain controller, open Administrative Tools | Active Directory Sites And Services and drill down to the site where the license server should be. You'll find an object for TS-Enterprise-License-Server there, as shown in Figure 3-33.

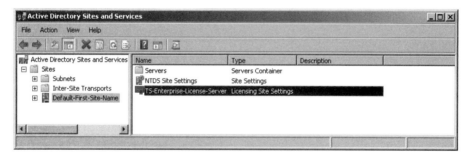

FIGURE 3-33 Find the Enterprise License Server object in the site.

Right-click on it and choose Properties from the context menu to open the dialog box shown in Figure 3-34.

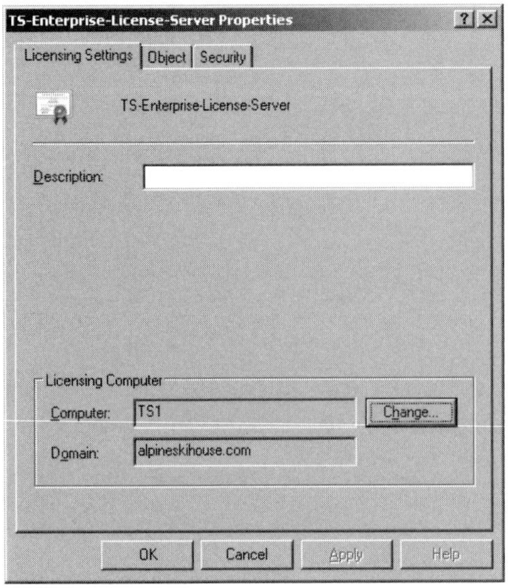

FIGURE 3-34 View the properties of TS-Enterprise-License-Server.

In the object Properties, click the Change button to select the license server you're adding to Active Directory. In the object picker, type the name of the server to add and click the Check Names button to ensure that it's a valid choice. Click OK to return to the Properties dialog box and then click OK again to exit back to Active Directory Sites And Services.

At this point, you can confirm that the license server is registered as an enterprise license server by opening TS Licensing Manager. The license server that previously had a Review link next to it should now say OK.

> **Note** Adding a second enterprise license server using the method detailed here can cause an existing enterprise license server to become uninstalled. If this happens (you'll know because a previously working enterprise license server in TS Licensing Manager will show up with a Review status instead of OK), then click Review to check the configuration. You'll see a button that allows you to publish the license server in Active Directory. Click it, and you're finished.

Reporting on TS CAL Usage

When users log onto a terminal server in per-user mode, the terminal server requests a TS User CAL for the user, and it will be assigned to their user account. You can't find evidence of this user CAL in the ADUC user account properties; this is not exposed in the UI. However, you can run a report on the license server to see how many user CALs have been allocated.

To run a terminal server User TS CAL report, open the Terminal Server Licensing Manager. Expand the server node, right-click on Reports, and select Create Report | Per User CAL Usage to open the dialog box shown in Figure 3-35.

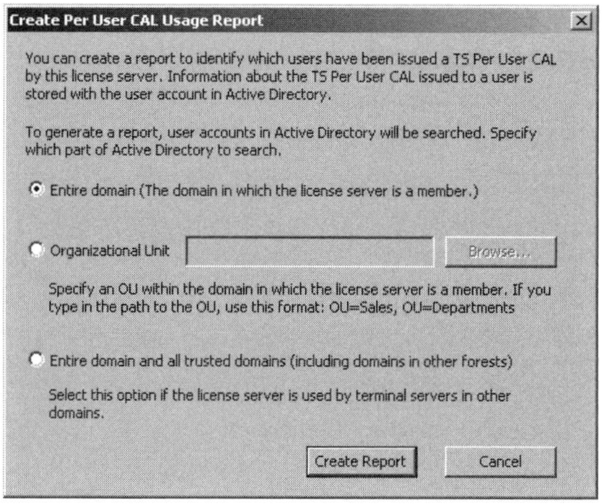

Create Per User CAL Usage Report

You can create a report to identify which users have been issued a TS Per User CAL by this license server. Information about the TS Per User CAL issued to a user is stored with the user account in Active Directory.

To generate a report, user accounts in Active Directory will be searched. Specify which part of Active Directory to search.

◉ Entire domain (The domain in which the license server is a member.)

○ Organizational Unit [_____]   [Browse...]

Specify an OU within the domain in which the license server is a member. If you type in the path to the OU, use this format: OU=Sales, OU=Departments

○ Entire domain and all trusted domains (including domains in other forests)

Select this option if the license server is used by terminal servers in other domains.

[Create Report]   [Cancel]

FIGURE 3-35 Choose a location for which to run the TS User Usage Report.

To generate the report, you need to specify the part of Active Directory to search for the data (remember the TS user licensing data is stored as part of the Active Directory user account). Select one of the following parts of Active Directory to search:

- **Entire Domain**   The domain that the license server belongs to.

- **Organizational Unit**   A particular OU where user accounts are stored that is also part of the domain where the license server resides. Choose this option to restrict a search to a particular OU, if you want to get usage for only a subset of users.

- **Entire Domain and all trusted domains**   Include domains in other forests in the search, but choosing this option will increase the time needed to generate the report.

Choose Entire Domain (the default choice) and click Create Report. After TS Licensing Manager creates the report, it appears in the right pane of the license manager, as shown in Figure 3-36.

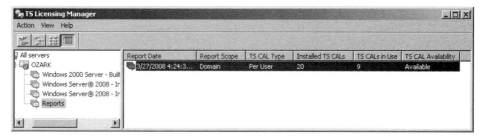

FIGURE 3-36 TS Per-User licensing usage report

To view the report, save the data to a file. Right-click on the report, choose Save As from the context menu, and provide a location to save the report to create a comma-delimited file at that location. Open the file in Notepad (or any program that can open .csv files) to view a report like the one shown in Figure 3-37.

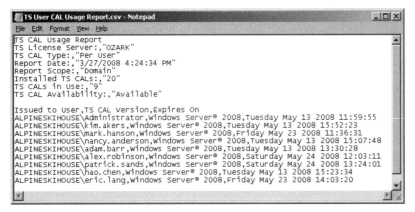

```
TS User CAL Usage Report.csv - Notepad                          _ □ ×
File  Edit  Format  View  Help
TS CAL Usage Report
TS License Server:,"OZARK"
TS CAL Type:,"Per User"
Report Date:,"3/27/2008 4:24:34 PM"
Report Scope:,"Domain"
Installed TS CALs:,"20"
TS CALs in Use:,"9"
TS CAL Availability:,"Available"

Issued to User,TS CAL Version,Expires On
ALPINESKIHOUSE\Administrator,Windows Server® 2008,Tuesday May 13 2008 11:59:55
ALPINESKIHOUSE\kim.akers,Windows Server® 2008,Tuesday May 13 2008 15:52:23
ALPINESKIHOUSE\mark.hanson,Windows Server® 2008,Friday May 23 2008 11:36:31
ALPINESKIHOUSE\nancy.anderson,Windows Server® 2008,Tuesday May 13 2008 15:07:48
ALPINESKIHOUSE\adam.barr,Windows Server® 2008,Tuesday May 13 2008 13:30:28
ALPINESKIHOUSE\alex.robinson,Windows Server® 2008,Saturday May 24 2008 12:03:11
ALPINESKIHOUSE\patrick.sands,Windows Server® 2008,Saturday May 24 2008 13:24:01
ALPINESKIHOUSE\hao.chen,Windows Server® 2008,Tuesday May 13 2008 15:23:34
ALPINESKIHOUSE\eric.lang,Windows Server® 2008,Friday May 23 2008 14:03:20
```

FIGURE 3-37 TS User Licensing usage report results

Although TS User CAL usage is not enforced, the data gained from this reporting feature will help you to demonstrate compliance with the TS End User License Agreement (EULA) requiring that users accessing the terminals server have a valid license assigned to them. The report contains the following data:

- The license server the report was run on

- The TS CAL type (which will be always per user since at this time Windows Server does not create reports on per-device TSCAL usage)

- The Report date

- The Report scope (domain, OU, etc.)

- The number of CALs installed on the server, how many are currently in use, and how many are currently available

- Which users have been issued a CAL, and when that CAL will expire and be returned to the pool

On the Companion Media This book's companion CD contains a TSCAL Reporting Tool that allows you to run license reports across multiple servers.

Revoking TS CALs

Unlike per-user licensing, per-device licensing is enforced. When a user logs on to a terminal server that is set to use TS Device CALs, the computer from which the user logged on is issued a TS Device CAL. The CAL is associated with a computer for a random interval of 52 to 89 days. It either must be renewed before it expires or the CAL goes back into the pool so the license server can allocate it to another client computer.

If you are replacing a few computers with new ones and have few enough CALs that you can't wait for the old allocations to expire, you might choose to revoke some TS CALs to fill in the gap.

You can't revoke all TS CALs at once. To reduce piracy, Microsoft has limited the ability to revoke TS CALs to 20 percent of the per-device TS CALs installed. For example, if your license server manages 100 Windows Server 2008 TS Device CALs and 200 Windows Server 2003 Device CALs, you can revoke 20 and 40 CALs respectively. Manual revocation is not intended to become effective concurrent-connection licensing by allowing you to revoke TS CALs on devices not currently being used.

To revoke a TS Device CAL, in the TS Licensing Manger, right-click on the CAL entry corresponding to the computer and choose Revoke CAL. The TS Licensing Manager will display a message confirming that the TS CAL has been revoked, and the TS CAL status in the Licensing Manager will be displayed as Revoked, as shown in Figure 3-38.

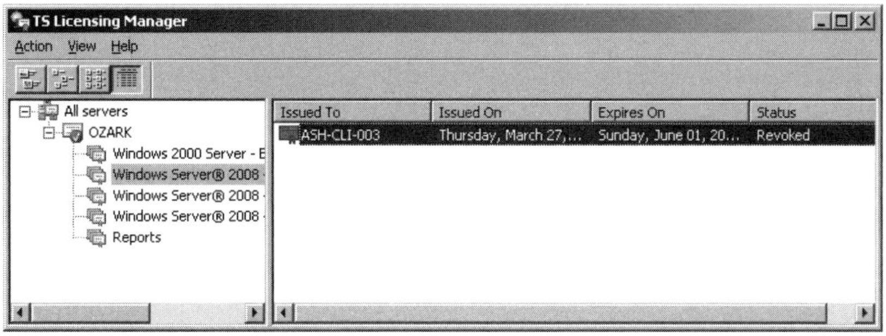

FIGURE 3-38 Revoked TS Device CALs have a status of Revoked.

This CAL is then available immediately in the device CAL pool and can be assigned to another computer. You may notice that you can still log on to the terminal server from a computer whose device CAL you have revoked, but its license will still be revoked in License Manager and the client device won't get a new one. The revocation worked; what you're seeing is the way the bookkeeping associated with revocation works. If you revoke a client computer's TS CAL, that computer can still connect until the TS CAL it formerly had expires. If you're following licensing guidelines, this should be a moot point, since the whole point of revoking licenses is to remove them from a computer that will no longer be used as a terminal server client. Just don't be surprised if that client PC can still connect to the terminal server for a while longer.

Restricting Access to TS CALs

TS CALs cost money. You probably want some control over who's able to use them. You may want to ensure that users don't set up terminal servers to experiment and use the production TS CALs, or that the department paying for the TS CALs is the one using them. If other departments want to use TS CALs, they can purchase their own.

If your license server is part of a workgroup, you probably don't have much to worry about, because only terminal servers in the workgroup can discover it. If the license server is in a domain, it's more easily discovered by terminal servers in the same forest, but there's also a way to ensure that only certain terminal servers can allocate licenses. If your license server is part of a domain, then you can enable a group policy to limit TS CAL disbursement to those terminal servers that are part of the license server's Terminal Servers local computer group. The Terminal Servers local computer group is created on the Terminal Server licensing server the first time the Terminal Services Licensing Service starts. By default this group is empty. To block rogue terminal servers from stealing TS CALs (or users in other departments from borrowing them), add terminal server computers to the Terminal Servers local group and then create a Group Policy object (GPO) and enable the TS License Server Security Group setting.

In Server Manager, expand Configuration | Local Users and Groups | Groups. In the Terminal Servers group, double-click, add the authorized terminal server(s) to the group, and click the OK button. You must add the terminal servers individually to this group—you can't group all the terminal servers together and then add that group to the Terminal Servers group.

On the domain controller, in the Group Policy Management tool, create a new GPO named something descriptive, such as TS License Server. Right-click on the new GPO and choose Edit. Navigate to Computer Configuration | Administrative Templates | Windows Components | Terminal Services | TS Licensing. Locate the License Server Security group setting, double-click it, select enable, and then click OK.

Note For more details on setting up a new GPO, see Chapter 4.

Finally, apply this policy to the license server:

1. Set the security filtering on the GPO to only include the license server. Choose the TS License Server GPO. In the Security Filtering section in the right pane, select Authenticated Users and click Remove.

2. Click Add, make sure the Computers selection is checked in the Object Type dialog box, add your license server, and click OK.

3. Apply this policy to the OU containing the TS License Server and then reboot the license server.

Using the Licensing Diagnosis Tool

After setting up licensing so that your terminal servers and license servers can find each other, you can double-check your work from the Licensing Diagnosis tool on the terminal servers.

On the terminal server, open the Terminal Services Configuration console, and then click on Licensing Diagnosis. The tool runs and produces a report like the one shown in Figure 3-39.

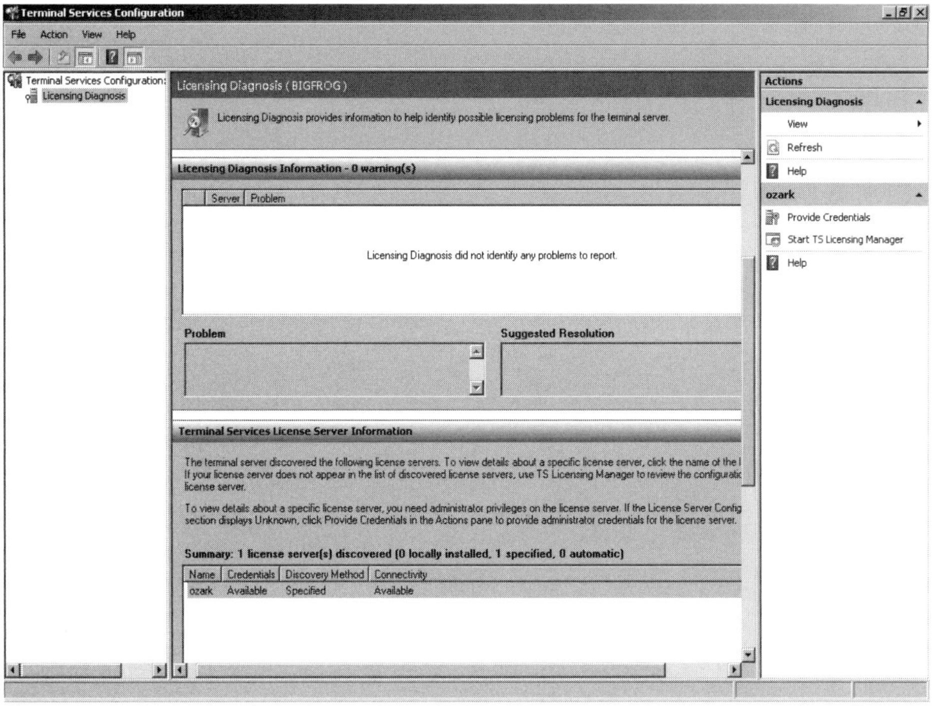

FIGURE 3-39 The Licensing Diagnosis tool gives TS Licensing specific information and details about problems.

The report shown in Figure 3-39 states that Licensing Diagnosis did not identify any problems. To get more details, click the entry for the license server located below the summary to show more details like those shown in Figure 3-40.

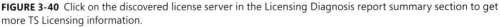

FIGURE 3-40 Click on the discovered license server in the Licensing Diagnosis report summary section to get more TS Licensing information.

As you can see, Licensing Diagnosis reports on a few other items you may find useful for troubleshooting licensing issues or for getting quick TS Licensing information. The report also shows:

- Discovery scope.

- "Prevent license upgrade" Group Policy setting. If enabled, this GPO defines how TS CALs are given to clients if no appropriate version of CAL is available for the client operating system version. If no earlier version TS CAL is available for a pre-Windows Server 2008 terminal server connecting to your license server, by default the license server will issue a TS CAL for Windows Server 2008. If you don't want this to happen, then enable this GPO.

- TS CALs installed and available. If you just want a quick glance at your TS CAL availability, you can view it here instead of using the License Manager on the TS License Server.

This report did not find any problems, but let's say that you had decided to put the group containing the terminal servers into the Terminal Server Computers local group on the license server, for use with the Licensing Server Security Group GPO setting. Therefore, all members of this group would now be members of the local license server security group.

You might expect that this would work, but it doesn't. You must add individual terminal servers to the Terminal Server Computers group, not the group containing them. If you add the group instead of specifying each server, you'll get an error.

Summary

This chapter has discussed the essentials of setting up a terminal server infrastructure: terminal server, license server, and licenses. By now, you should be familiar with how terminal servers create sessions, validate user logons, and issue licenses to authorized users or computers. You should also know how to set up a license server to support that terminal server and make sure it remains available.

Best practices for terminal server configuration include:

- Configure the terminal servers using Group Policy, not the Terminal Services Configuration tool. When adjusting settings on a per-server basis, it's too easy to introduce inconsistencies among servers, and inconsistencies now may lead to a lot of troubleshooting later.

- Install WSRM in per-session mode to evenly distribute processor time across user sessions.

- Install the Desktop Experience feature to enable Plug and Play redirection.

Best practices for license server management include:

- Wait to activate a server and install licenses on it until you are certain that that's the right license server. After you install the license packs, they'll be associated with that server, and it takes some effort to break that association.

- When using per-user licensing, always ensure that the license server's domain is trusted by the user account domains, or the license server will not be able to issue licenses.

- If installing a license server in a domain, use the Forest scope to make the server most easily discoverable. You can restrict access to the license server to only those terminal servers that should have it.

Additional Resources

The following resources contain additional information and tools related to this chapter:

- To learn more about setting up Group Policy objects for managing terminal server and user settings, see Chapter 4, "Creating the User Work Environment."

- To learn more about how to manage terminal server settings as a group, see Chapter 7, "Multi-Server Deployments and Securing Terminal Server Connections."

- For more details about how the license server issues TS CALs, see [MS-TSTS]: Terminal Services Terminal Server Runtime Interface Protocol Specification, available from *http://msdn2.microsoft.com/en-us/library/cc248570.aspx.*

- For more details about related Windows Server 2008 architecture, see Chapter 2, "Planning the Terminal Server Ecosystem."

Chapter 4
Creating the User Work Environment

After you have a terminal server installed, you can set up the user work environment so that users can be productive. This chapter and the next several chapters describe how to do this. In particular, this chapter discusses configuring profiles and folder redirection to work with Terminal Services.

The basic elements of a user workspace are the configuration settings in the user's profile and the default locations to save data. After reading this chapter, you will understand the following:

- How roaming, local, and mandatory profiles work

- Best practices for storing and managing profiles

- How to use folder redirection to unify user default locations between local and remote applications

- The benefits and drawbacks of using mandatory profiles to maintain a consistent look and feel

- How to secure the desktop to prevent users from saving files to it and why this is important

- How to support profiles when the client operating system is Windows XP

How Profiles Work

Apart from being the thing you see when you look at someone who's facing 90 degrees away from you, a *profile* is a collection of settings and documents that define a user's work environment. While a user is logged in, the collection of settings is stored in HKEY_CURRENT_ USER (HKCU) in the registry of the computer that user is logged on to; the documents are stored in the subfolders within the profile folder. How do these settings get into the registry and those files into the profile folder? Therein lies a tale—and that tale is good background for understanding some of the complications that arise in a terminal server environment.

> **Note** There are three types of profiles: local, roaming, and mandatory. Local profiles are stored on and used from a single computer. Roaming profiles are stored on and used from a network share, so they're available to any computer that can access that particular network share. Mandatory profiles are usually centrally located like roaming profiles, but whereas local profiles and roaming profiles are read-write, mandatory profiles are read-only.

User Profile and the Registry

The registry is organized into sections called *keys* that align with a particular configuration option. For example, computer-wide settings are stored in HKEY_LOCAL_MACHINE (HKLM), whereas user-specific settings are stored in HKEY_CURRENT_USER (HKCU). Windows Server 2008 maintains user-specific settings in HKCU while that user is logged on to the computer. You can see how HKCU works and reflects changes to the user environment by following the process outlined in the following sidebar, "See How the Registry Reflects Changes."

> ### See How the Registry Reflects Changes
>
> One easy way to watch how HKCU changes as you customize your environment is to make a change and watch the contents of the registry.
>
> 1. Run Regedit.exe and confirm that you want to run it when prompted.
>
> 2. Navigate to HKCU\Control Panel\Colors\Window. If you're using the default Windows Vista color scheme, the value of this entry should be 255 255 255. (Full saturation of red, blue, and green values show up as white on a monitor. Values of 0 for all three show up as black. If you ever had color theory classes, this is a demonstration of how black is the absence of color.)
>
> 3. Right-click the Desktop and choose Personalize from the context menu to open the Personalization window.
>
> 4. Click Window Color And Appearance. In the Appearance Settings dialog box, click Advanced to open the aptly named Advanced Appearance dialog box. From here, select Window from the Item drop-down list. Change Color 1 to light gray and click OK.

5. Click OK in the Appearance Settings dialog box. The screen will adjust for a minute and then the background color of windows will turn light gray.

6. If you examine the value of HKCU\Control Panel\Colors\Window, you'll see that it's now 192 192 192.

On Windows Server 2008 and Windows Vista, HKCU contains the subkeys explained in Table 4-1. (Even if you're logging on to a Windows Server 2008 terminal server from an older operating system such as Windows XP, the profile in the terminal session corresponds to the server platform, so these are still the registry keys that apply.) There may be more subkeys in this section—it depends on which applications you have installed.

TABLE 4-1 Subkeys of HKCU in Windows Vista and Windows Server 2008

Subkey	Description	Maps To
AppEvents	Sounds played on system events.	Control Panel\Sounds
Console	Command window settings such as window size, colors, and buffer size.	Command Prompt\Properties
Control Panel	User desktop appearance settings, mouse and keyboard settings, power policy, and accessibility.	Control Panel
Environment	Environment variable definitions.	Control Panel\System\Advanced
EUDC	Customized characters that end users install for viewing and printing documents when standard fonts don't support them. Applies to East Asian font sets.	Control Panel\Fonts
Keyboard Layout	Edits the keyboard layout. Useful if your operating system is displaying in one language but you want to use the keyboard layout of another one (for example, displaying in English but arranging the keyboard as though you were in Germany).	Control Panel\Regional and Language Options
Network	Network drive mappings and settings.	Control Panel\Networks
Printers	Printer connection settings.	Control Panel\Printers
Session Information	Information about the current session, such as how many applications are open.	Not stored—populated during the session
Software	Personal settings for all software installed for that user.	Individual applications
System	Contains the current control set for that user (drivers and services to run at startup).	Not stored—populated on startup

This information is in HKCU while the user it is associated with is logged on, but it can't stay there permanently; unlike HKLM, the current user settings are not persistent across logons. Most pieces of the registry are saved in files called *hives* and are loaded as necessary. When a hive file is opened, it's reloaded back into the registry. Therefore, HKCU is stored as a hive in a file called NTUSER.DAT. Each user logged on to the terminal server gets his own version of HKCU.

When you log on to a computer, the User Profile Service loads the hive file from the location specified in your user account properties and populates HKCU for that session. When you log off the computer, the hive file is written back to its storage location as NTUSER.DAT. If you happen to be logged on to more than one computer at a time, two copies of your profile will be open, populating the contents of HKCU on each computer.

> **Note** Profiles may be cached on the terminal server to speed up logons if you set the corresponding Group Policy. However, even if you enable caching, when a user logs off the terminal server, the corresponding branch of HKCU is cleared out. We'll talk more about caching user profiles in the section titled "Caching Roaming Profiles," which appears later in this chapter.

In addition to loading HKCU with the contents of your profile, logging on to a terminal server updates two parts of HKLM, the computer-wide registry. HKLM\Software\Microsoft\Windows NT\CurrentVersion\Profile List (Figure 4-1) contains a list of all currently logged on users and the profiles they're using. The users are identified by Security Identifiers (SIDs), but you can distinguish them by browsing the keys—they show the path to both the local cache (the ProfileImagePath key value shown in Figure 4-1) and to the roaming profile folder share (the CentralProfile key value shown in Figure 4-1), so it's not hard to map user names to profiles.

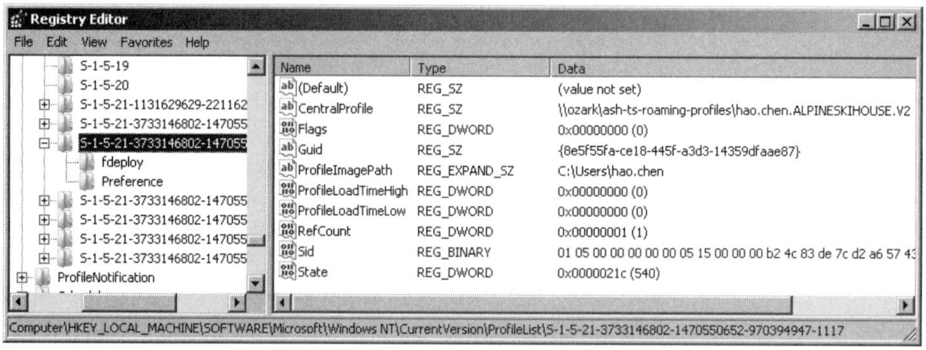

FIGURE 4-1 Loading a profile into a terminal session updates the Profile List key for the entire terminal server.

Another key in HKLM, shown in Figure 4-2, contains information about the Group Policy settings for that user. This registry key records the source of the Group Policy object (GPO) applied to this user, including its name and where it's stored.

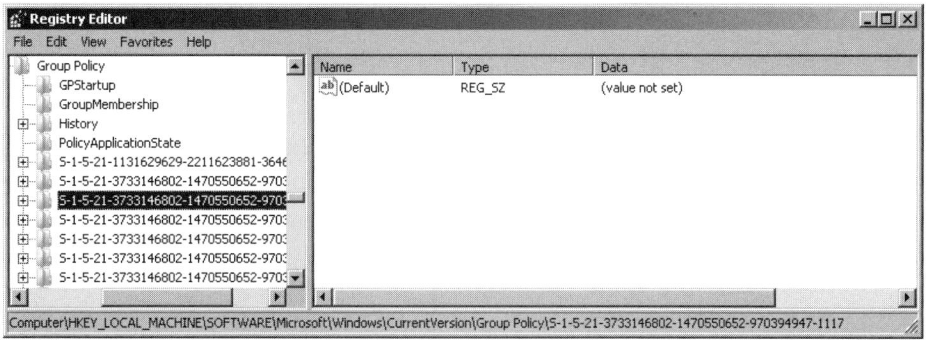

FIGURE 4-2 Logging on to a terminal session updates the Group Policy key for the terminal server.

When you log off from a terminal server, the two keys with your SID are locked. They don't actually go away, but if you attempt to open the key associated with a user who's currently logged off, you'll get an error message telling you that the system cannot find the file specified. Log on again, and the key with the same SID will be repopulated.

Although loading a profile adds two keys to the registry that never go away, most of the time it doesn't matter. As we'll discuss in the section titled "The Consequences of Deleting a Profile Folder from Explorer" later in this chapter, it *does* matter should you choose to delete a profile. Deleting the file doesn't delete the registry keys associated with it. Therefore, always use the correct tools to delete profiles.

How Profile Changes Are (Not) Merged

The operating system loads the contents of NTUSER.DAT into HKCU at logon and saves back to NTUSER.DAT at logoff, in the same way that you might open a Microsoft Office Word document when you log on, type in it for a while, and then save the document when you log off. This has some important implications for a terminal server environment.

As an example, imagine this scenario: You are logged on to two different computers and you open a new Microsoft Word document in each session. In Session 1, you type "Every Good Boy Does Fine." In Session 2, you type "All Cows Eat Grass." You save the file in Session 1 as Myfile.docx. Next you save the file in Session 2 as Myfile.docx in the same location, confirming that you want to overwrite the old file when prompted.

The next time you open Myfile.docx, the file will say only "All Cows Eat Grass." The phrase "Every Good Boy Does Fine" has been overwritten. In short, the files are not merged; they're written back to the save location, and the version last written to that location is the only one you'll see.

So it is with profiles, which are just another type of file. If you log on to two sessions, each of which is using the same roaming profile, you will have two copies of your profile open. If you make changes to the open profile, you'll see them at the time, but they won't be saved into NTUSER.DAT until you log off. (Unlike the Word .docx file, the file system won't ask if you want to overwrite the profile file.) As in the previous example, if you have a profile open in Session 1 and in Session 2, log off Session 1 and then log off Session 2, only the changes made to the Session 2 copy of the profile will appear when you log on again and reload that profile.

Note One implication of the way profiles work is that you shouldn't use the same profile for local sessions as you do for terminal sessions. If you do, then by definition every time you log on to your computer and then log on to a terminal server you will be opening two copies of your profile. You will almost certainly lose data this way.

You may be wondering whether opening two applications from a single terminal server opens one or two copies of your profile. In Windows Server 2003, you could create a Remote Desktop Protocol (RDP) session that would open a single application instead of displaying the entire desktop. (As noted in Chapter 1, "Introducing Terminal Services in Windows Server 2008," not many people did this because it wasn't terribly user friendly, but it was possible.) If you presented individual applications this way, then each time a user opened an application on the same server, she would open a separate session and therefore a separate copy of his profile. Windows Server 2008 improves on this design in two ways. First, it introduces RemoteApps. All RemoteApps launched from the same server run in the same session, so they only open a single copy of your profile. Second, when deciding where to route incoming connections to a terminal server farm, the TS Session Broker will check to see if a user already has an open session on a terminal server in the farm. If it does, then the user will be routed to that server to launch the application. End result: You have preference to the server where you already have an open connection, *and*, so long as you're only connecting to a single server, only one copy of the profile will be open.

Profile Contents External to the Registry

Not all parts of a profile are stored in HKCU. Folders for user data are stored in the profile folder, but separately from NTUSER.DAT. In Windows Vista and Windows Server 2008, the profile includes the folders listed in Table 4-2. (More folders may be available depending on which applications you have installed.)

TABLE 4-2 Folders Associated with a Windows Vista/Windows Server 2008 Profile

Folder	Description	Stored Separately in Windows XP
AppData	Default root location for user application data and binaries	No
Contacts	Used to store contact information and is also the address book for Windows Mail, the successor to Outlook Express	No
Desktop	All items stored on the desktop, including files and short-cuts	Yes
Documents	Default root location for all user-created files	Yes
Downloads	Default location for all files downloaded using Internet Explorer	No
Favorites	Bookmarked pages in Internet Explorer	Yes
Music	Default root location for all music files	Yes
Pictures	Default root location for all image files	Yes
Saved Games	Default location for saved games	No
Searches	Default location for saved searches	No
Videos	Default root location for all video files	Yes

As shown in Table 4-2, Windows Vista and Windows Server 2008 are a lot more granular about folder arrangements than Windows XP/Windows Server 2003 were. Rather than nesting folders, the operating system now organizes them at a top level. Unfortunately, this means that you can't use the same profiles for Windows Server 2008 terminal servers that you did for Windows Server 2003—the structure of the profiles doesn't match. We'll talk a bit later in this chapter about how to allow Windows Server 2003 and Windows Server 2008 profiles to coexist. (See the section titled "Sharing Folders Between Windows Server 2003 and Windows Server 2008 Roaming Profiles.")

> **Note** Windows Vista folder arrangements generally are more granular than those of Windows XP, but in other places, Windows XP top-level folders such as Nethood, Printhood, and a few others have been moved inside the AppData folder in Windows Vista.

Although these document folders are stored by default in the user's profile folder (see Figure 4-3, which has hidden files visible), they don't have to be. In fact, it's best if they aren't.

First, keeping user data within the profile folder increases the profile size. Assuming that you're storing profiles on a central share instead of on individual terminal servers (and, for reasons we'll discuss shortly, this is a good assumption), this can slow logons. A large profile increases the time it takes for users to log on and log off (since the data in the profile must be cached on the terminal server). A large profile can also impact the ability of additional users to log on to a terminal server. If profile caching is enabled, when the hard disk where the cache is stored fills up, no one else will be able to log on.

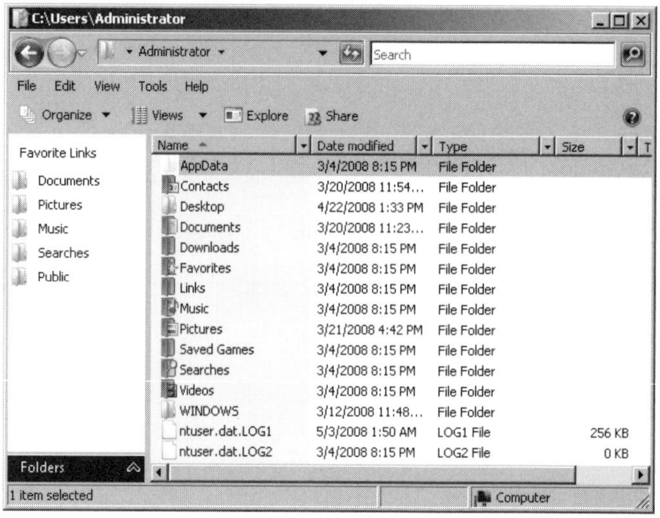

FIGURE 4-3 By default, a profile contains user data as well as user settings.

Second, if you're using mandatory profiles (more about these in the section titled "Choose Between Roaming and Mandatory Profiles" later in this chapter), and you don't redirect folders outside the profile folder, users will not be able to save files to the standard personal folders such as Documents. The files will look like they're saving, but they won't be saved. This will cause pain and agony and many unsolvable Help Desk calls.

> **Note** In previous versions of Windows, the Recycle Bin was stored on a per-computer basis. In Windows Vista and Windows Server 2008, the Recycle Bin is a hidden file in the root of the profile folder. You can't redirect it, and even if you're using mandatory profiles, you will still be able to recycle files.

For these reasons, it's good practice to use folder redirection with Terminal Services. We'll talk more about this in the next section.

Design Guidelines for User Profiles

Each of the following has an impact on the way you save user-specific configuration settings and data for use with terminal servers:

- Local profiles aren't generally suited to deployments of more than one terminal server, because the user experience will become different on every terminal server.

- For centrally stored profiles, the larger the profile, the longer it can take to log on or log off. The User Profile Service must copy the files to the terminal server and then copy them back to the profile when they're no longer needed.

- Profile settings aren't stored granularly; they're stored as a flat file. If more than one copy of the profile is open, the settings in the copy that were saved and closed last will be the ones reflected in NTUSER.DAT.

The following sections explain how these facts will impact your design.

Choose Between Roaming and Mandatory Profiles

Local profiles aren't a good fit for terminal services deployments larger than a single server. Storing local profiles on terminal servers in a multi-server environment will:

- Lead to an inconsistent user experience and may create problems that are hard to troubleshoot because they're linked to logging onto a specific terminal server.

- Fill up a terminal server hard disk with duplicate copies of a profile (that is, the profile will be stored on each terminal server a user logs onto).

- Require that you back up the terminal server because it now holds user data.

You have two remaining choices: roaming profiles and mandatory profiles. Neither choice is always appropriate. The option you pick depends on the amount of control you want and have authority to implement.

Roaming profiles may be freely edited by their owners within the limits defined by Group Policy (discussed in Chapter 5, "Fine-Tuning the User Experience"). That is, if you've defined the wallpaper for a user group via Group Policy, that will be the wallpaper every time anyone in that user group logs on. If you haven't specified the wallpaper using Group Policy, anyone is welcome to change the wallpaper when he connects to the terminal server. (The choices of wallpaper on the terminal server are admittedly not great, consisting as they do of either a logo backdrop or flat colors, but if users mapped drives to their terminal session, they could add wallpaper from any pictures stored on their computer.)

Mandatory profiles differ from roaming profiles in that their owners can edit them, but any changes they make will not be saved to the profile. This can speed up logoff times, since nothing is written back to the network share where you've stored the mandatory profiles. More insidiously, mandatory profiles don't save any data to folders stored within the profile folder. You *must* use folder redirection if using mandatory profiles for users to be able to save data to their personal folders. In fact, that's worth highlighting in a cautionary note.

> **Caution** If you use mandatory profiles, you must configure folder redirection in order to allow users to save files to their personal folders that are part of their profile.

The core choice between mandatory and roaming profiles is the tradeoff of flexibility versus control. Mandatory profiles make life easier for the terminal server administrator and eliminate the chance of a user erroneously making a profile configuration change that leads to

Help Desk calls (such as accidentally hiding the taskbar). Mandatory profiles also speed logoff times, but they don't allow users the degree of personalization that most have come to expect from Windows. More important, mandatory profiles don't allow other applications to save data to your profile either. This means that some security applications that require giving users a private key (the Encrypted File System is one) don't work with mandatory profiles. Your choice here will depend on your corporate culture, need to use applications that require private keys, and IT's ability to control the desktop.

> **Note** One option to the choice between roaming profiles and mandatory profiles is to not choose. Use mandatory profiles and combine them with a mechanism that allows users to save selected settings and have them applied at logon. Windows Server 2008 does not include this functionality, but several Terminal Services ISVs or consulting partners do. You can find an example of this functionality—a tool named Flex Profiles—from the following link on the companion CD: *http://www.immidio.com/flexprofiles*.

Use Folder Redirection

Whether you're using roaming profiles or mandatory profiles, it's best practice to use folder redirection.

If you're using roaming profiles, you want to make sure that the profile isn't getting too big, because a large profile will slow both logon and logoff times. People don't want to wait to log on to their computers. The fastest approach is to use local profiles, but for reasons we already discussed, you don't want to combine local profiles with terminal servers.

If you're using mandatory profiles, then you want to use folder redirection—but selectively. Any folders that you keep in the profile folder will become read-only. For some folders, this is very bad news—people won't be able to save their documents or pictures in their personal folders—so you'll definitely want to redirect those folders. But for some folders, this is exactly what you want. If you don't want people to remove icons from the Start menu, leave its folder in the profile folder.

Prevent Users from Losing Files

The Desktop folder contains everything you can see on the desktop—files and shortcut icons. Many users like saving documents to the Desktop. This is acceptable if you're seeing the full desktop, but if you're using RemoteApps, this isn't a great idea, because people don't see their desktop in the terminal server session and therefore can't easily browse it. (They could still open the documents if they moved to that path when opening a file, but they'd have to know to do this.) If you keep the Desktop folder in the profile folder and use mandatory profiles, then people can't save files to the Desktop . . . but if they try, it will appear as though they were able to do so. The file will be on the Desktop as long as they are logged on. Log off and log back on again, however, and the file will be gone.

You can use mandatory profiles to maintain a consistent look and feel for your users, prevent them from saving files to the Desktop, and give them an error message if they try. To do this, you'll need to:

- Redirect the Desktop folder to an external share.

- Set the permissions on this external share to read-only.

If you don't care if people save files to the Desktop (for example, if your users are connecting to a full desktop instead of to RemoteApps), then you can just redirect the Desktop folder.

> **Note** For instructions on implementing folder redirection, see "Centralizing Personal Folders with Folder Redirection" later in this chapter.

Speed Up Logons by Reducing the Data to Copy

People are sensitive to the amount of time it takes to log on to a session. If it takes too long, you'll have problems with people leaving their sessions open rather than logging off. This is a security risk, has the potential to lock files that more than one person may need to edit, and keeps open processes on the terminal server.

To encourage people to log off, you must therefore make the logon process as painless as possible. We already discussed using folder redirection to keep a profile's size down. To speed things up, you can also use the Group Policy that applies to the way a computer loads profiles to configure the following settings:

- Cache roaming profiles.

- Define the amount of time a terminal server will try to get the user profile.

- Set an upper limit on the size of a user profile.

> ### New to Windows Server 2008: Speeding Up Log*offs*
>
> Speeding up logons is important, but when it's Friday afternoon and you want to get out of the office fast, logoffs are just as important. There are two ways in which Windows Server 2008 helps logoffs take less time.
>
> You can limit the size of a profile using Group Policy (and help this limit by redirecting the folders out of the policy). This policy, Limit Profile Size, is set per user and is located in User Configuration | Policies | Administrative Templates | System | User Profiles.

Prior to Windows Server 2008, there was a nasty catch when it came to profile quotas in that previous versions of Windows were serious about enforcing this limit. If you made your roaming profile larger than Group Policy allowed, Windows would prevent you from logging off until you'd made the profile smaller. In Windows Vista and later versions, you can log off, but if the profile is larger than the size permitted by policy, the profile changes won't get written back to the roaming profile storage area.

Before Windows Server 2008, another issue that could delay logoffs (or prevent you from unloading your roaming profile altogether) was applications or drivers that left open handles to the registry (in other words, started to use it but never ended the connection to it). Microsoft had a separate tool called the User Profile Hive Cleanup Service (in an application called UPHClean) that checked for these open handles and closed them so users could log off. In Windows Server 2008, you no longer need to download this tool, because UPHClean functionality is handled by the User Profile Service.

Caching Roaming Profiles

To reduce the time it takes to log on to a terminal server, terminal servers cache the roaming profiles. Ordinarily, terminal servers attempt to retrieve the roaming profile from its central location. In cases when the network connection to the profile server is too slow or not working, however, being able to log on with a locally cached copy of your profile can at least speed things up. Caching stores a copy of the profile on the terminal server. This profile cache isn't used if the original roaming profile is available, but it can speed up logons in the case of slow or absent network connections.

Caching user profiles also means that you can use asynchronous processing of Group Policy, a policy processing model new to Windows Server 2008 that can speed up user logons. There are two ways that Group Policy can be applied. If you apply it synchronously (the default model for a server), logon doesn't complete until the Group Policy settings that apply to that user are applied. If you apply Group Policy asynchronously (the default model for a desktop), the user can log on while Group Policy is being applied. Asynchronous processing can lead to changes in the user environment after users have logged on but will speed up logon times if Group Policy processing is slowing things down.

All that being said, caching profiles does consume hard disk space on the terminal server. It can also prevent new users from logging on if the space allocated to cached profiles gets filled up. If you do cache profiles, make sure that you've got sufficient space for your user base and use the Group Policy and policy management tools described later in this chapter in the section titled "Removing Cached User Profiles on Terminal Servers" to delete profiles that aren't being used.

Caution Don't delete user profiles from the terminal server using Explorer or the delete command-line tools, because this does not clean up the registry entries associated with the profile and can affect the user's ability to log on again. The Delprof.exe tool does a complete job of cleaning up old user profile data. You can also configure the terminal servers using Group Policy to delete any profiles unused for a given period.

On the Companion Media To clean up old user profile data, download the Delprof.exe tool from the following location: *http://www.microsoft.com/downloadS/details.aspx?familyid= 901A9B95-6063-4462-8150-360394E98E1E&displaylang=en*. This link is available on this book's companion CD.

Storing Profiles

By default, when you log on to a computer for the first time, you'll create a new profile in its local profile directory (%SystemRoot%*Users*). This profile directory will have your name as a logon alias; it will contain your folders and NTUSER.DAT (which is a hidden file, so you won't see it unless you've enabled viewing hidden files). If left alone, thereafter you'll store every-thing in that location. Documents will default to Documents, images will default to Pictures, and where music is stored by default is left as an exercise for the reader. All will be well . . . so long as that's the only computer you use.

If it's *not* the only computer you use, life gets somewhat more complicated.

Thus far, we've set up only a single terminal server. However, in Chapter 1, we alluded to it being best practice to have multiple terminal servers organized into a farm. (In Chapter 7, "Multi-Server Deployments and Securing Terminal Server Connections," we'll discuss how to do this.) When a user logs on to a terminal server farm, a special kind of terminal server called a Session Broker looks at the terminal servers in the farm, picks the one with the low-est number of active sessions, and sends the user there, as shown in Figure 4-4. Each time a user connects, the Session Broker decides anew which server the user should connect to based on the number of connections each server is actively supporting and whether or not the user already has a session open somewhere. The user connects to the server with the fewest active connections or the one where the user already has an open session. It is likely (and highly recommended) that users will log off when not using their terminal server ses-sion, so if you use local profiles for terminal server sessions, then over time a user will have local profiles on all the servers in the farm.

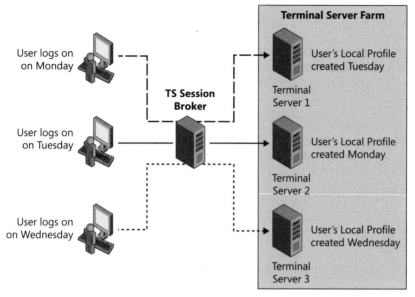

FIGURE 4-4 Over time, a user may have local profiles on every server in the farm.

This may not sound so bad. The user's logons will occur quickly, because the profile isn't loaded from the network but rather from the local computer. But when the user makes a change here and there, over time her desktop will look completely different depending on which terminal server she logs on to. (If user data is part of the profile—if you haven't redirected profile folders—the user will be even more confused, because the data she saved in one local My Documents folder won't be in another one.) If she makes a *bad* change, that change translates to a Help Desk call that can be tricky to figure out until you determine to which terminal server the user is connected. This is especially true because the problem might vanish if the user logs off and then logs back on and the Session Broker sends her to a different terminal server.

To avoid this scenario, all the terminal servers should use the same copy of the profile, which means that you need to use roaming profiles stored on a file share. When a user logs on, the User Profile Service looks at the user account properties to see where the profile reserved for terminal server sessions is kept and loads it from there.

When a user logs off, the profile is either deleted from the terminal server or retained in the local cache, depending on the Group Policy settings applied to the terminal servers. For faster logons, cache the profile but ensure that there's enough space on the hard disk holding the cache to support everyone who might need to cache their profile there.

Using Roaming Profiles with Terminal Services

This section discusses managing roaming profiles in a terminal server environment, including:

- How to convert an existing local profile to a roaming profile.

- How to use Group Policy to automatically set up the roaming profile storage area.

- How to create the Group Policy infrastructure that supports these policies, including security filtering and loopback policy.

- How to manage roaming profiles cached on the terminal servers.

Converting an Existing Local Profile to a Roaming Profile

In many cases, you won't start over with new roaming profiles but will have local profiles already in use that you must convert to roaming profiles.

Note It's very unlikely that you would convert a local profile that a user has been using on a desktop to be his Terminal Services roaming profile. The user may have administrative access to his personal computer, and could have installed numerous applications and made many customizations that don't apply to the shared (and more locked-down) world of terminal servers.

To do this, first you create a shared location to store Terminal Services user profiles. Give this folder the appropriate NTFS and share permissions. Tables 4-3 and 4-4 show the minimum share and NTFS folder permissions that need to be set.

TABLE 4-3 Share Permissions for a TS Roaming Profiles Storage Folder

User Account	Share Permissions
Everyone	Full control

TABLE 4-4 NTFS Permissions for a TS Roaming Profiles Storage Folder

User Account	NTFS Permissions
Creator owner	Full control, subfolders and files only
Local system	Full control, this folder, subfolders, files
User group that needs access	List folder/read data, create folders/append data, this folder only

Direct from the Source: How Profile Folders Are Named

The way that a user's profile folder is named depends on the circumstances in which it's created. The user My Name (with user name myname) with an account in Domain1 will store his profile in one of two places: \TS-Roaming-Profiles\myname or \TS-Roaming-Profiles\myname.Domain1.

The best case is that we add the domain name to the profile path; this disambiguates the path when there are two (or more) users with the same name living in different domains. For example, in a large corporate network, you might have Domain1\myname (that's me) and Domain2\myname (some other user). When Domain1\myname logs onto a legacy terminal server the profile created for him will be . . . \myname. If Domain2\myname later wants to store his profile on the same server, he will have a problem. That's why we added .domain to the profile path, so that users with the same name but from different domains would have different profiles. So ideally, we always want to add .domain to the profile path.

But then, what do we do with profiles that were created before we made this change and don't have .domain in the name? Leave them as is. But in this case, how do we know which user this particular profile belongs to? We use permissions to determine that. When the User Profile Service creates a new profile, it gives full control to the user whom this profile is created for. So, if Domain1\myname has explicit full control permission to the ...\myname folder, then this profile belongs to me and not to Domain2\myname. That's why we have this logic when creating profile names.

Here is the logic we use to create the profile path:

1. Attempt to locate the ...*username.domain* path. If it exists and the user has explicit permissions to it, then use it.

2. If the user does not have explicit Full Control access to ...*username.domain* or this folder does not exist, then try to access ...*username*.

3. If ...*username* exists and the user has explicit permissions to it, then use it.

4. If the user does not have explicit Full Control access to ...*username* or the folder does not exist, then use ...*username.domain*.

As you can see, by default we always create the folder with ...*username.domain*. Only when ...*username* folder exists and user has explicit Full Control access to it do we use it. Again, it's always best to include the domain name in the profile path so that two people with the same user name with accounts in different domains can store their profiles in the same central share.

Sergey Kuzin

Software Development Engineer II

To copy the local profile a user created on a terminal server to the designated file share, log on to the terminal server that contains the user's local profile using a domain admin account. Open the System Properties dialog box (in the Control Panel, or accessible by right-clicking Computer and choosing Properties). Click the Advanced tab and then click Settings under User Profiles, as shown in Figure 4-5.

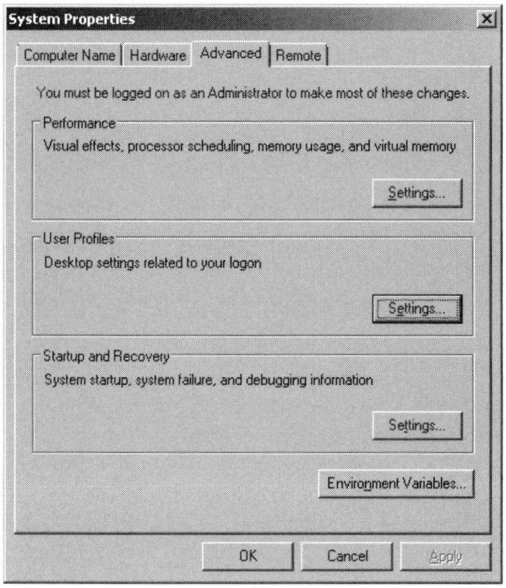

FIGURE 4-5 System Properties User Profiles Settings

Highlight the local user profile you want to make a roaming profile and click Copy To, as shown in Figure 4-6.

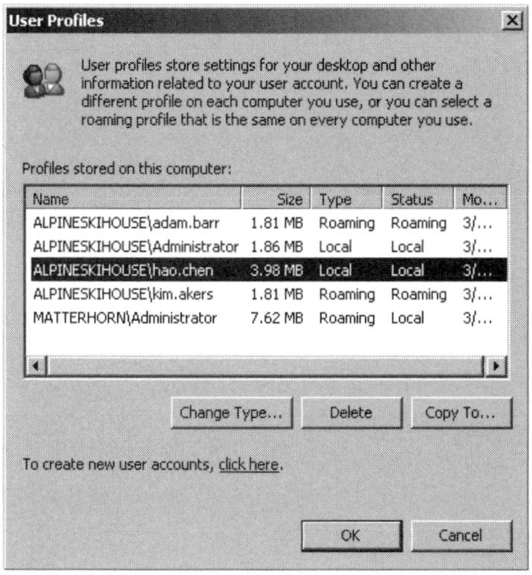

FIGURE 4-6 To move a local profile to a new location, highlight the user local profile and click Copy To.

You will see a dialog box like the one shown in Figure 4-7. Type or browse to the share location where you want to copy this profile.

FIGURE 4-7 Enter the location to copy the user profile and give the user permission to use the profile.

The location path should take this form: *Servername**Sharename**username.DomainName*.V2.

> **Note** Windows 2008 and Windows Vista profiles have a .V2 extension. Windows 2008 and Vista profiles are not compatible with Windows 2003 and Windows XP profiles.

To give the user permissions to use the profile, click Change and select the user's account from Active Directory. Click OK and then click OK again to exit. The profile will be copied to the designated location, with the folder name *username.DomainName*.V2.

Next, configure the user's Active Directory account to use this profile when logging into the terminal server. Open Active Directory Users And Computers and open the Properties dialog box for the user's account. Move to the Terminal Services Profile tab and type the Profile Path location using the format *servername**share name*\%*username*%.*DomainName* as shown in Figure 4-8.

Figure showing Hao Chen Properties dialog:

```
Hao Chen Properties                              ? X
  Member Of   | Dial-in |  Environment  |  Sessions
General | Address | Account | Profile | Telephones | Organization
   Remote control  |  Terminal Services Profile  |  COM+

Use this tab to configure the Terminal Services user profile. Settings in this
profile apply to Terminal Services.
 ┌ Terminal Services User Profile ─────────────────────┐
    Profile Path:
    [\\ozark\ash-ts-roaming-profiles\%username%.ALPINESKIHOUSE ]

 ┌ Terminal Services Home Folder ──────────────────────┐
    ⦿ Local path  [                                       ]

    ○ Connect:   [   ▼]  To: [                            ]

 ☐ Deny this user permissions to log on to Terminal Server

        OK        Cancel       Apply        Help
```

FIGURE 4-8 Type the Terminal Services User Profile path.

The variable %username% inserts the user account name into the profile path, so you don't have to customize the path for each person when adding new accounts manually or through a script. Nor do you need to add the .V2 extension to this path; it will be added automatically because the profile will be a 2008 version profile. The next time the user logs on to the terminal server, she will use her roaming TS profile.

On the Companion Media For tips on how to avoid the "duplicate link" problem you can introduce when converting a local profile to roaming, see *http://blogs.technet.com/ deploymentguys/archive/2008/05/01/dealing-with-duplicate-user-profile-links-in-windows-vista. aspx.* You can find the link on this book's companion CD.

As you can see, converting an existing local profile to a roaming profile involves some work. If you start over with a new roaming profile for users using the terminal server, you can skip most of the steps. Just specify the Profile Path as explained previously and then:

■ The User Profile Service will create a profile folder and profile in the specified path the first time the user logs on.

■ The user will be the owner of the folder and will therefore be the only one to have access to it.

If you copy a local profile to the correct share path *before* the user logs on, the Administrator will be the owner of the folder—not the user—and will be able to access the profile contents. Although a user profile folder is for the user's convenience, it is also useful for administrators to be able to access the contents of the folder to delete a corrupted profile or perform other maintenance. To permit this, give the Domain Admins group full control NTFS rights to the parent folder, and pre-create TS roaming profile folders for each user in the TS roaming profiles share. Make sure that the user has full control of his profile folder, subfolders, and files and that the user is also the owner of the folder.

Direct from the Field: Managing Roaming Profiles Without Admin Access to the File Server

To use roaming profiles, you need a file server to store them on. In a smaller deployment, you may have administrative rights to the file server as well as the terminal servers, but enterprise deployments often segregate ownership. If you aren't an administrator of the file server, you can't directly manage the folders—you'll need to ask the file server administrator. Even the Group Policy setting Add The Administrators Security Group To Roaming User Profiles will not help if the terminal server administrator is not a member of Administrators group on the file server. You could lobby to become a member of the Administrators group on the file server, but this is counter to Least Privilege Access principles.

You can resolve this situation with a logoff script. Use Icacls.exe to include TS administrators to the user profile's permissions during logoff from user's security context. This works because the user has full access permissions to his profile, so she can add necessary permissions for TS Administrators. For example, the Logoff script might look like this:

```
Icacls.exe \\<profile root>\%username%.%userdomain%.v2 /grant <TS Admins group>:
F /T /Q
```

Add this script to each user through Group Policy: User Configuration | Windows Settings | Scripts | Logoff Script. Now you can manage that profile folder.

There are two reasons to do this at logoff, not logon. First, if the user is logging on for the first time, the profile folder may not yet exist, so the settings wouldn't apply until the second time. If the user never logged in again, you couldn't delete his profile without the help of the file server administrators. Second, if the profile is large, it takes some time for icacls to go through the whole tree. Users do not like long logon times, so why make them wait to start working? Let the script process permissions when they're done working and less concerned about the time.

Bohdan Velushchak

Operations Engineer, MSIT

If you have your terminal servers in their own organizational unit (OU), you can also create a computer GPO with Loopback Processing enabled and give administrators access to profile contents by enabling the following GPO setting: Computer Configuration | Policies | Administrative Templates | System | User Profiles | Add The Administrators Security Group To The Roaming User Profile Share. For more information on using Group Policy to create and manage TS roaming profiles, see the section titled "Using Group Policy to Manage Roaming Profiles" later in this chapter.

Direct from the Field: Choosing the Right Local Profile to Convert

The number one problem is that most administrators are scared of Roaming User Profiles. They don't understand how they work, how to properly set them up on a file server, or how to set up the GPO to apply them to users, so instead they just use local profiles on the terminal servers. Then when they add a second server, they don't know why the users are complaining about all their settings being lost. After setting up their profiles, the next time the users log on, they access the original server and find their Outlook nickname file is missing entries. After adding a third or fourth server, the cycle repeats itself.

Now they finally decide to implement Roaming Profiles. OK, which local profile do they copy to the profile share on the file server? The network administrator may wonder what to do.

Since most people would rate their Outlook nickname file as most important to keep, copy the profile that has the most recent date or the largest size.

Carl Webster

Senior Enterprise Engineer, SARCOM

The preferred way to specify Roaming Profiles to use in a Terminal Services session is to create a GPO that dictates the terminal services roaming profile location for everyone that logs into any terminal server in a farm. The next section explains how to do this and how to set up the Group Policy infrastructure you'll need.

Using Group Policy to Manage Roaming Profiles

To create a GPO that dictates the Terminal Services Roaming Profile location for everyone who logs on to any terminal server in the farm, it's imperative to set up the terminal server environment OU and create the GPOs correctly. This is the single most important part of successfully using roaming profiles with terminal servers.

Group Policy has many different uses, but it all comes down to making changes to many computers or many users all at once, instead of individually configuring those computer user settings. Computer settings are applied when a computer boots up; user settings are applied when a user logs on. Because the settings are applied at logon, they don't have to be saved as part of a user's account properties.

Because computer settings are applied before the user policies, when managing terminal server settings you'll use an additional GPO to enforce *loopback policy processing*. We'll talk about loopback policies in the section titled "The Ins and Outs and Ins of Loopback Processing" later in this chapter. For now, the most important thing to remember is that this policy reapplies the user-specific settings that are placed on the OU where Loopback Processing is enabled after the normal user GPOs are applied, so the settings placed on the terminal server OU will always take precedence in case of a conflict.

There's some overlap between the computer-specific and user-specific settings in Group Policy, but you'll generally find that you'll need both to configure the users' working environment. When setting up a terminal server environment, where it's important not just that you are logging on but that you're using a terminal server, you'll definitely need both.

> **Note** The following explanations assume that you have permission to manage Group Policy for your terminal servers. If this is not the case, you'll need to provide the instructions to the administrator controlling Group Policy for your organization and let him fit them into corporate management policy. This is *one* way to organize your terminal server GPOs, but it is not the only possible model. GPO architecture is very individual to the particular situation. For example, for some organizations, blocking inheritance may not be an option for policy reasons. For more information on Group Policy modeling, see "Design Considerations for Organizational Unit Structure and Use of Group Policy Objects," located at *http://technet2.microsoft.com/ windowsserver/en/library/2f8f18cf-a685-48db-a7be-c6401a8fb6341033.mspx?mfr=true*. You can find the link on this book's companion CD.

Creating Group Policy Objects to Work with Terminal Server Users and Computers

To manage terminal servers using Group Policy, first create an organizational unit (OU) and place all the terminal servers you want to manage together in it. All terminal servers in the same farm should definitely be in the same OU. Computers can be in only a single OU. To create a new OU, open Active Directory Users And Computers, right-click the domain, and choose New | Organizational Unit. Name it something descriptive such as Terminal Servers and then drag and drop the terminal server computer objects into the OU (see Figure 4-9).

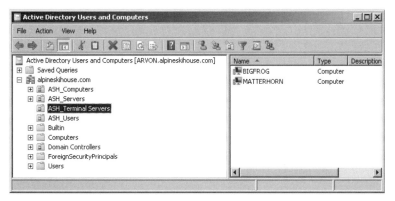

FIGURE 4-9 Create an OU for your terminal servers.

Next, block GPO inheritance for this OU so that only computer settings set by GPOs linked to this OU will apply to the computers in this OU, and only user settings set by GPOs linked to this OU will be applied to users logging on to the computers in this OU. Other GPOs set at the domain or site level will not be applied. To do this, open the Group Policy Management Console (Start | Programs | Administrative Tools | Group Policy Management), right-click the Terminal Servers OU, and choose Block Inheritance.

Next create two different types of GPOs: a computer GPO and a user GPO, as shown in Figure 4-10. Although one policy may contain both user-specific and computer-specific settings, it's best to isolate the two unless your environment is very small or your user base is very homogenous. This allows you to create a consistent model of terminal server management while still allowing you the flexibility to apply different policies to different groups of users.

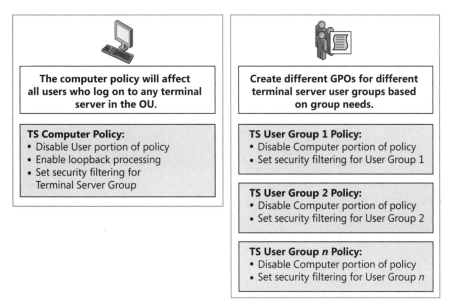

FIGURE 4-10 Creating separate user and computer GPOs for the Terminal Services environment

To create the GPOs for your terminal server environment, open the Group Policy Management Console (Start | Programs | Administrative Tools). Right-click the Group Policy Objects folder in the left pane, found under your domain folder, and choose New to show the dialog box in Figure 4-11. Name the computer policy something descriptive like TS Computer Policy.

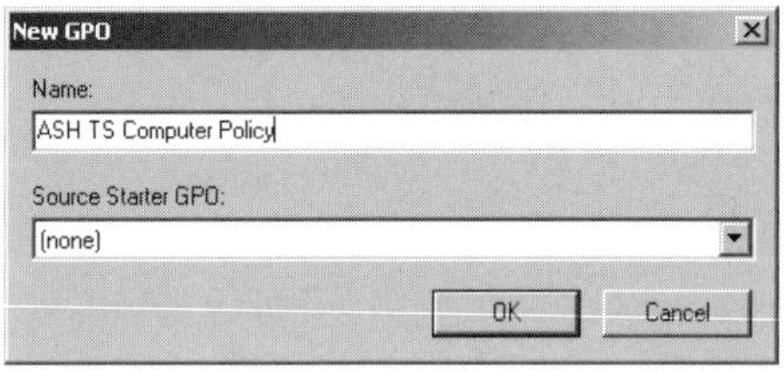

FIGURE 4-11 Create a terminal server computer policy.

Click OK, and you will be back in the Group Policy Management console, with a list of available policy objects—including the one you just created—in the right pane. When you click your Computer Policy, you will see a screen similar to the one in Figure 4-12.

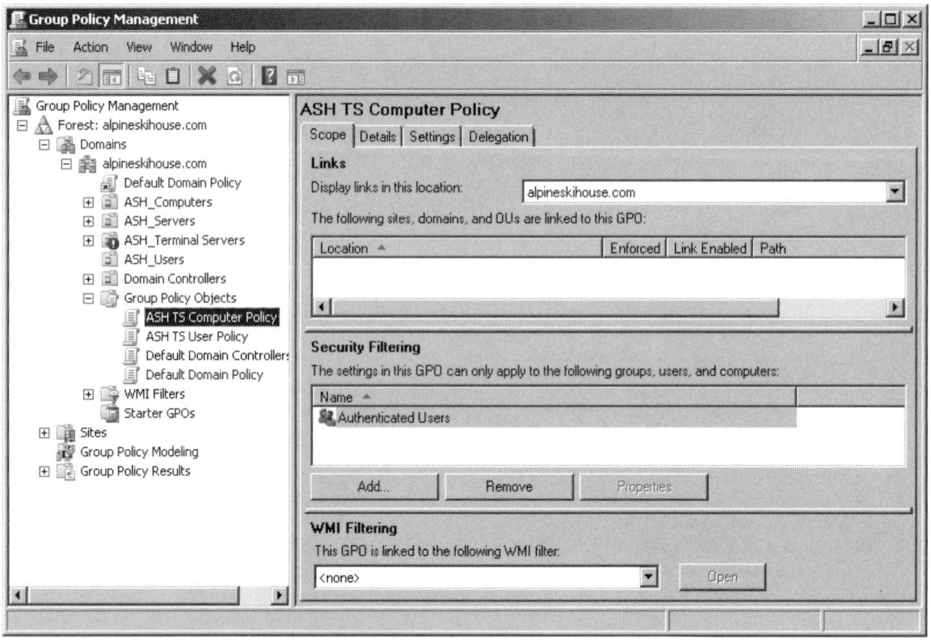

FIGURE 4-12 ASH TS Computer Policy default screen

Click the Details tab in the upper portion of the right pane. Here, there's a GPO Status drop-down list with four options: All Settings Disabled, Computer Configuration Settings Disabled, Enabled, and User Configuration Settings Disabled. To remove any user-specific settings from this GPO, select User Configuration Settings Disabled. This is important because you will use loopback policy to apply user GPOs placed on the terminal server OU after user logon. Making sure no user policies inadvertently set in a computer GPO get applied will help you better manage your environment.

> **Note** You can create and use multiple computer policies for terminal servers, but take special care to set the security on all computer GPOs exactly the same. Remember, the main goal here is to create a consistent environment across all terminal servers.

Follow the same process to create a new user-specific GPO. For the User Policy GPO (like the one shown in Figure 4-12), select Computer Configuration Settings Disabled from the drop-down menu on the Details tab. You can create more than one User Policy if you need to implement a different set of policies for different user groups.

Fine-Tuning GPOs with Security Filtering

A GPO works because by default anyone in the Authenticated Users group is allowed to use it—and Authenticated Users means "anyone who logged on to the domain." Computers actually log on to the domain, so they're members of this group.

To narrow the scope of to whom (or to what) these policies will apply, double-click the GPO in the Group Policy Objects folder and then turn to the Scope tab shown in the right pane. In the Security Filtering section on this tab, you can edit the users and groups to determine to whom the GPO will apply.

For your Computer Policy, you will want the settings to take place on all terminal servers. Add each terminal server computer object to the Security Filtering section (or if you have created a Terminal Servers group, then add it). Click the Add button to select the objects you wish to add and then click OK, as shown in Figure 4-13.

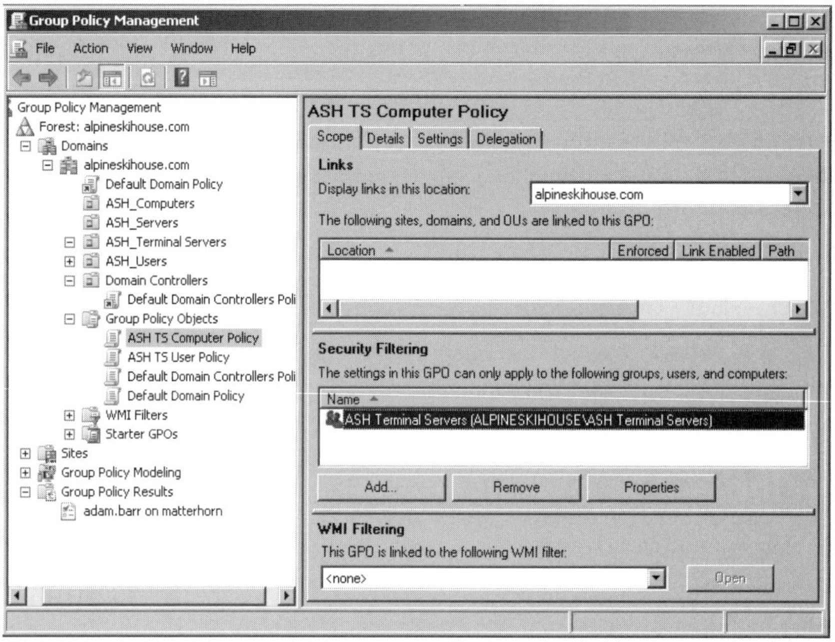

FIGURE 4-13 Add the terminal server computers group to the computer GPO security filtering.

Modify the Users Policy GPO Security Filtering to include the specific users group for which you want settings in the GPO to apply, as shown in Figure 4-14.

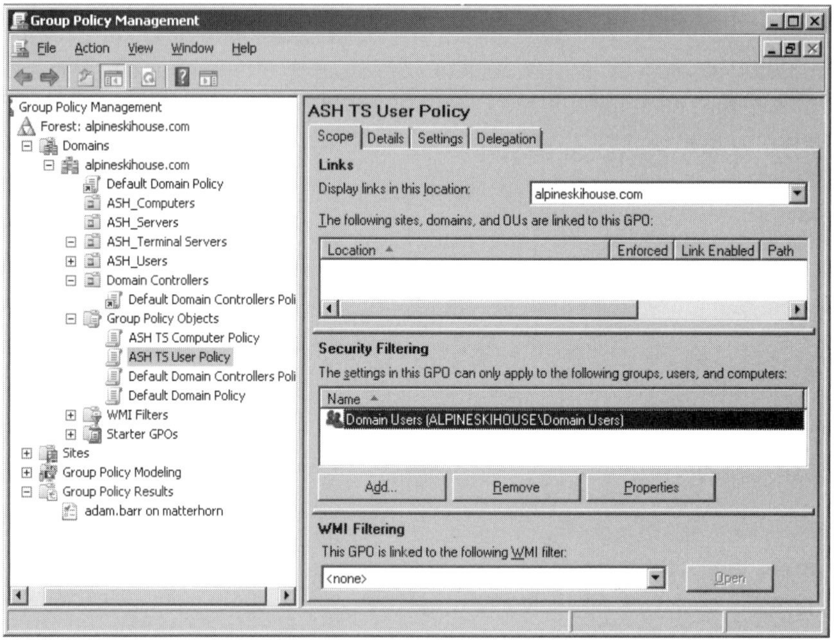

FIGURE 4-14 Add users to the GPO Security Filtering section of the ASH TS Users Policy.

Figure 4-14 shows the Domain Users group added to the Security Filtering section, but you can add any group here.

The Ins and Outs and Ins of Loopback Policy Processing

Outside a terminal server environment, you apply a lot of Group Policy based on the persona of the user logging on. If you don't want Adam Barr to open Control Panel, for example, you probably feel much the same way about this whether Adam Barr is logged on to his desktop computer or his laptop. Similarly, if you don't care about him running Control Panel on the desktop, then you continue not to care whether he's logged on to his desktop or his laptop. It's his space—let him mess it up. (The Help Desk may feel differently about this, but that's another matter.)

Enabling Loopback Policy Processing changes the order in which policies are applied. Normally, computer GPOs are applied when the computer starts up. Then user GPOs are applied when a user logs on. Therefore, the computer policy will always be applied first, then the user policy. If a user policy and a computer policy conflict, and the user policy is able to override the computer policy, the user policy will always win because it's applied last.

On a personal computer, it's perfectly acceptable to have the identity of the person logging on define the final settings for Group Policy. But a terminal server is one of the location-specific or context-specific situations in which *where* you are matters even more than *who* you are. For example, you might decide that it's acceptable for users to use clipboard redirection when connecting to remote desktops, but for security reasons you don't want them using clipboard redirection when connecting to a terminal sever farm hosting sensitive data. You need policies applied based on which computer you are logged on to. In this case, you will apply loopback policy processing to tell the Group Policy engine to apply the user GPOs that pertain to the computer (that are applied to the Terminal Server OU) after (or instead of) applying the user GPOs that are normally applied during logon. With loopback policy processing enabled, GPO processing will now work like this:

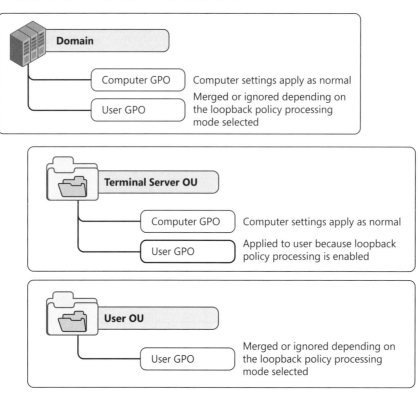

When the terminal server boots, computer GPOs are applied. When the user logs on to the terminal server, user GPOs are applied to their session (or ignored if loopback processing Replace Mode is selected). Then, because loopback policy processing is enabled, user GPOs that are applied to the terminal server OU are applied.

To enable loopback processing, right-click the Computer GPO applied to the terminal server OU and choose Edit. The Group Policy Management Editor opens the GPO. Go to Computer Configuration | Policies | Administrative Templates | System | Group Policy and find the policy User Group Policy Loopback Policy Processing Mode node in the pane at right. Double-click it and you will see the dialog box shown in Figure 4-15.

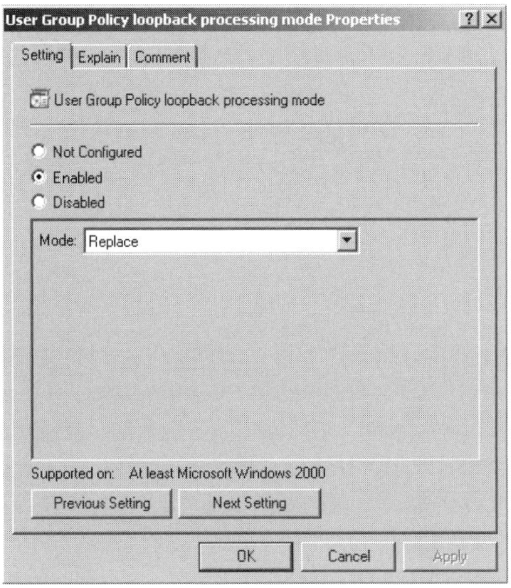

FIGURE 4-15 The User Group Policy Loopback Processing Mode Properties dialog box

How It Works: Applying Loopback Policy

Loopback policy can apply to users in one of two ways: Merge Mode and Replace Mode.

- In Merge Mode, Loopback Policy Processing will apply the user GPOs placed on the Terminal Server OU along with the normal user GPOs assigned to the OU where the user account resides. If there is a conflict, then the user GPOs applied to the terminal server OU will override.

- In Replace Mode, the Group Policy engine ignores the user's GPOs placed on the OU where the user account resides and applies only the user GPOs that apply to the terminal server.

Merge Mode or Replace Mode?

Whether you choose Merge Mode or Replace Mode (see the previous sidebar, "How It Works: Applying Loopback Policy") depends on your goals and how you've set up the rest of your environment.

If users are using the same GPOs to log on to the terminal servers and to their local desktops, their user settings may not mesh well with a shared environment. If that's the case, then you'd pick Replace Mode. If you want the user experience to be as similar as possible for both local and remote logons, then Merge Mode may be more appropriate for you, because it will preserve user-specific policies. The main thing you'll need to watch out for is that GPO settings from the GPOs applied to the user do not cause problems for your user when she is logged on to a terminal server. Using Merge Mode is more work, because it requires a lot of considering of individual policies and their effect on a remote workspace scenario.

Using gpupdate /force

Active Directory does not immediately send Group Policy changes down to the computers to which they apply. The Group Policy Engine on the computer (in our case the terminal server) actually pulls the GPO changes from Active Directory at specific intervals, called the *refresh interval*. By default, the refresh interval is 90 minutes (plus a random time ranging from 0–30 minutes). To immediately see the effects of changes you make to GPOs, you can force this refresh. Open a command prompt on your terminal server and type **gpupdate /force**. Rebooting the terminal servers has the same effect.

Using Group Policy to Define the Roaming Profile Share

After you have a Group Policy infrastructure set up, you can effectively create a policy to automatically create roaming profile folders in the proper folder share location.

The Group Policy setting to set the path for TS roaming profiles is in the Computer Configuration GPO folder. Right-click your TS Computer Policy GPO and choose Edit. Expand the GPO to Computer Configuration | Policies | Administrative Templates | Windows Components | Terminal Services | Terminal Server | Profiles. In the pane at right, double-click Set Path For TS Roaming User Profile, shown in Figure 4-16.

Note It may seem counterintuitive to set the TS roaming profile path for computers, not for users. But the terminal servers must know where to find the roaming profile so the User Profile Service can load it when a user logs on.

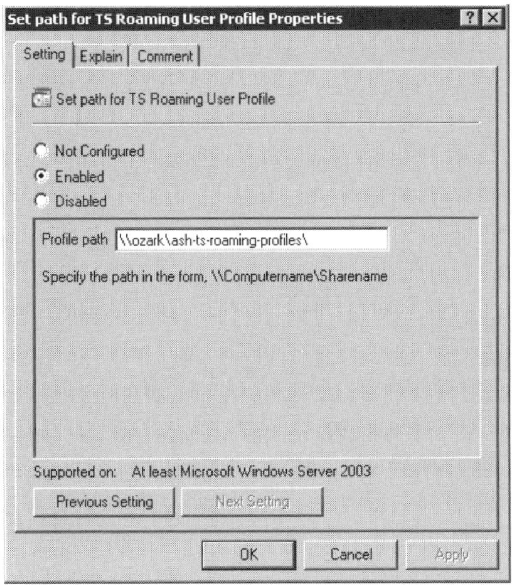

FIGURE 4-16 Set the path for Terminal Services Roaming User Profile storage.

Select the Enabled option and type the TS roaming profile share location in the Profile Path text box. If you use Group Policy to set the TS roaming profile path, then the profile folders that are created take the form of *username.domainname*.V2; you do not need to add the %username% variable, the domain name, or the .V2 extension. This is in contrast to defining the path to the Terminal Services profile folder by editing the user account properties through scripting or through Active Directory Users And Computers, where you must specify the *username* and *domainname* variables to create the folder properly.

> **Note** If you already have profiles stored in the profile path and the profile folders do not include the domain name (perhaps they take the form of *username*.V2), change the names to include the domain name. Otherwise, the existing profile will not be seen, and a new one will be created in the format *username.domainname*.V2.

If the profile folders are created automatically when the user logs on, then he gets sole access to his profile and is also set as the owner of the profile folder. To permit administrators to access the profile, enable the following GPO setting: Computer Configuration | Policies | Administrative Templates | System | User Profiles | Add The Administrators Security Group To Roaming User Profiles. With this GPO setting enabled, the following permissions are placed on newly created user folders:

- User—Full Control, owner of folder
- SYSTEM—Full Control
- Administrators—Full Control (This is the local administrators group of the server where the profiles are stored, which also contains the Domain Admins group.)

You can also pre-create user profile folders and set permissions as required. For more information about profile folder permissions, see the section titled "Converting an Existing Local Profile to a Roaming Profile" earlier in this chapter.

With this GPO setting set, users accessing the terminal servers in this OU will now have a roaming profile created and stored in the designated share.

Speeding Up Logons with Small Profiles

One of the biggest tasks that IT professionals face in a terminal server environment is to provide and maintain a consistent and efficient user experience. Users want to log on quickly, work steadily, get their job done, and get out. If they find that they have to wait longer to log on than they like, the IT department will hear about it.

Roaming profiles provide a consistent user experience across all terminal servers, following the user to whichever terminal server they log on to, instead of the randomization that local profiles stored on the terminal servers will produce. The roaming profile is also stored in a central location, where it's easy to back up. Roaming profiles definitely have some benefits. But if they are not well controlled and well-maintained, they can cause problems. As profiles are used over time, they grow in size. Recall the kinds of folders that are stored in a user profile: Documents, Desktop, Favorites, and more. If users add files to any of these places (and of course they will), the profile gets bigger. Over time, they can—and usually do—get a *lot* bigger.

When a user logs on to a terminal server, her roaming profile has to be copied to that terminal server, and when she logs out, changes must be copied back to the roaming profile storage location—and not just the changes, because writing profiles to their storage space is not writing the delta between the starting point and the ending point, but the entire file. Imagine if one of your users saved 30 gigabytes (GB) of data in his Documents folder. He would log on to the terminal server and then go get a cup of coffee. Or take lunch. Now imagine if all of your users had that much data stored in their Documents folder. If they all come in at 9 A.M. and try to log on to the terminal server, logons could quickly consume all of your network bandwidth. Soon the water cooler or break room would be very popular, and no one would get any work done.

Profile caching also suffers if you experience profile bloat. *Profile caching* saves a copy of the user profile on the terminal server, so that if the network is slow to retrieve the saved profile from its file share, the user can still log on using the cached copy. (When you log onto a terminal server, a copy of your profile is saved there as a matter of course. If you enable profile caching, the profile just isn't deleted when you log off.) However, if the profiles in the cache are too large, the space allocated for them will fill up, and people won't be allowed to log on, because there's no room to store their profile.

To speed logons, you have to control profile size. There are a few ways to do this, and you'll likely end up with some combination of them:

- Limit the size of the profile by policy.

- Trim cached profiles not used for a certain period of time so you have room to cache the profiles you really need.

- Use folder redirection to limit the amount of data in the profile.

Limiting Profile Size

One way to reduce the impact of caching profiles on the terminal servers is to limit the size of the profiles. Although too many profiles can still fill up the hard disk, smaller cached profiles have less impact. To limit profile size, open your TS User GPO and browse to User Configuration | Policies | Administrative Templates | System | User Profiles. Locate the policy Limit Profile Size and enable it.

> **Note** If you're redirecting folders, the size of the profile shouldn't be a major concern. NTUSER. DAT is a fairly small file. The exact size depends on the profile, but it's not much; check the size of one of your NTUSER.DAT files to adequately gauge the space needed to allocate space for profiles.

Removing Cached User Profiles on Terminal Servers

Another way to keep the size of the cache on the terminal server(s) from getting too large is to delete old copies of the user roaming (or mandatory roaming) profiles.

Using Group Policy to Delete Cached Profiles   You can use two computer Group Policy settings to automatically delete unused cached profiles on terminal servers in the Terminal Server OU. Both policies are located in Computer Configuration | Policies | Administrative Templates | System | User Profiles.

- **Delete Cached Copies Of Roaming Profiles**   Enabling this setting causes a user's cached profile to be deleted each time the user logs off. This setting ensures that the loaded profile is always the most recent. However, the cached profile provides a fall-back configuration to load if the actual profile isn't available due to network issues or an offline file server. If you delete cached profiles, then if the actual profile can't be loaded, the user will get a temporary profile and any changes they make to it will be discarded when the user logs off.

- **Delete User Profiles Older Than A Specified Number Of Days On System Restart**   Enabling this setting deletes cached profiles older than a specified number of days. But beware; the cached profiles are only deleted when you reboot the server. So if you don't restart your terminal servers regularly, don't expect this setting to do much deleting.

Manually Deleting Cached Profiles Manually deleting cached profiles sounds too simple to bother explaining, but it's more subtle than it may appear. Cached profiles are kept in the %SystemDrive%\Users directory. However, the seemingly easiest thing to do—look at the profiles, check the dates, note that some profiles haven't been used in a while and delete them—will prevent the owners of those deleted profiles from ever being able to log on to the terminal server and load their roaming profile again, at least without some work from you. See the section titled "The Consequences of Deleting a Profile Folder From Explorer" later in this chapter, for more information.

The problem is that cleaning up old profiles isn't just a matter of deleting the directories. The registry maintains a list of profiles in HKLM\Software\Microsoft\Windows NT\CurrentVersion\ProfileList. Sort through that key (see Figure 4-17) and you'll see entries for everyone who currently has a profile cached on the server. Although the keys themselves are identified by the SID of the user account, you can see the name of the profile path by examining the contents of each key.

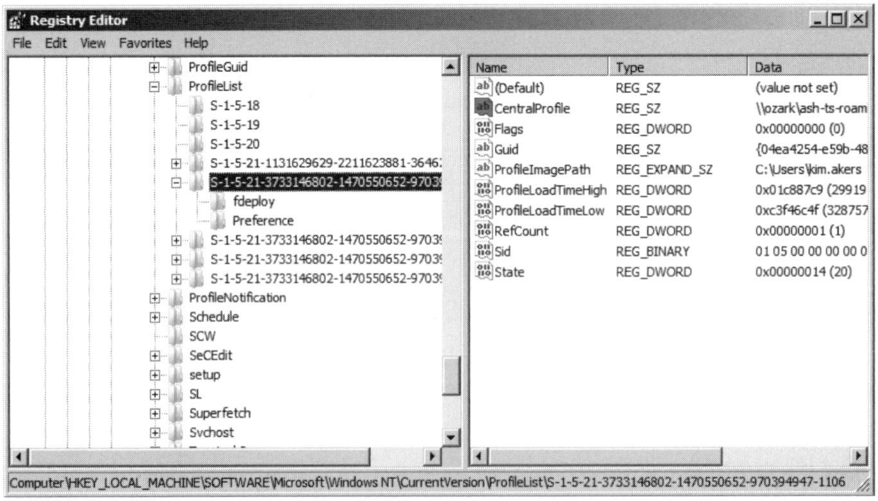

FIGURE 4-17 When you cache a profile on a server, it automatically creates a corresponding registry entry.

> **Note** Examining this key can also help you troubleshoot profile problems. If someone seems to be getting their standard profile to log on to the terminal server, check the contents of CentralProfile (see Figure 4-17). If this entry is blank, that person is using a local profile.

To safely delete a profile, use the User Deletion Utility, Delprof.exe, currently available for download from *http://www.microsoft.com/downloads/details.aspx?familyid=901a9b95-6063-4462-8150-360394e98e1e&displaylang=en*. This tool both deletes the entire contents of the profile and cleans up the registry so that there aren't any orphaned entries causing problems later. The link to this tool is available on this book's companion CD.

You don't need to install Delprof.exe on the terminal server to clean up profiles on that terminal server. You can download and install Delprof.exe on another server or a workstation and run the tool from there. By default, Delprof.exe installs to C:\Program Files\Windows Resource Kits\Tools. To use it, open a command prompt with administrative privileges, navigate to this directory, and run **delprof** with the necessary parameters.

> **Note** Add this path to your System Environment Path variable so you won't have to navigate to this directory each time you want to use the tool.

Table 4-5 lists the delprof parameter options.

TABLE 4-5 Delprof Parameters

Parameter	Description
/Q	Quiet, no confirmation
/I	Ignore errors and continue deleting
/P	Prompt for confirmation before deleting each profile
/R	Delete roaming profile cache only
/C	Remote computer name
/D	Number of days of inactivity

To delete the roaming profile cache on a specific server, run the command with the following arguments:

```
Delprof /R /C:\\servername
```

To be prompted to confirm the deletion, run the command with the following arguments:

```
Delprof /P /C:\\servername
```

You can also delete cached roaming user profiles from the User Profiles section of System Properties on the terminal server. Log on to the terminal server as a domain administrator. Go to Start | Control Panel | System and click Change Settings. The System Properties dialog box will appear. Move to the Advanced tab and then click Settings, located in the User Profiles section, to open the User Profiles dialog box shown in Figure 4-18.

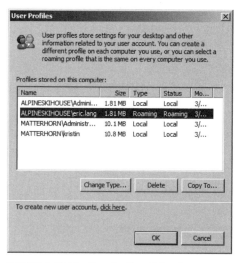

FIGURE 4-18 The User Profiles dialog box

Highlight the roaming profile you want to delete and then click Delete. When you see a dialog box confirming that you want to delete the profile, click Yes and the profile cache is deleted. Click OK.

The Consequences of Deleting a Profile Folder from Explorer

If you skip delprof or the graphical profile management tools and delete the unused profile folders from Explorer, the next time that user logs on, he will be unable to load his roaming profile. A temporary roaming profile will be created for him, and profile changes he makes will be discarded at log off. Event ID 1511 is logged in the Windows Application event log.

> **Note** Event ID 1511 states that Windows cannot find the local profile and is logging you on with a temporary profile. Changes you make to this profile will be lost when you log off.

Deleting that directory caused a problem because you didn't completely clean up the cached profile. For each cached profile stored in %SystemDrive%\Users\%UserName%, the User Profile Service creates a registry entry for this profile at HKLM\Software\Microsoft\Windows NT\CurrentVersion\ProfileList, shown in Figure 4-19. This registry key is named according to the user SID.

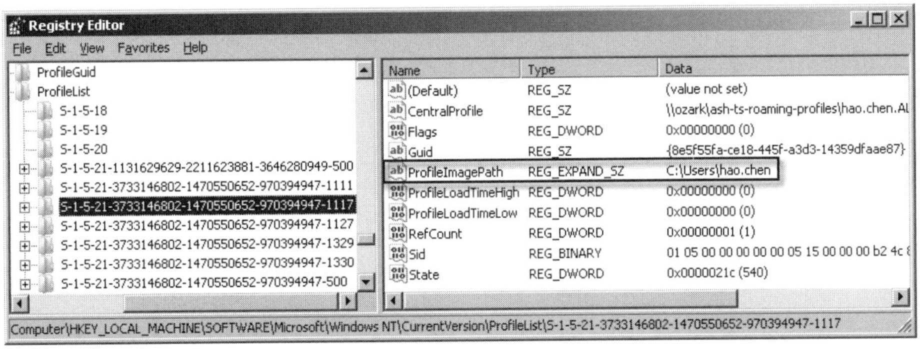

FIGURE 4-19 TS Roaming Profile cache registry entry for user hao.chen

The ProfileImagePath key in this folder indicates the cache location, by default in %SystemDrive%\Users\%UserName%. (The network location where the roaming profile is permanently stored is in the CentralProfile key.)

If you delete the user's locally cached profile folder and that user logs on to the terminal server, she will get a temporary profile. The registry entry corresponding to the user's cached profile is renamed. The SID part stays the same, but it is given an extension of .bak, and a new key is created in its place as shown in Figure 4-20.

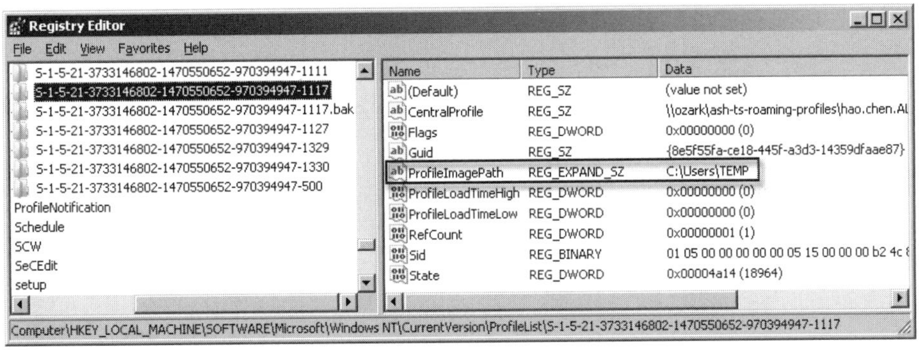

FIGURE 4-20 A new registry entry is created, but the ProfileImagePath key points to %SystemDrive%\Users\TEMP.

The newly created registry entry is named after the user SID just as before. However, the ProfileImagePath key inside the new folder now points to %SystemDrive%\Users\TEMP. So, the entry that used to work now has a .bak extension, and the one that is recognized is a temporary profile. When the user logs off, his temporary profile is not copied back to the central profile storage location on the fileserver. Delprof cannot help you here. It doesn't even recognize there is a problem with this user's profile now.

Deleting the rogue profile from the System Properties dialog box User Profiles section no longer works either. Most likely, the profile will not even be listed in the dialog box. If it is, it most likely means that the user has not completely logged off. If you do manage to select it and click Delete, you get the message shown in Figure 4-21.

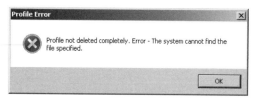

FIGURE 4-21 You can't use tools to clean up a partially deleted cached profile.

To correct this you must manually delete the abandoned registry entry that has the .bak extension. Only then can the user log on to the terminal server and have his roaming profile correctly cached once again on the server.

Centralizing Personal Folders with Folder Redirection

The biggest thing you can do to affect profile size is to not store user data in a user's profile. By default, user data folders such as Documents are in the profile, but they don't have to be. Instead you can create a pointer to a network share where the data actually lives. The user will still store files in their personal folders, but the user data won't be roamed so it will not impact the time required to load the profile to log on.

Not all profile folders can be redirected, but the ones with the biggest impact on profile size can be. These folders are:

- **AppData(Roaming)**   Contains a user's application settings that are not computer specific and therefore can roam with the user.

- **Desktop**   Contains any items a user places on his desktop.

- **Start Menu**   Contains a user's Start menu.

- **Documents**   Contains documents saved to the default location.

- **Favorites**   Contains a user's Internet Explorer favorites.

- **Music**   Contains a user's music files saved to the default location.

- **Pictures**   Contains a user's pictures saved to the default location.

- **Video**   Contains a user's video files saved to the default location.

- **Contacts**   Contains a user's contacts saved to the default location.

- **Downloads**   Contains a user's downloads saved to the default location.

- **Links**   Contains a user's Internet Explorer Favorite Links.

- **Searches**   Contains a user's saved searches.

- **Saved Games**   Contains a user's saved games.

Before you redirect these folders, you need a place to redirect them to. Create a shared folder on the server where you want to store the redirected folders and set permissions on this folder according to the user profile folder permissions stated in Tables 4-3 and 4-4.

To redirect the folders to this share, open the Group Policy Management Console, create or select an existing user GPO, right-click, and choose Edit. Go to User Configuration | Policies | Windows Settings | Folder Redirection, shown in Figure 4-22.

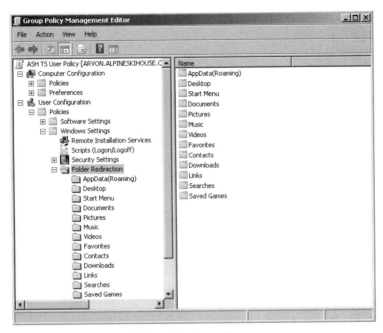

FIGURE 4-22 Setting the folder redirection policy

Right-click the AppData(Roaming) folder and choose Properties to open the dialog box in Figure 4-23.

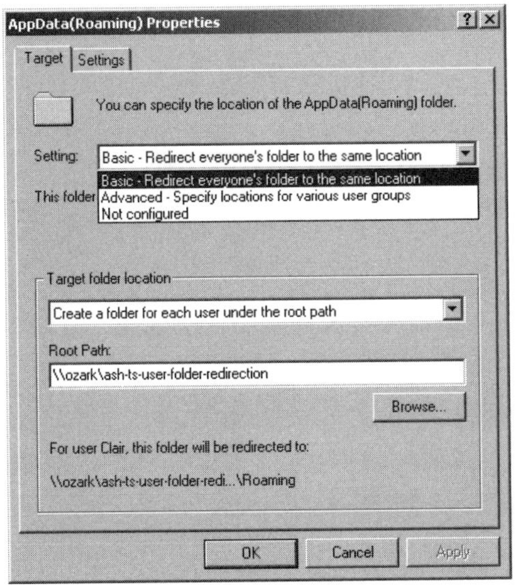

FIGURE 4-23 AppData(Roaming) folder redirection properties

To specify the location of the AppData(Roaming) Folder, choose between two options in the Setting drop-down menu.

- **Basic – Redirect Everyone's Folder To The Same Location** This means just what it says; all AppData(Roaming) folder data for every user will go to the same location.

- **Advanced – Specify Locations For Various User Groups** To store user data in different locations based on user group membership, choose this option.

Depending on which option you choose, the choices below that area change to adhere to your Setting choice. If you choose Basic, then you get a Target folder location drop-down menu with three choices:

- **Create A Folder For Each User Under The Root Path** Choose this option to put each user's profile data into a folder under the root path named according to their user name. In the Root Path text box, specify the location of your designated folder redirection share.

- **Redirect To The Following Location** Choose this option to redirect all user data to the same location. Do not choose this option if you want all users to retain their own settings. If you do, then the first user's data will get saved to the chosen location as expected, but subsequent users will attempt to save to the same location—unsuccessfully, since the first user will be the owner of the folder. Event error ID 502 will be logged in the Application event log, telling you that the specified path is invalid. However, this option does have a good purpose, as you will see in the section titled "Creating a Safe Read-Only Desktop" later in this chapter.

- **Redirect To The Local Profile Location** Your profiles roam, and you want your profile folders redirected to the network share, so do not choose this option.

Click the Settings tab shown in Figure 4-24.

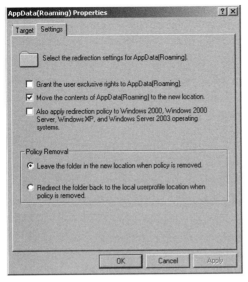

FIGURE 4-24 Clear the box for the option Grant The User Exclusive Rights To AppData(Roaming) to let administrators manage the redirected folder.

By default, Grant The User Exclusive Rights To AppData(Roaming) is enabled. If you leave it this way, then the user will own this folder and only she will be able to access this data. To enable managing this folder, clear this box so that the rights from the parent folder will be inherited. For example, if you give Domain Admins full control of the parent folder, then this group will have access to the redirected user folders as well.

If your users already have these folders before you set up folder redirection, then you must set up the existing folders in one of two ways, or else folder redirection will fail:

- The user needs to be the owner of the folder and can be granted exclusive rights to the folder.
- If the user does not need to be the owner of the folder, clear this box.

All of the folders listed in this GPO section have the same choices to pick from, except for the Pictures, Music, and Video folders. These folders have an extra setting that you can choose for the location of the folder: Follow The Documents Folder. This means that these folders will be stored in the user's Documents folder, wherever that folder is redirected to.

Sharing Personal Folders Between Local and Remote Environments

Because the TS RemoteApps in Windows Server 2008 are designed to blur the line between the remote computer and the local computer, it may make sense for you to help this along by using the same folder to store user-specific documents. This eliminates the problem of having to remember whether you were saving a file from a local or a remote application to know where the file would be stored.

Sharing Folders Between Windows Server 2003 and Windows Server 2008 Roaming Profiles

Note that 2003 profiles and 2008 profiles are not compatible. So, if you have some active 2003 terminal servers, you will need to keep two sets of profiles for your users—one to log on to the 2003 servers, and one to log on to the 2008 servers. However, folder redirection can be used to bridge the gap. Not all 13 folders that can be redirected in Windows Server 2008 can be redirected in Windows Server 2003—but some can. You can share the data in these folders between the 2003 profiles and the 2008 profiles. On the Settings tab of each folder in the Folder Redirection container is a check box option called Also Apply Redirection Policy To Windows 2000, Windows 2000 Server, Windows XP And Windows Server 2003 Operating Systems. For some folders, this option is available. On others (the ones that will not redirect for downlevel operating systems), it appears shaded and is unavailable. Table 4-6 shows which of the folders can be redirected for Windows 2000/XP/2003.

TABLE 4-6 Profile Folder Redirection Capabilities for Windows 2000/XP/2003 Operating Systems

Folder	Can the Folder Be Redirected for Downlevel Operating Systems?	Details
AppData(Roaming)	Yes	The following folders within AppData(Roaming) folder for 2000/XP/2003 will not be redirected: Cookies, network shortcuts, Printer Shortcuts, Recent, SendTo, Start Menu, Templates.
Desktop	Yes	
Start menu	Yes	In Windows Server 2003, the contents of the Start menu are not copied to the redirected location. It is assumed that the Start menu has been pre-created. Therefore, if you do not pre-create the Start menu and place it in the redirected location, the default Start menu located in the user's Windows Server 2003 roaming profile location is used instead.
Documents	Yes	
Pictures	Depends	If the check box is selected for Documents, this folder will follow the Documents folder for legacy operating system profiles. If Documents is not redirected, then this folder cannot be redirected for legacy operating system profiles.

TABLE 4-6 **Profile Folder Redirection Capabilities for Windows 2000/XP/2003 Operating Systems**

Folder	Can the Folder Be Redirected for Downlevel Operating Systems?	Details
Music	Depends	If the check box is selected for Documents, this folder will follow the Documents folder for legacy operating system profiles. If Documents is not redirected, then this folder cannot be redirected for legacy operating system profiles.
Video	Depends	If the check box is selected for Documents, this folder will follow the Documents folder for legacy operating system profiles. If Documents is not redirected, then this folder cannot be redirected for legacy operating system profiles.
Favorites	No	
Contacts	No	
Downloads	No	
Links	No	
Searches	No	
Saved Games	No	

On the Companion Media For more information on Windows Server 2003 Profiles and Folder Redirection, see *http://technet2.microsoft.com/windowsserver/en/library/06f7eebc-2ebb-47c5-8361-1958b58078cc1033.mspx?mfr=true*. You can find the link on this book's companion CD.

Setting Standards with Mandatory Profiles

One issue with roaming profiles is that users can change them. On the one hand, that's the point. On the other, change can cause problems. If users can change their profile, they can delete icons, accidentally resize their toolbar so that it disappears, add wallpaper that slows down their logon time, and so on.

One way to avoid this is to set policies controlling what users can and cannot do, and Chapter 5 explains how to do this. Another way to prevent users from making permanent changes to their profile is to make the user profile immutable. A user can change settings, but those settings will not be saved and will disappear with the next logon.

Profiles that don't change are called *mandatory profiles*. Mandatory profiles on a central store are copied to the terminal server at logon but are not copied back at logoff. Any profile changes that occur are discarded at the end of the user session. Many companies will not implement mandatory profiles because users find them too constricting, but combined with Folder Redirection, this option may give your users enough flexibility. All terminal server users can use individual profiles, or (since no one's writing to it) they can all use the same one. In this section, we'll show you how to support both scenarios.

Converting Existing Roaming Profiles to Mandatory Profiles

Setting up mandatory profiles is very similar to setting up roaming profiles using Group Policy. To convert a roaming profile to a mandatory profile, you first need to have roaming profiles working, either by setting the TS Roaming Profile path in the user's account properties in ADUC, or by using Group Policy. For information on how to set up roaming profiles, see the section titled "Using Group Policy to Manage Roaming Profiles" earlier in this chapter.

Assuming you have roaming profiles implemented, when a user logs on, her profile is stored in a subdirectory of the designated roaming profile share. To make the user's profile mandatory, in the user's profile folder, locate the file NTUSER.DAT and change its extension to .man (see Figure 4-25). The next time the user logs on, she'll be using a mandatory profile.

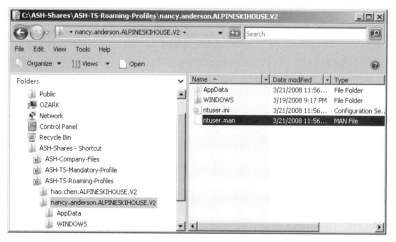

FIGURE 4-25 To convert a roaming profile to a mandatory profile, change its extension.

No changes the user makes to the profile will be saved. But combining mandatory profiles with Folder Redirection will give users some control over their TS environment and allow them to change their Favorites, Documents, Desktop, and so forth, without compromising the configuration data stored in HKCU.

Creating a Single Mandatory Profile

Mandatory profiles are easy to implement, but if you have many users, you probably won't want to manually convert each roaming profile to a mandatory one. To give everyone the same Terminal Services experience, you can create one mandatory profile for everyone as described in the following steps:

1. On a terminal server, log on as a local user with administrative rights. Use a local user account so that any Group Policy settings you have implemented on the Terminal Servers OU don't take effect. Customize the profile as appropriate and log off.

2. Create a network share to store the mandatory profile. Make sure the users who will use this profile have read access and SYSTEM has Full Control NTFS permissions. Administrators should be the Owner.

3. Set the GPOs. Edit the Computer GPO setting Set Path For TS Roaming Profile to point to the share created in step 2. Enable the Computer GPO policy setting Use Mandatory Profiles On The Terminal Server.

4. Run gpupdate /force on the terminal server(s) to update the policy.

5. Log on to a terminal server as a domain user. Log off. This will create a mandatory profile in the mandatory profile share inside of a new folder named .V2. Change the permissions on this folder to give users read access to the folder contents. Make Administrators the owner.

6. Log on to the terminal server used in step 1 as a domain administrator. Copy the local profile you created in step 1 to the .V2 folder created in step 5. Be sure to use the CopyProfile tool—do not do this manually, or it won't work. Set the permissions for the profile to be a group of users you would like to use the mandatory profile (a domain TS users group or domain users, for example).

7. After the profile is copied successfully, locate the NTUSER.DAT file in the .V2 folder in the mandatory profile share and rename it to NTUSER.MAN.

Creating a Safe Read-Only Desktop

One curious side effect to not being able to save anything to a mandatory profile is that any folders remaining in the profile (that is, not redirected) will not save changes either. For example, if you do not redirect the Desktop folder and if users save files to their desktops, those files will be discarded when they log off. There won't be any error and the file will be on the desktop during the session, but the files won't be there when the users log on again. To put it mildly, this could be confusing. However, if you're using TS Remote Apps, you don't really want people saving files to the Desktop, because not being able to see the Desktop will make those files hard to find.

To keep the Desktop read-only but make sure people know it is read-only, redirect the Desktop to a folder as described in the section titled "Centralizing Personal Folders with Folder Redirection" earlier in this chapter and make sure this folder is read-only. This will both prevent users from saving files to the Desktop (which you want) and alert them to the fact that they can't save files to the Desktop (which you also want). If they try, they will get an error. They still can't save anything to the Desktop, but at least they will *know* they can't.

Profile and Folder Redirection Troubleshooting Tips

Many people find the combination of terminal servers and profiles daunting. And it's true—things don't always work the way you expect them to. Table 4-7 describes some common errors, possible solutions, and the sections in the chapter where we discuss how to fix each problem.

TABLE 4-7 **Profiles and Folder Redirection Troubleshooting Tips**

Problem	Solution	Additional Information in This Chapter
Policies appear to be set correctly, but aren't being applied.	Force policy update via gpupdate or rebooting.	See the sidebar "Using gpupdate /force."
Folders are not being redirected to the proper location or roaming profiles are not being loaded.	Check event logs to make sure that share is available on the network and has appropriate permissions.	See "The Consequences of Deleting a Profile Folder from Explorer" and "Centralizing Personal Folders with Folder Redirection."
Group Policy settings aren't being applied to the right computers, groups, or users.	Check the security filters and make sure you've included the correct groups.	See "Fine-Tuning GPOs with Security Filtering."
Folders from downlevel profiles aren't redirecting properly, but Windows Vista profile folders are redirecting.	Make sure you've enabled downlevel folder redirection for that GPO.	See "Sharing Folders Between Windows Server 2003 and Windows Server 2008 Roaming Profiles."
Users cannot load their roaming profile when they log on and see a message that they will be logged on with a temporary profile.	You may have deleted the cached profile manually using Windows Explorer. Delete the old registry keys and use tools such as the profile management utility or delprof to delete profiles.	See "Removing Cached User Profiles on Terminal Servers."

Summary

Although roaming profiles (read-write or read-only) are the best model for storing user profiles in a terminal server environment, the complications involved in making them work well can be daunting. This chapter has explained how profiles work, including how the User Profile Service loads and saves configuration data. We've talked about best practices, including how to keep profiles manageable in size to speed user logons and how folder redirection and profile caching contribute to faster logons. We've explained how to set up Group Policy to enable automatic profile creation according to best practices and how to use security filtering and loopback policy processing to ensure that the policies are applied correctly to a terminal server environment. Finally, we've explained how to set up and use mandatory profiles with a terminal server environment and how to prevent users from losing files when using mandatory profiles.

Key points:

- Roaming profiles combined with folder redirection is generally the best way to store user data in TS environments. Folder redirection is very important for keeping logon times short and profile sizes small.

- Profiles don't merge, they overwrite. For best results, have open only one copy of the user profile at a time. For this reason, you should generally not use the same roaming profile for both local logons and terminal server logons.

- Implementing Group Policy correctly from the beginning is key to making roaming profiles work.

- Folder redirection is key to making profiles work properly.

  - Folder redirection keeps profiles small.

  - Using folder redirection, you can share folders between two profiles for better integration of the local and remote user experiences.

  - If using mandatory profiles, you must use folder redirection to allow users to save files to any of their normal document storage locations (e.g., Documents, Favorites, etc.).

Additional Resources

The following resources will extend your knowledge of topics addressed in this chapter. All links are available to you on this book's companion CD.

- For more information on user profile management (with or without Terminal Services), read the following:

    - "Managing Roaming User Data Deployment Guide," available online at *http://technet2.microsoft.com/WindowsVista/f/?en/library/fb3681b2-da39-4944-93ad-dd3b6e8ca4dc1033.mspx* and for download from *http://technet2.microsoft.com/WindowsVista/en/library/fb3681b2-da39-4944-93ad-dd3b6e8ca4dc1033.mspx?mfr=true.*

    - "Using User Profiles in Windows Server 2003," located at *http://technet2.microsoft.com/windowsserver/en/library/23ee2a30-5883-4ffa-b4cf-4cfff3ff8cb71033.mspx?mfr=true.*

- For more information about how to configure device redirection and how to lock down the server, see Chapter 5, "Fine-Tuning the Terminal Server Runtime Experience."

- For more information about application installation and publishing through TS RemoteApps and TS Web Access, see Chapter 6, "Installing and Publishing Applications."

- For more information about enabling terminal server farms with TS Session Broker and multi-server management, see Chapter 8, "Managing the Terminal Server Runtime Environment."

- For more information about how to enable secure access to the terminal server from inside the network—and from outside using TS Gateway—see Chapter 9, "Terminal Services Ecosystem Management."

- For more information about customizing the default profile (so that terminal server user profiles are customized upon creation), see *http://support.microsoft.com/kb/325364.*

Chapter 5
Fine-Tuning the User Experience

In the previous chapter, we discussed setting up profiles and folder redirection. So we'll assume that you're following best practices: your users now have a profile (mandatory or roaming) on a network share, and they are saving their documents on another network share to minimize the size of the user profile.

But those are simply the bare bones of creating the user work environment. Users have devices that they'd like to use in their terminal sessions; one of your jobs is determining what's possible, what the implications of permitting device and resource redirection are, and what you will and won't permit. And although Chapter 4, "Creating the User Work Environment," discussed setting up profiles with Terminal Services, what if mandatory profiles aren't an option? How will you lock down the terminal server so that one user can't affect others? How is it possible that client-side resources show up in the terminal session? As you can see, we're not yet done setting up the core user environment and answering basic questions.

In this chapter, we'll show you how to enable—yet control—your users' devices and desires, meaning that you'll understand how to map the client-side experience to the remote environment . . . but do so in a way that doesn't affect other users on the terminal server. You'll also learn how device redirection works. We'll discuss:

- The infrastructure in Windows Server 2008 that supports client resource redirection
- How you can use client resources in the remote session
- Locking down the terminal server (and why you have to do so)
- Optimizing the user experience
- Configuring remote control of a session
- Securing access to the terminal server

Remoting Infrastructure

Before delving too deeply into setting up the remote client experience, let's talk about the infrastructure that permits device and resource sharing between client and server, and how it's even possible for the client-side devices and settings to appear in the remote session.

Virtual Channels and the Remote Client Experience

The Remote Desktop Connection (RDC) client on the client computer and the terminal server session communicate with each other through *virtual channels*. Virtual channels are dedicated paths in the Remote Desktop Protocol (RDP) that carry particular kinds of data. For example, different channels support print jobs, Clipboard data, drive redirection, and so forth. In Windows Server 2008, virtual channels operate in both user mode and kernel mode. Remote audio and the Clipboard redirector both have virtual channels in user mode, while Plug and Play (PnP) devices communicate via kernel-mode virtual channels. To pass data between client and server, both ends of the channel must (a) exist and (b) be enabled. That's why it's possible to turn off drive redirection on a terminal server without being able to override this setting on the client—the terminal server just isn't listening on that channel. It's also why it's not possible to use a given virtual channel unless it is supported by both client *and* server. You can't, for example, use the RDP 6.1 client to enable PnP device redirection on a Windows Server 2003 terminal server. The client supports that channel, but the terminal server does not.

Note To be very clear about this, the RDC is the tool you use to connect to a terminal server. RDP is the protocol that enables communication between client and server.

Historically, virtual channels have been created at the beginning of the session and severed when the session was ended by client or server—these are *static channels*. Windows Server 2008 introduced a new kind of virtual channel called a *dynamic virtual channel* that an application can create after the session has begun, and it can also be severed before the session ends. This makes it possible to add new redirected devices to a session after it's started. If you relied on static channels entirely, then it would not be possible to plug in a camera (for example) to a remote session and have it show up. Instead, you'd have to plug the camera into the USB port before beginning the session.

Note Although it's possible to connect to a Windows Server 2008 terminal server using RDP 5.2 or later, applications using dynamic virtual channels require RDP 6.1 or later. The IWTSVirtualChannelManager interface that manages the connections has a minimum requirement of RDP 6.1. RDP 6.1 is included in Windows XP SP3 and Windows Vista SP1; it's also available as a separate download for Windows XP SP2 from *http://www.microsoft.com/downloads/details.aspx?FamilyId=6E1EC93D-BDBD-4983-92F7-479E088570AD&displaylang=en*. You can find this link on this book's companion CD.

Separating data into virtual channels is how this architecture allows you to disable client-side redirection selectively. It's possible to enable printing but disable drive redirection, or to enable Clipboard redirection but disable PnP devices.

Direct from the Source: Changing Bandwidth Allocation for Terminal Server Connections over RDP

When running applications in a remote connection, multiple applications send data from server to client. These applications compete for available bandwidth, and over a slow connection you may find that the session responsiveness suffers. This problem manifests itself most severely when printing a large document over a low bandwidth connection. The printer data competes for available bandwidth with the video rendering, thus deteriorating the graphics rendering significantly.

In Windows Server 2008 and Windows Vista, we fix this problem by allocating a fixed percentage of bandwidth to video updates to the client. The rest goes to virtual channel traffic for redirected devices. By default, this allocation is 70 percent for video and 30 percent for virtual channel data. When bandwidth usage is constrained, video data is guaranteed to get 70 percent of the available bandwidth so the session will remain responsive.

Although this scheme solves the problem effectively, there could be some scenarios in which you might want to tweak it a bit. You can adjust these settings by editing the registry. Please note that these edits are *not* supported, and you will need to reboot the terminal server to see the changes take effect.

View or add the following list of registry values that affect the bandwidth allocation behavior. These are all DWORD values under HKEY_LOCAL_MACHINE\SYSTEM\CurrentControlSet\Services\TermDD.

- **FlowControlDisable**—When set to 1, this value will disable the new flow control algorithm, making it FIFO (First-In–First-Out) for all packet requests. This provides results similar to Windows Server 2003. (Default for this value is 0).

- **FlowControlDisplayBandwidth/FlowControlChannelBandwidth**—These two values together determine the bandwidth distribution between display and virtual channels (VCs). You can set these values in the range of 0–255. For example, setting FlowControlDisplayBandwidth = 100 and FlowControlChannelBandwidth = 100 will make the bandwidth distribution equal between video and VCs. The default settings are 70 for FlowControlDisplayBandwidth and 30 for FlowControlChannelBandwidth, thus making the default distribution equal to 70–**30**.

- **FlowControlChargePostCompression**—This value, if set to 1, bases the bandwidth allocation on post-compression bandwidth usage. Default for this value is 0, meaning the bandwidth distribution is applied on pre-compressed data.

Makarand Patwardhan

Software Development Engineer //

One final point about virtual channels: They're used to send data between the client computer and the remote session, but they also pass data between the terminal server session and the system-wide components on the terminal server. This latter class of virtual channels isn't available to system administrators, however.

The Plug and Play Device Redirection Framework

In addition to dynamic virtual channels, PnP device redirection is also enabled through the new Device Redirection Framework introduced in Windows Server 2008, installed when you add the Desktop Experience feature. This framework makes it possible to redirect certain types of devices from a client computer to a remote session. (Right now, it only works for specific types of devices, but the framework is designed to support potentially any kind of PnP device.) Both local and remote applications can use the redirected devices, and the devices are visible only to the session in which they are started. Here's the really good part— this process works without installing drivers for those devices on the terminal server. The device redirection framework uses the client-side drivers to enable the devices.

So far as possible, you won't want to install drivers on a terminal server. Device drivers are not always reliable. If a driver crashes, it can affect the person using it (a user-mode driver) or crash the entire terminal server (a kernel-mode driver). Unfortunately, device drivers enable the operating system to communicate with hardware, so you don't have a choice about using them. Microsoft doesn't make all Windows drivers, so its control over this problem is limited.

Terminal Server in Windows Server 2008 is designed to minimize the dependency on device drivers. As you'll see (in the section "When TS Easy Print Isn't an Option: Distributing Drivers to Terminal Servers" later in this chapter), it's not always possible to avoid using device drivers to enable client-side devices, and we will explain how to support them when you can't avoid them. But PnP device redirection and TS Easy Print help reduce the problems associated with using drivers. They don't eliminate drivers entirely—you still need device drivers on the client computer. But they do keep the drivers off the terminal server, as long as the drivers support the framework.

On the Companion Media   Independent software vendors (ISVs) and driver writers who want to be sure that their drivers are compatible with the framework can use the Terminal Server PnP Device Redirection Framework Test Tool available online at *http://msdn2.microsoft.com/en-us/library/bb961229.aspx*. The guidelines for creating a conforming driver information file (INF) are located in "Device Driver INF Changes for Plug and Play Device Redirection on Terminal Server," located at *http://www.microsoft.com/whdc/driver/install/ts_redirect.mspx*.

The PnP Device Redirection Framework uses the components shown in Figure 5-1.

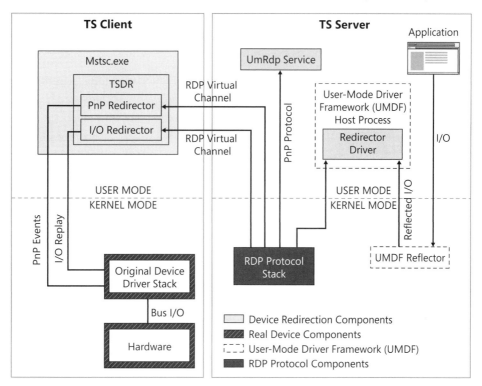

FIGURE 5-1 Architecture of the PnP Device Redirection Framework

On the client side is the new RDP client (Mstsc.exe), with a PnP redirector and an I/O redirector. These two components are visible on the client in the form of the Terminal Server Device Redirector (TSDR) in the System Devices section of the Device Manager. TSDR manages two aspects of communicating with client-side mobile devices:

- Inventory of which devices are present, their capabilities, and the data on them, handled by the PnP manager and passed to the PnP redirector

- Reads from and writes to those devices (I/O replay), handled by the input/output (I/O) manager and passed to the I/O redirector

The PnP manager and I/O redirectors both communicate with the driver stacks for the devices they're managing, which then communicate with the hardware. The TSDR sends this communication to the session on the terminal server via two virtual channels: one each for PnP-related traffic and I/O-related traffic.

On the server, the two virtual channels backed by TSDR both communicate with the Rdpdr.sys device driver in the RDP stack, which handles device redirection for RDP sessions. The PnP protocol passes the device management and I/O data between Termdd.sys in kernel mode and the Terminal Services User Mode Port Redirector service. This service, mentioned in Chapter 3, "Installing the Core Terminal Server Environment," is required to make device redirection work. By sending the data to the session, the PnP protocol and port redirection service allows the devices to show up in the session.

Communication with those devices is handled through the User-Mode Driver Framework (UMDF). The UMDF is part of the standard Windows operating system—it's not specific to terminal servers—and was originally developed to support devices such as cameras and portable music players. The UMDF has three components:

- Driver manager (user mode)
- Reflector (kernel mode)
- Host process (user mode)

The *driver manager* is a system-wide Windows service started when the first UMDF device is installed. It manages the host process and responds to messages from the reflector.

The *reflector* is the proxy for the kernel-mode stack for the drivers. It lives in the kernel, but is not a driver—its role is to send messages to the correct driver running in user mode. Every time an application makes an I/O request involving an application using the UMDF, the request goes through standard security vetting and is then passed to the reflector.

The *host process* is a child process of the driver manager (so that if it crashes, it won't bring down the driver manager). The host process accepts messages from the driver manager (to load drivers) and from the reflector (to accept requests to those drivers).

The three work together like this: An application makes an I/O request that requires a user-mode driver. (Which one isn't important for the general case we're describing.) The request goes to the reflector. The reflector passes this request to the UMDF framework within the host process. The framework either sends the job to the appropriate driver or sends it back to the reflector if no driver is available. Next, the reflector sends the request back to the driver manager to tell the host process to load an additional driver.

The UMDF host can manage any compatible user-mode driver. In this case, Terminal Services has implemented a redirector driver whose job is to communicate with Rdpdr.sys in the RDP protocol stack. Therefore, the redirector driver's job is to accept the messages passed to it by the reflector, which receives those requests from the application running in the remote session that's trying to access the redirected device.

As an example, the pieces can communicate something like this:

1. An application running in the remote session makes a request to copy a picture from a client-side media device.

2. The I/O request (to copy a file to the PnP device) goes to the kernel-mode UMDF Reflector.

3. The UMDF reflector passes the request to the UMDF host process, which determines that the request came from the terminal server session and uses the UMDF driver manager to route it to the user-mode redirection driver.

4. The redirection driver sends the request to Rdpdr.sys, in the protocol stack.

5. Via the virtual channels, Rdpdr.sys sends the request to TSDR on the client computer.

6. TSDR communicates with the I/O manager to satisfy the request.

Today, only devices supporting the Media Transfer Protocol (MTP) and Picture Transfer Protocol (PTP) may be redirected using the PnP Device Redirection Framework (and not all devices supporting those protocols are supported with Terminal Server). However, the framework is designed to be extensible so other types of devices can be redirected as well.

Printing Architecture

Printing is the primary device-redirection requirement for sessions on a terminal server. Windows Server 2008 supports two printing models: a new driver-free model for use with RDP 6.1, and a model for previous versions of the RDP client (also used with Windows Server 2003).

The Legacy Printing Model for Terminal Services

Printers available to applications running on a terminal server are usually not connected to the terminal server. For users to print from a remote session, two things must happen:

- The printer must show up in the remote session.
- The print job must get to the printer.

The following sections will explain how printer redirection works for RDP clients 6.0 and earlier.

Enumerating Printers in the Remote Session   Chapter 3 explained how session creation works. One component of session creation is enumerating any printers on the client computer so they can be redirected to the server. Several components are involved in the redirection:

- Winlogon.exe, the Windows Logon process in the client session
- Winsta.dll, used for configuring the session
- Termsrv.dll, the remote connection manager
- Rdpwsx.dll, a user-mode component on the terminal server that handles the connection sequence for remote connections using RDP
- Rdpdr.sys, the kernel-mode RDP device redirection driver

- Spoolsv.exe, the print spooler on the terminal server

- Usbmon.dll, which handles all the dynamic printer ports (dynamic because they are created and destroyed with the remote session) on the terminal server

- Mstscax.dll, the terminal server client, which enumerates the printers on the client and their names, drivers, and settings

- System Event Notification Service (SENS), which monitors system events such as Terminal Services session connects and disconnects and logon/logoff events and delivers them to the applications needing them

> **Note** Wlnotify.dll took this role in previous versions of Windows but was replaced with SENS in Windows Server 2008 and Windows Vista.

To automatically redirect client-side printers to the terminal session, these components cooperate in the following ways:

1. The client, Mstsc.exe, connects to a terminal server and goes through the connection and logon sequence. Winlogon.exe remains loaded in the user session, as does Winsta.dll, used for configuring the terminal session.

2. Via Winsta.dll and the remote connection manager, Rdpwsx.dll is notified of the new connection and notifies Rdpdr.sys.

3. Rdpdr.sys sends a packet requesting that the printers for the new session be enumerated.

4. The client collects the following information from the client computer and sends it to the session, where it is passed by Rdpwsx.dll to Rdpdr.sys:

   - Printer configuration data available, including name, driver name, paper orientation, default status, and so forth—everything standard for a Windows printer, but nothing contained outside the Windows printer configuration dialog boxes

   - Print queues and their port names

   - Manually created print queues created during previous logons (listed in subkeys under HCKU\Software\Microsoft\Terminal Server Client\Default\Add Ins\RDPDR on the client computer)

5. Rdpdr.sys creates a corresponding print port for each queue the client sends up, naming them TS*XXX*, where *XXX* is a number, counting from 001.

> **Note** A Group Policy controls whether all printers are redirected or just the client default printer. If it's the latter, then only the client default printer is created in the remote session.

6. Rdpdr.sys also tells the PnP application programming interfaces (APIs) that new print-ers are available. These APIs notify the spooler (Spoolsv.exe) of the new printers for that connection. The spooler has Usbmon.dll enumerate the available ports, as copied from the client and renamed on the terminal session. The spooler updates the client's regis-try to make the printers available to them.

> **Note** In Windows Server 2003, the spooler service was not session-aware and updated HKCU for everyone logged on to the terminal server, so that users ended up with print-ers in their profiles that belonged to other users. They couldn't use or see them, but they were recorded in the registry, and the CPU cycles the spooler service demanded to write to all the copies of HKCU on the terminal server strained the terminal server. This has been changed in Windows Server 2008 so that a user's printers are only written to the user's copy of HKCU.

7. Winlogon.exe notifies the System Event Notification Service (SENS) that the session is created. SENS waits for disconnect or logoff events so that it can tell Rdpdr.sys when to tear down the mapped ports.

8. SENS does the following:

   ❏ Ensures that the printer has a corresponding driver available on the terminal server.

   ❏ Sets the client's default printer to be the default printer in the terminal session.

   ❏ Adds the new printer queue to its list of devices.

   ❏ Sets the default security for the printer so that the logged-on user has read/write/print permissions to the printer queue and the Administrator has full control.

The printers should now appear in the remote session as TS001 to TS00n. If the printers are not appearing, check the following:

- Client printers are allowed to be redirected. This policy can be set in Terminal Services Configuration (in the RDP settings), in Active Directory Users And Computers, and in Group Policy. We'll discuss how to do this in the sidebar titled "Rules for Applying Settings" later in this chapter.

- Rdpdr.sys must be functioning properly. If no devices are being redirected and policy permits redirection, open Device Manager and inspect the contents of System Devices to find the Terminal Server Device Redirector and see if it's working properly.

- The Terminal Services UserMode Port Redirector service must be running. If it's not, then start it and disconnect and reconnect all sessions. Because printer queues are built at the beginning of the connection, simply restarting this service won't restore printer queues.

- The print spooler on the terminal server must be running.

Printing from a Remote Session Now that the printers are listed in the remote session, let's see how a print job gets to a redirected printer when Easy Print is not used. Printing involves a large number of moving parts, but this high-level view will show you how it works on a terminal server.

1. The application launches the print job. The user can see all the Win32 print options made available when Mstsc.exe notifies Rdpwsx.dll/Rdpdr.dll of the available printers.

2. When the application creates the print job with the help of the graphics device interface (GDI), it produces an enhanced metafile format (EMF) file that contains all the instructions needed to render that picture while maintaining the picture's original size, resolution, and layout. EMF metafiles are device-independent.

> **Note** It's possible to not use the EMF format (this is an option on your printer properties) and that option may be more efficient for pages that are all bitmaps, but for text-and-image printing, the EMF format is smaller and faster.

3. When GDI creates the EMF metafile, it passes it to the spooler. This metafile can be saved to disk if many print jobs are queued for a particular printer.

4. The spooled print job goes back to GDI. With the help of the user-mode printer drivers, GDI processes the print job so that it's in the RAW format the selected printer can accept (since EMF is device-independent).

5. Assuming that the print job is going to a redirected port (identified as TS*XXX*), the spooler sends the print job to the dynamic port monitor (Usbmon.dll).

6. The dynamic port monitor transfers the spool file to Rdpdr.sys, which sends the RAW data to the appropriate TS client where it's sent to the appropriate printer.

To sum up, most of the processing is done on the terminal server, the drivers must be present on the terminal server (so that the GDI can format the data stream appropriately for the selected printer), and there's a lot of data conversion (from GDI to RAW). Every time you convert data from one format to another, there's a risk of data loss.

The New Easy Print Architecture

The PnP Device Redirection Framework enables a new feature in Windows Server 2008 Terminal Services: PnP device redirection for media devices, cameras, and point-of-sale devices. Easy Print *fixes* a long-standing problem: printing from a remote session to a redirected printer. Before TS Easy Print, printing from terminal services was not an easy task. IT administrators had to deal with the following:

■ **Kernel-mode drivers** In the old days of kernel-mode drivers, a buggy driver could—and often did—crash the terminal server. For this reason, the use of kernel-mode drivers has been blocked by default since Windows Server 2003.

- **Driver name mapping**   When client and server were not running on the same kernel (e.g., clients running Windows 98 and the server running Windows 2000 Server), the drivers often didn't have the same name. You had to manually map them in an INF file to make printing to a redirected printer work at all.

- **Driver distribution**   You had to test drivers before installing them on the terminal server, and after they were tested, distribute them to all the other terminal servers.

- **Bandwidth usage**   Printing could take up a lot of bandwidth, which could slow the user session during print jobs.

In short, supporting printing has historically been a lot of work. Unfortunately, since the paperless office has yet to materialize, it's necessary to continue supporting the process.

It's been said that the definition of insanity is to keep doing the same thing and expecting different results. Since drivers on the terminal server are hard to support, Windows Server 2008 decided to leave the printing insanity behind by eliminating printer drivers on the terminal server as much as possible. Instead, Windows Server 2008 uses a new architecture based on the XML Paper Specification (XPS) print format to allow jobs printed to a redirected printer to use the client-side printer drivers. TS Easy Print is supported by clients running RDP 6.1 or later and .NET Framework 3.0 SP1 or later. The legacy format described previously is still supported for older versions of RDP, but TS Easy Print is the preferred method because of its lower management and bandwidth overhead.

Like legacy printing, Easy Print must render data into a WYSIWYG format and pass that data from the terminal server to the client where the printer is located. Where Easy Print differs is in the rendering and spooling process. Windows Vista and Windows Server 2008 (as mentioned previously) use XPS, which supports true WYSIWYG, greater color depth, and faster printing than GDI. When you print to XPS, you create an XML file that, like an EMF file, explains exactly what the desired output should look like. One major difference is that a native XPS file can be processed by an XPS-capable driver without being converted to the RAW format. Most of the time, an XPS spool file is smaller than an EMF one.

Basically, Easy Print takes a print job request and does only enough processing on the terminal server to get the print job to the client, as illustrated in Figure 5-2.

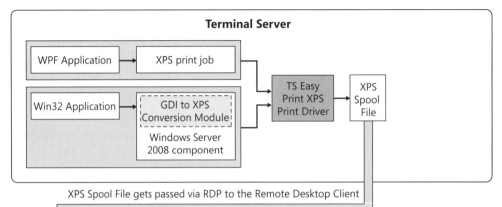

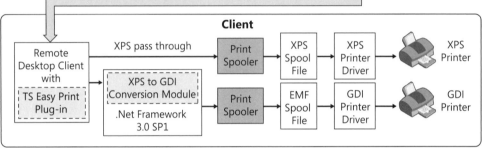

FIGURE 5-2 Easy Print uses client-side printer drivers to create print jobs.

The printing process works like this:

1. The user launches a print job from an application running in the remote session.

2. The print job is converted to an XPS file, whether from a Win32 application requiring initial conversion to GDI or directly from a Windows Presentation Foundation (WPF) application.

3. The XPS file is sent to the Easy Print plug-in in the Remote Desktop Connection client 6.1.

4. Unconverted XPS files go straight to the print driver as XPS spool files.

5. XPS files destined for a GDI printer are converted to EMF spool files.

6. The print job goes to the printer.

The most important concept to remember from this process is that you don't have to install printer drivers on the terminal server. TS Easy Print uses a proxy driver on the server to pass print jobs to the client for printing. Because of this, all client printers are available in the TS client session. By using TS Easy Print, you no longer have to match drivers on the terminal server with drivers on the client, and there is no risk of server crashes due to crashing kernel-mode print drivers.

Easy Print has another advantage over legacy printing models. As described earlier, the printer configuration information sent to the remote session was the same available to the Win32 interfaces on the client, and might not contain some driver-specific data.

TS Easy Print uses virtual channels to let you configure the printing properties application directly on the client computer. When a user clicks on a printer's preferences from a Terminal Services session, the TS Easy Print driver on the terminal server intercepts this call and sends the request to the TS Easy Print Plug-in on the RDC client. The client calls the client-side printer driver, which brings up the printing preferences dialog box on the client. Therefore, the preferences you get when you print from a client computer are the same preferences you get when printing from a Terminal Services session.

So far we've talked about how client device redirection works. Let's look now at how to implement it.

Moving the Client Experience to the Remote Session

It's been said of Terminal Services in Windows Server 2008 that it "makes it like being there, only better." Let's see what you can do to let users bring their personal work habits to the re-mote session, without causing trouble for you or the other users sharing that terminal server.

In the following sections, we'll discuss both per-user and per-computer settings that de-fine the client experience. Not all user-experience configurations can be managed at the user level in Group Policy. Where applicable, we'll include the settings in Terminal Services Configuration and Active Directory Users And Computers (ADUC), for those not using Group Policy to configure all settings.

Which Client Devices Can You Add to the Remote Session?

Most supported client devices require little setup to use in a remote session, as long as you meet the system requirements. For PnP redirection, make sure that you've installed the Desktop Experience feature on each terminal server. For Easy Print, make sure that you've installed RDP 6.1 and .NET Framework 3.0 SP1 or later on each client. Windows Vista SP1 and Windows XP SP3 both include clients that support RDP 6.1; you can also download RDC 6.1 for Windows XP SP2 from Microsoft's Web site. (The link is available on the companion media.)

Assuming that you've configured the server policy, most setup occurs on the client computer. Run the Remote Desktop Connection (RDC). To configure device redirection, turn to the Local Resources tab. The Printers and the Clipboard options are on this tab, but to choose to redirect other devices, you'll need to click the More button to open the dialog box shown in Figure 5-3.

FIGURE 5-3 Choosing to make PnP devices available in the remote session

If you use smart cards for user authentication in your environment, then smart cards must be redirected so users can use them to authenticate their remote sessions. As shown in Figure 5-3, smart cards are redirected by default.

Serial port devices are not remoted by default; not many devices use serial connections these days.

Drives are remoted by default. Expand the drives option to select particular drives to make accessible in the remote session. (One option is Drives That I Connect To Later, so you can opt to add USB drives to the remote session using dynamic virtual channels.)

PnP devices are not remoted by default, so you'll need to enable their redirection to use them in the session. In Figure 5-3, there is a camera plugged into the client computer. If you select the check box, when you connect to the remote session, the terminal server will install the redirector driver and then display the drive in My Computer as though it were locally attached, as shown in Figure 5-4.

FIGURE 5-4 Redirected devices appear in the remote instance of My Computer just as they do in the local instance.

Note If you don't see the PnP device automatically in the remote session—if instead the terminal server prompts you to install drivers—then you probably haven't previously installed the Desktop Experience, which is required to use the PnP Device Redirection Framework.

Redirected devices such as the camera in the example will disappear when unplugged and then will reappear when you plug them in. When the session ends, all redirected devices disappear from the terminal server.

Pros and Cons of Redirecting Resources

Providing remote access to resources has both benefits and drawbacks. The more remote devices you enable, the richer the client experience becomes, as it is more like the desktop client experience. But more redirected devices can lead to unintended consequences.

Obviously, redirecting drives opens a security hole. When a local drive is redirected to the remote session, it makes it easy to store data to the local drives. This is true from a desktop computer on the corporate network, of course, but a desktop or corporate-sponsored laptop is trusted. A personal laptop or a public computer in a hotel or coffee shop is not.

And even a trusted laptop can be lost or stolen. A laptop with corporate data on it is much more valuable than the cost of replacing the hardware. If you enable drive redirection, you're also vulnerable to data from the client computer making its way to the remote computer. In Windows Server 2008, drive redirection is full duplex—data can travel in both directions. It is not possible to restrict data to one direction. Therefore, it's necessary to make sure that you restrict remote user access to key drives from terminal sessions.

Perhaps less obviously, redirecting devices to a remote session may affect the experience for the person who's benefitting from the redirection. As discussed in the section titled "Restricting Device and Resource Redirection" later in this chapter, those remote devices must pass data back and forth between client and server. The more data you pass, the more competition there is for bandwidth between client and server. RDP compresses data well (see the How It Works sidebar titled "Tuning RDP Performance for LANs and WANs"), and it is quite responsive for LAN connections, but it can still be affected by large file transfers, like any other network—it's just that large file transfers don't affect the user's typing when working locally.

How It Works: Tuning RDP Performance for LANs and WANs

Remote work lives and dies by the responsiveness of the session. It doesn't matter how many features are available—if the session feels slow, then people won't use the terminal server. Therefore, it's important to do what you can to make RDP feel as responsive as possible when only limited bandwidth is available.

First, limit the unnecessary data traveling between client and server when bandwidth is at a premium. Don't map drives unless required, use TS Easy Print if possible, and consider the tradeoff between looks and performance when it comes to color depth, since more color depth means more data. You can configure the maximum color depth via Group Policy at Computer Configuration | Administrative Templates | Windows Components | Terminal Services | Terminal Server | Remote Session Environment | Limit Maximum Color Depth. Just enable the policy for your terminal server organizational unit (OU), and when clients connect, they will use the maximum color depth they support up to 32-bit color.

Second, choose your bulk compression algorithms carefully. RDP uses a version of the Microsoft Point-to-Point Compression (MPPC) Protocol described in RFC 2118. MPPC maintains a buffer for data to be sent between server and client. (Both the server and the client can use the bulk compression techniques to send data.) There are two main versions in Windows Server 2008 and Windows Vista SP1. The default compression algorithm uses an 8-kilobyte (KB) buffer to store data for each Protocol Data Unit

(PDU). Another compression algorithm uses a 64-KB buffer for each PDU and also implements Huffman encoding. Huffman encoding is, in short, a way to find out how often a given piece of data recurs and package the data as efficiently as possible based on that frequency. The algorithm with the 64-KB buffer is more appropriate for slower connections, but it uses more memory. To change the compression algorithm, enable the Group Policy at Computer Configuration | Administrative Templates | Windows Components | Terminal Services | Terminal Server | Remote Session Environment | Set Compression Algorithm For RDP Data. Because client and server will both use the same compression algorithm, when the client connects, it will tell the server what it can support.

Third, choose your features wisely. Windows Server 2008 enables ClearType remoting, which makes ClearType fonts look the same in a remote session as they do on the local terminal server. Unfortunately, performance is affected adversely when ClearType remoting is used. Ordinary text remoting displays fonts as characters—glyphs, to use the technical term. ClearType remoting displays fonts as bitmaps, as pictures of fonts. This reduces the likelihood that the client will be able to pull the right character from its cache where it stores recently received data. If it can't, then it will need the terminal server to send the character again. ClearType remoting is off by default and isn't recommended for WAN connections.

As you can see, the choices you could make depend on the amount of bandwidth available and are computer-wide. Users start feeling a noticeable lag in the response time at about 300 milliseconds. If you need to support both local and remote users, one option would be to define a parallel farm for use via TS Gateway only. (For more about TS Gateway, see Chapter 7, "Multi-Server Deployments and Securing Terminal Server Connections.") If you did this, then you could use the compression algorithm optimized for low-bandwidth scenarios and limit the color depth, then provide greater color depth and a memory-optimized compression algorithm on the terminal servers for local use.

Redirecting print devices may also ease management at the expense of performance. Because printing to redirected printers is much easier in Windows Server 2008 with Easy Print, it may be tempting to always print to redirected printers. This may be a good policy, but keep in mind the physical location of the printers. Every time the print job has to travel across the network, that's one hop across a relatively slow connection. (A LAN may be quite fast, but it's still slower than passing data between components on the same computer.) So if a client computer has a locally installed printer, that's one hop. If the client has a network connection to a TCP/IP printer, that's two hops (one to get to the client and one to get to the printer). If the client is connecting to a print server with connections to other printers, that's three hops: one to get to the client, one to get to the print server, and one to get to the printer.

Attaching the printers to the terminal server doesn't often work well. For one reason, this puts you right back to installing all the printer drivers on the terminal server, with the management overhead that entails. For another reason, terminal server clients may be nowhere near the terminal server—perhaps not even in the same country. But it's worth keeping the "hop" count in mind when designing the printer arrangement, balancing it against the management requirements.

The bottom line is that the decisions you make about device redirection will be based on the circumstances in which you're deploying terminal services and the scenarios you'll need to enable.

Note A good rule to follow is that it's generally better to be more restrictive than less so. A more restrictive approach reduces security holes and gives you the option of enabling functionality if you have to. Shutting down functionality that's been available is never easy or popular.

Rules for Applying Settings

You can apply some rules for configuring the user experience in multiple locations: Group Policy, user account properties in ADUC, and the TS Configuration Tool. It can be confusing to determine which ones you should set, and if you have conflicting settings, which takes precedence.

First, Group Policy always wins. If you're using Loopback Policy, user settings applied due to loopback processing win over regular user settings. But Group Policy always beats other settings. This is because Group Policy is applied not just at logon and computer startup, but also at intervals throughout the session.

If you're not using Group Policy and you're setting properties in both TS Configuration and user account properties, then under normal conditions, the settings defined from ADUC will always win. (You can override this, but that's the default behavior.)

This chapter shows you where settings are configured in the TS Configuration Tool, in ADUC user account properties, and in Group Policy. However, we strongly recommend that you use Group Policy to configure the user experience.

First, when Terminal Server was first released, all settings were available in the TS Configuration Tool. As the number of settings controlling the client user experience has proliferated, it's become impossible to keep them all in the dialog boxes for user or protocol settings. So, many new settings don't appear in TS Configuration or user account properties at all.

Second, Group Policy makes it infinitely easier to apply settings consistently, because TS Configuration only allows you to configure one server at a time. If you apply settings on a per-user basis using ADUC, then every time you add a new user account, you'll need to update the settings. With Group Policy, you'll only need to set the policies once and then add new accounts to the appropriate groups.

Third, Group Policy makes it easy to apply settings *inconsistently*, if you want to. Not all remote users are necessarily working under the same conditions. It's possible that you'll want to enable some forms of resource redirection for some people and not for others.

Finally, there are a couple of settings in the user account properties exposed through Active Directory that look like they do something, but they don't. On the Session tab in the user account properties, there's a setting that appears to controls which computer an end user may use to reconnect to a disconnected session. On the Environment tab, selecting the check box for connecting drives has no effect. Neither setting has any affect on terminal sessions using RDP.

> **On the Companion Media** If you'd like to configure Terminal Services attributes via Active Directory, then be sure to check out Quest Software's quaduser cmdlet, loaded when you load the Quest PowerShell provider with get-PSSnapin quest*. (The following link is provided on the CD: *http://www.quest.com/powershell/activeroles-server.aspx.*)

Run get-quaduser "UserName" format-list Ts* to retrieve the settings exposed through Active Directory for the given user. The only catch is that this tool will only allow you to get and set attributes exposed through Active Directory, and not all attributes are. For more examples of using quaduser to get and set TS user configuration data, see the Quest blog at *http://dmitrysotnikov.wordpress. com/2008/02/13/managing-terminal-services-attributes-with-powershell/.*

Direct from the Source: How TS Management Tools Have Evolved

Terminal Services provides a variety of tools for administration. They were designed from the beginning to accommodate scenarios based on the features we developed with each release.

TS NT4

In Windows NT, Terminal Server Edition, we had user properties allowing administrators to configure some of the TS properties per user in a simple deployment. At that stage, Terminal Services was just entering the market, so the feature set was limited: Users could connect to a server, they could have their roaming profile specific to TS sessions saved to a different location than the regular roaming profile, session limits could be set, administrators could get remote control, and the initial program could be set. Also, there were a few settings specific to Citrix that enabled administrators to use RDP and ICA clients in the same deployment.

Windows 2000 Server

With Windows 2000 Server, Terminal Services became a Windows component that could be installed in Remote Admin mode or Application server mode. This was the release that had the first version of Terminal Services Configuration and Terminal Services Manager. Terminal Services Configuration allows administrators to configure the server more effectively, providing server level settings as well as per connection. User properties were added to Active Directory as Windows shipped Active Directory. We started supporting printer redirection in this release. Terminal Services Manager enabled administrators to monitor activity on their deployed terminal servers. Additionally, we implemented a WMI provider for all settings in the configuration tools.

Windows Server 2003

Windows Server 2003 introduced Group Policy. Terminal Services added Group Policy settings for almost all settings present in User Properties as well as Terminal Services Configuration/WMI. Using Group Policy settings allows administrators to easily configure all terminal servers in an OU, by creating a Group Policy object (GPO) at the domain level. This is a great benefit because it is important to have all TS servers configured the same so that the user experience is the same, regardless of which server they are connecting. With Session Directory (now called Session Broker in recent releases), Terminal Services provided the first real multi-server solution.

We tried Windows Server 2003 Terminal Services first in our team by setting up a TS deployment with four Terminal Services servers in Application server mode, with applications installed and the environment configured to provide a good experience to our users. We added a profile server, a Session Directory Server and a Licensing Server and implemented session limits, TS Roaming Profiles, home directories, printer/drive redirection and joined our servers to the Session Directory. We had our challenges, because this deployment was in our corporate domain. Therefore, we needed to have our own Terminal Services OU, and we had to create the Terminal Services–specific GPOs, and at the same time, apply all corporate domain GPOs. But GPOs worked very well in this scenario. We did discover that the GPO for Session Limits did not allow granular setting to accommodate long weekends. This has been fixed in Windows Server 2008.

Windows 2008 Server

With Windows Server 2008, we improved our tools, providing even more settings in the user interface, in Terminal Services Configuration, as well as in GPOs. We introduced a TS RemoteApp Manager, a new tool to help administrators set up a TS RemoteApp server. We added more GPOs to configure terminal servers for Remote Applications Integrated Locally (RAIL) to enhance the remote client experience. Administrators can better identify Terminal Services GPOs because they are now grouped per TS role: Terminal Server, Session Directory Server, RDP settings (related to client), Session Experience Configuration, and so on. When it made sense, we added GPOs for all new features, because, based on our experience, Group Policy is the easiest in-the-box tool to use for terminal services environment configuration in large deployments. Also, the Terminal Services Configuration tool is now remotable: Administrators can connect to the terminal server they want to configure from their admin box, rather than connecting with a TS session and configure everything locally.

The corporate domain administrators gave us permission to administer our Terminal Services OU, so we were able to change our GPOs as needed. We can add/remove servers from our OU, which makes it very easy to expand or reduce our scope. The best part is that after the GPOs are created with all required settings, they don't require any maintenance or changes.

Geanina Andreiu

Software Development Engineer, Test

Printing from Terminal Services

The most important part of moving the client experience to the remote session lies in printing. The section titled "Printing Architecture" earlier in this chapter described TS Easy Print and the legacy printing model; here we'll talk about how to implement both methods of printing.

 Note Although the following discussions are about printing, they apply to faxing as well. Faxing works just fine with Easy Print—simply set up the fax on the client. When the client chooses to send a fax, the client-side dialog box opens to prompt the user for the contact information. Scanning is not supported in native Windows Server 2008, but it is enabled by several third-party products.

Using TS Easy Print

Making TS Easy Print work requires no setup on the client or the server as long as your clients meet the requirements. Observe TS Easy Print at work for some TS sessions in the following examples with a sample domain. Here's the domain breakdown:

- The domain is a Windows Server 2008 domain named Alpineskihouse.com.

- The Windows Server 2008 terminal servers are named MATTERHORN and BIGFROG.

- ASH-CLI-001 is a client PC running Microsoft Vista Sp1.

- ASH-CLI-002 is a client PC running Windows XP SP3.

.NET Framework 3.0 SP1 and RDC 6.0 both come with Vista Service Pack 1, so ASH-CLI-001 meets the requirements to use TS Easy Print. RDC 6.0 comes with XP SP3, but .NET Framework 3.0 Service Pack 1 (or later; version 3.5 is out as of this writing) does not—you must download and install it separately. RDC 6.0 includes support for RDP 6.1, which is required for TS Easy Print. Let's review the scenario: A user logs on to ASH-CLI-001. Four printers are available, as shown in Figure 5-5.

FIGURE 5-5 Printers are available on the client PC.

The user starts a Remote Desktop Connection (RDC) to the terminal server MATTERHORN. Opening the Printers console, you can see that all four printers have been redirected and are available in the terminal server session. The redirected printers are designated by the name of the printer plus the redirected session ID number (redirected 1), as shown in Figure 5-6.

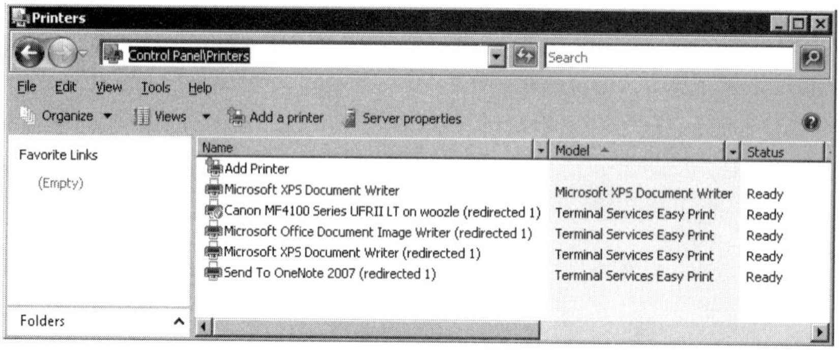

FIGURE 5-6 Redirected printers are designated by the session ID number.

> **Note** In the legacy printing model, redirected printers were named according to this format: Client Printer Name (from Client Computer Name) in session number *X*. Windows Terminal Server 2008 redirected printer names now follow this format: Client Printer Name (redirected session ID), and are therefore much easier to read and distinguish from other printers when many printers are available.

The user opens Notepad, creates a text file, and then chooses File | Print. The print dialog box appears, and the user selects the default redirected printer and then clicks the Preferences button in the upper-right quadrant of the printer dialog box. The printer properties dialog box appears. If the RDP session is open in full-screen mode, the printer properties dialog box appears to be part of the session. But if the Terminal Services session is viewed in a smaller window, as shown in Figure 5-7, the user can actually drag the printer dialog box out of the window. That is because this dialog box is launched not from the terminal server session, but from the local computer.

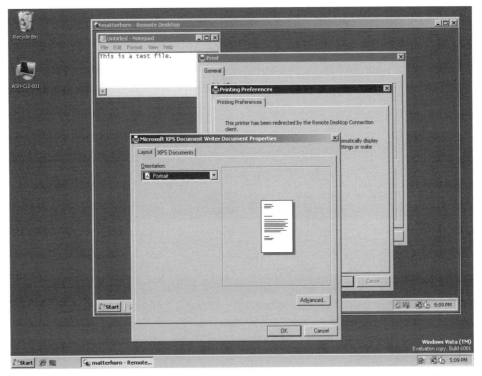

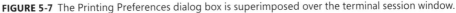

FIGURE 5-7 The Printing Preferences dialog box is superimposed over the terminal session window.

(Although you can't see it, printing to a redirected printer using TS Easy Print brings up another dialog box stating that the printer has been redirected by the RDC client and the printing preferences will display in a separate window.)

One Group Policy changes the way that TS Easy Print is applied. In Computer Configuration | Policies | Administrative Templates | Windows Components | Terminal Services | Terminal Server | Printer Redirection, there is a policy called Use Terminal Services Easy Print Printer Driver First. If this policy is enabled or not configured, the terminal server tries to use the TS Easy Print driver to install client printers first. Only if the TS Easy Print driver isn't available will it look for a printer driver on the terminal server that matches the printer driver on the client. If most of your clients depend on the legacy printing model, you can disable this policy. This does not disable Easy Print, but the terminal server will only use Easy Print if a printer driver is not available.

When TS Easy Print Isn't an Option: Distributing Drivers to Terminal Servers

Easy Print only works with RDP 6.1 or later and the .NET Framework 3.0 SP1 or later. Therefore, if you are supporting clients that can't run RDP 6.1, you'll need to install drivers on the terminal server as described earlier. The challenge here is how to get the drivers onto the terminal server (and distribute them to other terminal servers after they are tested).

To use legacy printing, you'll need to do the following:

- Distribute necessary printer drivers to the terminal servers.

- Use Group Policy to configure printer redirection appropriately.

You can use Group Policy or the Print Management Console (PMC) to distribute the drivers without touching every terminal server. In both cases, install the printers (so the drivers are installed) but then *delete the printers*. This second step is critical because it keeps users from being confused by printers they can see but don't have permission to print to.

Deploy Printer Drivers Using Group Policy   You can use Group Policy to deploy the printers to each terminal server and then remove the policy. When you apply and then remove the GPO, the printers get removed, but the drivers remain.

First, install the printers you need on your terminal servers on a print server and share the printers with the network. The printers don't have to work; you will only be using them temporarily.

Next, create a new GPO (in this example, it's called TS Printers). Edit the GPO, navigating to Computer Configuration | Policies | Windows Settings | Deployed Printers. Right-click Deployed Printers and choose Deploy Printer to open a dialog box like the one shown in Figure 5-8.

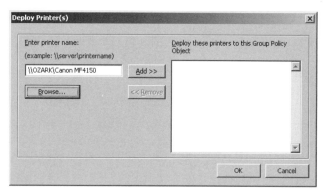

FIGURE 5-8 The Deploy Printer(s) dialog box

Enter the Universal Naming Convention (UNC) path for each printer whose drivers you need, click the Add button, and then click OK to exit. Back in the Microsoft Group Policy Management console (GPMC), ensure that the GPO security filtering will allow the GPO to be applied to your terminal servers. (The Authenticated Users group that is added by default includes the terminal servers, so you can leave it as it is.) Apply the GPO to the Terminal Servers organizational unit (OU).

Next, forcibly update the policies on the terminal servers by running the command *gpupdate /force* on each terminal server or by rebooting each terminal server. The printers are now installed.

Finally, after you've ensured that the printers are correctly deployed to the terminal servers, remove the printers by deleting the GPO from the terminal servers and forcibly updating the policy. The printer is removed from the terminal server, but the drivers are still available. (You can see this by checking the Server Properties of the Printers console (File | Server Properties | Drivers tab.)

The Print Management Console   You can also use the Print Management Console (PMC) to deploy printers. PMC is part of the Remote Server Administration Tools (RSAT) on Windows Server 2008 and installed as part of the Print Server role. As with Group Policy, you'll use the PMC to install the required printer types on all terminal servers (to lay down the drivers) and then delete the printers (to avoid confusing people while leaving the printer drivers in place).

First, use the PMC to install all the printer drivers you need on one of your terminal servers. Then delete them, removing the printers but leaving the drivers on the server. Next, use the PMC to export the printer drivers from that server to a file and import that file to the other terminal servers. You will need the printer drivers available to install on the first terminal server, so put them in a shared directory on your network that is accessible from the terminal server.

Install the necessary printers onto a network-accessible print server and then launch the PMC from Start | Administrative Tools | Print Management to open the console shown in Figure 5-9.

FIGURE 5-9 Print Management Console

Add the terminal servers to the Print Servers list by right-clicking on Print Servers and choosing Add/Remove Servers from the context menu. In the dialog box that appears, browse for the terminal servers in the network and choose Add to List. Click OK when you have added all terminal servers to the list.

Choose one terminal server in the list and add all printers to it. Right-click the server and choose Add Printer. Choose to search the network for printers and browse to the share location for all the printers.

After installing all of the needed drivers, right-click the server and choose Export Printers To A File from the context menu. The Printer Migration Wizard will start and provide a list of all the objects (printer queues and drivers) that will be exported to a file with the extension .printerExport. Click the Next button and choose a network-accessible location to store the file.

Using the PMC, import the exported file to the other terminal servers by right-clicking on each server and choosing Import Printers From A File in the context menu. Again, the Printer Migration Wizard will begin. Browse to the file location and navigate to the file. The wizard provides a list of objects it will import. Click Next to move to the next screen, as shown in Figure 5-10. From here you'll configure your import options.

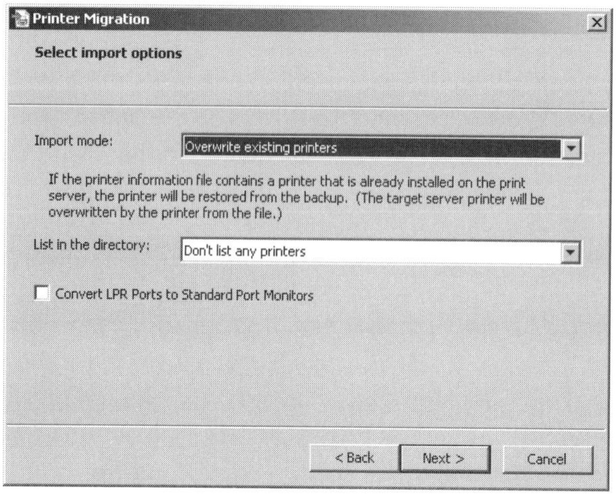

FIGURE 5-10 Printer Migration import options

You can choose either to overwrite existing printers or keep existing printers and import copies. To make the terminal servers homogenous, overwrite the existing drivers so that all servers are using the same printer drivers. Also in this dialog box, choose Don't List Any Printers from the List In The Directory drop-down list, as this will prevent you from publishing the printers in Active Directory (this is necessary because you only want the drivers). Click the Next button and you're done.

After importing the file to all of your terminal servers, you can delete the printers on each server. Expand each server's Printers folder, right-click each printer in the folder, and choose Delete.

> **Note** You can use the PMC to keep track of which terminal server has which printer drivers by clicking on the Drivers option located under each server.

Managing Print Settings with Group Policy

Group Policy for printer settings is configured in the following location: Computer Configuration | Policies | Administrative Templates | Windows Components | Terminal Services | Terminal Server | Printer Redirection.

- **Use Terminal Services Easy Print Printer Driver First**   If this policy is enabled or not configured, the terminal server tries to use the TS Easy Print driver to install client printers first. Only if the TS Easy Print driver isn't available will it look for a printer driver on the terminal server that matches the printer driver on the client. If most of your clients depend on the legacy printing model, you can disable this policy. This does not disable Easy Print, but the terminal server will only use Easy Print if a printer driver is not available.

  Other Group Policy settings located in the Printer Redirection folder may apply to your environment if you can't use TS Easy Print all the time.

- **Do Not Allow Printer Redirection**   If you enable this policy, users will not be able to redirect print jobs to their local computer printers. If you do not configure or disable this policy, printer redirection is allowed.

- **Specify Terminal Server Fallback Printer Driver Behavior**   Fallback printer driver behavior tells the terminal server that in the event that it cannot find a printer driver match to a printer driver on a computer, then it should attempt to use an alternate printer driver. Fallback printer drivers are the HP DeskJet 500, HP DeskJet 500C, HP LaserJet 4/4M PS, and HP Color LaserJet 5/5M PS. This setting is disabled by default.

- **Redirect Only The Default Client Printer**   Clients may have many printers installed on their client PCs; by default, all will be redirected to the Terminal Services session. To decrease resource usage on the terminal server, you can enable this policy so that only the default printer on the client PC will be redirected to the client Terminal Services session.

- **Do Not Set A Default Client Printer To Be The Default Printer In A Session**   By default, the client's default printer is the default printer for the remote session. If you enable this setting, there is no default printer for the remote session.

> **Note** The Use Terminal Services Easy Print Driver First and the Redirect Only The Default Client Printer settings can also be set in a User GPO at User Configuration | Policies | Administrative Templates | Windows Components | Terminal Services | Terminal Server | Printer Redirection.

Redirecting Time Zones

If all users are accessing Terminal Services from the same building, they are all working within the same time zone. If the work force is mobile or spread over a wide geographic area, trying to work from a non-local time zone can get disorienting for the end users. This isn't uncommon; many large companies are spread out over a country, and quite a few—even small companies—must support people outside their own country and even outside their own continent. If the data center is in New York but one part of the development team is working from California and accessing remote applications to keep project logs, using the New York time zone can be very confusing.

Starting with Windows Server 2003, Terminal Services has been able to redirect the client's time zone to the terminal session. The server does the math, subtracting or adding time according to the relative time zones, and then presents the adjusted time in the client session. The time *zone* is sent to the terminal server, not the actual time. If the users manually adjust their time on their computers but don't change the time zone, then the difference will not show up in the terminal session. In Windows Server 2008, this setting is available as a user policy as well as a computer policy, so you can selectively redirect time zone information.

The Group Policy setting controlling time zone redirection is Allow Time Zone Redirection. If you want to configure it for users or groups of users, it's located at User Configuration | Policies | Administrative Templates | Windows Components | Terminal Server | Device And Resource Redirection. Configure this setting on a computer-wide basis by enabling the same policy in Computer Configuration | Administrative Templates | Windows Components | Terminal Server | Device And Resource Redirection. By default, time zone redirection is turned off. To turn it on, enable the policy. All clients capable of returning the client computer's time zone (RDP 5.1 and later) will do so.

> **Note** Although time zone redirection has been supported since Windows Server 2003, the user policy controlling it is new in Windows Server 2008. In Windows Server 2003, you could only enable or disable this setting on a computer-wide basis.

Locking Down the Terminal Server

One of the new features in Windows Server 2008 Terminal Services is TS RemoteApps. TS RemoteApps blur the line between client and desktop by displaying remote applications alongside locally running applications, rather than in a separate desktop window. This makes it easier to avoid losing applications and can simplify training, because you don't have to teach inexperienced users how to find the applications they need. No one ever sees a desktop; they just see the application they need to run. When the user closes the last TS RemoteApp they have open, the session ends.

Why, if no one sees a desktop, would you need to lock down the terminal server?

The answer goes back to Chapter 3, explaining the component pieces of a terminal server environment and how sessions are launched and supported. Even if you're viewing only a TS RemoteApp, an entire session is still running. A savvy end user can find out pretty easily that Ctrl+Alt+End opens Task Manager on the remote session. And when you have Task Manager open, you can get to Run. When you can get to Run, you can run nearly any application or command on the terminal server that isn't locked down.

As Yoda might say, "Ctrl+Alt+End leads to the Task Manager. The Task Manager leads to Run. Run leads to suffering."

Displaying only a single application is no replacement for locking down the terminal server. In this section, we'll talk about the Group Policy settings you can apply to accomplish this.

As we go through the process of locking down the terminal server, you'll need to keep your personal situation in mind. This is not a complete list of what you *must* do. This is a description of what you *can* do.

First, some of these settings will overlap—the same goal may be accomplished using different settings, so it will be up to you to choose what settings or methods of lockdown work for your circumstances.

Second, for practical reasons, you may not be able to set every setting we talk about in the next pages. Shutting down Internet Explorer will close one back door to the terminal server, but if the main reason you run a terminal server is to provide access to a browser-based application, then blocking access to Internet Explorer may not be a viable option. Test all policies before deploying them to make sure that the combinations you've chosen haven't disabled any functionality you need.

Restricting Device and Resource Redirection

Drive and resource redirection are large parts of making a remote application feel like a local application. It allows users to open their local files in remote applications (or save remote files to their local computer easily) and makes it easy to copy bits of data between local and remote sessions, hear audio from a remote session on a local computer, print from a terminal services session, and so on.

Integration between local and remote computer sounds great . . . until you really need to enforce security on corporate data. For example, by default, client drives and the Clipboard are visible in a remote connection, but both open a security hole from the data center to a remote computer. This allows users to copy or even save sensitive data from the corporate network to an unsecured computer.

The rule of thumb for device and resource redirection is that more is not necessarily better. Disable redirection that you don't need. Doing so cuts down on bandwidth resources that may be used for other functions and also reduces server and sensitive data exposure.

Disable drive and resource redirection in one of four ways:

- Using Group Policy
- Using Active Directory Users And Computers on a per-user basis
- Using the Terminal Services Configuration Tool on a per-server basis
- Using the RDC on a per-connection basis

Remember, Group Policy settings are always the best choice compared to the others, with ADUC settings next, then TS Configuration Tool, and finally, RDC settings.

Restrict Device and Resource Redirection Using Group Policy

We recommend using Group Policy to control device and resource redirection for the reason you will read about over and over throughout this book: You can control device and redirection from one source, which is consistent for every terminal server and Terminal Services session within the environment.

Device and resource redirection can be disabled or enabled by setting the corresponding device or resource Group Policy settings to the appropriate state (either to enabled or disabled, depending on the setting).

The following computer policies are located at Computer Configuration | Policies | Administrative Templates | Windows Components | Terminal Services | Terminal Server | Device And Resource Redirection:

- **Allow Audio Redirection**   Users can redirect audio from the terminal server by setting the Remote Computer Sound on the Local Resources tab of the RDC, and by default audio is redirected to the client computer. You may want to disable audio redirection if you're not running any applications that require it. Disabling the computer Group Policy setting overrides the RDC settings. If this setting is left unconfigured, it is not controlled by Group Policy but can be controlled using the TS Configuration Tool on a per-server basis.

- **Do Not Allow Clipboard Redirection**   Enable this setting to disable Clipboard redirection. It is possible to turn off Clipboard redirection from the RDP client, but if you're serious about keeping data off the local computers, it's better to use Group Policy or the Terminal Services Configuration Tool. Otherwise, the enterprising user will just open the Advanced Properties on the client, click the Local Resources tab, and check the box to enable Clipboard redirection.

You can also turn off Clipboard redirection using a user policy located at User Configuration | Policies | Administrative Templates | Windows Components | Terminal Services | Terminal Server | Device And Resource Redirection. It is unconfigured by default.

What if you'd generally like to enable Clipboard redirection but have one or two sensitive applications? Because RemoteApps running on the same server are all running within a single session, it's not possible to disable Clipboard redirection on a per-application basis. To create that kind of granularity, you'll need to isolate the applications requiring the higher level of security on separate terminal servers and disable Clipboard redirection on those servers.

- **Do Not Allow COM Port Redirection**   By default, COM port redirection is allowed for Terminal Services sessions. If your users don't need it, stop COM port redirection by enabling this setting. If you disable this setting, then COM port redirection is always allowed. If this setting is left unconfigured, COM port redirection is not specified by Group Policy but can be specified using TS Configuration Tool on a per-server basis.

- **Do Not Allow Drive Redirection**   Redirecting user drives to the terminal session enhances the feel of the session but opens a security hole. Drive redirection is a two-way street: Any data that users can access from the terminal session can be copied from it, and they can copy data to any drive they have access to. To turn off drive redirection for users or computers, enable the Do Not Allow Drive Redirection computer policy.

> **Note** Although you can disable drive redirection using TS Gateway, this setting will be ignored if the end user enables drive redirection from the Remote Desktop Connection client, and the terminal server itself permits drive redirection. You must turn off drive redirection at the terminal server to strongly enforce this policy.

- **Do Not Allow Client Printer Redirection**   Drive redirection is an obvious security hole, but printing can also create a security problem. To disable all printer redirection, enable this policy, found in the computer Group Policy settings: Computer Configuration | Policies | Administrative Templates | Windows Components | Terminal Services | Terminal Server | Printer Redirection. By default it is not configured; if unconfigured, printer redirection can be controlled via ADUC, RDC, or TS Configuration Tool.

- **Do Not Allow LPT Port Redirection**   This setting does not redirect LPT printers. However, it will have no effect if you're using Easy Print, because that's not redirected— just sent to the client for processing. This setting may be configured from either ADUC or the Client Settings tab for RDP of the Terminal Services Configuration Tool.

- **Do Not Allow Supported Plug And Play Device Redirection**   By default, this setting is not configured at all (using RDC, TS Configuration Tool, or Group Policy). Stop redirection of PnP devices such as media players and cameras by enabling this setting. If you do not configure this setting, then you can control PnP device redirection using the RDC or the RDP settings available on the Client Settings tab of the TS Configuration Tool. (This setting is not exposed in ADUC.)

- **Do Not Allow Smart Card Device Redirection**   By default, smart card redirection is enabled for RDP 6.1. Override this by enabling the Do Not Allow Smart Card Redirection Group Policy setting. This setting is available only through Group Policy.

Restrict Device and Resource Redirection Using ADUC

Only printer redirection can be controlled via ADUC. To do so, open Active Directory Users And Computers, double-click a user account, click the Environment tab, and select or clear the boxes next to Connect Client Printers At Logon. This setting is enabled by default.

There is also an option for Connect Client Drives At Logon; it is checked by default. However, this setting has no effect. It was originally designed to be used by the Citrix MetaFrame add-on to Windows 2000 Terminal Services (before RDP supported drive redirection), and it isn't used by RDP.

Restrict Device and Resource Redirection Using TS Configuration Tool

You can also disable device and resource redirection from the Terminal Services Configuration Tool, but remember that this means configuring each server separately.

To disable drive and resource redirection from Terminal Services Configuration, open the RDP client properties by opening the RDP-Tcp Properties dialog box visible in the Connections setting of the TS Configuration Tool. Click the Client Settings tab shown in Figure 5-11 and clear the boxes corresponding to the type of redirection you want to disable. Click Apply, then click OK, and you're done.

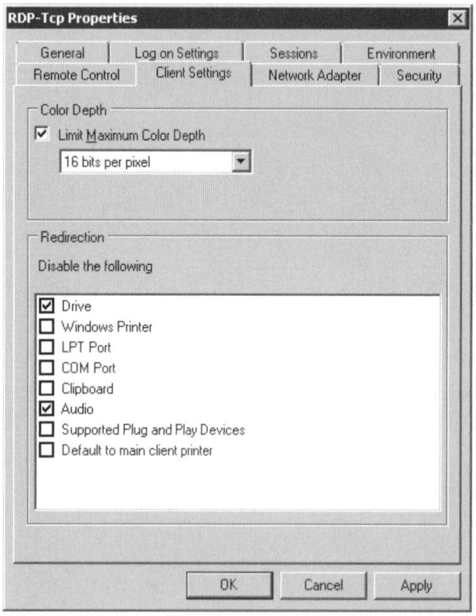

FIGURE 5-11 Restrict redirections by checking the boxes on the Client Settings tab of the RDP-Tcp Properties dialog box.

Because of the different ways you can control device and resource redirection, the options can be confusing. Table 5-1 is a summary of the types of devices and resources that can be redirected, whether they can be controlled by ADUC, RDC, TS Configuration Tool, or Group Policy, and what that controlled state is set to by default.

TABLE 5-1 Default Drive and Resource Redirection Settings for ADUC, RDC, TS Configuration Tool, and Group Policy Settings

	ADUC User Environment Tab	Remote Desktop Client 6	Terminal Services Configuration Tool	Computer Group Policy
Audio		Enabled	Disabled	Not configured
Printers	Enabled	Enabled	Named Windows printer; not configured	Not configured
LPT port			Not configured*	Not configured
Clipboard		Enabled	Not configured	Not configured
Smart cards		Enabled	Not configured	Not configured
Serial ports/ COM ports		Not configured	Not configured	Not configured
Drives	Has no effect**	Not configured	Not configured	Not configured
Drives connected to later		Not configured		
PnP devices		Not configured	Not configured	Not configured
Devices plugged in later		Not configured		

*In the Terminal Services Configuration Tool, LPT port redirection will be disabled and not able to be edited (the check box will be shaded and unavailable to check) if this Group Policy setting, Use Terminal Services Easy Print Printer Driver First, is enabled. The setting is located at Computer Configuration | Policies | Administrative Templates | Windows Components | Terminal Services | Terminal Server | Printer Redirection.

** Although there is a setting on the Environment tab in the user account properties available from ADUC, this setting has no effect. It was originally designed to be used by the Citrix MetaFrame add-on to Windows 2000 Terminal Services (before RDP supported drive redirection), and it isn't used by RDP.

Prevent Users from Reconfiguring the Server

The last thing you need is for unknown changes to occur on a terminal server, let alone a terminal server farm that you are trying to keep consistent. Because you have multiple users accessing the same server, allowing users to reconfigure the server at the least would render any change management efforts completely ineffective and may even lead to disaster. Set the following Group Policy settings to help limit server changes to the ones you know about and authorize.

Restricting Access to the Control Panel

User Configuration | Policies | Administrative Templates | Control Panel

- **Prohibit Access To Control Panel**   Users should have no need to access the Control Panel. Enabling this setting removes Control Panel from the Start menu and Windows Explorer, and users won't have access to Control Panel, nor will they be able to run any of the Control Panel items.

> **Note** When you enable this setting, you prevent administrators from installing any Windows Installer MSI package onto the terminal server, even if the explicit Deny is set for the Administrator account. Therefore, to install applications you'll need to disable this policy. At the same time, disable remote logons.

Restrict Printer Driver Installation

Computer Configuration | Policies | Windows Settings | Security Settings | Local Policies | Security Options

- **Devices: Prevent Users From Installing Printer Drivers**   Enabling this setting prevents users from adding printer drivers to a terminal server as part of adding a network printer. This policy does not affect Administrators and does not pertain to adding a local printer.

Prevent Access to the Registry

At first, thinking that users might run Regedit.exe leads to worst-case scenarios. The truth is, on a terminal server, domain users are restricted to writing to their own keys. That said, you don't want users wandering through HKCU. To prevent access to tools that enable direct edits to the registry, use the following two policies:

User Configuration | Policies | Administrative Templates | System

- **Prevent Access To Registry Editing Tools**   By default, access to the registry (on a limited basis) is allowed. Enable this setting to prevent access to the registry.

- **Disable Regedit From Running Silently**   Enable this setting to prevent users from running regedit with the /s switch. For instance, a user could run **regedit /s *Filename*.reg** from a command prompt and import a file into the registry even though the previous policy is enabled.

Prevent Access to Windows Automatic Updates

To prevent Windows updates from being automatically applied to production terminal servers, disable Windows Automatic Updates. This lockdown isn't about users so much as it is about making sure that changes aren't made without full intention and testing. The policies are:

User Configuration | Policies | Administrative Templates | System

- **Windows Automatic Updates**   Enabling this setting prevents Windows from automatically searching for and downloading and installing updates. If this setting is not configured or disabled, Windows will automatically download updates to the server.

User Configuration | Policies | Administrative Templates | Windows Components | Windows Update

- **Remove Access To Use All Windows Update Features**   Enabling this setting blocks access to the Windows Update Web site and removes the Windows Update link from the Start menu and from the Tools menu in Internet Explorer. Notifications about updates will cease and automatic updating is disabled.

Close Back Doors to Executables

Much of locking down the terminal server involves closing back doors into the server. This minimizes unintended consequences caused by users running the command prompt, browsing the network, or browsing the computer.

Restrict Access to Start Menu and Networking Items

Windows Server 2008 Start menu enables access to the terminal server. Figure 5-12 outlines the Start menu program areas, which are important to understanding how the policies we're discussing work and interact. (The policy effects may appear obvious, but they are much less so when you apply them.)

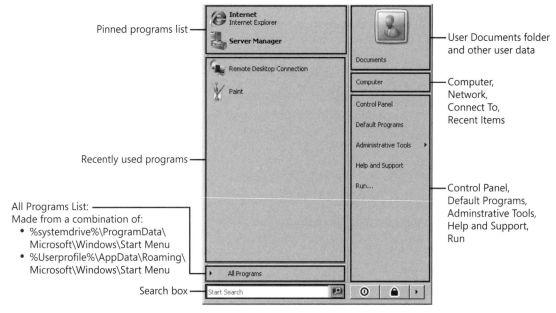

Pinned programs list

User Documents folder and other user data

Computer, Network, Connect To, Recent Items

Recently used programs

Control Panel, Default Programs, Adminstrative Tools, Help and Support, Run

All Programs List:
Made from a combination of:
- %systemdrive%\ProgramData\ Microsoft\Windows\Start Menu
- %Userprofile%\AppData\Roaming\ Microsoft\Windows\Start Menu

Search box

FIGURE 5-12 Windows Server 2008 Start menu areas and their sources of data

The taskbar is also a back door to the operating system, offering easy access to the QuickLaunch, Address, Links, and Desktop toolbars. Unless you restrict access to the Start menu and taskbar, you've left many windows open on the terminal server. To lock down the Start menu and taskbar, use these Group Policy settings:

User Configuration | Policies | Administrative Templates | Start Menu And Taskbar

- **Prevent Changes To Taskbar And Start Menu Settings**   Being able to make changes to the taskbar and the Start menu gives users the opportunity to access programs such as Internet Explorer, e-mail programs, network shares, and Internet Web sites via the Address bar, Links, and so on. Enabling this setting blocks access to the Properties dialog box users get when they right-click the taskbar. It also removes the Taskbar and Start menu items from the Taskbar And Settings Menu Properties dialog box. It does not stop users from turning on taskbar toolbars.

- **Show QuickLaunch On Taskbar**   By default, the QuickLaunch toolbar is shown on the taskbar when a user logs on. This can be helpful if you want to place application links for your users on this bar, for instance, by preconfiguring the default user pro-file. But be aware that users can delete icons from the QuickLaunch toolbar, and this might generate Help Desk calls. Users can also turn this toolbar on and off. Hide the QuickLaunch toolbar and prevent users from turning it on by disabling this setting.

- **Remove Access To The Context Menus For The Taskbar**   Enabling this setting pre-vents users from turning Taskbar Toolbars on and off.

- **Remove Programs On Settings Menu**   Enabling this setting removes access to Control Panel, Printers, and Network Connections folders from the Start menu.

- **Remove Common Program Groups From The Start Menu**   Enable this setting to display in the Start menu only items pulled from the user's profile. Items from the Public User profile will not be merged and available on the user's Start menu in the All Programs list or on the desktop.

- **Remove The Pinned Programs List From The Start Menu**   Enabling this setting removes the pinned programs list from the Start menu and prevents users from pinning programs to the Start menu. By default, Internet Explorer and an e-mail client may be pinned to this menu; this setting removes their links by clearing the corresponding boxes on the Simple Start menu customization control panel.

- **Remove the All Programs List From The Start Menu**   All Programs is normally made up of a combination of the public users' programs and an individual user's programs portion of their profile. Enabling this setting removes the All Programs menu from the Start menu. This includes links to Accessories, the Startup folder, and other program links that you may not want to be accessible.

- **Remove Network Connections From Start Menu**   Enabling this setting denies users access to the Manage Network Connection link in the Network And Sharing Center.

- **Remove Network Icon From Start Menu**   Enabling this setting removes the Network icon from the Start menu; however, it still appears and is accessible in Control Panel and Windows Explorer.

- **Remove Favorites Menu From The Start Menu**   Although the Favorites menu is not shown by default, enabling this setting prohibits users from displaying the Favorites menu via the Properties of the Start menu, thus prohibiting easy access to URLs from the Start menu.

- **Remove Run Menu From The Start Menu**   Enabling this setting removes the Run option from the Start menu, Task Manager, and Windows Explorer. Additionally, users will not be able to enter a local file path or a UNC path into the Internet Explorer address bar. The key combination Windows Logo+R no longer brings up the Run box if this setting is enabled.

- **Remove Drag And Drop Context Menus On The Start Menu**   Enabling this setting prevents users from dragging and dropping links to the Start menu. However, it does not prevent access to the Start Menu Properties.

- **Do Not Search Internet**   Enabling this setting prevents the Windows Search box from searching Internet history or Favorites. This can decrease user access to URLs that could point to executables or other potentially harmful script files.

- **Do Not Search Programs**   Enabling this setting keeps users from searching for programs on the terminal server. This will prevent searching the terminal server for programs that users may not need to run.

Remove Icons from the Desktop

Placing icons on the desktop is a very easy and direct way to access some information if you're displaying full desktops instead of individual applications. However, you may not want users looking at the System properties of My Computer or mapping a drive so easily. You can remove icons from the desktop with these settings:

User Configuration | Policies | Administrative Templates | Desktop

- **Hide And Disable All Items On The Desktop**   Enabling this setting hides and disables all items on the desktop, including the Recycle Bin and My Computer. Users will not be able to access My Computer from the desktop and gain access to unauthorized data and programs by mapping a network drive. However, these programs are still available from other locations, such as the Desktop toolbar on the taskbar.

- **Remove Computer Icon From The Desktop**   This policy removes the Computer icon from the desktop as well as within Windows Explorer, and from the Desktop toolbar on the taskbar, preventing users from right-clicking on My Computer and mapping a drive.

Restrict Access to CD-ROM and Floppy Drives

CD-ROM and floppy drives (assuming your servers have floppy drives) on the terminal server should not be a large security risk if you have any level of physical security on the terminal server, because people won't be able to insert their own CDs and floppy disks into a server behind a locked door. In the interest of blocking a back door, however, you can enable these policies that limit access to these external drives except from local connections.

Computer Configuration | Policies | Windows Settings | Security Settings | Local Policies | Security Options

- Devices: Restrict CD-ROM Access To Locally Logged-On User Only
- Devices: Restrict Floppy Access To Local Logged-On User Only

Prevent Access to the Command Prompt

The command prompt isn't a back door so much as a front door; if you can get to the command prompt, you can run any executable to which you have access.

User Configuration | Policies | Administrative Templates | System

- **Prevent Access To The Command Prompt**   Enable this setting to prevent users from using the command prompt.

Remove Access to Task Manager

The Task Manager is only one step removed from the command prompt, as it has access to the Run button.

User Configuration | Policies | Administrative Templates | System | Ctrl+Alt+Del Options

- **Remove Task Manager**   Enable this setting to prevent users from executing new tasks (starting programs) or changing the priority of processes via the Task Manager.

Restrict Access to Internet Explorer and the Internet

Blocking access to Internet Explorer browser takes away the ability to easily connect to the Internet, because there is no browser to use (at least not one you have provided). To completely block access to Internet Explorer, create a Software Restriction Policy (more about this later in the section titled "Using Software Restriction Policies") that denies Internet Explorer from running.

You can also inhibit access to Internet Explorer by hiding the icon and removing access to Windows Updates.

User Configuration | Policies | Administrative Templates | Start Menu And Taskbar

- **Remove Links And Access To Windows Update**   Although the Windows Update Web site is only available to administrators, users can use Windows Update from the Control Panel (if you have not blocked access to it) to open Internet Explorer. If you are not blocking Internet Explorer access, enable this setting.

User Configuration | Policies | Administrative Templates | Desktop

- **Hide Internet Explorer Icon On Desktop**   This policy does not prevent users from launching Internet Explorer another way, but it removes the Internet Explorer icon from the desktop and also from the QuickLaunch toolbar on the taskbar.

To limit access to Internet Explorer, you can set a proxy setting on the browser to point to an internal Web page telling users that Internet access has been blocked, and disable the ability to change the proxy settings. This will allow access to intranet sites while keeping users off the Internet. To do so, configure the following policy:

User Configuration | Policies | Windows Settings | Internet Explorer Maintenance | Connection

- **Proxy Settings**   Set the proxy settings to a false internal address or to an internal Web site telling users that Internet access is forbidden from Terminal Services. Select the check box next to Do Not Use Proxy Server For Local (Intranet) Addresses.

User Configuration | Policies | Administrative Templates | Windows Components | Internet Explorer

- **Disable Changing Proxy Settings**   Enable this setting so users can't disable or change the proxy setting you defined.

If users need to access Internet Explorer to reach the Internet, you can at least stop them from changing browser settings by enabling the following settings controlling the display of the tabbed Tools dialog box:

User Configuration | Policies | Administrative Templates | Windows Components | Internet Explorer | Internet Control Panel

- **Disable The Advanced Page**   Enabling this setting blocks access to the Advanced page defining the security settings for Internet Explorer. (The Advanced page has other functions, but the security settings are most important to the safety of your terminal servers.)

- **Disable The Connections Page**   Enabling this setting blocks access to the Connections page, where users can configure VPN and proxy settings.

- **Disable The Content Page**   Enabling this setting blocks access to the Content page, where ratings and certificates are managed.

- **Disable The General Page**   Enabling this setting blocks access to the General page, where the home page settings, display settings, and browsing history are managed.

- **Disable The Privacy Page**   Enabling this setting blocks access to the Privacy page, which defines settings for blocking pop-up windows and the security settings for pages.

- **Disable The Programs Page**   Enabling this setting blocks access to the Programs page, where e-mail clients, default browser notifications, and browser add-ons are managed.

- **Disable The Security Page**   Enabling this setting blocks access to the Security page, where zone trust levels (and zone memberships) are set. This is another important page to lock down.

Restrict Access to System Drives

The goal is to keep users out of drives on the terminal server. Users aren't storing data on the terminal server, so they don't need to be able to do anything other than run the applications allotted to them. By default, ordinary users can't do much to the system drives—if they try to delete important files or published applications, they are prompted for administrative credentials. If they run management tools such as Terminal Services Configuration, they can view options but can't edit them. However, there's no reason for users to be poking around the system drive, so you need to know how to keep them from doing this.

User Configuration | Policies | Administrative Templates | Windows Components | Windows Explorer

- **Remove Map Network Drive And Disconnect Network Drive**   Enabling this setting removes the ability to map a network drive by right-clicking on My Computer or from the Tools menu in Windows Explorer and Network Sharing Center.

- **Remove Windows Explorer Default Context Menu**   Enabling this setting removes the window users get when they right-click an item in Windows Explorer; for instance, right-clicking My Computer provides users with a menu with the option to map a network drive or manage the computer.

- **Hide These Specified Drives In My Computer**   This setting does just what it says; it hides the drive letters you specify. It does not block access to the drives via other methods such as Run. Limit this setting to specific drive letters if you have mapped drives that users must have readily available. To really prevent access, use it in combination with the following policy:

- **Prevent Access To Drives From My Computer**   Enable this setting for drives A through D to prevent access to those drives, which are most likely the system drives, the floppy drive, and the CD-ROM drive. Users will see the drives but cannot open or search them. Limit this setting to specific drive letters if you have mapped drives that users need to access.

Prevent Users from Running Unwanted Applications

Your goal is to prevent users from running any applications to which you have not granted them access. As we'll discuss in Chapter 6, "Installing and Publishing Applications," publishing applications via the RemoteApp Manager adds them to the *allow list* of applications that may be launched locally. However, after a user makes a connection to the terminal server, the allow list has no further effect. In this section, we'll talk about the default ways to restrict program access.

Direct from the Field: The Simplest Way to Lock Down a Terminal Server

What's the simplest thing you can do to lock down a terminal server? Remove the "execute" permissions from everywhere they don't need to be. Do users really need to be able to execute programs from their home drives, temporary Internet files, or the outlook attachment cache folder? Of course not! And by preventing them from doing so using this method, you remove about 99.99 percent of all possible ways to execute "rogue" software on your terminal server.

Whether you remove these permissions via Group Policy (with a Software Restriction Policies disallowed path rule) or via good old-fashioned editing of NTFS permissions depends largely on your environment and what else you might be doing. But the bottom line is that there are only a few instances in which users actually must be able to run programs (such as the "Windows" and "Program Files" folders, for example). For everything else on a server (and the network), remove those permissions!

Brian Madden

Independent Technology Analyst, Author, Terminal Services MVP, and Editor in Chief of BrianMadden.com

User Configuration | Policies | Administrative Templates | System

- **Don't Run Specified Windows Applications**   This is the blacklist approach—starting with everything and then defining applications that are not allowed to run. Blacklists aren't the most effective way to manage applications, because executable names change (or new executables are created) and blacklists don't take changes into account.

  This policy does not stop users from copying the executable file from another computer, renaming it, and running the same application under another name. A better way to block application execution is to implement Software Restriction Policies.

- **Run Only Specified Applications**   This is a white-list approach—starting from nothing and then adding programs that are allowed to run. This approach is more secure than the blacklist approach because it does restrict even new executables, but it can be difficult to implement because of unexpected application dependencies.

Enabling this setting and adding executables to the corresponding list prevents all programs except the ones on the list from running. However, it does not stop users from copying an executable file from another computer, renaming it to match an application known to be exempt, and running it that way.

Computer Configuration | Policies | Administrative Templates | Windows Components | Terminal Server | Connections

- **Allow Remote Start Of Unlisted Programs**   When disabled, this policy prevents users from launching any application via RDP other than the ones specified in the allow list. Again, be aware that this does not affect locally run programs. If you log on to the terminal server and are presented with a desktop, then you can still run other programs that are not on the RemoteApps list.

Because the Group Policy settings don't check for anything except the filename, a better approach to blocking application execution is to implement Software Restriction Policies.

Using Software Restriction Policies

Software Restriction Policies block unauthorized applications, scripts, macros, or any other executables from running on a terminal server. They're implemented through Group Policy on the terminal server that's checked every time a piece of software is run. It can be set as a user or a computer policy (or both), which means that administrators have the flexibility to allow or deny software for groups of users or for everyone who logs on to a terminal server.

Depending on how you set up the policy, one of two things happens. Either the software is expressly denied or not allowed by the policy and it does not run, or the software is specifically allowed or not denied by the policy and it executes. The reason software can be seen as either expressly allowed or not denied and vice versa is because there are three ways to set up the policy.

A Software Restriction Policy is made up of two parts: a security level and additional rules. The security level is an overall rule that reflects the method you will use to restrict software access. You have three choices:

Computer Configuration | Policies | Windows Settings | Security Options | Software Restriction Policies | Security Levels

These GPO settings will be available after you create a policy.

- **Unrestricted**   This is the least secure method. It allows all programs to be executed except those you specifically deny.

- **Basic User**   This method is considered an intermediate level of security. Unless there is an exception found for this rule, software will run as a normal user (without administrative privileges).

- **Disallowed**   This is the strictest, but also the most secure, method. It does not allow any programs to run except those you specifically allow. If you choose to use this method, take care to fully test the policy before activating it on production computers, so you find all software dependencies.

When you have chosen your security level, you then make exceptions to this overall rule for specific applications or types of applications or code by creating additional rules with a different default rule applied. There are four types of additional rules you can create to make exceptions to the security level:

Computer Configuration | Policies | Windows Settings | Security Settings | Software Restriction Policies | Additional Rules

These GPO settings will be available after you create a policy.

- **Hash Rule**   A *hash* is like a digital fingerprint of a piece of software. Using the piece of software as an input to an algorithm, the algorithm then creates a representation (a hash) of the piece of software based on its contents instead of other ways, such as its location or its name. If you change anything about the software, its hash is no longer valid and it will not execute.

- **Certificate Rule**   A certificate rule uses code-signing digital certificates to identify software. You can issue code-signing certificates to your software and use them to identify the software on the terminal server by checking the digital signature in the certificate.

 Note Basic User security level is not supported for certificate rules.

- **Path Rule**   This rule identifies a specific path of an application and only the application in that path can be allowed or denied. A specific piece of code (such as Winword.exe) can be expressed in the path or the path can point to a folder. If the latter, all code in the folder is allowed or denied. For example, if you host Microsoft Office 2007 applications on your terminal server, you can point to the Microsoft Office installation directory. All code in that directory will be allowed or denied depending on the policy security level and additional rule settings. Environmental variables, UNC paths, registry paths, question marks, and asterisk wildcards can be used in path rules.

- **Network Zone Rule**   This rule only applies to .msi files, so is probably not very useful in locking down a terminal server except when installing software. The network zone rule allows or denies software installation (.msi files only) based on which Internet zones it was downloaded from.

These rules are applied from the most specific to the most general in nature. Certificate rules are extremely specific about the software they represent, followed by hash rules, then path rules, and finally, Internet zone rules are the least specific. Any software not covered by one of these additional rules is controlled by the default security level (default rule).

As an example, let's create a software restriction policy that will affect domain users in the following ways when they log on to your terminal server(s):

- Domain users can run Microsoft Office 2007 applications.
- Domain users cannot run Internet Explorer.
- Domain users cannot run Cmd.exe or Control.exe (Control Panel).
- Domain users cannot run any software on the terminal server that is not installed on the terminal server. For instance, if a user copies Cmd.exe from her local computer to her roaming profile desktop and then tries to launch this application from the terminal server, you want the action to fail.

This example assumes you have your terminal servers placed in their own OU, and if you have multiple terminal servers, that they are configured identically.

Because you want to affect the domain users group when they log on to the terminal server, create a software restriction policy in the user section of a GPO, located here:

User Configuration | Policies | Windows Settings | Security Settings | Software Restriction Policies

Note   The Software Restriction Policy setting for Computers is located at: Computer Configuration | Policies | Windows Settings | Security Settings | Software Restriction Policies.

Open the Group Policy Management console (GPMC), and create a new GPO; in this example it is named TS Software Restriction Policy. Then navigate to the Software Restriction Policies folder, right-click the folder, and choose New Software Restriction Policies.

To keep software not installed on the terminal server from running on the terminal server, you need to disallow all software from running on the terminal server, and then make exceptions to this rule for software located in specific places on the terminal server.

Click the Security Levels folder, and in the right pane, right-click Disallowed and choose Set as Default. Now you need to create the exceptions to this default rule. So you don't lock yourself out and so you can run applications installed on the terminal server, Microsoft creates two exceptions to the Disallowed security level and places them in the Additional Rules folder when you create a new software restriction policy. They are:

- %HKEY_LOCAL_MACHINE\SOFTWARE\Microsoft\WindowsNT\Current Version\SystemRoot%

  The security level for this additional rule is set to Unrestricted; it allows access to items in the server system root folder (C:\Windows). Users need access to some items in the Windows folder to log on, so keep this setting.

- %HKEY_LOCAL_MACHINE\SOFTWARE\Microsoft\Windows\Current Version\ProgramFilesDir%

  The security level for this additional rule is set to Unrestricted and allows access to the items in the Program Files Directory. Internet Explorer happens to be installed to this directory, so delete this rule, because one of the goals is to block access to Internet Explorer.

Users currently have unrestricted access to Cmd.exe and Control.exe because of the additional rule that allows unrestricted access to the Windows folder; Windows contains the System32 folder, which is where these applications reside. Therefore, you need to make additional rules to deny access for these specific applications. Right-click the Additional Rules folder and choose New Path Rule. Enter the path to Cmd.exe in the Path text box (C:\Windows\System32\Cmd.exe), change the Security Level to Disallowed, type a description of the rule, and click OK. Then do the same thing for Control.exe.

To allow Microsoft Office software to run, create another path rule, type the path to Microsoft Office (typically C:\Program Files\Microsoft Office), and change the Security Level to Unrestricted. Type a description of the rule and click OK. To apply this GPO to the Domain Users group, change the Security Filtering on the GPO by removing Authenticated Users Group and adding the Domain Users group. Apply the GPO to the OU where the terminal server(s) reside, and you are done.

Now, if you don't already have loopback policy processing enabled, create a computer GPO, apply loopback processing, and then apply the GPO to the terminal server OU. This applies the user software restriction policy to the users specified in the user software restriction policy security filtering.

If you set Software Restriction Policies (SRPs) using a computer GPO, you will likely want to forgo applying this policy to the local administrator account. To do this, click the Software Restriction Policies folder, double-click the Enforcement setting, and choose to Apply Software Restriction Policies To The Following Users: All Users Except Local Administrators. Click OK.

Keeping the Terminal Server Available

Finally, some Group Policy settings allow you to improve the user experience through limiting access or shortening logon times.

Allow or Deny Access to the Terminal Server

Although users cannot log on to the terminal server unless they are members of the local Remote Desktop Users group on that terminal server, you can also control the ability to log on via Group Policy.

- Computer Configuration | Policies | Administrative Templates | Windows Components | Terminal Server | Allow Users To Connect Remotely Using Terminal Services

  This setting controls whether or not users can remotely access the terminal server. A terminal server will not accept any user logons until its Remote Desktop Users group is populated. This policy gives you more granular control over who has access to the terminal servers and will allow you to keep some users from using up licenses you'd intended for other users. You can also use this policy to block access to a terminal server so you can perform maintenance on it.

> **Note** It's also possible to prevent logons to the terminal server via ADUC; one option in the user account properties defines whether or not users are allowed to log on to the terminal server (they are, by default).

Limit the Number of Terminal Server Connections

For application licensing reasons or performance reasons, you may want to limit the number of simultaneous connections to the server.

- Computer Configuration | Policies | Administrative Templates | Windows Components | Terminal Server | Limit Number Of Connections

  Enable the Limit Number Of Connections setting to limit the total number of simultaneous connections that can be active on a terminal server. If you have 100 users, and each user is limited to one session, you know that you can limit the number of connections to approximately 100 and not interfere with user access. This also ensures you won't allow more connections than are needed.

Setting Session Time Limits

Setting session time limits can be a delicate balancing act. For example, the longer that disconnected sessions are available before being terminated, the more time users have to reconnect. Reconnecting to an existing session is faster than creating a new session, and reconnecting to an existing session keeps the user locked into a particular terminal server.

However, disconnected sessions still require some memory. Not much is needed, because when a session is disconnected, the data stored in physical memory is high on the list to be paged to disk, but it does require some memory. If the terminal server is memory-constrained, disconnected sessions may have an effect on performance.

You can set session limits defining how long sessions may be active or idle before they're disconnected. However, you can't set session time limits on a granular basis for individual RemoteApps. All RemoteApps using the same session will follow the same rules.

Remote Control of User Sessions

You've probably experienced this. You have a problem with your computer or with an application. Something just isn't right—for example, you can't format the spreadsheet the way you want even though you're sure you're doing it properly. Someone stops by your desk and asks why you're beating your head against the monitor. When you explain that the spreadsheet isn't working properly, your co-worker asks you to show him what's not working. You do it again, and it works perfectly this time.

You can enable this phenomenon on a terminal sever even without someone standing behind you. One way in which remote sessions on a terminal server can be useful is that it is simple to troubleshoot problems by shadowing a user's session. Client desktop systems support Remote Assistance, but sessions running on a terminal server are even easier to monitor using the Terminal Services Manager tool. We'll talk about how to use Remote Control later in Chapter 8, "Managing the Terminal Server Runtime Environment," but for now we'll focus on the permissions options and how to set them.

> **Note** Only members of the Administrators or Domain Administrators group are allowed to shadow sessions on the terminal server, so you don't need to worry about users spying on each other. Remote Control is only supported with full desktops, not with TS RemoteApps.

You can define the way Remote Control works from the terminal server, from the user account properties in ADUC, or using Group Policy on either a per-server or per-user basis.

There are two levels of interaction with a Remote Control session. First, you can use it to view the user setting. This setting allows both the user and the administrator to see the session at the same time, but only permits the user to interact with it. The other option is to allow the administrator to interact with the user's session.

There are three options for Remote Control:

- You can disable it entirely. This setting will prevent administrators from using Remote Control on user sessions. This is the most secure option, but the least helpful.

- You can enable it but require the user's permission for an administrator to connect to the session.

- You can enable it and not require any notification.

Of the three, we prefer the second option, to require user permission. That makes it very clear that the Remote Control session has begun and gives users a feeling of privacy while still allowing administrators to help them. This option also makes it less likely that an administrator will mistakenly pick the wrong session to shadow, since the user they pick in error will see a notification message and the correct user won't see anything.

To configure Remote Control Settings for individual terminal servers, go to Start | Administrative Tools | Terminal Services and open Terminal Services Configuration. In the Connections sections at the top of the middle pane, you'll see an entry for RDP-Tcp. Double-click it to open the RDP-Tcp Properties dialog box and go to the Remote Control tab shown in Figure 5-13.

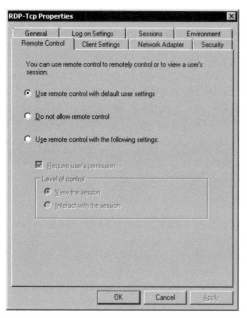

FIGURE 5-13 Configuring computer properties for Remote Control

As you can see, the default settings allow the per-user settings to override. To configure Remote Control settings on a per-user basis, open Active Directory Users And Computers and open a user's account properties as shown in Figure 5-14.

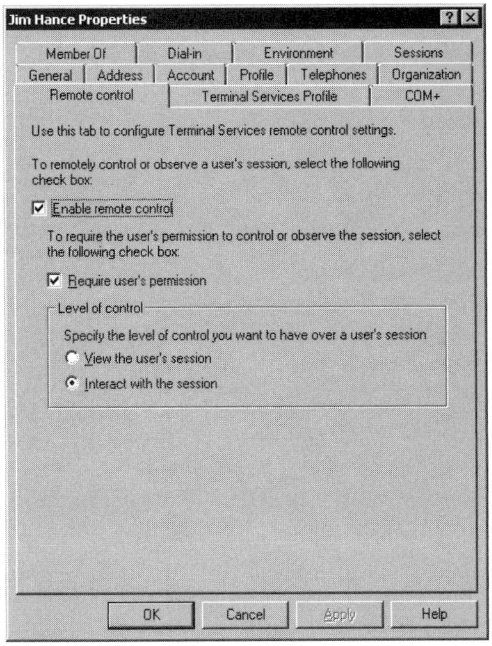

FIGURE 5-14 Configuring user account properties for Remote Control

To set remote settings using Group Policy, configure Set Rules For Remote Control Of Terminal Server User Sessions. You can set the policy on a per-computer or per-user basis. For computers, the policy is located in Computer Configuration | Policies | Windows Components | Terminal Services | Connections. For users, it's in User Configuration | Policies | Windows Components | Terminal Services | Connections. Enable the policy and then edit the settings to pick the appropriate option shown in Figure 5-15.

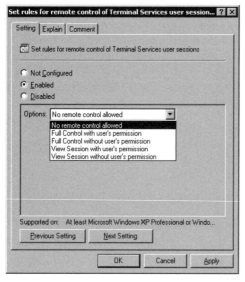

FIGURE 5-15 You can edit the Remote Control Group Policy for users or for all terminal servers.

If you don't configure the policy or any remote control settings, then the settings in ADUC will control by default, and Remote Control sessions will be allowed with the user's permission, with administrators allowed to interact with the session.

Unless there's a really good reason to configure Remote Control settings differently for discrete sets of people, you should configure them for all terminal servers in the same way. Having different policies for different people could easily confuse administrators and render the Remote Control option less useful.

Summary

Effective use of redirected devices is important in making the remote experience feel local. In this chapter, we've discussed the components of Windows Server 2008 that enable device and resource direction to a remote session, including virtual channels, the PnP Device Redirection Framework, the legacy printing architecture, and the new Easy Print architecture. This chapter has also explained how to lock down components of the terminal server so that you can enable the richest possible experience while protecting the terminal server from malicious or careless users.

Here are some of the best practices covered in this chapter:

■ To maximize session responsiveness, consider available bandwidth. For low-bandwidth scenarios, adjust the bulk compression algorithm to use less bandwidth and more memory.

- Use Group Policy to configure user settings if possible. All settings are in Group Policy and not all are represented in either ADUC or the Terminal Services Configuration Tool.

- Use TS Easy Print wherever possible. If it is not available, use the Printers Console to distribute drivers so all terminal servers are using identical print drivers

- Lock down the terminal server by removing the ability to browse the operating system and permitting only authorized executables to run.

- Limit usage of the terminal servers and limit session counts to keep control of licensing for applications licensed on a per-connection basis and optimize performance on the terminal servers.

Additional Resources

The following resources are related to topics covered in this chapter. You can find the links on this book's companion CD.

- For more information about the User-Mode Driver Framework, see *http://msdn2.microsoft.com/en-us/library/aa510983.aspx*.

- To find out what the Terminal Services Team Blog has to say about device redirection, see *http://blogs.msdn.com/ts/archive/tags/Device+Redirection/default.aspx*.

- For more information about XPS and to see some applications that use XPS, go to *http://www.microsoft.com/whdc/xps/default.mspx*.

- The enhanced metafile format (EMF) specification from Microsoft is available online at *http://download.microsoft.com/download/a/e/6/ae6e4142-aa58-45c6-8dcf-a657e5900cd3/%5BMS-EMF%5D.pdf*.

- For more information about Software Restriction Policies, see *http://go.microsoft .com/fwlink/?LinkID=92567*.

- To download Quest Software's PowerShell provider, go to *http://www.quest.com/ powershell/activeroles-server.aspx*. This link is also provided on the companion CD.

- For examples of how to use Quest Software's PowerShell provider to check Terminal Services user attributes, see *http://dmitrysotnikov.wordpress.com/2008/02/13/ managing-terminal-services-attributes-with-powershell/*.

- To download RDP 6.1 for Windows XP SP2, go to *http://www.microsoft.com/downloads/ details.aspx?FamilyId=6E1EC93D-BDBD-4983-92F7-479E088570AD&displaylang=en*. This link is also provided on the companion CD.

Chapter 6
Installing and Publishing Applications

Terminal servers are essentially centralized personal computers (PCs) shared by many users. As such, they're not very interesting without user applications installed on them. This chapter discusses the process of installing applications on a terminal server and publishing those applications through Terminal Services RemoteApps (TS RemoteApps), one of the core features of Terminal Services in Windows Server 2008. In this chapter, we'll cover:

- How applications install on a terminal server

- How installation settings are added to user profiles

- How TS RemoteApps work

- Publishing applications

- Signing Remote Desktop Protocol (RDP) files

- Best practices for distributing TS RemoteApps

- Best practices for TS RemoteApp management

- Integrating TS RemoteApps and Terminal Services Web Access (TS Web Access)

Installing Applications on a Terminal Server

Installing an application on a terminal server is different from installing the same application on Windows Vista. When you install an application on Windows Vista (or Windows Server 2008 when not configured as a terminal server), you're generally prompted to choose whether you want to install that application for all users of the computer or just for the user who is currently logged on. The installation performed for all users differs from the installation performed for a specific user. The differences between these choices are explained in Table 6-1.

TABLE 6-1 Installation Options for Windows Server 2008/Windows Vista

Option	All Users	Current User
Shortcuts	Installed in All Users profile	Installed in current user's profile
Listing in Programs and Features in Control Panel	For all users	For the current user only
COM registration	HKLM\Software\Classes	HKCU\Software\Classes
Run with executive privileges	Yes	Optional
Storage location for icons and transform files	%WinDir%\Installer\ {ProductCode}	%UserProfile%\AppData\Microsoft\ Installer\{ProductCode GUID}

There are few surprises here: the per-user installation stores all relevant data in the user's profile. An all-users installation stores the relevant data on a per-computer basis (or in All Users so that the terminal server is ready to add more users to the application).

Which Applications Will Work?

Most newer applications will run on a terminal server, but you can't assume that every application will perform successfully. As you know if you've used Terminal Services in the past, not all applications, especially older applications, work on a terminal server. Sometimes the problem is that the application is too resource-intensive to share, or it may require too many graphical updates to update the client-side display properly (rendering applications come to mind). But sometimes the problem is more subtle than that. Fundamentally, most applications were designed originally with the assumption that they would be running only on a single computer—DOS applications were even designed to assume that they were the only program running on the computer at a given time—and the way they store data and the permissions they need may reflect that assumption.

Broadly speaking, most application compatibility problems come from one of five sources:

- Installation
- Concurrent resource usage
- Privacy issues
- Performance issues
- Device redirection

Let's look at each of these in more detail.

Application Installation

Many application installations are designed for a single-user computer. This means that such an application was created with certain assumptions, for example, that it's acceptable to store settings in HKCU, which would render them inaccessible to other users, or to store settings in INI files in the Windows directory.

One application-compatibility setting that is available to developers to avoid these kinds of problems is the */TSAWARE* option, which is in a program's header file. For example, applications designed to be multi-user aware should not use INI files to store settings. The */TSAWARE* switch provides a workaround for applications that were not necessarily designed for a multi-user environment so that if an application does use INI files, the terminal server will accommodate this during installation by creating virtual Windows directories for each user in which to store the INI files. Without this option, applications using INI files will have a single configuration file, and everyone using the application will have the same settings.

Unfortunately, there's no way for an administrator to check to see if the */TSAWARE* option has been set in an application. If you have a homegrown application that depends on INI files, however, you can check with the developer to see if it is TS-aware so that INI files will be stored on a per-user basis.

Concurrent Resource Usage

Many instances of the same application run concurrently on a terminal server. If the applications want to use the same physical port, write to the same files, or write to the same portions of the registry, they won't work on a terminal server. If two applications attempt to write to the same file at the same time, this can lead to data corruption; if they write to the same file at different times (perhaps to the same INI file, as in the previous section), then this can lead to unexpected behavior.

Privacy Issues

Although the architecture of a terminal server session is designed to keep session memory areas separate, applications also must honor this in the way they share files. If those files store any private data (for example, the Web pages a user has viewed), then the applications can't use the same files.

Performance Issues

By definition, applications running on a terminal server must share disk I/O, processor time, and physical memory. If an application needs a lot of any of those, then it's probably not a good fit for a terminal server. (Even the CPU throttling discussed in Chapter 3, "Installing the Core Terminal Server Environment," only divides CPU time more evenly—it doesn't make more of it.) Similarly, if an application's screen updates can't refresh quickly enough given the available bandwidth, then it may not be a good candidate for remote execution.

Device Redirection

As discussed in Chapter 5, "Fine-Tuning the User Experience," Windows Server 2008 terminal servers can redirect new kinds of resources. They can't, however, redirect *everything*—or at least, they can't support all features (e.g., ActiveSync) if they do. Some devices will not work in a remote session.

What can you do about these limitations of applications and device redirection? First, you can do some checking ahead of time so that you will know which applications will work and which will not. One option is search some Web sites to find out what applications have been packaged to work on a terminal server, because if someone else has been able to make the application work, then at least you know that it can be done. (The software provider visionapp, for example, maintains a list of this kind at *http://visionapp.com/1701.0.html?&ftu=7074772b28*.) Another option is to analyze the applications themselves, using the Application Analyzer tool available on the Resource Kit CD and described in the following sidebar.

> ### Direct from the Source: Introducing the TS Application Analyzer
>
> TS Application Analyzer is a tool for administrators who are using terminal services and want to determine the compatibility of an application with TS before deploying it.
>
> The TS Application Analyzer uses the Microsoft Application Verifier as the back end. When you analyze an application, the tool intercepts function calls from that application into the operating system and notes the calls and the parameters that have been passed. Depending on the function call and the parameters passed, it decides whether this call is going to cause problems in the TS environment and categorizes the results as warnings or problems.
>
> The full documentation for TS Application Analyzer is available on this book's companion CD, but following are a few things to keep in mind when running the analyzer:
>
> - This tool primarily focuses on issues relating to concurrent usage and privacy. The potential problems it highlights may not always manifest. Understanding this is critical to interpreting the results correctly and effectively using the information they provide. Simply because an application generates no errors does not mean, for example, that it is not resource intensive.
>
> - The problems that the TS Application Analyzer identifies are not necessarily insurmountable. This tool breaks down issues into several categories by issue

type, such as File, Registry, and so on. The tool also breaks down the issues into two levels of severity: Warnings and Problems. Most of the time you should focus on the problems, unless you are actually trying to pinpoint a problem source (which a developer or tester might do).

- It's important to understand that when the TS Application Analyzer identifies a problem, the tool has detected that the application has made a non–TS-compatible API call, but this call itself can be a part of a condition in the application. For example, it may say, "Try to open this file as an administrator, but if you can't do that, then just open it as a normal user." In this case, the TS Application Analyzer would still see that the application tried to open a file as an administrator and it would flag this as a problem. Therefore, just because something shows up as a problem, you may find that it needs interpretation to determine if it's a real problem.

Anubhav Kushwaha

Program Manager II

Storing Application-Specific Data

Installing applications on a terminal server is somewhat different from both the per-user or all-users installation options performed on a PC or server without terminal services installed. The situation is different; in this case, you want all users who access the terminal server to be able to use the application, but you also want them to be able to maintain their settings in their profiles so those settings will follow them between terminal servers. Therefore, when you install applications on a terminal server, the operating system combines the two approaches. Application binaries are stored to be accessible to anyone connected to the terminal server, but the operating system stores some settings in a particular part of HKLM called the *shadow key*. The location of this key will vary with the operating system and application type:

- 32-bit versions of Windows Server 2008 store shadow key information for 32-bit applications in HKLM\Software\Microsoft\Windows NT\CurrentVersion\Terminal Server\Install\Software. (Obviously, you can't install or run 64-bit applications on a 32-bit operating system.)

- 64-bit versions of Windows Server 2008 store shadow key information for 32-bit applications in HKLM\Software\Wow6432Node\Microsoft\Windows NT\CurrentVersion\ Terminal Server\Install\Software.

- 64-bit versions of Windows Server 2008 store shadow key information for 64-bit applications in HKLM\Software\Microsoft\Windows NT\CurrentVersion\Terminal Server\Install\Software.

The shadow key stores configuration settings for all the applications installed on the terminal server, divided by publisher. When a user logs on, the contents of this key are copied to her profile, as long as the contents of the key are newer than the contents in the profile. The operating system determines the relative age of the configuration data in the user profile and in the shadow key by comparing the values of two registry keys, both of which record last write-time in seconds since 1970. The key in the user profile is LastUserIniSyncTime, stored in HKCU\Software\Microsoft\Windows NT\CurrentVersion\Terminal Server; the date of the shadow key is stored in LatestRegistryKey in HKLM\SOFTWARE\Microsoft\Windows NT\CurrentVersion\Terminal Server\Install\IniFileTimes. If the profile is newer, the settings aren't copied; if the configuration in the shadow key is newer, the user profile is updated with the data in the shadow key. You don't want to update the central data source, so the user profile will *never* update the shadow key.

How It Works: 32-Bit Applications in a 64-Bit World

It's important to separate registry data for 32-bit and 64-bit applications so that they don't load the wrong DLLs or overwrite each other's configuration data. Therefore, 64-bit applications on a 64-bit server use the keys and values stored in HKLM\Software, and the 32-bit applications use the keys and values stored in HKLM\Software\Wow6432Node. Under each key, the structure is approximately the same.

It would be impossible to support 32-bit applications on a 64-bit operating system if all 32-bit applications had to be rewritten to support this compatibility key. Instead, to make this work, 64-bit versions of Windows use *registry redirection* to intercept calls to the registry. If a 32-bit application (or component, for that matter) tries to read from or write to the registry, then the operating system WOW64 subsystem intercepts the request and redirects it to the appropriate path of the registry. If 64-bit applications attempt to access the registry, the WOW64 subsystem ignores the call.

Sometimes both 32-bit and 64-bit applications need the same data, but they must read from their own section of the registry. For data that both versions need, the operating system employs *registry reflection*. Registry reflection updates both the 32-bit section and the 64-bit section. This is done mainly for operations such as file association (HKLM\Software\Classes) to ensure that the same application always opens a file with a particular extension. Registry reflection ensures that the contents of the Classes key are maintained in parallel for both the 32-bit and 64-bit sections of the registry.

For our purposes here, the implications of this are that 64-bit versions of Windows maintain two areas for shadow keys: one for 32-bit applications and one for 64-bit applications.

Avoiding Overwriting User Profile Data

The decision to overwrite or not overwrite the user profile is done solely by the relative age of the data in the profile and the shadow key. If you add more servers to the farm, the new servers will have a newer date than the older servers. This can lead to problems, as the newer terminal servers overwrite the user-updated data in the user profile because it's apparently newer. As an example of how this could affect the user, let's say that you had a terminal server with Microsoft Office 2007 installed on it. You allow users to customize their application experience, so they change which toolbars are visible. When you introduce a new terminal server, the default settings on the new terminal server will have a newer time stamp than the user profile time stamp. When the user logs onto the new terminal server, the changes the user had made and grown to rely on would be overwritten with the default options on the new server. You can get around this problem in one of several ways:

- Create new servers from images of old servers.
- Ensure the shadow key time stamps on the new servers are older than the user profile.
- Remove the keys from the shadow key.
- Prevent updates to existing profile data.

Edit the Shadow Key Time Stamps

Since the decision to write or not is based on whether the information in the user profile is older than the data in the shadow key, one approach is to ensure that the shadow key is always older than any data in the user profile. You can set the clocks back on new servers before installing applications. The number of seconds since 1970 is determined by the clock on the operating system, not the system clock on the motherboard, so it's not hard to fool. You just need to ensure that you're consistent about the date you set the terminal servers to.

An after-the-fact approach could be to change the time stamps on the registry keys. Terminal Server MVP Brian Madden has posted two Microsoft Product Support Services (PSS) tools for Windows 2000 Server on his Web site that allow you to set the registry time stamp (Sdt.exe) and check dates for the shadow keys programmatically (Rdt.exe). The tools are easy to use; Sdt.exe allows you to supply new dates for the registry as sdt *day month year*, and Rdt.exe outputs the data in a human-readable form that looks like this snippet:

```
Key: Software\Microsoft\Windows NT\Current Version\Terminal Server\Install\
Software. Subkeys 1, timestamp 5:22:18:882 on 3/12/2008
Key: Microsoft. Subkeys 3, timestamp 19:25:38:51 on 3/12/2008
Key: Multimedia. Subkeys 1, timestamp 19:25:35:316 on 3/12/2008
Key: Audio. Subkeys 1, timestamp 19:25:35:379 on 3/12/2008
Key: WaveFormats. Subkeys 0, timestamp 19:25:35:379 on 3/12/2008
Key: Office. Subkeys 1, timestamp 19:25:38:51 on 3/12/2008
Key: 12.0. Subkeys 1, timestamp 19:25:38:51 on 3/12/2008
Key: Common. Subkeys 1, timestamp 19:25:38:51 on 3/12/2008
```

```
Key: LanguageResources. Subkeys 0, timestamp 19:25:38:51 on 3/12/2008
Key: Windows. Subkeys 1, timestamp 5:22:18:882 on 3/12/2008
Key: CurrentVersion. Subkeys 4, timestamp 21:8:11:851 on 3/12/2008
Key: Explorer. Subkeys 2, timestamp 19:51:42:384 on 3/12/2008
Key: FileExts. Subkeys 1, timestamp 19:51:42:384 on 3/12/2008
Key: DDECache. Subkeys 1, timestamp 19:51:42:384 on 3/12/2008
Key: IExplore. Subkeys 1, timestamp 19:51:42:384 on 3/12/2008
Key: WWW_OpenURL. Subkeys 0, timestamp 19:51:42:400 on 3/12/2008
Key: MountPoints2. Subkeys 3, timestamp 19:51:41:212 on 3/12/2008
Key: {dbca535b-ea4c-11dc-939f-806e6f6e6963}. Subkeys 0, timestamp
19:51:41:212 on 3/12/2008
```

However, because Rdt.exe was written for Windows 2000, it is not 64-bit aware and reads only the main shadow key; you can't see or edit the time stamps on the HKLM\Software\ Wow6432Node that 32-bit applications refer to. (No, the tool doesn't take arguments for the registry key to read or edit.) For 64-bit operating systems, you will need either to be proactive about setting the system time beforehand or take one of the following approaches: remove the sections or disable writes to the profile.

> **Note** If you're interested in trying out these tools for 32-bit environments, see Brian Madden's blog entry on the subject: *http://www.brianmadden.com/content/article/Finally-Shadow-Key-Timestamping-Utilities-from-Microsoft.*

Removing Sections from Shadow Keys

Another way to prevent the keys from being updated in the user profile is to delete them from the shadow key. If you do so, of course they won't be added to the user profile, and you'll need to apply them with logon scripts.

The advantage to this approach is that it ensures that the keys won't overwrite the user profile. The disadvantage, of course, is that it takes some work to set this up and more to maintain it. You need to delete the contents of the shadow key on all terminal servers, and you must ensure that all users get the keys added to their session. Additionally, if you add more applications, you must update the logon scripts.

Selectively Disabling Registry Writes

Rather than removing the contents of the shadow key, you can selectively control registry propagation. Go to HKLM\Software\Microsoft\Windows NT\CurrentVersion\Terminal Server\ Compatibility\RegistryEntries*PathName*, where *PathName* is the path to the key you don't want updated (located in HKCU\Software). For example, if you examine the contents of this path, you'll see that Microsoft\Windows\CurrentVersion\Explorer\Shell Folders is already there.

Note For 32-bit applications on a 64-bit operating system, edit the path to HKLM\Software\
Wow6432Node\Microsoft\Windows NT\CurrentVersion\Terminal Server\Compatibility\
RegistryEntries*PathName*.

The tricky bit here lies in the value assigned to this key to control propagation. By default,
Microsoft\Windows\CurrentVersion\Explorer\Shell Folders has a value of 108 hex. This value
is actually the result of compatibility bits. A value of 8 hex means that the path points to a
32-bit application. The 100 part comes from the configuration of registry mapping. If this bit
is set (which means it has a value of 100), then new entries from the system master registry
image will be added to the user profile when the application is started, but no existing data
will be deleted or changed. If this bit is not set (has a value of 0, or isn't present), the operating system deletes and overwrites the user's registry data if it is older than the system master
registry data.

Therefore, to prevent a Win32 application registry settings from being updated in the user
profile, provide the path to the key in HKEY_USERS where that application data is stored and
give it a value here of 108 in hex.

Populating the Shadow Key

How does this data get into the shadow key in the first place? The answer depends on the
type of application installation. Applications that install from Microsoft Windows Installer
files (MSIs) work differently from applications that install from EXE files, and the changes can
have real implications for the way the shadow key captures registry settings.

Direct from the Source: Two Models for Application Installation on Windows Server 2008

Not all applications install in exactly the same way. The following information describes
how MSIs differ from applications that do not install from MSIs.

The Pre-MSI Model

In the pre-MSI model, applications are typically installed by running a custom Setup.exe
file or a common installation tool such as InstallShield. Such setups do not visibly
distinguish per-user configuration from per-machine configuration, so there is no easy
way for terminal servers to capture the per-user related changes and propagate such
changes to each user's hive. Hence, what's called "install mode" is used, which puts the
session (not the machine) into install mode. This records any registry key operation in
that session, no matter what process makes the changes. For example, if the administrator decides to change his home page while installing an application in install mode,
that change will also be recorded. Therefore, it is important not to take any actions

while an installation is ongoing that do not pertain directly to the installation. When the installation finishes, the session should be put back into the execute mode.

Related commands are *change user /install* and *change user /execute*. The "recording" of registry key changes is saved in the registry under HKLM\SOFTWARE\Microsoft\ Windows NT\CurrentVersion\Terminal Server\Install\Software.

While in install mode, changes to the Start menu are also tracked, and then those changes are moved to the all-users menu so that shortcuts are visible to all users.

When a user logs on, Userinit.exe checks to see if the user's hive under HKCU\Software has or is missing keys from the equivalent path above. If anything is added, or changed, it compares the two paths and takes appropriate action by adding keys/values from the HKLM path.

The MSI Model

Applications with MSI-based setup install differently. Since the advent of MSI, a centralized service is now responsible for installation, so there is no need to track registry key changes made by any or all programs in a session. Instead, we need to track only the registry key changes made by the MSI infrastructure. Additionally, MSI has options to make per-user installation appear as a global installation for all users (although this is mostly limited to user interface elements such as the Start menu or Desktop shortcuts). Since applications continue to install registry keys (in HKCU) during installation, we need to record such changes and propagate them to every user. We must track these changes, but the scope is limited to changes made by the MSI infrastructure. Therefore, there is no need to put the session into install mode. Instead, we have a private contract with the MSI service to capture the HKCU-related changes.

MSI detects that it is running on a terminal server and makes all per-user changes in the system context instead of a user's context, which means that instead of changes to installer's HKCU, changes go into System's HKCU (which is HKU\.DEFAULT\ Software). Before MSI makes any per-user changes, it makes a reference copy of HKU\. DEFAULT\Software, after which MSI runs and makes all the required changes while installing the application package.

When MSI has finished the installation, it signals the end of this transaction, which runs a side-by-side comparison of the before and after states of the HKU\.DEFAULT\ Software trees. When the comparison is complete, MSI saves the delta in HKLM\ SOFTWARE\Microsoft\Windows NT\CurrentVersion\Terminal Server\Install\Software. When a user logs on, the same model as before is used to copy registry keys into the user's hive.

One final note: MSI permits a model of installation called *custom actions*, which is a type of installation that MSI doesn't support natively, but which is implemented by a custom DLL that has been loaded by a vendor. This custom action can do whatever it wants, including rebooting the machine. Therefore, on terminal servers, MSI is hard-coded to refuse a per-user installation by a regular (nonadministrator) user.

Ara Bernardi

Senior Software Development Engineer

When you run an MSI file to install an application, this action sends a message to TSAppCompat component to prepare for installation. This component then creates a snapshot of HKCU\.Default\Software and saves it. When the MSI is done installing and making changes, the operating system blocks further installations.

Now, the TSAppCompat component walks the contents of HKCU\.Default\Software to compare the before and after, including all insertions, deletions, and changes. Having done so, it creates a delta of all the changes. This delta is what now populates the shadow key.

Only the contents of HKCU\.Default\Software are monitored. If the MSI launches another DLL (an infrequently used option), then the effects of that DLL will be ignored.

The *change user* command that comes with Windows Terminal Services and used when you run an installation routine such as Setup.exe is another matter. When you put the terminal server session into Install mode with the command change user /install, a different component named advapi32 monitors all registry changes—everything, not just changes that have anything to do with installing the application. So long as the terminal server session is in Install Mode, then the changes are recorded and copied to the user profile when they log on. For example, if you change the home page for Internet Explorer, you'll be recording this data and changing it for everybody.

Understanding TS RemoteApps Internals

TS RemoteApps work a little differently from applications displayed from a full remote desktop, because they must integrate with the locally installed applications. In essence, the server sends the entire desktop to the client. The client-side components create their own application windows to mirror those in the remote session.

Chapter 3, "Installing the Core Terminal Server Environment," explains the processes and startup mechanism for a remote session. With TS RemoteApps, the process is a little different; the client and server must be even more closely aligned (see Figure 6-1). When a client computer launches its first TS RemoteApp, it works as illustrated in Figure 6-1.

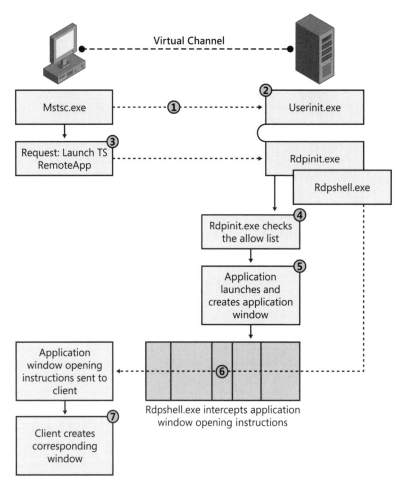

FIGURE 6-1 Starting a TS RemoteApp

The following steps explain this launch process:

1. Client connects to the server and starts TS RemoteApp session (but does not yet launch the application).

2. The session is created. Userinit.exe is launched, and it launches Rdpinit.exe, which manages Rdpshell.exe, the TS RemoteApp shell (in lieu of Windows Explorer).

3. The server-side and client-side components connect via a virtual channel used especially for TS RemoteApp communication.

4. Rdpinit.exe checks the allow list for the application. If the application is in the allow list, the terminal server launches the application.

5. The application launches and creates an application window.

6. Rdpshell.exe intercepts the application window opening instruction and sends it to the client.

7. The client creates a corresponding window to match the one on the terminal server.

From here, the user interacts with the remote session as usual.

As you can see, communication between the terminal server session and client is key to making this work. Let's explore TS RemoteApp components in more detail.

Server-Side Components

On the server, several components must cooperate to ensure the following:

- Only applications currently in the allow list may be launched as TS RemoteApps.

- The client-side proxy window must open and close in tune with the invisible application window on the terminal server.

- The components making this possible are:

  ❑ Rdpinit.exe

  ❑ Rdpshell.exe

  ❑ Rdpdd.dll

  ❑ The application window

Figure 6-2 depicts how the RemoteApps components work together to create the user experience. For more information about how this fits into the entire terminal server architecture, see Chapter 3.

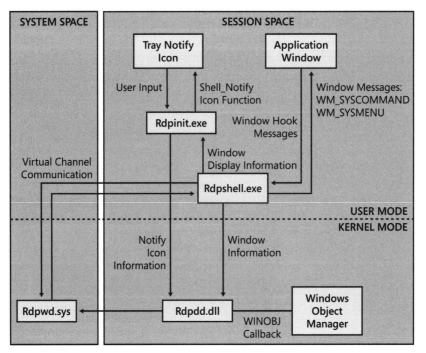

FIGURE 6-2 Server-side components enabling TS RemoteApps

Rdpinit.exe is the TS RemoteApp equivalent of Userinit.exe, which launches logon scripts and starts the user shell. Rdpinit.exe is the component responsible for launching the Rdpshell.exe and implements Shell_NotifyIcon to update the client-side taskbar via Rdpdd.dll. Rdpinit.exe also handles the logoff logic: When there are no more TS RemoteApps application windows open and no processes running in the user session that haven't exited, Rdpinit.exe disconnects or logs off the session in accordance with the rules set in Group Policy. (You can't configure this setting on the terminal server.)

Rdpshell.exe is the TS RemoteApp equivalent of Explorer.exe. It keeps track of changes to application windows (e.g., opening and closing) and sends them to the client-side components so that the application window visible to the client behaves exactly like the application window in the invisible shell. Rdpshell.exe also keeps track of any connect/disconnect/reconnect events to the remote session, so the application window on the client side disappears or reappears as appropriate.

Rdpdd.dll is the kernel-mode RDP display driver in the session. This component receives the windowing and system tray icon notifications from Rdpinit.exe and Rdpshell.exe and updates the display accordingly. It also sends all display updates to the terminal server to be sent to the session.

Client-Side Components

On the client side, other components cooperate to make the TS RemoteApp visible on the desktop and update the application window in the remote session (see Figure 6-3). These components include:

- Microsoft Terminal Service Client (MSTSC), including:
    - The RAIL plug-in
    - The windowing plug-in
    - The input and drawing orders handlers
- The RAIL proxy window
- The notify icon

> **Note** TS RemoteApps is the feature. The technology powering TS RemoteApps is called RemoteApps Integrated Locally (RAIL).

MSTSC is the RDP client. Its components specific to TS RemoteApps have the following jobs:

- The windowing plug-in collects the window positioning information from the remote session and passes it to the RAIL plug-in.
- The drawing orders handler collects the window appearance information and feeds it to the shadow bitmap.
- The shadow bitmap sends bitmaps to the RAIL plug-in to draw the application window.
- The RAIL plug-in receives all the drawing and positioning information and collects all the input for that window to send back to the terminal server. It also collects user feedback on the window state and position and sends it to the remote session to update the application window there.

The rest is easy. The RAIL proxy window is the window for the TS RemoteApp; it is positioned using the data fed by the windowing plug-in, and it is drawn using the shadow bitmap. The notify icon displays the TS RemoteApp in the taskbar.

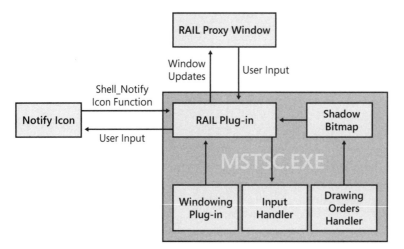

FIGURE 6-3 Client-side components enabling TS RemoteApps

TS RemoteApps and Monitor Spanning

One of the new features of Windows Server 2008 is *monitor spanning*, wherein a session on a terminal server expands to fit all the monitors connected to the client computer. When the client connects to the terminal server (for any monitor configuration), it tells the RDP display driver (Rdpdd.sys) the size of the monitor attached to it, adding the monitor resolutions together (see Figure 6-4). Rdpdd.sys accepts this and treats the multiple monitors as one big monitor. It's not aware that multiple monitors are connected; it simply uses the size of the total display area, up to 4096 × 2048 pixels, for the display. (If you exceed the total display area on your monitors, the display will only be up to 4096 × 2048.) Session shadowing is not affected, because the monitors are all seen as a single entity. To enable monitor spanning, connect to the remote server by using the /span option with Mstsc.exe like this: `mstsc.exe /span`, or add the entry `span monitors:i:1` to the RDP connection file. In the absence of this entry, monitor spanning is disabled for desktop connections.

> **Note** Generating video display takes some processor power and memory on the terminal server; the larger the display, the more power it takes. If everyone using the terminal server uses monitor spanning to its full capacity, this could affect performance.

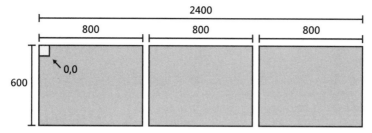

FIGURE 6-4 Individual monitors add up to a single large monitor sized 2400 × 600.

Because all the monitors are seen by the RDP display driver as a single entity, there are some restrictions on configuration. First, all the monitors must be set to the same resolution, because to the server, they're all the same monitor. If you don't set all the monitors to the same resolution, then even if monitor spanning is enabled the desktop will be confined to your primary monitor. Second, the monitors must be set up in a horizontal configuration, as in Figure 6-4; the spanning is intended to go from left to right. Third, the leftmost monitor must be the primary monitor, so that both client and server start counting in the upper left as 0,0 when deciding how to arrange pixels on the screen.

One limitation of monitor spanning is that it really isn't a multi-monitor solution so much as a way to support a large display. The desktop extends across the entire space (meaning that you may want to use an odd number of monitors to avoid dialog boxes being split between two monitors). And maximized applications maximize across the entire space, which can make them inconveniently wide. TS RemoteApps makes monitor spanning more multi-monitor-like by exploiting what it knows about the monitor window size to maximize applications to the monitor you've got them in, at the same time making it possible to move them around. As an example, launch Microsoft PowerPoint as a TS RemoteApp while two monitors are connected to your client computer. Both monitors are set to 1280 × 800. A newly launched TS RemoteApp will appear maximized on Monitor 1. To move it, click its Restore Down button it and drag the window to Monitor 2. When you maximize it again, the TS RemoteApp will appear in the confines of the second monitor instead of being spread across every monitor connected to the client computer. If you position a TS RemoteApp across two monitors, it will maximize the one in which more of its window is displayed, as shown in Figure 6-5.

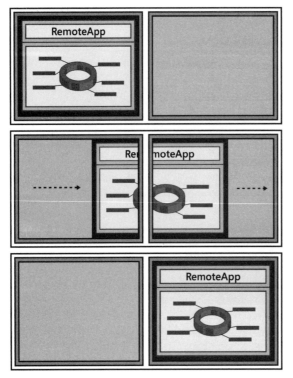

FIGURE 6-5 A TS RemoteApp will maximize to the monitor on which more of its window is displayed.

How does TS RemoteApps know where to draw the application window? When running TS RemoteApps, as you modify the application window on the client (maximize it, minimize it, and so forth), these changes are sent to the application window on the terminal server. Although the server doesn't know that there are multiple monitors, the client does. When you maximize a TS RemoteApp in a client-side monitor, it maximizes to the monitor on which you have it displayed. It then reports its new size to the remote application window. The result is that the application window is sized for a single monitor, not the entire spanned area.

Before connecting to the TS RemoteApp, you must configure the monitors to the same resolution. If you don't, you'll see some odd behavior. TS RemoteApps displayed on one monitor may "leak" into the display on another one. (For example, a File | Open menu may partially display on Monitor 1 when the application's primary display is on Monitor 2.) For best results, configure the monitor resolution before connecting.

Publishing Applications on a Terminal Server

In previous versions of Windows Terminal Services, you couldn't launch single applications, just a desktop. To run an application, you launched a remote desktop and launched the application from there. For complete desktop replacement (as with thin clients) this was fine, but for PC environments in which users might be (and usually were) running both local and remote applications, it meant remembering which window an application was running in. It was a bit like using a multi-monitor computer where you could see only one monitor at a time.

Windows Server 2008, of course, adds TS RemoteApps, but TS RemoteApps do not just happen automatically. To enable them, you must add the installed applications to the allow list, and then package them for distribution. To do that, you'll use the TS RemoteApp Manager.

Using TS RemoteApp Manager to Create TS RemoteApps

To make installed applications TS RemoteApps, you must:

1. Add those applications to the allow list of programs that may initiate a remote session, including the appropriate parameters.

2. Package those applications.

3. Distribute those applications.

The next sections will look at these steps in more detail.

Adding Applications to the Allow List

It's important to understand what adding applications to the allow list is and isn't. It *isn't* a form of software restriction policy, as we discussed in Chapter 5. Adding an application to the allow list only enables that application to be launched as a TS RemoteApp; after the remote session has begun, it's possible to launch any other application on the terminal server to which you have access. Do not consider the allow list a method of locking down the terminal server.

Adding applications to the allow list also isn't the same as packaging them. Doing so makes it *possible* to package them, but the packaging is still a separate step, whether it is done manually from TS RemoteApp Manager or automatically using TS Web Access.

So what *is* it? Adding an application to the allow list makes it possible to launch that application remotely and defines the conditions under which the application will be launched (in TS Web Access, with or without command-line parameters, and so forth). If you add an application to the allow list, package it, give that RDP file to someone, and *then* remove the application from the allow list, that TS RemoteApp file will no longer work. Additionally, if you previously configured the application to work with TS Web Access, it will no longer appear in the portal after you remove it from the allow list.

To add applications to the allow list, open the TS RemoteApp Manager (see Figure 6-6) from Start | Administrative Tools | Terminal Services | TS RemoteApp Manager. This tool controls which applications are available as RemoteApps and how those RemoteApps are accessed.

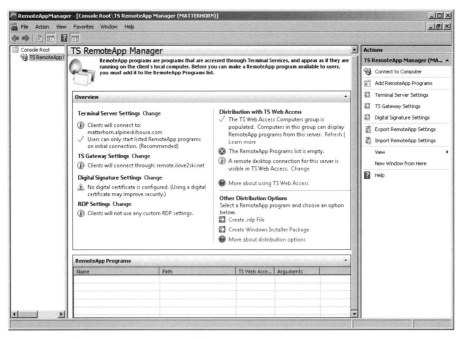

FIGURE 6-6 The TS RemoteApp Manager interface

Take a look at the options in the middle pane; you'll use them when adding applications to the allow list. If you click any of the *Change* hyperlinks here, you'll open the tabbed dialog box shown in Figure 6-7.

RemoteApp deployment settings apply globally to all applications that you add to the allow list when packaging the files (unless you explicitly change the settings during creation), but will not affect packages you've already created.

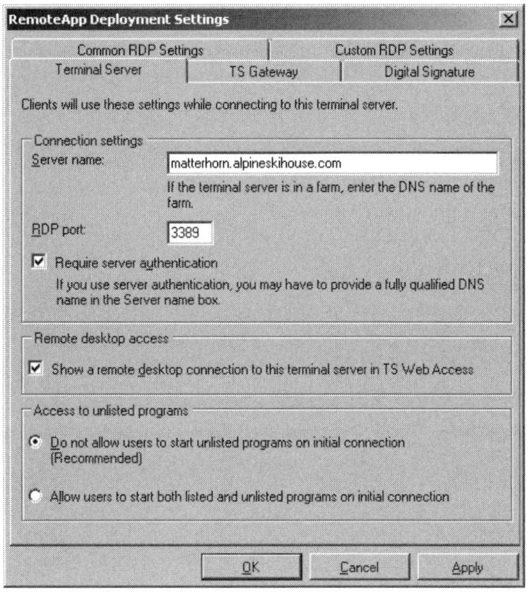

FIGURE 6-7 The RemoteApp Deployment Settings dialog box

> **Caution** If you're distributing TS RemoteApps manually or via Group Policy, decide on your settings before doing so. Only the dynamically created RDP files created when a user launches an application from TS Web Access reflect the most current server, TS Gateway, and RDP settings. RDP files that you distribute through e-mail or a file share, or those distributed through Group Policy as MSIs, will not automatically update.

The following list gives an overview of the settings and functionality available on the tabs in the RemoteApp Deployment Settings dialog box. These settings will be discussed in detail in the section titled "Editing Distribution Options" later in this chapter.

- The Terminal Server tab controls the server connection settings, including the name of the server or farm the RDP files should point to, the port to use, whether TS Web Access should show a connection to the terminal server desktop, and whether users are restricted to the allow list when it comes to launching TS RemoteApps.

- The TS Gateway tab controls the TS Gateway settings that will be applied to the RDP files you create, such as whether the TS Gateway should be automatically detected or specified, when TS Gateway should be used, and whether TS Gateway and the terminal server should use the same credentials.

- The Digital Signature tab shows the certificate you're using to sign RDP files (if applicable).

- The Common and CustomRDP Settings tabs control device redirection, font smoothing, and session color quality.

The remaining sections in the middle pane of the TS RemoteApp Manager don't allow you to configure anything but show you the current status or surface actions you can take.

- The Distribution With TS Web Access section shows whether any applications are available through TS Web Access (or, more precisely, whether they can be based on the current contents of the allow list).

- If you choose an application in the allow list (under RemoteApp Programs), you'll have the option of creating an RDP file or MSI package.

None of this applies, however, until you populate the allow list. To add an installed application to the allow list, you must add it to the RemoteApp Programs list located in the lower section of the middle pane (shown previously in Figure 6-6) by following the next set of steps.

> **Note** You can add only applications on a Windows Server 2008 terminal server to the allow list. Windows Server 2003 terminal servers cannot support TS RemoteApps or back a TS Web Access Server, except to connect to a full desktop.

1. Click the Add RemoteApp Programs button in the Actions pane or right-click in the RemoteApp Programs section and choose Add RemoteApp Programs to start the RemoteApp Wizard. Click Next.

2. Choose the application(s) that you want to publish by selecting the corresponding check box in the RemoteApp Programs list (see Figure 6-8). If an installed application does not appear in the list, locate it by clicking the Browse button and navigating to the executable file.

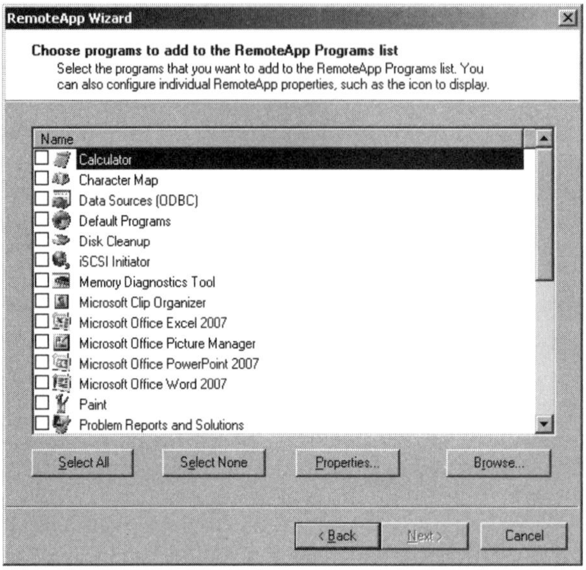

FIGURE 6-8 Choose one or multiple installed applications to add to the allow list.

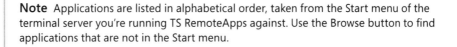

Note Applications are listed in alphabetical order, taken from the Start menu of the terminal server you're running TS RemoteApps against. Use the Browse button to find applications that are not in the Start menu.

3. If required, edit the application settings by clicking the Properties button. The Properties section is discussed in the following section, titled "Editing RemoteApp Properties." If you've selected more than one application from the list, you can't edit the properties.

4. Click Next, review the settings you have chosen, and click Finish. The application is now on the allow list.

Editing RemoteApp Properties

Those are the steps at a high level. The Properties section deserves detailed mention.

You can edit a setting for a TS RemoteApps either while adding it to the allow list or after you've added it by right-clicking its entry in the list and choosing Properties. When you open the properties of a published application, you'll see a dialog box similar to the one shown in Figure 6-9.

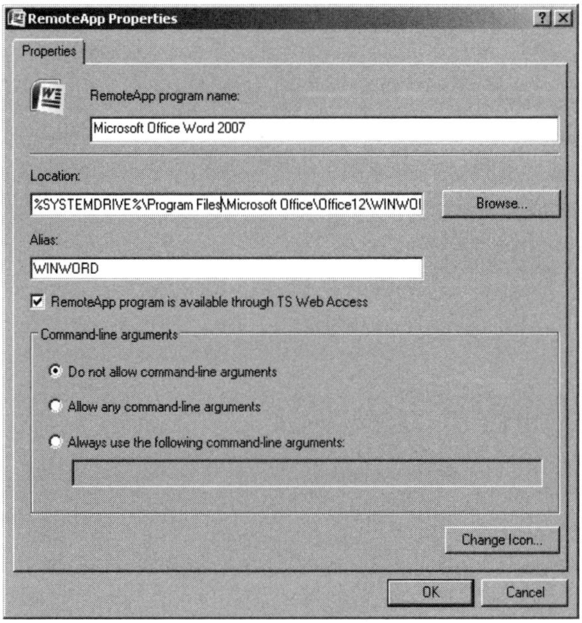

![RemoteApp Properties dialog box showing the Properties tab with RemoteApp program name "Microsoft Office Word 2007", Location "%SYSTEMDRIVE%\Program Files\Microsoft Office\Office12\WINWOI" with a Browse button, Alias "WINWORD", a checked checkbox "RemoteApp program is available through TS Web Access", a Command-line arguments section with three radio options (selected: "Do not allow command-line arguments", "Allow any command-line arguments", "Always use the following command-line arguments:"), a Change Icon button, and OK/Cancel buttons.]

FIGURE 6-9 RemoteApp Properties dialog box

Choose an Appropriate Program Name The RemoteApp program name will be used as the application link in TS Web Access, the RDP file name of created RDP files, and as the shortcut link name resulting from a published MSI file that appears on a user's Start

Menu or desktop. If you're publishing the application only once, you're unlikely to edit this. However, you can publish the application more than once, each time with individual settings, and you can name it according to its settings. For example, if you want to make it easy for members of the Accounting team to open their monthly reports, you can hard-code the TS RemoteApp to open the report file using the command-line arguments. If you do so, it makes sense to edit the RemoteApp program name to show the name of the report instead of the name of the file.

Enable Integration with TS Web Access   Make the RemoteApp available via TS Web Access by selecting the option Remoteapp Program Is Available Through TS Web Access. Doing so makes it possible to display this application for launching through a Web site. You'll still need to do a little work to enable TS RemoteApps through a Web site. (See the section titled "Terminal Services Web Access" later in this chapter for more details about this.)

Don't Change the Alias   The Alias of the program is a unique identifier for the application, defaulting to the application screen name. Although you can edit this property, it's best that you don't. The TS RemoteApp Manager, like most Terminal Services tools, is built on top of Windows Management Instrumentation (WMI) interfaces—in this case, for TS RemoteApps. The class *Win32_TSPublishedApplicationList* lists all TS RemoteApps in an array, identifying them by their alias. If you change the alias, the class will not be able to find the TS RemoteApp in its list. TS Web Access populates its list of applications by querying WMI, so editing the alias may cause the TS RemoteApp to not work with TS Web Access.

The alias also names the RDP file you create from that allow list. If an RDP file with that name already exists, then the RDP file will adjust its name as appropriate.

Adding Command-Line Arguments   Although it's easy to miss because we're so used to opening applications from the graphical user interface (GUI), many applications support a number of command-line parameters. You can use them to automatically open files, to disable the splash screen, or even to open a document and highlight a particular section—it all depends on the application. For instance, to tell a TS RemoteApp instance of Microsoft Office PowerPoint 2007 to open Mydoc.pptx (stored on file server OZARK) as a slideshow when the PowerPoint application launches, we add this command-line argument to the PowerPoint TS RemoteApp: `/S \\ozark\ash-company-files\mydoc.pptx`.

By default, command-line arguments are not enabled for RemoteApps because no arguments are universally appropriate. By allowing end users to specify their own arguments, you expose the terminal server to attack, for example, through rogue Web sites. If you must enable arguments, select one of the following choices:

- **Allow Any Command-Line Arguments**   Choose this option to allow users to assign parameters to a RemoteApp. Users can then open the RDP file in a text editor and add the arguments they want to use for that connection, as shown in Figure 6-10.

```
POWERPNT.rdp - Notepad
File Edit Format View Help
redirectclipboard:i:1
redirectposdevices:i:0
redirectprinters:i:1
redirectcomports:i:1
redirectsmartcards:i:0
devicestoredirect:s:*
drivestoredirect:s:*
redirectdrives:i:1
session bpp:i:32
span monitors:i:1
prompt for credentials on client:i:1
remoteapplicationmode:i:1
server port:i:3389
allow font smoothing:i:0
promptcredentialonce:i:1
authentication level:i:0
gatewayusagemethod:i:2
gatewayprofileusagemethod:i:1
gatewaycredentialssource:i:0
full address:s:farm.alpineskihouse.com
alternate shell:s:||POWERPNT
remoteapplicationprogram:s:||POWERPNT
gatewayhostname:s:remote.ilove2ski.net
remoteapplicationname:s:Microsoft Office PowerPoint 2007
remoteapplicationcmdline:s:/S \\ozark\ash-company-files\test.pptx
```

FIGURE 6-10 Add a command-line parameter to a RemoteApp RDP file

Note If you digitally sign your RDP files, don't allow users to specify command-line arguments. If they edit the arguments, they'll corrupt the file.

- **Always Use The Following Command-Line Arguments**   If you choose this option and specify arguments, they'll be applied when that TS Remote App is launched.

Note For best performance on a terminal server, it's always best to disable unnecessary images. For example, to remove the splash screen from the opening of any Microsoft Office application, add the /q switch to the list of required command-line arguments. See the Additional Resources section at the end of this chapter for pointers to command-line arguments for some sample applications.

Treat command-line arguments as one more kind of Terminal Server setting—but one that applies to a particular TS RemoteApp. It's analogous to drive mapping. On a terminal server, you can either disable drive mapping or enable it. If you disable it, then no matter what changes users make to the client-side settings, they can't map drives. If you enable it, then users have the option to map drives or not map them, as they see fit.

The command-line arguments to TS RemoteApps take this one step further.

- You can enable arguments—whatever the end user wants to add—just as you can enable drive mapping.
- You can disable arguments, just as you can disable drive mapping. If the user edits the RDP file to add arguments, those arguments won't be processed.

- You can enable arguments that you specify. Whatever settings you choose for a particular TS RemoteApp will apply every time that RemoteApp is launched—they're not dependent on a particular instance of an RDP file, any more than drive mapping is. (This option has no counterpart in drive mapping, but it would be equivalent to a setting that allows only certain drives to be mapped, or for data to flow only from client to server instead of both ways.)

The settings you pick will always apply to that TS RemoteApp when it's launched, because they're defined on the server.

Editing the Application Icon   To change the icon that will represent the application, click the Change Icon button in the lower-right corner of the screen and choose a different icon. The path to the icon file must be a Universal Naming Convention (UNC) path so that the TS RemoteApp can be exported to another server, and the path will remain valid. For example, if you edit the TS RemoteApp to open a document, you can change its icon to one that represents a document (Word has many alternate icons), not the application.

Editing Distribution Options

After adding applications to the allow list, you must get the RDP files to users so they can launch those applications. You can do this in one of three ways:

- Create RDP files and make them available to end users from a file share or by sending them in e-mail.

- Create MSI files (which are installable versions of the same RDP files) and distribute them to users via Group Policy.

- Enable the applications in the allow list for display via TS Web Access as explained previously in the section titled "Editing RemoteApp Properties" and dynamically create the RDP files on demand when users access the TS Web Access server.

This section will discuss the first two options; the third will be discussed in the later section titled "Using TS Web Access."

The middle pane of the RemoteApp Manager shows all the applications currently in the allow list and the options for configuring the terminals server, TS Gateway, and digital signing options. Click the Terminal Server Settings in the Actions pane to edit global settings used to configure RemoteApp RDP and MSI distribution files. These settings also apply to RDP files created on the fly when a user clicks a RemoteApp icon in TS Web Access.

> **Note** You can't edit these settings from created RDP and MSI distribution files nor from TS Web Access. To make changes to these settings, first make the changes in the RemoteApp Deployment Settings dialog box and then redeploy RDP and MSI files. TS Web Access creates RemoteApp sessions on demand and so uses the current settings automatically.

Click the Terminal Server Settings Change link located in the Overview pane to open the tabbed RemoteApp Deployment Settings dialog box shown in Figure 6-11. From this dialog box, you can edit the settings for the terminal server, TS Gateway, common RDP settings, custom RDP settings, and digital signature.

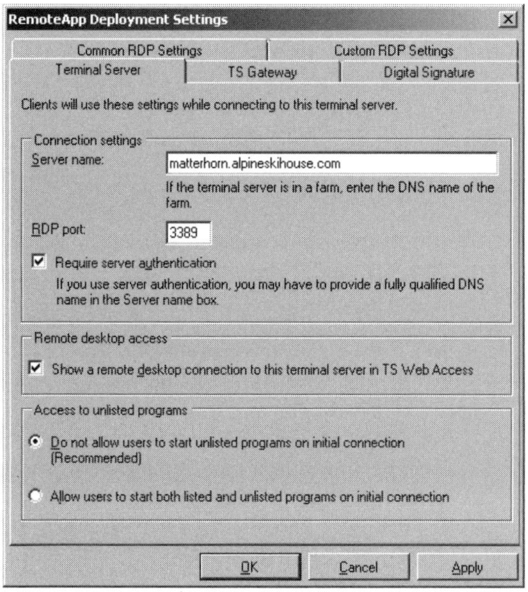

FIGURE 6-11 The RemoteApp Deployment Settings dialog box

Terminal Server Tab   The Terminal Server tab contains three sections:

- **Connection Settings**   Specify the server name and port that clients will connect to when using RemoteApps. If you have a terminal server farm, specify the farm name. By default, the server name is the fully qualified domain name of the server, and the port is 3389, the default RDP port. Be sure to edit this setting to display the farm name (as a FQDN), if appropriate.

- **Remote Desktop Access**   You can make a remote desktop connection to the terminal server(s) available to users on the TS Web Access Web site by selecting the option Show A Remote Desktop Connection To This Terminal Server In TS Web Access.

- **Access To Unlisted Programs**   By default, Do Not Allow Users To Start Unlisted Programs On Initial Connection is selected. This setting does not prevent an application from launching after the remote connection has been made, but it prevents users from launching TS RemoteApps that are no longer on the allow list.

TS Gateway Tab   As described in Chapter 7, "Multi-Server Deployments and Securing Terminal Server Connections," you can deploy TS Gateway to give users secure access to RemoteApps from outside the company intranet. If you do so, then the settings specified on the TS Gateway tab are applied when users launch TS RemoteApps.

> **Note** You can also open the TS Gateway tab from the Change link next to TS Gateway Settings in TS RemoteApp Manager.

Enable Automatically Detect TS Gateway Server Settings to have the TS Gateway server settings gathered from Group Policy. This setting is defined in User Configuration | Polices | Administrative Templates | Windows Components | Terminal Services | TS Gateway. There is no corresponding computer policy to link terminal servers or farms with a particular TS Gateway server.

If you're not dividing TS Gateway usage according to user identity, you can specify the TS Gateway server to use in this section. You can also define the type of authentication that must be used when using TS Gateway. For example, for greater security, you could require smart card authentication. To use the same user credentials to access TS Gateway and the terminal server, select the corresponding check box. Otherwise, users will be prompted for credentials to access TS Gateway and then again to access the terminal server.

> **Note** You may notice that the authentication method used by TS Gateway is NTLM, not Kerberos, although Kerberos is the default authentication method for Windows Server 2008. This is because you can't use Kerberos for Internet scenarios. Kerberos requires that both client and server be domain-joined so that they can contact the authentication service. Therefore, for TS Gateway, you'll rely on either NTLM or smart card access. One major difference between NTLM authentication and Kerberos authentication is that NTLM validates only the computer's domain membership, whereas Kerberos validates its full name.

Digital Signature Tab   Code-signing is probably familiar to you: You sign code to validate that you are authorizing its execution and are willing to state that it isn't malware. Running an RDP file only launches code that's already present on the client computer: MSTSC. Why do RDP files need to be signed when they're executing trusted code? An RDP file looks innocuous, but has one major vulnerability. If you get an RDP file in an e-mail message and are told to run it when you want to use an application, then you're not necessarily going to open this file to see where it's sending you. It's trivial to alter an RDP file to send it to a different server from the one originally specified. Once there, when you present your credentials, those credentials can be intercepted. Users who execute TS RemoteApp RDP files need assurance that the RDP file they execute is created by a trusted source and that it has not been altered. Digitally signing an RDP file provides users with the author's identity so they can make an informed decision when executing the RDP file. If a user does not recognize the publisher of the code, she doesn't have to execute it. Digital signing also proves that the code is authentic; in other words, it has not been tampered with or changed in any way after publishing. If a signed RDP file is altered in any way that changes how it's secured, the file is corrupted and won't launch.

How It Works: Background on Digital Certificates

The digital certificate used to sign an RDP file is an electronic file that contains proof that the subject of the certificate (the Web server, the user, the application, the entity) is indeed who or what it claims to be. Digital certificates are used for a variety of purposes, like authenticating servers, signing e-mail, or authenticating users on a network.

When used to sign RDP files generated by RemoteApp Manager, the digital certificate provides the software publisher identity to users of the RDP files. This gives users assurance that they will connect to a trusted terminal server. It also assures that the RDP file code has not been altered in any way after it was published and signed using the certificate.

To prove that the subject of the certificate is real, the issuer of the certificate (the certificate authority, or CA) must verify the subject's identity. The CA does a background check to be sure that the user requesting the certificate is who he says he is. (The result is that you can't get signing certificates from a company that you don't belong to, or even to a company that you do belong to if you don't have authority to get them.) After the CA has verified the requestor's identity, the CA signs the certificate with its digital signature to show that the appropriate checking has taken place and to verify that the certificate subject is valid.

You can obtain a digital certificate from a public company such as VeriSign or thawte. Alternatively, your company can maintain your own public key infrastructure (PKI, the system that maintains CAs and other systems related to digital certificates) and can issue and maintain your own digital certificates. In either case, a digital certificate is verified as legitimate by verifying the issuing CA signature used to sign the certificate. To verify the issuing CA signature, that CA certificate—which contains its digital signature—needs to be installed on the client computer in the Trusted Root Certificate Store. Users can add CA certificates to this store for every source they trust.

Microsoft operating systems come with some certificate authority CA certificates already installed in the Trusted Root Certification Authorities store, as part of the Microsoft Root Certificate Program. Member certificates can be downloaded and installed using Windows Update. What this means is that users do not need to install anything to trust one of these CAs. This is important if users will be running RemoteApp RDP distribution files on public or remote computers, where they may not have the permissions to install certificates (or don't know how to do so).

On Windows Vista, when an application needs to verify a certificate that has been signed by a CA, and that CA is not directly trusted (its certificate is not installed in the Trusted Root Certification Authorities store on the computer), then the computer checks with Windows Update to see if the CA has been added to the Microsoft list of trusted authorities. If it has, then the certificate is automatically downloaded and installed in the Trusted Root Certification Authorities store on the computer.

> **Note** Computers running Windows XP and earlier operating systems can update their trusted root certificates by downloading the latest root update package from the Microsoft Updates Catalog. For more information about the Microsoft Certificate Update Program, go to *http://www.microsoft.com/technet/archive/security/news/rootcert.mspx?mfr=true*.

If users run TS RemoteApp RDP files from public or remote computers, sign RemoteApp distribution files using a digital certificate obtained from a public CA that is a member of the Microsoft Root Certificate Program so the certificate can be verified. If you sign the RDP file with a privately created certificate, the trusted root certificate store won't know anything about it unless told, and the certificate will be rejected. You can use a certificate issued by an in-house CA, but the recommendation is that the CA certificate be co-signed by a public CA in the Microsoft Root Certificate Program.

To digitally sign RDP files, select the option Sign With A Digital Certificate. Then click the Change button and choose a digital certificate from the certificates installed on the terminal server.

To sign RDP files, you may use a code-signing certificate or an SSL certificate issued from a public CA or an enterprise CA maintained in-house. If you maintain your own enterprise CA, you can also configure the CA to issue RDP signing certificates. The certificate must be installed in the local computer or user personal certificate store to be available as a certificate choice for RDP file signing.

When a user opens a signed RDP file, he will be presented with the screen shown in Figure 6-12.

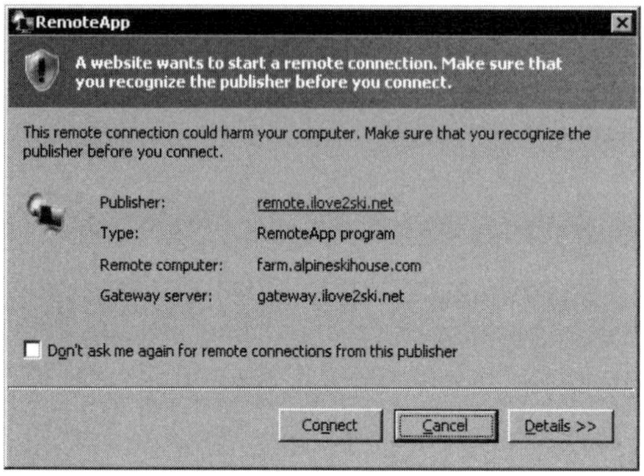

FIGURE 6-12 Signed RDP files present the user with the publisher identity before the code executes.

The user can then verify the publisher and be assured that he is executing the intended code from the correct source. The user can then execute the code by clicking the Connect button, or he can choose to click the Cancel button and not execute the file.

If you do not use digital signatures to sign RDP files, when users open a published RDP file they will receive a warning (shown in Figure 6-13) stating that the publisher of the RDP file can't be identified.

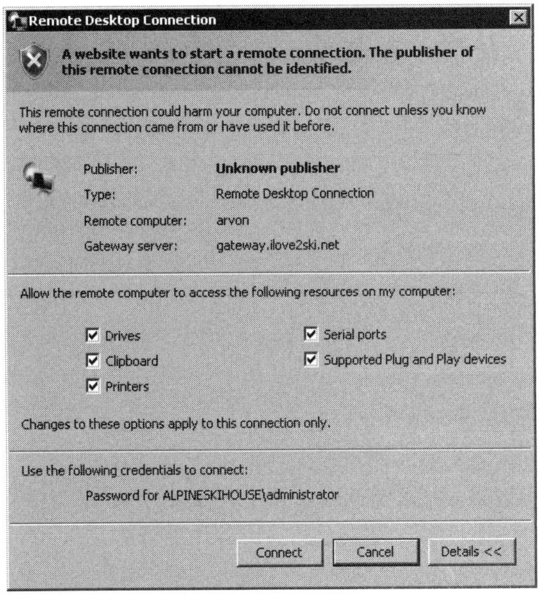

FIGURE 6-13 If a digital signature is not used to sign an RDP file, the user receives a warning that the publisher of the Remote Connection can't be identified.

The user either connects anyway by clicking the Connect button or clicks the Cancel button to cancel the connection.

Common RDP Settings Tab   Configure display settings and device redirection settings on the Common RDP Settings tab. These settings will be set in the RDP file and will be used as long as these settings are not specified through Group Policy. See Chapter 5 for more details on controlling device redirection.

> **Note** For best performance, do not allow font smoothing if the TS RemoteApps will be available via the Internet. Font smoothing works by converting the glyphs (characters) to bitmaps—basically, they're pictures of letters instead of the letters themselves. This makes the letters look good, but it can really impact the connection performance over high-latency connections. The issue is that by converting the glyphs to bitmaps, the cache on the client is now much less useful; it's harder to match bitmaps than glyphs. The hit rate will drop and the screen updates will slow.

Custom RDP Settings Tab   Add custom settings that are not specified in the common deployment settings of RemoteApp Manager by typing the settings in this tab. (See the following sidebar, titled "Understanding RDP File Settings," for more details about available RDP settings.)

Understanding RDP File Settings

Not all options for an RDP file are exposed through the graphical user interface (GUI) of Mstsc.exe. To change the way a TS Remote App (or desktop) launches, you can edit the contents of the RDP file by opening it with a text editor such as Notepad. See Table 6-2 for more details. Most of these are reasonably self-explanatory, but it's good to examine what you can and can't control with an RDP file. (Not all settings here will be present in all RDP files, and desktops may have additional options.)

TABLE 6-2 Sample RDP File Content Settings

Settings	Details
redirectclipboard:i:1	Enables Remote Clipboard, which is required for copying and pasting text between local and remote settings.
redirectposdevices:i:0	Redirects Point of Sale Devices.
redirectprinters:i:1	Redirects printers to the remote session.
redirectcomports:i:1	Redirect COM ports to the remote session.
redirectsmartcards:i:0	Enables smart cards to use smart cards for single sign-on.
devicestoredirect:s:*	Specifies the devices to redirect to the remote session.
drivestoredirect:s:*	Specifies the devices to redirect to the remote session. Possible values may include drive letters and the string "Dynamic Drives", which means the drives you connect.
redirectdrives:i:1	Specifies whether drives are redirected.
session bpp:i:32	Specifies the color depth to use.
span monitors:i:1	Enables monitor spanning (on by default for TS RemoteApps).
prompt for credentials on client:i:1	Corresponds to the Always Ask for Credentials option in the RDP file.
remoteapplicationmode:i:1	Specifies that the RDP file will display a TS RemoteApp.
server port:i:3389	Specifies the port the server listens on for incoming RDP connections.
allow font smoothing:i:0	Enables font smoothing, which is disabled by default because it disables glyph caching by showing all glyphs as bitmaps. This can drastically slow performance over slow connections.
promptcredentialonce:i:1	Prompts the user for credentials only once if the credentials for TS Gateway and the terminal server are the same.
authentication level:i:0	Controls whether server authentication is used to verify a server identity before the connection is made.

TABLE 6-2 Sample RDP File Content Settings

Settings	Details
gatewayusagemethod:i:	Specifies if and how TS Gateway is used. Valid values include 0 (Do not use TS Gateway), 1 (Always use the TS Gateway, even for local connections), 2 (Use the TS Gateway if a direct connection cannot be made to the terminal server), 3 (Use the default TS Gateway settings), and 4 (Do not use TS Gateway). 0 and 4 have the same effect; the only difference is in the user interface (UI), wherein the option to bypass TS Gateway is selected or cleared.
gatewayprofileusagemethod:i:1	Determines the TS Gateway authentication method a user can use, whether the defaults are specified by the administrator (0) or user-specified (1).
gatewaycredentialssource:i:0	Specifies the credentials that should be used to validate the connection. Values may be 0 (ask for password, uses NTLM), 1 (use smart card), or 4 (allow user to choose).
full address:s:farm.alpineskihouse.com	Specifies the name of the farm or server the RDP file points to.
alternate shell:s:||WINWORD	Indicates the application to start for TS RemoteApps.
remoteapplicationprogram: s:%path%\winword	Specifies the alias of the TS RemoteApp; don't change it or you may prevent the TS RemoteApp from working with TS Web Access.
gatewayhostname:s:remote. ilove2ski.net	Specifies the name of the TS Gateway.
remoteapplicationname:s:test document	Specifies the name of the TS RemoteApp as displayed in TS Web Access or at connection time.
remoteapplicationcmdline:s: /q /t \\everest\griffin-anderson\ _Terminal Server Book 2008\ Chapters\test.docx	Provides command-line arguments for this TS RemoteApp.

Some settings should not be changed if the RDP file is signed, because this will break the signature, corrupt the file, and render it unusable.

You can also copy and paste settings from another RDP file configuration. To do so, configure an RDP connection as needed and save the file. Then open the file in a text editor (as shown previously in Figure 6-10), copy the settings needed from that file, and paste them into the Custom RDP Settings text box.

Maintaining Allow List Consistency Across the Farm

It is technically possible to configure TS Remote Apps on each server in your farm. However, doing so is extra work and prone to error. Even if you manage to create exactly the same allow list on each terminal server (without which TS RemoteApps won't execute against that server), the chances are good that you won't edit all properties and icon settings correctly if you attempt to set up all the servers manually. If the properties are inconsistent across servers, then you may end up with odd behavior, such as an application launching a file from one server but not from another.

The good news is that you don't need to try to maintain the RemoteApp settings manually. Although Windows Server 2008 does not have a centralized RemoteApp management tool, it has the next best thing: the ability to export the allow list and associated settings from one server and import them to another. You don't need to move the RDP files around; just make sure that the terminal servers can all launch the appropriate TS RemoteApps with the same settings.

> **Note** Designate one terminal server to act as a kind of RemoteApp settings management server. Configure the RemoteApp settings as needed on this server and create the allow list on that server and then export the settings to the other terminal servers. The server you designate as the settings management server for RemoteApp settings is the one that the TS Web Access Server should point to.

To export the allow list and associated settings, click the Export RemoteApp Settings link in the Actions pane of TS RemoteApp Manager to open the dialog box shown in Figure 6-14.

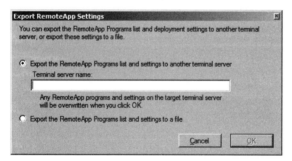

FIGURE 6-14 Export RemoteApp Settings dialog box

For terminal servers on the same network, choose the first option and give the terminal server DNS name. Click OK and the settings will appear in the TS RemoteApp Manager of the chosen server. Import RemoteApp programs and settings to a server by clicking the Import RemoteApp Settings link in the Action pane of TS RemoteApp Manager, and specifying the DNS name of the server from which to import the settings.

If the terminal servers aren't on the same network or the secondary terminal server isn't currently online, save the allow list and settings as a file. Select Export The RemoteApp Programs List And Settings To A File and then choose the name and location to store the file. The created file will have an extension of .pub. On another terminal server, open TS RemoteApp Manager and click the Import RemoteApp Settings link in the Actions pane. Locate the .pub file and click Open.

One caution about importing and exporting the allow list: If you are digitally signing the files, you won't be able to create RDP or MSI files from a secondary server. Although it will appear that the signing settings have been exported for you to use when creating RDP files, this is incorrect. The required *certificate* will not be stored in the secondary server certificate store. Therefore, trying to create RDP files or MSI files from the server that imported the settings will fail, because the certificate is not valid for that server. It's best practice to designate one terminal server as a management server. Create the RDP and MSI files from the designated management server, point the TS Web Access server to this server, and just import the allow list to the secondary servers. Alternatively, you can obtain a certificate for each of the other terminal servers and manually edit the RemoteApp digital certificate settings on each terminal server to reflect the correct certificate. However, this is a lot more work and not usually necessary.

Distributing RemoteApps

After adding applications to the RemoteApp Programs list and tweaking global TS RemoteApp settings, you make TS RemoteApps available to users by distributing RDP files or MSI files, or users can launch RemoteApps via links provided through TS Web Access.

Distributing RDP Files   RemoteApp RDP distribution files are self contained—the user does not install them. The user double-clicks the file, provides valid user credentials, an RDP session launches, and the application opens. Because the files are self-contained, you can distribute them to users via network share, Web site, e-mail, CD-ROM, and so on. To use RDP files from computers outside the corporate LAN, you need to deploy TS Gateway to provide secure access to terminal servers in the network.

> **Note** For information about TS Gateway, refer to Chapter 7.

When users double-click a RemoteApp RDP file, they see a connection screen (refer to Figures 6-12 and 6-13) that either reveals the software publisher identity (so users know they are executing code from a trusted source) or indicates that the publisher is unknown. Users can click the Details button and change which device types are redirected for the session. (If device redirection is already configured on the terminal server or through Group Policy, those settings take precedence over user-defined settings. Changes to device details will have no effect.)

Distributing MSI Files   You can also put MSI files on a file share or e-mail them to users, but their main purpose is to deploy TS RemoteApps via Group Policy. To use Group Policy to deploy RemoteApp MSI files, create a Group Policy object (GPO) and link it to an organizational unit (OU) for the users or client computers for which the Group Policy should apply. Navigate to either Computer Configuration | Policies | Software Settings or User Configuration | Policies | Software Settings, as appropriate. Right-click Software Installation and choose New Software Package.

Deploying RemoteApp MSI files using a computer policy results in the application being assigned and installed automatically when the user boots the computer. Only administrators can uninstall the application.

> **Note** Although you can normally assign applications (installing them automatically) or publish applications (making them available for installation), it's best practice to assign MSIs containing RDP files. Otherwise, the file associations linked with those TS RemoteApps won't work properly.

Ending TS RemoteApp Sessions

All TS RemoteApps from the same server run in the same session for greater efficiency. Therefore, when a user closes one TS RemoteApp, this doesn't close the entire session if other TS RemoteApps are still running. There is no option to log off or close a session from a RemoteApp—and for good reason, since doing so would simultaneously terminate all TS RemoteApps the user launched from that server.

Second, with RemoteApps, users are no longer launching and using applications from within another desktop. Instead, they open and close RemoteApps from their own desktop, and they no longer make a definitive decision about the state of their session by either disconnecting or logging off. Rather, they open and close RemoteApps as needed and do not have to think about the session. This is good from a user perspective, but it makes knowing when to disconnect a Terminal Services session a bit more complicated.

Since a TS RemoteApp session depends on the presence or absence of its TS RemoteApps, the logic for determining when the session should end is different from that of a desktop. The section titled "Understanding TS RemoteApps Internals" earlier in the chapter explained the communication paths between the client-side application and the remote session. When the very last TS RemoteApp in a session is closed (signaled through a windowing event showing that the window is closed), and key processes are no longer running in the remote session, the connection determines that the session is complete and can be disconnected. The time that the session remains in a disconnected state depends on how you configure the Group Policy setting Set Time Limit For Logoff Of Remoteapp Sessions, located in Computer Configuration | Policies | Administrative Templates | Windows Components | Terminal Services | Terminal Server | Session Time Limits.

> **Note** RemoteApps and system tray icons that the user launches indirectly are included in this determination. As an example, let's assume a user opens a Microsoft Office Word document with a Word RemoteApp and the document contains a link to a Microsoft Office Excel spreadsheet. If the user also uses Excel as a RemoteApp, then clicking on the link indirectly opens the Excel RemoteApp. Both of these RemoteApps need to be closed for the session to be disconnected.

You don't necessarily *want* to terminate a session as soon as the last TS RemoteApp is closed. It's much faster to reconnect to an existing session than to recreate a new one (the process of loading all the processes to support the session is expensive). Therefore, you may want to edit the user or computer Group Policy to prolong the interval between disconnection and termination of TS RemoteApp sessions. This gives users a little time to realize that they have one more e-mail to send and launch Outlook from the existing remote session, rather than waiting for a new session. To do so, enable the following GPO setting: Computer (or User) Configuration | Administrative Templates | Windows Components | Terminal Services | Terminal Server | Set Time Limit For Logoff Of Remoteapp Sessions. Select the Enabled radio button and choose a time setting from the RemoteApp Session Logoff Delay drop-down menu, as shown in Figure 6-15.

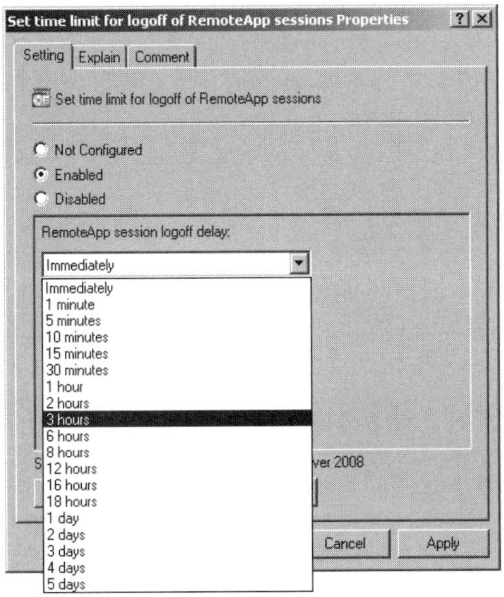

FIGURE 6-15 The Set Time Limit For Logoff Of RemoteApp Sessions Properties Group Policy setting

Note If you also enable the GPO setting Set Time Limit For Disconnected Session, then choose a time for that GPO that is longer than the time specified for Remoteapp Session Logoff Delay. Otherwise sessions will always be terminated before the Remoteapp Session Logoff Delay Time limit is reached, thus rendering that GPO moot.

There's a tradeoff between keeping responsive sessions and not overloading the terminal server. If you choose to retain sessions for a long time (which has other benefits in a farm; see Chapter 7 for more details), you'll affect the terminal server, because the disconnected sessions remain active. Be sure that you have sufficient page file space to accommodate the disconnected sessions when they're not in use.

Terminal Services Web Access

Terminal Services Web Access (TS Web Access) provides access to TS RemoteApps and remote desktops to users via a Web site. The TS Web Access server points to a terminal server with an allow list that allows applications to be displayed in TS Web Access (one of the properties of an application added to the allow list). The Web site contains a Web part that is populated with the contents of the allow list enabled for TS Web Access, using the icons you specified when adding the application to the allow list. When users open the TS Web Access Web site, they are provided with links to available RemoteApps. When a user clicks an application icon, this will launch an RDP file from the terminal server and the RemoteApp executes as described in this chapter. If you remove an application from the allow list, the application is no longer displayed in the Web part.

One of the biggest advantages of deploying RemoteApps using TS Web Access is that the RDP files created on the fly are done so using the current settings specified in the RemoteApp Manager of the associated terminal server. Therefore, they are always up to date. You don't need to redistribute RDP files to users whenever a change occurs in the TS RemoteApp Manager.

Note The TS Web Access server must be a member of the TS Web Access Computers local security group on the terminal server to query it for applications.

You can also use TS Web Access to provide remote desktop access to computers that have Remote Desktop enabled. This is useful for users who need access to their desktop computers from other locations, or for users who need access to more than one computer. A user provides the name of the computer to connect with, and an RDP file is dynamically created and opened. The user provides proper credentials, and the remote desktop session is started.

Note The user needs to be a member of the Remote Desktop Users group of the specified computer in order to successfully remote to that computer.

Installing and basic configuration of TS Web Access is really simple, as explained below.

Installing the TS Web Access Role

Implementing TS Web Access installs the TS Web Access Web site to the TS virtual path of the Internet Information Services (IIS) Default Web site. The install directory is located at %WinDir%\Web\Ts. To install TS Web Access on a Windows 2008 server, open Server Manager and follow these steps:

1. If the Terminal Services role is not installed, right-click Roles, click Add Roles, and then choose the Terminal Services Role. Then add the TS Web Access role service.

2. If the server already has the Terminal Services role installed, right-click Terminal Services Role in Server Manager, click Add Role Service, and choose the TS Web Access role service.

3. Because this server acts as a Web server, you must install IIS 7 for it to work. If IIS 7 is not installed already, you will be prompted to add the role service. Click Add Required Role Services. You will see a screen with an introduction to IIS 7. Click Next, review the Web Server role services that will be installed for IIS, and click Next.

4. Confirm the installation instructions and then click Install.

5. When the installation completes, the installation results will show that the TS Web Access role service and the IIS role installed successfully. Click Close.

> **Note** Alternatively, you can use the Servermanagercmd.exe command-line utility to install TS Web Access like this:
>
> ```
> servermanagercmd.exe -install TS-Web-Access
> ```
>
> If you choose to install via the command line, then any needed components like IIS 7 that are not installed already will be installed automatically.

Associating TS Web Access with a Terminal Server

TS Web Access creates RDP files using the settings provided in the RemoteApp Manager of a single terminal server that you associate with TS Web Access. It populates this Web part by querying the Windows Management Instrumentation (WMI) interfaces on the terminal server to see what applications are on the allow list and are configured to be shown in the portal.

Enabling Secure WMI Access

Because the Web part is populated via WMI, you must open communication for WMI between the TS Web Access server and terminal server. If they're on the same network, you don't need to do anything special. If they're not—if the TS Web Access server is outside the firewall, for instance—you'll need to open a WMI communication port. In Windows Vista and Windows Server 2008, you can configure a specific port to use for WMI traffic.

To specify a port, stop the WMI service on the TS Web Access server from the Services tool in Administrative tools or from the command line with `net stop "Windows Management Instrumentation"` (with the quotes included). Then, define the communication port in this way (making sure you choose one that isn't already being used): `netsh firewall add portopening TCP` *portnumber* `WMIFixedPort`. Restart the WMI service.

Like RDP files created using the RemoteApp Manager, the dynamically created RDP files from the TS Web Access RemoteApp Programs page tab adhere to the configuration settings specified in TS RemoteApp Manager. For example, if TS RemoteApp Manager global settings specify connecting to a terminal server farm, then the RDP files created by TS Web Access RemoteApp Programs tab will also contain this setting. Likewise, if RemoteApp Manager contains TS Gateway settings, then TS Web Access RDP files are also set up to connect through TS Gateway.

> **Note** The connection options used when RDP files are created from the Remote Desktops tab do not adhere to TS RemoteApp Manager. Instead, the options are set in IIS. We discuss this in the section "Configuring TS Web Access Remote Desktop Connection Options" a little later in this chapter.

To create this association between TS Web Access and a single terminal server, log on to the TS Web Access Web site as a member of the TSWA Administrators group and add the name of the terminal server to the Editor Zone on the TS Web Access Web Site Configuration section. (If the terminal server and TS Web Access server are the same server, then point to localhost or the server name.) Give the TS Web Access server access to the terminal server by adding the TS Web Access server computer account to the terminal server TS Web Access local security group.

Access TS Web Access by opening Internet Explorer and connecting to *http://server_name/ts*, or go to Start | Administrative Tools | Terminal Services | TS Web Access Administration. Click the Configuration link, and the Configuration section appears as shown in Figure 6-16. This tab is available only to members of the TSWA Administrators group, and the only configuration option is the terminal server that the Web server is pointing to.

FIGURE 6-16 The TS Web Access configuration page

In the Editor Zone pane on the right side of the page, add the name of the terminal server to use to populate the Web Part (or localhost, if they're the same server), and click Apply. If you mistype the name of the server in the Terminal Server Name input box, the applications in TS Web Access will disappear and you'll see an error message; but they'll reappear as soon as you point to the correct server.

Then on the terminal server specified in the TS Web Access Properties, add the TS Web Access computer object to the TS Web Access local security group.

TS Web Access Web Site Placement and Access Options

TS Web Access is a good way to make TS RemoteApps available to users in situations in which it may be difficult to distribute RDP files directly. To provide secure access to TS RemoteApps via TS Web Access to users outside your network, you should implement either TS Gateway, with or without ISA Server, or another VPN solution. Also, if you have a perimeter network, then it is advisable to place the TS Web Access server there to minimize your attack surface. Then if your Web server is compromised, your internal network should not be.

Whether or not you place TS Web Access server in the perimeter network or on the internal network (i.e., if you don't have a perimeter network), it's a good idea to install an SSL certificate on the TS Web Access server and configure the site to use HTTPS so that users can connect securely to the Web site.

Depending on how you want internal and external users to access the Web site, you can set up access in a few different ways:

- You make only an internal URL available.

- You have an external URL that is used by both internal and external users.

- You provide one URL for internal access and another for external access to the TS Web Access Web site.

Internal-Only URL

If you want external users to connect to the TS Web Access Web site using an internal URL, then they must first obtain access to the internal network to get to the TS Web Access Web site. You can use any method to get the users securely onto the network, such as VPN, TS Gateway, or so forth.

External-Only URL

You can provide the same external URL to both internal users and external users to access the Web site. But if the DNS for this external address is resolved by an external DNS server, then you will need to enable DNS doctoring in your firewall. At a high level, DNS doctoring creates a mapping of internal and external addresses (you'll need to make sure your firewall supports this). An internal network client connects to an external DNS server for DNS resolution, and the external DNS server responds to the query. The firewall sees that the external DNS resolution IP Address really translates to an IP address on the internal network. The firewall intercepts the DNS resolution response from the external DNS server and replaces it with the internal address. The internal Active Directory DNS will cache this result, so the client won't need to hit the external DNS server whenever it attempts to connect to the external URL.

Note Links to information on DNS doctoring are provided in the Additional Resources section at the end of this chapter.

Both Internal and External URLs

Let's say that you want internal users to use an internal URL to connect to the TS Web Access Web site, and you want external users to use an external URL. Additionally, you want both external users and internal users to use HTTPS when connecting to the Web site to ensure a secure connection. To accomplish this, you can obtain a Subject Alternative Name (SAN) certificate. A SAN certificate (also known as a Unified Communications Certificate or UCC certificate) contains multiple subjects.

Applying the SAN certificate to the Web site means that the certificate will match both internal and external URLs, so a user won't get warning messages when trying to connect. For instance, our test environment internal domain name is alpineskihouse.com, but for users outside of our internal network, we use the domain name ilove2ski.net. So we use a SAN SSL certificate on the TS Web Access Web site with the following two subjects: apps.alpineskihouse.com and apps.ilove2ski.net.

You can get SAN certificates from a public certificate authority (CA), or you can create your own if your company maintains its own PKI. As of this writing most public CAs are commonly charging a lot more money for SAN certificates than they do for regular SSL certificates; in some cases, they may cost three times as much.

If your budget will not accommodate a SAN certificate, you could use a standard SSL certificate (with one common name), allow HTTP and HTTPS access to the Web site, and then block port 80 at the firewall. This means that internal users could access an internal unencrypted HTTP address (no SSL certificate needed), and external users would still have to use an encrypted HTTPS address. Of course, this assumes that your company security policy allows unencrypted access to intranet sites from inside the corporate network.

For more information on SAN / UCC certificates, refer to the Additional Resources section at the end of this chapter.

Using TS Web Access

To launch TS Web Access RemoteApp Programs, users must have RDC 6.1 installed as part of Windows Vista SP1 or Windows XP SP3 or available as a standalone installation for Windows XP SP2. Users access the TS Web Access Web site by browsing to *http://servername/ts*. The RemoteApp Programs page appears, as shown in Figure 6-17.

For these pages to work, the Microsoft Terminal Services Client ActiveX control must be enabled. Vista SP1 clients logging onto the Web site for the first time should see a pop-up message that asks for permission to install the ActiveX control. The user must right-click the Information Bar (a yellow bar) to install the control. A user running Windows XP SP3 may not see this pop-up message. To install the control, such a user would need to click Tools | Internet Options, select the Programs tab, and click the Manage Add-ons button at the bottom of the dialog box. Then the Windows XP SP3 client would find the Microsoft Terminal Services Client Control in the list of add-ons, click it, select the Enable radio button, and click OK.

FIGURE 6-17 The TS Web Access RemoteApp Programs page

The Remote App Programs page provides links to all TS RemoteApps available from TS Web Access. When a user clicks on a TS RemoteApps icon in TS Web Access (or chooses a desktop to connect to, as discussed in the next section, "Connecting to Other Desktops from TS Web Access"), the TS ActiveX control in the browser creates a temporary RDP file in the user's Temp folder on the client computer. The RDP file will have a randomly generated name, beginning with TSPORTAL and including a five-digit number. Next, the ActiveX control calls Mstsc.exe and points it to the path of the new RDP file, as in this example for an RDP file named TSPORTAL#12345:

```
mstsc.exe /web/ webfilename:%userprofile%\AppData\Local\Temp\TSPORTAL#12345.rdp
```

This launches Mstsc.exe exactly as if you'd pointed it to any other RDP file, creating the connection.

Connecting to Other Desktops from TS Web Access

A popular feature of TS Web Access (especially when combined with TS Gateway, discussed in Chapter 7) has nothing to do with TS RemoteApps at all. Rather, it's the ability to connect to a computer desktop (such as *your* computer desktop) from the Internet. This is great for telecommuting and working from the road.

To get to your desktop, first make sure that the TS Web Access site is one of your Trusted Web sites. Then click the Remote Desktop link to open the Remote Desktop page shown in Figure 6-18.

FIGURE 6-18 The Terminal Services Remote Desktop Web Connection page

From here, users can connect to servers—and other computers that have Remote Desktop enabled—by typing in the name of the computer, selecting the screen size, and clicking the Connect button. When a user clicks the Connect button, an RDP file pointing to the computer specified is created on the user's computer, using the settings defined in Web.config on the TS Web Access server.

> **Note** A user must be a member of the computer's Remote Desktop Users security group to log on remotely.

The Options button provides a set of RDP settings that the user can adjust, including device and resource redirection, whether to allow keyboard shortcuts in the remote desktop session, and what the speed of the connection is. However, if these options are specified using Group Policy or TS Configuration, then the settings specified by the user are ignored.

Configuring TS Web Access Remote Desktop Connection Options

Whereas with TS RemoteApps you'll configure settings from the RemoteApp Manager, the settings for Remote Desktops made available through TS Web Access are configured using settings on the IIS server hosting the Web site. We recommend using TS Gateway (described in Chapter 7) to provide secure access to desktops from the Internet.

To use TS Gateway with the TS Web Access Remote Desktops tab, you will need to provide the name of the TS Gateway server in IIS on the server that hosts the TS Web Access Web site.

On the TS Web Access server, open IIS. Expand the default Web site (or the Web site where you installed TS Web Access), select the TS folder, and then, in the ASP.NET section in the pane on the right, double-click Application Settings. Double-click Default Gateway Server, add the name of your TS Gateway server, and click OK. Then choose the TS Gateway authentication method by double-clicking GatewayCredentialsSource and specifying the corresponding number value:

- 0 – NTLM (password)
- 1 – Smart Card
- 4 – User Chooses Later (the default)

Now external users will access the Remote Desktops tab of TS Web Access Web site and type in the name of the computer to which they want to connect, which will allow them to make the connection securely through TS Gateway.

If you do not want users to be able to use the Remote Desktop capabilities from the TS Web Access Website, double-click Show Desktops and change the default True entry to False. This will hide the Remote Desktops tab.

Enable or disable the following resource redirection options by double-clicking each option and changing the value for the entry to true (enable) or false (disable):

- Clipboard redirection
- Drive redirection
- PnP redirection
- Port redirection
- Printer redirection

The changes take place immediately, so if the Web page is open, refresh the page to see those changes.

Alternatively, you can use a text editor such as Notepad to directly modify the Web.config file for the TS Web Access Web site located at %WinDir%\Web\ts\Web.config. Locate these entries and change "true" to "false" as needed and then refresh the browser:

```
<add key="xPrinterRedirection" value="true" />
<add key="xClipboard" value="true" />
<add key="xDriveRedirection" value="true" />
<add key="xPnPRedirection" value="true" />
<add key="xPortRedirection" value="true" />
```

> **Note** If PnP, Port, and Drive redirection options are shaded and unavailable, add the Web site to the Web browser's Trusted Sites list and they will become available.

By design, if you connect to a Remote Desktop through TS Web Access, the RDP file will bypass TS Gateway if the terminal server and client are on the same network. What if you *don't* want to bypass TS Gateway when connecting to a Remote Desktop via TS Web Access? TS Web Access uses Web.config to provide RDP settings to the client so the client can create its own RDP file for connecting to the terminal server. None of those settings force the use of TS Gateway.

You can get around this by editing the Web page presenting TS Remote Desktops. The *GatewayUsageMethod* property to the *IMsRdpClientTransportSettings* interface has five possible values. To force clients connecting to Remote Desktops via TS Web Access to use TS Gateway, change the value of this property from 2 (which selects the check box for the Bypass TS Gateway Server For Local Addresses option in the Remote Desktop Connection UI) to 1 (which clears the check box for the Bypass TS Gateway Server For Local Addresses option in the Remote Desktop Connection UI). See the following sidebar for more details.

Direct from the Source: Forcing the Use of TS Gateway for Remote Desktops

Let's say that you're attempting to access a Remote Desktop via TS Web Access. Although the client computers attempting to access the TS Web Access page are all on the same subnet as the TS Web Access server, you've configured the network so that they're actually connecting via the Internet, not the intranet. Therefore, you'd like to require that these clients use TS Gateway.

There's no check box on the Remote Desktops page to force the use of TS Gateway, but you can make it happen by editing Desktop.aspx from this:

```
if ((DefaultTSGateway != null) && (DefaultTSGateway.length > 0)) {
    RDPstr += "gatewayusagemethod:i:2\n";
```

To this:

```
if ((DefaultTSGateway != null) && (DefaultTSGateway.length > 0)) {
    RDPstr += "gatewayusagemethod:i:1\n";
```

All Remote Desktop connections initiated from that TS Web Access site should now go through TS Gateway.

Rob Leitman

Senior Software Development Engineer

Direct from the Source: Why Do I See "Unknown Publisher" When Connecting to Remote Desktops?

RDP file signing lets you put some user protection in place by allowing an RDP file's publisher to sign the file with a digital certificate. So, if you trust the publisher, you know you can trust the RDP connection. Unsigned files will show a warning label when launched.

If you're using TS Web Access to make both TS RemoteApps and full remote desktops available, you may notice something odd if using RDP file signing. When you launch the TS RemoteApps, their dialog box will indicate that the files are signed (i.e., they will identify the publisher of the file). When you launch a connection from the Remote Desktops page, the dialog box will warn that the Publisher is not known, meaning that the file is unsigned.

Whether you click an icon on the RemoteApp Programs page or the Connect button on the Remote Desktops page, doing so creates an RDP file. There's one important difference between these approaches, however: When you click an icon on the RemoteApp Programs page, an RDP file that has been created from settings on the terminal server is channeled to the client. When you click Connect on the Remote Desktops page, the client creates the RDP file. The following illustrations show this.

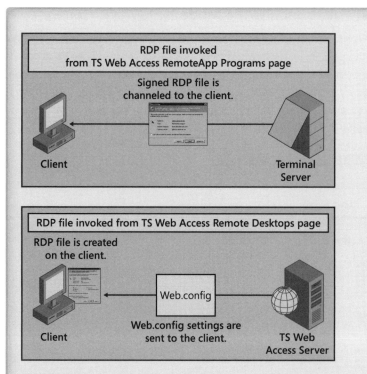

RDP signing is available for TS RemoteApps but not for connections to full desktops. Here's why: The RDP file created when you launch a TS RemoteApp from TS Web Access is created on the terminal server using the configuration settings set in TS RemoteApp Manager. You can specify a digital certificate in TS RemoteApp Manager with which to sign TS RemoteApps. If you have specified a digital certificate, the RDP file will be signed when it's created and then channeled to the client. Thus, the publisher of the RDP file will be identified to the client.

In contrast, an RDP file is created *on the client* when you click the Connect button on the Remote Desktops page, combining the settings specified in the Web.config file and Desktop.aspx on the TS Web Access server, along with any input from the user. There's no setting on the client to specify a digital certificate to use to sign RDP files it creates. The client does not sign the file, and the publisher is shown as unidentifiable.

Janani Venkateswaran

Program Manager

Understanding Public and Private Mode

The RemoteApp Programs page and the Remote Desktop page each contain a check box at the bottom of the page specifying whether or not the computer used to access TS Web Access is a private computer that complies with the user's organization security policy. This box is selected by default, so when a user opens a RemoteApp via TS Web Access, she has the option to save her credentials on the computer from which she is accessing the RemoteApp, as shown in Figure 6-19.

FIGURE 6-19 Users are given the opportunity to save their credentials.

If users are on a public computer, they should clear this box. Doing so will remove the option to remember the user's credentials used to connect to the RemoteApp or Remote Desktop. Unfortunately, you can't use single sign-on (SSO) with TS Web Access because IIS does not use the contents of CRED.SSP.

Customizing TS Web Access

TS Web Access lends itself to customization. While a complete description of how to create a custom portal is outside the scope of this book, let's take a look at some of the options.

Customizing the RDC Client Update Settings

So far, this chapter has assumed that the client machine already has RDC 6.1 installed, so it can launch TS RemoteApps from TS Web Access. But what if the correct version *isn't* installed?

Normally, the portal displays an error message pointing you to a Terminal Server team blog entry that explains what you're seeing and tells you that you need RDC 6.1 to use TS Web Access. This blog entry doesn't make it easy to fix the problem, however—it just tells you what's happening. To make it easier for users to get the correct version of the client, you can customize the link to point to an internal page hosting the required clients and service packs. This allows you to support users connecting to TS Web Access from an intranet with no Internet Web Access or to standardize on a version of the client that you think appropriate.

> **Note** A standalone installation of RDC 6.1 for Window XP SP2 is available, so you don't have to upgrade to the next service pack just to get the latest client. You can get this client at *http:// www.microsoft.com/downloads/details.aspx?FamilyId=6E1EC93D-BDBD-4983-92F7-479E088570 AD&displaylang=en*. Vista SP1 is available from *http://www.microsoft.com/downloads/details .aspx?FamilyID=b0c7136d-5ebb-413b-89c9-cb3d06d12674&DisplayLang=en*, and Windows XP SP3 is available from *http://www.microsoft.com/downloads/details.aspx?FamilyID=68c48dad-bc34-40be-8d85-6bb4f56f5110&DisplayLang=en*.

To modify the target URL, log on to the TS Web Access server as an administrator and follow these steps:

1. Open IIS Manager (Start | Administrative Tools | Internet Information Services (IIS) Manager.

2. In the navigation pane of IIS Manager, expand the server name, expand Sites, expand Default Web Site, and then click TS. (By default, TS Web Access is installed to this location. If you installed TS Web Access to a different site, locate it and then click the site name.)

3. Under ASP.NET, double-click Application Settings. In the Actions pane, click Add and then, in the Add Application Setting dialog box, do the following:

    a. In the Name text box, type **rdcInstallUrl**.

    b. In the Value text box, enter the target URL for the link.

> **Note** To restore the link to point to the default URL, right-click the rdcInstallUrl application set-ting and then click Remove.

Alternatively, you can use a text editor such as Notepad to directly modify the Web.config file for the TS Web Access Web site. By default, the path of the configuration file is %WinDir%\ Web\ts\Web.config. To modify the file, under the *<appSettings>* section of the file, add an entry like this one, where *URL* is the target URL for the link: `<add key="rdcInstallUrl" value="http://URL" />`.

This will update the page to the new location.

Changing TS RemoteApp Display

The default TS Web Access RemoteApp Programs page is pretty basic—it shows the applica-tion icons, and that's about it. However, you can customize this Web site to suit your needs. For instance, you may want to provide other links to Web-based applications, documents, Web sites, or any other Web-based content. TS Web Access doesn't have any easy way to add more data, but other frameworks, such as SharePoint, do.

> **Note** One advantage of the way that TS Web Access works is that any portal Web parts can query WMI on the terminal server. Several TS ISV partners have created solutions on top of WMI to extend the capabilities of the TS RemoteApps platform. The Additional Resources section at the end of this chapter points you to some free options.

For example, the TS Web Access Web part that makes TS RemoteApps available on the TS Web Access Web site can be integrated into a SharePoint Web site, as shown in Figure 6-20.

To integrate the TS Web Access Web part with SharePoint, download the step-by-step guide "Customizing TS Web Access by Using Windows SharePoint Services" available at *http:// download.microsoft.com/download/b/1/0/b106fc39-936c-4857-a6ea-3fb9d1f37063/Step_by_ Step_Guide_to_Customizing_TS_Web_Access_by_Using_Windows_SharePoint_Services.doc.*

FIGURE 6-20 Adding TS Web Access support to SharePoint

Summary

A terminal server is only as interesting as the applications it makes available. This chapter has discussed how to install applications on a terminal server, and how settings for those applications make their way to the user profiles as they launch applications. We've also discussed best practices for making sure that the default application settings don't override user profile data, and we have examined some of the alternative approaches.

After the applications are installed, it's time to create TS RemoteApps. This chapter has explained how TS RemoteApps integrate with the local shell and how to enable them by populating the allow list. We've discussed the pros and cons of the various distribution methods and how to edit the configuration settings for the applications. Finally, we've shown how to populate TS Web Access with TS RemoteApps and desktop connections and how TS RemoteApps are launched from the portal.

Additional Resources

TS RemoteApps and TS Web Access enable a lot of customization. The following resources are related to topics covered in this chapter. You can find the links on this book's companion media.

■ For more information about how to use command-line arguments to open applications, see the product documentation at these Web sites:

❑ For Microsoft Office Word, see *http://office.microsoft.com/en-us/word/HP101640101033.aspx*.

❑ For Microsoft Office PowerPoint, see *http://office.microsoft.com/en-us/powerpoint/HA101538891033.aspx*.

❑ For Microsoft Internet Explorer 7, see *http://blogs.msdn.com/petel/archive/2007/01/19/internet-explorer-7-command-line-arguments.aspx*.

❑ For Adobe Acrobat, see *http://partners.adobe.com/public/developer/en/acrobat/PDFOpenParameters.pdf*.

■ For more information on customizing TS Web Access, see the documentation provided at the following Web sites:

❑ To integrate the TS Web Access Web part with Windows SharePoint Services, download the step-by-step guide "Customizing TS Web Access by Using Windows SharePoint Services" at *http://download.microsoft.com/download/b/1/0/b106fc39-936c-4857-a6ea-3fb9d1f37063/Step_by_Step_Guide_to_Customizing_TS_Web_Access_by_Using_Windows_SharePoint_Services.doc*.

- ❏ For a free add-on to Windows Server 2008 that enables per-user application filtering, see the Ericom Web site at *http://www.ericom.com/WS08.asp* or vision-app's Web site at *http://www.visionapp.com*. Both applications are also available on this book's companion CD.

- ❏ For an example of another customization of TS RemoteApps in a portal using Microsoft Silverlight technology, see *http://narenda.mvps.org/coolts*. As of this writing, the beta version of the application is available, and you can download it from *http://wss-id.org/blogs/narenda/archive/2008/01/03/ts-web-access-with-silverlight-beta.aspx*.

- ❏ Want to write your own custom display? See the TS RemoteApps documentation at *http://msdn.microsoft.com/en-us/library/bb736360(VS.85).aspx*.

- ■ For more information on SAN/UCC certificates, see "How to Configure SSL Certificates to Use Multiple Client Access Server Host Names" at *http://technet.microsoft.com/en-us/library/aa995942.aspx*.

- ■ For information on installing an SSL Certificate on IIS 7, see *http://learn.iis.net/page.aspx/144/how-to-setup-ssl-on-iis-7/*.

- ■ For more information on DNS Doctoring, consult the following Web sites:

  - ❏ *http://www.cisco.com/en/US/products/hw/vpndevc/ps2030/products_tech_note09186a0080094aee.shtml#backinfo*.

  - ❏ *http://www.cisco.com/en/US/products/ps6120/products_configuration_example09186a00807968c8.shtml*.

Chapter 7
Multi-Server Deployments and Securing Terminal Server Connections

No terminal server is an island.

Terminal servers do not operate independently of other terminal servers or of outside considerations. One of the key parts of a successful terminal server deployment is making it interact with other terminal servers and with the outside world—and doing all this securely. That's the focus of this chapter. We'll discuss the following:

- Key technologies Terminal Services uses for connection security and the features they support

- Why server farms are important for even small deployments

- The Terminal Services Session Broker role and how to install and configure it

- Using Terminal Services Gateway to provide secure communication from the Internet

- Creating a fault-tolerant Terminal Services Gateway architecture

Securing RDP Connections

Chapter 5, "Fine-Tuning the User Experience," discussed some approaches to locking down the terminal server to protect it from unintended consequences. Isn't that enough?

Locking down the terminal server is important, but it assumes that you've *already* made a secure connection to the terminal server. That assumption leaves out the possibility of the connection—or the communication between the client and server—being compromised in some way. For example:

- The connection could be intercepted at logon and the logon credentials could be stolen.

- An existing connection could be intercepted and the data flow could be compromised.

- The user could connect to a malicious server and type his logon credentials.

- A computer infected with a virus could connect to the terminal server.

- A client computer not authorized to connect to the terminal server could repeatedly attempt to connect, tying up resources on the terminal server as it attempts to authorize the connection, thus preventing authorized users from connecting.

The catch to mitigating all these connection vulnerabilities is that the logon experience is a critical part of a successful terminal server deployment. If the connection experience is bad, then the users accessing the terminal server will be unhappy with the service. Therefore, you must keep the data stream secure but as fast as possible. In the next sections, we'll talk about the key Windows components that tackle this dilemma, including:

- Remote Desktop Protocol (RDP) encryption levels

- Server authentication mechanisms

- The Credential Security Service Provider

- Network Access Protection policies

Core Security Concepts

Communication security in Windows Server 2008 and Windows Vista depends on three core pieces:

- Transport Layer Security (TLS) for authenticating the server identity

- Network Access Protection (NAP) policies for checking a computer's state of health before it connects to the terminal servers

- The Credential Security Service Provider (CredSSP) for enabling single sign-on (SSO) and network-level authentication.

RDP Encryption Levels

Because there's a lot of open network between the user running the application on a terminal server and the server running the application, it's important to encrypt the traffic going between them so that it can't be intercepted. By default, RDP traffic will be encrypted as strongly as the client can support it—128-bit, if you're using RDP 5.2 or later. By default, both the terminal server and the client are configured to let the client and the server negotiate the highest level of encryption both can support.

RDP clients support three levels of encryption: Low, High, and FIPS-compliant.

Low Security   Low security uses only a 56-bit key to encrypt traffic and will not support server authentication (see "Authenticating Server Identity" in this chapter). It also encrypts only traffic going from client to server, not that moving from server to client. This security model is workable only if data is flowing in just one direction, and is therefore not suitable for any features enabling bidirectional data flow, such as client drive mapping. (Even in this case, the video stream sent to the client could be intercepted.) As you can see, Low security is the level of last resort.

High Security   High security uses a 128-bit key to encrypt data going between client and server; it encrypts traffic going in both directions. You can use High security to support TLS-based server authentication. High security supports server authentication.

You can configure the terminal server to use High security for RDP encryption from TS Configuration or from Group Policy (Computer Configuration | Administrative Templates | Windows Components | Terminal Services | Terminal Server | Security).

FIPS-Compliant Security   FIPS-compliant security uses FIPS-compliant algorithms for encrypting the data flow between the client and the server. FIPS (Federal Information Processing Standard) describes the standards for key generation and key management. There's no such thing as FIPS encryption, but many encryption mechanisms are FIPS-compliant. Only algorithms submitted to the National Institute of Standards and Technology (NIST) may be considered FIPS-compliant. FIPS-compliant security supports server authentication for RDP connections.

When you require FIPS compliance through the Terminal Services Configuration tool, you're defining the security algorithms the server may use. For example, it defines the way that TLS works. As of this writing, it will use Triple Data Encryption Standard (DES) for encrypting the TLS traffic, RSA for the public key exchange, and the Secure Hashing Algorithm (SHA-1) for the TLS hashing.

Even if you don't choose to use server authentication, when FIPS compliance is required via Group Policy, RDP encryption will use the Triple DES algorithm. The server uses FIPS algorithms for more than just establishing secure communications between RDP client and server. Again, the FIPS-compliant algorithms will change with time as more algorithms are tested and determined to be compliant. On Windows Server 2008, the encrypted file system (EFS) behavior won't change regardless of this setting; the default algorithm is the FIPS-compliant 256-bit Advanced Encryption Standard (AES) algorithm. On previous versions of Windows, requiring FIPS compliance would make EFS fall back to Triple DES.

You can configure the terminal server to use FIPS-compliant algorithms either from Group Policy or from Terminal Services Configuration. If you set Group Policy to require FIPS compliance, this will override the Terminal Services-specific Group Policy that sets the RDP Encryption level to High.

> **Note** Because NIST (National Institute of Standards and Technology) certification takes some time, it is possible that the FIPS-compliant algorithm may not be the strongest available algorithm. More recent algorithms may not have been certified yet.

Authenticating Server Identity

One danger of communicating with a remote computer that requires you to supply your credentials is that the server may not be who you think it is. If it's a rogue server impersonating a real one, you could inadvertently type your credentials into the server, thereby giving an attacker everything they need to connect to your domain or server.

RDP includes encryption, but does not have any means to authenticate the server. NTLM authentication can verify a remote computer's domain membership, but not its actual identity. To alleviate this problem, Terminal Services supports Transport Layer Security (TLS), introduced for Terminal Services in Windows Server 2003 SP1. TLS communication, which is very similar to Secure Sockets Layer (SSL) communication, allows the client to authenticate the server's identity and then creates a session key for the remainder of the communication between client and server.

> **Note** TLS is the Internet Engineering Task Force (IETF) standard based on Secure Sockets Layer (SSL) v3, published by Netscape. Although TLS is based on SSL, the two aren't compatible. However, both TLS and SSL v3 implement a mechanism by which they can fall back to the appropriate protocol if necessary.

To establish communication using TLS between client and server, the client and server go through the following process. (This isn't specific to RDP connections; RDP just has the option of using TLS.)

1. A client computer connects to a TLS-enabled terminal server and requests a secure connection, telling the terminal server the ciphers and hashes it supports.

2. The terminal server picks the strongest cipher and hash function from the client's list and tells the client which one it has chosen. (If there's a minimum set on the terminal server and the client can't meet this minimum, the connection will fail.)

3. The terminal server sends a digital certificate (commonly called an SSL certificate) to the client, naming the terminal server, the trusted certificate authority who signed the certificate, and the server's public key.

4. The client verifies that the certificate is valid. (For this to work, the client must have the certificate authority in its list of trusted authorities. This means either using a public authority that the client already trusts, or if you've created your own certificate authority, importing the root certificate onto the client.)

5. The client picks a number at random, encrypts it with the server public key, and then sends the result back to the terminal server to decrypt with the private key. When it has been successfully decrypted, this randomly chosen number is the session key for the remainder of the connection between client and server. The session key is used to encrypt and decrypt the communication for this session.

Note The level of encryption the client is configured for controls the level of encryption used to generate the session key. To use TLS/SSL to authenticate server identity, the client must be configured to use either High or FIPS-compliant security. You can't use SSL with Low encryption.

TLS uses asymmetric encryption to verify the server identity and, after it is authenticated, to share the session key used to secure the connection. The session key is valid only for the duration of the session.

If any step of this sequence doesn't work, the connection has not been fully secured. What happens then depends on the settings on the client. In the case of authentication failure, you can choose to:

- Connect anyway without notifying the client that there was a problem authenticating the server.

- Warn the client but still allow the connection.

- Deny the connection outright if it can't be verified.

Authenticating Client Identity with Network Level Authentication (NLA)

Authenticating the server protects the client from connecting to a malicious terminal server masquerading as a legitimate one, but what about protecting the terminal server from malicious connections? As discussed in Chapter 3, "Installing the Core Terminal Server Environment," the process of starting a connection—even just presenting a logon screen—requires the server to create many of the processes required to support a session (e.g., Csrss.exe and Winlogon.exe). Session creation is expensive, so creating even this much of a session—only to be told that the user trying to access the terminal server doesn't have the required credentials—is both a security vulnerability and a performance hit.

One way to reduce both the security hit and the performance hit is to enable connections only from computers that support Network Level Authentication (NLA). You may have noticed that, with the RDC 6.x client, when you connect to a terminal server you don't connect to the terminal server logon screen to provide your credentials. Instead, a local dialog box pops up to take your credentials on the client. This dialog box is the front end to CredSSP (see Figure 7-1).

FIGURE 7-1 The Windows Security dialog box is the user interface to CredSSP.

When you type your credentials into this dialog box, even if you don't choose to save them, they go to the Credential Security Service Provider (CredSSP), which then passes the credentials to the terminal server via a secure channel. Only if the terminal server accepts the credentials will it begin building a session for this user.

> **Note** You may also see NLA referred to as *frontside authentication*. It's the same thing, with a different name.

On clients that support CredSSP and RDP 6.x, the clients will always use NLA if it's available. You can also configure the terminal server to permit connections only from computers that support NLA, using Group Policy or Terminal Services Configuration. Because CredSSP, the technology that supports NLA, is part of the operating system, not part of RDP, the client OS must support CredSSP for NLA to work. Therefore, although there is an RDC 6.0 client available for Windows XP SP2, this doesn't enable Windows XP SP2 to use NLA.

> **Note** Although remote connections to Windows Vista desktops are somewhat outside the scope of this book, it's worth mentioning that you can also restrict Windows Vista to accept connection requests only from clients that support NLA. To do so, go to Control Panel | System | Remote Settings. From the Remote tab of the System Properties dialog box, select the option restricting incoming connections to those that can support NLA.

Speeding Logons with Single Sign-on

Time spent typing credentials into a dialog box is wasted time, in the eyes of the user who is less concerned about system security than in getting his work done; after all, security is not his job. It's acceptable to present credentials once to a terminal server, but when you access multiple servers, it's much more irksome.

Single sign-on enables domain-joined clients to store their credentials and present them automatically each time they connect to a new terminal server. After you provide your user name and password once, you won't have to do so again as long as you're connecting via the same credentials. SSO saves credentials according to the terminal server you're connecting to, so connections to individual terminal servers will still prompt you for connections in a way that connecting to a farm via its farm name will not.

The Credential Security Service Provider

Two of the new security features of Windows Vista and Windows Server 2008 depend on the ability to cache credentials so that end users don't have to provide them, either because they don't want to (as in the case of single-sign on), or because they're given no opportunity to provide them (as in the case of NLA). The piece that makes credential caching work is the Credential Security Service Provider (CredSSP). CredSSP is available on Windows Vista, Windows Server 2008, and Windows XP SP3. Again, it is not linked to RDP 6.1. CredSSP is part of the operating system, not part of RDC.

> **Note** Although CredSSP is available on Windows XP SP3, it's disabled by default. To enable it, you'll need to modify two registry keys. Go to HKLM\SYSTEM\CurrentControlSet\Control\Lsa, and in Security Packages, data type REG_MULTI_SZ, append **tspkg** to the list of security providers already present. In HKLM\SYSTEM\CurrentControlSet\Control\SecurityProviders, make sure that Credssp.dll is present. You can't use Group Policy to configure SSO on Windows XP SP3.

CredSSP delegates user credentials to a trusted server via a secure channel using TLS. After it has those credentials, the trusted server can impersonate the user and log on to itself without waiting for a user to present credentials.

How Terminal Servers Use CredSSP   CredSSP comes into play in several terminal server scenarios:

- For network-level authentication, CredSSP provides the framework that allows a user to be authenticated to a terminal server before fully establishing the connection.

- For single sign-on, CredSSP stores user credentials and passes them to the terminal server to automate logon.

> **Note** Because Internet Information Services (IIS) doesn't use CredSSP, this functionality can't be used to enable SSO to a TS Web Access Web site. If you require users to log on to the TS Web Access portal, they won't be able to use their stored credentials for this purpose. They'll need to authenticate against both portal and terminal server.

- For reconnecting to a session within a farm, CredSSP speeds the process of passing the connection to the correct server by allowing the terminal server to see who's logging on without having to create an entire session (using NLA in a slightly different scenario).

How It Works: How CredSSP Authenticates Server and Client

CredSSP enables mutual authentication of server and client as shown in the following illustration:

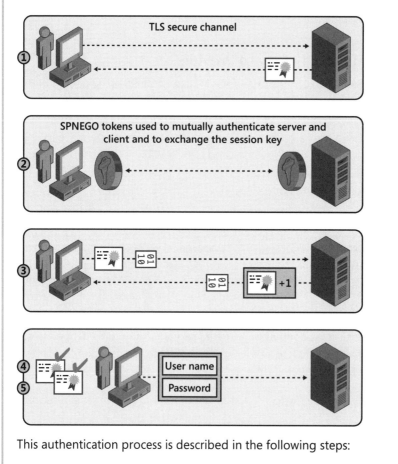

This authentication process is described in the following steps:

1. The client initiates a secure channel with the server using Transport Layer Security, and the server passes back its certificate with its name, certificate authority, and public key. Only the server is identified; the client remains anonymous at this point.

> **Note** Although the client uses TLS to establish the secure connection, this isn't full server authentication, because at this point of the transaction the client and server don't need to have a mutually trusted certificate authority. At this stage of communications, the server could present a self-signed certificate.

2. When the session has been established and a session key is created, CredSSP uses the Simple and Protected Negotiate (SPNEGO) protocol to mutually authenticate server and client, so they know they can trust each other. Basically, this mechanism lets the client and server agree on an authentication mechanism they both support, such as Kerberos or NTLM.

3. Mutual authentication complete, CredSSP on the client encrypts the server's certificate with the session key created during Step 2 and sends it to the server. The server receives the encrypted certificate, decrypts it using its private key, and then adds 1 to the most significant bit of the certificate number. It then encrypts the result and sends it back to the client.

> **Note** The point of performing a function on the certificate is to ensure that no one can intercept the exchange between client and server and spoof the server.

4. The client reviews the encrypted certificate that it gets from the server and compares it to the certificate it has.

5. Assuming the results match, CredSSP on the client sends the user credentials to the server.

Managing the CredSSP Store   Users can save, edit, and delete credentials in the CredSSP store. To initially save the credentials to use with SSO, select the Remember My Credentials check box in the Windows Security dialog box shown in Figure 7-2.

FIGURE 7-2 Storing credentials in CredSSP

After they're saved, and you have made an initial connection, you can edit them (for example, if you change your password, as CredSSP will not automatically update password changes) by clicking the Edit link in Figure 7-3.

FIGURE 7-3 You can edit or delete stored credentials.

If you choose to edit the saved credentials, you'll see a dialog box like the one used to log on. Your domain and user name will be displayed and your password credentials will be left blank. If you choose to save credentials using another user name, you can also click the Use Another Account button to completely start over. Use this option to update a stored password after you've changed it.

If you click the Delete link, you'll remove that stored credential from the CredSSP store. A dialog box will prompt you to confirm the action and then clear that saved user name and account information from the cache. Use this option to delete credentials you accidentally saved or which are no longer needed.

Understanding Network Access Protection

TS Gateway, which we'll discuss in detail later in this chapter, makes it easy to enable people to securely connect to internal network resources via the Internet. One trouble with allowing computers outside the network onto the network to use terminal servers is that you don't know where those computers have been. More to the point, you don't know what they bring with them.

You can enforce certain policies on computers that are frequently attached to the corporate network: you can update virus signatures, check for application updates, and so forth. But computers connecting to terminal servers from outside the network, not updated according to the policies of that network, pose a different problem: How do you keep computers you don't control from infecting the network? You certainly don't want those computers to infect the terminal servers and possibly lead to mass infection of all personal computers that attach to them.

One way is to check those computers before they join the network and make sure they conform to the organization health policies before they're allowed access. The Windows Server 2008 technology that makes this possible is Network Access Protection (NAP).

Network Access Protection is a big topic that covers a lot more than working with TS Gateway to prevent computers not meeting minimum health requirements from accessing terminal servers. NAP policies are used to determine whether a client computer is permitted to use the wireless network or to get an IP address from a Dynamic Host Configuration Protocol (DHCP) server, for example. NAP works with TS Gateway in this way: In addition to implementing Connection Authorization Policies (TS CAPs) (which define *who* is allowed to access the network via TS Gateway) and Resource Authorization Policies (TS RAPs) (which define which network resources those users can access after they connect), you also set policies on a Network Policy Server (NPS) to determine the minimum requirements for the client computer's state of health before it connects to the terminal servers the TS CAPs and TS RAPs permit it to use. The client reports, the NPS sees how the client fares, and then TS Gateway tells the client whether it's allowed to connect to the terminal servers via TS Gateway or not.

Core NAP Concepts   To understand NAP, you must be familiar with the following concepts:

- Statement of Health (SoH) and system statement of health (SSoH)
- System health agents (SHAs)
- Network Policy Server (NPS)/Health Policy Server

The TS Gateway installation installs and uses a local NPS but it can also access a centralized NPS. The configuration mainly depends on (a) whether you're clustering the TS Gateway servers and don't want to maintain CAPs on both servers and (b) whether you're planning to use NAP for controlling access to any other network resources. For example, if you also use it to govern access to the wireless network, you'll most likely set up a central NPS to handle both cases. For details on how to set up TS Gateway to use a central server, see the section titled "Using a Central NPS to Store TS CAPs" later in this chapter.

How NAP Supports TS Gateway   Now that you have the background, let's look at the details of how NAP supports TS Gateway.

1. The client requests access to a terminal server or desktop connection via RDP and TS Gateway.

2. Each System Health Agent collects the client data for its area (e.g., antivirus) and creates a Statement of Health for that area.

3. The NAP agent for TS Gateway on the client (there's a NAP agent for each kind of connection NAP supports) collates the reports from the various SHAs on the client and creates a single System Statement of Health (SSoH). NAP supports independent software vendors (ISVs) replacing the SHA on the client, but the native SHAs will report on the policies shown in Table 7-1.

TABLE 7-1 Contents of the Statement of Health

System Health Agent	Example Information Reported
Firewall	Whether the firewall is enabled and currently running.
Automatic Updates	Whether automatic updates are enabled, and whether the client is configured only to check for updates, automatically download updates, or both download and install discovered updates. It will also report when the client was last updated. If a Windows Software Update Services (WSUS) server is defined for the client, the SHA will also report the name of this server.
Antivirus/Antispyware	Whether antivirus and antispyware software is installed, enabled, up to date, and currently running.
Security Updates	The current security state of the client, according to the security updates currently installed.
Client version	Windows XP, Windows Vista RTM, or Windows Vista SP1.

4. The client sends this SSOH to the TS Gateway, which processes it locally if it's acting as its own NPS, or forwards it to the central one, as appropriate.

5. The NPS evaluates the SHA report against its policies. Based on these policies, it sends a message back to the client with its report on the client health status as compared to the policy, and tells the client how it fared. This report can include details such as the following:

   ❑ The client conforms to all policies.

   ❑ The client requires security updates.

   ❑ The client isn't running antivirus software, or this software needs to be updated.

Note The NPS does not save any SHA-reported client data, so every time the client reports on its state of health, the HPS will be looking only at the latest information. There's no cache to be out of date.

The report also tells the client whether it's allowed access to the terminal servers or not.

6. The client then acts according to the report. If it's following policy, then it is able to get on the network in accordance with the TS CAPs and TS RAPs defined by TS Gateway. If it's not, then it is denied access to the network. Because the client is connecting from outside the network and the TS Gateway is its only route in, it can't connect to a remediation server to fix the problems that make it out of compliance with policy. In other NAP scenarios, the client may be able to get to a restricted area of the network to fix the reported problems before trying again.

Configuring the Security Settings on the Terminal Server

The section titled "Core Security Concepts" earlier in this chapter explains the details of using various connection-security mechanisms. This section explains how to configure those settings using the Terminal Services Configuration tool and Group Policy.

Configuring Connection Security Using the Terminal Services Configuration Tool

All per-server connection security settings are configured from the General tab of the protocol listener properties. To get here, go to Administrative Tools | Terminal Services | Terminal Services Configuration, then double-click RDP-TCP in the Connections section of the middle pane. The General tab is shown in Figure 7-4.

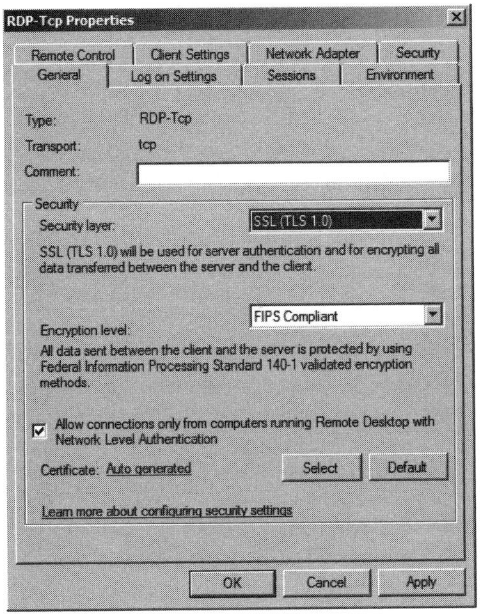

FIGURE 7-4 Edit connection security from the General tab of the RDP-TCP listener.

Server Authentication   Set the server authentication settings from the Security Layer section. The default is Negotiate, meaning that client and server will both use TLS for server authentication if it's supported. There's no real reason to mandate using RDP Security Layer, which does not support server authentication, but you can edit this setting to force server authentication using TLS. If the server can't be authenticated, then the client behavior can be set from the client RDP file settings configured on the Advanced tab of the RDC: Do Not Connect If Authentication Fails, Warn Me If Authentication Fails, and Always Connect, Even If Authentication Fails.

You can choose the certificate that the server should use to authenticate itself by clicking the Select button near the bottom of the screen. In this example, the terminal server is using a self-signed certificate. If you click the Select button, you can get more details about the certificate, including what it's used for, the name of the certificate authority backing it, and when the certificate expires.

Encryption Levels   Set the encryption level, noting that you must use either High or FIPS-compliant encryption to support server authentication. High encryption uses the strongest key strength of the server; FIPS-compliant encryption uses an encryption algorithm that has been tested by NIST on Windows Server 2008.

> **Note** FIPS-compliant algorithms are not necessarily stronger than High security on all platforms; it depends on what's installed and what's been tested. The point of FIPS compliance is to serve as a policy measure for networks that must conform to these guidelines.

Network Level Authentication   To permit only client computers supporting NLA, select the appropriate check box on this page. Doing so will prevent any client computers that do not support NLA (any client running RDC prior to 6.x and any operating system not supporting CredSSP) from connecting to the server. Only Windows Vista and Windows XP SP3 support CredSSP.

Configuring Connection Security Using Group Policy

Terminal Services Configuration only edits security settings for a single server. To edit settings on multiple servers, you'll need to use Group Policy. Group Policy also includes security options not available through the Terminal Services Configuration graphical user interface (GUI).

Server Authentication   To configure server authentication policies, go to Computer Configuration | Policies | Administrative Templates | Windows Components | Terminal Services | Terminal Server | Security. To require server authentication, enable Require Use Of Specific Security Layer For Remote (RDP) Connections and choose SSL (TLS 1.0) from the list of security layers. (RDP, you may recall, does not support authentication; choosing this option encrypts the traffic but does not authenticate the server.) If you leave the setting at Negotiate (the default), the clients will attempt to use TLS, if they support it.

Group Policy allows you to control the template used for server authentication to make sure that the terminal server presents the right one. In Computer Configuration | Policies | Administrative Templates | Windows Components | Terminal Services | Terminal Server | Security, you can enable Server Authentication Certificate Template and provide the name of the template to use. If you do, then the server will choose only from among certificates using that template with a name matching the server name. If there's more than one certificate to choose from, the server will choose the certificate with the latest expiration date. If you've already specified a certificate to use for server authentication, the terminal server will ignore this setting.

Encryption Levels   The policy you use to set RDP encryption levels depends on the level of security you're setting. By default, the client and server will negotiate the most complex algorithm they both support. You can change the encryption to Low or, far more likely, require all connections to use High or FIPS-compliant encryption algorithms. If you do so, clients that do not support these algorithms will not be able to connect to the server.

To set the minimum encryption level, go to Computer Configuration | Policies | Administrative Templates | Windows Components | Terminal Services | Terminal Server | Security and enable the Set Client Connection Encryption Level policy, choosing Low Level, High Level, or Client Compatible from the drop-down list.

To require FIPS using Group Policy, go to Computer Configuration | Policies | Windows Settings | Security Settings, Local Policies | Security Options. Find The System Cryptography: Use FIPS Compliant Algorithms For Encryption, Hashing And Signing setting and enable it.

> **Caution** Enabling this policy causes the terminal servers to use FIPS-compliant algorithms for *everything*, not just for RDP connections, so be aware that requiring FIPS may cause problems with some Web sites and applications that require inter-server communication.

Understanding Session Broker

Creating a Terminal Services environment consisting of one terminal server may work for a small business, but it has some drawbacks. First, the company can outgrow the hardware capabilities of a single server. Second, there is no built in redundancy; losing that one server means no one can work. Implementing a server farm provides a scalable and redundant application hosting platform.

A terminal *server farm* consists of two or more terminal servers with the same software configuration (e.g., security settings) and application sets, all represented under a single farm name so they appear to the client as a single entity. Server farms are combined with load balancing so that the workload is distributed evenly among all farm members. Because the servers are homogenous in configuration, it does not matter to users which server they get directed to, because all servers should provide the same user experience.

Even when terminal servers are clustered into a farm, the final connection is always between a client computer and a single terminal server. When you're connecting to individual servers, connecting is simple: The RDP file or RDC client points to a specific server, and assuming that the user is authorized to connect, the connection is made. There's no ambiguity about where the connection should go. A multi-server deployment adds a layer of complexity because the user session must be directed to a particular server. You need two mechanisms to determine which server a connection request should ultimately go and to get it there: a load balancer and a session broker.

Distributing Sessions in a Farm

A load balancer spreads incoming workload evenly among a group of servers (or, in other scenarios, routers or other network appliances). Load-balanced resources should always be configured identically, to avoid connection-specific errors that can be hard to troubleshoot.

Load balancers can be implemented in software or hardware, and their balancing algorithms vary widely. For example, round robin DNS is a very simple software-based load balancing technique where multiple host records are created for the same host name. Each time a request for that host name is made, the DNS server returns the host records in consecutive order. (The catch to this method is that, if a host goes offline, DNS continues routing people to that server as long as the host record remains in its database.) Microsoft Network Load Balancing (NLB) works by sending a percentage of incoming connections to each load-balanced server, on the principle that if the incoming requests are evenly distributed, the traffic should be, too. (For this reason, NLB is better for load balancing servers when the connections are very short, like Web servers. Terminal server load will not necessarily distribute evenly according to the number of connections coming in.) Therefore, if you're looking for a simple means of balancing connections across terminal servers, your best bet is likely not random distribution of incoming connections but sending the new connection to the server that has the lowest number of connections. More sophisticated load balancers can use complex rules to disperse traffic based on processor load, memory load, client IP address, and so forth.

That's the load balancing part. The brokering capability part comes in when it matters where the incoming connection goes. For Web services, for example, if you're connecting to a server it really doesn't matter which one you connect to, since your connection retains no state and won't last very long. For terminal server sessions, though, it matters a great deal. It's far better for you to maintain all connections belonging to the same user on a single server—and in a single session—for the following reasons:

- Only one copy of your profile will be open (see Chapter 4, "Creating the User Work Environment," for more details).

- The overhead on the terminal servers will be reduced, since session creation is expensive and there's a minimum set of processes needed to support a Terminal Services session (see Chapter 3 for more details).

With NLB, you can define affinity for a particular server so that all incoming requests from a client will go to a particular server, but this isn't quite what's wanted either. That server may not always be the best server for the purpose—the server may be offline, for example.

Therefore, you need a brokering option that can answer two questions about incoming connections and route connections accordingly:

- Does the user attempting to make this connection already have a session open on a terminal server in the farm?

- If not, which server has the lowest number of connections?

Session Broker, the new Terminal Services role service replacing Session Directory, makes those decisions about how to distribute incoming connections to a farm.

How It Works: Session Broker Routing Methods

Session Broker can support two kinds of load balancing redirection: IP address redirection and routing token redirection. DNS round robin and Network Load Balancing use IP address redirection; hardware load balancers such as Cisco's Content Switching Module may use routing token redirection.

IP address redirection, used when clients can connect directly to servers in the farm and the default for Session Broker, works like this:

1. The client connects to the initial load balancer and is routed to a terminal server, where the client is authenticated.

2. The terminal server queries Session Broker for the terminal server to which this client should be redirected.

3. Session Broker returns the answer to the terminal server, which passes the encrypted load balance packet to the client. The packet contains the IP address of the chosen terminal server.

4. The client connects directly to the terminal server IP address specified in the load balance packet.

When the load balancing configuration requires that all traffic go initially to the load balancer, clients can't connect using IP addresses. In that case, the load balancer must support TS Session Broker routing tokens. Clients get routed to the appropriate terminal server like this:

1. The client connects to the initial load balancer and is routed to a terminal server, where the client is authenticated.

2. The terminal server queries Session Broker for the terminal server to which this client should be redirected.

3. Session Broker returns the answer to the terminal server.

4. The terminal server tells the client to connect again to the load balancer, but this time it gives the client a routing token to give to the load balancer.

5. The routing token contains the IP address of the chosen terminal server.

6. The client connects directly to the terminal server IP address specified in the routing token.

What Is Session Broker?

In Windows 2008, the Session Directory feature from Windows 2003 is renamed to Session Broker. Session Broker includes the capabilities of the Windows 2003 Session Directory and also contains new functionality. Session Broker provides:

- Session Reconnection, reconnecting users to their disconnected sessions.

- Session based load balancing, which evenly distributes Terminal Services sessions to servers in the farm according to the server capabilities and the number of connections it's hosting.

- Session draining, slowly draining sessions from a terminal server that must go offline by not allowing new connections to the server.

Unlike its predecessor, Session Broker can run on Windows 2008 Standard Edition as well as on Windows Server 2008 Enterprise and Data Center Editions. Windows 2003 servers can take advantage of the session reconnection feature, but to take part in the new load balancing feature, terminal servers must run Windows Server 2008. Clients need a minimum of RDC 5.2 to use Session Broker Load Balancing.

Note Although Session Broker is designed to route connections to terminal servers, it exposes some application programming interfaces (APIs) that allow its behavior to be modified so that it can route connections to blade PCs, virtual machines, or even desktops. For more information, see "Extending Terminal Services Session Broker" on MSDN at *http://msdn.microsoft.com/en-us/ library/cc644953(VS.85).aspx*.

How Does Session Broker Work?

Connections made to a terminal server farm that is participating in Session Broker Load Balancing (SBLB) go through these steps (shown in Figure 7-5):

1. The client requests a connection to a terminal server farm. A load balancer (external to Session Broker) determines how to route this initial request.

2. The client connection is sent to the terminal server specified by the initial load balancing mechanism; the user authenticates to that terminal server. If the client supports NLA, it is used here to reduce the overhead on the terminal server. The terminal server can authenticate the client without creating an entire session.

3. The terminal server passes the user's credentials to Session Broker to find out which terminal server is the best choice to host the connection (for example, if the user already has a session open).

4. Session Broker checks its database, which stores the information shown in Table 7-2, to see if the user already has a session open and, if so, which server it's on and what the Session ID is. It can also tell whether the session is displaying a full desktop or TS RemoteApps. This is important because, as discussed in Chapter 3 and in Chapter 6, "Installing and Publishing Applications," the two sessions have different shells.

5. If a user already has a session established on a terminal server, Session Broker routes the connection to that terminal server, and the user is reconnected to the existing session (or reconnected to the disconnected session, if applicable). If the user does not have an existing session, Session Broker determines the server with the fewest sessions and sends the connection to that terminal server.

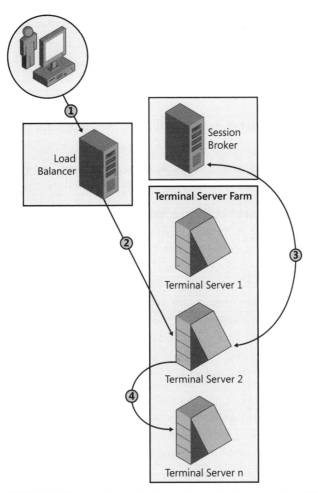

FIGURE 7-5 How sessions get directed to terminal servers using TS Session Broker

Note To avoid new terminal servers from being overwhelmed with sessions (because they have the fewest sessions), Session Broker permits a maximum of 16 pending connections to a server.

TABLE 7-2 Routing Information Stored by Session Broker

Session Broker DB Field	Description
Source-server-ID	Name of the server that the session resides on
Session-ID	Session ID which is determined by the server on which the session originated
Username	User name of the user logged on to the session
Domain	Domain to which the user belongs
TS-Protocol	Protocol used to connect the session
session-creation-date-and-time	Time and date the session was created
disconnection-date-and-time	Time and date that the session was disconnected (if applicable)
application-type	Session type (displaying desktop or TS RemoteApps)
resolution-width	The resolution width of the RDP session (e.g., 1024)
resolution-height	The resolution width of the RDP session (e.g., 768)
color-depth	The color depth in the session

Choosing Between Round Robin DNS or Network Load Balancing for Initial Routing

Session Broker Load Balancing doesn't come into play for the first step in this process, in which a client is routed to a terminal server in order to be sent to the Session Broker.

A third-party load balancing solution is an option, but Windows Server 2008 has two load balancers you can implement for no additional cost. Round robin DNS is the simplest to implement. Basically, each host name in DNS has multiple host records backing it. Every time a connection to that host name is attempted, DNS sends the connection to the host records in rotation. Its downfall is that client-side DNS caching can result in clients resolving DNS requests with cached records instead of receiving a reply from the DNS server. This means that round robin DNS is bypassed completely. Also, round robin DNS does not know when a server goes offline, so it will continue to reply to requests with the host record of the unavailable server, resulting in 30-second delays for clients who receive this reply.

For these reasons, you may choose to use another type of network load balancer such as Network Load Balancing (NLB), which distributes incoming connections evenly across the load-balanced servers. Although NLB is not ideal for load balancing among terminal servers, it's fine for creating the initial connections because they don't last long.

You may be wondering how Session Broker keeps track of the terminal servers. What happens if one goes offline, and how will the Session Broker know if it does? For that matter, what will it *do* if a server goes offline?

To keep track of terminal server status, the Session Broker keeps track of whether the connections it redirects to the terminal servers in the farm actually go through. If a redirection attempt succeeds, then great—the terminal server is available. If a redirection attempt fails, then there *might* be a problem with the terminal server or the network—but it's not definite, since it was only one attempt. Therefore, 60 seconds after the initial redirection request, the Session Broker starts pinging the terminal server that didn't respond. If the terminal server does not respond to a set number of pings (a default of 3, at a default interval of 10 seconds) then the Session Broker removes that terminal server from its database.

This back and forth means that, about 2–3 minutes from the time the Session Broker attempts to send a connection to an unavailable terminal server, the Session Broker will stop looking for the server. Removing a terminal server from the farm by deleting it from the TS Session Directory Computers group will not delete it from the Session Broker's database. If you take a server offline, you can speed up the process of purging the database by shortening the intervals at which it looks for the terminal server. These are controlled by three registry keys located under HKLM\SYSTEM\CurrentControlSet\Services\Tssdis\Parameters in the Session Broker's registry. Conveniently, all these values are in decimal, so they're easy to interpret. The three that you need to concern yourself with are these:

- TimeBetweenPings (default value of 10, the value is in seconds)
- NumberFailedPingsBeforePurge (default value is 3)
- TimeServerSilentBeforePing (default value is 60; the value is in seconds)

To decrease or increase the interval between the time a Session Broker attempts to connect and when it purges the terminal server from the database, edit these settings. Just be aware that a connection problem or the server being offline isn't the only reason why a terminal server might not respond.

> **On the Companion Media**   The SBDatabaseDump.vbs script found on the companion media is a sample you can use to dump the contents of the Session Broker database.

Direct from the Source: How NLA Speeds Session Broker Routing

Before Windows Server 2008, when a terminal server in a farm received a connection request, it created a temporary session to authenticate the user and load user policies. If no local disconnected session was present, it queried the TS Session Broker to see if there was a disconnected session for the user on another computer in the farm. If a disconnected session was found, a redirection request was sent to the client to connect to the other server instead. The temporary session was then discarded.

The temporary session creation resulted in significant delay in completing the connection because a full logon occurs in the session. Also, the user experience was unpleasant because the user saw two welcome screens, first for the temporary session and then again for the redirected session. The new technique addresses these drawbacks when a connection is made using the new Terminal Services client with CredSSP.

Windows Server 2008 introduced a new technique to improve the redirection scenario. Clients that support Network Level Authentication can pass their credentials to the terminal server. The terminal server hosting the temporary connection can use those credentials to authenticate that the user is allowed to log on to the farm and can pass those credentials to the Session Broker to help it look for an existing connection associated with those credentials. If Session Broker finds a disconnected session on another computer in the farm, it immediately sends a redirect packet to the client, and the client subsequently connects to the redirected server. Hence no temporary session is created before the connection is redirected. This change improves security, since the client must be authenticated even before it makes the connection, and it also improves performance since the first terminal server doesn't have to create a temporary session.

Munindra Das
Software Development Engineer II

Setting Up Session Broker

To set up Session Broker, you must install the TS Session Broker role service, join the terminal servers to a farm, permit them to use TS Session Broker, and optionally configure the terminal servers to accept more or fewer connections relative to other servers in the farm.

Installing the TS Session Broker Role Service

You must install TS Session Broker on a domain member; it can be on a domain controller or member server. The server does not need to be a terminal server. To install TS Session Broker, follow these steps:

1. Open Server Manager. If the server does not contain any other Terminal Services role services, click the Roles item in the left pane and then click Add Roles. The Add Roles Wizard starts. Click Next on the Before You Begin page.

2. Select the Terminal Services role and click Next. On the Introduction to Terminal Services page, click Next. If the server already has a Terminal Services role installed, click the Terminal Services in the Roles Summary section and then click Add Role Services.

3. Select the TS Session Broker role service and click Next.

4. On the Confirmation Installation Selections screen, click Install.

5. The Installation screen will show that the installation succeeded. Click Close.

> **Note** You can also install TS Session Broker from an elevated command prompt with the following command: Servermanagercmd.exe -install ts-session-broker. To remove TS Session Broker, type Servermanagercmd.exe -remove ts-session-broker -restart.

Installing Session Broker creates a new local security group named Session Directory Computers. You must add terminal servers to this group to permit them to work with the Session Broker.

> **Note** If Session Broker is installed on a domain controller, the Session Directory group will be a Domain Local Group and is accessible via Active Directory Users And Computers (ADUC) Users container.

Configure Terminal Servers to Work with Session Broker

To join terminal servers to a farm and let them work with Session Broker, you must do the following:

- Add the terminal servers to the Session Directory Computers group on TS Session Broker. Even if you have multiple farms, they can all be supported by the same TS Session Broker. Add the terminal servers regardless of the farm they belong to.

- Set up initial load balancing among the terminal servers so they can route temporary sessions through TS Session Broker.

- Configure the terminal servers to be members of a farm.

To add terminal servers to Session Directory Computers group on the TS Session Broker, open Server Manager, expand Configuration | Local Users And Groups | Groups, and then double-click the Session Directory Computers security group in the right pane. On the Members tab, Click Add, type the terminal server computer accounts, click OK, and then click OK again.

> **Note** If the TS Session Broker server is also a domain controller (DC), you can't use Server Manager to add terminal servers to the Session Directory Computers group; use ADUC to do this instead.

For terminal servers that will participate in load balancing, set up an initial load balancer to disperse the initial connection.

You can join terminal servers to a farm via Terminal Services Configuration or Group Policy.

Using Terminal Services Configuration to Join a Farm   To join a farm using Terminal Services Configuration, open the tool on the terminal server. In the Edit Settings section on the middle pane, double-click Member Of Farm In TS Session Broker to open the dialog box shown in Figure 7-6. Select the box next to Join A Farm In TS Session Broker and the options will be available for configuration.

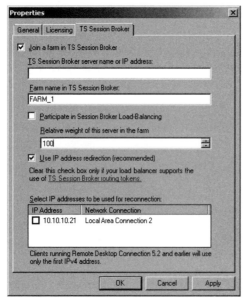

FIGURE 7-6 TS Session Broker tab settings

The options on the TS Session Broker tab are described as follows:

- In the TS Session Broker Server Name Or IP Address field, provide the server name or IP address of the server where TS Session Broker is installed.

- In the Farm Name In TS Session Broker field, type the name of the farm that this terminal server will join (FARM_1 is the default). This name does not have to correspond to an existing DNS entry.

- Select the Participate In Session Broker Load-Balancing check box to engage this terminal server in TS Session Broker load balancing. Optionally, you can give the server a relative weight, which describes its capacity relative to the other terminal servers in the farm. Although all terminal servers should be configured identically, not all may have the same amount of memory or the same number of processor cores. For example, if a server is only 75 percent as powerful as other servers in the farm, then you can reduce its weight to allow it only 75 percent as many connections as the other servers. The default value is 100.

- Choosing to use IP Address Redirection depends on the capabilities of the initial load balancer. If the initial load balancer allows clients to connect directly to terminal servers in the farm, then select this box to use IP address redirection.

> **Note** Unless you know otherwise, always use IP address redirection. Some initial load-balancing configurations require all terminal server traffic to be routed through the load balancer. Therefore, clients do not communicate directly with terminal servers in the farm, as they won't know their IP addresses. Instead, they talk to the load balancer, and the load balancer passes the communication to the appropriate terminal server. In these situations, the load balancer must use routing token redirection instead of IP address redirection.

Using Group Policy to Join a Farm   Managing farm membership settings on each terminal server isn't best practice because it's too hard to keep all the settings consistent. If you mistype the farm name on a terminal server, for example, you'll create a new farm and that server will not be load-balanced with the other terminal servers you'd intended to group it with. The easiest way to configure a terminal server farm and TS Session Broker Load Balancing is to use Group Policy. The settings are located in Computer Configuration | Policies | Administrative Templates | Windows Components | Terminal Services | Terminal Server | TS Session Broker.

Create a GPO and apply it to the organizational unit (OU) where the terminal servers reside. Set the policies as described here:

- **Configure TS Session Broker Farm Name**   Enable this setting and specify a farm name. Session Broker can keep track of multiple farms, so this setting specifies a farm name, not a server. Because the Group Policy object (GPO) is applied to an OU holding the terminal servers, all terminal servers will know this farm name.

- **Configure TS Session Broker Server Name**   Enable this setting and type the IP address, the fully qualified domain name or the NetBIOS name of the server where TS Session Broker is installed. Terminal servers in the farm will be serviced by this Session Broker.

- **Join TS Session Broker**   Enabling this setting joins the terminal servers to the farm specified in the TS Session Broker Server Name policy setting.

- **Use TS Session Broker Load Balancing**   Enable this setting and the terminal servers will participate in TS Session Broker Load Balancing. For this to work, the three previous policy settings must be enabled and configured.

All of these policy settings, if not configured or disabled, can be configured using Terminal Services Configuration, although the settings in Group Policy take precedence if there is a conflict. One exception to this rule is the Join TS Session Broker policy setting; if it is disabled in Group Policy, it cannot be configured via Terminal Services Configuration.

Enabling Remote Access Using TS Gateway

Prior to Windows Server 2008, administrators had two choices to provide access to terminal services using the tools in the box:

- Enabling VPN support.

- Exposing the terminal sever to the world by opening port 3389 to listen for incoming RDP connections. (In a variation, some administrators configured RDP to listen on a different port so that the terminal server would at least not be listening on a known port. This wasn't much security against attacks and required administrators to edit the RDP files to point to the correct port.)

Both approaches have their downsides. Virtual private networks (VPNs) give remote users the same connectivity outside the network as they have inside, which isn't necessarily appropriate for all situations. VPNs also require a VPN client on the client computer. Opening the terminal server to the outside world—even on a non-standard port—is asking for trouble. Because those were the only two options available in the box, most administrators who needed to enable extranet access to the terminal servers used helper products from TS ISV partners.

TS Gateway, a new role service in Windows Server 2008, makes it possible to enable remote access to the network using only built-in components with the following conditions:

- Only specified users can use the TS Gateway to access the network—not all terminal server users need to be granted this access.

- Those specified users can use only specified resources, so they're not necessarily getting access to the entire corporate network.

- Those users can connect using any computer that's able to be a TS Gateway client.

In a nutshell, TS Gateway acts as a proxy to the terminal servers. Incoming connections come in on port 443, used for SSL traffic. It takes those connections and routes them to the appropriate terminal server, or even desktop computer, using RDP tunneled through the SSL connection. Implementing TS Gateway means that:

- VPN tunnels are no longer needed to provide secure RDP access to terminal servers and computers with remote desktop access enabled.

- Port 3389, and any other hole punched in a firewall for use with RDP connections, can be closed. Now only port 443 is needed.

- Users in larger corporate environments who may have been blocked from connecting via RDP to resources across Network Address Translation (NAT) devices (resources may be separated by firewalls that blocked port 3389 for security reasons) are no longer hindered; connections established by TS gateway use SSL port 443, commonly opened on firewalls.

You can use TS Gateway either on its own or in combination with TS Web Access (discussed in Chapter 6). TS Gateway, in combination with TS Web Access, allows remote users to securely access corporate RDP-based resources (terminal servers, remote desktops, and RemoteApps) via a Web browser.

How TS Gateway Works

TS Gateway is the middleman for remote users making RDP connections to resources located inside the corporate network. This is how it works:

1. A user wanting access to an internal RDP resource launches the RDP file pointing to that resource, whether from a saved RDP file or from TS Web Access.

2. The RDP file is configured to use TS Gateway for extranet connections (this is part of packaging an RDP file for TS RemoteApps, for example) and first establishes an SSL tunnel to TS Gateway.

3. TS Gateway checks its connection access policies (TS CAPs) to authenticate the client and to verify that the client is authorized to make this connection.

4. When authenticated and authorized, the client requests access to a specific internal RDP resource: a RemoteApp, a terminal server desktop, or a client computer with remote access enabled. TS Gateway checks its resource authorization policies (TS RAPs) to verify that the client is allowed to connect to the requested resource.

5. If the client is allowed, TS Gateway establishes an RDP connection to the resource. Thereafter, all traffic for this connection flows through TS Gateway, as shown in Figure 7-7. TS Gateway forwards packets back and forth from the terminal server and the remote client, sending RDP packets over port 3389 to the internal RDP resource, and SSL encapsulated packets over port 443 to the remote client.

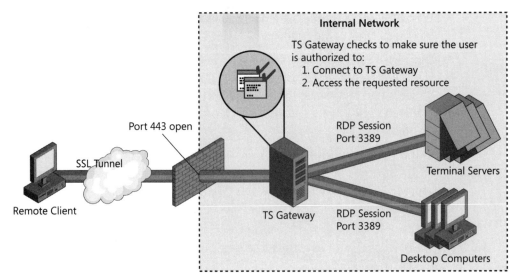

FIGURE 7-7 TS Gateway acts as the middleman for connections to RDP resources.

Enabling TS Gateway Authorization Policies

TS Gateway uses authorization policies to control connections to internal RDP resources. Different authorization policies enable user access to TS Gateway and the internal resources beyond the gateway.

TS Connection Authorization Policies (TS CAPs) define:

- Which user groups can connect to TS Gateway
- From which computers users can connect (optional)
- Supported authentication methods (smart card or password)
- Which client devices will be redirected to the remote session

TS CAPs are stored in a Network Policy Server (NPS), part of the Network Policy and Access Services role. You must install this role with TS Gateway; optionally, you can elect to store the TS CAPs on a central NPS to allow multiple TS Gateway servers to draw their TS CAPs from the same server. (This also makes sense if you're using NPS for other reasons.) We'll talk about how to set up the centralized TS CAPs in the section titled "Using a Central NPS to Store TS CAPs" later in this chapter.

TS Resource Authorization Policies (TS RAPs) specify which internal resources (specified by computer groups) user groups allowed by the TS CAPs are allowed to connect to after connecting to TS Gateway.

Think of TS CAPs and TS RAPs as specifying *who* can get to *what*. TS CAPs define *who* can connect to TS Gateway and TS RAPs define *what* internal resources user groups can connect to after they connect to TS Gateway. Therefore, users must meet the requirements specified on at least one TS CAP and one TS RAP to first connect to TS Gateway and then to do anything after that.

Defining multiple TS CAPs and TS RAPs allows you to granularly grant network access based on the needs of the clients, instead of giving clients full access to every RDP-enabled device on the network. This means you can even define a terminal server farm solely for outside access that is isolated from any sensitive data, if that is required. As part of the TS Gateway installation, you can create an initial TS CAP and TS RAP. But you may need more than one TS CAP and TS RAP to control access to TS Gateway and to network resources more explicitly.

For instance, you can use two TS CAPs and two TS RAPs to specify connection requirements such as these:

- Company Accounting Team Remote Access Authorization Policies
    - TS CAP: Accounting user group members can establish a connection to TS Gateway, but only when they are using computers that belong to the Accounting computer group. These users can only connect using smart cards, and device redirection will be disabled.
    - TS RAP: Accounting group users can then only connect to Accounting computers as well as the company TS farm.
- Company Sales Team Remote Access Authorization Policies
    - TS CAP: Sales user group members can connect to TS Gateway from any computer. They can use password authentication, and clipboard and printer redirection are allowed.
    - TS RAP: Sales user group members can connect to computers that are members of the Sales computer group.

> **Note** The next section will show you how to create a TS CAP and TS RAP as part of the TS Gateway installation procedures. For information on creating TS CAPs and TS RAPs post-installation, see the section titled "Creating and Maintaining TS Gateway Authorization Policies" later in this chapter.

Preparing to Install TS Gateway

Before launching the Add Roles Wizard, you should be familiar with the following requirements.

For TS Gateway and remote client computers to establish an encrypted connection to one another, you must obtain and install a server authentication certificate in the TS Gateway server computer certificate store. You can get the certificate from a public certificate authority (CA); server authentication certificates are often referred to as SSL or Web server certificates. Or if you maintain your own Public Key Infrastructure (PKI), you can generate your own server authentication certificate. No matter where you get the certificate, remote computers connecting to the TS Gateway server will attempt to verify the validity of the TS Gateway certificate. They do this by searching their own trusted root certificate store for the root CA certificate of the CA that signed the TS Gateway certificate. If the root CA certificate is there, the client trusts the root CA, and therefore can trust the TS Gateway server (this is called the chain of trust). If not, then the connection will not be established.

You may not have control over the remote computers used to connect to TS Gateway if they're not company assets or computers belonging to the users connecting via the Internet. Therefore, either purchase a server authentication certificate from a public CA that is part of the Microsoft Root Certificate Program, or have your root CA certificate co-signed by a public CA that is part of this program. Members of this program have their root CA certificates already installed on Windows operating systems (and they can be updated by Windows Update), so you will decrease the chance of user connections failing due to certificate validation issues. If you use certificates that aren't already in the client's trusted store, users will need to install them before they can connect to TS Gateway.

Note For more information on the Microsoft Root Certificate Program and certificates, see Chapter 6.

To work with TS Gateway, the server authentication certificates must have the following attributes:

- The certificate must be a computer certificate, because users will be authenticating with a server, not a person.

- The extended key usage for the certificate must be Server Authentication (OID 1.3.6.1.5.5.7.3.1).

- The certificate Subject name should match the DNS name that the client will use to connect. For instance, if remote users will connect to remote.alpineskihouse.com, this needs to be the subject on the certificate. You can also use a wildcard certificate to work for all subdomains (for example: *.alpineskihouse.com).

Note To specify multiple alternative names for a certificate, use a certificate that uses the Subject Alternative Name (SAN) attribute. For example, if you use both the .com and .net variations of your domain, you can specify both remote.alpineskihouse.net and remote.alpineskihouse.com. If the certificate uses the SAN attributes, then users can only connect using RDP 6.1 (available in Windows Vista SP1, Windows XP SP3, or Windows Server 2008).

Installing and Configuring TS Gateway

To install the TS Gateway Role Service, log on with an Administrator account and proceed through the wizard as described in the following steps.

1. Open Server Manager, add the Terminal Services role, and choose the TS Gateway Role Service when prompted. If the Terminal Services role is already installed, then select the Terminal Services Role, click Add Role Service in the right pane, choose TS Gateway, and click Next.

2. You will be prompted to install any required role services and features required for TS Gateway as shown in Figure 7-8. TS Gateway requires IIS 7, which includes the required RPC over HTTP Proxy feature, and Network Policy and Access Services, used to store TS CAPs. Click Add Required Role Services and then click Next.

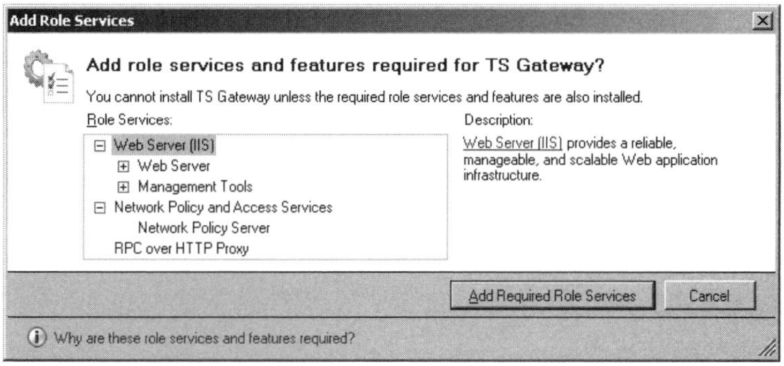

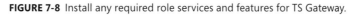

FIGURE 7-8 Install any required role services and features for TS Gateway.

3. You will be prompted to provide a server authentication certificate to use for establishing SSL connections. If you have already installed the required server authentication certificate in the server computer certificate store, it will appear in the list of certificates to choose from, as shown in Figure 7-9.

   Otherwise you can create a self-signed certificate (you should only use this type of certificate for testing in a non-production environment). If you don't currently have a certificate installed, you can skip this step by selecting Choose A Certificate For SSL Encryption Later. Click Next.

   > **Caution** If the TS Gateway server has more than one server authentication certificate installed, the Wizard will configure TS Gateway with the first one it finds. This may not be the one you intend to use. If you have more than one server authentication certificate installed on the server, check to make sure TS Gateway is configured with the intended certificate.

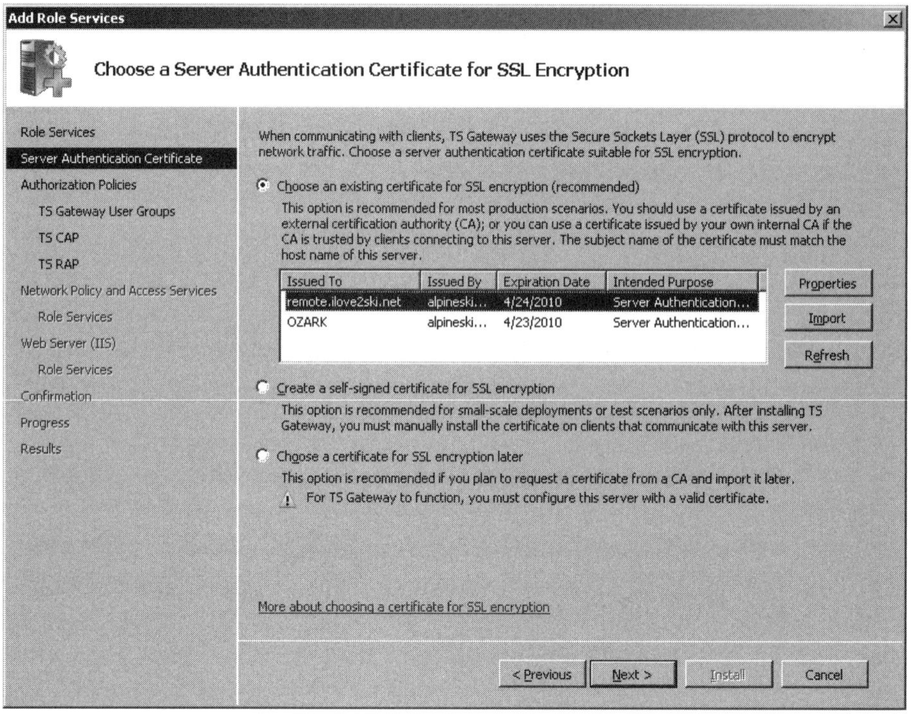

FIGURE 7-9 Choose an SSL certificate to use with TS Gateway.

4. Choose to create the required TS CAP and TS RAP authorization policies by selecting the option Now and then clicking Next. (You can also opt to do this later using the TS Gateway Management Console, but remember that you must have at least one TS CAP specified before users can be authorized to connect to TS Gateway, and at least one TS RAP to enable users to get to resources.)

5. Add the local or domain user groups that will be associated with both the TS CAP and the TS RAP. By default, the local Administrators group is already added. Members of the user groups added here are allowed to connect to TS Gateway. They can also connect to computer groups listed in the TS RAP that you create as part of the installation process. To add multiple user groups, type them and separate them with a semicolon or click the Add button to add each group. If the user groups you want to add are located in different domains, you must use the Add button to add each one. Click Next.

6. Specify the name for the TS CAP (the default is TS_CAP_01) and choose the Windows Authentication method for users to connect to TS Gateway by selecting the box next to Password, Smart Cards, or both. Click Next.

7. Enter the name of the TS RAP (the default is TS_RAP_01) and add a local or domain computer group that contains the resources to which user groups will connect. Alternatively, you can give users full access to internal terminal servers and computers with remote desktop enabled by choosing Allow Users To Connect to Any Computer On The Network. Click Next.

8. If you are installing Network Policy Server (NPS), the Network Policy And Access Services introduction page appears. Click Next and then click Next to install Network Policy Server.

9. If you previously chose to install IIS, then the IIS introduction page appears. Click Next and then click Next again to install the selected IIS role services.

10. Confirm the installation selections and click Install. When the installation is complete, you will see an Installation Results page showing that the installation is successful. Click Close.

Installing TS Gateway from the Command Line

You can install TS Gateway via command line by typing `servermanagercmd.exe -install ts-gateway.`

If you install TS Gateway this way, you are not prompted to install any dependency components; they are automatically installed as needed. Also, a TS CAP and TS RAP are not created, so you must configure the policies manually before users can use TS Gateway. If a certificate that can be used with TS Gateway is found, the installation adds it to this configuration. If the installation does not find a valid certificate, you will need to install an appropriate certificate and manually configure TS Gateway to use it.

Configuring TS Gateway Options

To manage TS Gateway, open the TS Gateway Management Console by going to Start | Administrative Tools | Terminal Services | TS Gateway Manager, as shown in Figure 7-10.

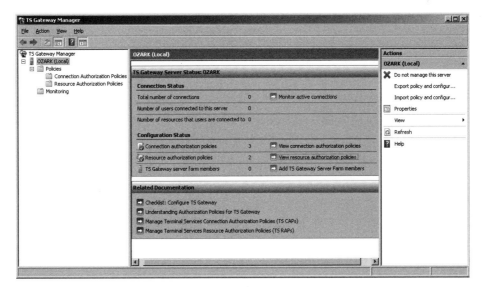

FIGURE 7-10 The TS Gateway Management Console

Click the server in the left pane to view the Connection Status and Configuration Status details in the middle pane. This pane contains three sections, each of which contains information and links to configuration pages in TS Gateway. The three sections are:

- The Connection Status shows you how many connections are currently established with TS Gateway and how many resources users are connected to.

  You can monitor and disconnect active connections here. Open the Monitor Active Connections page by clicking the corresponding link.

- The Configuration Status section tells you how many TS CAPs and TS RAPs are presently configured. If you have set up a TS Gateway farm, this section indicates how many servers are in that farm.

  You can configure or modify TS CAPs and TS RAPs here by clicking the View Connection Authorization Policies link and View Resource Authorization Policies link, respectively.

  Create or modify a TS Gateway farm by clicking the Add TS Gateway Server Farm Members link.

- The Related Documentation section provides links to TS Gateway configuration Help files.

To configure the TS Gateway settings, right-click the TS Gateway server in the left pane and choose Properties. The server Properties dialog box appears, as shown in Figure 7-11.

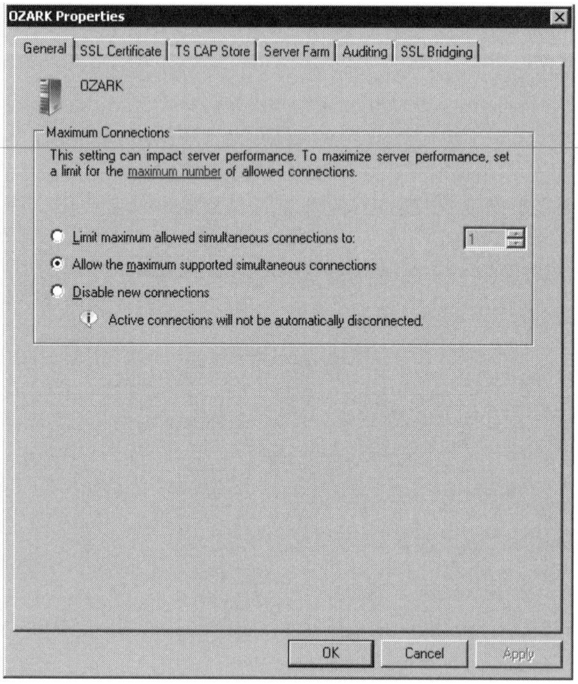

FIGURE 7-11 TS Gateway server Properties dialog box

From here, you can edit the settings as described in the following sections.

Creating and Maintaining TS Gateway Authorization Policies

TS CAPs and TS RAPs work together to give remote users access to internal resources. Although the end result relies on both of these items being configured, TS CAPs and TS RAPs are not tied to each other. TS CAPs define who is allowed to connect to the network via TS Gateway. TS RAPs define what computer resources those users who do connect to the network via TS Gateway are allowed to access.

When a user needs to get to a resource and tries to connect to TS Gateway, the TS Gateway first checks the TS CAPs to find an allowed group that the user belongs to. After TS Gateway finds an allowed group of which the user is a member, the user connects to the gateway. Then, to allow the user to connect to the requested resource, TS Gateway checks all TS RAPs to find a policy that allows access. If one is located the user connects. Otherwise, the connection isn't allowed.

Obviously, if you allow a user access to TS Gateway but do not give permission to connect to any resources, the result is that the intended access will fail. Make sure that the TS CAPs and TS RAPs, although independent, complement each other.

> **Note** Using the installation wizard to create TS CAPs and TS RAPs makes it appear that the two are more linked than they are. The user groups you specify in the TS CAP are merely supplied in the corresponding user group entry box for both TS CAPs and TS RAPs, but a user group can be associated with more than one TS RAP.

You have the option of configuring a TS CAP and TS RAP when you install TS Gateway from the wizard (the command-line installation doesn't give you the opportunity). However, you'll need to know how to configure TS CAPs and TS RAPs post-installation as well, as your access strategy and needs develop over time.

Creating a TS CAP   Creating a TS CAP after installation is similar to doing it during the installation routine. However, there are some differences; we'll point them out as we go through these steps.

1. Expand the Policies folder in TS Gateway Manager, right-click the Connection Authorization Policies folder, and choose Create New Policy to start the Authorization Policies Wizard.

> **Note** Since we haven't yet added a central Network Policy Server (NPS) role, this assumes the TS CAPs are locally managed and stored. When TS CAPs are stored on a centralized NPS, you can only create a TS RAP from TS Gateway.

2. The Authorization Policies Wizard will appear. You still have the option to create both a TS CAP and a TS RAP or to create only one or the other. If you choose to create both, the wizard will run through both the TS CAP and TS RAP wizards consecutively. Choose Create Only A TS CAP and click Next.

3. Enter a name for the TS CAP (to help you distinguish TS CAPs, make the name distinctive), and click Next.

4. Specify the windows authentication method (password, smart card, or both) and then add the users groups and the computer groups that are authorized to connect to TS Gateway.

   Notice that this step differs from the TS Gateway installation wizard. The installation wizard asks you to supply local or domain user groups that will be associated with both the TS CAP and TS RAP. This wizard does not do this. Instead, it asks to supply user groups for only the connection authorization policy. Click Next.

5. By default, the TS CAP allows all device redirection. Here you can disable device redirection for clients using this policy (except for smart cards, which may be users' only way to log on). Or, you can select Disable Device Redirection For The Following Client Device Types and then select the boxes next to the devices that should not be redirected.

   This differs from the TS Gateway installation wizard, which does not give you the option to disable or limit device redirection at all. Instead, the initial TS CAPs created with the installation wizard will have device redirection enabled for all client devices. Click Next.

> **Note** Disabling drive redirection from the TS CAP will have no effect if drive redirection is enabled on the destination computers protected via TS Gateway and the RDP client enables drive redirection.

6. Review the Summary page to make sure you chose the right settings and click Finish.

> **Note** If you are familiar with the process of creating a TS CAP, you can skip the wizard and just fill in the requirements for the authorization by right-clicking the Connection Authorization Policies folder in TS Gateway and choosing Create New Policy | Custom. This will open a tabbed New TS CAP dialog box that you can use to fill in the same settings for which you're prompted in the wizard.

This new TS CAP defines a group of people (and/or computers) allowed to access TS Gateway, but it doesn't get them any further than the TS Gateway, because you haven't yet defined any resources for them to use. To define resources associated with user policies enabled through TS CAP, create a TS RAP.

Creating a TS RAP   Creating a TS RAP from TS Gateway Manager is also very similar to creating one using the installation wizard, except that you are asked to associate user groups with the TS RAP. You also can create and use TS Gateway specified computer groups in the TS RAP. Again, we'll highlight these differences in the following steps to creating a TS RAP.

1. Expand the Policies folder in TS Gateway Manager, right-click the Resource Authorization Policies folder, and choose Create New Policy | Wizard to start the Authorization Policies Wizard.

> **Note** Even if you're using a centralized NPS, you still create TS RAPs on the local TS Gateway. NPS does not support TS RAPs.

2. Again, you can choose to create both a TS CAP and a TS RAP or to create only one or the other. If you choose to create both, then the wizard will run through both the TS CAP and TS RAP Wizards consecutively. Choose To Create Only A TS RAP and click Next.

3. Enter a name for the TS RAP (again, choose something descriptive) and click Next.

4. Add local or domain user groups associated with this TS RAP that can access the resources specified in it. To specify multiple user groups, separate them with a semicolon or click the Add button again to add another group. If the groups you want to add are in different domains, you must use the Add Group button to add each one. Click Next.

5. Now choose the computer group that contains the resources that the specified user groups are allowed to connect to. You can allow users to connect to any network resource, specify a domain computer group, or specify a TS Gateway-managed computer group if this TS RAP will control access to a terminal server farm. If you are allowing access to a terminal server farm, you have to choose An Existing TS Gateway-Managed Computer Group, Or Create A New One. (We'll discuss the details of this option in the section titled "Enabling Access to a Terminal Server Farm" later in this chapter.) For now, choose Allow Users To Connect To Any Network Resources. Click Next.

> **Note** When creating a TS RAP during the installation, you won't have the option of choosing a TS Gateway-managed group.

6. Remember that TS Gateway acts as a proxy to the network resources. In the next page, specify the port that people are able to use via TS Gateway. By default, the gateway will only allow connections via port 3389, which is the default port for RDP. You can opt to configure another port (for example, if you've edited the port that RDP uses). Most of the time, you'll choose 3389. Click Next.

7. In the final page of the wizard, you'll see a summary of the settings you've configured. Click Finish, and the new TS RAP will be visible in the Resource Authorization Policies Folder.

> **Note** If you are familiar with the process of creating a TS RAP, you can skip the wizard and just fill in the requirements for the authorization by right-clicking the Resource Authorization Policies folder in TS Gateway and then choosing Create New Policy | Custom. This opens a tabbed New TS RAP dialog box that you can use to fill in the same settings for which you're prompted in the wizard.

Modifying an Existing Authorization Policy   To modify an existing TS CAP or TS RAP in TS Gateway Manager, select the Connection Authorization Policies folder or the Resource Authorization Policies folder, respectively. You'll see the according authorization policies in the center pane. Double-click the policy you want to edit. Edit the policy properties as appropriate and then click OK to save and close the policy.

Using Group Policy to Control TS Gateway Authentication Settings

Three User Policy Group Policy settings will help you control when clients use TS Gateway to connect to RDP resources and which TS Gateway server they use. The policies are located at User Configuration | Policies | Administrative Templates | Windows Components | Terminal Services | TS Gateway.

- **Set TS Gateway Authentication Method**   This policy specifies the authentication method clients must use to connect to TS Gateway, as specified in the TS RemoteApps settings on the terminal server, on the client in saved RDP files, or from the RDC. The choices are:

    - Ask For Credentials, Use NTLM Protocol

    - Ask For Credentials, Use Basic Protocol

    - Use Locally Logged-On Credentials (enables single sign-on with TS Gateway)

    - Use Smart-Card

    You can allow users to change this setting by selecting the box next to Allow Users To Change This Setting, or you can enforce the setting you choose by clearing this box. If users cannot change this setting, it will be in effect for all connections to that TS Gateway.

- **Enable Connection Through TS Gateway**   Enabling this setting means that when users cannot create an RDP connection to a computer, they try to connect via a TS Gateway that you specify (or they discover). You can enforce this setting or allow users to change it by clearing or selecting the Allow Users To Change This Setting check box.

- **Set TS Gateway Server Address**   This setting specifies the TS Gateway that users use. If you chose to enable the previous setting, you need to specify the TS Gateway server to use by enabling this policy and entering the TS Gateway server address. Enforce this setting or allow users to change it by clearing or selecting the Allow Users To Change This Setting check box.

Enabling Access to a Terminal Server Farm

To allow user groups to connect to a terminal server farm, you need to create a TS CAP and a TS RAP to support this access as described in the section titled "Creating and Maintaining TS Gateway Authorization Policies" earlier in this chapter. However, the TS RAP in this case is different; to enable access to a terminal server farm, the TS RAP must either allow access to any network resource, or it must specify a TS Gateway-managed computer group that represents the terminal server farm. The TS Gateway-Managed computer group is created and maintained by TS Gateway.

To create a TS Gateway-managed computer group when creating a TS RAP using the wizard, you'll be prompted to determine whether the access should extend to:

- A specific domain computer group
- All computers with the specified port open
- Members of a TS Gateway-managed computer group

If you select the last option, you'll open a new page in the Authorization Policies Wizard where you create or select an existing TS Gateway-managed computer group. Select Create A New TS Gateway-Managed Computer Group, enter a descriptive name for the group, and add the NETBIOS and FQDN names of the farm.

You can also edit an existing TS RAP so that is uses a TS Gateway-managed computer group. In TS Gateway click the Resource Authorization Policies folder then double-click the TS RAP you wish to edit. Select the Computer Group tab and select the option to Select An Existing TS Gateway-Managed Computer Group Or Edit An Existing One. Click the Browse button and choose an existing group, or click Create New Group button to open the New TS Gateway-Managed Computer Group dialog box. Enter a name for the new group, then on the Network Resources tab, add the NetBIOS and FQDN names of the farm, and then click OK.

Note You can specify the farm name as an IP address, a NetBIOS name, or an FQDN, or enter all three so users can connect using any of these name options.

Setting up the TS RAP to enable farm access is required to allow users to use TS Gateway to get to the terminal server farm, but you still must enable access to the individual terminal servers in the farm. There are two ways to allow access to the farm members:

- Option 1: Add the terminal servers individually to the TS Gateway-managed computer group.
- Option 2: Put the terminal servers into an Active Directory computer group and add that computer group to the TS Gateway-managed computer group.

For Option 1, add the terminal servers to the TS Gateway-managed computer group you created for the farm. In order for users to use both NetBIOS and fully qualified domain names (FQDNs), add them both to the list. For example, if you have terminal servers named TS1 and TS2 that belong to the domain called mydomain.local, add the following names to the TS Gateway Computer Group:

- ❏ ts1 and ts1.mydomain.local
- ❏ ts2 and ts2.mydomain.local

For Option 2, create another TS RAP and add the same user groups you did in the TS RAP you created previously and add an Active Directory computer group containing the terminal servers. Using this method adds a level of security and manageability; terminal servers are only in the managed group if they are added to the Active Directory security group. If you add or remove terminal servers from the domain, then as long as you update the Active Directory computer group, you won't have to adjust TS Gateway to accommodate the change.

> **Note** If you have more than one farm, include servers from only one farm in each TS Gateway-managed computer group so that you can keep your resource permissions straight. The name of the farm must be part of the managed computer group.

To create, modify, or delete TS Gateway-managed computer groups, click the Resource Authorization Policies folder in TS Gateway. Choose Manage Local Computer Groups from the Actions menu in the right pane to open the dialog box in Figure 7-12.

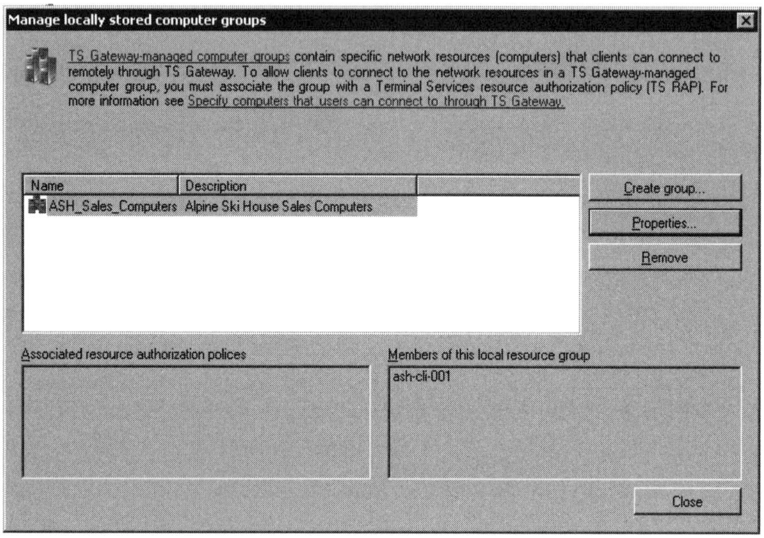

FIGURE 7-12 The Manage Locally Stored Computer Groups dialog box

Clicking on existing computer groups reveals the TS RAPs they are associated with in the lower section of the left pane and the computer group members in the lower section of the right pane (in Figure 7-12, the group has only one member).

To create a new computer group, click the Create Group button. On the General Tab, enter a name for the computer group. On the Network Resources tab, enter the name or IP addresses of the terminal servers or computers you want to add to the group. Click OK.

To edit an existing group, click the Properties button and adjust the computer group name or the servers in the group as necessary. To delete a TS Gateway-managed computer group, click the group, and click the Remove button.

Limiting Simultaneous Connections to TS Gateway

Windows Server 2008 Standard Edition supports a maximum of 250 simultaneous connections to internal resources through TS Gateway and by default is set to allow this maximum. Other Windows Server 2008 editions have no limit and by default allow an unlimited amount of simultaneous connections to internal resources through TS Gateway. You can specify a different limit, or you can disable new connections to prepare for taking a TS Gateway server offline.

To set a specific number of simultaneous connections (for optimization purposes or other security-related reasons), in TS Gateway Manager, right-click the TS Gateway server in the left pane and click Properties. On the General tab, choose Limit Maximum Allowed Simultaneous Connections To. Then specify a number in the corresponding selection box. To drain connections from this server (for maintenance), choose Disable New Connections. Doing so does not allow any more new connections to TS Gateway, but it leaves the existing ones undisturbed.

Choosing an SSL Certificate to Use with TS Gateway

Go to the SSL Certificate tab on the TS Gateway Properties window to select an SSL certificate to use with TS Gateway. This certificate will be used to create a secure connection with client computers so that the communication between the client and TS Gateway will be encrypted.

> ### How It Works: How an SSL Session Is Established Between the TS Gateway Server and the Connecting Client
>
> The following illustration shows how SSL communication works between the TS Gateway server and the RDC client.

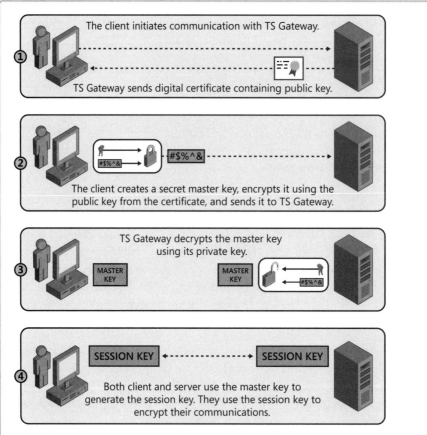

The following steps describe this process in detail:

1. The client starts communication with TS Gateway by either browsing to the TS Web Access Web site or by executing an RDP file. TS Gateway sends its digital certificate (which contains its public key) to the client.

2. The client verifies the certificate by checking its time stamp, making sure the TS Gateway address matches the subject provided in the certificate, and making sure the certificate has not been revoked. It also makes sure it trusts the certificate by checking to see if the CA certificate that was used to sign the TS Gateway server's certificate is located in the client's certificate store.

3. The client then creates a secret master key and uses the server's public key to encrypt it. The client sends the encrypted secret to the server.

4. TS Gateway decrypts the secret master key with its private key that only it has. Now server and client use the master key to generate a symmetric session key which they will use to encrypt their communications for this session. When the session is terminated, the session key is discarded. For more information on how SSL works, see *http://support.microsoft.com/default.aspx?scid=kb;EN-US;q245152*.

For the client computer to be able to establish the SSL session with the server, it needs to validate the server's certificate. To do this the client computer must have the CA certificate used to sign the server's certificate installed in its trusted root certificate store. For this reason, it's best practice to purchase your TS Gateway SSL certificate from a public CA that is part of the Microsoft Root Certificate Program. Alternatively, if you maintain your own PKI, you should have your CA certificate signed by a CA that is a member of the Microsoft Root Certificate Program. CAs that are part of this program have their CA certificates already installed on Microsoft operating systems or can have their certificate installed via Windows Update. This is important if your clients will be connecting to TS Gateway from computers that you do not control.

Note For more information about the Microsoft Root Certificate Program, see the sidebar in Chapter 6 titled "How It Works: Background on Digital Certificates."

If you have already configured TS Gateway to use a certificate, the certificate information is displayed on this tab. You can choose another certificate by clicking the Browse Certificates button and choosing from the certificates listed. SSL certificates that are installed to the server's Computer Certificate Store Personal folder will be available on the SSL certificate tab.

If you do not have an SSL certificate installed on this server, you can create a self-signed certificate to use with TS Gateway. Use this certificate for testing purposes only; if it's used in a production environment, you will have issues with users who are not able to validate the certificate because it's not in their trusted root certificate store.

To create a self-signed certificate, choose Create A Self-Signed Certificate For SSL Encryption on the SSL Certificate tab and click the Create Certificate button. The Create Self-Signed Certificate dialog box will appear, as shown in Figure 7-13.

Enter the common name of the certificate (the name users enter to access TS Gateway). Because the certificate is self-signed, it is its own root certificate. Clients must have this certificate installed on their computers to validate this same certificate used by TS Gateway. Therefore, the Store The Root Certificate check box is selected by default; this allows you to store the file so you can install it to your test clients. Click the Browse button, navigate to the chosen location, and type a filename, or type the location and filename in the File name box, and then click OK.

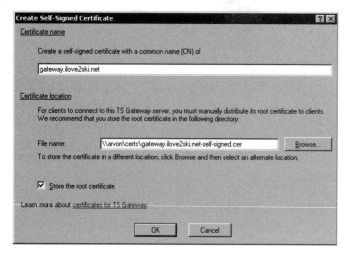

FIGURE 7-13 Create a self-signed certificate for TS Gateway.

> **Note** To install the certificate on your test clients, open an MMC on the client computer and add the Certificates snap-in. Expand the Certificates store tree and then right-click the Trusted Root Certification Authorities. Choose All Tasks | Import and follow the steps in the wizard to import the self-signed certificate file you created from TS Gateway Manager.

Bypassing TS Gateway for Internal Connections

It's understandable that you want remote users to establish secure encrypted connections to desktops and servers located on the internal network. But for local users accessing resources on the same internal network, you may choose to bypass TS Gateway and allow them to connect directly to the resource. There are two places to do this:

- **Remote Desktop Client**   Open the RDC and click the Options button. Click the Advanced tab and then click the Settings button in the Connect From Anywhere section. Select Use These TS Gateway Server Settings, supply the server name, and then select the box next to Bypass TS Gateway Server For Local Addresses.

- **TS RemoteApp Manager**   Use this setting to bypass TS Gateway for RemoteApps and for RDP files created by TS Web Access. Open TS RemoteApp Manager, click the TS Gateway Settings link, select Use These TS Gateway Server Settings, supply the server name, and then select the box next to Bypass TS Gateway Server For Local Addresses.

> **Note** To see how to force Remote Desktop connections initiated from TS Web Access to use TS Gateway, see Chapter 6.

Auditing TS Gateway Events

For troubleshooting and planning purposes, auditing connection events is a good idea. The TS Gateway Auditing tab shown in Figure 7-14 allows you to specify the TS Gateway events you want to log.

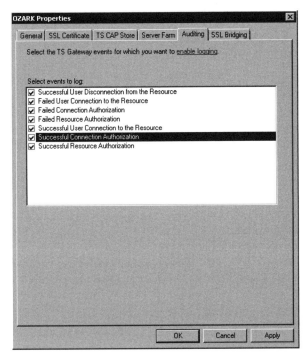

FIGURE 7-14 The TS Gateway Event Auditing tab

These events are logged in the Event Viewer under Application And Services Logs | Microsoft | Windows | Terminal Services-Gateway. By default, all available TS Gateway connection and authorization events are logged. To modify which connection and authorization events are audited, select or clear the boxes corresponding to the available events in the Select Events To Log dialog list. Generally, failed events are more interesting than successful ones, since they can signal unauthorized attempts or annoyed users.

Monitoring and Managing Active TS Gateway Connections

When troubleshooting failed connections or making sure that your load balancing is working properly, it's very helpful to be able to see what connections have been made. You can see all active TS Gateway connections from the Monitoring folder of TS Gateway Manager, shown in Figure 7-15.

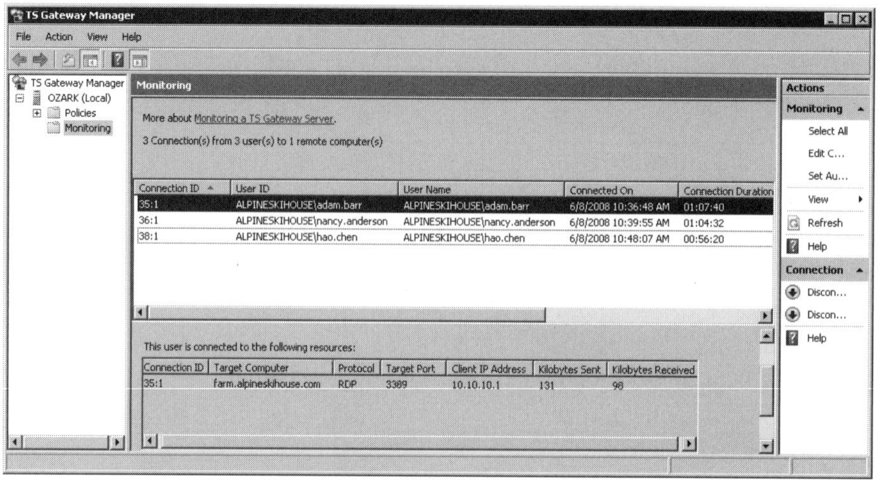

FIGURE 7-15 TS Gateway Monitoring folder

Click the Monitoring folder in the left pane to view detailed information about all active TS Gateway connections. The specific data reported for each connection includes:

- **Connection ID** The Connection ID is formatted as <A:B> where A is the Tunnel ID and B is the Channel ID. The tunnel ID shows you how many connections have been made to TS Gateway since the service started. If you restart the Terminal Services Gateway service, the Tunnel ID count restarts at 1.

- **User ID** The User ID shows the domain and username of the user who established the session, taking the form *domain\username*.

- **User Name** The session user's full name as specified in Active Directory.

- **Connection On** When a session was established.

- **Connection Duration** How long a session has been active.

- **Idle Time** How long a session has been idle.

- **Target Computer** The computer that the session is connected to.

- **Client IP Address** The IP address of the client computer that is connecting. If you are connecting to TS Gateway from the other side of a firewall, the IP address listed will be the address of the firewall.

- **Target Port** The port to which the user is connected.

Clicking on any of the active sessions will show you most of the same information as the preceding list, but will also reveal the total kilobytes (KB) sent and received in that session.

By default, TS Gateway updates this data every 30 minutes. To change this interval, right-click the Monitoring folder, choose Set Automatic Refresh Options from the context menu, and specify the new interval. Don't refresh too often; sampling takes processor cycles, so a high refresh rate can affect server performance. You can also disable automatic data refreshing by choosing the option Do Not Refresh Automatically. Click OK for the settings to take effect.

You can also disconnect sessions from this folder, according to the following rules:

- To disconnect a session, right-click the session and choose Disconnect This Connection.

- A user can establish more than one TS Gateway session. To disconnect all of the user's sessions, choose Disconnect This User.

- Disconnect all TS Gateway sessions at once by right-clicking the Monitoring folder, choosing Select All, then right-clicking any of the highlighted sessions and choosing Disconnect These Connections.

> **Note** To slowly drain TS Gateway sessions, configure the TS Gateway to stop accepting new connections, as described in the section titled "Limiting Simultaneous Connections to TS Gateway" earlier in this chapter.

You can also edit the TS Gateway connection limit from the Monitoring folder. Right-click the Monitoring folder and choose Edit Connection Limit from the context menu. This brings up the General Tab of the TS Gateway server Properties dialog box. Limit the sessions to a specific number, or put the TS Gateway into drain mode and click OK.

Implementing TS Gateway

Depending on your network capabilities and security requirements, you can position TS Gateway and the firewall differently to achieve higher levels of network security. For the sake of simplicity, these scenarios assume a single TS Gateway storing its own TS CAPs and TS RAPs.

TS Gateway: Inside the Private Network

If you do not have a perimeter network, you can put TS Gateway in the internal network, as shown in Figure 7-16, with only port 443 opened in the firewall. The firewall permits incoming traffic to the TS Gateway on port 443 (SSL), and the gateway processes the incoming connections to make sure that they're permitted to access the network. Once complete, the TS Gateway routes the connections to the terminal servers or remote desktops via port 3389 (RDP), as described earlier in this chapter.

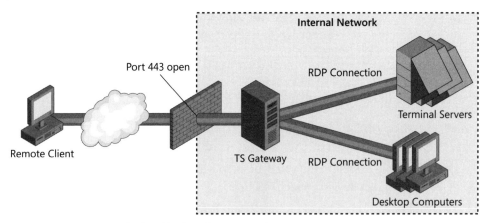

FIGURE 7-16 TS Gateway is placed in the private network.

Choosing this option allows TS Gateway to communicate directly with Active Directory, so it can pull its user and computer groups from a central location. (Without this ability, you'll need to set up local user groups and can't use the domain computer groups to form TS CAPs and TS RAPs.) However, it also means that when an incoming connection is permitted, the gateway is wide open. You can restrict connections to 3389 for their remote connections, and you can restrict the list of servers that the incoming connections can use. However, you can't define a set of permitted ports to use. More important, if the TS Gateway is compromised, the private network is wide open.

To have a bit more control over which ports are open, you can use an additional firewall, as shown in Figure 7-17. This way, you can be sure that only port 3389 is open; or you have the option of not limiting the ports that TS Gateway will permit and using the firewall to control the kinds of traffic that are available. The first firewall will have port 443 open. The second will have port 3389 open to permit RDP traffic to pass to the private network.

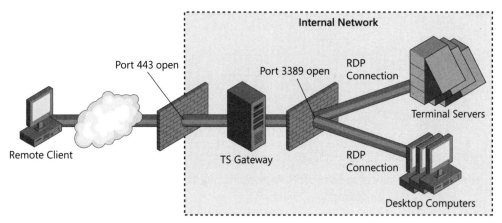

FIGURE 7-17 TS Gateway is placed in the perimeter network.

Using TS Gateway with SSL Bridging

For additional security, you can deal with both these issues by using Microsoft Internet Security and Acceleration (ISA) Server (or another SSL bridging device) to bridge incoming SSL connections in the perimeter network (shown in Figure 7-18) to TS Gateway on the internal network.

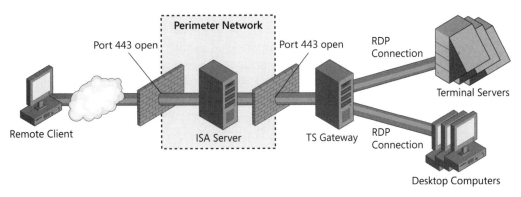

FIGURE 7-18 Use ISA Server or other SSL bridging device for SSL connection termination and packet inspection in the perimeter network.

The first bridging method is called HTTPS-HTTPS bridging. By bridging SSL traffic, you gain further control of the communication to and from TS Gateway. The bridging product (ISA Server in this scenario) acts as a policeman by decrypting SSL connections coming from outside the network, inspecting them for malicious code, and then re-establishing the SSL session with TS Gateway if the packets pass inspection. All traffic flowing to and from TS Gateway goes through ISA Server.

You can also bridge HTTPS-HTTP communications between the ISA server (or other bridging device) and TS Gateway, also called *SSL offloading and termination*. Reasons for choosing HTTPS-HTTP bridging include:

- **Saving processor cycles**   SSL packet processing generally takes more CPU cycles than regular HTTP traffic. By offloading the SSL communication to ISA or other bridging device, you save processing power.

- **Smart card authentication**   Smart card authentication requires that IIS be configured for HTTP and not HTTPS. Therefore, for secure communications, you need something to handle the SSL traffic before passing it to IIS on TS Gateway.

To do so, HTTPS-HTTP bridging must be enabled in TS Gateway. Open TS Gateway Manager, right-click the server, and choose Properties. On the SSL Bridging tab, select the box next to Use HTTPS-HTTP Bridging (Terminate SSL Requests And Initiate New HTTP Requests). Click OK.

> ## How It Works: Does SSL Bridging Offer Performance Benefits?
>
> The short answer is that it depends on what kind of bridging you're doing.
>
> When deployed with a simple firewall, the TS Gateway server is still processing all the incoming SSL traffic. As you may recall from our earlier discussion about how SSL communication works, a lot of back and forth happens to establish a secure communication between client and server. The client must initiate the connection, and the server's digital certificate must be validated by the client. Then a secret session key must be established in order to encrypt the communications. While it's doing all this, the TS Gateway server must still act as a proxy for the incoming connection requests. On a busy server, this can consume a lot of processor cycles.
>
> HTTPS-HTTPS SSL bridging adds an additional layer of security to the SSL communication by examining the contents of the SSL traffic and ensuring that it contains no malicious packets before sending it to the TS Gateway. However, HTTPS-HTTPS bridging does not offload the SSL processing; it only decrypts the HTTPS traffic to examine it before encrypting it again to send to the TS Gateway. The TS Gateway must still do all the SSL communication processing—it just knows that it is safe to do so. For any performance benefit, you must implement SSL offloading and termination with HTTPS-HTTP bridging. The catch is that you must balance the performance benefit of not processing the SSL traffic with the fact that, after it leaves the ISA server, the traffic is no longer encrypted. The traffic should be passing over the private network at this point, but for some implementations this may still be a consideration.

Creating a Redundant TS Gateway Configuration

For the most part, previous sections have tacitly assumed that you have one TS Gateway. As with terminal servers, however, one is not enough. The trouble isn't the number of simultaneous connections (the TS Gateway job isn't very taxing; one server can handle hundreds of simultaneous connections), but rather that a single TS Gateway server means the possibility of a single point of failure. The job TS Gateway performs is critical: Lose the gateway and you lose remote access into your corporate network (exclusive of other VPN solutions).

So you need two (or more) instances of TS Gateway. In this section, we'll discuss how to make this possible without unnecessary effort on your part, including:

- Configuring TS Gateway to work with Network Load Balancing for load balancing and failover.
- Centralizing the connection authorization policies.
- Centralizing the resource authorization policies (yes, this is possible).

Creating a Fault-Tolerant TS Gateway Farm

Implementing TS Gateway means that all remote sessions must connect to the TS Gateway server to establish RDP connections to internal network resources. If the TS Gateway server dies, so does remote access to terminal server farms and other remote desktop computers. To address this problem, add a second TS Gateway server, cluster the two, and load balance the incoming connections.

TS Gateway doesn't have any load-balancing logic; another component such as Network Load Balancing (NLB) must provide the load-balancing functionality. If you set it up properly, NLB will load balance the connections between the TS Gateway servers in the farm and provide redundancy. If one TS Gateway goes offline, any connections for which it was acting as a proxy will be disconnected. However, when the users automatically reconnect, they are sent to the working TS Gateway server and will be reconnected to their previous sessions. In the absence of the load-balanced farm, those connections would be completely severed.

NLB load balances based on incoming network traffic to a virtual IP address, or *cluster IP address*, as shown in Figure 7-19.

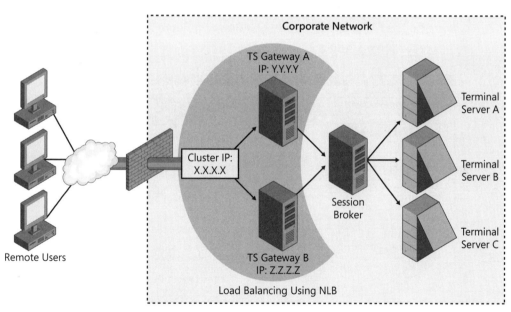

FIGURE 7-19 Scenario of NLB load balancing TS Gateway servers

In this case, network traffic to port 443 doesn't go to a specific TS Gateway server. Instead, it goes to the cluster IP address representing the collection of TS Gateway servers. When it is there, the load balancing determines which TS Gateway the connection should go to, generally based on the current load.

> **Note** If you configure session affinity for a server, connections for that session will continue to route through the same TS Gateway server, even if the other server has fewer sessions at the time.

To use NLB you need two network interface cards (NICs) installed on each TS Gateway computer. One NIC will support incoming connections for management purposes, and NLB will use the other for load balancing. Even if you choose to use DHCP for the management NIC (we recommend using static addressing for both NICs), the one for NLB use must be configured with a static IP address. Also, the NLB NIC does not need a gateway address, because it is not going to send traffic off the network.

When you have installed the NICs on your TS Gateway servers, next install NLB on each TS Gateway server that will become part of the cluster. Either use Server Manager or install from the command prompt like this: `servermanagercmd -install nlb`.

After installing Network Load Balancing, create a server cluster and add the TS Gateway servers as members. Open the Network Load Balancing Manager from Start | Programs | Administrative Tools | Network Load Balancing Manager or by typing **nlbmgr** in the Start | Run box. The NLB Manager appears, as shown in Figure 7-20. Complete the following steps to create a server cluster.

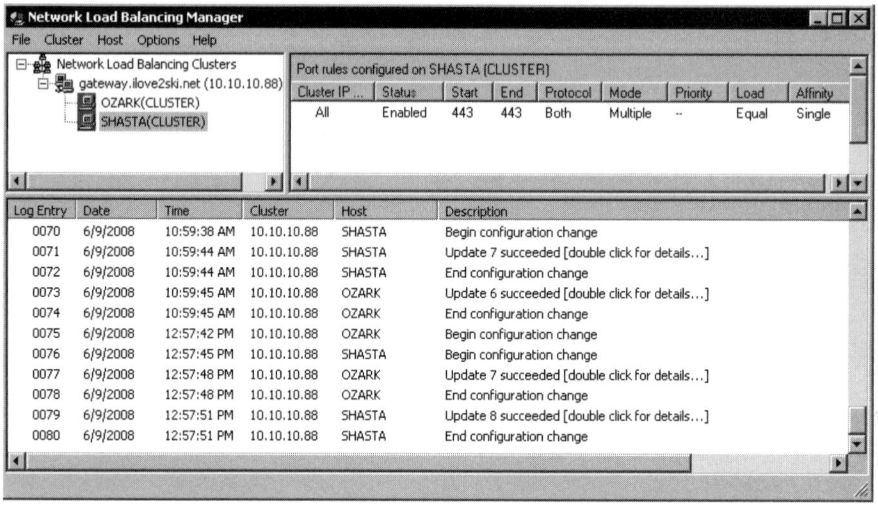

FIGURE 7-20 Set up the server cluster from the Network Load Balancing Manager.

1. Click Cluster and select New.

2. In the Host input box, enter the name of one of your TS Gateway servers and click Connect. NICs available to use with NLB will appear in the lower text box. Select the dedicated NIC you have configured to use with load balancing (remember, it must have a static IP address) and click Next.

3. The IP addresses assigned to the NIC will appear. The priority number is a unique number that differentiates the servers. Accept the default value. The IP address in the lower text box will be dedicated to load balancing. It's possible that both NICs will show up in the text box (assuming you have dual NICs); if so, you can delete the extra IP addresses, edit them, or add the correct one using the Add, Edit, and Remove buttons. Leave the Initial Host State as Started and click Next.

4. Specify the cluster IP address by clicking the Add button and specifying the IP address. When users request access to TS Gateway, they will be sent to this address instead of a specific TS Gateway server address. Then the connection is sent by the load balancer to the appropriate TS Gateway server. Click Next.

5. Enter the full Internet name that remote users use to access TS Gateway and choose the cluster operation mode (Unicast or Multicast). All host adapters must use the same operation mode or NLB will not function. Click Next.

> **Note** Unicast replaces the MAC address of the load balancing adapters with the cluster virtual MAC address that is generated by the NLB software. Therefore, to communicate with the cluster nodes, you need another NIC. With Multicast, the cluster MAC is added to the NIC, so each NIC has two MAC addresses. Either of these modes can cause switch port flooding, so you must get your network team involved to address this properly. For instance, if you use Multicast, you can add static maps to the switch for the NLB nodes. If you use Unicast, you can use a VLAN to contain NLB traffic.

6. For the NLB to do its job, you need to indicate the ports it should listen on for traffic. By default, it listens on ports 0 to 65535, and load balances the connections if the traffic appears on one of those ports. However, it only needs to listen on port 443 to accept incoming SSL connections. Edit the default rule to make the range 443 to 443.

7. You can also change the rule Filtering Mode and Affinity. Choose Multiple Hosts to allow multiple hosts to handle traffic for this port rule. Now you have three Affinity choices:

   ❑ **None**   Choosing this option means that multiple connections coming from the same IP address can be spread among the farm members.

   ❑ **Single**   Choosing this options gives affinity to connections coming from the same IP address; they will be terminated on the same TS Gateway farm member.

   ❑ **Network**   Choosing this option means that client connections within the same Class C address space are terminated on the same TS Gateway server.

   Single is almost always the best choice. Otherwise, you may find that TS RemoteApp connections in a single RDP session may be distributed among more than one TS Gateway server. Troubleshooting connection problems is easier when the connections for each session are coming through one TS Gateway server. More important, each session connection requires two SSL connections: one from the client to the TS Gateway server and, one from TS Gateway to the client. Without server affinity, it's possible for a session's SSL connections to get split between two servers. Since both the incoming and the outgoing connections are necessary to support the session, splitting the session between two servers doubles the chances that the session will be lost due to a downed TS Gateway server. The only time you don't want to enable single affinity is if all connections appear to be coming from the same IP address because they're passing through a proxy server or a firewall that shows incoming connections as coming from the internal IP address of the proxy server or firewall.

8. Choose Single and click OK. Then click Finish.

Now add the other TS Gateway farm members by right-clicking the cluster and choosing Add Host To Cluster. Give the name of the server and then choose the dedicated IP address you will use for this host, just as you did when setting up the first host. Because this server will be joining this cluster, you do not get to choose any other settings. Do this for each cluster member.

Direct from the Field: Why You Should Use Affinity

If SSL connections of a session get split between two servers, it actually reduces the resilience of the TS Gateway farm for failover. Here's how it happens. Imagine you have many clients sharing a single SSL session to server A and another to server B. If either of the servers fails, clients connected through the failing server need to reconnect, but so do all those who have the split connection between servers A and B. The only circumstance under which you should not set affinity is if many clients are coming in from one IP address (e.g., are working through a proxy server).

Not setting affinity adds complexity to the environment in several ways: You can have SSL connections split up and redirected to different servers, and as the administrator, you have no control over this. Second, in case of a failed server, more clients suffer (those who go through this server *plus* those who have single SSL session served on the failed server). Third, in general, it reduces the predictability.

When you have any IP-based affinity on the NLB, the Server Farm feature is simply not used. There will be no situation when different SSL connections from the single client (so, from the same IP) will be sent to different TS Gateway servers, as IP affinity is set on NLB. So, it doesn't matter if the Server Farm setting in TS Gateway is configured or not.

Don't use the affinity option included with some hardware load balancers. It does not provide any additional benefits to TS Gateway over using IP affinity, and it still requires the Server Farm setting to be configured.

Bohdan Velushchak
Operations Engineer

After you've created the cluster and added all TS Gateway cluster hosts, the Network Load Balancing Manager should look similar to Figure 7-21.

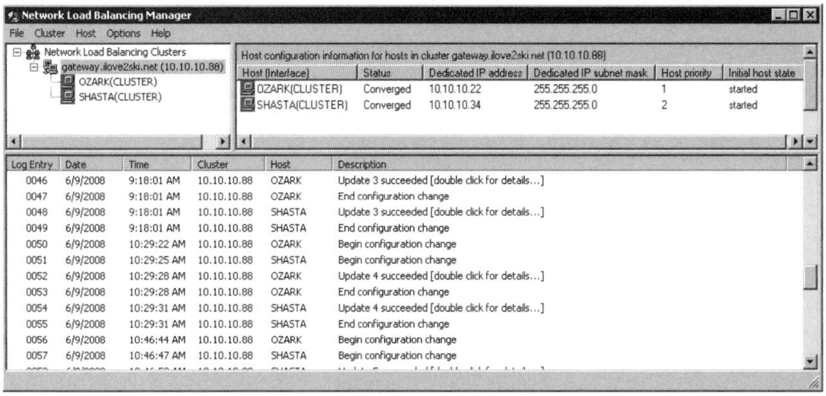

FIGURE 7-21 Network Load Balancing Manager with a cluster created and hosts converged

All hosts should converge (note that hosts appear with a green square around the computer icons). If NLB can't hear a server heartbeat, the server state will display as "unreachable" with a red X on the computer icon. When the heartbeat resumes, the server reconverges. The details of the changes show in the bottom pane.

Dealing with TS Gateway Split SSL Connections   Setting affinity in a load balancer is the ideal, but it won't always work. For instance, if a large number of the TS Gateway connections will be coming from users behind a proxy, their IP addresses will all appear to be the same, and they will all get routed to one TS Gateway farm member. If you can't use IP affinity, then you must set up a TS Gateway Farm on each TS Gateway farm member to stop splitting up incoming and outgoing SSL connections for each session. By setting up the farm on each TS Gateway server, you're telling all the TS Gateway servers about all the other ones. Doing so ensures that connections supporting the same connection can all be routed through the same TS Gateway.

Open TS Gateway Manager, right-click the server, and choose Properties from the context menu to open the server Properties dialog box. Click to the Server Farm tab, shown in Figure 7-22.

Add a server farm member to the TS Gateway Server Farm Member text box and click Add. Do this for all server farm members and then Click OK. Repeat this process for each TS Gateway server farm member. Connections supporting the same session should now be sent through the same TS Gateway server.

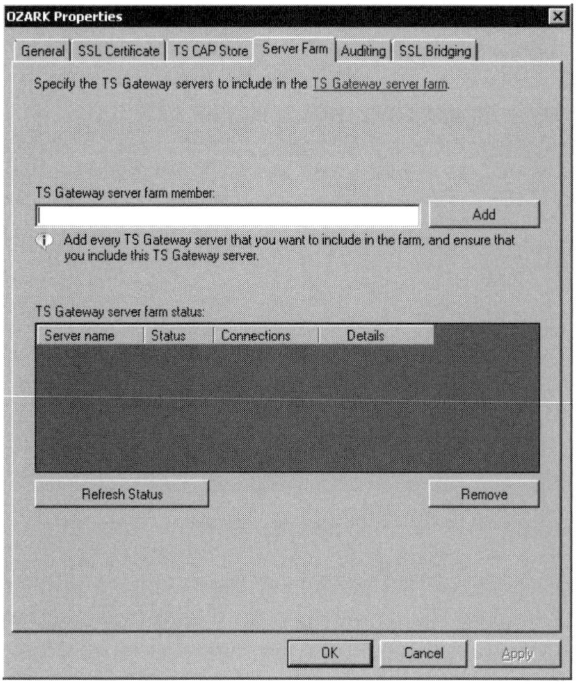

FIGURE 7-22 The Server Farm tab

Maintaining Identical Settings Across a TS Gateway Farm   All TS Gateway servers in the server farm need to have identical TS CAPs and TS RAPs, or you'll get inconsistent experiences depending on which gateway server you connect to. To make sure the server settings match, you can export the settings from one TS Gateway server to a file and then import those settings to the other farm members.

To export TS Gateway policy and configuration settings, open TS Gateway Manager, right-click the server, and choose Export Policy And Configuration Settings. Specify a name for the XML file and then type a storage location or use the Browse button to browse to the location; click OK. To import TS Gateway server settings, right-click the TS Gateway server and choose Import Policy And Configuration Settings. Then specify the file you want to import by typing the location or browsing to the file and then click OK.

Using a Central NPS to Store TS CAPs   Exporting and importing settings is one way to maintain consistency across TS Gateway servers. This requires some work to make sure that you not only make the gateway servers consistent in the first place, but that they stay that way over time. To do so, you can create a central NPS either on one of the TS Gateway servers or on a different server altogether and set all TS Gateway servers to use the central NPS to store TS CAPs. You might also do this if you already have an NPS running in your environment for other reasons and you decide to consolidate NPS functions onto one server.

The TS CAP Store tab in the TS Gateway Properties dialog box, shown in Figure 7-23, allows you to choose where to store TS CAPs.

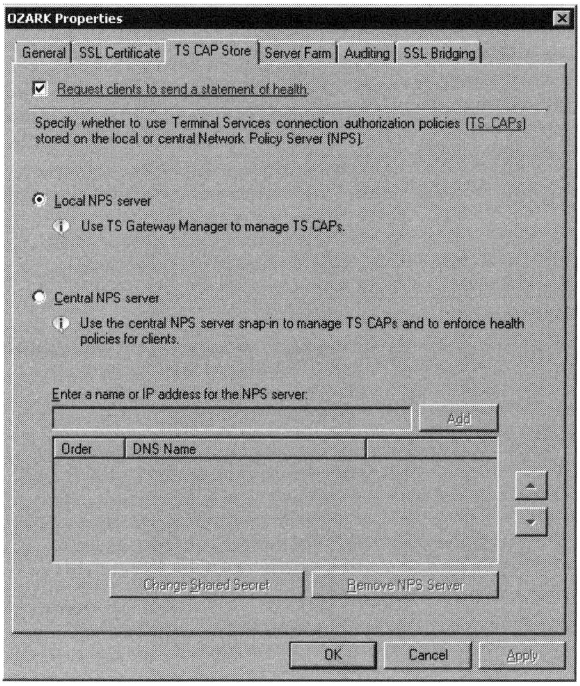

FIGURE 7-23 The TS Gateway Properties TS CAP Store tab

If you choose to use a central NPS, the new NPS will act as a Remote Authentication Dial-In User Service (RADIUS) server to the TS Gateway servers, and the TS Gateway servers will act as RADIUS clients to the NPS, as shown in Figure 7-24.

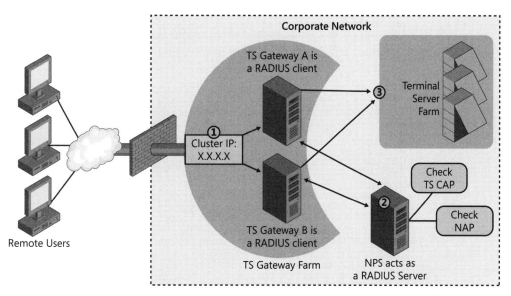

FIGURE 7-24 TS Gateway servers act as RADIUS clients when you store TS CAPs on a central NPS.

If you set up a central NPS for storing TS CAPs, the process to connect to a terminal server via TS Gateway will work like this example:

1. A remote user starts a TS RemoteApp from a published RDP file that has a TS Gateway server configured in it.

2. The TS Gateway servers forward the requests to the new NPS, which checks the TS CAPs (and possible network access policies) and either allows or denies access based on whether or not the requester meets policy criteria.

3. If the requestor meets policy requirements as defined in the connection and resource authorization policies, then the user gets connected to a terminal server, and the TS RemoteApp launches.

To use TS Gateway with a centralized NPS, you need to set up the NPS (or use an existing one), tell it about the TS Gateway servers, tell the TS Gateway servers to forward network access requests to the new NPS, and recreate new TS CAPs on the designated NPS, as described in the following sections.

Install NPS   On the designated server, install the Network Policy And Access Services role via Server Manager, or run this command from an elevated command prompt: `server-managercmd.exe -install NPAS`.

Direct the TS Gateway Servers to the NPS   When the NPS is ready, point the TS Gateway servers to the centralized TS CAP storage location. On each TS Gateway Server:

1. Open TS Gateway Manager, right-click the server, and click Properties. Select the TS CAP Store tab and choose Central NPS Server. Type the name or IP address for the NPS, and click the Add button.

2. The NPS must trust the TS Gateway to allow it to use its authorization policy store. Enter a shared secret password to use in validating the connection to the new Network Policy Server, and click OK.

> **Note** After you specify another NPS, you can no longer create TS CAPs using TS Gateway Manager so long as the gateway points to it. These options are unavailable, and the TS CAP folder is replaced with a Central Network Policies folder that shows which Network Policy Server TS Gateway now uses to store TS CAPs. In this case you create and edit TS CAPs on the centralized NPS server instead.

Configure TS Gateway Servers As RADIUS Clients   Next, configure each TS Gateway server as a RADIUS client and point each of them to the RADIUS server. On each TS Gateway server:

1. Open Network Policy Server (Start | Programs | Administrative Tools | Network Policy Server).

2. Expand RADIUS Clients And Servers and select Remote RADIUS Server Groups.

3. In the right pane, double-click TS GATEWAY SERVER GROUP. Click Add, type the name or IP address of the NPS, and click OK. If there are any other servers listed, remove them by selecting them and clicking the Remove button. Then click OK.

Enable Access Request Forwarding   Next, make sure the NPS installed on each TS Gateway computer (the RADIUS client) forwards network access requests to the new centralized NPS (the RADIUS server). On each TS Gateway server:

1. Under Policies, click the Connection Request Policies Folder, right-click TS GATEWAY AUTHORIZATION POLICY, and click Properties.

2. On the Overview Tab, make sure the policy is enabled and that the Type Of Network Access Server is Terminal Server Gateway.

3. On the Conditions Tab, make sure that the condition NAS Port Type with a value of Virtual VPN is added. If it is not, click the Add button and then scroll down and select NAS Port Type. Click the Add button and then select the box next to Virtual (VPN) in the Common Dial-Up and VPN Types box. Click OK.

4. On the Settings tab, click Authentication and select Forward Requests To The Following RADIUS Server Group For Authentication. In the drop-down list, choose the TS GATEWAY SERVER GROUP you created earlier.

5. Click Accounting and select the box next to Forward Accounting Requests To This Remote RADIUS Server Group. In the drop-down list, choose the TS GATEWAY SERVER GROUP you created in Step 3.

Enable NPS to Trust the TS Gateway Servers   Next, configure the NPS to respond to requests from the TS Gateway servers.

1. On the designated NPS, open the Network Policy Server management console, right-click RADIUS Clients, and choose New RADIUS Client from the context menu.

2. Enter the name of a TS Gateway server and its IP address.

3. In the Vendor Name drop-down list, accept the default and enter the shared secret that you specified on TS Gateway servers. Then click OK.

4. Repeat this for each TS Gateway server that will act as a RADIUS client.

The RADIUS clients will show up in the right pane, as shown in Figure 7-25.

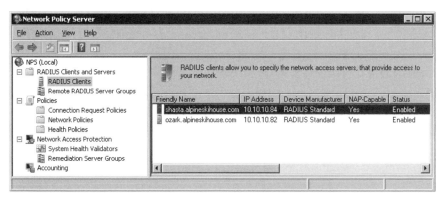

FIGURE 7-25 Add each TS Gateway server as a RADIUS client on the NPS.

Next, create a connection request policy to allow TS Gateway to establish a connection to the NPS.

1. Right-click Connection Request Policies (shown in Figure 7-25) and choose New.

2. Give the policy a descriptive name, select Terminal Server Gateway from the Type Of Network Access Server drop-down list, and click Next.

3. Add at least one connection for which this policy will be evaluated (and for which TS Gateway will pass). For example, add the Client IPv4 Address of the TS Gateway server. Click OK.

Recreate TS CAPs on the NPS   TS CAPs do not get transferred to a new NPS when you choose to use a central NPS, so your next step is to recreate the TS CAP(s) on the new NPS.

A TS CAP is really a Network Access Policy; TS Gateway provides a specific user interface to make it easier for you to create a policy with the settings that will work with TS Gateway. If you create a TS CAP on TS Gateway and then open the Network Policy Server console on the TS Gateway server, you will find that the TS CAP is created and stored under the Network Policies folder. Creating a network policy can accomplish the same thing as a TS CAP, and more. Although the intricacies of network policy creation on an NPS are outside the scope of this book, here is an example of how to create a simple policy that allows access to TS Gateway based on user group membership.

1. In the Network Policy Server Management Console, right-click Network Policies and choose New.

2. Give the policy a name, and for Type Of Network Access Server, choose TS Server Gateway from the drop-down list. This specifies the type of network access server that will send connection requests to the NPS. Click Next.

3. At least one condition is required for this policy to be evaluated when a connection request is sent to NPS. Add one by clicking the Add button and then choosing a condition category. In this case, choose User Groups and click Add.

4. Click Add Groups, type a User Group, and click OK. You can add multiple groups by clicking the Add button again and adding another group. Click OK and then click Next.

5. Accept the defaults on the next four screens and click Finish.

Configuring a Central TS RAP Store

TS CAPs, as you've seen, are really NPS Network Authorization Policies in a different guise. TS RAPs can't be managed by NPS; they're actually implemented through the Authorization Manager (sometimes known as AZMan). The Authorization Manager supports role-based access, so it's a good fit for TS RAPs. There is one failing from the point of creating a load-balanced farm: it does not support remote connections.

However, you can tweak TS Gateway to point to a remote location to view its TS RAPs so that both TS Gateways in the same load-balanced farm can have the same resource authorization policies without making you regularly export and import the TS RAPs. There's no UI in the TS Gateway manager to do this, but you can change the location of RAP.XML (the file containing the TS RAP settings) from the registry.

Open the Registry Editor and go to HKLM\SOFTWARE\Microsoft\Windows NT\CurrentVersion\ TerminalServerGateway\Config\Core\RAPStore. Edit the value of this key to point to a network location. Set the permissions on this share properly so that only TS Gateways are allowed write/read access. Otherwise, someone can easily circumvent the TS RAPs.

Using Network Access Protection with TS Gateway

Earlier in this chapter, we discussed how network access protection (NAP) works. This section explains configuring TS Gateway to use NAP to keep client computers not meeting system health policies away from terminal servers and other computers with remote desktop enabled. A full discussion of NAP is outside the scope of this book, so we'll concentrate on using NAP with TS Gateway to create secure and safe remote access to internal resources.

For a broader discussion of NAP, see the book *Windows Server 2008 Networking and Network Access Protection (NAP)* (Microsoft Press, 2008), by Joseph Davies and Tony Northrup. (The link to more information about this book is located in the Additional Resources section at the end of this chapter.)

> **Note** When it is used with TS Gateway, NAP can only *prevent* client computers from logging on to the network; it can't *fix* them. TS Gateway, unfortunately, does not support the remediation server groups that other enforcement models do. By definition, the clients in need of remediation are outside the network.

Using the wizard is the easiest way to create a NAP. In the Network Policy Server console, from the Standard Configuration section in the middle pane, choose Network Access Protection (NAP) from the drop-down list and click the Configure NAP hyperlink to open the Configure NAP Wizard shown in Figure 7-26.

First, choose the type of NAP policy you want to configure from the drop-down list. Here, choose Terminal Services Gateway (TS Gateway). Name your policy and click Next.

From the dialog box shown in Figure 7-27, choose the TS Gateway servers that will use this NAP. In this example, we'll keep it to a single server; redundant configurations are discussed in the section titled "Creating a Fault-Tolerant TS Gateway Farm," earlier in this chapter. For now, be aware that you *could* add a second server here. Click Next.

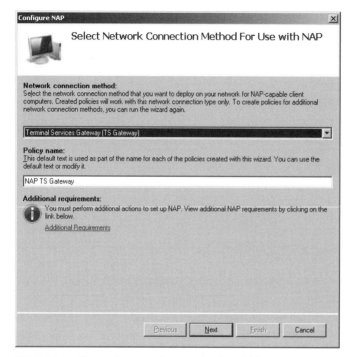

FIGURE 7-26 Choose the type of connection for which you're configuring NAP.

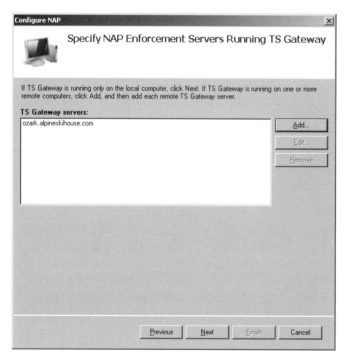

FIGURE 7-27 Choose the servers to which this NAP will apply.

Next, choose the device redirection policies to apply to the redirected clients and select the authorization methods they're allowed to use. For example, in the dialog box shown in Figure 7-28, you could clear the box for password authentication and select the one for smart cards to require use of smart card authorization from TS Gateway. Click Next.

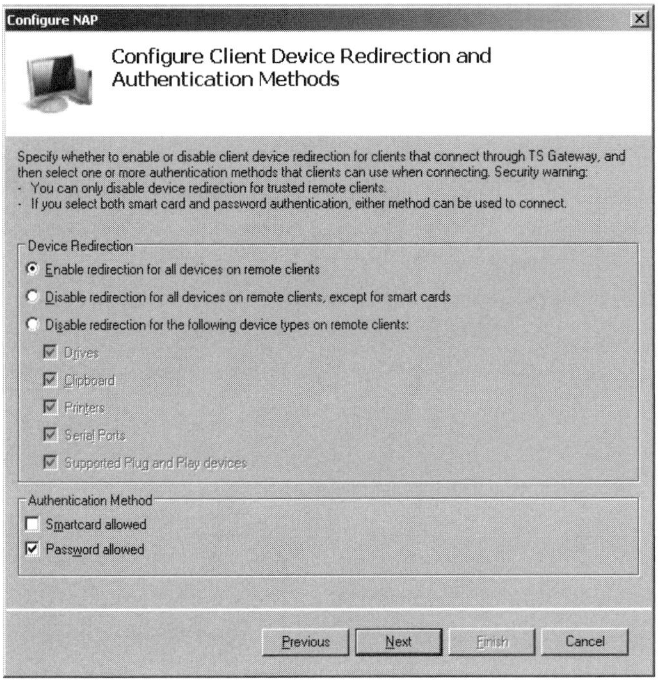

FIGURE 7-28 Configure the client device redirection and authentication methods.

Next, configure a user or computer group allowed to use the TS Gateway; in other words, create a TS CAP. Click the Add User or Add Machine buttons to choose user or computer groups. Click Next.

Now, choose the health policy to apply. As you can see in Figure 7-29, there's only one option: the Windows Security Health Validator.

Note Although Windows Server 2008 comes with only one health policy, the NAP model is extensible. ISVs can write their own sets of rules to cover conditions not accounted for in the default health validator.

On this page, choose what should happen when computers that are NAP ineligible attempt to connect. By default, they're denied access, but you can permit access and log the connection. Notice that NAP through TS Gateway does not ask you to specify a remediation server group, as other NAP configurations do. Remediation servers are not supported with TS Gateway because the clients never get to the network. Click Next.

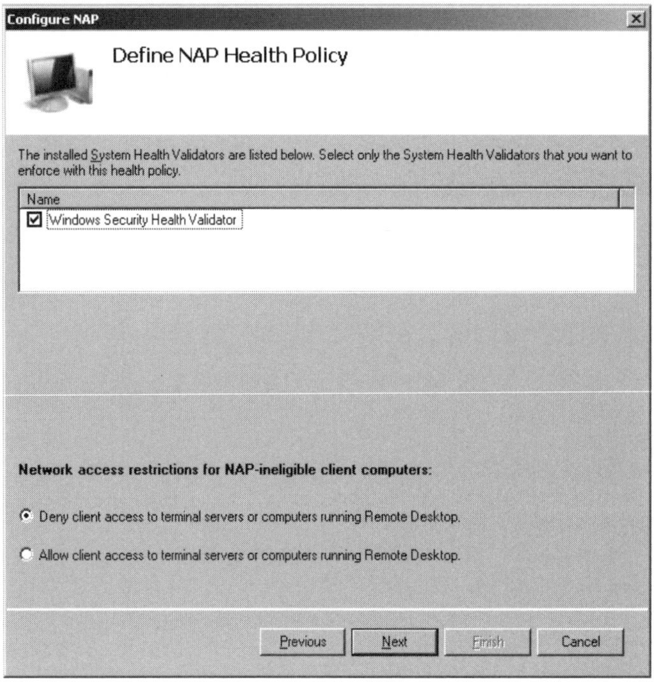

FIGURE 7-29 Choose the health validator and behavior for noncompliant clients.

Finally, the wizard will show your options for review. If they're what you intended, click Finish.

After the NAP Creation Wizard finishes, you will find that it created one connection request policy, three network policies, and two health policies. These policies work together, first to accept connection information from TS Gateway, and then to evaluate whether or not clients requesting a connection should be allowed or denied based on the health of the computer from which they are connecting. Figure 7-30 shows the relationship between these policies.

This is what each type of policy does:

- The Connection Request policy allows TS Gateway to send connection requests to the NPS.

- Each of the three Network Policies allows either full or limited access to the network, depending on which Health Policy the requesting computer meets or if the client is not capable of providing a Statement of Health.

- The two Health Policies, one a "passing" policy, the other a "failing" policy, determine the fate of a computer requesting connection to TS Gateway. Using specifications that are set in the Windows Security Health Validator, the computer requesting a connection is checked out and will always meet the requirements of one of these policies.

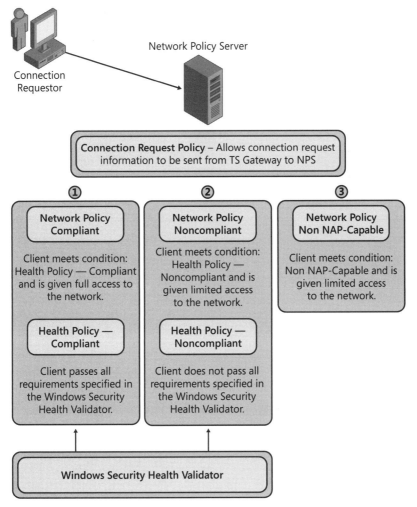

FIGURE 7-30 The relationships of policies created by the NAP Wizard

NAP clients will always fall into one of three scenarios shown in Figure 7-30. The client computer will meet the conditions specified in the Compliant or Noncompliant network policy, or they will not be NAP capable and therefore meet the condition of the Non NAP-Capable network policy. The computers that meet the requirements for the Compliant network policy will be given full access to TS Gateway. Those computers that meet the requirements for either of the other two policies will not be given access to TS Gateway.

The Windows Security Health Validator (WSHV) is where you set the health requirements you want computers to meet. To edit the WSHV in the NPS console, expand Network Access Protection, click System Health Validators, and then double-click Windows Security Health Validator in the middle pane. You can change the default outcomes for the specified error codes you may receive from the system health validator or the system health agent on the client. Now click Configure. As shown in Figure 7-31, WSHV includes tabs that pertain to configuration for Windows XP and Windows Vista operating systems.

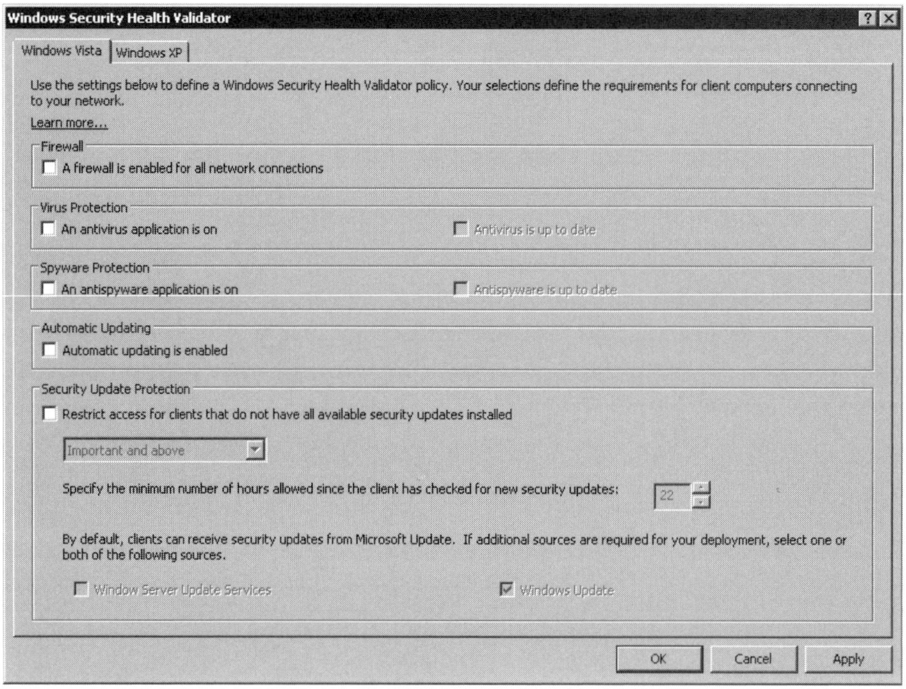

FIGURE 7-31 Windows Security Health Validator

Select the boxes next to items you want to include as requirements for clients to gain access to TS Gateway. If you have both Windows XP and Windows Vista, then you need to set requirements on each of the pertaining tabs. Then click OK.

Configuring NAP Clients

In order for client computers to be checked against NAP policies, you must take the following steps:

1. Enable the NAP client.

2. Enable the TS Gateway Quarantine Enforcement client (this tells the client to communicate the computer health status to the NPS).

3. Add the TS Gateway to the Trusted Gateways list on the client. Only Windows Vista and Windows XP SP3 can be NAP clients.

Note Although online documentation on whether Windows Server 2008 can be a NAP client is conflicting, it cannot be a NAP client for TS Gateway using only components that come with the OS. This is because the Windows System Health Agent (WSHA) (the default client agent that is used to pass the Statement of Health to the NPS server) is not supported on Windows Server 2008. It is possible that you could integrate a third party SHV and SHA and then use Windows Server 2008 as a NAP client for TS Gateway.

Windows Vista has the NAP client enabled by default. Windows XP SP3 does not. Enable it by starting the Network Access Protection Agent service and then restarting the computer.

For Windows Vista, enable the TS Gateway Quarantine Enforcement client by adding the NAP Client Configuration snap-in to an MMC. Click Enforcement Agents, right-click the TS Gateway Quarantine Enforcement client, and click Enable. An easier way to do this is to open an elevated command prompt and run `netsh nap client set enforcement ID = "79621" Admin = "Enable"`.

There is no NAP Client Configuration snap-in for Windows XP, so enable the TS Gateway Quarantine Enforcement client by using the command line.

For Windows Vista or Windows XP, add the TS Gateway to the Trusted Gateways list by opening Regedit.exe and navigating to HKLM\SOFTWARE\Microsoft\Terminal Server Client \TrustedGateways. Add a new string value: GatewayFQDN. Then double-click GatewayFQDN and enter the FQDN name of the TS Gateway.

On the Companion Media Easier yet, Microsoft provides a script that performs all of these tasks. Download the text file Tsgqecclientconfig.txt (*http://www.microsoft.com/downloads/ details.aspx?familyid=cb986639-20e5-4f16-8e48-be68d23dc888&displaylang=en*) and rename it to Tsgqecclientconfig.cmd. You will need to run the script with elevated privileges. Open an elevated command prompt, navigate to the directory where the script resides, and type `tsgqecclientconfig <TS Gateway FQDN>`. Restart the computer, and you're done.

Troubleshooting Declined Connections to TS Gateway

After setting up TS CAPs, TS RAPs, and NAPs, you may find that you can no longer establish a connection to TS Gateway. All too often, the error messages you receive for a denied logon are cryptic, so you know that a user was denied a connection to TS Gateway, but you don't know why. The Event Logs on both the TS Gateway server(s) and the NPS can help you find the source of the problem.

For instance, if you have a fundamental problem between the RADIUS client (TS Gateway) and the NPS (if run on a separate computer), you will receive an error telling you that the connection was denied because the client did not meet the connection authorization requirements. Naturally you will suspect that a TS CAP is blocking access. But in some cases, a problem between the RADIUS client and server may exist. To determine the real reason for a blocked connection, correlate the event logs in these three places:

- In the TS Gateway server Event Viewer:

  Application Logs and Security | Microsoft | Windows | TerminalServices-Gateway | Operational: The denied connection will show up in this log as event ID 201. You can see who tried to log on and generally why they were denied. Correlate this with the following log.

  Windows Logs | Security: Look for Audit Failure log entries (event IDs 6273 and 6274) that correspond to the attempted logon time. Scroll to the bottom of these logs to find a reason code and a reason for the blocked connection.

- In the NPS Event Viewer:

  Check the system log for event IDs coming from source NPS. For instance, if your radius clients have dual NICs and they start communicating with the NPS from an IP address not specified in the RADIUS Client field in the NPS Console, you will see Event ID 13 in your event logs.

Connections that are blocked due to TS RAP policies are straightforward. If a user is blocked by a TS RAP, she simply doesn't belong to a group that has access to the requested resource. The event is logged at Application Logs and Security | Microsoft | Windows | Terminal Services-Gateway | Operational.

Connections that are blocked due to NAP policies are also fairly straightforward. The log files are found in two places:

- On the NPS, open Event Viewer and expand Custom Views | Server Roles and click Network Policy And Access Services. This custom event log view contains all of the event logs pertaining to NPS, including accounting events that occur on this server.

- By default NPS logs accounting and authentication requests to a log file located at %SystemRoot%\System32\LogFiles. To adjust which events are logged, or other settings like the log location, open the Network Policy Server console, click Accounting, and then click the Configure Local File Logging link.

Summary

Setting up a single terminal server takes some effort. Moving beyond the single-server model to support multiple servers, and to support them—not only from inside but also outside the network—increases the complexity dramatically. However, it is really necessary to support a fault-tolerant configuration. Therefore, this chapter has shown how to incorporate TS Session Broker and TS Gateway with the terminal servers.

This chapter has introduced you to a number of best practices:

- Load balance TS Gateway servers to increase gateway uptime.

- When using a TS Gateway farm, centralize the TS CAP and TS RAP sources to simplify configuration. If centralizing isn't possible for some reason, use the export and import capabilities on the TS Gateway servers to maintain servers with identical settings.

- Enable server affinity to keep all SSL connections for a single session on the same TS Gateway server and to reduce the risk that a downed server will take down the session.

Additional Resources

The following resources are related to topics covered in this chapter. You can find the links and scripts on this book's companion media. A lot of this chapter has focused on the various conditions under which connections are made, and you'll see resources here related to that as well.

- Event codes and resolutions for TS Gateway issues are on Microsoft's Web site at *http://technet2.microsoft.com/windowsserver2008/en/library/d7bc8841-ff0a-4c73-9144-6e9a2a475ab91033.mspx?mfr=true*.

- For the specifics of using Microsoft ISA server with TS Gateway, see *http://technet2.microsoft.com/windowsserver2008/en/library/9f293f18-b0fd-48f8-b103-957fad92d70b1033.mspx?pf=true*.

- To learn more about NAP, see *Windows Server 2008 Networking and Network Access Protection (NAP)*, by Joseph Davies and Tony Northrup with the Microsoft Networking Team, available at *http://www.microsoft.com/mspress/books/11160.aspx*.

- Session Broker inventory script (SBDatabaseDump.vbs).

- NAP client configuration tool (Tsgqecclientconfig.cmd) *http://www.microsoft.com/downloads/details.aspx?familyid=cb986639-20e5-4f16-8e48-be68d23dc888&displaylang=en*.

- For more information about CredSSP, see *http://www.wipo.int/pctdb/en/wo.jsp?IA=WO2007033087&DISPLAY=DESC*.

- For more about how the connection sequences work, see "Remote Desktop Protocol: Basic Connectivity and Graphics Remoting Specification," available for download from *http://msdn.microsoft.com/en-us/library/cc240445.aspx*.

- "Terminal Services Gateway Server Protocol Routing Specification," available for download from *http://msdn.microsoft.com/en-us/library/cc248485.aspx*.

- "Windows Security Health Agent (WSHA) and Windows Security Health Validator (WSHV) Protocol Specification," available for download from *http://msdn.microsoft.com/ en-us/library/cc215773.aspx.*

- "Statement of Health for Network Access Protection (NAP) Protocol Specification," available for download from *http://msdn.microsoft.com/en-us/library/cc212976.aspx.*

Chapter 8
Managing the Terminal Server Runtime Environment

Previous chapters explored how to set up and configure a terminal server and the subordinate roles. Setting up the terminal server puts users in a position to log on and use it . . . but administrators need a tool to keep track of what those users are doing and to help them, if necessary. That tool is the Terminal Services Manager.

This chapter will explore how to use the session management tools—both command-line and graphical—to view and interact with running terminal server sessions. We'll discuss:

- The tools available in Windows Server 2008 to help you manage sessions

- How to find and manage sessions on a terminal server

- How to find and manage processes on a terminal server

- How to get remote control of user sessions

- How to create custom server management groups in Terminal Services Manager

- How to use the command-line tools, scriptable interfaces, and Windows Management Instrumentation (WMI) to get information the graphical user interface (GUI) doesn't offer

Introducing Terminal Server Management Tools

Windows Server 2008 has a set of tools for managing the user runtime experience: Terminal Services Manager graphical user interface (GUI) and command-line tools to supplement it and enable scripting. Before delving into their usage, let's take a quick tour so that you can see what's possible.

Terminal Services Manager

Let's start by getting oriented. The Terminal Services Manager tool is similar to the same tool in previous versions of Windows but has some new functionality to reflect the new Terminal Services roles such as TS Session Broker. After you install the Terminal Services role, the Terminal Services Manager tool in Figure 8-1 is accessible from Start | All Programs | Administrative Tools | Terminal Services | Terminal Services Manager. Using this tool, you can:

- Display real-time data about current users, sessions, and processes.

- Monitor, disconnect, and reset sessions.

- Remotely control a user's session.

- Send messages to users.

- Terminate sessions and log off users.

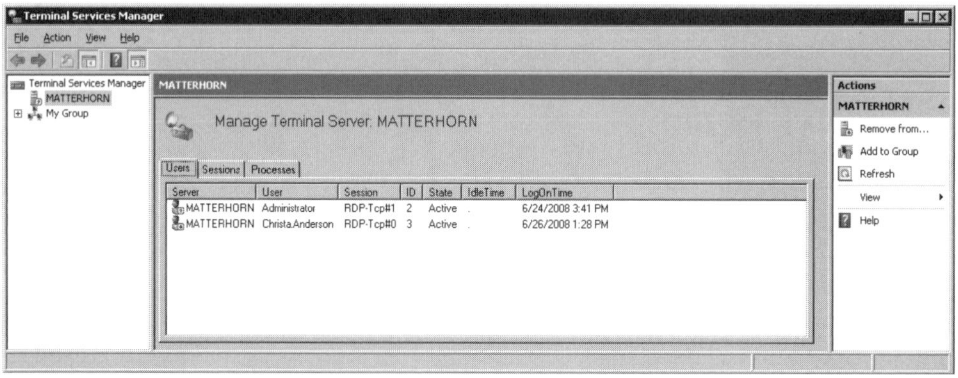

FIGURE 8-1 Terminal Services Manager

The left pane displays the available terminal servers for you to manage. Although you can only manage one server at a time, you can add additional servers to this pane from TS Session Broker or by searching Active Directory. We'll talk about *how* to do this later in this chapter, in the section titled "Organizing Terminal Servers in Terminal Services Manager."

The center pane displays the information for the currently selected server, including connected users, the sessions on the server, and the processes running on the server. Some of this data may be redundant, as it's just different ways of displaying data about those logged onto the terminal server, what they're doing there, and which sessions are open.

The right pane displays the context-sensitive actions you can take depending on the item you've selected in the left or center panes.

The Users tab (see Table 8-1) contains current data pertaining to the users connected to the terminal server and the associated Terminal Services sessions.

TABLE 8-1 **Terminal Services Manager Users Tab Data**

Data	Description
Server	The server the user is logged onto.
User	The user account name of the user who launched the session.
Session	The session associated with the user.
ID	The Session ID that the terminal server uses to identify sessions. Each Session ID is unique to its terminal server.
State	The current state of the session (active, disconnected, reset, or idle).
Idle Time	The number of minutes since the last keyboard stroke or mouse movement in the session.
LogOnTime	The date and time the user logged on.

Much of the data located on the Sessions tab (see Table 8-2) mimics the data on the Users tab. However, the Sessions tab displays a few more session details, allowing you to determine the protocol used to connect to the terminal server and the names of the computers that users connect from (if the session is active).

TABLE 8-2 **Terminal Services Manager Sessions Tab Data**

Data	Description
Server	The terminal server on which the session is running
Session	The session type
User	The user name associated with the session
ID	The number that identifies the session to the terminal server
State	The current state of the session (active, disconnected, reset, idle, etc.)
Type	The type of client used in the session (i.e., RDP client or console connection)
Client Name	The name of the client computer that established the session
IdleTime	The number of minutes since the last keyboard stroke or mouse movement in the session
LogonTime	The date and time the user logged on
Comment	An optional field that can give other information about the session

The Processes tab (see Table 8-3) displays details about the processes currently running on the terminal server, the associated sessions, and the users that invoked them.

TABLE 8-3 **Terminal Services Manager Processes Tab Data**

Data	Description
Server	The terminal server on which the process is running
User	The user account that launched the process
Session	The session number associated with the process
ID	The ID that identifies the session to the terminal server
PID	The ID that identifies the process to the terminal server
Image	The executable associated with the process

Terminal Services Manager displays similar information in many different ways to support various starting points you may take to gather needed information. For example, if user Kim Akers has a problem with a runaway program in her session, you can use the Processes tab to stop the process and be sure that you picked the instance that belongs to her. If Kim needs help with her session, you can highlight the root of Terminal Services Manager to find out which server she is logged onto, shadow her session, and assist her. Fundamentally, though, the information you can get about sessions is pretty straightforward: which users are logged on, whether they're using their session, which applications they're running, and which terminal server they're connected to.

When you understand what information you can get from Terminal Services Manager, you can answer many questions, even if the GUI doesn't anticipate those questions. For example, you can find out how many users are logging on during a particular interval in the morning or how many people are using a particular application. Knowing either of these pieces of information, you can take appropriate action: end processes, terminate sessions, or (outside the Terminal Services Manager tools) purchase more licenses or add more servers to meet demand.

This chapter will cover all of the actions you can perform using Terminal Services Manager. However, when you automate queries or changes, you'll want to know about the command-line tools and sometimes combine them with the Windows Management Instrumentation (WMI) interfaces via Windows PowerShell. Unfortunately, the GUI does not always refresh well, even in a small farm. To get the most reliable information about session status, the command-line tools may be more reliable.

On the Companion Media You can run the Terminal Services Manager tool from Windows Vista with the Remote Server Administration Tools (RSAT), which includes both Terminal Services Manager and Remote Desktops. Download RSAT from the Microsoft Web site at *http://www.microsoft.com/downloads/details.aspx?FamilyId=9FF6E897-23CE-4A36-B7FC-D52065 DE9960&displaylang=en.*

Direct from the Source: Using the Status Dialog Box in Terminal Services Manager

If you right-click an active remote connection in the Sessions or Users tab, you'll see a Status option in the context-sensitive menu. Click it, and you'll see a dialog box like the one shown below.

In reality, you can learn the following information from this dialog box:

- The User Name field, populated only when you open the Status dialog box from the Sessions tab, shows the name of the currently logged in user.

- Network Adapter tells you the name of the network adapter the user is connected to on the terminal server. The information here is the same as what's in the Terminal Services Configuration | RDP-Tcp | Network Adapter tab, so if you choose a specific NIC for RDP connections, that's the one that will appear here.

- Client Address tells you the client computer's IP address for local connections. If the connection was launched through TS Gateway, this address will not display.

- Client Build Number tells you the build number (like the version) of the client operating system.

- Client Directory points you to the location on the client where the DLL supporting the RDP client is stored.

- Client Color Depth indicates the color depth used in the RDP session.

- Encryption Level shows you the encryption setting managed through Group Policy or in Terminal Services Configuration, showing not the actual encryption setting but what option the client computer sets the encryption level

- Client Resolution shows the resolution of the remote session.

- The Input/Output Status section shows the traffic passing between the remote session and the client computer.

Notice that I left out a couple of the settings that you can see in the dialog box. Both the Client Hardware ID and the Client Product ID are hardwired fields that will be the same for all client computers. (They're here for legacy reasons.) Therefore, they don't give you any useful information.

Apart from those two fields, however, this dialog box shows you some information about the client experience that you can't get anywhere else. Want to understand why a user is saying that their application looks grainy? Check the screen resolution here. Need to know the IP address that a client computer is using to connect to the terminal server? Check it here. Beta-testing a new version of the client operating system? You can tell here who's using the beta version by checking the build number. You can even use the Input/Output Status data to confirm that a session is not frozen; when the user moves the mouse, the number of incoming and outgoing bytes should update.

James Baker

Program Manager II

Command-Line Tools

In addition to the graphical tools, Windows Server 2008, like previous versions of Windows Server, has command-line tools you can use to view session information, manage a session's contents, remotely control a user's session, and so forth. These command-line tools are built on the same interfaces as the graphical tools, so any information you get from one (e.g., Process ID) can be used in another.

It is also worth noting that Windows Server 2008 and Windows Vista both support the Terminal Services command-line tools; they are part of the operating system (OS) and you don't need to install Remote Server Administration Tools (RSAT) or the Terminal Services role to use them. Table 8-4 lists the available command-line tools.

TABLE 8-4 Terminal Services Command Reference

Command	Description
change logon or chglogon	Enable, disable, drain, or query information about logons from Terminal Services sessions.
change port or chgport	Lists or changes the COM port mappings to be compatible with MS-DOS applications.
logoff	Logs off users and deletes their session from the terminal server.
msg	Sends a message to a user or multiple users on a terminal server.
query process or qprocess	Displays information about all the processes currently running on a terminal server.
query session or qwinsta	Displays information about sessions on a terminal server.
query termserver or qappsrv	Lists all the terminal servers on a network.
query user or quser	Displays information about the users connected to a terminal server.
reset session or rwinsta	Terminates a session on a terminal server.
shadow	Enables an administrator to remotely control an active session of another user on a terminal server. You must run this command from within an RDP session for it to work.
tscon	Connects to another session on a terminal server (you have to be in a remote session in order to connect to another remote session).
tsdiscon	Disconnects a session from a server.
tskill	Terminates a process running on a terminal server. You can identify the process by image name or Process ID.
tsprof	Copies the Terminal Services user profile from one user to another.

Note The following command-line tools have been removed in Windows Server 2008:

- **tsshutdn** This command was used to shut down a terminal server. Use the shutdown command instead.
- **register** This command was used to register a program.
- **cprofile** This command was used to remove wasted space in a user profile and to delete file associations from the registry that were made to certain applications.

Connecting Remotely to Servers for Administration Purposes

When using the TS Session Broker to load balance terminal server connections, you may find it challenging to connect to a server for administrative purposes. Obviously, when connecting for management purposes, the logic should be different: You don't want to connect to the terminal server on which you already have a session or the terminal server with the lowest number of connections. Instead, you want to connect to the specific terminal server that you need to manage. You also don't want to use a Terminal Services client access license (TS CAL) just to do maintenance on the server.

In previous versions of Terminal Services, you made an administrative connection (one that bypassed TS Session Broker and did not require a TS CAL) by launching the connection with the /console switch. In Windows Server 2008, this behavior remains pretty much the same, but in Windows Server 2008 and Windows Vista (and RDP 6.1), the /console switch has been replaced with /admin. Functionally, /admin is equivalent to /console.

It's functionally equivalent, but it is not syntactically equivalent. If you use the /console switch when connecting from Windows Server 2008 or Windows Vista to a server in a farm, you may not notice that it doesn't work, meaning, the /console switch is ignored—you still log on, but you will use up a TS CAL.

To start a remote session for administrative purposes, you must launch the RDC from the Run dialog box or command prompt and add the /admin switch there like this:

```
mstsc /admin
```

You can also specify the /admin switch when adding connections to the Remote Desktops Remote Server Administrative Tools (RSAT).

That said, the /console switch still works when connecting from an older RDP client to a Windows Server 2008 terminal server. Plug in /admin when working from Windows XP client, and Mstsc.exe will open a dialog box that explains the proper syntax for the command, because that version of the RDC client has never heard of the /admin switch. Unfortunately, this means that you'll need to change the connection syntax depending on whether you're connecting from a current or older version of Mstsc.exe.

One reason for the revision is the change to the session architecture. As Chapter 2, "Planning the Terminal Server Ecosystem," explains, the session architecture has changed so that there is now one session for services, with which humans do not interact. You no longer connect to the console; rather, you connect to an administrative session.

There's one other difference with administrative connections. In Windows Server 2003, you could make two remote administrative connections and one console connection from the physical console, all without using a TS CAL. Windows Server 2008 permits two simultaneous administrative connections. This may look like a reduction in licensed connections, but the previous model was also a convenience. That's because it was possible for two administrators to make connections, leave them connected, and effectively block anyone else from making an administrative connection to the terminal server because the remote logon count was at capacity. You had to have the console connection just to reset one of those remote connections. In Windows Server 2008, you can choose to disconnect an administrative connection if you need to make one and the number of admin connections is already at capacity. The other administrator will find his session as it was left, and you are not forced to log on from the console to disconnect the session.

Managing Terminal Servers from Windows Vista

If you have only one terminal server, you can probably do everything you need to do with Terminal Services Manager from the console; if you have multiple terminal servers, you can even add them to one instance of the tool so that you can do everything from one place. But if you don't have physical access to a terminal server, you can still get the same functionality from Windows Vista to work from your laptop or workstation. The Microsoft Remote Server Administration Tools (RSAT) are a collection of tools used to manage Microsoft Windows Server 2008 servers.

> **Note** For those who have worked with Windows Server 2003, RSAT is the next rendition of the Windows 2003 Server Administration Tools Pack (Adminpak.exe).

RSAT is compatible with 32-bit and 64-bit Windows Server 2008 and 32-bit and 64-bit Windows Vista SP1 clients running Windows Vista Business, Enterprise, or Ultimate editions. RSAT is not compatible with previous versions of Windows.

RSAT contains many more tools than we will discuss in this chapter, as it encompasses tools to manage other Windows Server 2008 roles. We will concentrate on the Terminal Services specific RSAT tools:

- **Terminal Services Manager**   Used to manage terminal servers
- **Remote Desktops**   Used to connect to remote desktops from one window

Both of these tools get installed on Windows Server 2008 when you install the Terminal Services role. They work the same way when installed on a computer running Windows Vista.

To install RSAT on a Windows Vista client, download the Microsoft Remote Server Administration Tools for Windows Vista (KB941314) from the Microsoft Web site. Be sure to download the correct version (32-bit or 64-bit) of the RSAT MSU file. You can find the following links on the companion media:

- For x86 Windows Vista clients download: *http://www.microsoft.com/downloads/details. aspx?FamilyId=9FF6E897-23CE-4A36-B7FC-D52065DE9960&displaylang=en*
- For x64 Windows Vista clients download: *http://www.microsoft.com/downloads/details. aspx?familyid=D647A60B-63FD-4AC5-9243-BD3C497D2BC5&displaylang=en*

Install the tool by double-clicking the Microsoft Update Standalone Package (MSU) file and clicking OK to install the Update For Windows (KB941314).

After you've installed RSAT, you will need to enable it, as the installer does not enable all of the tools by default. Open Control Panel and double-click Programs and Features. Then click Turn Windows Features On Or Off. Select the check box next to Remote Server Administration Tools, expand Role Administration Tools, and then expand this selection and select the check boxes next to Terminal Services Tools. Then click OK.

When you have enabled the tools, you will find a Terminal Services folder now visible in Administrative Tools that contains links to the Terminal Services Manager and Remote Desktops tools.

Note Although installing and using RSAT Terminal Services tools from a Windows Vista client can be helpful, you will not be able to shadow sessions via Terminal Services Manager directly from the Windows Vista client. You can only shadow a session from another remote session. Therefore, you will need to remote into a Windows 2008 Server or onto your own computer with RSAT tools installed and then use the *shadow* command-line tool or Terminal Services Manager from there.

Organizing Terminal Servers in Terminal Services Manager

When you first start Terminal Services Manager, it will show you only the local terminal server—not very useful if you're managing a server farm. You can add more servers to the console view in a couple of ways: by creating a custom group (or populating an existing group) or by importing all known terminal servers from a farm.

Note After you add terminal servers to a particular group, they're there unless you manually delete them. You can't drag terminal servers to a new group, although you can add one server to multiple groups if you wish.

To create a new group, right-click the Terminal Services Manager icon in the left pane and choose New Group from the context menu. In the dialog box that appears, type the name of the new group and click OK. This group will now appear in the left pane.

Terminal Services Manager starts with one default—and empty—group named My Group. To populate an existing group, right-click its icon in the left pane of Terminal Services Manager and choose Add Computer from the context menu. This will open the Select Computer dialog box you may have seen before when working with the Microsoft Management Console. From here, you can add computers to the group in one of three ways:

- If you know the name of the terminal server you want to add to the console, select Another Computer, type the name into the text box, and then click OK. The terminal server will appear in My Group.

- If you are fairly certain but not totally positive of the name of the terminal server, click the Browse button. In the dialog box that opens, type the name of the terminal server and click Check Names. If the name is accurate, it will appear in the Enter The Object Name To Select text box with an underline.

- If you have no idea of the name of the terminal server, here's how to proceed: From the second Select Computer dialog box, click the Advanced button to search Active Directory. Click the Locations button to specify the organizational unit (OU) the terminal servers are in and then click Find Now to list all servers in that OU. From there, you can select servers one at a time to appear in the Select Computer dialog box.

> **Note** To add more than one server at a time from the Select Computer dialog box, type the names and separate them with semicolons. If you select a second computer from Active Directory, you'll overwrite the first choice you made.

Manually populating groups is time-consuming if you aren't sure of the names of the servers. Operating on the principle that you'd like to manage the terminal servers in your farm, regardless of their names, you can import server information from the TS Session Broker. To do this, simply right-click Terminal Services Manager and choose Import From TS Session Broker. Enter the name or IP address of the Session Broker server from which you want to import and click OK. A new server management group will be created named TS Session Broker (*servername*), and another group beneath it will be named after your farm name, as shown in Figure 8-2.

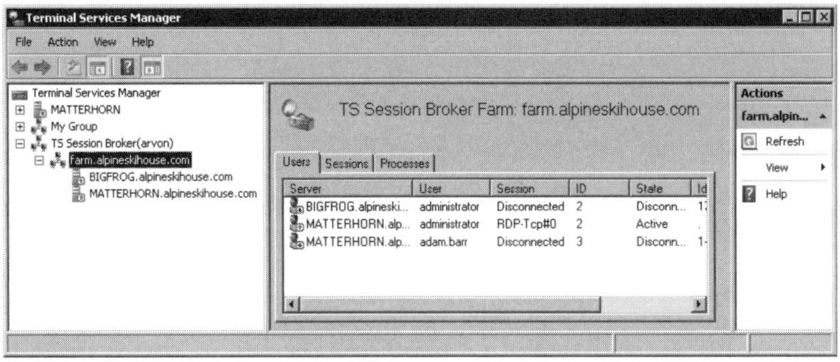

FIGURE 8-2 Import TS Session Broker farm members into Terminal Services Manager

After adding the TS Session Broker Group to Terminal Services Manager, you must connect to each server in order to glean any useful data. This is a one-time process; after this, they will be connected when you open this tool on this particular server or workstation. Right-click each server and choose Connect. After all servers are connected, you can highlight the group (in Figure 8-2, this is farm.alpineskihouse.com), and user, session, and process data for all servers in the group appear together in the middle console pane. You can also click each server in the group and view just the data for that server.

Monitoring and Terminating Processes

One of the basic questions about remote sessions is what processes are executing inside those sessions. As we've discussed in previous chapters, some processes are common to all sessions, but other processes tell you what users are doing in their remote session. You can even use processes to determine whether a user is connected to a full desktop or to a TS RemoteApp. Additionally, you may need to terminate a hung process in a session or terminate all instances of a specific application.

Monitoring Application Use

You can monitor processes on a terminal server from Terminal Services Manager or by using the *query* command-line tool with the *process* parameter as shown here:

```
query process
```

From Terminal Services Manager, connect to the server you want to monitor and then select the Processes Tab in the middle pane to display all processes running on that terminal server. You can then sort the table by clicking on the column headings (Server, User, Session, ID, PID, or Image).

You can accomplish the same thing at the command prompt by running the *query process* or *qprocess* command against a terminal server. The syntax for both of these commands follows:

```
QUERY PROCESS [* | processid | username | sessionname | /ID:nn | programname] [/SERVER:
servername]

   *               Display all visible processes.
   processid       Display process specified by processid.
   username        Display all processes belonging to username.
   sessionname     Display all processes running at sessionname.
   /ID:nn          Display all processes running at session nn.
   programname     Display all processes associated with programname.
   /SERVER:servername The Terminal server to be queried.
```

You can get a list of all processes running on a terminal server. For example, the following command returns all processes running on terminal server MATTERHORN:

```
query process * /server:matterhorn
```

You can also get more granular information by specifying different parameters. For instance, to find all the processes running under sessions started by the user nancy.anderson on server MATTERHORN, the command and data returned would look like this:

```
query process nancy.anderson /server:matterhorn
 USERNAME               SESSIONNAME        ID    PID  IMAGE
 nancy.anderson         rdp-tcp#2           4   3296  taskeng.exe
 nancy.anderson         rdp-tcp#2           4   3736  rdpclip.exe
```

```
nancy.anderson          rdp-tcp#2              4   2680  dwm.exe
nancy.anderson          rdp-tcp#2              4   3700  explorer.exe
```

Another example of getting specific process-related information from the command line is to find all instances of a particular application running on a terminal server. For instance, to find all sessions in which users are running Excel.exe on server MATTERHORN, the command and results would look like this:

```
query process excel.exe /server:matterhorn
 USERNAME                SESSIONNAME        ID    PID  IMAGE
 adam.barr               rdp-tcp#1           2   3156  excel.exe
 nancy.anderson          rdp-tcp#2           4   3044  excel.exe
 kristin.griffin         rdp-tcp#3           5   4088  excel.exe
 christa.anderson        rdp-tcp#4           6   3176  excel.exe
```

If you've used Windows PowerShell, you may be familiar with the *Get-Process* cmdlet. It's a useful tool that tells you a lot about the processes running on a computer, including working set, CPU time, and more much more information than *qprocess* can convey. Unfortunately, *Get-Process* is not multi-user aware and only reports on the processes running in the current session. Similarly, you can't use the *Stop-Process* cmdlet very well on a terminal server, because it is only aware of the processes running in the same session it is.

Terminating Applications

When you know where an application is running, you can terminate it if you need to. A user's application may be unresponsive or a user may get past your lockdown schemes (see Chapter 5, "Fine-Tuning the User Experience"). It's even possible to terminate a process for one user so that another user can use it without violating your application licensing. To terminate a process from Terminal Services Manager, connect to the server where the process is running, select the Processes tab, right-click the process, and choose End Process.

You also can end a process from the command line by running the *tskill* command. The syntax is:

```
TSKILL processid | processname [/SERVER:servername] [/ID:sessionid | /A] [/V]

    processid           Process ID for the process to be terminated.
    processname         Process name to be terminated.
    /SERVER:servername  Server containing processID (default is current).
                           /ID or /A must be specified when using processname and /SERVER
    /ID:sessionid       End process running under the specified session.
    /A                  End process running under ALL sessions.
    /V                  Display information about actions being performed.
```

Notice that you can kill either a specific instance of an application on a terminal server or all instances. To terminate an application running in a specific session, use the */ID:sessionid* parameter to specify that session. You need to know the session ID where the process is running, so you must first run *query session* to find out what the session ID is.

To illustrate, let's combine these two commands to effectively shut down one instance of an application. This example will terminate the Excel.exe process running in the session for user adam.barr on server MATTERHORN. First run the *query session* command to find the correct session ID:

```
C:\windows\system32>query session /server:matterhorn
 SESSIONNAME         USERNAME             ID  STATE  TYPE        DEVICE
 services                                  0  Disc
 console             Administrator         1  Active
 rdp-tcp#1           adam.barr             2  Active rdpwd
 rdp-tcp#0           administrator         3  Active rdpwd
                     nancy.anderson        4  Disc
                     kristin.griffin       5  Disc
                     christa.anderson      6  Disc
 rdp-tcp                               65536  Listen
```

Then terminate Microsoft Excel by specifying the process name, the server, and the session ID:

```
C:\windows\system32>tskill excel /server:matterhorn /ID:2
```

 Note Notice that the process name is equivalent to the name of the executable minus the extension. Leaving off the extension is important; although image names normally include the extension, the command won't work if you include it.

What if you forget to disable installations and discover a Mahjong tournament taking place among the users on a terminal server? You can also terminate a process running in all sessions on a terminal server by using the */A* switch in this way:

```
tskill mahjong /server:matterhorn /A
```

Monitoring and Ending User Sessions

Before you start monitoring and ending sessions in Terminal Services Manager, you should recognize the different session types you will see and what they are for. Four types of sessions appear in Terminal Services Manager:

- **Console**   Session supporting someone logged on locally
- **RDP-Tcp**   Remote RDP session
- **Services**   Session used by server services
- **Listener**   Session listening for incoming connection requests

For our purposes, you're going to work most often with the RDP-Tcp sessions.

Switching Between Sessions

Let's say you have logged onto your Windows Vista or Windows XP desktop via RDP with your domain credentials so that you can work on that computer from a remote location. When you do so, the console session switches to the RDP session and the console goes back to the logon screen. The same functionality is behind the ability to move between sessions on a terminal server, using Terminal Services Manager or the *tscon* command. You can switch between your own sessions if you have more than one, or (if you know the password) you can connect to another user's session and disconnect your own. (Connecting to a session using this functionality automatically disconnects the session you started from.)

There are a few caveats to using the Connect functionality:

- It only works to connect to an RDP-Tcp session from another RDP-Tcp connection on the same server. You can connect to an active or a disconnected session.

- Although you can connect to another session from an administrative (/admin) connection, you can't connect to an administrative connection from another RDP-Tcp connection.

- When prompted for a password while connecting to a session from Terminal Services Manager, the password is obscured on the screen. When you supply the password to the command-line tool, the password may optionally be displayed on the screen, in clear text. Therefore, be careful how you use *tscon* when anyone is standing behind you!

Note If you attempt to connect to a local logon session from *tscon*, you'll get an error code 31, telling you that A Device Attached To The System Is Not Functioning. If you attempt to connect to an */admin* remote connection, you'll get an error message that access is denied.

Chapter 3, "Installing the Core Terminal Server Environment," and Chapter 7, "Multi-Server Deployments and Securing Terminal Server Connections," walked through the process of what happens when you type your credentials into the RDP client to log on, but what about the session connection functionality through *tscon* and the Terminal Services Manager tool? How does this work? See the following Direct from the Source sidebar for details.

Direct from the Source: What Happens to the Password I Type into *TSCON*?

The Connect tool (whether implemented from the command line or the GUI) implements this functionality through the WTSConnectSession function described on MSDN at *http://msdn.microsoft.com/en-us/library/bb394782(VS.85).aspx*. For the purposes of the IT Pro, this function takes three important parameters: *logonID, targetlogonID,* and *password.*

> Basically, what happens is that this function accepts the domain name and user name of the person initiating the request. If these do not match, then the person initiating the request must type in the password of the account who owns the target session. One key fact to note is that Connect only works on the same terminal server—you can't connect to a session on another terminal server. Therefore, the credentials don't go over the network except when you type them into the RDP window, and then they're protected by RDP encryption.
>
> The bottom line is that, when you connect to another session, the credentials you provide are protected. They never leave the terminal server and they are removed from memory as soon as the function is finished with them.
>
> *Al Henriquez, Software Development Engineer II*
>
> *Meher Malakapalli, Senior Development Lead*

To use the Connect functionality from Terminal Services Manager or *tscon*, follow these steps:

1. Launch an RDP session to the terminal server hosting the session to which you want to connect.

2. Find the correct session. From Terminal Services Manager, find the correct session from the Users or Sessions tab in the center pane. From the command prompt, find the session ID by typing **query session**.

3. Connect to the session. From Terminal Services Manager, right-click the session and choose Connect from the context menu. From the command prompt, type **tscon** *sessionID* **/password:***password* to enter the password with the command or **/password*** to be prompted for the password. You'll need to include all this information in the command.

> **Note** You must supply the password when connecting from the command prompt or the command will fail. When connecting from Terminal Services Manager, you are prompted for the password if connecting to a session not your own.

4. Assuming you provide the correct password and the session can be connected to, you will connect immediately to the new session. If the password isn't valid, you'll see an error message.

So why do this? The functionality is most useful if TS RemoteApps isn't in the picture. In Windows Server 2003 and before, the only way to publish individual applications was by limiting a session to a single application. By using Connect, it was possible to move between individual applications on the same terminal server. Today, this command isn't applicable to most situations, since the only sessions you should be able to connect to (assuming reason-ably secure domain password protection) are your own. One possible scenario for using Connect in this present version on Terminal Services is if you were logged onto a terminal server as both a user and an administrator, using two different accounts. You could switch to your administrator persona by connecting to the session.

Closing Orphaned Sessions

An *orphaned session* is one that is no longer being used. An orphaned session can occur for a number of reasons, for example, if you do not limit users to one session and don't set a time limit for resetting idle and disconnected sessions, you may encounter sessions that were left open by users. You may also find orphaned sessions if users get disconnected from their ses-sion and you are not implementing the session directory service (that will reconnect users to disconnected sessions). In this instance, when the users reconnect to the farm, they might open a new session and unknowingly abandon the other session.

There are many ways to decrease orphaned sessions. You can configure Group Policy objects (GPOs) to automatically end idle and disconnected sessions after a certain period of inactivity, or you can implement the session directory service to reconnect users to their disconnected sessions. However, if these avenues are blocked for you, you should know how to terminate orphaned sessions.

First, you must determine which sessions are really abandoned. A good way to tell if a ses-sion is not being used is to look for active and disconnected sessions that have been idle for a certain period of time, such as if you have shift workers and a session is idle for longer than the normal daily shift hours. Check the Terminal Services Manager Users or Sessions tab or use the *query user* command to figure out which sessions to terminate by finding out how long sessions have been idle. For example, to check the Idle Time setting for all sessions on server MATTERHORN, you can run this command:

```
C:\windows\system32>query user /server:matterhorn

 USERNAME              SESSIONNAME        ID  STATE   IDLE TIME  LOGON TIME
 administrator         console             1  Active      none  7/26/2008 6:51 PM
 adam.barr            rdp-tcp#1            2  Active         7  7/30/2008 4:55 PM
 administrator         rdp-tcp#0            3  Active         .  7/27/2008 6:37 PM
 nancy.anderson       rdp-tcp#2            4  Active         7  7/30/2008 4:55 PM
 kristin.griffin      rdp-tcp#3            5  Active         7  7/30/2008 4:56 PM
 christa.anderson     rdp-tcp#4            6  Active         6  7/30/2008 4:56 PM
```

 Note See the section titled "Auditing User Logons" later in this chapter for more examples of how to use the *query user* command.

The results will show the state, idle time (if applicable), and logon time of each session.

At this point, you have a couple of options: you can disconnect the session or terminate it. Disconnecting the session causes it to use fewer resources on the server while leaving open the applications and data in use in the session. Terminating the session (also called resetting the session) will completely end the session. Disconnecting is not invasive; users can get back to where they were by logging on again, but it does continue to use resources on the terminal server. Terminating frees resources but may lead to file locking issues, because it's an ungraceful exit and files may not close properly.

> **Note** Terminal Services does not support concurrent user licensing. Therefore, if you're using a native Terminal Services environment with no add-ons licensed on a concurrent-user basis, it's immaterial from a licensing perspective whether you disconnect or terminate a session. However, this is a consideration if using Citrix's XenApp, which is licensed on a concurrent-user basis.

Disconnecting Sessions

Disconnecting a session using Terminal Services Manager is easy. Find the session to disconnect, right-click it, and choose Disconnect from the context menu. You must be connected to the same server as the session you're disconnecting.

To disconnect a session from the command prompt, use *tsdiscon*. The syntax is simple:

```
TSDISCON               [sessionid | sessionname] [/SERVER:servername] [/V]
  Sessionid            The ID of the session.
  Sessionname          The name of the session.
 /SERVER:servername  Specifies the terminal server (default is current).
 /V                   Displays information about the actions performed.
```

As you can see, when using the command-line tool, you can specify the terminal server on which you want to disconnect a session. One caution: If you run *tsdiscon* without arguments, you'll disconnect your own session even if you're sitting at the console. You won't lose any data, because the session will continue running and you can just reconnect, but disconnecting yourself is disconcerting.

Terminating Sessions

You can easily terminate a session from Terminal Services Manager or the command prompt.

To terminate a session from Terminal Services Manager, highlight the session on the Users or Sessions tab, right-click, and choose Reset. You'll see a dialog box telling you that you're resetting this user's session. Click OK, and the session will reset. All processes belonging to that user will be immediately terminated.

You can also terminate active and disconnected sessions from the command line using one of these three utilities (their syntax is shown here):

```
RESET SESSION {sessionname | sessionid} [/SERVER:servername] [/V]
RWINSTA {sessionname | sessionid} [/SERVER:servername] [/V]
LOGOFF [sessionname | sessionid] [/SERVER:serverna me] [/V]
```

Reset Session and *rwinsta* are functionally the same in that they terminate the connection ungracefully. *Logoff* is a little different in that, although it won't save open files, it will at least write back changes to the profile.

The syntax for all three commands requires that you use the session name or session ID to identify the session you want to close, so you will need to get this information from Terminal Services Manager or from the command line by using the *query user* command. The syntax is:

```
QUERY USER [username | sessionname | sessionid] [/SERVER:servername]
```

For instance, to reset a disconnected session for user paul.koch on server MATTERHORN, run these commands:

```
C:\Users\Administrator>query session paul.koch /server:matterhorn
 SESSIONNAME        USERNAME              ID STATE   TYPE        DEVICE
                    paul.koch              5 Disc
C:\Users\Administrator>reset session 5 /server:matterhorn
C:\Users\Administrator>query session paul.koch /server:matterhorn
No session exists for paul.koch
```

Providing Help with Remote Control

In addition to the methods just described, another way to interact with user sessions is to shadow them. Inevitably, every user at one time or another calls the Help Desk to get assistance from the IT staff. And as helpful as staff can be, and as willing to describe their unfortunate circumstances as users can be, sometimes, it is best to experience the problem to solve it efficiently. Windows Server 2008 (like its predecessor) gives you the ability to observe the user session or even take control of the session so that you can act as the user and experience the difficulties a user has. Hopefully, this experience provides a clearer picture of the situation and leads to a speedy resolution of the Help Desk ticket.

There are three places in which Remote Control settings are controlled:

- **Group Policy**   Used to specify Remote Control settings for all terminal servers in a farm

- **Terminal Services Configuration**   Used to specify Remote Control settings on a per-server basis

- **Active Directory Users And Computers (ADUC) User account properties**   Used to specify Remote Control settings on a per-user basis

The ability to remotely control or *shadow* a user's session is enabled by default in ADUC on the Remote Control tab of each user account as shown in Figure 8-3.

> **Note** Even though Remote Control is enabled by default in ADUC user account properties, these settings are only used when Terminal Services Configuration (instead of Group Policy) is used to stipulate Remote Control settings, and only when Terminal Services Configuration is set to Use Remote Control With Default User Settings. We will look at Terminal Services Configuration Remote Control settings later in this section.

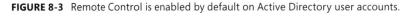

FIGURE 8-3 Remote Control is enabled by default on Active Directory user accounts.

If you do not want to be able to remote control sessions opened by the user, clear the Enable Remote Control check box.

By default, the user's permission is required for you to interact with the user's session. When you invoke remote control of a user session, the user receives a prompt similar to Figure 8-4 requesting that she grant you permission to control the session.

FIGURE 8-4 If the user's permission is required for shadowing the session, the user will see this notice.

If Require User's Permission is not enabled, then you can gain remote control (for viewing or interacting, depending on the level of control option selected) of the user session without her knowledge or permission. When you attach to the session, the user sees nothing and is not aware of your presence, unless of course you interact with the session, for example, if you move the mouse, open a file, or close a window. Then your presence will be obvious, or the user will think something is wrong with the computer. Unless you have specific reasons for viewing sessions without user awareness, we recommend that you require the user's permission to interact with the session. This procedure preserves user trust, and your presence will not confuse users (which could end up in another Help Desk call). It also helps to safeguard against accidentally choosing the wrong session to shadow, as the user needs to accept the request.

> **Note** If you decide to interact with user sessions without user knowledge or permission, check with your company's legal and human resources (HR) departments first, to make sure that the company is legally protected and HR policies reflect this need.

By default, administrators have full control of the user session. This means you can manipulate the session (use the keyboard and mouse, etc.) as if you are the user. This level of control can be changed to allow only observation by selecting the option View The User's Session. At this level, you can observe the user's session, but you cannot control it in any way.

Remote Control settings can also be set using Terminal Services Configuration on each server or by using Group Policy. Group Policy settings taking precedence over Terminal Services Configuration settings.

Enabling Remote Control via Group Policy

Control of this functionality can be set with either a user Group Policy (to affect certain groups of users) or a computer Group Policy (to affect all users who log on to a server or server farm). These settings are located at:

- Computer Configuration | Policies | Administrative Templates | Windows Components | Terminal Services | Terminal Server | Connections | Set Rules For Remote Control Of Terminal Services User Sessions

- User Configuration | Policies | Administrative Templates | Windows Components | Terminal Services | Terminal Server | Connections | Set Rules For Remote Control Of Terminal Services User Sessions

> **Note** If both of these Group Policy settings are enabled, the computer policy settings will take precedence.

Opening either of these Group Policy object (GPO) settings reveals the screen shown in Figure 8-5.

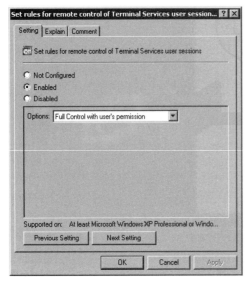

FIGURE 8-5 The Set Rules For Remote Control Of Terminal Services User Sessions GPO setting dialog box

Enable the GPO setting and then specify whether user permission is required for interaction with the user session and what level of control will be allowed. Do this by choosing the appropriate option from the Options drop-down menu. The options available are:

- **Full Control With User's Permission**   With the user's permission, you can take action in the session just as if you were the user.

- **Full Control Without User's Permission**   Without the user's permission and without the user receiving any notification, you can take action in the session just as if you were the user.

- **View Session With User's Permission**   With the user's permission, you can view the session but not interact with the session in any way.

- **View Session Without User's Permission**   Without the user's permission and without the user receiving any notification, you can view the session but not interact with the session in any way.

If these Group Policy settings are set to Not Configured, then Remote Control settings are controlled by Terminal Services Configuration. However, enabling either of these Group Policy settings relinquishes control of Remote Control from the Terminal Services Configuration, and thus the setting options there will not be available.

To disable remote control of user sessions, choose the No Remote Control Allowed option from the Options drop-down menu.

Note You might think that disabling either of these Group Policy settings would disable remote control of user sessions. This is not the case. Disabling either of these GPO settings means only that Remote Control is not specified via Group Policy and is specified using Terminal Services Configuration.

Enabling Remote Control via Terminal Services Configuration

Terminal Services Configuration is used to set Remote Control settings on a per-server basis. On a terminal server, open Terminal Services Configuration, double-click the RDP-Tcp connection, and then click the Remote Control tab shown in Figure 8-6.

There are two ways to enable remote control:

- Enable remote control and specify whether user permissions are required to shadow the user session and the level of control (view only or interact) permitted when shadowing the session.

- Enable remote control and use the Remote Control settings set in each user's ADUC account properties to specify whether shadowing that user's session is allowed, whether the user's permission is required, and the level of control (view only or interact) permitted when shadowing the session.

- Disable remote control of user sessions created on the server by choosing Do Not Allow Remote Control.

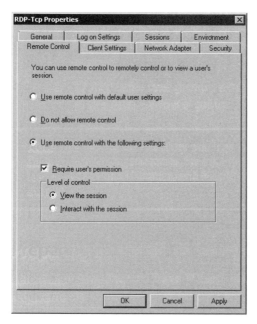

FIGURE 8-6 Configure Remote Control via Terminal Services Configuration RDP-Tcp Properties

Shadowing a User Session

Before you try to shadow a session, there are two things to keep in mind. First, you can only shadow a session from another RDP session, because you're basically intercepting the shadowed session and sending it to your own session. You can't send RDP updates to a local logon, just as you can't connect to an RDP session from a local logon. (You'll see this when you start Terminal Services Manager from the console session; there's a warning that these tools will be disabled.)

Somewhat more insidious, you can't shadow all remote sessions. To be precise, you can only shadow sessions connecting to a full desktop. It will appear that you can shadow other sessions, because nothing in the user interface (UI) prevents you from connecting to a session hosting TS RemoteApps, and you won't see any warnings. However, shadowing TS RemoteApps isn't supported. The problem is that, as you may recall from Chapter 6, "Installing and Publishing Applications," TS RemoteApps requires some detailed communication between server and client to position the window correctly. This communication doesn't extend to both the computer from which the administrator is shadowing the session and the original client computer. If the administrator shadowing the session moves the application window, it may disappear from the session when the administrator restores control, or it may just render the application unresponsive. Therefore, although it is technically possible to shadow a TS RemoteApp session, it's not a good idea. Before shadowing, be sure that you're connecting to a full desktop session.

> **Note** The tricky bit is that neither Terminal Services Manager nor the command-line tools distinguish between full desktops and TS RemoteApps. To learn how to distinguish between sessions running TS RemoteApps and those running a full desktop, see the section titled "Differentiating RemoteApp Sessions from Full Desktop Sessions" later in this chapter.

Shadowing a session is simple. Create an RDP connection to a server or desktop with Terminal Services Manager installed and then open Terminal Services Manager. On the Users tab in the middle pane, right-click the user whose session you want to shadow and select Remote Control. If the user's permission is required, the user will receive a remote control request and can accept or deny your request.

Meanwhile, on the server you will see a dialog box asking you to specify a key sequence to end the shadow session (shown in Figure 8-7). Ctrl+Tab is the default choice, but you can choose other options if the default doesn't work for you.

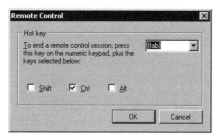

FIGURE 8-7   Choose a hot key sequence to end a shadow session.

 Note The dialog box says that the first key in the sequence should be typed on the numeric keypad. In reality, some of the choices are not on the numeric keypad but are found on the other sections of the keyboard.

Your screen may freeze briefly while the user is alerted to your shadow request (and the user's screen may blink once when you connect).

After the user grants you permission to shadow the session, your session will be replaced with the user's session desktop. If settings permit you only to view the session, then you will be able to see the user's actions, but you won't be able to interact with the session. Otherwise, you can take part in the session as if you were the user. To stop shadowing, simply press the hot key sequence you selected when establishing the session; the shadow session will disappear and you will be back to your desktop. The user's session will continue as normal.

You can also start a shadow session from the command line. Again, you'll need to establish an RDP session first and run the command from it. To get remote control of a session from the command line, use the *shadow* command and provide the name of the user or the session ID to which you want to connect. To shadow a session on a remote computer, use the following syntax:

shadow /SERVER:*servername*

When you start a shadow session from the command line, there is no prompt for you to choose a key sequence to end the shadow session. To end the shadow session, use the key sequence Ctrl+*.

 Note The asterisk above the number 8 does not work to stop shadowing. Use the asterisk on your numeric keypad.

Troubleshooting Session Shadowing

If you try to shadow a user session and can't, there are a few steps you can take to trouble-shoot the problem. First, make sure that the user's session is allowed to be shadowed. This setting can be configured through Group Policy (for users or computers), the user account properties, or in Terminal Services Configuration.

If you find that the settings in these areas are set correctly and you are still being denied, check with the user. It may be that the user is mistakenly answering "No" to the request to let you remote control the session.

Error messages you may receive when trying to shadow a session are most helpful when you're trying to shadow a session from the same terminal server as the session you're trying to shadow is connected to. For instance, if you are trying to shadow a user session from the same server that the user is logged onto, and Terminal Services Configuration is set to not allow remote control, you will receive a message like this:

```
shadow 3
Your session may appear frozen while the remote control approval is being negotiated.
Please wait...
Remote control failed. Error code 7051
Error [7051]:The requested session is not configured to allow remote control.
```

However, if you are initiating the shadowing operation from a computer other than the one that hosts the session that you want to shadow, you will not get such a straightforward message. Instead, if there's a problem, you will receive a cryptic message like this:

```
shadow 3 /SERVER:matterhorn
Your session may appear frozen while the remote control approval is being negotiated.
Please wait...
Remote control failed. Error code 2
Error [2]:The system cannot find the file specified.
```

Typically, if you get an error code 2, it means either the user denied your request to shadow the session or shadowing the session is not allowed.

If you'd like to save yourself the trouble of trying three different tools to find the current Remote Control settings and where they're set, query the *Win32_TSRemoteControlSetting* WMI class from Windows PowerShell.

> **Note** The methods and properties for this class can be found online at *http://msdn.microsoft .com/en-us/library/aa383817(VS.85).aspx*.

To view the Remote Control settings for a computer, open Windows PowerShell and enter the following command:

```
get-wmiobject -namespace "root\cimv2\terminalservices" -class Win32_TSRemoteControlSetting
```

The important bit of the output is at the bottom, where you'll see values such as this:

```
Caption                     :
Description                 :
InstallDate                 :
LevelOfControl              : 0
Name                        :
PolicySourceLevelOfControl  : 0
RemoteControlPolicy         : 1
Status                      :
TerminalName                : RDP-Tcp
```

The key properties *LevelOfControl*, *PolicySourceLevelOfControl*, and *RemoteControlPolicy* provide answers to the following questions: Do you have permission to shadow this session? Where is this policy set?

> **On the Companion Media**   The Windows PowerShell script, shadowcheck.ps1, helps automate the commands detailed here.

LevelofControl can have values from 0 to 4, with the following meanings:

- 0 = Remote control is disabled.
- 1 = Administrator has full control; user must grant permission to be shadowed.
- 2 = Administrator has full control; user permission is not required.
- 3 = Administrator can view the shadowed session; user must grant permission to be shadowed.
- 4 = Administrator can view the shadowed session; user permission is not required.

The *PolicySourceLevelOfControl* shows where the value of *LevelOfControl* comes from. A value of 0 means that this value is set on a per-user basis, a value of 1 indicates that it's set by Group Policy, and a value of 2 means that it's the user account policies.

The value of the *RemoteControlPolicy* property indicates whether Remote Control settings are configured on a per-use basis (1) or per-server (0).

You can observe the changes to these settings by editing the Remote Control settings from Terminal Services Configuration. Try editing the settings to see how the value of the *LevelOfControl* property changes when you disable remote control, and you'll see the value change when you run the script.

Preparing for Server Maintenance

When you need to patch a terminal server or update an application, you certainly don't want users to be connected to it at the time. Therefore, you'll need some method of keeping users off the server when necessary. This is generally known as putting the terminal server into *drain mode*, where existing connections are allowed to continue but no new ones are allowed in (and the TS Session Broker won't route any connections there).

When preparing for maintenance, there are three steps you should perform, in order:

1. Disable new logons.
2. Inform users of the planned downtime.
3. Programmatically shut down the terminal server.

Disabling New Logons

You can put a server into drain mode via Terminal Services Configuration or the command line.

From Terminal Services Configuration, move to the Edit Settings area in the middle pane and double-click User Logon Mode. This will open a dialog box presenting three options:

- **Allow All Connections**   This is the default user mode. All connections are allowed.

- **Allow Reconnections, But Prevent New Logons**   This is drain mode. Users with existing sessions are allowed to reconnect or to stay connected to the terminal server, but new connections are blocked.

- **Allow Reconnections, But Prevent New Logons Until The Server Is Restarted**   This is temporary drain mode. The terminal server will not accept new connections (and the TS Session Broker will not route connections to it) until the server is rebooted. After the server has rebooted, this setting will revert to Allow All Connections.

Choose the option that suits your needs and click OK.

To change user logon mode from the command prompt, you'll use the *change logon* command. You must execute this command from the terminal server whose user logon mode you're changing; the tool does not offer a remote option. The *change logon* syntax is pretty simple:

- **/query**   Returns the state of the server
- **/enable**   Enables logons that had been disabled
- **/disable**   Disables all incoming connections, including reconnections

- **/drain**   Puts the server into drain mode

- **/drainuntilrestart**   Puts the server into temporary drain mode

If you're familiar with this tool from previous versions of Windows Server, you may notice the new options for enabling drain mode and temporary drain mode. Otherwise, the syntax hasn't changed from Windows Server 2003.

Notice that *change logon* offers an option that the GUI does not: /disable. Drain mode prohibits new connections but does allow users to reconnect to existing sessions. If you're serious about removing users from the terminal server, use `change logon /disable` to prevent any incoming connections, even reconnections. However, use this option with care. Disabling logons when users have existing sessions open can result in lost data or profile changes in the orphaned sessions. Drain mode combined with reminders to users that you will be shutting down the server and requests to users to log off their sessions is a safer option.

Each of these options only allows you to configure one terminal server, though. To set the logon mode on more than one terminal server at a time, use either Group Policy or script the logon mode via WMI. To edit the User Logon Mode via Group Policy, go to Computer Configuration | Policies | Administrative Templates | Windows Components | Terminal Services | Terminal Server | Connections | Allow Users To Connect Remotely Using Terminal Services.

Group Policy is most useful for longer-term changes affecting many servers (you shouldn't edit Group Policy for a temporary change to two servers), whereas WMI is better for faster or more directed changes. Group Policy isn't practical for, say, changing the logon mode for two terminal servers in the farm while the other two keep accepting logons, but WMI works well for this.

One way to check for the current logon mode via WMI on the local computer is to run the following Windows PowerShell script. To run this script on a remote computer, change the value of *$strComputer* to the name of the other computer.

```
$strComputer = "."
$termserv = get-wmiobject -class "Win32_TerminalServiceSetting" -namespace ` "root\CIMV2\
terminalservices" -computername $strComputer
switch ($termserv.AllowTSConnections)
{
   0 {"User logons are disabled."}
   1 {"User logons are enabled."}
   default {"The user logon state cannot be determined."}
}
switch ($termserv.SessionBrokerDrainMode)
{
   0 {"Allow all connections."}
   1 {"Allow incoming reconnections but prohibit new connections."}
   2 {"Allow incoming reconnections but until reboot prohibit new connections."}
   default {"The user logon state cannot be determined."}
}
```

For example, this script will return the following message if the server is in temporary drain mode:

```
User logons are enabled.
Allow incoming reconnections but until reboot prohibit new connections.
```

> **On the Companion Media** This script is on the companion media as checklogon.ps1.

Notice that this script has to query two properties to return all the information. The *AllowTSConnections* property corresponds to the */enable* and */disable* switches, and *SessionBrokerDrainMode* corresponds to the */drain* and */drainuntilrestart* switches. As before, we're using the switch statement to evaluate the actual values and make interpreting the output easier. The efficiency of running a script to get the information you need is somewhat reduced if you have to look up the return values on Microsoft Developer Network (MSDN) to know what they mean.

Sending Messages to Session Users

Shutting down a terminal server without telling users is apt to annoy them. Even if you plan to start maintenance after work hours, it's still a good idea to let users know that they should completely shut down their sessions, not just disconnect them. You can also send messages for less drastic reasons, such as telling a user to resend a print job or warning users to shut down an application.

One way to communicate with your user base is by sending messages from the Terminal Services Manager or the *msg* command-line tool. Using these tools, you can communicate with individuals, selected groups, or everyone logged into the terminal server. You can even wait for acknowledgement of your message.

From Terminal Services Manager, right-click a session and select Send Message. You will get a screen similar to Figure 8-8.

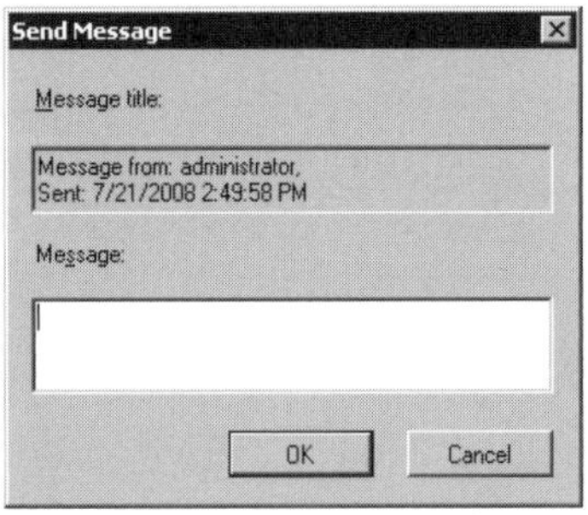

![Send Message dialog box with fields for Message title, Message from: administrator, Sent: 7/21/2008 2:49:58 PM, Message text area, and OK and Cancel buttons.]

FIGURE 8-8 Send a message to Terminal Services session users by filling in the Send Message dialog box.

The message contains the sender's user name and the time the message is sent. Type your message in the Send Message dialog box and click OK. The user will receive your message dialog box, which will look like Figure 8-9.

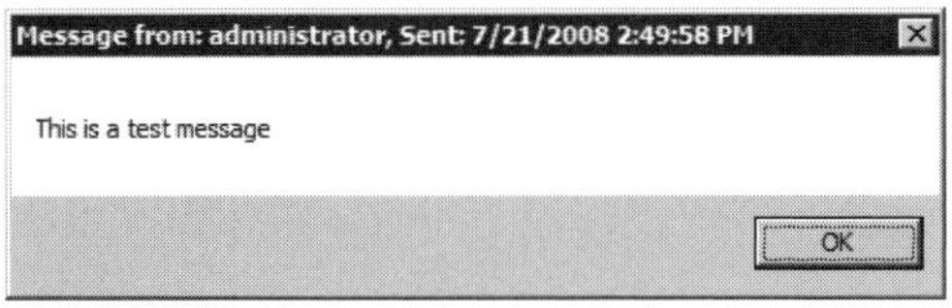

FIGURE 8-9 Users receive messages in a pop-up window.

Unlike the shadowing feature, sending messages is supported for RemoteApps. Users running RemoteApps or full desktop sessions receive the same message dialog box; the only difference is that RemoteApps users get a message dialog box on their desktop, whereas users running a full desktop session receive the message in that session window.

You can also use the *msg* command-line utility to send a message to a Terminal Services session like this:

```
msg nancy.anderson /SERVER:matterhorn Nancy, Tech Support has reviewed your case, and will
be with you in 5 minutes.
```

If you are not running the command from the terminal server where the session is active, then you must specify the server as the preceding command does.

You can specify sessions based on user name, session ID, or session name. Use the *query* command or Terminal Services Manager to get any of these data points.

If you have not limited users to one Terminal Services session per server, then you may need to send a message to every session that user has open. If you provide the user name as an argument, the message will appear in all sessions belonging to that user.

To send a message to all sessions on a server, use the * argument. For example, to send a message to every session on server MATTERHORN, run this command:

```
msg * /SERVER:matterhorn This server will be rebooted at 3pm.  Please close your RemoteApps.
```

You can also send a message to all users, session IDs, or session names contained in a file. Using a file to specify who should receive a message can be helpful if you need to communicate with a group of users, but not every single person using the terminal server. For instance, maybe you need to tell all accounting department users on server MATTERHORN to shut down the accounting application. To do this, first create a file containing the user names of the accounting department users. This is most easily done from Windows PowerShell with the following script that gets the users in the ASH_Users OU and adds them to a file named c:\scripts\ashusers.txt. (Obviously, you'll need to modify the Lightweight Directory Access Protocol (LDAP) paths and filename for your purposes.)

> **Note** Use getnames.ps1 any time you want to get the names in a collection. It can be easily modified to return computers as well as users, and to point to different locations.

```
$OU = [ADSI] "LDAP://OU=ASH_Users, DC=alpineskihouse, DC=com"
$UserList = "c:\scripts\ashusers.txt"
foreach ($child in $ou.psbase.children)
{
out-file -filepath $UserList -append -inputobject $child.name
}
```

> **On the Companion Media:** The script to get the names of members of an OU and dump them to a file is on the companion media as getusers.ps1.

When you have the names, then just run the *msg* command as shown here:

```
msg @ c:\scripts\ASHUsers.txt /SERVER:matterhorn Please close the accounting application.
```

Shutting Down and Restarting Terminal Servers

When you've drained the server of users and notified anyone who remained connected to the server, you can shut it down. You've probably shut down a server from the GUI; shutting down a terminal server is no different. However, since you may not have shut it down from the command prompt, we'll focus on that option.

> **Note** The *tsshutdown* command used in Windows Server 2003 is no longer available in Windows Server 2008 and Vista. Use the *shutdown* command instead. You must be an administrator to shut down or reboot a terminal server. In Windows Server 2008, users in Terminal Services sessions do not get access to the Shut Down, Restart, Hibernate, or Sleep options in the Start menu. Regular users cannot execute the *shutdown* command.

Shutting down and rebooting a terminal server from the Start menu is no different than shutting down or rebooting a Windows 2008 server (without Terminal Services installed) or a Vista client. Go to Start and then click the arrow to the right of the lock button on the lower right of the menu. A menu pops up and you choose either Restart or Shut Down.

When you choose to shut down or restart a server, you will see a pop-up window similar to the one shown in Figure 8-10.

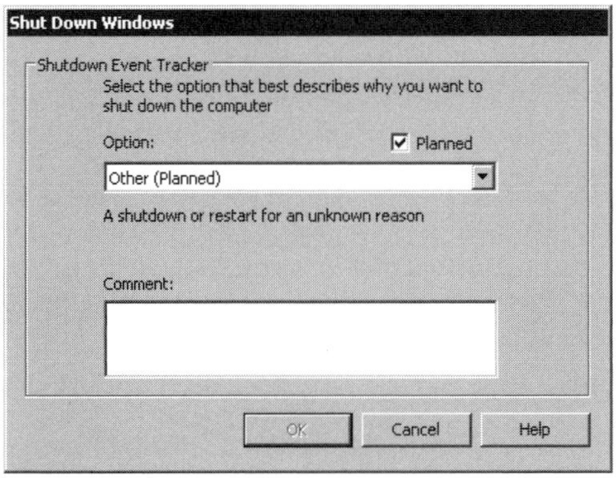

FIGURE 8-10 The Shut Down Windows dialog box

Here, you need to choose a reason for the shut down/reboot from the Option drop-down menu. Also, indicate whether the action was planned or unplanned, type any comments you want to add in the Comments window, and click OK. This information is recorded in the server System Event Log (Event ID 1074). This logging is helpful for keeping track of who rebooted or shut down a server, and why they did so. Giving detailed information in the Comments area can make it easier for another administrator to figure out the exact reason for a reboot. For instance, if you install an application update, you can add a comment in the Shut Down Windows dialog box indicating exactly which one it was, which saves time if someone else needs the details later.

You can also use the *shutdown* command to shut down or restart a server from the command line. This command can be run from a Windows 2008 server or even a Windows Vista client. The command syntax is:

```
shutdown [/i | /l | /s | /r | /g | /a | /p | /h | /e] [/f] [/m \\computer][/t xxx][/d
[p|u:]xx:yy [/c "comment"]]
```

> **Note** Typing *shutdown* at a command prompt gives you the same command syntax and arguments as typing *shutdown /?*.

Table 8-5 shows a list of the command-line arguments available for the *shutdown* command.

TABLE 8-5 *shutdown* Command Arguments

Argument	Input	Details
No arguments		Displays the command syntax and arguments. This is the same as typing /?.
/?		Displays the command syntax and arguments.
/i		Displays the graphical user interface (GUI). This must be the first option if used with other options. Use this option to shut down or reboot more than one computer at a time.
/l		Log off the computer. This cannot be used with /m or /d options.
/s		Shuts down the computer.
/r		Restarts the computer.
/g		Restarts the computer and then starts registered applications.
/a		Aborts a system shutdown but can only be used against the *shutdown* command given with a timeout period (/t *xxx*).
/p		Turns off the local computer with no timeout or warning. Can be used with /d and /f options.
/h		Hibernates the local computer. Can be used with the /f option.
/e		Supposed to be used to document the reason for an unexpected shutdown of a computer, but it does nothing. Use the /c argument instead.
/m	\\computername	Specifies the target computer to shutdown or reboot.
/t	*xxx*	Set the timeout period before shutdown or reboot to xxx seconds. The valid range is 0–600, with a default of 30. Using /t xxx implies the /f option.
/c	"comment"	Add a comment about the reason for the restart or shutdown. Maximum of 512 characters allowed.
/f		Forces running applications to close without forewarning users; /f is automatically set when used in conjunction with /t xxx.
/d	[p|u:]xx:yy	Indicates the reason for the restart or shutdown; *p* indicates that the restart or shutdown is planned; *u* indicates that the reason is user defined. If neither *p* nor *u* is specified, the restart or shutdown is unplanned; *xx* is the major reason number (positive integer less than 256); *yy* is the minor reason number (positive integer less than 65536). (See Table 8-6 for a reason code reference.)

We won't run through every option the *shutdown* command offers, but we will highlight some options applicable to a Terminal Services environment.

Using the command-line utility means you can shut down or reboot a server remotely. For instance, to shut down the server MATTERHORN from a remote Windows Vista client, the command looks like this:

```
shutdown /m \\matterhorn
```

Use the /r command to reboot a server like this:

```
shutdown /r /m \\matterhorn
```

As with shutting down or rebooting from the GUI, it's good to document why the event is occurring. Use the /c argument to add a comment to the event to get recorded in the event log. For example, this command shuts down MATTERHORN and adds a comment to explain the reason for the shutdown:

```
shutdown /r /m \\matterhorn /c Installed accounting application update.
```

To document the planned reason for a shutdown or to restart via the command-line interface (CLI), use codes that correspond to the Option drop-down menu in the Windows Shut Down dialog box. The syntax for choosing a reboot code is `shutdown /d [p|u:]xx:yy`. The letters *p* and *u* indicate a planned action or user-defined action, respectively. The letter combination *xx* indicates the major reason number code; *yy* indicates the minor reason error code. Table 8-6 shows the reasons and corresponding code numbers.

TABLE 8-6 Major and Minor Number Codes Corresponding to Reasons for a Server Shutdown or Reboot

Type	Major	Minor	Title/Explanation
Types:			
E = Expected			
U = Unexpected			
P = Planned			
U	0	0	Other (Unplanned)
E	0	0	Other (Unplanned)
E P	0	0	Other (Planned)
U	0	5	Other Failure: System Unresponsive
E	1	1	Hardware: Maintenance (Unplanned)
E P	1	1	Hardware: Maintenance (Planned)
E	1	2	Hardware: Installation (Unplanned)
E P	1	2	Hardware: Installation (Planned)
P	2	3	Operating System: Upgrade (Planned)
E	2	4	Operating System: Reconfiguration (Unplanned)
E P	2	4	Operating System: Reconfiguration (Planned)
P	2	16	Operating System: Service pack (Planned)
	2	17	Operating System: Hot fix (Unplanned)
P	2	17	Operating System: Hot fix (Planned)
	2	18	Operating System: Security fix (Unplanned)
P	2	18	Operating System: Security fix (Planned)
E	4	1	Application: Maintenance (Unplanned)
E P	4	1	Application: Maintenance (Planned)

TABLE 8-6 Major and Minor Number Codes Corresponding to Reasons for a Server Shutdown or Reboot

Type	Major	Minor	Title/Explanation
E P	4	2	Application: Installation (Planned)
E	4	5	Application: Unresponsive
E	4	6	Application: Unstable
U	5	15	System Failure: Stop error
E	5	19	Security issue
U	5	19	Security issue
E P	5	19	Security issue
E	5	20	Loss of network connectivity (Unplanned)
U	6	11	Power Failure: Cord Unplugged
U	6	12	Power Failure: Environment
P	7	0	Legacy API shutdown

For instance, to reboot the server MATTERHORN and document the reboot as due to application maintenance, the command is:

```
shutdown /r /m \\matterhorn /d p:4:1
```

Running the preceding command remotely produces event ID 1074 in the System Event Log on the server that is rebooted, with a description of the action that occurs. The data includes the username that initiated the request, the IP address of the computer the request comes from, and the reason for the request:

```
The process wininit.exe (10.10.10.23) has initiated the restart of computer MATTERHORN
on behalf of user ALPINESKIHOUSE\Administrator for the following reason: Application:
Maintenance (Planned)
```

Shutdown.exe is also helpful if you need to reboot many servers. To do so, run the following command:

```
shutdown /i
```

This command brings up the dialog box named Remote Shutdown Dialog shown in Figure 8-11, which gives you the ability to specify more than one computer to shut down or restart.

Click the Add button and type the name of the computer you want to shut down or restart. Do this for all computers you want to shut down or restart. Then choose the action you want to perform from the What Do You Want These Computers To Do drop-down menu:

- Restart

- Shutdown

- Annotate Unexpected Shutdown (This option works only if you previously had an unexpected shutdown or restart.)

Choose the reason for this action by selecting the appropriate choice from the Option drop-down menu and add any comments in the Comment text box. Then click OK.

As an example, if you perform scheduled server maintenance such as running some updates every Sunday and include a reboot, you can automate the reboot process by creating a scheduled task with the Windows Server 2008 Task Scheduler or by using the command-line tool *schtasks*. For example, to reboot the server MATTERHORN every Sunday night at midnight, use *schtasks* as shown here:

```
schtasks.exe /create /SC WEEKLY /D SUN /RU administrator@alpineskihouse.com /RP password /
TN RebootMatterhorn /TR "C:\windows\system32\shutdown.exe /m \\matterhorn /r /c Matterhorn-
WindowsUpdates-Reboot" /ST 24:00
```

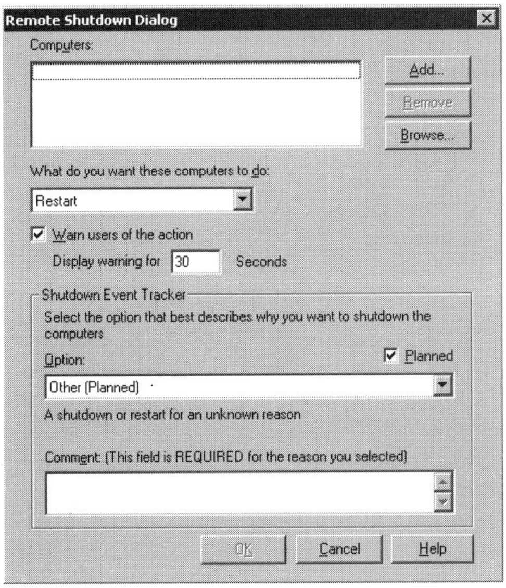

FIGURE 8-11 The Remote Shutdown Dialog dialog box

> **On the Companion Media** This scheduled task is located on the companion media as schedreboot.bat.

If a shutdown or reboot attempt fails, Event ID 1073 is logged in the System Event Log of the server that fails to reboot. The log won't tell you why the action failed, but it will at least let you know it did fail and which user account issued the command. Optionally, you can use Schtasks.exe to create a task that performs an action such as running a script that e-mails you every time the event ID appears. The details of server-reboot-failed.vbs are in the next sidebar, "Direct from the Field: E-Mail Yourself When a Reboot Fails."

```
schtasks.exe /Create /TN EventLog-1073 /TR "cscript \\ozark\it$\server-reboot-failed.vbs"
/SC ONEVENT /EC System /MO *[System/EventID=1073]
```

On the Companion Media This scheduled task is located on the companion media as emailonfail.bat. The scheduled task executes server-reboot-failed.vbs, which you can access from *http://theessentialexchange.com/blogs/michael/default.aspx*. This link is on the companion media.

Direct from the Field: E-Mail Yourself When a Reboot Fails

When performing remote reboots, you're not present to see whether the reboot works . . . and it can waste a lot of time if you think a server reboots when it doesn't. One solution is to e-mail yourself when a shutdown or reboot fails. You'll need a Simple Mail Transfer Protocol (SMTP) server running in your domain (you can install the SMTP server feature built into Windows Server 2008 or you can use another SMTP server) and a script to do the e-mailing. You can edit this sample script to conform to your needs.

```
Option Explicit
'''----- script configuration area
Const strSMTPServer = "arvon.alpineskihouse.com"
Const strFrom       = "alerts@alpineskihouse.com"
Const strTo         = "adam.barr@alpineskihouse.com "
'''----- end configuration area

Dim objMail              ' the CDO object
Dim objWSHNetwork        ' windows-script-host network object
Dim strNetBIOSComputer   ' the netbios name of our computer

''' get the NetBIOS computer name
Set objWSHNetwork  = CreateObject ("WScript.Network")
strNetBIOSComputer = objWSHNetwork.ComputerName
Set objWSHNetwork  = Nothing

''' do the real work to send the message
Set objMail = CreateObject ("CDO.Message")
objMail.Configuration.Fields.Item ("http://schemas.microsoft.com/cdo/
configuration/sendusing")      = 2
objMail.Configuration.Fields.Item ("http://schemas.microsoft.com/cdo/
configuration/smtpserver")     = strSMTPServer
objMail.Configuration.Fields.Item ("http://schemas.microsoft.com/cdo/
configuration/smtpserverport") = 25
objMail.Configuration.Fields.Update
objMail.From     = strFrom
objMail.To       = strTo
objMail.Subject  = "Critical error!! " & strNetBIOSComputer & " failed to reboot
" & Now
objMail.Textbody = "Critical error!! " & strNetBIOSComputer & " failed to reboot
" & Now & vbCRLF
objMail.Send
Set objMail = Nothing
```

Michael Smith

Exchange MVP, Smith Consulting

> **On the Companion Media** A link to the preceding code is provided on this book's
> companion media. You can access it from the blog at *http://theessentialexchange.com/blogs/*
> *michael/default.aspx.*

Applying TS Management Tools

Thus far, the examples in this chapter have focused on the tools themselves. In this section,
we'll take a step back from the tools and show you how to combine tools to get the information you need when it's not supplied directly by the tools themselves.

Differentiating RemoteApp Sessions from Full Desktop Sessions

One good example of applying the terminal server management tools lies in determining whether you can shadow a session. As explained earlier in this chapter, shadowing TS
RemoteApps sessions isn't supported and can lead to some very odd behavior. Therefore,
it's good to avoid shadowing a TS RemoteApps session. Unfortunately, this is easier said than
done, because Terminal Server Manager doesn't spell out the difference. You can find the TS
RemoteApps sessions, but it requires knowing what you're looking at.

From Terminal Services Manager, the User tab and Session tab reveal no differences between
desktop and TS RemoteApps sessions. Go to the Processes tab, however, and you can see
one difference: the shell processes for the two types of sessions are different, as discussed
in Chapters 2 and 6. As you may remember, desktop sessions use Explorer.exe as a shell and
Userinit.exe to launch Windows Explorer; TS RemoteApps sessions use Rpdshell.exe and
Rdpinit.exe, respectively. Therefore, if user Hao Chen calls you to ask for help, you can check
the Processes tab to determine if Hao is running a desktop session that you can shadow.

> ### How It Works: Identifying Full Desktop Sessions
> You can find TS RemoteApp sessions from the command line using *query.* The *query*
> *session* command will help you find the sessions hosting Rdpinit.exe/Rdpshell.exe, and
> *query process* will help you find out whether a user's session contains those processes.
>
> To find out which sessions on terminal server MATTERHORN are running Rdpshell.exe,
> run this command:
>
> ```
> query process RDPshell.exe /SERVER:matterhorn
> ```

The results show that Paul Koch is running a RemoteApp and therefore should not be shadowed:

```
USERNAME              SESSIONNAME        ID   PID  IMAGE
paul.koch             rdp-tcp#1           3    3132 rdpshell.exe
```

Let's say you know the user whose session you want to shadow. You can ask the user to describe the session appearance and figure out if he is running a TS RemoteApp, but that's slow and unreliable. The better alternative is to query Terminal Services Manager for the processes the user is running. To query the processes running for user Kim Akers on server MATTERHORN, run this command:

```
query process kim.akers /SERVER:matterhorn
```

In this example, Kim Akers is not running Rdpinit.exe or Rdpshell.exe, so shadowing the session is supported.

```
USERNAME              SESSIONNAME        ID   PID  IMAGE
kim.akers             rdp-tcp#1          3    2276 taskeng.exe
kim.akers             rdp-tcp#1          3    3480 rdpclip.exe
kim.akers             rdp-tcp#1          3    3884 dwm.exe
kim.akers             rdp-tcp#1          3    3560 explorer.exe
kim.akers             rdp-tcp#1          3    2660 winword.exe
kim.akers             rdp-tcp#1          3    3676 splwow64.exe
kim.akers             rdp-tcp#1          3    3880 powerpnt.exe
kim.akers             rdp-tcp#1          3    3436 excel.exe
```

The preceding command also reveals the session ID, which you need to shadow Kim's session like this:

```
shadow /SERVER:matterhorn 3
```

Auditing Application Usage

Many administrators want to know if their application licensing is in compliance. Unfortunately, this isn't easy to determine. First, application licensing for a terminal server can be tricky—you need to read the fine print for the application, and if you must be able to demonstrate compliance for legal reasons, you may need to clarify the details with the application Independent Software Vendor (ISV). (Not all license agreements are written with terminal servers in mind, and the application vendor—not Microsoft—owns the design for application licensing on terminal servers.) Second, Windows Performance Monitor doesn't offer a way to keep track of how many instances of a process are open on a server other than adding a process counter and manually counting how many processes have the same name except for the number at the end.

You *could* count application instances from Terminal Services Manager by counting processes on each one and adding the results for all terminal servers, but why would you? The *query process* or *qprocess* command provides a way to do the same thing programmatically. With a little help from some other scripting objects, the *query process* command can be the basis of a rudimentary application metering tool.

> **Note** The *Get-Process* Windows PowerShell cmdlet isn't session-aware, so it will return only processes in the current session.

This series of scripts will do the following:

- Find all terminal servers in an OU
- Query all terminal servers to get a list of the processes running on each one
- Ignore all processes that aren't the application we want to count
- E-mail you if more people are using the application than you have licenses
- Keep a log file of this data for trending

> **On the Companion Media** Some of these tasks also apply to other inventory tasks. To make it easier for you to reuse the code, we've included them on the companion media as tsnames.vbs, processes.bat, runbatch.vbs, proccleanup.vbs, checkfile.vbs, and count-email.vbs. Appaudit.vbs is the entire application metering script.

Because this script involves a bit of data wrangling and error handling, we decided to put the full script on the TS Resource Kit blog for those who want to walk through the code and understand how it works. This section will highlight the pieces that use the command-line tools for managing terminal servers. The URL is located on the companion CD: *http://blogs.technet.com/tsresourcekit/default.aspx*.

> **Note** Use this tool not only to keep track of your licensing, but also to let you know if an application's usage is decreasing. If you're considering retiring an application, recording how many instances are running over time can give you the data you need to know about how many people are still using it.

Get the Terminal Server Names

First, you'll need the names of all the terminal servers. How you do this depends on whether the terminal servers are in a domain or a workgroup. (The workgroup model will support both domains and workgroups, but the domain model doesn't work for workgroups since it depends on reading OU memberships.) In both cases, you'll collect the names of the terminal servers and put them into a file.

Assuming that all identically configured terminal servers are in the same OU, one way to do this is to query that OU and return its members, writing the names to a file. The companion media contains a Windows PowerShell script that does this (see getservers.ps1), but you can also do this with VBScript as below (tsnames.vbs on the companion media). The comments in the script explain how it's used.

```
Option Explicit
Const ForWriting = 2

' Get Terminal server computer list from AD terminal server OU
' Write terminal server names to terminalservers.txt

Dim objFSO 'File System Object
Dim objTSOU 'Terminal Server OU
Dim objTSItem 'Each item in OU
Dim strTSComputer 'Each terminal server
Dim strTSTextFolder 'folder to hold text file
Dim strTSTextFile 'list of terminal servers in the OU
Dim strTSLDAPPath 'Path to terminal server OU
Dim objTSTextFile 'created text file

    ' =====Configuration Area================
strTSTextFile = "terminalservers.txt"
strTSTextFolder = "\\ozark\it$\"
strTSLDAPPath = "LDAP://OU=ASH_TerminalServers, DC=alpineskihouse, DC=com"
    ' =====End Configuration Area============

Set objTSOU = GetObject(strTSLDAPPath)
objTSOU.Filter = Array("Computer")

    '=======================================
' If file exists add data, if not, then create file and add data

Set objFSO = CreateObject("Scripting.FileSystemObject")
If objFSO.FileExists(strTSTextFolder & strTSTextFile) Then
'do nothing
Else
Set objTSTextFile = objFSO.CreateTextFile(strTSTextFolder & strTSTextFile)
objTSTextFile.Close
End If

Set objTSTextFile = objFSO.OpenTextFile(strTSTextFolder & strTSTextFile, ForWriting)
For Each objTSItem in objTSOU
```

```
    strTSComputer = objTSItem.CN
    objTSTextFile.WriteLine strTSComputer
Next
objTSTextFile.Close
WScript.Quit
```

This won't work in the workgroup scenario, because workgroups don't have OUs. In that case, you'll need to rely on the *query termserver* command as in the following example. This is a bit more complicated, because the command-line tool returns some extra data and you'll need to remove it from the file. This section relies on both termserv.bat and queryts.vbs on the companion media.

```
Option Explicit

Const ForReading = 1
Const ForWriting = 2

Dim objFSO ' File System Object
Dim objTSFile ' Gets and opens terminal servers text file
Dim objNewTSFile ' Gets and opens terminal servers text file
Dim objTSBATfile ' TS Batch file location
Dim strTSFile ' Terminal Servers text file
Dim strTSLines ' lines in text file
Dim strFileContents 'Contents of text file
Dim strEndofString ' Last line in text file
Dim intLength 'Length of contents
Dim WSHShell 'Script shell to run batch file


' =====Configuration Area================
objTSBATFile = "\\ozark\it$\BAT\termserv.bat"
' =====End Configuration Area============


' ========================================
' Run batch file query termserv
' requires batch file
' batch file code is: query termserv >\\ozark\it$\terminalservers.txt

Set WSHShell = CreateObject("Wscript.Shell")
WSHShell.Run (objTSBATFile),0, True


' =========================================
' Query termserv command adds two lines of header info to file
' This removes this extraneous information

' =====Configuration Area================
strTSFile = "\\ozark\it$\terminalservers.txt"
' =====Configuration Area================

Set objFSO = CreateObject("Scripting.FileSystemObject")
Set objTSFile = objFSO.OpenTextFile(strTSFile, ForReading)
```

```
Do until objTSFile.AtEndOfStream
objTSFile.SkipLine
objTSFile.SkipLine
strTSLines = objTSFile.ReadAll
Loop

objTSFile.close


'  ===========================================
' Remove carriage return at end of file

Set objNewTSFile = objFSO.OpenTextFile(strTSFile, ForWriting)
objNewTSFile.Write strTSLines


Set objNewTSFile = objFSO.OpenTextFile(strTSFile, ForReading)
strTSLines = objNewTSFile.ReadAll
objNewTSFile.close

strFileContents = strTSLines
intLength = Len(strFileContents)
strEndofString = Right(strFileContents, 2)
If strEndofString = vbCrLf Then
              strFileContents = Left(strFileContents, intLength - 2)
              Set objNewTSFile = objFSO.OpenTextFile(strTSFile, ForWriting)
              objNewTSFile.Write strFileContents
              objNewTSFile.Close
End if

Set objTSFile = Nothing
Set objNewTSFile = Nothing

wscript.quit
```

List Processes on the Terminal Servers

When you know the names of the terminal servers in an OU, query each server by typing
query process <executable> /server:<server name>. To make it easy, automate this
process by running a batch file that runs the *query process* command against the saved server
list and pipes that data to a file, as shown here:

```
< FOR /F %%G IN (c:\scripts\ASHTSServers.txt) DO query process * /server:%%G >>\\ozark\it$\
processes\processes.txt
```

Why use a batch file? Mostly because it's easy. There's no reason to reinvent the wheel and
try to pull all the process data from all the terminal servers when *query process* does the
same thing so succinctly. This batch file is on the companion media as processes.bat.

Extract the Application Name

When you have a list of all processes running on all terminal servers in an OU saved to a file, you will need to focus on the particular process for which you need a usage count. Run this script to keep only lines in the text file that contain the application name. In this script, we are looking for Excel.exe, but you can edit the script to adjust the application name as required. The script is on the companion media as proccleanup.vbs.

```vbscript
Option Explicit
Const ForWriting = 2
Const ForReading = 1

' Remove the unneeded lines from the file

Dim objFSO ' File System Object
Dim strSearchString 'Each line in the file
Dim strNewContents ' New contents of processes.txt
Dim colMatches ' Collection of matches
Dim strMatch ' Each match
Dim objFindApp 'Regular Expression
Dim objProcessesFile ' path to processes.txt file
Dim objTextFile ' Open processes.txt file

' =====Configuration Area=================
objProcessesFile = "\\ozark\it$\processes\processes.txt"
' =====End Configuration Area============

Set objFindApp = CreateObject("VBScript.RegExp")

' =====Configuration Area=================
objFindApp.Pattern = "excel.exe"
' =====End Configuration Area============

Set objFSO = CreateObject("Scripting.FileSystemObject")
Set objTextFile = objFSO.OpenTextFile(objProcessesFile , ForReading)

Do Until objTextFile.AtEndOfStream
   strSearchString = objTextFile.ReadLine
   Set colMatches = objFindApp.Execute(strSearchString)
   If colMatches.Count > 0 Then
      For Each strMatch in colMatches
      strNewContents = strNewContents & strSearchString & vbCrLf
      Next
   End If
Loop
objTextFile.Close

Set objTextFile = objFSO.OpenTextFile(objProcessesFile, ForWriting)
objTextFile.Write strNewContents
objTextFile.Close

WScript.Quit
```

> **On the Companion Media** The text file contents produced by the preceding script contains a carriage return at the end of the file, which for line counting purposes will increase the count by one. We delete this carriage return in checkfile.vbs, located on the companion media.

Record Application Instances and E-Mail Alerts

Now run count-email.vbs (on the companion media) to count the lines left in Processes.txt (the file produced by the preceding script) and send an e-mail to a specified e-mail address if the count is higher than the number of licenses you own. This section will also record the count to a text file each time you run the script so that you can tell how application usage changes over time.

```
Option Explicit

Const ForWriting = 2
Const ForReading = 1
Const ForAppending = 8


'=======================================
'Check if processes.txt file exists in specified directory

Dim objFSO 'File System Object
Dim strFileContents 'Contents of processes.txt
Dim intLength 'Length of contents
Dim strEndofString ' Last line in file
Dim objProcessesFile 'Path to processes.txt file

' =====Configuration Area=================
objProcessesFile = "\\ozark\it$\processes\processes.txt"
' =====End Configuration Area============

Set objFSO = CreateObject("Scripting.FileSystemObject")

If objFSO.FileExists(objProcessesFile) Then

'do nothing

Else
    Wscript.Echo "Error - Processes file missing."
    WScript.Quit
End If


'=======================================
'Count the lines in the file processes.txt

Set objProcessesFile = objFSO.OpenTextFile(objProcessesFile, ForReading)
objProcessesFile.ReadAll


'=======================================
' If the count > licenses owned then email alert
```

```
Dim objLicensesOwned 'The number of application licenses owned

' =====Configuration Area================
objLicensesOwned = 1
' =====End Configuration Area============

' WScript.Echo objProcessesFile.line & " " & "objects still counted"
If objProcessesFile.line > objLicensesOwned then

' =====Configuration Area================
Const strSMTPServer = "arvon.alpineskihouse.com"
Const strFrom       = "alerts@alpineskihouse.com"
Const strTo         = "kristin.l.griffin@alpineskihouse.com"
' =====End Configuration Area============

Dim objMail              ' the CDO object
Dim objWSHNetwork        ' windows-script-host network object
Dim strNetBIOSComputer   ' the netbios name of our computer

'========================================
' get the NetBIOS computer name

Set objWSHNetwork    = CreateObject ("WScript.Network")
strNetBIOSComputer = objWSHNetwork.ComputerName
Set objWSHNetwork  = Nothing

'========================================
' do the real work to send the message

Set objMail = CreateObject ("CDO.Message")
objMail.Configuration.Fields.Item ("http://schemas.microsoft.com/cdo/configuration/
sendusing")       = 2
objMail.Configuration.Fields.Item ("http://schemas.microsoft.com/cdo/configuration/
smtpserver")      = strSMTPServer
objMail.Configuration.Fields.Item ("http://schemas.microsoft.com/cdo/configuration/
smtpserverport") = 25
objMail.Configuration.Fields.Update
objMail.From    = strFrom
objMail.To      = strTo
objMail.Subject = "Licensing Check!! " & Now
objMail.Textbody = "Licensing Check!! "  & " The application count in use is " &
objprocessesFile.line & " which is higher than number of licenses purchased " & Now
objMail.Send
Set objMail = Nothing
                End if

'========================================
' Create or append data to log file

Dim strProcLogDir ' Path to Reports folder
Dim strProcLogFile ' Log file
Dim objApp 'Specified application
Dim objProcLogFolder 'Processes Log Folder
Dim objProcLogFile 'Processes Log File
Dim strProcLogText ' Text to write to Processes Log File
```

```
' =====Configuration Area================
objApp = "excel.exe"
strProcLogDir = "\\ozark\it$\reports"
strProcLogFile = "\processcountlog.txt"
' =====End Configuration Area============

    Sub subAppend
    ' Append count to the log file processcountlog.txt

    Set objProcLogFile = objFSO.OpenTextFile(strProcLogDir & strProcLogFile,
ForAppending, true)
    strProcLogText = NOW & " | The # of instances of " & objApp & " running is " &
objProcessesFile.Line
    ' Writes strText to processcountlog.txt
        objProcLogFile.WriteLine(strProcLogText)
    objProcLogFile.close
    End Sub


'=======================================
' Check that the directory folder exists, if not create file

If objFSO.FolderExists(strProcLogDir) Then
'do nothing

Else
    Set objProcLogFolder = objFSO.CreateFolder(strProcLogDir)
objProcLogFolder.close
End If


'=======================================
' If log file exists append data, if not, then create file and append data

If objFSO.FileExists(strProcLogDir & strProcLogFile) Then
    call subAppend
Else
    Set objProcLogFile = objFSO.CreateTextFile(strProcLogDir & strProcLogFile)
objProcLogFile.Close
    call subAppend
End If

WScript.Quit
```

On the Companion Media The appaudit.vbs script found on the companion media is a sample you can modify to count instances of other applications and send e-mail to yourself with any violations. This sample is designed for our environment, so you'll need to edit it to work for your specific situation. Areas to change are highlighted in the script as Configuration Areas.

Auditing User Logons

Like application usage auditing, you can use the built-in tools to get you some information to help with capacity planning. One part of capacity planning, after all, is knowing how many people are using the terminal server and how these numbers are increasing over time. That way, you can scale the hardware before users start wondering why the server is slow. It's also helpful to review logon patterns. As we discussed in Chapter 2, there is a great deal of process creation associated with establishing a user session. If many users log on to the server at the same time, you may need to adjust the amount of memory available to support this pattern. Starting up a process requires two to three times the memory that it takes to keep it running.

It's hard to plan for intense logon periods or increasing numbers of users if you don't know about them. Using the *query users* command, you can create a rudimentary user auditing tool.

To find out how many users have a session open on a terminal server, open Terminal Services Manager and select the Users tab. All users with sessions will be listed there. You can also get this information by running the following command from a Windows Vista client or a Windows 2008 Server:

```
query users /server:SERVERNAME
```

That is fine for getting real-time data to help you solve a real-time issue, such as determining if your server is overloaded with user connections and performing poorly. But to get a sense of the average number of users logging onto a server, you will need to compile a user count over time.

You can run this command and pipe the data to a file like this:

```
query users /server:SERVERNAME > c:\userlogons.txt
```

Closing Unresponsive Applications

If a user's application hangs, one way to handle the problem is to stop the process for that application. How you do this depends on whether you want to stop all instances of that process on the terminal server or just the one that's causing trouble.

In this scenario, the user's application is not responding. You must terminate the process associated with the application. If you have a farm, first you will need to find out which server hosts the user session.

Do this by opening Terminal Services Manager and adding the servers for a Session Broker farm. Then for each server, look on the Users tab and find the user. If you have not limited users to one session, then you will need to check all servers and find all sessions the user might have established. After you know where the user is connected, you must locate the hung application.

If you support only one session per user, then all you need to do is click the Processes tab on the server that hosts the user session containing the hung application, sort by Image, find the process associated with the user and the hung application, right-click anywhere in the line entry, and choose End Process.

If your user has multiple sessions, then you need to check the processes on each server, locate the specific server and user session in which the process is running, and terminate the process.

You can also accomplish all of this from the command line.

In this example, hao.chen, a user in the alpineskihouse.com domain, has been running the Microsoft Excel RemoteApp. It has become unresponsive and needs to be terminated. This domain has a terminal server farm and limits users to one session at a time.

First you need to locate the server that hosts hao.chen's session. Run the *qprocess* command against every server in the farm until you find hao.chen.

```
C:\windows\system32>qprocess excel.exe /server:bigfrog
 USERNAME          SESSIONNAME       ID    PID  IMAGE
 paul.koch         rdp-tcp#1          4   2720  excel.exe
 adam.barr         rdp-tcp#2          5   3228  excel.exe

C:\windows\system32>qprocess excel.exe /server:matterhorn
 USERNAME          SESSIONNAME       ID    PID  IMAGE
 hao.chen          rdp-tcp#1          4   2776  excel.exe
 nancy.anderson    rdp-tcp#3          5   3392  excel.exe
 alex.robinson     rdp-tcp#4          6   3532  excel.exe
```

Now stop the Excel.exe process associated with hao.chen. Do this by specifying the PID associated with the process shown in the preceding query.

```
C:\windows\system32>tskill 2776 /server:matterhorn
```

Note You can also specify the process by using the *session ID* and *process name* switches. Refer to the section titled "Monitoring and Terminating Processes" earlier in this chapter for other examples of terminating processes.

Then run *qprocess* against MATTERHORN again to see that the process for hao.chen has been terminated:

```
C:\windows\system32>qprocess excel.exe /server:matterhorn
 USERNAME                SESSIONNAME      ID    PID  IMAGE
 nancy.anderson          rdp-tcp#3         5   3392  excel.exe
 alex.robinson           rdp-tcp#4         6   3532  excel.exe
```

If other users also complain, and it is apparent that all instances of Microsoft Excel are hung, terminate them all by running *tskill*, but use the *processname* parameter (the image name minus the executable extension) and the switch */A* (tells *tskill* to kill all instances of the *processname*):

```
C:\windows\system32>tskill excel /server:matterhorn /A
```

Then run *qprocess* again and see that there are no longer any instances of Excel.exe running.

```
C:\windows\system32>qprocess excel.exe /server:matterhorn
No Process exists for excel.exe
```

Summary

This chapter has explained how to manage current Remote Desktop Protocol (RDP) sessions using the graphical and command-line tools. Some of the best practices we've covered include the following:

- For the most accurate information across multiple servers, use the command-line tools.

- For best password security, do not use *tscon*, because it displays the password on the screen in clear text.

- If you must forcibly remove a session from a terminal server, use the *logoff* command rather than resetting the session. Although *logoff* won't save user data, it will write profile changes back to the profile server, whereas resetting the session does not.

- Don't try to shadow TS RemoteApp sessions. Use Terminal Services Manager or *query session or query process* to determine whether a session is displaying a full desktop or a TS RemoteApp.

- When preparing for user maintenance, use the */drain* switch with the *change logon* command to slowly drain users from the terminal server, rather than using the */disable* switch.

- You can use the command-line tools to help you learn patterns of application usage and user logons and save those inventories to a log file.

Additional Resources

This chapter includes a number of tools for checking settings and running inventory, all of which are on the companion media.

- For more details about how there can be multiple instances of the same process on a terminal server, see Chapter 2, "Planning the Terminal Server Ecosystem."

- For more details about the session startup process, see Chapter 3, "Installing the Core Terminal Server Environment."

- To learn how to configure Remote Control settings via Group Policy, see Chapter 5, "Fine-Tuning the User Experience."

- For details about how TS RemoteApps are drawn on the client computer, see Chapter 6, "Installing and Publishing Applications."

- For guidelines to life-cycle management of Terminal Services roles, see Chapter 9, "Terminal Services Ecosystem Management."

Chapter 9
Terminal Services Ecosystem Management

Most of this book has examined the individual Terminal Services roles in great detail. In this final chapter of the Terminal Services Resource Kit, we'd like to show you the big picture. You've built a server farm including terminal servers, session broker, license server, portal, and gateway. Now, assuming your plan is not to put this in a box and never touch it again, you'll need some way to keep it running and allow it to grow with your needs. This chapter will address how to keep your terminal server farm running reliably, addressing such questions as:

- What do I need to back up?

- What are the principles of change management?

- How can I implement these principles?

- How do I demonstrate a computer's configuration for compliance reasons?

- How do I know when I need to add more capacity for the various server roles?

- How do I back up and restore Terminal Services role services?

- Which roles can I virtualize successfully?

The Case for Standardization

Diversity is a good thing if you're a forest, even if you're an organization. It's a terrible thing if you're a load-balanced server farm.

The whole point of diversity is to shake things up and make results less predictable. If you're part of a company trying to come up with creative ideas, diversity helps you. But Information

Technology (IT) infrastructure is—or should be—the steady sea on which your ship of creative ideas sails. If it's not, then creative efforts get lost while your company is trying to stay afloat. A diverse server farm will make your IT department underperform in these ways:

- Troubleshooting
- Cost management
- Quality of service
- Responsiveness to changing needs

Troubleshooting becomes an issue because with a diverse server ecosystem, you don't know what to expect. Every problem requires an investigation if you don't know for sure that all the application servers are running the same versions of the application (especially an issue if you're supporting in-house applications), they're not all configured to use the same licensing model, or they don't all have the same profile caching rules. In a worst-case scenario, the administrator troubleshooting a problem must walk through the "What changed?" litany to attempt to discover why a server isn't working when it used to. If all the servers are identical, then it is simpler to compare the broken server with the working ones and discover the differences. Finally, you can't easily automate the provisioning of servers if they're all different.

Cost management is difficult with a diversity of servers for a couple of reasons. First, it may eliminate some efficiencies of scale. If you're maintaining a wide variety of hardware, it takes more research to be sure you're getting the right part if you need more memory or must replace a network card, for example. Even more important, cost management is difficult when troubleshooting servers requires basic research to find the starting point.

Diversity is also the enemy of service level agreements (SLAs). How can you guarantee uptime if you don't know the basis of this guarantee? The less predictable the servers are, the less weight an SLA carries because it's resting on too many unknowns. You can't guarantee a system if you don't know its configuration, and you can't predict the outcome of a change if you don't know the baseline. Additionally, it's hard to say how long a service outage will be if you're not sure how long it will take you to find out why the problem occurred.

Finally, diversity is the enemy of responsiveness to change. The more time you spend solving problems, the less you have to spend on planning improvements or implementing those improvements. Working in reactive mode is hard on everybody—IT staff and end users alike. The IT staff professionals get worn out from troubleshooting all the time, and the end users can't rely on a stable platform to do the work that they're paid to do.

The case for diversity is that it encourages the rock-star image of the IT pro who has seen it all—and therefore has a pretty good idea how to fix problems. But while being a star is fun and lucrative for that person, it's better for the IT department and the company if you don't need an expert in that capacity to get you out of trouble. And if you are the expert, a bit less troubleshooting can give you more time for learning something new and thinking about how to improve the server infrastructure instead of how to fix it.

Principles of Change Management

Most service outages are caused by change. Most of the time spent recovering from a service outage is spent trying to figure out what caused the problem.

Change is inevitable. Without change, you'll never update applications, never change server lockdown policies, and never apply security patches, to name a few. So even though change is risky, it's going to happen. You must prepare for it, only make planned changes, and keep track of those changes so you can reduce troubleshooting time.

The hard part isn't updating the terminal servers. The hard part is updating the servers so that:

- You can map the changes you make to a business need so that all stakeholders understand why the change is important.

- All the changes get made consistently to all like servers.

- You can reverse the change if you must.

- You can map the change you made to the original business requirements so that management can evaluate the success of the change going forward.

- The system keeps working.

Being able to make changes in a controlled fashion so that you meet the above criteria is called *change management*. In this section, we'll examine some principles of change management as they apply to terminal servers. More general references appear in the "Additional Resources" section at the end of this chapter.

Change management is a catchphrase for the practices that allow you to not only maintain working computers, but also have a reasonable degree of certainty that they will remain in working order. It's not about knowing which button to push or which registry key to edit. It's about:

- Pushing that button only when necessary

- Having a good understanding of what pushing that button will do

- Having a high degree of confidence that pushing the button will lead to an improvement in performance

- Being able to demonstrate to an auditor that you *did* push the button

- If required, being able to roll back the change—to unpush the button

The idea of change management is not specific to terminal servers by any means. What we're going to talk about in this section applies to any kind of server—even any kind of *computer*—for the team in charge of desktop maintenance. But terminal servers are definitely helped by change management processes. The following three points are good reasons to implement change management practices in a Terminal Services environment.

First, terminal servers support many users. If one workstation goes offline, then one user can't work. If one terminal server goes offline, then depending on the load that terminal server is supporting, it could prevent dozens or even hundreds of users from working.

Second, all of the Terminal Services roles have a lot of moving parts. Terminal servers, for example, provide a host of applications that may be tuned specifically for running on a terminal server, and for times when Terminal Services Easy Print (TS Easy Print) isn't an option, may have printer drivers as well. Recreating this delicate structure will take some time if the terminal server goes down.

> **Note** Group Policy helps you manage all the moving parts of the Terminal Services ecosystem and, as we'll see later in this section, is key to one tenet of change management: automating configuration management.

Third, the Terminal Services role services interact with a lot of other server roles. Not only does each one of the five Terminal Services role services interact with the others, they also interact with Active Directory, possibly certificate servers if you have an internal Public Key Infrastructure (PKI), file servers, mail servers, and so forth. Any change to a piece of this intricate web can affect many other server roles.

Change Management Challenges

Change management best practices are inherently deliberate so that no change is made unless it is necessary, understood, and recordable. Therefore, there are several conditions that can make change management hard to implement. To list a few:

- Crisis makes deliberate change management hard, because there's a lot of pressure to work quickly. If the TS Gateway is offline and no one can log on to the network from the Internet, then having to work within the doctrines of change management procedures may not be as appealing as wielding a quick fix.

- Accolades for the single expert who saves the day don't encourage change management. If the person who walks over to the downed TS Gateway sits down, fiddles with something all night, then comes out of it with a working TS Gateway is a hero—even if no one knows exactly what he did or really knows why it worked—then that encourages people to make changes without adhering to change management practices. Making everything work is good, but it's even better if the fix is easily reproducible and known not to interfere with other working components.

- Too many controls can also make good change management impossible. If you're monitoring every single file change on a server, you'll drown in data and won't be able to see the changes that really matter.

- Fear of making a mistake discourages users and administrators from following change management best practices. You may recognize that if a change you make turns out badly, you might get blamed. In that case, you might either forgo making the change or log on as an anonymous administrator—more about this shortly—so no one can prove you made the change.

- Lack of budget for preparation work can cause problems later. Particularly if your business model is built around servicing clients, it's not always easy to charge clients for time spent on best practices of change management, even if that could reduce downtime later.

- The time requirement and the delay in seeing full results also make it difficult to implement change management practice. Setting up a change management system across multiple departments and disciplines (IT operations professionals aren't the only ones who need change management procedures) takes a long time. According to the October 2007 Gartner Group report, "How to Navigate IT Change From Development to Production," implementing a federated, integrated IT change management process can take three to five *years*.

The hardest part of change management is that it's fundamentally about policy, not about technology. To a degree, technology can provide tools to help you follow change management best practices. But for the technology to be effective, it must be backed by policy. You will have to:

- Get management approval for the idea of change management, because without a company-wide commitment to it, it will never happen.

- Teach administrators how to use the tools to follow the change management best practices and also teach them why they should follow these practices.

- Educate administrators about data-retention policies for audit logs.

- Establish rules for change management and penalties for not following those rules.

- Enforce the penalties consistently.

If you don't follow any one of these five steps, all the technology in the world can't help you. Your first step in the process, however, is to commit to change management.

Implementing Change Management Best Practices

As outlined in *The Visible Ops Handbook: Implementing ITIL in 4 Practical and Auditable Steps* (see "Additional Resources" at the end of this chapter), there are four main stages to good change management. Slightly reworked for our situation here, they are:

1. Don't change anything yet—just figure out how you'd like this system to work.

2. Take inventory of hardware, software, and business assets.

3. Establish a process to reliably build these assets.

4. Develop metrics to make improvements.

Easily said, but this will take a while. The next sections will discuss these steps in more detail as they apply to terminal servers. For in-depth books on how to implement Information Technology Infrastructure Library (ITIL), see the "Additional Resources" section at the end of this chapter.

First, Do No Harm

The first step to effective change management is to stop making changes haphazardly. (It may not feel haphazard, but unless you are fully confident that you have recorded every change that everyone has made to the servers in the past month or two, your system could use structure.) Freeze changes to the servers to give you some time to draft the first version of your change management policy.

Now that you've frozen the servers, it's time to define policies for how change is executed, including, for example:

- Who can make changes?

- Who authorizes changes?

- What is the change review process?

- When can changes be made?

- How do you test changes prior to deployment in production?

- How will you revert a change if required?

- How will you determine the success or failure of a change, and how will you track this?

Who Can Make Changes?

The question of who can make changes will depend on the size of the organization and how it's structured. Smaller businesses may spread IT responsibility across roles, so the same person can install a new application on the terminal server and also update domain security policy. Larger companies may specifically assign responsibilities so that terminal server administrators may not be able to change all aspects of the terminal server ecosystem. This is a good time to examine your access policies.

> **Note** For best change control, don't use the Administrator account, or else limit its use to one person. If just anyone can log on as Administrator, then it is very hard to tell who's actually made a change. Even if you can find the change event in the event log, you can't know for certain if the person who made the change was authorized to do so. The Administrator account should be protected just like a named account.

Direct from the Field: The Human Factor

In many cases, it's not technical details that matter most to a successful Terminal Services project, but policies. Good examples of this are deployment processes, compliance requirements, and capacity planning.

Automated Deployment Policies

Automated deployment and maintenance procedures are essential parts of keeping servers in a large load-balanced farm consistent. The spectrum of deployment tools starts with simple scripts and ends with high-end management products and frameworks; however, all cover the full deployment process from operating system installation and system configuration to application deployment and adaptation of the users' workspaces. A terminal server administrator should never have to do any installation manually.

A policy of using automated deployment systems remains useful after the original deployment. Server management automation also reduces the pain of routine maintenance and enables easy documentation. Automatic deployment also enables *staging*, which is another best practice for terminal server environments. In staging, a server (often a virtual server) is used as a stage to test changes before they are made live. Large environments may have up to four stages: development, test, acceptance, and production. Smaller environments most often have two stages: test and production.

Compliance Requirements

In many countries, IT organizations are increasingly required to support government and regulatory compliance initiatives, including the Federal Information Security Management Act (FISMA), the Health Information Portability and Accountability Act (HIPAA), the Gramm-Leach-Bliley Act (GLBA), the Sarbanes-Oxley Act (SOX), and the Control Objectives for Information and Related Technology (CobiT). Beyond the software deployment automation described previously, compliance requirements may include that companies establish a comprehensive information security plan based on establishing a monitoring solution that allows enforcing compliance with legal and regulatory policies.

Capacity Planning Based on User Experience

There is no universally applicable formula to calculate the resources needed for a terminal server farm. The criteria matrix derived from user requirements, application requirements, and server requirements is just too unpredictable and too complex.

The human factor can help with capacity planning. It is based on comparing the number of real users you can get on a terminal server using well-known system and application settings with the number of synthetic test users on a server using the same characteristics. For example, if 15 real users can work well on a terminal server you monitor over several days, it may be the case that you can have 60 synthetic users on the very same server using scripted user session sequences. The ratio, however, will probably be different in other environments. The example environment introduced previously implies a 1:4 ratio of real users to synthetic users. If you modify one of the characteristics—such as server hardware, system tuning settings, application set, or operating system version—you need to run the same synthetic user tests. The test result and the real user to synthetic user ratio from the first comparison give you a good indicator of how many real users you will be able to host on the new or updated system. This means that test procedures following a simple but reproducible methodology are a key element to successful and predictable capacity planning. But never change the test methodology and never change more than one of the server or application set characteristics at a time.

When introducing Terminal Services in a corporate environment, always focus on the human aspect including business managers, IT administrators, and, of course, users. If any of these three groups do not accept the strategy, even the best technical plan will lead to unsatisfactory results.

Dr. Bernard Tritsch

Vice President for Research and Development, Immidio

Who Authorizes Changes?

How are changes authorized in your organization? Is there a formal sign-off procedure when, for example, someone decides to change the scope of backups based on a new understanding of how essential system data is stored? Or does the administrator in charge of that element make the change, because it doesn't seem to affect anyone else and he understands it best?

For good change management, all stakeholders in a change should sign off on a change before it's made. If they can't sign off on it because its impact isn't fully understood, that may be a good argument for not making the change, particularly if the change represents significant risk. (Even changes to a backup represent risk—changes to the backup model affect the data available to restore.) The team of stakeholders should collectively understand the business reasons for making the change as well as the following technical considerations:

- What is the priority of this change relative to other proposed changes?
- What resources are needed and available to make this change?
- What are the security implications of this change?

- How will this change affect other parts of the infrastructure?

- How will this change affect IT customers?

What Is the Change Review Process?

If you're going to have a change review, it makes sense to have a structure in which to execute that review. Even critical changes—*especially* critical changes—need review to make sure that they're fully understood. If a suggested change is truly time-sensitive, then it may need an accelerated change review meeting, but all changes must be understood before being authorized. Otherwise, you'll have no chance of tracking change impact and success, and the impact of the critical change may have ramifications that you didn't anticipate. Many change management models recommend a weekly change review meeting, with the option of emergency sessions for proposed changes that are too urgent to wait for the scheduled meeting.

When Can Changes Be Made?

When you have determined that a change must be made, then the change needs to be scheduled. Time-sensitive modifications can have an emergency window scheduled, but scheduling allows timing to be planned. For example, without planning the timing, it's hard to be sure that the asset being modified isn't being used at the time and that the change administrator A is making won't conflict with the change made by administrator B.

Establishing a change window has a few advantages. It allows for planned downtime at a time when the servers are least utilized and reduces the number of reboots, because multiple changes can be made at the same time. A change window also makes it easier to catch unauthorized changes, if there's a known window for editing configuration. By definition, any change made outside the window is not approved.

How Do You Test Changes?

You've got an administrator authorized to make changes, the appropriate approval to make the change, and you've designated and gotten sign-off for a deployment window . . . you're all set, right?

Almost. You weren't planning to deploy a change in production without having a plan for testing it and a way to back it out if required, were you?

The test platforms that organizations use range from the essentially nonexistent (e.g., deploy the change when no one's using the server and then try connecting) to the sophisticated model of duplicating the production configuration in the test lab so that the tests you make are as realistic as possible. But for any change, you need some mechanism to find out what's going to happen when you deploy it, preferably before the Help Desk telephones start ringing.

The best test platform closely mimics the production platform. Realizing this goal is much easier with a good change management system supported by automation technology. We'll talk more about this in the section titled "Create a Provisioning Process" later in this chapter, but the basic idea is that a test computer should be built using the same processes—and the same binaries—that your production servers use. Whether you're working from a golden image (a standard image used for building every instance of a specific kind of server) or building servers through technology that layers server roles on top of operating systems like a layer cake, the same principle applies. That principle is: If you can automate building a production server, you can automate the building of a test server using the same building blocks, and the testing will be more accurate for it.

How Do You Revert Change?

There will be times when even tested changes will need to be reverted—unforeseen complications are not 100 percent avoidable. Backing out some changes could be as easy as uninstalling the hotfix or patch. Other changes could lead to reverting the earlier snapshot (for virtual machines), restoring all changed items from backup, or completely restoring the operating system. We strongly recommend testing your procedures for rolling back changes before you need them to make sure they work as expected.

How Do You Track Change Success and Failure?

This final step is extremely important, because it allows you to see over time how the change decisions you're making are affecting service uptime. If more changes fail than succeed, then something is wrong with the review and testing processes. On the other hand, if every single change you make succeeds, either things are running extremely smoothly or the failures aren't being recorded.

Tracking changes—and their rate of success or failure—can help you when something does go wrong. If you know what changes have been made recently to the asset that's having problems and can include that information in the bug or trouble ticket, you're closer to being able to solve the problem. The first troubleshooting question is always "What's different?" If the answer is "I have no idea," or "Nothing," that's not much of a starting point.

All this said, designing a change management system according to the previous guidelines isn't easy. Setting up a system like this generally represents a big change in culture. Implementing the process will require cooperation at the highest levels of your organization or else someone might see the time spent on deliberately reviewing changes as wasted time.

Even if the change management system is agreed on in principle, in practice it may look like it would be easier to circumvent, and enforcement can be tricky. Preventing people from using the Administrator account is relatively easy if you change the password and make it policy that everyone must use their own account to log on the servers. Except for deliberate exceptions for critical fixes—which must be approved and documented as exceptions—enforcing change approvals and change windows to ensure that only authorized changes get done may be more difficult. Once again, this will never work without management approval for implementing change management processes.

Inventory the Terminal Servers

While determining the change management policies, you've got another important task: inventorying your terminal servers. You may find surprises, such as a rogue terminal server set up in a lab that is allocating Terminal Services client access licenses (TS CALs) from the license server or a third TS Gateway that isn't part of the load balancing and has Terminal Services connection authorization policies (TS CAPs) and Terminal Services resource authorization policies (TS RAPs) different from those of the officially sanctioned TS Gateway servers. But even without surprises, for effective change management, it's important to know what you've got, including the hardware in the servers supporting those roles, the software installed on those servers, and the TS CALs and certificates supporting their operation. The more details that you have about all of these, the easier it will be to determine what effect changes will make.

Role Inventory   At a high level, knowing what server roles you've got and how they communicate can help you keep track of what you need. This inventory doesn't take the detailed look of a hardware or software inventory, but lets you get a big picture of the Terminal Services ecosystem, which servers are authorized, and which roles are redundant. For example, you might ask yourself:

- How many approved terminal servers do I have?

- Are there any terminal servers that aren't approved?

- Are all the terminal servers in the same farm? If not, how are they distributed?

- If there is more than one server farm, why is this necessary?

- How many TS Gateway servers do I have? If there is more than one, are they load-balanced?

- How many TS Session Broker servers do I have? Are they load-balanced?

- What license servers are available?

- What is the licensing model?

- How are my TS CALs distributed? Are they on a single server or on multiple servers, and are they divided evenly?

- What type of TS CALs (per-device or per-user) is installed on the license servers?

- What roles, if any, are housed on the same server?

- What are the IP addresses and names of each role server?
- Where is the TS Gateway server in relationship to the firewall(s)?

Doing this kind of inventory can result in a system map like the one shown in Figure 9-1. This map makes it easy to determine which server you need to connect to for particular kinds of management tasks (this can save a lot of time) and can even help with troubleshooting, since the big picture for your network is laid out before you.

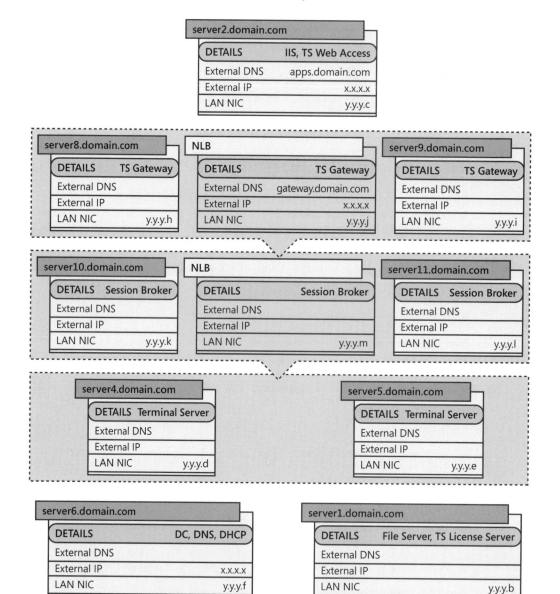

FIGURE 9-1 Use a system map to create a high-level Terminal Services role inventory.

> **On the Companion Media** A Microsoft Office Visio diagram much like the one in Figure 9-1 is available on the companion media. The detailed boxes are linked to a Microsoft Office Excel spreadsheet that is also included on the companion media. To use it in your environment, simply update the spreadsheet and re-establish the external data link in the Office Visio file.

By inventorying system roles, you can make sure that you're conforming to your own best practices, including:

- Are all the terminal servers associated with the right farm? (That is, are the farm names intentional, or did you accidentally misspell a farm name and inadvertently create a single-server farm?)

- Have you divided the TS CALs among two license servers according to best practices?

- Have you made redundant all roles that can be made redundant?

- Are all TS Gateway servers using a centralized Network Policy Server (NPS) configured to be Remote Authentication Dial-In User Service (RADIUS) clients?

- Are there any unauthorized role servers that need to be either managed or decommissioned?

- Is one terminal server designated the management server for creating signed Remote Desktop Protocol (RDP) files?

- Have you clustered the TS Session Broker servers?

> **On the Companion Media** Each inventory system is explained below. On the companion media, a simple spreadsheet for inventorying terminal servers in a low-complexity environment is included on the media as ServerInventory.xls.

Hardware Inventory Hardware inventory tells you what hardware resources support each terminal server role. This step may sound simplistic, but it's really important to troubleshooting. If you have more than a few terminal servers, the chance of every terminal server in the farm being physically identical to each other is low and gets lower over time. You may have assembled the farm from a combination of new and existing servers. Or, as you've added capacity, you may have purchased the latest and greatest hardware each time—but "latest and greatest" can mean different things over the course of a year if you aren't deliberately ordering the same configuration you already have. (Obviously, the more structured your purchasing or leasing habits, the closer the hardware configuration will be to identical for each server.)

So start by doing an inventory of the computer, using a form like the one shown in Table 9-1.

TABLE 9-1 Sample Hardware Inventory Sheet for TS Server01

TS Server 01	Description
Server role	
BIOS version	
Processor speed	
Processor sockets and cores	
Motherboard	
RAM	
Page file size and location	
Number of hard drives and sizes	
RAID configuration	
Power supply(s)	
Video card	
CD-R/RW	
DVD	
NIC type and MAC address	
IP Address	
Computer location (e.g., site, building, and room)	
Machine serial number	
Machine owner	

Armed with this knowledge, you are in a better position to know whether you've got the correct server roles on the correct hardware, and you can evaluate how similar the terminal servers are. It reduces the chance that you'll overload an underpowered terminal server if you know that it's relatively underpowered, for example. If you find that one terminal server has less memory than others, you can add more memory or reduce its weight among the load-balanced servers. (For more information on Session Broker and load balancing, see Chapter 7, "Multi-Server Deployments and Securing Terminal Server Connections.")

Software Inventory   Role inventory tells you what kind of server roles you have deployed, and hardware inventory tells you about the hardware supporting each role. Software inventory gets into more of the details about the software supporting each role.

For all servers, the software inventory should tell you the version of the operating system and the patches and service packs you've applied. Other software inventory may be more role-specific:

- Installed applications (including versioning) and any edits to the applications (terminal servers)

- The name of the administrator who installed the software and the date it was added to the list of approved applications

- Contents and locations of TS RAPs, TS CAPs, network access policies if applicable, and mapping to the business justifications for each policy set (TS Gateway)

- The locations of TS RAPs (TS Gateway)

- Available RDP/Microsoft Windows Installer (MSI) files (Terminal Server)

Business Asset Inventory   Finally, keeping track of the business assets linked to terminal servers is important so you know where they are and can recover them if required. These assets may include:

- Application license numbers

- TS CALs and TS License Server activation information

- Certificates (and the paperwork used to generate them) for RDP file signing, TS Gateway authenticating, and so forth

If you ever need to restore TS CALs to different hardware, you may need to call the Microsoft Clearinghouse to do so. The process will go much more smoothly if the data used to activate your license server is easy to find. Also be sure to document which server you installed the TS CALs on.

> **Note** For more details about backing up and restoring a license server, see the section titled "Backing Up and Restoring TS License Server" later in this chapter.

> **On the Companion Media** One way to determine the issued license count is by running a report using the TS License Server Report Tool (TS License Server Report.exe). The reporting tools in Windows Server 2008 only work against a single-license server. If you run inventory against all license servers, you can determine which servers have TS CALs installed, what kind, and how many are in use across all servers—important if you've split the licenses between multiple-license servers to make the licensing model more fault-tolerant.

To maintain certificate records, you need the original certificate request, a copy of the certificate, the name of the certificate authority (CA) you purchased it from, the account information if you used the CA Web site, and the name of the server that requested the certificate. (To reduce the amount of cross-referencing you need to do, note both the server name and its role, so you can tell why it had the certificate.) Armed with that information, you should be able to tell which servers have certificates, know that the ones that need them have them, and be able to get them again from the CA if required.

Create a Provisioning Process

What if you abandon the idea of troubleshooting and just rebuild because it is easier and faster? On the one hand, you won't feel the glow of accomplishment that comes from troubleshooting a really tricky configuration problem. On the other hand, you might avoid having to stay up all night to troubleshoot and instead, you could get the glow from a brisk walk around the block.

In all seriousness, the goal of troubleshooting is to get a server working again. Given that, sometimes the best option is to restore or replace it rather than spending time figuring out why the server is not working properly. That way, you return service to the users who depend on it. Then, if you have time and it seems like more than a one-time error, you can troubleshoot offline while everyone is still happily productive on the replacement server. Skipping real-time troubleshooting in favor of quick recovery (and then troubleshooting at your leisure) is not an easy goal, but with a lot of planning and some specialized software, it's possible.

An automated provisioning process enables better testing. If you can reproduce a server, you also can create a realistic test environment in the same way that you'd build a server. That means that your testing is more likely to reveal problems that might only manifest themselves under particular conditions.

To pick the right approach, keep in mind what you need to know about a server that is specific to that type of server (or that server in particular) to replace it quickly. See Table 9-2 for some of the key data that makes a Terminal Services role server able to do its job.

TABLE 9-2 Key Terminal Services Role-Persistent Data

Server Role	Key Data	Storage Locations	More Data
Terminal Server	Application customizations, RDP/MSI files, user environment settings	Application packages/scripts, Group Policy, Registry, files on terminal servers, user profiles	Chapters 3–6
TS Session Broker	Which terminal servers are in the farm	Registry	Chapter 7
TS Web Access	Web page customizations, terminal server providing icons to Web page	Web.config, Desktop.aspx, Default.aspx	Chapter 6
TS Gateway	TS CAPs, TS RAPs, NAP policies (optional)	Files (by default on TS Gateway), NPS configuration data	Chapter 7
TS Licensing	LServer directory, Licensing registry keys, certificate from Clearinghouse	System state data, registry, LServer directory	Chapter 3

There's a variety of approaches you can take to automatically recreate Terminal Services roles, giving you a greater or lesser recovery time. These approaches might include:

- Group policy combined with automated server builds
- Golden images
- Automated provisioning tools

You're likely going to use a combination of approaches to replace a server, not just one of those described below. The more complex your deployment scenario, the more likely you'll need a flexible rebuilding system.

Group Policy   Out of the box, Windows Server 2008 can get you part of the way there with automated deployment solutions and Group Policy.

Group Policy is the simplest mechanism for reconfiguring terminal servers and adding capacity. It's not a complete rebuild, obviously, because it requires you to reinstall the server operating system, install any required patches, and install applications.

One of the limitations of Group Policy for configuring the Terminal Services ecosystem is that it applies mainly to the terminal servers. Here are a few examples: It doesn't configure TS Gateway servers to be load-balanced or to use a centralized network policy server (NPS). It doesn't support per-NIC configuration. You can't use it for certificate management. Nor can you use Group Policy for management tasks such as installing TS CALs or publishing TS RemoteApps. It's a configuration tool, not a full management tool.

Group Policy also doesn't fully link server roles to each other. For example, although you can use Group Policy to specify the licensing server a terminal server should use, you can't use it to specify the TS Gateway server the terminal server should point to for creating RDP files, or the terminal server a TS Web Access server should point to in order to get its RemoteApp display information. (You can use it to add computers to security groups required for the various Terminal Services role services to work together, however.)

Group Policy also doesn't log. You can see where you *are* with Group Policy using Gpresults. exe, but you can't see where you *were*. That is, you can always see current settings, but Group Policy does not automatically record changes that you make. This can sometimes make troubleshooting complicated when you're trying to determine why a setting didn't take, and in a lower-security environment it can potentially lead to configuration changes that are harder to detect (see the section titled "Who Can Make Changes?" earlier in this chapter).

Finally, another potential complication with Group Policy is the administrative privileges that configuring it requires. In less complex environments, the terminal server administrators and Group Policy administrators may be the same people, but this isn't always the case. (See Chapter 6, "Installing and Publishing Applications," for more information about this and one approach to working around this limitation.)

On the plus side, Group Policy allows you to consistently apply operating system and Terminal Services–specific policies to servers just by adding them to the organizational unit (OU) to which the policy is applied. It also allows you to record the configuration of the terminal servers for auditing purposes or comparing settings in different environments (for example, test and production environments). Therefore, it is very good for configuring most of the settings on a terminal server and some of the key settings on other TS roles.

Finally, using Group Policy allows you to assert with confidence that all servers are conforming to the established configurations (so far as they are controlled via Group Policy), since enabled Group Policies trump per-server configuration and apply to all members of an OU unless you make an explicit exception as described in Chapter 4, "Creating the User Work Environment." So while Group Policy isn't a complete solution for server farm management, it's a very good way of enforcing standards as long as Group Policy changes are carefully vetted and approved.

Golden Image Libraries   Another approach to change management is the use of golden images. Golden images are the usual name for a library of server images that are perfectly tuned. You only use these images to build more servers.

The simplest way to store and duplicate golden images is as virtual machines. As discussed in Chapter 2, "Planning the Terminal Server Ecosystem," you can't, practically speaking, virtualize terminal servers for a production environment due to the overhead. However, you can virtualize many Terminal Services role services with good effects, since they are lightweight and don't have the same I/O demands that terminal servers do.

Virtualizing servers have many advantages for change management. For one, they make it very easy to reverse changes; for example, if you don't like the current version of the TS Gateway configuration, you can always restore a previous snapshot of the virtual machine. Virtualizing servers make it easy to duplicate (or clone) an exact copy of a server because the servers are file-based.

If you have a wide variety of servers, golden images may be hard to maintain for storage reasons. But the likelier case for many terminal server farms running Windows Server 2008 without additional management software is that the variety among servers is low. Even if you have a lot of servers, it doesn't matter as long as you don't have too many variations of each.

The biggest trick with golden images lies in making sure that the golden image always contains the latest version of the server operating system and patches and that production environments and the image library are always in synch. There are a lot of tools for managing golden images, but you're looking for:

- Tools that make it easy to update current images with any approved production changes

- Tools that make it easy to update the test environment to ensure that it matches production

- Spare virtual machine (VM) host capacity to run the virtualized computers while the original equipment may be offline

Direct from the Field: Using Virtualization Technology to Enable Disaster Recovery

Kroll Factual Data provides business information to mortgage lenders, consumer lenders, property management firms, and other businesses. We have been a part of the Microsoft Technology Adoption Program for virtualization products for the past several years, and we have about 1,500 virtual machines (VMs) across our computing environment.

As companies experiment with server virtualization, one of the benefits that is seemingly overlooked (or is not emphasized as often as it should be) by those discussing virtualization technologies is the impact that virtualization can have when creating and maintaining a disaster recovery environment.

Put simply, the more that your production environment is virtualized, the easier it is to build a disaster recovery environment using the golden images created for your production systems.

For years, I worried about my company's ability to recover from a catastrophic disaster. But over the last 18 months, we have utilized Microsoft Virtual Server to create the situation that we are in today.

We have a production data center environment that is 85 percent virtualized. All of the golden images are replicated to our disaster recovery (DR) site (the golden image store is constantly updated to the DR site, and the updated/patched/modified golden images are automatically replicated to DR as soon as they are changed). We have standing VM hosts awaiting a VM image (these machines are running and used for testing). Our Internet circuits and vendor connections are "hot" and tested constantly. Databases and all other non-VMs are already duplicated and maintained at the DR site (we're talking a couple dozen machines, not the 600 that are located in our production environment today).

Were we to experience a major disaster, the IT staff at our DR site would immediately start the process of copying VM images to selected hosts. We would change our circuit routing and externally hosted Domain Name Service to the DR IP range. After the VMs are copied to the host machines, we would start to bring up the "new" data center. Our testing has shown that this can realistically be completed in less than a day, but we have a 24-hour Recovery Time Objective (RTO).

Our DR site is populated by our legacy hardware. But with server virtualization, this is not a problem. Sure, you may not be able to run 20 VMs on a single host due to the older hardware configurations, but even if you can only run a quarter of that number, you are gaining additional life out of "end-of-life" equipment. You are also getting your production systems up and running in pretty much the same condition that they were running in your real production environment.

I still worry about business continuity situations. (Who doesn't?) But the DR plan that we have established for our core technology finally lets me rest a little bit better. And using the Microsoft virtualization software and Microsoft System Center management tools has made the entire disaster recovery project more cost effective, not only from a licensing and equipment side, but also from staffing and administrative perspectives.

As you embrace a virtualization technology, keep disaster recovery in the back of your mind as another solution in your DR maintenance plan.

Chris Steffen

Principal Technical Architect, Kroll Factual Data

Server Provisioning Tools   For more complex environments that may be hard to support with golden images, you can design servers, not as complete images, but as collections of building blocks that can be combined according to the type of server you need to create. For a simple example, if you maintain two server farms with different applications, you don't need to maintain one golden image for each farm. Instead, use the same building blocks for each terminal server until you get to the application sets, then use the appropriate applications to build each server type. Another example might be building a test server with a new version of an application under development, but which is completely identical to the production servers in every way.

On the Companion Media One example of this approach is taken with visionapp Server Management, part of the visionapp Application Delivery Management Suite. See the companion media for a link to a free version of this tool.

The main idea behind this approach is to break apart the steps needed to provision a server and create installation packages for each of these steps. Then you create scripts to run the packages one after the other to build a server. Figure 9-2 shows the six typical steps and package types that are built and stacked to create servers.

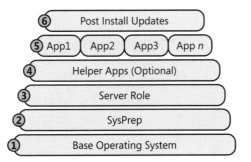

FIGURE 9-2 Creating a terminal server in a series of steps

Each step in this process consists of prebuilt packages that include application binaries and scripts to set specific parameters for that package. Packages are combined and run in a predefined manner in order to build servers to precise specifications. After the servers are built, they are also maintained by building new packages and applying the new packages to the working server. For instance, you might build packages that include monthly updates and then apply the packages to your servers each month. Any new servers that are added to your infrastructure can now be built to the same specification by applying all packages in the same predefined manner that was used to build the existing servers.

For example, as Figure 9-3 shows, to build a terminal server farm in our alpineskihouse.com domain to host Microsoft Office 2007, we would choose a base image package, a SysPrep package (to add the server to the domain, set an IP address, and other identifying information), a server role package, and all necessary application and update packages. These packages would then be methodically applied to each server in the farm, resulting in identical terminal servers, with the exact same OS build, applications, and patches, but each with its own necessary uniqueness (e.g., computer name, IP address, and so forth).

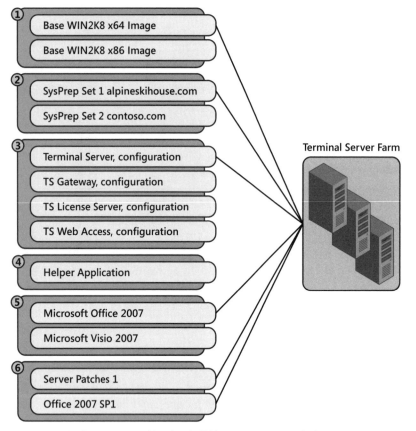

FIGURE 9-3 Packages are combined to build homogenous terminal servers.

Packages are assembled into installation scripts, as shown in Figure 9-4. The packages are combined with scripts that define the installation sequence, including any necessary reboots. Next, packages and installation script combinations are coordinated into a set and run in sequence to create predetermined server configurations. Figure 9-4 shows only one such script set, but you can make many different script sets from many installation script packages, depending on all the package combinations you need to build the different servers in your environment. For instance, a single-application package or an operating system package can be part of many different installation scripts, because by themselves each is one generic piece of the whole puzzle. The unique puzzle made up of those component pieces is the set.

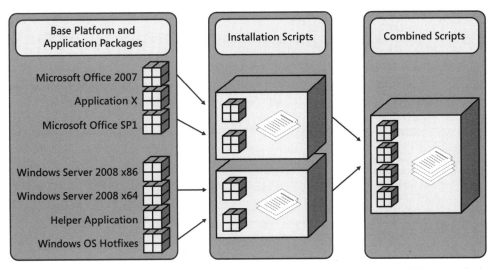

FIGURE 9-4 Packages are combined into scripts, which are combined into script sets, which get applied to servers.

This kind of repeatable process is great for provisioning servers in a systematic fashion, and it provides a mechanism to provision multiple servers at once. It also serves as excellent documentation as to exactly how the servers were configured, what server parameters and settings have been set on each server, and which patches and service packs have been applied. Automated provisioning processes like the one described here are usually well detailed in provisioning and engineering documents.

Enable Improvement

Enabling improvement is the final part of the process; it builds on every aspect of what you've done before:

- By tracking changes and the change success or failure, you can see whether previous changes have worked as planned. You also can evaluate the likelihood of similar changes having the desired effects.

- By creating a repeatable process, you've made a way to build test platforms that you can use to stage and test changes.

- By creating change management policies, you've established a process by which improvements can be reviewed and approved.

- By creating a way to add changes programmatically, you've made it easier to include approved changes in the base platform so they become part of the testing platform.

Backing Out Changes

One important question of change management is how to back out changes that have unforeseen consequences. One way to avoid this is to test. But if your test environment doesn't quite duplicate your production environment or more users stress the servers in ways that your pilot didn't anticipate, you may need to reverse a change.

Even changes that are fairly simple to reverse may be more far-reaching than you think. If you make a business decision to change the terminal server license model from per-user to per-device, this requires two changes. Most obviously, you'll need to change the terminal server license mode from per-user to per-device. Perhaps less obviously—because it's not a technical change—someone will need to contact the Microsoft Clearinghouse to get new licenses issued using the original paperwork. Doing the first step and not doing the second will eventually lead to users no longer being able to log in.

Backing out a change programmatically is sometimes simplest to do by returning to an earlier build version. Backing out changes requires knowing which registry keys and binary files were updated by a change and restoring them to a previous version. But if you have a backup of a previous version of that system, you can just restore the backup. Again, we strongly recommend testing the procedures you will use to make sure they work as expected.

Demonstrating Configuration Compliance

Whether you need to demonstrate compliance for an external audit or an internal one, following change management best practices makes it easier to demonstrate that you have done so. Every change has been formally approved, and every change is recorded.

You can't prepare for a compliance audit in the week before it happens. If compliance audits are part of your organizational culture, then you'll need to get a system in place that's effectively self-documenting through these practices:

- Know the scope of the audit—what are the questions being asked?

- Keep a software and hardware inventory.

- Document your control mechanisms including the change management process, the meeting minutes from when changes were approved, and the records of the changes made so you can map the requested change against the technical adjustments made.

- Document any known exceptions to change management policies. If you don't document this, then it's hard to argue that no exceptions are ever made—you can't prove that you would know of any.

- Document all downtime—scheduled and unscheduled—so that you can demonstrate uptime metrics. Again, if you don't document it, you can't prove that you would know about the downtime.

What Server Roles Need to Be Backed Up?

Let's start with one basic piece of maintenance: backups. What roles need to be backed up, and why?

Generally speaking, two server roles shouldn't need to be backed up at all. Terminal servers should not have any per-user data on them. Ideally, you should be able to bring servers online quickly if they're needed, but there shouldn't be anything on them that needs to be backed up as such—just restored from the saved configuration so they're identical to all other servers. Profiles may be cached, but the main profile is on a network share (that you should be backing up), and folders are also redirected so that users leave no personal data on the terminal server. TS Session Brokers are also unlikely candidates for backup. The TS Session Broker database doesn't persist any data other than the terminal servers in the farm, so you don't need to back up the servers.

Other role services do persist data and will require backups:

- TS Web Access
- TS Gateway
- TS Licensing

This section will first provide a quick overview of backup and recovery tools in Windows Server 2008, since they're different from the ones in previous versions of the operating system. Next, it will review which data need to be backed up for each role service and where that data is stored.

A Quick Overview of Backup Tools in Windows Server 2008

Although this isn't the place for a full discussion of system backups (see the *Windows Server Backup Step-by-Step Guide for Windows Server 2008* at *http://technet.microsoft.com/en-us/library/cc770266.aspx* for details—the link is located on the companion CD), this is a quick guide to get you started backing up and restoring critical data on Terminal Server roles.

If you're accustomed to launching the backup tools by opening Run and typing **ntbackup**, you may have some trouble starting backups. Ntbackup.exe has been replaced in Windows Server 2008 and Windows Vista with Windows Server Backup and the Wbadmin.exe command-line utility. Windows Server Backup works a little differently from Ntbackup.exe. Rather than a file-based backup system like its predecessor, Windows Server Backup takes snapshots of the volumes you specify. Windows Backup is launched from the Administrative Tools program group and can be used to take full volume backups, which can be used both to perform a bare metal restore and also to restore individual files and folders.

Wbadmin.exe is the Windows Server Backup command-line utility. It can take full volume or system state backups and can perform full system restores or system state restores. You can only run Wbadmin.exe if you're a member of the Administrators or Backup Operators groups, and you must launch it from an elevated command prompt. Right-click Command Prompt and choose Run As Administrator from the context menu.

On its own, typing **wbadmin** doesn't do anything—it's the starting point for a number of subcommands, which are listed in Table 9-3.

TABLE 9-3 Wbadmin Subcommands

Subcommand	Description
Wbadmin enable backup	Configures and enables a daily backup schedule. This subcommand applies only to Windows Server 2008.
Wbadmin disable backup	Disables your daily backups. This subcommand applies only to Windows Server 2008.
Wbadmin start backup	Runs a one-time backup. If used with no parameters, uses the settings from the daily backup schedule. This command works for both Windows Vista and Windows Server 2008.
Wbadmin stop job	Stops the currently running backup or recovery operation. This command works for both Windows Vista and Windows Server 2008.
Wbadmin get versions	Lists details of backups recoverable from the local computer (by default) or the location specified in the command. This command works for both Windows Vista and Windows Server 2008.
Wbadmin get items	Lists the items included in a specific backup. This command works for both Windows Vista and Windows Server 2008.
Wbadmin start recovery	Runs a recovery of the volumes, applications, files, or folders specified. This subcommand applies only to Windows Server 2008.
Wbadmin get status	Shows the status of the currently running backup or recovery operation. This command works for both Windows Vista and Windows Server 2008.
Wbadmin get disks	Lists disks that are currently online. This subcommand applies only to Windows Server 2008.
Wbadmin start systemstaterecovery	Runs a system state recovery. This subcommand applies only to Windows Server 2008.
Wbadmin start systemstatebackup	Runs a system state backup. This subcommand applies only to Windows Server 2008.
Wbadmin delete systemstatebackup	Deletes one or more system state backups. This subcommand applies only to Windows Server 2008.
Wbadmin start sysrecovery	Runs a recovery of the volumes containing the operating system's state. This subcommand applies only to Windows Server 2008, and it is only available if you are using the Windows Recovery Environment.

TABLE 9-3 Wbadmin Subcommands

Subcommand	Description
Wbadmin restore catalog	Recovers a backup catalog from a specified storage location in the case where the backup catalog on the local computer has been corrupted. This subcommand applies only to Windows Server 2008.
Wbadmin delete catalog	Deletes the backup catalog on the local computer. Use this subcommand only if the backup catalog on this computer is corrupted and you have no backups stored at another location that you can use to restore the catalog. This subcommand applies only to Windows Server 2008.

Each one of these options has multiple subcommands within it. To get help with any topic, type **wbadmin subcommand /?** for a full listing of options for that subcommand. For additional information on Wbadmin, visit *http://technet.microsoft.com/en-us/library/cc754015.aspx*.

For our purposes, here are a few tips:

■ You can't back up system state data to the same drive it came from.

■ System state data will be gigabytes in size, so plan accordingly for backups.

■ Network-accessible backup locations must be Universal Naming Convention (UNC) paths, not mapped drives.

■ You can't back up single files or folders (use Xcopy or Robocopy to copy single files), but you can restore single files with Windows Backup.

Note Xcopy has been deprecated, but it's still available on Window Server 2008 (and Windows Vista) along with Robocopy.

The next sections will show you what data you need to back up for the Terminal Services roles that persist data and where it's located (in case you don't want to do an entire system restore).

Making Roles Redundant

The fastest way to keep a server role online is to make multiple servers support it. That way, if one server goes offline, then other servers will keep supporting that role.

To make terminal servers redundant, create a server farm with at least two servers in it. That way, users will never need to know which servers are online, or even if you add new capacity. That's because the TS Session Broker will send the incoming connection to the correct server based on existing connections or the number of concurrent sessions on a terminal server, if the user doesn't already have an existing connection. (If a terminal server suddenly fails while users are connected to it, those users may lose data if they haven't saved recently, but they will be able to reconnect to another server and continue working.)

You can't really make the terminal server that's the source of information for the TS Web Access server redundant, because TS Web Access points to a specific server rather than a server farm. (However, as noted in the section titled "What Roles Can You Virtualize?" later in this chapter, if you arrange your terminal server capacity correctly, you may be able to keep a backup data source.)

Clustering works for other Terminal Services roles: TS Web Access (treat it as an Internet Information Services [IIS] server), TS Session Broker, and TS Gateway, as described in detail in Chapter 7.

As you can see, building redundancy into the Terminal Services ecosystem is generally possible. The exception to this is the TS Licensing Server. This is one of the more fragile pieces of your Terminal Server ecosystem because it's (a) essential, (b) can't be clustered, and (c) can only be rebuilt without outside assistance from the Clearinghouse under specific circumstances. The TS CALs on the license server are tied to that license server, so you can't just reinstall them on a new license server if the original one goes to That Great Datacenter in the Sky. After users have licenses, you don't need daily access to the license server, because it's not part of the license check. However, when you must be able to issue per-device TS CALs, not having access to a license server can prevent new users from logging on to a terminal server at all.

Tables 9-4 and 9-5 summarize the effects of a downed license server on per-user and per-device enabled environments and the effects on connecting clients.

TABLE 9-4 Per-User Licensing Enabled, and the Lone TS License Server Goes Offline

Status of Client	Redundant License Servers?	Impact on Client
New, needs TS CAL	No	Client is not affected
Existing, has TS CAL	No	Client is not affected
Expired, needs TS CAL	No	Client is not affected

TABLE 9-5 Per-Device Licensing Enabled, and the Lone TS License Server Goes Offline

Status of Client	Redundant License Servers?	Impact on Client
New, needs TS CAL	No	Client is denied access
Existing, has TS CAL	No	Client allowed access until TS CAL expires
Expired, needs TS CAL	No	Client denied access

> **Note** For details about how and when the terminal server will access a license server, see Chapter 3, "Installing the Core Terminal Server Environment."

The best way to achieve redundancy with license servers is to have multiple-license servers and split the TS CAL license packs among them. That way, you avoid both the possibility of a terminal server not being able to reach a lone license server and the lone license server being unable to issue a license. Recall from Chapter 3 that a terminal server only keeps looking for a license server until it finds one that responds to its request—even if that license server doesn't have any licenses. If the license server can't fulfill the request, then it forwards the request to other license servers that it can discover. Therefore, if you split the licenses, you double the chances that the terminal server will reach a license server with TS CALs installed, and if the license server that it does reach happens to be out of licenses, then it can forward the request to the other server. To avoid relying on discovery, you can tell the terminal servers about all the license servers available, using Group Policy or by editing the list of approved license servers through Terminal Services Configuration on each terminal server. Because the TS Licensing role service is lightweight (it does not use much processing power or memory), it can easily be combined with other roles on one computer. For that reason, it's not hard to find a place to put this role service.

If one license server goes down, clients have a better chance of getting a permanent TS CAL assigned to them because the other license server is still up and will most likely have TS CALs that it can issue. Users or computers with expiring TS CALs will be able to get a new permanent TS CAL assigned to them (provided that the license server has one to give). New clients will still get a temporary TS CAL the first time they access the terminal server and will get a permanent TS CAL the second time they access the terminal server, providing one is available. And even if the license server runs out of device CALs, a new client will still be able to get a temporary CAL and connect for 120 days. This is plenty of time to get the downed license server back online and also to get more licenses.

> **Note** Putting the terminal servers into per-user mode can help you avoid outages because per-user licensing isn't enforced. It's actually okay to run in per-user mode, even if you have purchased device TS CALs. For that reason, in an emergency, flip the switch. You won't be able to use the License Server application to keep track of how many device TS CALs are used, but as long as you have enough licenses to accommodate your connecting devices, this is in compliance with the end user license agreement (EULA). Then you can fix your downed license server.

The Alternate Redundancy Model for TS Licensing Servers

There's been a lot of controversy in the past about the best way to support high availability for a license server (including, confusingly, on some places on the Microsoft Web site), so it's worth mentioning the other option that is sometimes suggested. The alternate suggested model is to put all the TS CALs on one license server but maintain two license servers so the empty one can forward the request if the terminal server gets to it first.

We (and the product team) recommend splitting the TS CALs between two servers because this model is less likely to lead to a service outage, as illustrated in Tables 9-6 and 9-7. The alternate model will lead to a user being locked out if the license server containing the TS CALs goes offline and if no licenses are available on the other server. Of course, if both servers are out of licenses, the user will be denied access, but that's true of any licensing arrangement—that's just a function of not having as many TS CALs as you need.

TABLE 9-6 Bad Effects of Grouping All TS CALs on One Server

Status of Client	Redundant License Servers?	Split TS CALs?	Impact on Client
New	Yes	No	Client gets temporary TS CAL and can access terminal servers for up to 120 days
Existing	Yes	No	Client is not affected
Expired license	Yes	No	Client is denied access

TABLE 9-7 Splitting the Per-Device TS CALs Maintains Service Availability in All Cases

Status of Client	Redundant License Servers?	Split TS CALs?	Impact on Client
New	Yes	Yes	Client is not affected
Existing	Yes	Yes	Client is not affected
Expired license	Yes	Yes	Client is not affected

Backing Up and Restoring TS Web Access

Recovering a TS Web Access server is fairly straightforward, because this role does not store information so much as present data from other server roles and present a conduit to them. Unless you have other roles on the server, or you have customized the Web site displaying TS RemoteApp icons and Remote Desktops, there isn't any personalized data on this role. It might actually take you longer to restore a TS Web Access server from backup than it would to reinstall and reconfigure the role service. That said, you should still document the following information about the server to make it easier to recreate:

- Which terminal server the TS Web Access server uses as its source of data

- Whether there's any customization in Web.config or Desktop.aspx files (even if there isn't, then this information will inform others that there are no backups to restore)

If you do customize the Web page, you will need to back up the edited files. For example, if you configure TS Web Access to work with SharePoint, you will need to back up the Web.config located at: %SystemRoot%\Inetpub\wwwroot\.

If you customize any of the TS Web Access Web pages, you will need to back up those pages located by default at: %SystemRoot%\Windows\Web\ts\en-us (in our case; yours may be in a different language folder). We recommend backing up the entire %SystemRoot%\Windows\Web\ts folder.

You can restore these files to any TS Web Access server; they're not specific to the hardware in any way.

Backing Up and Restoring TS Gateway

The recommended way to back up a TS Gateway is to take a full backup of the server. The harder way is to back up the individual TS Gateway–related files, which can then be restored to a new TS Gateway server. The upside to doing it the hard way is that these files are not hardware dependent. The TS Gateway critical information consists of:

- TS Gateway configuration settings

- The SSL certificate (This certificate is tied to the server that requested it, so if you are recovering to a new instance of the operating system, you will need to request a new certificate.)

- TS Resource Authorization Policies (TS RAPs)

- TS Connection Authorization Policies (TS CAPs)

To back up the configuration settings, you can export those settings to a file, just as if you were going to export your configuration and import it to another TS Gateway server. This will include your TS CAPs and TS RAPs (if configured locally). It will also include server farm settings, auditing settings, CAP Store location, and whether or not clients will send a Statement of Health. It does not include Secure Sockets Layer (SSL) bridging settings or SSL certificate settings.

Make sure you back up your digital certificate file and all pertinent information you use to obtain the certificate; if you need to get the certificate reissued, this information will come in handy. This pertinent information may include:

- The certificate itself

- The certificate request

- Company name

- Domain name

- Corporate contact

- Technical contact

- Billing contact

- Domain registrar

- Company tax ID or other data you gave to the CA in order to verify your business identity

- Account information you used to set up an account on the issuing CA's Web site

If you store your TS RAPs in a centralized location, then back up the Rap.xml file in that location. (As explained in Chapter 7, you may choose to edit the location of this file to centralized storage of the TS RAPs for load-balanced TS Gateway servers.)

Because TS CAPs are really just network access policies, they are actually stored in the NPS server, either locally on the TS Gateway, or on the centralized NPS server. If you centralize your TS CAPs, then exporting the TS Gateway configuration will not export the centralized TS CAPs, but only the setting that points to the centralized location.

Backing Up NPS and Centralized TS CAPs

You can back up centralized TS CAPs by exporting the NPS server settings to a file. Open the NPS Server tool, right-click the NPS Server, and choose Export Configuration Settings. Using this method will export any shared secrets used to facilitate communication with TS Gateway servers to the XML file in plaintext.

You can also use the *netsh nps export* command. Every time you make a configuration change to the TS CAPs, you should export this configuration data. This export includes all Network Policy Server data, not just TS CAPs, but as you can see from the snippet below, the TS CAP data is part of the export file data.

```xml
<TS_CAP01 name="TS CAP01">
- <Properties>
  <Policy_Enabled xmlns:dt="urn:schemas-microsoft-com:datatypes" dt:dt="boolean">1</
Policy_Enabled>
  <Policy_SourceTag xmlns:dt="urn:schemas-microsoft-com:datatypes" dt:dt="int">1</
Policy_SourceTag>
  <msNPAction xmlns:dt="urn:schemas-microsoft-com:datatypes" dt:dt="string">TS CAP01</
msNPAction>
  <msNPConstraint xmlns:dt="urn:schemas-microsoft-com:datatypes" dt:
dt="string">MATCH("NAS-Port-Type=^5$")</msNPConstraint>
  <msNPConstraint xmlns:dt="urn:schemas-microsoft-com:datatypes" dt:dt="string">USERN
TGROUPS("S-1-5-21-3733146802-1470550652-970394947-513;S-1-5-21-3733146802-1470550652-
970394947-512")</msNPConstraint>
```

```
    <msNPConstraint xmlns:dt="urn:schemas-microsoft-com:datatypes" dt:dt="string">MATCH
("Called-Station-Id=UserAuthType:(PW)")</msNPConstraint>
    <msNPSequence xmlns:dt="urn:schemas-microsoft-com:datatypes" dt:dt="int">1</
msNPSequence>
    </Properties>
    </TS_CAP01>
```

To back up the NPS using the netsh command-line utility, open a command prompt with elevated privileges and run **netsh nps export filename = "pathtofile"**. For example, we keep our backup configurations on a central server named OZARK, and we use the date as the backup name, so the command is:

```
netsh nps export filename = "\\ozark\ash-nps-storage\07042008.xml"
```

Backing up the shared secrets is optional with the command-line utility, so if you do not want them contained in plaintext, then this is the tool to use. Optionally, to export the shared secrets used by RADIUS clients, add the *exportpsk* parameter to the command like this:

```
netsh nps export filename = "\\ozark\ash-nps-storage\07042008.xml" exportpsk = yes
```

But again, be aware that this will include the shared secret in plaintext, as shown below:

```
- <IP_Address xmlns:dt="urn:schemas-microsoft-com:datatypes" dt:dt="string">ozark.
alpineskihouse.com</IP_Address>
    <NAS_Manufacturer xmlns:dt="urn:schemas-microsoft-com:datatypes" dt:dt="int">0</NAS_
Manufacturer>
    <Quarantine_Compatible xmlns:dt="urn:schemas-microsoft-com:datatypes" dt:dt="boolean">
1</Quarantine_Compatible>
    <Radius_Client_Enabled xmlns:dt="urn:schemas-microsoft-com:datatypes" dt:dt="boolean">
1</Radius_Client_Enabled>
    <Require_Signature xmlns:dt="urn:schemas-microsoft-com:datatypes" dt:dt="boolean">
0</Require_Signature>
    <Shared_Secret xmlns:dt="urn:schemas-microsoft-com:datatypes" dt:dt="string">your
shared secret will be here in plain text</Shared_Secret>
```

Effects of Losing a TS License Server

Losing your TS License Server (due to hardware or software failure) could have different results on Terminal Services clients, depending on the licensing model in effect and the current TS License status of the Terminal Services client.

If you have your terminal servers set for per-user licensing, the situation may not be critical: If you lose your license server and a client attempts to connect to the terminal server, the terminal server will allow the connection. This is because per-user licensing is not enforced.

As explained in Chapter 3, per-user TS CALs are not really given out; usage is just tracked by TS License Manager. After the 120-day grace period, as long as the terminal server has contacted a working license server once, it will still allow connections if the license server goes offline. Therefore, your clients will not feel the impact of a TS License Server outage.

> **Note** Just because per-user licensing isn't enforced doesn't mean you don't need the license server—or the TS CALs it stores. It just means that a license server outage won't prevent users without TS CALs from logging on to terminal servers in per-user mode.

If you have your terminal servers set for per-device licensing, it's good to know that a client that already has a TS CAL will not look for another license until seven days before the expiration date, when it starts trying to renew the TS CAL. Should you lose your license server, you have a minimum of seven days to get your TS License Server back online before existing clients could be denied access due to an expired license. The potential to affect the client experience comes into play when you have per-device licensing enabled and you lose your license server. A new client requesting access to a terminal server would be denied access if no license server is available.

Backing Up and Restoring TS License Server

You can restore most server roles to another server by simply installing the role service and restoring the data used by that role service. A good example of this is restoring TS Web Access to another server. You can't do this with a license server, because when you install TS CALs, they are tied to the operating system–specific information you gave to the Clearinghouse upon activation.

In order to back up and properly restore a license server, you need to understand how the TS CALs are bound to the server and how communication occurs between the TS License Server, the terminal servers, and the Terminal Services clients.

Background: How TS CALs Are Tied to a Server

When you activate a TS License Server with the Microsoft Clearinghouse, the Clearinghouse issues an X.509 digital certificate to the TS License Server. It is used to encrypt communications with the Clearinghouse. Figure 9-5 depicts the process of activating a TS License Server and installing TS CALs.

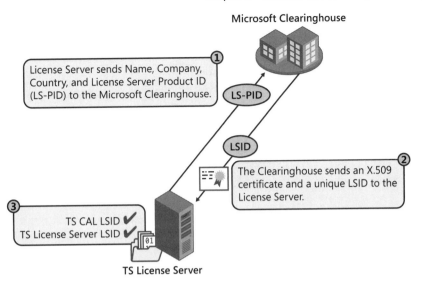

Microsoft Clearinghouse

① License Server sends Name, Company, Country, and License Server Product ID (LS-PID) to the Microsoft Clearinghouse.

LS-PID

LSID

② The Clearinghouse sends an X.509 certificate and a unique LSID to the License Server.

③ TS CAL LSID ✔
TS License Server LSID ✔

TS License Server

FIGURE 9-5 The Microsoft Clearinghouse issues an LSID to the TS License Server, which is matched to the LSID contained in the TS CALs.

1. You activate the TS License Server. The TS License Server sends information to the Clearinghouse identifying the TS License Server. This information includes:

    ❑ Name

    ❑ Company

    ❑ Country

    ❑ License Server Product ID (LS-PID)

    The LS-PID is server-specific because it is created from the Windows Product ID (PID), a unique identifier created when you install the operating system. It contains the Microsoft Product Code (MPC) that identifies the OS product and the Channel ID that specifies the channel through which you purchased your Windows operating system (Retail, Original Equipment Manufacturer [OEM], Volume Licensing Programs, Evaluation, or Checked Build).

2. The Clearinghouse issues an X.509 certificate to the TS License Server. The certificate is used to establish secure communications between the TS License Server and the Microsoft Clearinghouse. The Clearinghouse also sends a unique License Server ID (LSID) to the server.

    This certificate is not stored in the regular computer certificate store on the server. Instead, it is stored in the registry at HKLM\SYSTEM\CurrentControlSet\Services\TermServices\Parameters.

3. You install TS CAL packs. TS CALs are created based on a 35-character alphanumeric representation of the digital certificate that was issued to the TS License Server. This

35-character sequence contains the LSID. When TS CALs are installed, the TS License Server matches the LSID in the 35-character sequence with its own LSID that was issued by the Clearinghouse. If they match, then the TS CALs are installed. If they do not match, the server rejects the installation.

The key point is that *the LSID issued to the TS License Server is created from the LS-PID*. The LS-PID is created from the unique operating system PID. This process ties the TS CALs to the TS License Server operating system installation.

Communication from the terminal servers and the clients is encrypted based on the TS License Server certificate as shown in Figure 9-6.

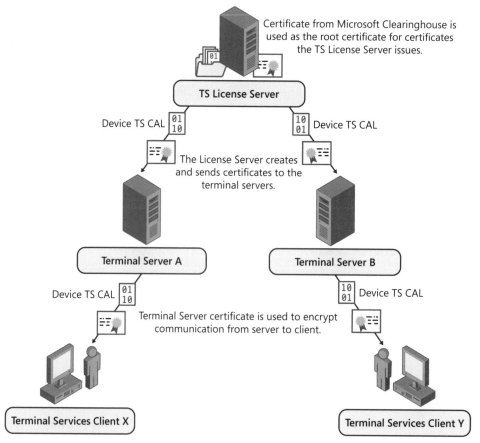

FIGURE 9-6 The TS License Server issues certificates to the terminal servers.

1. The license server gets a X.509 root certificate from the Clearinghouse based on its PID.

2. The license server creates digital certificates signed with its own certificate and issues them to the terminal servers (terminal servers request TS CALs on behalf of the users or computers connecting to them).

3. The terminal servers use their digital certificates to establish secure communications with clients in order to check for and to issue TS CALs.

The result is that in order to establish secure communication, the TS client verifies the terminal server certificate by checking the signature on the certificate. The terminal server certificate is signed by the TS License Server certificate. If you change the TS License Server, the certificates handed down to the terminal servers will no longer be valid and new ones will be issued.

> **Note** For per-user licensing, the terminal server doesn't have to send anything to or get anything from the client computer, since all the TS CAL usage information is stored in Active Directory.

Because the TS License Server and TS CALs are tied to the operating system installation, we recommend maintaining a full backup of the TS License Server. At a minimum, you will need to maintain a backup of the following TS License Server components:

- The server system state (this contains the registry, and therefore the X.509 certificate issued to the TS License Server and the licensing registry keys).

> **Note** The TS License Server database is located by default at: %SystemDrive%\System32\ Lserver. (This is actually contained in the system state when a server runs the TS Licensing role service). To confirm the TS License Server database location, start the TS Licensing Manager, right-click the License Server, and choose Review Configuration.

- Optionally, the system repair directory (%SystemRoot%\Repair).

- The information you gave to the Microsoft Clearinghouse when you activated your TS License Server. You will need this if you have to call the Clearinghouse to get your TS CALs reissued. This is the information the Clearinghouse uses to identify you.

In some circumstances, you will be able to recover your TS License Server, but you won't be able to recover your TS CALs. If this is the case, then you must call the Microsoft Clearinghouse in order to get your TS CALs reissued.

> **Note** For more information on contacting the Clearinghouse, see *http://technet.microsoft.com/ en-us/library/cc754677.aspx*. This link is included on the companion CD.

If you need to rebuild your TS License Server, your recovery method will determine whether or not you have to contact the Microsoft Clearinghouse to get the TS CALs reissued.

TS License Server Recovery Methods Requiring TS CAL Reissuance

Each operating system installation uses server-specific encryption that is unique to that installation. Every new installation of the OS changes the crypto keys used in the server-specific encryption.

To be fully functional without requiring a call to the Clearinghouse, the TS License Server restore needs three things:

- TS License Server database directory.
- Licensing registry keys.
- Crypto keys from the OS (those that crypto application programming interfaces [APIs] use; these are machine specific). This is required to prevent piracy.

If your license server is still operational and you restore the system state (which will include the LServer folder), your TS License Server will be fully functional. Unissued TS CALs will be available to new devices.

If you use imaging software to make backups of your license server and then restore this image to new or existing hardware, you will have a fully functioning TS License Server. Unissued TS CALs will be restored and available.

Although Microsoft does not support restoring a system state to another server, even if the hardware is identical, we have had success doing this in our test environment (we will do this using Windows Server Backup later in this section). Situations in which you would need to get your TS CALs reissued are those in which you are unable to restore the system state and the LServer folder successfully. For instance, Microsoft also does not support restoring the system state to dissimilar hardware. In this case, it's possible that you will need to start over with a new license server and therefore will need to get your licenses reissued.

> **On the Companion Media** See *http://support.microsoft.com/kb/249694* for more information on requirements for restoring a system state to different hardware. The link is located on the companion media.

If you only have a backup of the LServer folder, you can restore it and recover your reports. Also, issued TS CALs will still work. However, any unissued TS CALs will not be restored. You will see that your licenses are recovered, but none will be available for issue. Contact the Clearinghouse to have them reissued.

Finally, if you do not have a working backup of your license server, you can install a new license server and call the Clearinghouse to get your TS CALs reissued to the new server.

Table 9-8 summarizes the restoration process you may go through and when you will need to contact the Microsoft Clearinghouse to get your TS CALs reissued.

TABLE 9-8 TS License Server Recovery Methods and When to Get TS CALs Reissued

Action	Hardware	Type of Backup Restored	Have to Get CALs Reissued?
Install new OS	Existing or identical hardware	Restore full backup of old TS Licensing Server.	Restore will be successful, no need to contact the Clearinghouse.
Install new OS	Existing or identical hardware	Restore only the LServer folder and the System State.	Restore will be successful, no need to contact the Clearinghouse.
Install new OS	Existing or identical hardware	Restore only the LServer folder.	Your licenses will be viewable and your issued count will be accurate, but unissued TS CALs will not be available. Call the Clearinghouse and get your TS CALs reissued.
Keep old OS	Existing hardware	Restore only the LServer folder and the system state.	Restore will be successful, no need to contact the Clearinghouse.
Restore from backup	Existing, identical, or dissimilar hardware	Restore server image (bare metal restore). This is best practice way to recover a TS License Server.	Restore will be successful, no need to contact the Clearinghouse
Install new OS	New or existing hardware	No recovery available, start from scratch.	Call the Clearinghouse and get your TS CALs reissued.

Recovering a TS License Server Using Windows Server Backup

As we said previously, Windows Server Backup replaces Ntbackup.exe in Windows Server 2008 and uses block-based backup technology to back up whole volumes instead of individual files and folders. To be clear, you can only back up whole volumes, but you can choose to restore whole volumes or individual files and folders. Windows Server Backup also uses file-based technology to back up and restore the system state only (use the Wbadmin command-line tool to back up and restore the system state).

> **On the Companion Media** For more information on Windows Server Backup, see *http://technet.microsoft.com/en-us/library/cc770266.aspx* and *http://technet.microsoft.com/en-us/library/cc754015.aspx*. Both links are available on the companion media.

Windows Server Backup supports system state recovery only on the same operating system installation where the backup was taken. Performing a system state restore on another OS instance is not supported even if the other operating system is on similar or the same hardware. That being said, we were successful in restoring full functionality of our TS License Server in our environment using Windows Server Backup in this fashion. It may work for you, but we can't guarantee that it will always work.

Direct from the Source: Supported System State Recovery Scenarios

Windows Server Backup supports system state recovery only on the same operating installation where the backup was taken. Doing system state recovery on another operating system instance is not supported, even if the other operating system is on similar or the same hardware.

System state recovery does not restore the entire Windows operating system or Windows directory, but only a subset of it. What constitutes system state and what should be recovered when doing system state recovery is documented in the MSDN article at *http://msdn.microsoft.com/en-us/library/aa381498(VS.85).aspx.*

To improve the reliability of the system state recovery process from Windows Server 2003, more Windows files were included as part of the system state backup and recovery process in Windows Server 2008. Although this increased the reliability of the recovery itself and that of the recovered server, it coupled the recovery process much more tightly with the specific operating system instance and also with the physical hardware.

A fresh operating system install (even if it's on the same hardware) may not have the same set of files as the server that was backed up. For example, the server that was backed up may have programs *A*, *B*, and *C* installed, whereas the fresh operating system that is installed on the same hardware may just have program *A* installed at the time of recovery. The differences may not be restricted to the applications that are installed but may extend to drivers, services, updates, server roles, server features, and so forth.

Since system state recovery is a partial recovery of Windows files, there is no way to guarantee that the server on which recovery is being attempted is in a state similar to or compatible to the server that was backed up.

All this said, in controlled environments where administrators know that the operating system state is very similar to or the same as the server that was backed up, chances are high that system state recovery will succeed and that the system integrity will be preserved. For this reason and for a couple of advanced requirements from Microsoft Product Support group, Windows Server Backup allows you to recover the system state on a different OS install. It's a best case effort anyway and hence is not a supported scenario.

The highly recommended and most reliable way to protect any server—including TS—against unbootable or disaster scenarios is to take a bare metal restore backup of your server. For the cost of a few extra gigabytes (GBs) of disk space allocated for backup, you can get complete protection of your server including data protection, system state protection, and disaster recovery features. You can still use the same backup to perform a system state recovery from the running operating system as you could with a system state–only backup. As always, to ensure that an operating system recovery does not affect other server data, it's recommended that other server data and application data be stored on a volume other than the critical volumes.

Prabu Ambravaneswaran

Program Manager II

As we stated earlier in this chapter, you cannot make a backup to the system volume. You will need to have either another volume available for storage, or you can target a UNC path. Windows Server Backup does not support backing up to tape.

In the following examples, we will show you how to back up your TS License Server. Then we will show you how to restore a bare metal backup to a different server and also how to restore only the system state (identical hardware is assumed).

Windows Server Backup is not installed by default; you must install it via Server Manager or by using the Servermanagercmd.exe command-line utility. The following code shows the installation of both Windows Server Backup and the Wbadmin command-line utility (and subsequently the Windows PowerShell dependency):

```
C:\Users\Administrator>servermanagercmd.exe -install backup-features
.........................................
Start Installation...
[Installation] Succeeded: [Windows Server Backup Features] Windows Server Backup.
<100/100>
Success: Installation succeeded.
C:\Users\Administrator>servermanagercmd.exe -install backup-tools.
Start Installation...
[Installation] Succeeded: [Windows PowerShell].
[Installation] Succeeded: [Windows Server Backup Features] Command-line Tools.
<100/100>
```

To back up the critical volume, you can use the graphical user interface (GUI) or the Wbadmin command-line tool. For this example, we use the command line. We have a USB drive E connected to our TS License Server OZARK. The following command backs up the critical volume to drive E:

```
C:\windows\system32>wbadmin start backup -allCritical -backuptarget:e:
wbadmin 1.0 - Backup command-line tool
(C) Copyright 2004 Microsoft Corp.
Retrieving volume information...
This would backup volume Local Disk(C:) to e:.
Do you want to start the backup operation?
[Y] Yes [N] No y
Backup to E: is starting.
```

In this example, the TS License Server OZARK crashes due to a hardware failure. First, we do a bare metal restore to another system. The system does not have an operating system installed yet. We connect the USB drive used to store OZARK backups to the new server.

1. On the new system, place the operating system CD in the CD-ROM drive and start the server. Press any key to boot to the CD/DVD.

2. The Install Windows GUI starts. Make necessary adjustments for Language, Time, Currency Format, and Keyboard choices; click Next.

3. On the next page, instead of clicking the Install Windows button, click Repair Your Computer in the lower-left portion of the screen. This initiates the Windows Recovery Environment (WinRE).

4. Click Windows Complete PC Restore, as shown in Figure 9-7.

FIGURE 9-7 To perform a bare metal restore, choose the Windows Complete PC Restore tool.

The wizard finds the backup drive automatically and then finds the latest available backup, as shown in Figure 9-8.

FIGURE 9-8 The wizard finds the latest backup located on attached drives.

5. The next page allows you to add drivers to the recovery process. Because we are restoring to identical hardware, we do not need to install alternate drivers (but if you are attempting to recover to dissimilar hardware, here is where you add needed drivers). Click Next.

6. Confirm that you want to format the disks and restore the backup by checking the corresponding check box and clicking OK, as shown in Figure 9-9.

FIGURE 9-9 Confirm that you want to format the disks and restore the backup.

The restore process will run. When the server reboots, your server will be restored, and your TS License Server will be fully functional.

Regarding this next example, even though restoring a system state backup to new hardware is not supported, we had success in our test environment. We will recover only the system state data to a new server. This server has identical hardware and a new OS installation has been completed. The server is currently in a workgroup. It is named OZARK, the same name as the server we are replacing.

1. Install the Terminal Server role and the TS Licensing role service. Because the server is in a workgroup, the discovery scope for this license server can only be This Workgroup. This is okay—it will get changed when the system state data from the original license server is restored.

2. Install Windows Server Backup on the new server and attach the USB drive used to store the license server backups.

3. Because multiple backups can be stored in one location, we need to obtain the version of the backup we want to restore. We do so by running the following command:

```
wbadmin get versions -backuptarget:e:
wbadmin 1.0 - Backup command-line tool
(C) Copyright 2004 Microsoft Corp.
Backup time: 9/4/2008 2:09 PM
Backup target: Fixed Disk labeled ozarkbu(E:)
Version identifier: 09/04/2008-21:09
Can Recover: Volume(s), File(s), Application(s), Bare Metal Recovery, System State
```

The data returned shows all of the backups located on the backup target. In our example, there is only one, but there could be several. The version identifier is what we use to specify the backup we want to use for recovery. To restore the system state data to the new server, run this command:

```
wbadmin start systemstaterecovery -version:09/04/2008-21:09 -backuptarget:e:
wbadmin 1.0 - Backup command-line tool
(C) Copyright 2004 Microsoft Corp.

Do you want to start the system state recovery operation?
[Y] Yes [N] No y
```

Here we choose *Yes* to start the system state recovery operation, and we get a warning letting us know that we are recovering to a different machine.

```
WARNING:
The specified backup is of a different machine than the current one.
Restoring the backup to an alternate machine is not recommended as it might put the
machine into an unstable state.
Are you sure you want to use this backup for restoring the current machine?
[Y] Yes [N] No
Y
```

The restore runs, and when it is done, it tells us to reboot. Upon reboot, a command-line window appears and indicates that the restore finished successfully. Pressing the Enter key on the keyboard finishes the restore. If all went well, the server now is joined to the domain, has the same PID as the failed server, the contents of the LServer folder are restored, and the TS License Server is fully functional.

We show this example using Windows Server Backup because this backup option comes with the operating system. But it's worth noting that backup software from companies such as Acronis and Symantec can perform bare metal restores to dissimilar hardware. So your recovery abilities ultimately will be a function of the backup technology you use. Third-party backup software may yield different results.

Caution Thoroughly test your disaster recovery methods before relying on them in a production environment.

Virtualizing your TS License Server also can break the ties to specific hardware. Because Windows Backup is VSS-aware, when you run a backup of the host server, it in turn backs up the child virtual machines (VMs), which you can restore if need be. If you use Windows Server 2008 Hyper-V and only restore the .vhd file, then you will need to recreate the VM settings, such as the amount of RAM to use and the network adapter settings. However, the .vhd is restorable, and your TS License Server will be functional. If you use third-party backup software, check with your vendor to determine the capabilities of the software for backing up virtual environments.

> **On the Companion Media** Microsoft System Center Data Protection Manager (DPM) should be able to back up single Hyper-V virtual machines in the future (look for the release of DPM 2007 SP1). For information on DPM, see *http://www.microsoft.com/systemcenter/ dataprotectionmanager/en/us/protect-virtual-environments.aspx* (the link is available on the companion media).

Adding Capacity

If the experiment with Terminal Services goes well, at some point you'll find that demand is outstripping what the terminal servers can supply. In this section, we'll talk about how you can keep tabs on the increasing load on the terminal servers at key times, and we'll discuss virtualization options that let you keep spare capacity on hand.

Measuring Server Stress

Before adding capacity, you need to know how much stress the servers are under. One way to determine this is to measure connections in two contexts: the rate of new connections added during logon times and the number of connections each terminal server sustains at a time when you'd expect users to be already logged on and working. Both numbers are important for different reasons.

You need to know the rate of logons to help determine one kind of server stress. Process creation is expensive in terms of resources; the beginning of a session requires a lot of process creation, as you can see from the description of the per-session processes in Chapter 3.

You need to know the number of concurrent logons to help you see trends in server usage. Are more or fewer users utilizing each terminal server, or is the rate of usage staying steady? This can help you both in hardware planning and in business planning, as you may see that you need to purchase more TS CALs to remain in compliance with the licensing requirements explained in Chapter 3.

> **Note** Another way to derive similar information is to run license reports against the license server to see how quickly you're using up TS CALs.

Both questions—the rate at which users are logging on and the number of them using the terminal servers—can be answered using the script here, which creates a file with entries like the entries shown in Figure 9-10. Basically, what we're doing is accessing the Active Sessions counter of the Terminal Server object at a given time and date and then writing that information to a comma-separated value (CSV) file.

```
# This script gets the number of active sessions
# for a named server and writes the date and the count to a CSV file.
######Configuration Area########
$PerfObj = "Terminal Services" # Performance Object
$PerfCounter = "Active Sessions" # Performance Counter
$PerfCounterInst = "" # Performance Instance
$Server = "HELEN" # Server
$LogPath = "\\ozark\it$\Logs\"
$LogFileNAme = "-ActiveSessions.csv"
##############################
$LogFile = "$LogPath$Server$LogFileName"
$MonthDay = get-date -format "ddMMM"
$Year = get-date -format yyyy
$Time = get-date -format "HH:mm:ss"
$objPerfCounter = New-Object
System.Diagnostics.PerformanceCounter($PerfObj,$PerfCounter,$PerfCounterInst,$Server)
$objPerfCounterData = "$MonthDay" + "," + "$Year" + "," + "$Time" + ","
+$objPerfCounter.NextValue()   | out-File "$LogFile" -append
```

On the Companion Media The preceding script is available on the companion media as ActiveSessions.ps1.

Every time you run the script, it appends a new line to the file in the location specified in the script. Opening the report in Office Excel, you will see data similar to that shown in Figure 9-10.

	A	B	C	D
1	9-Sep	2008	8:30:00	26
2	9-Sep	2008	9:00:00	43
3	10-Sep	2008	8:30:00	27
4	10-Sep	2008	9:00:00	40

FIGURE 9-10 Sample output from the ActiveSessions.ps1 script

To get a good picture of the logon speed and sustained concurrent sessions, you need to run this script at least three times a day. Run it twice (or more often) during the time you expect most users to log on, separated by a reasonable interval to help you see the rate of logons during that time. You may need to adjust this interval to get the shape of the curve; the more often you run the script during this period, the more data points you'll get to draw the curve accurately.

Run it an additional time during a period when you expect most users to be logged on, such as mid-afternoon on a day midweek. (Obviously, you'll need to experiment with the timing according to the way your organization works, but that's the basic idea of what you're trying to do. Find a time that users are not logging on, but rather are working steadily. Check the number of sessions at that time.)

> **Note** Create two versions of the script, one to store logon rates and one to store concurrent connections when the server is working. This will make it easier for you to find the data you need.

To run the scripts automatically at the same time every day, open Task Scheduler, located in the Administrative Tools program group, and follow these steps:

1. From the Action menu, choose Create Basic Task to start the Create Basic Task Wizard.

2. Give the new task a name and description.

3. For the Trigger, specify the interval at which you want to run the script. Choose Daily.

4. Specify the time at which you want to run the script. Provide the time for the first check.

5. For the Action, choose Start A Program from the list.

6. Provide the path to the script.

7. Click Finish to complete the task creation.

Repeat as required to get the correct intervals to tell you how quickly users log on to the server in the mornings and how many users are using the terminal servers during the day.

You can find out similar information for the TS Gateway with a similar script that uses another set of performance counters, as shown in the following example. Again, this script gets the number of concurrent connections for a TS Gateway server and sends the report to a file, appending it each time you run the script. This will help you not only determine how many users are logging on using the TS Gateway (which is interesting for observing how users are working) but also can help you demonstrate that connections are being distributed evenly among load-balanced servers.

```
# This script gets the number of current connections to a TS Gateway server
# for a named server and writes the date and the count to a CSV file.
######Configuration Area######
$PerfObj = "Terminal Service Gateway" # Performance Object
$PerfCounter = "Current Connections" # Performance Counter
$PerfCounterInst = "" # Performance Instance
$Server = "OZARK" # Server
$LogPath = "\\ozark\it$\Logs\"
$LogFileNAme = "-TSGCurrentConnections.csv"
#############################
$LogFile = "$LogPath$Server$LogFileName"
$MonthDay = get-date -format "ddMMM"
$Year = get-date -format yyyy
$Time = get-date -format "HH:mm:ss"
```

```
$objPerfCounter = New-Object
System.Diagnostics.PerformanceCounter($PerfObj,$PerfCounter,$PerfCounterInst,$Server)
$objPerfCounterData = "$MonthDay" + "," + "$Year" + "," + "$Time" + ","
+$objPerfCounter.NextValue()  | out-File "$LogFile" -append
```

On the Companion Media The preceding script is available on the companion media as TSGCurrentConnections.ps1.

Again, use Task Scheduler to run this script at regular intervals to let you build a pattern of usage.

You may have noticed that both of the preceding scripts look very similar to each other. They are identical except for two areas:

- The names of the performance counter category, object, counter, and instance
- The name of the output file

When you know the names of the objects, counters, and instances for which you want to gain performance data, you can plug them into the script, run it, and pipe the data to a file. Follow these steps to get the category, object, counter, and instance names you need. In this example, we will set the script to get the Memory: Committed Bytes from terminal server OZARK.

Note For the performance counters you should be monitoring to determine a baseline and to reveal any increasing stress, see Chapter 2.

List the available performance counter categories formatted into a list (so you can read all of the data).

```
PS C:\windows\System32>[System.Diagnostics.PerformanceCounterCategory]::GetCategories() |
format-list
```

When you know the name of the category, create a new object and assign it to a variable. Place the category name in the parentheses as we do here with the category "memory":

```
PS C:\windows\System32>$category = new-object System.Diagnostics.PerformanceCounterCategory
("memory")
```

Become familiar with the different parameters of a performance counter; assign a performance counter object to a variable, and take a look:

```
PS C:\windows\System32>$perfcounter = new-object system.diagnostics.PerformanceCounter
PS C:\windows\System32>$perfcounter
```

```
CategoryName    :
CounterHelp     :
CounterName     :
CounterType     : (this is how the data is formatted)
InstanceLifetime : Global
InstanceName    :
ReadOnly        : True
MachineName     : .
RawValue        : (This is the raw, unprocessed data retrieved by this counter)
Site            :
Container       :
```

Next, get the instance names available for the specified category. There may or may not be any instances depending on the counter you have chosen.

```
$category.GetInstanceNames()
```

If the counter has instances, then add the instance name (in quotations) between the parentheses of the following command. This will yield the counters for that instance. If there are no instances, then run the command with no instance entered between the parentheses:

```
$category.GetCounters()
```

Find the counter name in the listed results. Now you have all of the pieces necessary to fill in the script Configuration area that follows, along with the server name and the log file name. Run the script, and the processed data will be appended to the specified file.

> **Note** RawValue data is unprocessed; get the processed data from the NextValue property, as shown in the last line of the following script.

```
# This script gets Committed bytes for a named server
# and writes the date and the count to a CSV file.
######Configuration Area#######
$PerfObj = "Memory" # Performance Object Category
$PerfCounter = "Committed Bytes" # Performance Counter
$PerfCounterInst = "" # Performance Instance
$Server = "OZARK" # Server
$LogPath = "\\ozark\it$\Logs\"
$LogFileNAme = "-Memory-Committed-Bytes.csv"
############################
$LogFile = "$LogPath$Server$LogFileName"
$MonthDay = get-date -format "ddMMM"
$Year = get-date -format yyyy
$Time = get-date -format "HH:mm:ss"
$objPerfCounter = New-Object System.Diagnostics.
PerformanceCounter($PerfObj,$PerfCounter,$PerfCounterInst,$Server)
$objPerfCounterData = "$MonthDay" + "," + "$Year" + "," + "$Time" + ","
+$objPerfCounter.NextValue()   | out-File "$LogFile" -append
```

On the Companion Media This script can be found on the companion media as CommittedBytes.ps1. Another example script that gets the Percent Process Time of a named server is also included on the companion media as PercentProcTime.ps1.

What Roles Can You Virtualize?

When it comes to adding capacity quickly or recovering quickly from a failed server, it's hard to beat virtualizing. Particularly with the availability of the new Hyper-V platform in Windows Server 2008, it's tempting to want to virtualize server roles. It's true that virtualizing has a lot of advantages:

- Backing up a server means backing up a file.
- Backing out changes is easy if you snapshot a server before making any change.
- Less physical space is required in the data center, and a VM not currently running can be stored in an image library.

Functionality-wise, there is no reason why you can't run any Terminal Services role inside a VM. Any problems that you will have come from two places: user load and saved state data.

- VMs, almost by definition, force multiple computers to compete for resources. Since VMs also have a lot of I/O to read from the virtual hard disk, and terminal servers also require I/O to read from the page file or user files, the combination can create a bottleneck.
- If you save a backup of a server role that maintains state data—even server patches—then you need to keep updating that backup to truly bring the environment back up exactly the way you left it.

For an example of what can happen with persistent data, let's take a look at what happens if you virtualize a TS License Server. To keep the math simple, let's say that you have 10 TS CALs. You load the TS CALs on a VM named TLS01. You run TLS01 for a while, long enough to issue five TS CALs, then decide that you'd better back up the VM, saving the VHD file as TLSBAK.

TLS01 runs for a while longer, long enough to issue licenses 6–10. Then it crashes, and you bring up TLSBAK so you have a working license server. TLSBAK has no record of TS CALs 6–10 being issued. This is where things may become a little weird. The TLSBAK response depends on whether you have per-user licenses or per-device licenses.

If the licenses are per-user, then the situation is actually pretty simple. Per-user TS CALs are not assigned, as you may recall from Chapter 3. Instead, when a user is issued a license, her user account object (recall, per-user licensing requires Active Directory) is updated to show that she is using a TS CAL. When you run a report to show TS CAL usage, the report does a Lightweight Directory Access Protocol (LDAP) query against Active Directory to see how many user accounts have the "I am using a TS CAL" property set. So long as you have purchased enough per-user TS CALs to account for all the users who need them, the reporting works, because allocation data isn't stored on the license server.

Per-device TS CALs don't work out quite so well with virtualization, because the license allocation database is on the license server. Going back to our example, TS CALs 1–5 were allocated to devices A–E before you backed up the VM, so TLSBAK will know about them. TS CALs 6–10 were issued to devices F–J while TLS01 was working, but TLSBAK didn't know about that. When TLSBAK comes online, it will issue TS CALs 6–10 to devices K–O, so TS CALs 6–10 have been issued twice.

So far everything works, because once the license server has assigned a TS CAL to a device, it does not get involved again so long as the license remains valid: The terminal server asks the client for a TS CAL, and the client computer produces it. But seven days before the license is due to expire, the terminal server will note that it's coming to the end of its license period and will present the TS CAL to the license server for renewal. The licenses allocated to devices F–J will come up for renewal first. The license server will be unable to renew those license assignments, because it has no record of them being assigned to those computers. The licenses will expire. At this point, client computers F–J no longer can connect, because they have no license; they can't get one because TLSBAK is out of licenses. And unless you check the reports carefully, you think you are in compliance, because every computer had a license.

The moral? Virtualizing license servers is simpler if you use per-user licensing, because none of the bookkeeping is kept on the terminal server.

> **Note** Virtualizing license servers does not allow you to violate the terms of your EULA. Only one copy of a TS CAL may be issued.

Although a TS Gateway server may maintain some state data in the form of TS CAPs and TS RAPs, it doesn't have to. As discussed in Chapter 7, load balancing TS Gateway servers reduces your risk of one failing and rendering your terminal servers inaccessible from the Internet. Put the TS CAPs and TS RAPs on a central server, and you can virtualize the TS Gateway servers that point to the central location.

TS Session Broker maintains no state data at all (its connection database is temporary) and can be clustered and virtualized.

The Case for Virtualizing a Terminal Server

We've said it repeatedly: Don't virtualize a terminal server. Not only will the terminal server have to compete with other virtual machines for processor cycles and RAM, the disk I/O bottleneck of VMs will exacerbate the issues of disk I/O associated with terminal servers. Nope, just don't do it.

All that said, there *is* a situation in which virtualizing a terminal server makes sense: when creating a TS RemoteApp management platform and backer for TS Web Access, as described in Chapter 6.

There are a couple of reasons to do this. First, we recommend assigning one terminal server to sign all RDP files and to be the definitive source of all allow-list definitions. That way, there's no question about which applications should be allowed and presented on the TS Web Access server: One server is authoritative, and one server signs all the RDP files and exports its allow list to other servers. So one server becomes the TS RemoteApp management server, but that server has its own server-specific certificate for signing RDP files. If this computer goes offline, you'll need another certificate.

Second, each TS Web Access server points not to a farm, but to a specific server that tells the Web page which applications to display. If that server isn't available, then TS Web Access won't work.

For both these reasons, it makes sense to designate one terminal server as the TS RemoteApp management server, put it into drain mode (see Chapter 8 "Managing the Terminal Server Runtime Environment," for more about this), and virtualize it. Then you can back up the .vhd file holding the drive data and spin up the backup if anything happens to the original. Because the TS RemoteApp management server is in drain mode, it won't be affected by the I/O bottleneck of ordinary terminal servers running in VMs.

Summary

After you have the Terminal Services ecosystem set up, you will need to keep it working. That means both careful change management and knowing how to keep server roles available and restorable. In this chapter, we've discussed how to do this and some of the approaches you may want to follow for increased server uptime.

Some best practices include:

- Follow good change management practices so that you always know who has made what changes to the servers and what the effects of those changes were.

- If possible, use an automated deployment system to make it easy to restore capacity and duplicate servers.

- Be careful to update golden images and scripted installations with approved changes to make sure that the servers you rebuild follow the latest guidelines.

- Virtualize server roles where possible to simplify backups.

- Split installed TS CALs among at least two license servers to avoid service outages with per-device TS CALs.

Additional Resources

Ongoing terminal server ecosystem health is improved if you have a good understanding of how the pieces of the ecosystem work. Here are some pointers to other chapters that explain the background of these server roles:

- For more details on the role of processor, memory, and disk I/O in supporting terminal servers, see Chapter 2, "Planning the Terminal Server Ecosystem."

- To learn what processes the server must create every time it creates a new session, see Chapter 3, "Installing the Core Terminal Server Environment."

- For details on what licenses are required for accessing a terminal server and how to run usage reports, see Chapter 3.

- For background on how TS Gateway supports user connections to a terminal server or other endpoint, see Chapter 7, "Multi-Server Deployments and Securing Terminal Server Connections."

There's a lot of theory around how to build an effective change management system. For some examples, see the following resources.

- *The Visible Ops Handbook: Implementing ITIL in 4 Practical and Auditable Steps,* by Kevin Behr, Gene Kim, and George Spafford (Information Technology Process Institute, 2005), offers good advice about change management best practices.

- There's a lot of interest in combining Information Technology Infrastructure Library (ITIL) best practices and Six Sigma process improvement. For one high-level look, see "Combining ITIL® and Six Sigma to Improve Information Technology Service Management at General Electric" at *http://documents.bmc.com/products/documents/67/60/46760/46760.pdf.*

- Explanations of and texts of the latest Information Technology Infrastructure Library (ITIL) is online at *http://www.itlibrary.org/index.php?page=ITIL_v3.* For change management purposes, two of the most important volumes are *Service Transition* and *Continual Service Improvement.*

Part of system management involves tools that don't have anything to do with Terminal Services but are important to keeping the Terminal Services infrastructure available.

- For more information about backing up and restoring data with Windows Server 2008, see the Wbadmin.exe documentation at *http://technet.microsoft.com/en-us/library/cc754015.aspx.*

- For more information about backing up and restoring single files with Windows Server 2008, see *http://technet.microsoft.com/en-us/library/cc733145.aspx* for Robocopy documentation. Xcopy documentation is at *http://technet.microsoft.com/en-us/library/bb491035.aspx.*

- For more information on the *System.Diagnostics* Namespace, see *http://msdn.microsoft.com/en-us/library/system.diagnostics.aspx.*

- For more information on *PerformanceCounterType* enumerations, see *http://msdn.microsoft.com/en-us/library/system.diagnostics.performancecountertype.aspx.*

About the Authors

Christa Anderson

Born a military brat, Christa lived in various places in the western United States until a visit to Virginia ended in a 20-year stay. She returned to Seattle in 2007, where she enjoys traveling, photography, theater, cooking, boating, making stained glass, and spending time with her family of humans, canines, felines, and avians. Christa's interest in travel and environmental issues contributed to her enthusiasm for presentation remoting, beginning with Citrix WinFrame in the middle 1990s. A former Terminal Services MVP and freelance technical author and speaker for over a decade, she is now a program manager on the Presentation Hosted Desktop Virtualization team at Microsoft. She promises to talk about something other than the book now.

Kristin L. Griffin

Kristin was born in California and grew up a military brat, part of a loving and happy family. She has worked with Terminal Services since Windows 2000 and has implemented Terminal Services for a diverse set of customers, including distributors, law offices, and commercial contracting firms. Formerly a senior consultant for a Virginia-based Internet and application service provider, she is now a Seattle-based independent consultant and author. She enjoys photography, computer graphics, camping, traveling, stained glass, woodworking, and buying more tools from the hardware store. Most of all she enjoys being with her family. She takes her dog, Nani, with her wherever she goes.

Index

A

Get Certified—Windows Server 2008

Ace your preparation for the skills measured by the Microsoft® certification exams—and on the job. With 2-in-1 *Self-Paced Training Kits*, you get an official exam-prep guide + practice tests. Work at your own pace through lessons and real-world case scenarios that cover the exam objectives. Then, assess your skills using practice tests with multiple testing modes—and get a customized learning plan based on your results.

EXAMS 70-640, 70-642, 70-646
MCITP Self-Paced Training Kit: Windows Server® 2008 Server Administrator Core Requirements
ISBN 9780735625082

EXAMS 70-640, 70-642, 70-643, 70-647
MCITP Self-Paced Training Kit: Windows Server 2008 Enterprise Administrator Core Requirements
ISBN 9780735625723

EXAM 70-640
MCTS Self-Paced Training Kit: **Configuring Windows Server 2008 Active Directory®**
Dan Holme, Nelson Ruest, and Danielle Ruest
ISBN 9780735625136

EXAM 70-647
MCITP Self-Paced Training Kit: Windows® Enterprise Administration
Orin Thomas, et al.
ISBN 9780735625099

EXAM 70-642
MCTS Self-Paced Training Kit: Configuring Windows Server 2008 Network Infrastructure
Tony Northrup, J.C. Mackin
ISBN 9780735625129

ALSO SEE

Windows Server 2008 Administrator's Pocket Consultant
William R. Stanek
ISBN 9780735624375

EXAM 70-643
MCTS Self-Paced Training Kit: Configuring Windows Server 2008 Applications Infrastructure
J.C. Mackin, Anil Desai
ISBN 9780735625112

Windows Server 2008 Administrator's Companion
Charlie Russel, Sharon Crawford
ISBN 9780735625051

Windows Server 2008 Resource Kit
Microsoft MVPs with Windows Server Team
ISBN 9780735623613

EXAM 70-646
MCITP Self-Paced Training Kit: Windows Server Administration
Ian McLean, Orin Thomas
ISBN 9780735625105

Windows Server 2008—
Resources for Administrators

Windows Server® 2008 Administrator's Companion

Charlie Russel and Sharon Crawford
ISBN 9780735625051

Your comprehensive, one-volume guide to deployment, administration, and support. Delve into core system capabilities and administration topics, including Active Directory®, security issues, disaster planning/recovery, interoperability, IIS 7.0, virtualization, clustering, and performance tuning.

Windows Server 2008 Administrator's Pocket Consultant

William R. Stanek
ISBN 9780735624375

Portable and precise—with the focused information you need for administering server roles, Active Directory, user/group accounts, rights and permissions, file-system management, TCP/IP, DHCP, DNS, printers, network performance, backup, and restoration.

Windows Server 2008 Resource Kit

Microsoft MVPs with Microsoft Windows Server Team
ISBN 9780735623613

Six volumes! Your definitive resource for deployment and operations—from the experts who know the technology best. Get in-depth technical information on Active Directory, Windows PowerShell™ scripting, advanced administration, networking and network access protection, security administration, IIS, and more—plus an essential toolkit of resources on CD.

Internet Information Services (IIS) 7.0 Administrator's Pocket Consultant

William R. Stanek
ISBN 9780735623644

This pocket-sized guide delivers immediate answers for administering IIS 7.0. Topics include customizing installation; configuration and XML schema; application management; user access and security; Web sites, directories, and content; and performance, backup, and recovery.

Windows PowerShell Step by Step

Ed Wilson
ISBN 9780735623958

Teach yourself the fundamentals of the Windows PowerShell command-line interface and scripting language—one step at a time. Learn to use *cmdlets* and write scripts to manage users, groups, and computers; configure network components; administer Microsoft® Exchange Server 2007; and more. Includes 100+ sample scripts.

ALSO SEE

Windows Server 2008 Hyper-V™ Resource Kit
ISBN 9780735625174

Windows® Administration Resource Kit: Productivity Solutions for IT Professionals
ISBN 9780735624313

Internet Information Services (IIS) 7.0 Resource Kit
ISBN 9780735624412

Windows Server 2008 Security Resource Kit
ISBN 9780735625044

microsoft.com/mspress

System Requirements

To use this book's companion CD-ROM, you need a computer equipped with the following minimum configuration:

- Microsoft Windows Server 2008, Windows Vista, Windows Server 2003, or Windows XP
- 1 GHz 32-bit (x86) or 64-bit (x64) processor (depending on the minimum requirements of the operating system)
- At least 1 GB of system memory (depending on the minimum requirements of the operating system)
- A hard disk partition with at least 1 GB of available space
- Appropriate video output device
- Keyboard
- Mouse or other pointing device
- Optical drive capable of reading CD-ROMs

Some items on the companion media have specific requirements.

The companion CD-ROM contains numerous links to scripts, tools, Knowledge Base articles, and other information. To view these links, you will need a Web browser and Internet access.

The companion CD-ROM also includes scripts that are written in VBScript (with a .vbs file extension), Windows PowerShell (with a .ps1 file extension) and a few batch files. The Windows PowerShell scripts require that you have Windows PowerShell 1.0 installed and that you have set the Windows PowerShell execution policy to "RemoteSigned." To run these scripts, your system must meet the following additional requirements:

- On Windows Server 2008, install the Windows PowerShell feature.
- Scripts intended for execution on the local server that depend on specific counters and interfaces will not execute correctly unless the appropriate Terminal Services role service is installed. (For example, a script that queries TS Gateway interfaces will not return results unless the TS Gateway role service is installed.)
- Windows XP SP2, Windows Server 2003 SP1, or Windows Vista: To install Windows PowerShell on these operating systems, download and install Windows PowerShell from the "How to Download Windows PowerShell 1.0" Web page located at *http://www.microsoft.com/windowsserver2003/technologies/management/powershell/ download.mspx*.

The scripts on the CD are not signed. To run them on your computer, we recommend setting the Windows PowerShell Execution Policy to "RemoteSigned." To do this, start Windows PowerShell and type **Set-ExecutionPolicy RemoteSigned**. This setting will allow you to run the scripts on the CD, and it is more secure than setting this policy to Unrestricted..

> **Note** For more information on using the Set-ExecutionPolicy cmdlet see: *http://www.microsoft .com/technet/scriptcenter/topics/msh/cmdlets/set-executionpolicy.mspx.* This link is available on the companion CD.

When you run a Windows PowerShell script, you need to provide the full path to the script. To use the VBScript scripts and batch files, double-click them, or execute them directly from a command prompt.

Finally, the CD contains a network diagram and sample files created in Excel 2007 and Visio 2007, so you will need to have those two applications installed to use these samples. The network diagram Visio file pulls data from the network diagram Excel file; therefore, in order to fully utilize the network diagram Visio file, you will need to update the data in the Excel file and refresh the data in the Visio file. For more information on refreshing external data in Visio 2007, see the Visio Help files. You can download free viewers or trial versions of Microsoft Office 2007 at *http://office.microsoft.com/en-us.*

What do you think of this book?

We want to hear from you!

Your feedback will help us continually improve our books and learning resources for you. To participate in a brief online survey, please visit:

microsoft.com/learning/booksurvey

...and enter this book's ISBN-10 or ISBN-13 number (appears above barcode on back cover). As a thank-you to survey participants in the U.S. and Canada, each month we'll randomly select five respondents to win one of five $100 gift certificates from a leading online merchant. At the conclusion of the survey, you can enter the drawing by providing your e-mail address, which will be used for prize notification only.*

Thank you in advance for your input!

Where to find the ISBN on back cover

Example only. Each book has unique ISBN.

Stay in touch!

To subscribe to the *Microsoft Press* Book Connection Newsletter—for news on upcoming books, events, and special offers—please visit:

microsoft.com/learning/books/newsletter